# The Token-Ring Management Guide

## Other McGraw-Hill Communications Books of Interest

BALL • *Cost-Efficient Network Management*
BERSON • *APPC: A Guide to LU6.2*
BERSON • *Client/Server Architecture*
BLACK • *Network Management Standards*
BLACK • *TCP/IP and Related Protocols*
BLACK • *The V Series Recommendations*
BLACK • *The X Series Recommendations*
BOAR • *Implementing Client/Server Computing: A Strategic Perspective*
CHORAFAS • *The Complete LAN Reference*
COOPER • *Computer and Communications Security*
DAYTON (RANADE, ED.) • *Integrating Digital Services*
DAYTON • *Telecommunications*
FEIT • *TCP/IP: Architecture, Protocols, and Implementation*
FOLTS • *McGraw-Hill's Compilation of Open Systems Standards*
FORTIER • *Handbook of LAN Technology, Second Edition*
GRAY • *Open Systems: A Business Strategy for the 1990s*
HELDMAN • *Global Telecommunications*
HUGHES • *Data Communications*
INGLIS • *Electronic Communications Handbook*
KESSLER • *ISDN*
KIMBERLEY • *Electronic Data Interchange*
KNIGHTSON • *Standards for Open Systems Interconnection*
MCCLAIN • *The Open Systems Interconnection Handbook*
NAUGLE • *Local Area Networking*
NEMZOW • *The Ethernet Management Guide*
PECAR • *The McGraw-Hill Telecommunications Factbook*
RADICATI • *Electronic Mail*
RORABAUGH • *Communications Formulas and Algorithms*
ROSE • *Programmer's Guide to Netware*
SARCH • *Integrating Voice and Data*
SCHLAR • *Inside X.25*
TERPLAN • *Effective Management of Local Area Network*
WATERS • *Computer Communications Networks*
WHITE • *Interworking and Addressing*

# The Token-Ring Management Guide

**Martin A. W. Nemzow**

**McGraw-Hill, Inc.**

New York San Francisco Washington, D.C. Auckland Bogotá
Caracas Lisbon London Madrid Mexico City Milan
Montreal New Delhi San Juan Singapore
Sydney Tokyo Toronto

The Token-Ring Management Guide *is dedicated to my children, Sophie Esther Wiesel Weingrod Nemzow and Gabriel Charles Wiesel Weingrod Nemzow, and especially for Carol.*

**Library of Congress Cataloging-in-Publication Data**

Nemzow, Martin A. W.
The token-ring management guide / Martin A. W. Nemzow.
p. cm. — (McGraw-Hill series on computer communication)
Includes bibliographical references and index.
ISBN 0-07-046321-2
1. IBM Token-Ring Network (Local area network system) I. Title. II. Series.
TK5105.8.I24N46 1993
004.6′5—dc20 92-43721
CIP



2 3 4 5 6 7 8 9 0 WHT WHT 9 0 9 8 7 6 5 4 3

ISBN 0-07-046321-2

*The sponsoring editor for this book was Jeanne Glasser, the editing supervisor was Kimberly A. Goff, and the production supervisor was Donald F. Schmidt.*

# Contents

# Preface

Data communications and networks are often promoted as a "competitive weapon" and the means to solve computer problems and lower data processing expenses. Such approaches often misfire unless the network is carefully and intelligently administered. In today's competitive environment the lack of data communications is tantamount to failed data processing. An ordinary Token-Ring network can meet basic data processing requirements and furnish an organization with the means to maintain parity with the competition. Outstanding uses of Token-Ring technology are required to create a sustainable competitive advantage.

This book presents the practical knowledge needed to design, build, grow, and maintain a Token-Ring data communications network for most vendor equipment and software, whether Andrews Systems, BICC, Cabletron Systems, Hewlett-Packard, IBM, Madge, Microsoft, Novell, Thomas-Conrad, or many others. Issues such as interconnecting networks to form enterprise-wide networks and successfully achieving interoperability are addressed, as are the cost and benefits achieved through host mainframe downsizing and installation of client-server networks.

*The Token-Ring Management Guide* is designed primarily to answer questions facing a consultant, network manager, and the network team. The specifications of the Institute for Electrical and Electronics Engineers (IEEE) 802 committee and the International Standards Organization (ISO) network standard are used as a base for definition of key terms because most vendors try to adhere to these standards. Vendor-supplied Token-Ring documentation is supplemented and explained, and its practical ramifications are discussed. In addition, the nuts and bolts of planning for installation and wiring, capacity planning, physical maintenance, and statistical tracking are presented for the busy network administrator. Concise and specific illustrations and descriptions prepare even the novice for all stages of network administration to clarify the ambiguous and sparse vendor Token-Ring documentation.

This preface presents the organization of *The Token-Ring Management Guide*. As an acknowledgment of the reader's limited time, Figure P.1 illustrates the design and flow of the knowledge contained within this book.

Chapter 1 presents the network in light of its connective power as a strategic resource in today's competitive resource-limited environment and suggests how to make a persuasive argument for network technology.

Chapter 2 speculates on the future of Token-Ring as a viable networking protocol for local area networking, distributed processing, and connectivity to enterprise-wide networks.

Chapter 3 discusses in overview the benefits of networking and describes what Token-Ring is, how it works, the variations in Token-Ring protocols, and the types of problems that can be encountered in a production environment.

Chapter 4 broaches health risks facing network personnel and users.

Chapter 5 presents the standard OSI networking model and the variations in Token-Ring. It describes standard twisted-pair variations, transmission speed options, and other protocol enhancements.

Chapter 6 describes the hardware and the mechanical process of Token-Ring. The components of a Token-Ring network are described and illustrated to help the reader understand the ingenious simplicity of a Token-Ring network.

Chapter 7 explains the Token-Ring process. This includes the transmission methodology and characteristic features of network-level software.

Chapter 8 details the planning procedures for the mechanical components of Token-Ring networks, completing what spartan vendor instructions omit. This chapter outlines those issues that an experienced network manager considers before building or expanding a Token-Ring network.

Chapter 9 explains the installation procedures for the mechanical components of Token-Ring networks, supplementing incomplete vendor instructions. This chapter suggests what steps an experienced network manager takes for testing and benchmarking a newly installed network.

Chapter 10 explains why bridges, gateways, and repeaters are necessary on a large Token-Ring, and how these units are installed. Since organizational growth is likely to outstrip the capacity of any original network, bridges, gateways, and repeaters are also presented as solutions to overloaded networks.

Chapter 11 addresses the concept of the enterprise-wide network. Internetworking and network software issues are gaining importance.

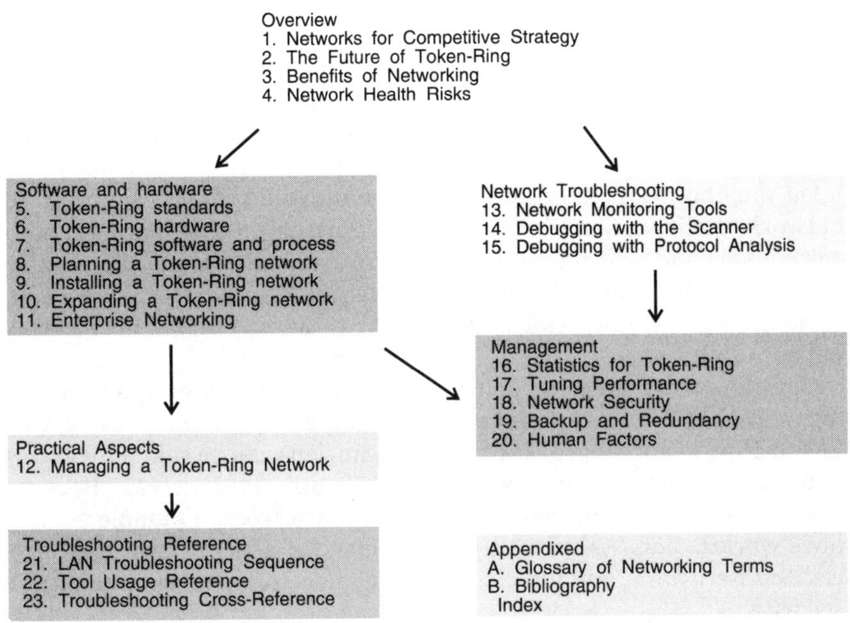


**Figure P.1** The organization of *The Token-Ring Management Guide.*

Client-server computing is displacing downsized mainframe data processing, and local area networks are becoming integrated into distributed computing and enterprise-wide environments.

Chapter 12 presents practical rules of thumb and suggestions for sucessfully using Token-Ring. The formal IEEE and ISO specifications do little to explain the hows and whys of success and failure with Token-Ring; therefore Chapter 12 concentrates on operational management.

Chapter 13 suggests practical tools that test, monitor, and analyze network status. When the network fails there are various techniques to identify, locate, and repair problems. Some techniques require specialized tools like a multimeter, a twisted-pair wiring scanner or time domain reflectometer, and a network analyzer.

Chapter 14 details the usage of a time domain reflectometer and twisted-pair scanner as well as the practical steps to check the usability of network hardware and to verify correct installation. These tools also provide a highly desirable method to benchmark a network.

Chapter 15 describes the necessity for network management software [such as Simple Network Management Protocol (SNMP), Common

Management Information Protocol (CMIP), or CMIP over TCP/IP (CMOT)] and the network protocol analyzer and how to identify, locate, and isolate suspected network problems.

Chapter 16 calculates the statistics of Token-Ring transmission protocols. This information is useful in order to understand why bottlenecks and slowdowns occur and why performance becomes suboptimal.

Chapter 17 shows how to tune network performance. This builds upon the knowledge from the chapters on installation, configurations, network traffic, and statistics. It also discusses optimal planning, network loads, and alternative solutions for overloaded rings. This single chapter can be invaluable when network trouble occurs, when no solutions are self-evident, and there appear to be no options for locating network failures.

Chapter 18 discusses security issues and explains why the networking model contains no reference to either data or physical security, why Token-Ring is not secure, and what precautions can be taken to protect a network from outside prying and unauthorized access. Because Token-Ring is a public network, packets are freely readable by any node workstation. As such, it is dependent on network software, specialized hardware, and judicious management procedures to maintain security.

Chapter 19 explains backup procedures and suggests what hardware, software, or operational procedures can be implemented to produce a nearly fault-tolerant network. Issues and redundancy for the important network services—file storage, printing, tape backup of network data, and shutdown of failed segments—are discussed in this chapter.

Chapter 20 illustrates why trained and qualified people are an important resource for network administration. Token-Ring depends on people with expertise and experience. Without knowledgeable people, the network will perform below capacity, cause severe operational problems, constrain organization growth, and in extreme cases even fail to function.

Chapter 21 is a detailed troubleshooting manual that describes techniques to isolate hardware, software, and network overloading problems.

Chapter 22 summarizes the contents of this book with a Token-Ring tool usage manual. This chapter supplies ideas and information on when to analyze the indicator lights or use the multimeter, a TDR, the transceiver tester, or a protocol analyzer to solve network problems.

Chapter 23 iconically describes the network components and then, using tables with four different formats, matches symptoms of common network problems with the possible causes. This information is not available cross-referenced, nor completely accessible from other sources, including vendor documentation, the IEEE 802.5, or OSI specifications.

The Appendices include a glossary with network and Token-Ring terms defined and cross-referenced by the all-too-common acronyms.

*Martin A. W. Nemzow*

# Acknowledgments

My sincere thanks and gratitude to the following people. Without their help and support this book would never have been publised.

Teresa Barensfeld, McGraw-Hill, Inc.

Diane Barry, Cabletron Systems, Inc.

Scott Cutler, SE Area Manager, Microcom

Steve Dauber, Product Marketing Manager, Network Analysis Products

Barry Eggers, Major Accounts, Business Development Manager, Cisco Systems

Daniel Endy, SEI Corp.

James Fetterolf, AMP Inc.

Peter Galvin, LAN Products Marketing Manager, Andrew Corp.

Brian Garafallo, Headquarters Sales Representative, Novel LANalyzer Group

Jeanne Glasser, Sponsoring Editor, McGraw-Hill, Inc.

Kimberly Goff, Senior Editing Supervisor, McGraw-Hill, Inc.

Elizabeth Grieser, Triplett Corp.

Jeanne Kilker, PR Manager, Microtest

Scott Kirby, Area Support Manager, Cisco Systems

Ronald Lee, Senior Consultant, Novell, Inc.

Kevin MacLean, Cabletron Systems, Inc.

John O'Brien, Nova University

Perry Rohan, Cabletron Systems, Inc.

Charles Schachter, Network General Corp.

Laura Schlafly, David Browns Group, Network General Corp.

Chuck Sparks, Area Sales Manager, Cisco Systems

Dave Turner, Senior Technical Consultant, Cabletron Systems, Inc.

Jeff Wallach, Sales Representative, Network General Corp.

Carol Weingrod, M.D.

I am also grateful to SST Associates for the use of the *LAN and Enterprise Network Performance Queueing Model* and to the people at Network Performance Institute, Inc. (product successor to SST Company).

*Martin A. W. Nemzow*

# Part 1
## Overview

This section presents an overview of Token-Ring networking. Chapter 1 presents the network in light of its connective power as a strategic resource in today's competitive resource-limited environment and suggests how to make a persuasive argument for network technology. Chapter 2 speculates on the future of Token-Ring as a viable networking protocol for local area networking, distributed processing, and connectivity to enterprise-wide networks. Chapter 3 discusses in overview the benefits of networking and describes what Token-Ring is, how it works, the variations in Token-Ring protocols, and the types of problems that can be encountered in a production environment. Chapter 4 broaches health risks facing network personnel and users.

Chapter

# 1

# Networks for Competitive Strategy

This chapter is intended to provide the sparks for new ideas so that readers can better utilize networking technology. It is also included to address and counter the threats that top management may perceive to be arising from the diffuse, complex, critical, and rapidly expanding technology of communications. In addition, this chapter discusses the new emphasis upon interconnectivity and host mainframe access, workgroup tools, and data sharing issues.

Networking technology includes the simplest local area networks to those enterprise-wide endeavors that span large, multiple-site organizations. Although this book contains specific, hands-on information for managing Token-Ring local area networks, most readers doubtlessly will be deeply immersed within Token-Ring and already understand its potential. This chapter is here when management must be sold a specific course of action, local area network (LAN) investment decisions, or technological change. This chapter is included when technical knowledge is insufficient to make a purely business or strategic decision; it is useful to frame equipment acquisition decisions in other terms when asking top management to sign the big check.

Networks in corporations, government organizations, and not-for-profit associations no longer provide an unassailed advantage over competitors—even if used well. Local area networks (LANs) are necessary in virtually all organizational activities today. The economics of data processing (DP) are such that mainframes perform either specialized functions, process huge volumes of transactions, provide massive data repositories, or are being phased out with "downsized" operations. Terminal service with minicomputers or LANs connecting personal computers (PCs) and workstations provide adequate and cost-efficient technology for all but the most specialized processing requirements. The UNIX minicomputer or engineering workstation supports large databases. LANs support most DP functions.

Today, LANs provide mission-critical processing for daily accounts payable, accounts receivable, sales analysis, brokerage account tracking, and function as windows into distant data sources. When designed and managed properly, LANs are reliable. Uptime without a single hardware, software, or management failure can exceed three months; backup channels, spanning trees, and hot servers can provide 100 percent uptime.

The cost and quality of standardized software for PCs and workstations has dramatically shifted the cost efficiency from singular central processing units (CPUs) to distributed computing environments. The availability of specialized database servers and "superservers" on networks has supplanted much of the traditional mainframe operations. The inherent value provided by the LANs include the distribution of information, selected and controlled access to data, and access to tools usable by people who are less than computer-literate. The computer processing technology is being pushed to the people who thus have the most need for it, but at the same time, this technology is also being given to those with the least computer skill and with the least available time for learning it. In other words, the technology is being simplified and disseminated in that new format. LANs are providing the rudiments to construct the assembly lines for information manufacturing. The air drills and screwdrivers, power presses, rivet guns, and conveyer belts of this century will be paralleled by the spreadsheets, word processing, image preparation, voice generation, and groupware of the next century.

While LANs once may have provided a strategic advantage for an organization, they are a virtual necessity today. Organizations are thus at a strategic *disadvantage* to be without LANs. There is a DP cost disadvantage without LANs. There is a tool quality disadvantage without LANs. There is a steeper user training cost and less access to planning, tracking, and processing tools without LANs. Nonetheless, there are still some strategic advantages available through LANs when combined with local area networks (WANs) and telecommunications. These new advantages relate to cost-cutting, labor reduction, consolidation of services, and improved operating efficiency. Specifically, downsizing DP operations and distributing resources is cost-efficient. Labor costs are reduced when paper files are optically scanned, centrally stored, always locatable for review or photocopies, and quickly available throughout an organization via LAN and WAN. Facsimile (FAX), voice, data, and video can be converted to analog signals for transmission on X.25, T-1, fractional T-1, or can even be packetized for delivery by frame relay and regional optically-based data services. Transmission can be prioritized and queued subject to available bandwidth for service cost reductions.

The complex business environment is challenging organizations to discover new ways to retain any competitive advantage. In addition to traditional physical and monetary assets such as equipment, buildings, and cash reserves, an organization has information and particularly networking data communications assets. Information management is better understood by most private-sector business administrators through the context of the value chain, market dynamics, distribution channel, and price points than it is through the context of computer technology, networking, management of information systems, or data processing. However, those represent information with a time value; those who can sift through them and craft good decisions survive and thrive. An organization also can leverage the creative uses of information and networking technology for strategic benefit. The aim of networking strategies is to move an organization to its potential while locking out its competitors and providing a sustainable competitive advantage which those competitors will find difficult to copy.

There is a continuum of complexity with computer and communications technology. For a small company, networking just the inventory system might be considered a strategic necessity, while a larger company might implement a network to serve all workers at all locations for electronic mail, software disk storage consolidation, optical storage and retrieval, and shared access to corporate databases. Some might even include customers and suppliers. There is a learning curve attached to information and communications technologies. Even while the key to success is to learn faster and implement sooner than the competition, the networking trend is continuing. Each success raises the ante; more complex and intuitive applications of networking are required to sustain a competitive parity. The ante today is any network.

This proliferating new communications technology has redefined the marketplace because it has altered the competitive game for all organizations. Communications have become integral to most computer and business activities. Some organizations will fail to recognize the available opportunities, and others will fail to recognize how to adapt them to the new possibilities in their strategic planning. Technological changes improve the efficiency and enhance implementation of communication. Networking, in particular, is a sophisticated and deliberate strategy that can lower data processing costs, improve profits, productivity, market share, product distribution, and work environments by facilitating quick decisions, improving information flow and accuracy, and communicating such information and decisions rapidly to those who would benefit from them.

Specifically, networking provides an economy-of-scale through downsizing and distributing complex mainframe data processing operations to smaller, less expensive, and more responsive personal computers interconnected by means of an enterprise-wide network. Networking also provides communal access to information and other networked resources. Additionally, networking provides a new shared access to previously unavailable corporate data in (database) views for many users. Furthermore, the technology vanguard shifts from powerful Unix workstations to common personal computers. The sophistication and ease-of-use of generic software means that specialized data applications are available in days rather than months or years.

If information and networking technology appear to be strategic solutions, this technology must be applied with foresight, forethought, and a critical understanding of the market. Clearly, the risk is not only to those who try new technology with its potential for clumsy and inefficient results; too many organizations have learned the painful consequences of limiting the reach and coverage of information exchange. The risk is also to those who watch and wait while others succeed first.

With the accelerating pace of change, the complexity of technology, and the increasing sophistication of those applying networking technology, there is little ascertainable difference between strategic initiative and a "hare-brained" idea; for a strategy to be effective it must be implemented correctly before the competition understands what that strategy is. Of necessity, effective strategies must precede the complete understanding of the applicable technology.

## Advantages of Networks

Networks yield significant advantages that can overwhelm a non-networking competitor. Networking power can provide better service with fewer resources. Specifically, downsizing from mainframe technology to distributed personal computers (PCs) is very cost-effective for many common organizational functions like bookkeeping, billing, and payroll. Networking can also provide a medium in a research and development environment for cross-fertilization of ideas. This concept is presented in more detail in Chapter 11.

Networking can streamline processes that are inherently slow or inherently fragile, and automate these processes for higher integrity. While the financial planner is often severely challenged to quantify these benefits in terms acceptable to stockholders, trustees, and bankers, it has been proven that networks do generate cost-effective benefits, create significant economies of scale, boost worker productivity, and create unanticipated and imaginative results. Examples are presented later in this chapter. Networks thus offer an applicable competitive strategy. Furthermore, as a business reaches beyond borders of states, countries, or continents, network communication is a critical component to success. The competitive parities created through networking and replacing mainframes are summarized in Figure 1.1.

It has been known for years that data processing is a viable competitive tool. Such systems have generated information that managers have applied to pare costs, simplify product design, identify excessive or expensive procedures, locate cost variances, reduce inventory, target

- Higher worker productivity
- Integration of process and information
- Lower installation cost per device or user
- Sharing of expensive resources
- Consolidation of scarce resources
- Creation of critical channels for communications
- Increases in the speed of contact and transactions
- Global access to information
- Higher resource utilization
- R&D discovery
- Interaction between information workers
- Lower communication costs
- Globalization
- Acquisition integration and standardization
- Concurrent activities

**Figure 1.1** Networks provide competitive parities.

customer preferences, and provide strategic product information required to capture a market segment. Data processing is most useful in capturing cost, inventory, pricing, and production information.

More sophisticated uses of computer networking power have been integrated directly into marketed products and services, and these products and services sell better because of that informational content. While computer-related products—hardware, software, information, published works, or research & development (R&D)—are often presented as products and services that strategically benefit from computer networking, many "unlikely" products and services benefit as well by providing wider information exchange and faster response, and by opening new areas and new sources. Examples that this book highlights include airline flights, hospital supplies, air conditioners, and cosmetics.

## Networks Reduce Costs

The desktop metaphor has blossomed with the advent of MS Windows 3.0. Two major new categories of products, network fax and optical storage and retrieval (sometimes called *automated image management*), show great potential for many organizations. Network fax simplifies fascimile delivery by eliminating the printing and manual fax cycle. Network fax provides literally the ability to "print to a fax number" from a computer. Additionally, incoming fascimiles can be routed to individuals, thus minimizing security leaks and lost faxes, while providing online copies, an automated storage facility, and optical character recognition capabilities, while eliminating curling, yellowing, and fading thermal output. Optical storage provides the ability to scan documents and store them on magnetic disks or optical drives. The LAN provides the means for a user to retrieve individual pages or entire documents. Once a document is scanned and filed, it is rarely lost. Users can review multiple copies simultaneously; whereas folders are often misplaced or lost. Copies are easily printed or faxed. When documents (scanned or received as fascimiles) include important text, this text is optically scanned for character content. The text can be imported into WordPerfect, WordStar, MS Windows, or any word processor or database.

DST of St. Louis created Optifile for in-house use to minimize the paper costs associated with handling mutual fund transactions. PS-2s running the OS/2 operating system, the native OS/2 SQL database, and presentation manager access clustered IBM AS/400 systems running the DB2 database. The client network operating system is LAN Manager and the OS/2 LAN. Each page image is stored as a single binary data record compressed to a 20:1 ratio. The image is decompressed at the client station to minimize network traffic. Access from the client PCs to the host AS/400 is via IBM Token-Ring at 16 Mbits/s, or via dial-up WAN from remote offices.

The choice for Token-Ring was predicated by the choice of the host IBM database and image servers, by the native networking support in OS/2, and because of the limited choices for microchannel adapter (MCA) network interface cards (NICs) and AS/400 NICs at the time this project was initiated. Furthermore, IBM provided a single focus for the hardware, software, network interconnection, maintenance, and technical support. Since the organization had a great deal invested in the vendor relationship and existing equipment, they felt that this choice was the safest. This is also a common direction for large corporations; the cost advantages for less expensive networking protocols and vendors are often perceived as insignificant in light of the risk involved in the transition to client-server-based online transaction processing.

Mutual fund transactions are paper intensive, particularly when there are nearly twenty million customers. Furthermore, the SEC requires that all share purchases, conversions, custody transferships (401K and IRA), and redemptions be retained for seven years. Since customer paper files are easily misfiled, lost, and often retained offsite in bulk warehouse facilities and not quickly accessible, optical storage and retrieval is extraordinarily cost-effective. Although retrieval may be slow—about twenty seconds initially for the first page, ten seconds thereafter, the ability to locate a person by cross-referenced name, address, telephone number, social security number, fund name, or employer is a boon. Locating a physical file requires a platoon of file clerks. Furthermore, with optical storage, customer records are accessible not only from the processing site, but also almost instantly at any regional sales office via WAN. Data sharing and interconnectivity simplifies the supplanted manual procedure of photocopying source documents from microfiche and sending the paper by fax or express delivery.

Daily operations and labor requirements are simplified. Microfiche document copying for offsite backup is no longer needed. Manual folder creation and filing is no longer necessary. Documents are fed into a sheet feeder and coded by an operator as each document is scanned. Three people now perform the job of sixty. The benefits do not end there. Auditing is simplified since any transaction is directly supported by available evidence and documentation. Optical storage devices—not to be confused with optical storage and retrieval—provide a write-once permanent laser-burned record that meets SEC qualifications for security and permanence.

## Networks Create Monopolies

TWA built the APOLLO flight reservation system, while American Airlines constructed the SABRE network. These two reservation systems were integrated into the travel agent's selling cycle. They surpassed expectations because they offered precise and readily available information about flight times, seating availability on a selected flight, and connecting links. Once these flight reservations had widely replaced the mediocre travel agent, reinforced the knowledgeable agent, and circumvented other information channels, these systems monopolized the purchasing decisions by preventing travelers from seeing alternatives to TWA and American flights.

Cost information was filtered at the time of the presentation to the benefit of the airlines and detriment of the traveler. The reservation system bypassed alternative purchasing processes by providing time-critical information otherwise unavailable to the true decision maker, the agent, not the traveler. Figure 1.2 contrasts the functional simplicity of the flight reservation system with more complicated preprinted information schedules.

Competitors have not been idle in the ten years of SABRE operation. Two examples are presented here. Certified Vacations, which assembles packaged tours from unfilled transportation seats, vacant accommodations, and empty cruise cabins, also seeks to improve upon its data processing capabilities. Just as DST shifted to client-server processing, Certified Vacations, is installing PCs to access new host-based database servers and provide simultaneous online information for many different categories of services (that is, airline flights, cruise cabins, hotel rooms, tours, and local services). The impetus is not to reduce costs. Rather, there is a lack of parts for aging traditional (or *legacy*) mainframes. Furthermore, these systems can not provide the desired graphic user interface, the application development tool kits, the simultaneous access and automated updates of information desired. The impetus is to

| **Preprinted Flight Schedules** | **Online Reservation System** |
|---|---|
| Determine source and destination | |
| Locate flight option | Query terminal for |
| Direct flights | Flight times |
| Indirect flights | Seating |
| Connection flights | Lowest fair and/or most commission |
| Competitors' connecting flights | Flight plan |
| Repeat for each airline | |
| Confirm with airline | |
| Determine seating availability | |
| Determine pricing (many options) | |
| Check alternatives | |
| Select option | Select option |
| Confirm with airline | Confirm with airline |

**Figure 1.2** Flight reservation purchasing process.

provide more and better information to the telemarketing sales representatives in order to either provide a less expensive vacation package, *upsell* the customer and provide a more luxurious vacation, or capture last-minute vacancies and opportunities otherwise lost with adequate information systems.

Similarly, a cruise company called Carnival Cruise Line is seeking to bypass this network for its niche market. The cruise line company is building its own system to track customers and provide point-to-point plane reservations, hotel accommodations, and the actual cruise itself. The company seeks to optimize its revenue, share of the market, and control over the quality of its packaged vacations. Both organizations are enduring the transition from traditional IDMS, CICS, and COBOL host applications to graphically-based OS/2 PM and MS Windows environments with Token-Ring networks.

It is important to realize that the benefits offered by networking technology should not be viewed merely in terms of how much it will benefit the organization to the detriment of the competition. In as much as it is necessary today to truly be competitive and figuratively wage a business war against the competition, it is also important to realize that technology exposes opportunities which can bring about enormous benefits for the consumers as well.

Consider how better information provided faster and in a more coherent format can yield a far superior vacation deal at a reduced cost. In effect, Certified Vacations is creating an arbitrage position whereby it finds services that otherwise have no value to their providers, and it finds the consumers who view them as an outstanding opportunity. Note that Certified Vacations creates this new value without incurring any holding or brokerage costs, or maintaining a position in actually making a commitment on services until such time as it receives payment for those services. It manufactures nothing, provides no actual performance with regard to the vacation or travel services, and it is not really responsible for providing actual travel services. The only costs which it incurs are its information gathering and processing operations. As such, this organization demonstrates how information has become a precious commodity and the recombination of information yields sustainable business opportunities.

## Networks Focus Distribution Channels

Hospital Supply Corporation of America (HSC) supplied hospitals with free video display terminals and dial-up WAN connections to its headquarters. Not only were the connections mechanical, but also administrative. This computer link-up provided hospitals with information on both hospital and HSC inventory levels, product prices, alternative products, and an instantaneous ordering process with known delivery times. Hospitals were able to reduce in-house inventory, pare costs, and uniformly locate better products at better prices.

HSC planned its own inventory levels with more efficiency and analyzed what hospitals needed and when, thus offering automatic deliveries of basic commodities. Competitors of HSC who tried to install terminals for their inventory lines found desktop space lacking, users unwilling to learn a new computer ordering system, and hospital administrations unwilling to cover training costs for small improvements offered by HSC competitors. Once the ordering system was installed and proven successful, competitors lacked a sufficient infrastructure to compete.

When these systems were integrated into the daily workings of the hospitals and buying economies were passed along to them, then HSC raised prices and substituted higher priced products for commodity items. This yielded a stunning price advantage for HSC, an advantage that is both legal and sustainable. The influence of the computer purchasing systems in the buying process is presented in Figure 1.3.

In similar ways, organizations can link vendors, suppliers, and even customers into communications networks. Information Data Exchange (IDE) is inevitably replacing paper transactions. High delivery costs, the increasing expense of forms and subsequent paper handling and storage costs, and the errors introduced through transcription of customer purchase order numbers and ordering information only encourages more organizations to consider more efficient alternatives. This represents the installation of online network systems such as HSC's, or direct transfer of electronic data in compatible and standardized formats. The vital need for interchangeable formats initiated the concept of IDE.

- Automate inventory
- Determine product shortages
- Locate new and/or improved products
- Search for lowest price
- Locate sufficient quantity to complete order
- Order
- Backorder
- Expedite emergency shipments
- Arrange delivery
- Bill
- Return

**Figure 1.3** The influence of computerized purchasing.

## Networks Improve Information Flow

Fedders, Incorporated, which supplies environmental cooling and heating systems for large commercial and industrial buildings, gave large customers personal computers with software. Architects and building engineers use this software to configure the cooling and heating needs for a planned building. The building engineer transmits this information to Fedders offices for processing, and naturally, the results specify selected Fedders components. Not only are the architects hard-pressed to gather similar specifications from competitors, but Fedders gains early knowledge of building plans. As a result, Fedders vigorously sells components to the contractors before the competition even knows about the proposed building and promotes architectural specification of Fedders equipment at the design stage.

Competitors of Fedders, like competitors of HSC, find themselves locked out of similar strategies because of the reluctance of architects to learn and simultaneously use a second though necessarily superior computer product. Figure 1.4 positions this critical influence of a computer on the architect's decision-making cycle.

## Networks Add Value to Products

Cosmetic companies are using computers to learn about potential customers from a data entry questionnaire process at department store counters. The questionnaire seeks such information as skin color and tone, skin dryness, skin problems, specific cosmetic color preferences, clothes style preference, and lifestyle. An "expert system," a computer program that simulates the skills of an expert cosmetologist, generates a report containing details about, and categorizing problems facing, the customer. A salesperson can use this focused and highly personalized information to make a good sale and suggest specific products for the customer.

- Accept plan
- Design building per architect's concept
- Configure cooling and heating systems
- Determine equipment components and prices
- Search for lowest price
- Accept configuration and/or redesign
- Verify quantities and performance by vendor
- Select vendor
- Arrange delivery

**Figure 1.4** Computers influence the architectural design cycle.

Often the report contains specific instructions for the customer on product usage. This report sells products more successfully than other methods because the products are bundled into proper combinations and proper quantities. Not incidentally, the sales ticket is often higher. After a successful sale, customer data are sent to headquarters, and customers are contacted periodically by phone or mail, or in person, solicited for reorders, plied with new products that may appeal to them, and tracked for all future purchases. Figure 1.5 demonstrates how an integrated sales system augments the initial buying process, and later the remarketing programs.

## Bulletin Boards Shift Purchasing Decisions

Online bulletin boards like the IBM and Sears joint venture, called Prodigy, or prior bulletin boards, including The Source and CompuServe, are dial-in computer services. This replicates for consumers what HSC did for hospitals. These bulletin boards services (BBSs) provide exchange of information

- Determine customer preferences stated subconscious
- Determine customer requirements
- Determine customer criteria for satisfaction
- Determine price ranges for sales ticket
- Determine customer impulse buying habits
- Generate a qualified lead
- Increase average sales ticket
- Information data exchange (IDE) decrease transaction costs
- Customers receive faster response
- Suppliers implement just-in-time (JIT) deliveries
- Inventory storage costs are reduced
- Inventory obsolescence and wastage is minimized

**Figure 1.5** Integrated computer systems improve sales procedures.

in specialized forums, games, current news and weather, and consumer buying services. While the concept of the community bulletin board is alive and well primarily in order to list used and unneeded items for sale, it also advertises services, airline tickets, catalog sales, cars, and even homes.

These listings supplement the usual channels for goods and services advertising. TV, newspapers, magazines, and radio advertising encroaches on everyday life. This online service presents the image that the consumer can pick and choose what advertising to see; it is not an unwanted bombardment. This advertising medium is perhaps more insidious than that. Just as the Home Shopping Club suggests to TV viewers that an item is unique, limited in quantity, or at a bargain price, and also make it very easy to make a purchase painlessly by credit card, these online services simplify the process and monopolize the consumer's time. The online service maintains up-to-date credit card information; press a few keys and a purchase is made. Delivery is by U.S. Postal Service, United Parcel Service, or over-night Federal Express.

The time online must displace something else. This includes TV time, listening to the radio, or reading periodicals. The user is shifting where advertising is gathered and analyzed. The potential for locating the lowest prices should be available on these huge consumer product databases. Instead, the strategic advantage for the merchandisers is higher or parity pricing. The merchandisers take from local retailers. This is a very significant advantage.

Figure 1.6 lists the business advantages of online marketing as provided through wide area networks. Because these services are on computers, advertising viewing preferences and actual purchase information can be explicitly tracked. While it is not clear to date whether these online services sell credit card sales information, they have yet to intelligently target online consumers with personalized sales pitches. Just as HSC could establish automatic deliveries and promote good deals for their customers, these online services do have the potential to send online electronic mail (or have merchandisers send mail) containing focused sales pitches.

## Information Distribution Supplants Processing

All these computer-aided product sales are billed as "data processing" coups. The technology of the times has extended from corporate support services to front-line product enhancement. Additionally, process information converts the product marketing cycle into a value added at the time of sale. While, in fact, these computer information systems do apply data processing operations, a key component of their success is dependency upon data transmission networks.

The flight reservation systems coordinate global information over wide area telecommunication networks. The flight operations network lowers

- Online advertisement displaces other media
- Pricing need not be competitive
- Novelty increases sales
- Purchase and delivery is convenient
- Potential to track individual consumer preferences
- Potential ability for targeted marketing
- Online sales displaces local or other catalog sales

**Figure 1.6** The benefits of online marketing.

operating costs and provides significant economic return with local networks and enterprise-wide access. The hospital supply ordering system relies upon leased lines to connect hospitals with corporate computers. Both the air conditioning and cosmetic supplier initially used mail delivery of superior customer-supplied information to corporate headquarters for analysis and eventual targeted marketing. The air conditioning and cosmetic suppliers have since integrated on-site data collection with corporate in-house data processing. The online merchandising systems use technology to simplify the purchase and delivery of a product and have extraordinary potential for targeted marketing. In all phases of these processes, a network provides data transmission.

The information that made these results feasible was always available but difficult to accumulate in accurate or useful formats. Data processing made data collection possible, and networks made the information readily and easily available; this becomes the strategic necessity. Information that is readily gathered within a focused and familiar content with a clearly identified benefit to the end users (consumers) is apt to be more accurate than any information gathered from shopping mall or telephone surveys. Data can be delivered, without filtering, directly to the people who process such information and distributed to those who implement products or services.

## Networks Are Fundamental to Wall Street

Financiers value information highly. Stock prices represent a forecast view of the future; they are information. Therefore, effectively, financiers buy and sell information. Not only does information have extraordinary value in terms of identifying takeover targets and estimating the purchase price range for an entire company, or a portion of its capital stock; information has become an important commodity in its own right. As a consequence, financiers are becoming more familiar with the data processing methodology and networking since better information is their strategic necessity.

Information processing and distribution systems provide the data with which the Wall Street brokers and bankers price stocks, anticipate the financial health of a company, and assign value to a company for the purpose of making loans. As price-arbitrage becomes a more readily accepted method for outperforming the market, brokers and bankers want faster systems, more data, and better integration of the information processing and distribution channels. They need networks to survive.

As an example, the New York Stock Exchange (NYSE) processes during peak days over 300 million shares representing 500,000 individual transactions. The buying and selling of stock takes place at kiosks within the pit area of the exchange. Increasingly, exchanges are made in block transactions. These transactions are negotiated between buyer and seller in other buildings, in other cities, and need to be "posted" on the NYSE to provide the transaction price data for other buyers and sellers. A device called the *Universal Floor Device Controller* (UFDC) routes the data all over the the stock exchange floor, and exports it to ticker-tape machines and information brokers. The UFDC is a network of data entry points, displays, and printers that provides sales confirmations—it automates the outdated brokerage system first introduced in the cattle mercantile exchanges of Chicago in the 1880s. See Figure 1.7.

On October 19, 1987, when the market fell 508 points, the transaction volume exceeded the planned peak by 250 million shares. Some of the panic that day, and on subsequent days, can be directly attributed to delays in the processing and distribution of information. Because there were delays in communicating verbal information in the usual way, by telephone, brokerage firms found it difficult to predict stock prices and execute orders. Because trades failed to occur as rapidly as expected the price information was delayed.

Because trade confirmations were delayed or lost as the price dropped, brokers and consumers feared further price decreases and tried to sell more stock. This cycle deepened the panic; it was alleviated when the NYSE management halted trading early each day for 2 weeks to unbur-

- List buy and sell orders
- Announce transaction prices
- Print transaction confirmations
- Calculate transaction volumes
- Announce bid and ask prices
- Segregate odd lots
- Transmit confirmations to brokerage houses
- Transmit all information to distribution channels
- Disseminate corporate news and rumors

**Figure 1.7** The functions of the Wall Street networks.

den the data processing facilities before the system could become undermined beyond repair. The stock transaction network was saturated with trades, and the solution was to reduce transmission volume and off-load the transactions to hours when the exchange was closed.

Various commissions have since determined that computer trading and its associated networks were a fundamental cause in the market panic; Wall Street now accepts the fundamental importance of data processing and these data transaction networks which bind together the financial fabric. Telephone networks cannot handle the information efficiently or accurately, and confirmation on paper has become a bottleneck as well; computer trading, trade processing, and distribution of transaction prices is now critically dependent on data networks. Not only was the telephone as a transaction medium effectively made obsolete in October 1987; the importance of the computer network was firmly and irrevocably established as the telephone's successor.

It is also worthwhile to note that the speed and complexity of financial transactions allowed many corrupt brokerage houses and workers to reap enormous gains by parking stock in computerized accounts. Others took advantage of trade delays and inside information masked in layers of computer systems, computerized paper trails, minor technical opportunities, and glitches in the flow of networked information to cheat. Although networks provide significant opportunity for legitimate economic gains, the leading edge of any technology also provides the knowledgeable insiders with an illegitimate opportunity for fraud.

The dark side of networking technology exists, too. Private or privileged information is more widely available and dispersed. Although security has always been a concern in the data processing (DP) community, downsizing DP operations, distributed processing with client-server networks, enterprise-wide networks, and global networks remove the limiting walls of physical security. Networks remove boundaries. While this is of extraordinary significance because it creates economic benefits, it also constitutes a new risk.

Another sign that the financial community is aware of the value of networks is illustrated by an example of a recent takeover. Scandia Airlines (SAS) decided to acquire British Caledonia (BC). The usual first step in a takeover attempt is for the acquiring company to purchase a large block of stock in the target company. This stock represents the power to change the board of directors and make new policy for the target company. In this example, SAS orchestrated a preemptive strike and hired many key British Caledonia DP managers and computer programmers prior to purchasing any of BC's stock.

Perhaps, even more interesting, as the financial service sector consolidation continues, many DP operations are no longer necessary. The acquired "lights out" shops with their virtually unlit and automated computer rooms are closed, their workload acquired and processed by the new parent company. Mainframes are disappearing, downsized and replaced by LANs and wide area linkages. Any local networks can be folded into the new corporate structure. While it is perceived that the cost advantage is with the LANs, the real benefit is the reduced application development time and improved tools for LAN-based client-server sites.

As the APOLLO and SABRE networks demonstrate, information and networking are the key control, management, and marketing tools in today's information-based economy. SAS manipulated the outcome of this takeover because BC was stripped of vital value; other companies which had sought to acquire BC clearly saw that BC was severely weakened by the loss of the DP department. In some ways, this maneuver was the ultimate "poison pill," although perpetrated by the aggressor in this case. Future takeover targets might consider the desire of selling a DP department to thwart acquisition.

Ultimately, whether these aggressive tactics are legal and acceptable will be determined by judges and legislators. In the interim, other corporate acquisitions will start with a purchase of corporate information, and the acquisition of the information department and the networks that distribute corporate information.

## Strategic Necessity of Networks

Token-Ring is strategically necessary. There are economic advantages to Token-Ring, as well as process and informational improvements. More difficult to justify as advantages are interconnection, intercommunication, and project-worker interrelationship. Figure 1.8 outlines these six "I"s.

The economic arguments are straightforward. Token-Ring is a low cost installation, less expensive than a PBX system utilizing switching networks and modems, that encourages sharing of expensive resources and constructs a critical communications channel. Furthermore, data storage and printing services can be consolidated; data storage is usually cheaper in bulk units, and printing services are usually sporadic so that one printing unit can usually provide adequate service for many users. Peripheral devices, specialized processors, and other services can

- Integration of process
- Information
- Interconnection
- Intercommunication
- Interrelationship
- Influence (in the organization through access to data)

**Figure 1.8** The strategic advantages of Token-Ring.

be shared enterprise-wide with ease of access to yield higher utilization rates and similar shared economies.

Networking provides a recognized cost minimization integrating disparate steps into a continuous cycle. This process improvement is often observed in automated production and manufacturing environments. It is also an advantage where information is gathered, processed, stored, and sold. Networks integrate software design processes, accounts processing, and computer-aided design (CAD) into computer-aided manufacturing (CAM). Electronic and desktop computer-aided publishing (CAP) gathers text and graphic components together in a single place—the computer—and integrates an awkward, time-consuming, and time-constrained process into a streamlined cycle.

A strategic network advantage includes the networked access to optical storage and retrieval systems that lessen the storage cost and access times while providing more effective use of the information. Memory-intensive multimedia, which is the inclusion of sound and video information within an application, sees improved performance and utility when it is networked. This streamlining of design, accounting, production, manufacturing, quality assurance, and ultimately the marketing process amplifies labor to increase worker productivity. Figure 1.9 shows production cycle steps, typically time-consuming, that are streamlined by Token-Ring networking.

- Plan
- Determine data collection requirements
- Collect data
- Filter and correct data
- Process data
- Generate reports
- Analyze
- Make decisions
- Produce results, develop Information products
- Assure quality
- Market
- Sell
- Package and direct for shipment
- Deliver
- Bill
- Analyze the financial results

**Figure 1.9** The steps streamlined by Token-Ring network integration.

## Shared Network Resources

Shared resources is a catch-all phrase that means everybody accesses all the equipment, a concept usually perceived from the resource-rich viewpoint. However, the reverse is also true. A resource not purchased because it is too expensive, too specialized, or marginally utilized by a single person or group may be highly desirable when viewed as a global network resource. A marginal resource on a network can be used to capacity, rather than remaining idle and wasted. Processes and methods not otherwise attempted can be tried and perfected because these resources are accessible.

Shared information has value in three ways. The first of these is that information otherwise duplicated is consolidated for data collection, storage, and processing. Data are inherently inaccurate, but single sources of information tend to be more accurate than succeeding information. As data are duplicated, so are their inherent errors multiplied by the number of copies distributed and modified by the processing operations as errors that become second, third, or more generations removed from the original errors. EDI minimizes distribution errors. The second value of shared information is that information otherwise difficult to gather becomes readily available for planning, processing, analyzing, and decision-making. It might not otherwise be generated, but because it is available, it can be applied. Two people sharing information may uncover novel possibilities when they chance to meet and discuss their different views of the shared data. The value of users all sharing the same version (and release) of a spreadsheet program is that the information retains a shared and accessible format. The third of the ways that shared information is strategically important concerns its value in innovation, accidental discovery, and incidental research and development.

## Business Arguments for a LAN

Data communications is an organizational Tower of Babel. The challenge, as senior-level personnel perceive it, is to regain control of data processing, desktop computing, and networking without exceeding already tight budgets. The goals of the network manager and the administration team are to maintain the network, resolve any complaints from the user community, keep pace with the ever-changing technology, and enjoy their work. Since senior management increasingly questions the productivity gains from information technology, a convincing case is necessary.

Local area networks can create order from chaos, as Figure 1.10 shows. LANs clearly interconnect a diverse array of machines, including personal computers, terminals, mainframes and minicomputers, CAD/CAM and CAP equipment, and specialized peripheral devices. A local area network coalesces the information and processing systems into a coherent environment with minimum duplication of resources;

- Interconnection
- Integration
- Automation
- Control
- Economy
- Utility
- Stability
- Strategic value
- Supplemental values (voice and video channels)
- Resource sharing
- Flexibility
- More efficient communications
- Shared access to information

**Figure 1.10** The business case for networking as provided by Token-Ring.

therefore, networks enable better management of resources. Additionally, a network streamlines connections, thus making separate or duplicate wiring systems unnecessary; creates new electronic mail pathways for interpersonal communication that are faster, efficient, and egalitarian; and also readily constructs an infrastructure for process integration.

A network aids in process control, resource allocation decisions, daily maintenance and operations, accessibility and monitoring workloads, faster results, and reduction of unwarranted activities. Control is centralized under one network manager or *information officer* in the newest terminology. The simplicity of network wiring saves on personnel moves and new equipment installation. Because many resources can be shared, a network is economical and utilitarian.

When resources are shared, data processing is independent of location, and machines and information become interchangeable for stability; most fault-tolerant systems rely upon networking technology. Any node station could, if necessary, provide access to information anywhere on the network. This flexibility is part of the attraction of networking technology. Valuable information can be duplicated.

These shared benefits and strategic values are nebulous. They are more difficult to quantify with hard financial evidence than they are to qualify with words and examples. Some of these reasons, like data accuracy and integrity, can be economically determined and become the logical arguments for justifying network costs, while an argument for a network based on accidental discovery and possible innovation is often emotional and instinctual. How does one prove that a worthwhile invention, a future finding, some as yet unknown data discovery, will recoup all the network expenses? How does one justify the value of a telephone system and a "network" of industry contacts, or the value of friendships?

Networks can never be fully justified, nor proven to be a complete solution. Incidental benefits may provide adequate reasons for new peripheral devices and networks in a research and development organization, a think tank, or a university setting. However, budgetary constraints create pressure for careful selection of such projects as a network installation. As a consequence, the cross-fertilizing power is an argument stated as an aside, and carefully skirted thereafter. This benefit is too intangible to justify with economic arguments.

Whenever you are considering new network projects, communicate the idea to superiors, subordinates, and peers throughout the organization. This has the benefit of letting others plug into your idea and plan to accommodate it or benefit from it. You find yourself with new allies (or, unfortunately, new enemies). Not only does a network project have an effect on other groups—for example, it could require significant floor space for new file servers—it could also fulfill and solve their needs as well. Networks often provide and promote synergy. Frankly, one network is cheaper than two, and better advanced planning can reduce internetworking costs when that becomes necessary.

## Presenting Networking

The reasons listed in Figure 1.10 are a good starting point for framing a convincing economic argument to top management. The key function of a manager is communications. A network's key function is to promote communications. A presentation coordinating these two—the problem and the solution—is an appropriate strategy to win acceptance of a new (or expanded) network. Networking transforms the way an organization does its job by improving the quality and effectiveness of marginal communications. In those cases where such a proposition may frighten upper-level management, the analysis is best replaced by economic approaches.

For example, suggest that it is better to be the "bankrupter" than the "bankruptee." Successful exploitation requires creative management, thus aggressive leadership from the top of the organization. Therefore, the leaders must accept the plan and promote it. Shift the burden of the decision-making. As stated in later chapters, consensus rather than the lone-wolf attack is a powerful tool for accomplishing goals. A straightforward economic argument is also applicable.

Talk costs, not technology. Technology is often perceived as a solution in search of a problem. Instead, present clearly the financial expenses to be incurred, the initial investment outlay, reliability, service, and cost containment. Demonstrate that networking provides cost-effective efficiency. Present the risks of the operations involved, the risks of failure. Present the vendors, their equipment, why their equipment is the most cost-effective solution. Since Token-Ring is a generic and widely supported networking standard, explain why Token-Ring does not tie the networking technology to a specific vendor, or to a volatile industry. Extrapolate what transformations are required, what impact the network will have on the people of the organization. Talk benefits, not technology. Present the savings to be accrued with the networking technology. Indicate the benefits, whether soft or hard. Explain where the organization will gain short term and long. Make clear the risk of not maintaining competitive information and communication technology, as well as the need for a strong posture in the marketplace. Figure 1.11 contrasts the costs and benefits of installing a new technology.

It is insufficient to tally up the numbers for the business managers who sign the checks. Blue-sky intangibles do not carry much weight when money can be spent on something else. Check signers want sophisticated cost-benefit analyses. Demonstrate the short-term payback. Calculate the net present value of the network over time. Show how downsizing DP operations by replacing the host mainframe and 200 terminals with three file servers, 250 PCs, plus the network interface cards and cables will actually generate money in the present year. Show how the return on the networking project exceeds the organization's cost of capital.

Contrast the costs and the benefits. The standard methodology is to outline a cost-benefit relationship. Quantify both costs and benefits within the same framework, usually economic, and make a direct comparison. Ascribing a monetary value in current dollars (all present and future income and expenses relating to a project, a present value formulation) is also an effective method to justify a network. However, many benefits are financially intangible. Justify one absolute improvement and explain the additional "free" resources acquired as well. This strengthens the argument because the tenuous benefits are not erroneously subjected to the same stringent analysis as that of the basic design solutions.

Management acceptance for a networking project is not complete despite an approved budget and the proper go-ahead. Acceptance is

| Costs | Benefits |
|---|---|
| Financial | Financial |
| Risk of failure | Cost savings |
| Downtime | Flexibility |
| Human disruption | Strategic gains |
| Time | Reliability |
| Change | Efficiency |
| Security | Service |
| | Support |
| | Control |
| | Better communications |

**Figure 1.11** The costs and benefits for Token-Ring networking.

always contingent; it could be revoked at any time and the project canceled. While you might have convinced management that the project is critical to the long-term strategic success of the organization, tenure can be a short-term event. Carte blanche funding does not mean nor imply carte blanche development. Be receptive. Bewildered people may marvel at the idea, agree with the concept, and provide just enough leeway for you to construct an incomplete and nonfunctioning network. Understand that new technology frightens, more so when it appears to be a black art. Recognize that strategic networking projects that are too complex for users to understand and utilize will fail.

Avoid projects that cannot be demonstrated at discrete steps. Implement in small steps. For example, install the LAN for a client-server database and ensure that the database meets users' needs. Install the mail systems. Do not forget to train the users and respond to their complaints. Add more networks. Lastly, interlink the many networks that are required for the enterprise-wide finale. Each step represents a discrete success than can be evaluated for its own merits. Realize that projects must be justified as viable at all times. Progress reports and demonstrations maintain credibility, an important aspect in showing that the networking concept remains sound, viable, desirable, and beneficial.

Most strategic advantages are soft and intangible until someone bushwhacks the way. The path is murky, uneven, dangerous, anxious for those at the cutting edge. This is why there is little ascertainable difference between strategic initiative and a "hare-brained" idea. It has been said that for a strategy to be effective it must be implemented correctly before the competition even begins to understand what that strategy is and how the technology can be applied.

When the path is jungle clear—if the explorers have been successful—the results may already have been achieved, thus frustrating the hopes of those who follow in safety. Innovation is risky, benefits and opportunities shadowy except to the visionary few. The strategic advantages provided by networks inhabit this same jungle world. The dangers are clearly seen, the simple economic benefits are quantifiable and justifiable, whereas the more intangible aims—securing a market niche, accessing critical information before a competitor, automating production processes, simplifying the purchasing process for a customer, and capturing that customer's business—are available only for those willing to risk innovation. The alternative is a weak parity with your competitors. It is a floating crap game with rules tempered by experience, changing costs, performance, and technological breakthroughs. Seize the opportunity on your own terms rather than being driven to it by others' successes and pressures.

Chapter

# 2

# The Future of Token-Ring

This chapter is included here merely to help network administrators, *management of information services* (MIS) directors, and other managers make sound arguments for specifying a particular network architecture, selecting a hardware and software vendor, and choosing Token-Ring. All too often, choices are second-guessed and vociferously questioned after the fact. It is important to know how to justify and quantity LAN benefits and expenses. Olof Soderblom obtained a patent for token ring in 1967. IBM developed the "Zurich Ring" during 1983 and 1984 as an alternative to *Institute of Electrical and Electronic and Engineers* (IEEE) proposal 803.2 (Ethernet) then under initial consideration. Token-Ring networking technology continues to gather momentum for both the initial 4 Mbits/s standard and the more robust 16 Mbits/s enhancement.

Part of the success can be attributed to the strength of IBM marketing. The simplicity derived from standardization and multiple platform and protocol support provided by the IEEE 802.5 Token-Ring architecture has boosted Token-Ring beyond the IBM world. The sheer marketing power of what once was the largest single computer firm provided the Token-Ring inroads into corporate DP operations. This success is in contrast to the lack of vendor conformity within other network protocols, including the early versions of Ethernet or StarLan, ARCNET, MPB, AEGIS, PRONET-10, and other proprietary networks. This success ensues in spite of the multiplicity of *network operating systems* (NOSs) supported by this architecture including IBM Token-Ring, Novell NetWare, OS/2 LAN, LAN Manager, and LAN Server. The utility of Token-Ring partially results from the wide acceptance of IBM PS/2 personal computers, the simple star-based architecture, and the marketing savvy of IBM. Part of the success also can be attributed to the development and economics of twisted-pair and improved transmission speeds, which have extended the lifespan of Token-Ring. Emergence of vendors providing compatible Token-Ring network cards that will work with host-based, proprietary SNA addressing schemes has encouraged MIS directors to commit to this now more accessible technology.

Furthermore, the high costs of choosing the wrong emerging network technology may encourage users of networks to opt for the more conservative path of known and generally accepted technologies. However, demands for higher software performance, enormous distributed data files, channel clogging multimedia sound, images, and video beg for faster protocols, such as Fiber Data Distributive Interchange (FDDI). This technology is already relevant and gathering momentum for use in these premier applications and as a backbone to interconnect distributed buildings and university campuses. The economics will certainly improve. Just as Token-Ring hardware originally cost upward of $5000 and now is available at 20 percent of that cost, $1400 FDDI connections can be expected to show a similar cost curve.

Do not discount the future of Token-Ring and assume that it will merely be bypassed by technological change. Token protocol networks provide inherently consistent response time and reasonable throughput, although with higher overhead than ARCnet or Ethernet. A slower response time (usually measured in ms) is provided in exchange for consistency and predictability of token protocols. Possibilities include an Token-Ring transport mechanism of 100 Mbits/s or more. The Open Systems Interconnection (OSI) communication structure provides the means to alter layers independently of the others. Since Token-Ring is literally a description of physical media interconnections and the data transport mechanism, definitions can be supplemented and extended to encompass a faster transport media. Therefore, it is theoretically possible to retool Token-Ring for a higher bandwidth. It is also likely that Token-Ring processes will soon be separated from the underlying medium much as NetBIOS is a transmission-layer protocol independent from the physical transmission process.

While many forward-thinking product developers and strategic planners might be aghast at this blasphemy, it is also important to realize that applications and user work flow patterns are very difficult to upgrade. Installed bases of software, computer equipment, and dedicated processes provide a conservative drag on the quickening pace of technical development. Retraining and retooling people is more difficult, expensive, and time-consuming than replacing hardware. Furthermore, personal preferences endure as many network managers can attest as they install yet another character-based word processor into *graphical user interfaces* (GUI) such as X Windows and MS Windows.

Yet, this very conservatism is a major reason for the success of Token-Ring and its continued applicability. As many organizations realize the value and necessity for comprehensive data communications, the merit of enterprise-wide networks emerges. Unfortunately, the diversity of installed bases of PCs, workstations, and file servers, as well as mainframes precludes most organizations replacing all existing systems. In fact, that is absurd and unnecessary. Token-Ring and Novell NetWare provide a foundation for routing linkage, because Novell natively supports both protocols. Although Token-Ring protocols do not run on the physical Ethernet *yet*—the other predominant LAN protocol—Novell easily supports client linkages between Token-Ring, ARCnet, FDDI, and Ethernet. That is a sufficient and efficient method to connect disparate computers, operating systems, and network protocols. Furthermore, IBM and other vendors provided tools to interconnect traditional mainframes with PCs for data access and interchange.

The future shows us that the divisions seen in the early data communications protocols is fast disappearing. The differences between transmission media has virtually vanished–most networks now work with unshielded twisted-pair—and the desire to maintain disparate protocols is vanishing. This does not mean that Token-Ring, or any existing protocols, will vanish soon. The entrenched facilities and sunk costs for networks is too large to accept the widespread transition to the newest, fastest protocol.

While most people may view new technology as a threat to an existing one, sometimes, instead, it can amplify the value of older technology. For example, the *MS Windows Resource Kit* and the new network-ready *MS Windows for Workgroups* provides MIS with the necessary tools to create applications for a Token-Ring environment. Although *Dynamic Data Exchange* (DDE) was designed to be an MS Windows tool for linking data within a single PC, various software vendors have created extensions for full network DDE data access and linkage. This includes network data and even data accessible through automated phone connections, remote linked sites, and enterprise-wide networks. *Object Linking* and *Embedding* (OLE) provides a means not merely to link specific data cells but also to include the latest versions of entire documents, graphic images, full-motion video, and sounds. The sudden availability and prominence of interconnectivity, and interoperability, and development of user-level tools only increases the importance of existing networks. Existing Token-Ring networks are unlikely to be replaced very quickly by faster or merely new technology; instead, they will be integrated into organization-wide networks. This data access and linkage process has opened many eyes to utility of PC and MS Windows or X Windows-based GUIs. These tools provide uniform front ends for users to gather, construct, and process networked data. This, too, drives efforts to downsize data processing operations.

Similarly, while Novell predominantly supports *interpacket exchange/sequenced packet exchange* (IPX/SPX) protocols, Novell also created the *Network Device Independent Specification* (NDIS) which allows software vendors to build applications that are virtually independent from the underlying network protocols, including Token-Ring. Corporate end users prefer Token-Ring because of the vendor relationships and the existing MIS infrastructure. Things that work endure longer than shrewdly expected. IBM Token-Ring will not go away any faster than 40 year-old COBOL programming code can vanish. Just as COBOL with GUI tools encourages many to persist with legacy mainframe systems, Token-Ring persists for its installed base, emergence of secondary product vendors, and extended support for 16 Mbits/s transmission speed on unshielded twisted-pair (UTP), burst mode and early token release enhancements.

Furthermore, a major stumbling block to all network technology is the difficulty to manage and control the communication channels and the attached resources. This is particularly the case with some common network protocols that lack some network management control features. Network management is in its infancy and tools exist merely to capture information. Few tools provide assessments or intelligently help analyze this information, and fewer yet can make automated decisions. Despite the codification of *Simple Network Management Protocols* (SNMP) or the long-awaited *Common Management Information Protocol* (CMIP), management remains in its infancy. The nature of compound networks, backbones, interconnectivity, bridging, and routing and the problems of ensuring network reliability and balancing performance without doubt will increase with FDDI. While better throughput may solve some traffic bottlenecks, faster speeds and additional protocols merely increase the complexity of networks and the importance of resolving bottlenecks at network interconnections. The infrastructure must be developed to manage network complexity.

Token-Ring remains in a growth mode because of the new availability of UTP Token-Ring components. Furthermore, the tools, experience, and compatibility issues are expanding. It will not be replaced for years, but will be supplemented when specific situations demand higher transmission speeds. FDDI is positioned as just one supplement. Other supplements are just "vapornets." Do not discount Token-Ring. The installed base ensures its survival for some more years. Also, Token-Ring, per se, has been repackaged to delay its obsolescence. For example, the 16 Mbits/s and "ringing tank" jitter reduction technology improves throughput and signal quality. Networks utilizing available telephone wiring to simplify installation, lower costs, and minimize network management will give a new lease to Token-Ring.

Additionally, the OSI structuring of most high-level protocols allows software developers to rethink, rebuild, and rebundle network services. We might see Token-Ring delivery serviced by faster *TPDDI* (FDDI on twisted-pair) rings. This repackaged Token-Ring technology also provides a good starting point for small network installations that can gradually expand to routed rings connecting concentrations of other installations. Networks were once the domain of software developers, universities, and large corporations. Small businesses now use LANs as an efficient alternative to minicomputer-based applications and for enterprise-wide communication. Token-Ring networks supporting client-server processing also provide an important downsizing opportunity since it is less expensive than mainframe data processing. This is a driving force for effective and interoperable networks, such as TCP/IP and Novell. The range of applicability and accessibility has increased the need for lower-end technology. Furthermore, connectivity is still king; Token-Ring provides a wealth of plug-and-play intercompatibility otherwise unavailable. Its major limitation is the 16-Mbits/s transport speed and effective throughput with 50 nodes per database server. While FDDI promises a faster standard, it provides perhaps only a transitional product because it is limited to 100 Mbits/s. That is not a great difference in the scheme of the computing world and may be insufficient to warrant wholesale replacement of existing networks. Networks providing 1000 Mbits/s, such ATM, will soon be deployed and may find a wider audience cost permitting.

There are FDDI implementations that encapsulate Token-Ring packets for faster delivery. Implementations of routers, packet switches, and gateways in hardware will boost the integration of small networks into enterprise-wide endeavors. Furthermore, high-bandwidth optical links will add credibility to construction of effective enterprise-wide networks, while electronic exchange of data and online storage and retrieval of documents will supplant more paper transactions. Additionally, the requirements of internetworking, distributed databases will change the emphasis from peer-to-peer networking to client-server models.

Although Ethernet, Token-Ring, and FDDI all support peer-to-peer and client-server processing, the winner in any network protocol race will be the one providing the most effective management and control tools. TCP/IP-based Ethernet now has that advantage in terms of cost and management tools. FDDI is as yet an expensive technology becoming fractured into many proponents and variants. Token-Ring is the clear winner in the corporate world where is provides an easier transition from the legacy mainframe into distributed computing. The emergence of the OSI model has helped vendors realize that interconnectivity, interoperability, and network management are crucial to technology sales. As a result, more quality network management tools are available which provide architecture- and protocol-independence and support for large architectures.

Chapter

# 3

# Benefits of Networking

This chapter describes Token-Ring in overview. It defines the concepts of networks and local area networks, then describes the benefits of the networking environment. Common network configurations and transmission protocols are expounded upon and compared to Token-Ring configurations and protocols. The final section of this chapter describes the problems with Token-Ring.

## Definition of a Local Area Network

A *processor* is anything with computing power such as a microcomputer, a mainframe computer, or an intelligent workstation. A *device* is anything that performs processing, input and/or output services, such as a computer, a printer, a terminal, or a plotter.

A *network* exists whenever two or more processors are connected to one another with a cable and with networking software (software that directs the flow of information between processors and that monitors requests for access to devices). A network connects processors that may have been isolated from one another. Each processor or device on a network is called a *node*.

A *local area network* (LAN) transmits large amounts of data at high speeds over limited distances. A local area network generally services a single room, a single floor, a building, or a two-building facility, as shown in Figure 3.1. The LAN is generally limited to a compact geographic area (perhaps a 1500-m circumference).

A mainframe servicing remote terminals provides centralized processing while a LAN is decentralized. On a LAN, the network processing power is distributed among all the processors and peripheral devices. While a mainframe that serves remote terminals may structurally look like a local area network, the LAN differs because each workstation and processor operates independently. Usually, an inexpensive and general-purpose cable provides a trunk cable that forms the network's *ring* or

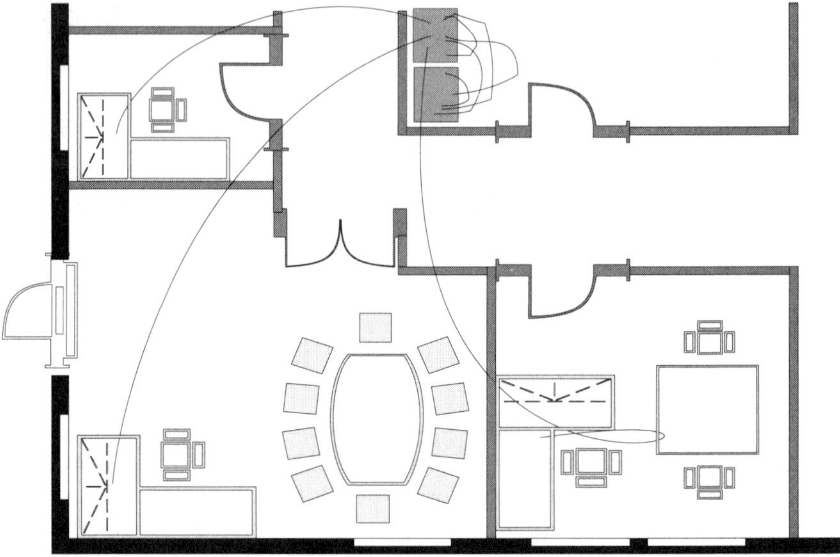

**Figure 3.1** A local area network (LAN) services a "local area."

*backbone*. In fact, the network is only a utility that uses all the devices. See Figure 3.2 for a definition of a LAN.

A LAN is oriented to benefiting a group with a common cause, common equipment, and similar and shared needs. A local area network should interconnect equipment from different manufacturers, as shown in Figure 3.3. This capability is termed *peer-to-peer exchange*.

A LAN interconnects equipment with many specific functions, allowing resources to be shared by all network users as shown in Figure 3.3. Information can be shared across the network and stored on disk. Programs can be stored in a single location and made available to multiple users, thus saving expensive disk space and increasing availability of data and tools.

Peer-to-peer exchange is also used to refer to a network with nodes of equal capacity. *Client-server* exchange refers to the network situation

- Limited geographic area [0.1 to 1 kilometer (km)]
- Moderate to high data rate (0.1 to 100 Mbits/s)
- Inexpensive medium ($0.60 to $10.00 m)
- High interconnectivity and access
- Decentralized control
- Interconnectivity between manufacturers

**Figure 3.2** The definition of a local area network.

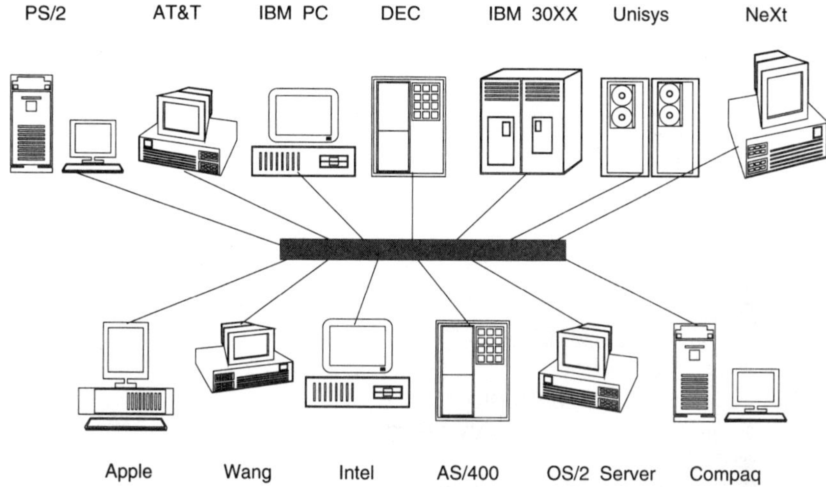


**Figure 3.3** LANs provide peer-to-peer vendor intercompatibility.

where a server computer provides specialized services not available (or configured to be available) on the client computers, as shown by Figure 3.4. *Servers* provide various concentrated functions like printing, file storage, application software storage, database data storage, optical storage and retrieval, network facsimile, electronic mail functions, and gateways to other networks. Figure 3.5 lists typical server functions. Chapter 11 discusses client-server processing in the context of enterprise-wide networks.

An *internetwork* is a network of networks. An internetworks is typically more complex than a single network because it must service numerous topologies, protocols, transmission media, and a larger number of devices and nodes. Internetworks are represented by wide area networks and enterprise-wide networks.

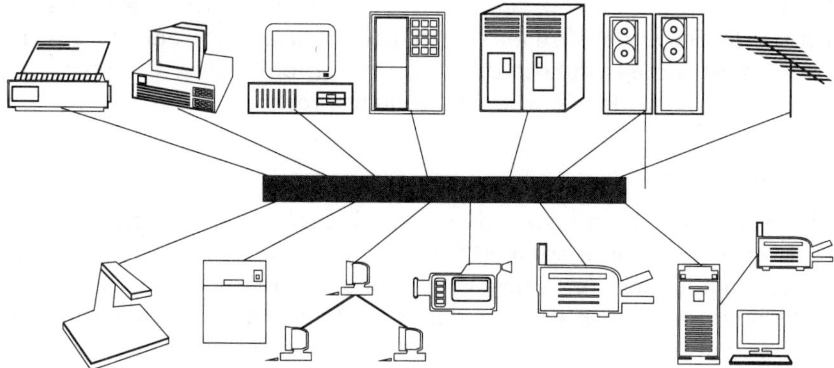

**Figure 3.4** A local area network provides many services.

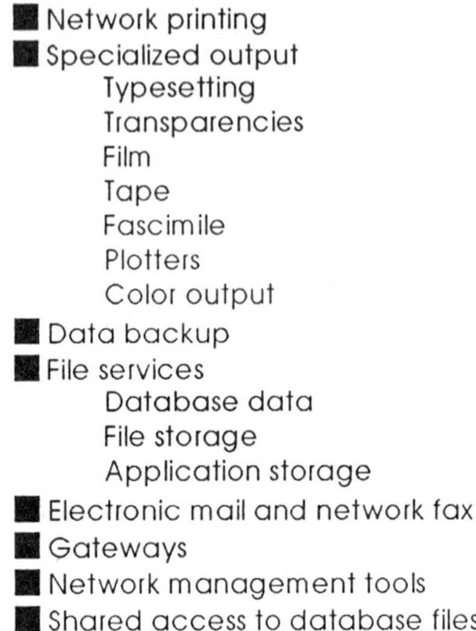


**Figure 3.5** Client-server functions.

A *wide area network* (WAN) represents the interconnection of multiple local area networks. This usually refers to the connection of LANs within different buildings, but it could easily refer to the connection of LANs within the same building. WAN connectivity is often provided by dial-up phone lines (analog signaling), public data networks (digital signaling), private branch exchanges and lease lines (usually digital networks), microwave transmissions, packet switching and routing, optical fiber, and satellite communications. *Metropolitan area networks* (MANs) represent the interconnection of users and LANs within a campus-wide area. Such networks are indeed common for college campuses, universities, large commercial facilities, and government installations. Both of these wider geographically distributed networks fall within the definition of an *enterprise-wide network*. The enterprise-wide network also may connect dispersed geographic sites. Chapter 11 is devoted to the issue of enterprise-wide networks.

## Benefits of Establishing a Network

There are both operational and economic benefits to setting up a network that replaces either distributed processors that can connect only through telecommunications, or a host mainframe. Operational benefits include wider access to devices, more productive software, greater access to shared information, and reduced transmission errors. Economic benefits include few equipment purchases, more equipment available to each user, decreased warranty costs, and lower cost per device. See Figure 3.6.

- Wider access to devices
- Greater independence
- Faster access to devices
- Shared information
- Reduced transmission errors
- Specialized communications
- Fewer purchases
- Extra processing power

**Figure 3.6** A local area network provides many services.

## Operational Benefits

A network provides wider access to peripheral devices because all devices become available to all processors on the network. On a network, a user whose workstation is running off processor A can use a printer on processor B. Printers, plotters, typesetters, CAD/CAM workstations, facsimiles, scanners, video entry systems, and specialized disk and tape storage devices can be shared.

Network access can facilitate remote usage of a peripheral device otherwise accessible only through data transfer by magnetic medium, a slow and irksome process. A network therefore provides faster access to devices.

With a network, distributed processing permits stand-alone microcomputer workstations to function undisturbed by such things as remote failures, peak loads, and limited resources; the processors are not dependent on the availability of one mainframe. Note, however, that clients of a client-server processor are completely dependent upon that server. The distribution of workload requires at least the same aggregate central resources as any mainframe environment, but with networking the processing occurs at greater speeds, with more flexibility and greater independence. The distribution of peripheral loads also frees the central mainframe for more important jobs.

Many distributed processing sites that are not on a network experience problems in providing data file backup, in sharing information, or in coprocessing. Tasks that were formerly isolated on individual processors can be consolidated to improve operational efficiency. For example, computer-aided design, publishing, and manufacturing processes can reside on one network. Programs can be made available to more users with less disk space across a network, and specialized processors are easily accessible. Networks make possible electronic mail for internal communications. Electronic mail is a "free" network service that provides rapid delivery, high success of delivery, message broadcasting, and automatic reply options. Network facsimile minimizes paper handling, prints incoming faxes to LAN printers, and adds security features.

Telecommunications via *private branch exchange* (PBX) modems is inherently slow and error prone unless expensive error-checking and correcting equipment is used, whereas a network has fewer transmission errors. Telecommunications is also a *simplex* (unidirectional) transmission in that only one workstation can talk at any time to only one other workstation, in one direction. A local area network allows *duplex* (two-way), simultaneous connection to all facilities from all facilities, at transmission speeds thousands of times faster. Networks with optimized architecture provide high data rates on tuned channels that often interconnect supercomputing processors or scientific data acquisition equipment, offering access to specialized communications.

## Economic Benefits

Rather than support each workstation with local data storage and local printing, plotting, typesetting, and tape facilities, a network permits sharing of these resources among multiple processors and users. This is the function and justification for the client-server configuration. Fewer purchases are necessary and there is some consolidation of resources. In a distributed processing environment that does not use networking, growth means that many basic resources like printers, storage media, and modems need to be duplicated whereas networks provide these critical services more economically. Resources that might not be cost-effective to purchase for a single purpose may become attractive when a network makes them available to multiple network users. Often, extra processing power, which is like an empty airplane seat because it has little value, can be accessed across a network and used.

The economics of LANs are similar to those of any mainframe environment. There is a high fixed cost for initial installation but an increasing economy for additional nodes. An example of this economy is presented in Figure 3.7. The shape of the curve emphasizes the decreasing costs for marginal additions. The basic network wiring cost is a fixed asset that must be provided independently of the number of nodes. While the initial network wiring installation costs $10,000 and the first node costs $8000 with printer, modem, and local data storage, the tenth unit costs a marginal $3000 for a total expenditure of $80,000; peripheral devices are shared rather than duplicated for each additional unit and network costs are amortized over a wider base, as the concave graph indicates. The effect is a lower cost per additional workstation and a cost that is less than that of a centralized processing environment such as a host mainframe.

In summary, networking logically divorces the workstation from the file structure, the disk storage, and the CPU. A novel application of this concept is network computing, which means that underutilized CPUs will broadcast their status and provide automatic parallel computer power; this technology is available with specialized Unix workstations.

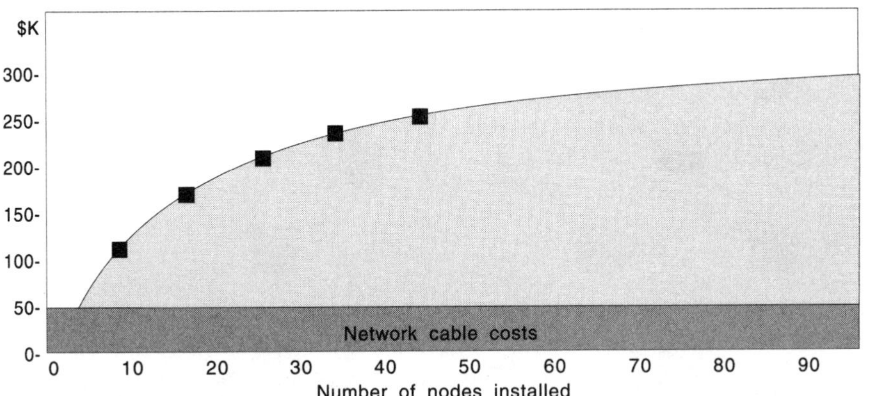


**Figure 3.7** Networks provide economies-of-scale.

Network databases are a specialized application of network computing. The IEEE parallel processing group seeks to define a Network Interface Definition Language (NIDL) to promote parallel processing and logical process partitioning, although the complexity to date defies solution on even single CPU processors.

## Network Topologies

A *topology* describes the geographic relationship of the network nodes. The three most prevalent topologies include the bus, ring, and star configurations. See Figure 3.8 for representations of these architectures.

### Star Topology

The star network is often the choice where many units are dependent upon a single processor, as in a typical mainframe situation where personal computers require frequent access to a mainframe. In this situation all cable connections are separately wired to a centralized patch panel. Although the mainframe environment is not strictly a "network," most mainframe computer wiring is handled in such a manner.

Multiplexing units, hub concentrators, and wiring pairs only reduce wiring requirements without eliminating them, and this topology provides few economies unless it is wired in parallel with a phone system. It is cheap when well-planned, but increasingly expensive for each additional node, particularly for any nodes that exceed planned capacity, as each added unit will require wiring from the node location to the central location. Physical movement of a node can be a very simple process since changes can be performed at a central patch panel. It is, however, a stable design in that any failed node would affect few, if any, other nodes; although centralized failure would affect all nodes.

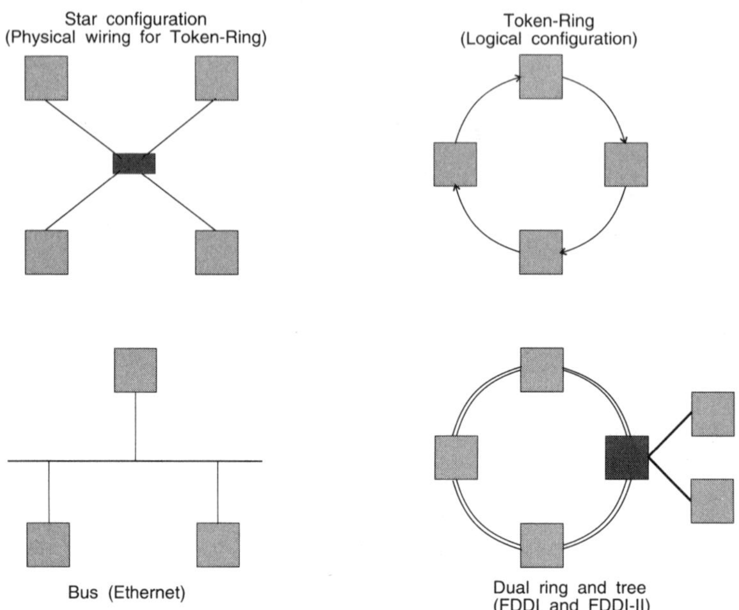


**Figure 3.8** Common local area network topologies.

In fact, the twisted-pair Token-Ring technology uses this topology. The hubs, or concentrators, provide multiple ports that are wired with the standard *voice-grade* telephone cable or special data *data-grade* communications cable. The data-grade wire is preferable. Since this twisted-pair cable is often available and underutilized, twisted-pair Token-Ring seems to be a cost-effective and desirable idea. The downside to using standard voice-grade twisted-pair for Token-Ring is very real and should be considered carefully. New installations might consider installing *category 5* twisted-pair, which is qualified for the emerging 100 Mbits/s FastNet and FDDI on twisted-pair, in order to provide a simpler transition to faster protocols. A secondary benefit of category 5-qualified wire is that is more immune to external noise and crosstalk, and may also minimize the broadcast of undesirable electrical radiation.

Radio-frequency or infrared concentrators eliminate any need for point-to-point wiring. The nodes on the star configuration transmit with radio waves or invisible light through the air without physical cable. There is no need for traditional wiring. This wireless technology is notable where networks need to be quickly installed or frequently moved, and it may actually lower overall installation costs by reducing cabling costs. In fact, unlike with wireless networks, the data communications wiring often gets left behind either as part of a leasehold improvement or because it is too difficult and expensive to recover. Conferences, training sessions, and tradeshows are good examples where this technology is very desirable. Some limitations exist for air transmission. Dirty or smoky environments impair infrared network performance, while the radio-frequency networks transmit within narrow frequencies, thus limiting the available number of nodes. Security concerns with single frequencies are being addressed with spread-spectrum transmission. The health consequences from application of either of these two wireless technologies are unknown; their purported risks remain to date unsubstantiated, as Chapter 4 explains.

### Ring Topology

The ring configuration is designed as just that, a circular architecture with each node directly connected to two other nodes. All network traffic passes through each node in series on the ring until it reaches the intended receiver. This wiring scheme demonstrates few economies over the star design. It is also complicated and requires meticulous care to wire correctly. The ring is easily expanded to insert more nodes, although this process is disruptive since the ring is broken while a new unit is installed.

Also, physical movement of a node requires two separate steps: disconnection to remove a node and again to install the node in its new location. Likewise, should any single node fail, the network fails just as the failure of one decorative tree light causes the whole string to fail. It is a fragile design despite the addition of various automatic mechanisms designed to bypass failed cable sections or nonresponsive nodes. Token-Ring is in fact a ring structure, although it is actually wired in a star for simplicity, as Figure 3.9 illustrates. Furthermore, Token-Ring includes

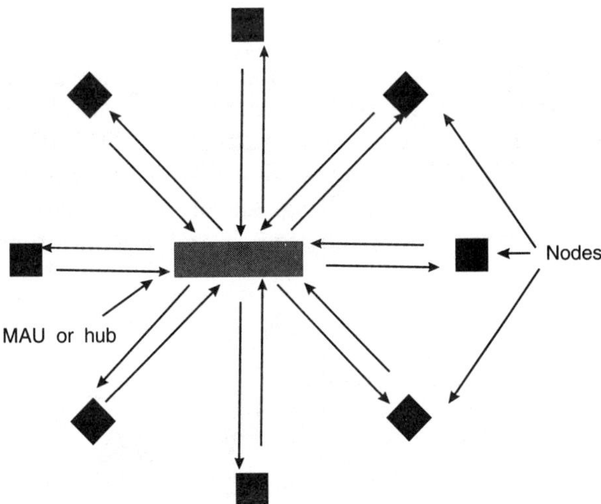


**Figure 3.9** Token-Ring is a logical ring, although wired as a physical star.

*ring wrap* and *lobe isolation* techniques to somewhat minimize the fragility of the ring. Ring wrap occurs when a node fails and the wiring hubs attempt to exclude any device–usually a multiport hub–that provides network attachment to that failing node. Lobe isolation occurs when the hub can exclude just one failing node.

The FDDI optical technology and FDDI on twisted-pair is based upon a dual-ring topology. Two rings with counterrotating transmission channels to some degree overcome the basic limitations of the ring design. When a node fails, as in Token-Ring, it is supposed to remove itself, that is, "self-heal" from the ring until repair. The dual ring becomes a single ring at the failure point. Additionally, physical failures in a segment of fiber are supposed to be removed from service by applying this fail-safe mechanism. FDDI or CDDI is useful for interconnecting individual Token-Rings across a campus.

### Bus Topology

The bus design is an open architecture. All nodes connect in parallel on a single cable section and it is perceived as a simple architecture that is more difficult and expensive than star-wired twisted-pair. It is a common configuration, often used for Ethernet. One or more coupled sections and the nodes on it form a complete stand-alone network segment. One single segment usually forms a backbone and connects to all other segments and individual or multiple Token-Ring rings. While this division of the network into separate segments improves traffic flow and increases reliability, it also allows all nodes to reach all other nodes. A bus technology is useful for providing interconnectivity between many Token-Rings.

## Available Protocols

The last section described physical topologies. Networks also vary by transmission protocol, which is the method used to transmit data. The common networking protocols include RS-232, CSMA (Carrier-Sense Multiple-Access), CSMA/CD (Carrier-Sense Multiple-Access with Collision Detection), token bus, Token-Ring , and optimized token bus. Figure 3.10 shows which protocols can be used on each network topology.

| Configuration | Available Protocols |
|---|---|
| Bus | CSMA, CSMA/CD, token, optimized token |
| Star | CSMA, CSMA/CD, RS-232, polling |
| Ring | CSMA, token, polling, priority enforcement, OSI |

**Figure 3.10** Available network protocols.

Protocols range from simple one-way or two-way transmissions, as on an RS-232 network, to controlled token-passing and polling schemes or statistical broadcasting schemes. Token-Ring is a token passing protocol, and this protocol will be described in explicit detail. Each protocol has certain benefits and efficiencies as well as limitations. Benefits include simplicity, speed, and compatibility. Efficiencies are reflected in computer processor overhead, transmission timing, and loading factors. Limitations lie in the lack of a class of computers to accept that protocol, the relative difficulty of installing or maintaining a specific protocol, relative speed, and relative cost.

RS-232 is generally run on twisted-pair, which is better known as *telephone wire*. RS-232 often can run on existing telephone cabling, and if not, this common wire is simple to install. Modems (sound *mo*dulator/*de*-*mo*dulator) alter digital voltage changes into an analog sound pattern that is transmitted over twisted-pair. RS-232 is often used for mainframe-to-dumb-terminal communications, because such communication is relatively low load and slow speed. Two-way connections are established between a destination and a source, and this link is inflexible during the transmission session. RS-232 is often bundled into a T-1 network framework. T-1 is a dedicated high-speed digital link that connects distant locations. This wide area network (WAN) differs from the LAN because of the lack of distance limitations between nodes. T-1 is served via PBX and common carriers like AT&T. Speeds of communication range from 300 baud up to 120,000 baud. This corresponds to approximately 30 to 600 characters per second. Generally, a limit of 9600 baud is achieved on voice-grade phone lines due to limitations inherent in this technology. New bit compression with error detection and correction technology is bringing higher speeds (14,000 and 24,600 baud) to market, although higher speeds often create disproportionately higher error rates.

*Carrier-sense multiple-access with collision detection* (CSMA/CD) is the protocol for Ethernet and 10Base-T. The conflict from interfering signals is termed a *collision*. *Collision detection* is a euphemistic description of a busy network unable to handle the transmission volume. Collisions occur when two or more units transmit simultaneously, a factor usually indicative of the significant two-way transmission delay over the full network length, or, of channel overloading. This protocol *saturates* when the traffic level becomes too high, thereby preventing any communications whatsoever. Collisions are handled by rebroadcasts. Figure 3.11 outlines how CSMA/CD works.

Token protocols are more orderly than Ethernet CSMA/CD protocols. If the analogy of CSMA/CD is the swinging door, token passing is analogous to a revolving door. Token protocols provide a consistent and controlled network load. No matter the traffic volume on the network, all nodes get equal access to the network. The network will remain functional under the

| **CMSA**/CD | **Characteristics** |
| --- | --- |
| Carrier sense: | Listen before transmitting |
| Multiple access: | Transmit when channel Is free |
| Control process: | Persistent |
| | Signal speed allows collisions |
| | Collision detection and retry transmission |
| | Delays a random length of time |
| | Equal access (no priorities) |
| | Algorithm generates delay |
| Advantages: | Efficient with workload less than 30 percent capacity |
| Disadvantages: | Nondeterministic; jams under heavy loads |

**Figure 3.11** Carrier-sense multiple-access with collision detection protocols (CSMA/CD) as used for Ethernet.

heaviest load. The delays waiting for permission to transmit will increase linearly with loading. Figure 3.12 charts how the token protocol works.

Rather than each transmitter competing for a window in which to broadcast a message, a token is passed from one node to the next. The token conveys the permission to transmit; no workstation can transmit without the token. Figure 3.13 illustrates the token-passing protocol and the mechanics of token permission in operation.

While the token passing scheme in Figure 3.13 seems more orderly, it suffers from certain inefficiencies. For example, the token can get lost and not be regenerated for a time long by communication protocol standards, or duplicate tokens could be mistakenly generated. Token-passing protocols limit the maximum time a workstation can actually hold the token, and this scheme assumes a uniform traffic level and penalizes high-volume users. Unfortunately, too, a workstation with a defective network access interface can hog the signal and "jabber" useless noise. Also, time is lost in the protocol of passing and accepting the token when a workstation may simply pass the token along without a need to communicate. This protocol

| **Token passing** | Characteristics |
| --- | --- |
| Carrier sense: | Ring poll; token acquisition; repeated signal |
| Channel access: | Acquire token for permission to transmit |
| Control process: | Non-persistent |
| | Ring poll |
| | Maximum token hold time |
| | Equal access (no priorities) |
| Advantages: | Does not saturate under ultimate loading |
| Disadvantages | High overhead; transmission slows with load |

**Figure 3.12** Token passing protocols.

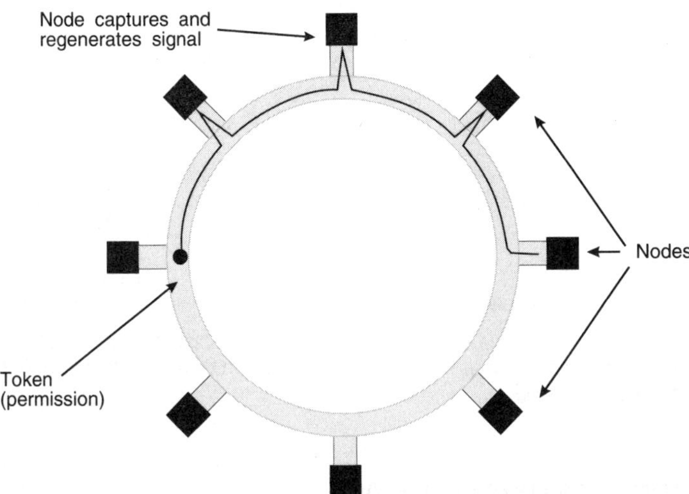


**Figure 3.13** Token grants transmit permission to only one node at a time.

is effective at very high traffic loads since it does not saturate; it is predictable and merely gets slower. All the protocols have best uses. Sometimes the choice is dictated by the higher initial expense of one protocol and the equipment it requires, a protocol's incompatibility with existing equipment, the cost of retrofitting an existing building for one type of network, the recommendations of an equipment vendor, or the availability from a vendor of a specific protocol. Other times, the software, production, and intercompatibility issues dictate the choices. A protocol is usually chosen in conjunction with many competing considerations.

Token-Ring has a higher initial cost than RS-232. However, RS-232 cannot provide adequate file transfers in the necessary time frame, support the overhead for the pixelated screen pagination necessary for most desktop workstations, or service graphic manipulation at transmission rates consistent with current technology. These two, and several other protocols, are compared for speed, cost, and installation flexibility in Figure 3.14.

Token-Ring is often selected because it is flexible, very expandable, and compatible with the equipment of many manufacturers and software vendors. Additionally, the extended topologies of the radio-frequency and twisted-pair star provide flexibility in network design, extension, maintenance, and preferences. Not only are communications possible among different vendors; often different machines can "talk" and share information in a transparent manner. This magic is possible because Token-Ring is an official networking standard and also conforms to the structure of the generic network design specified by the ISO communications model, as described in Chapter 5.

| Protocol | Rate (Mbits/s) | Cost per node in dollars | Flexibility |
|---|---|---|---|
| RS232 | 300 to 120,000 | 200 to 600 | Low |
| X.25 (star) | 300 to 19,200 | 200 to 600 | Low |
| Ethernet (bus) | 10 | 950 | High |
| Ethernet (star) 10BASE-T | 10 | 800 | Medium |
| Token-Ring | 4 to 16 | 800 | Medium |
| FDDI Ring | 100 | 2250 | Low |
| TPDDI (CDDI, SDDI) | 100 | 1250 | Medium |

**Figure 3.14** Comparisons of various protocols in common usage. Note the additional cost per node, not including workstation or amortized network backplane expenses.

## The Problems of Token-Ring

The problems with Token-Ring include the lack of built-in resources for debugging and testing in spite of industry acceptance of network management protocols. These problems encompass the likelihood of electrical failure, the inability to track network traffic and predict overloading problems in advance, and the difficulty in expanding network capacity. The Novell NetWare SNA gateway and similar products are unlikely to work with any network interface card but the IBM 4/16 Token-Ring card; this is not a fault of other vendors, but rather a result of the proprietary implementation of SNA addressing. These are common problems often created in the initial installation or by creeping growth of a network or internetwork. It is prevalent for the far-reaching, strategically implemented enterprise-wide network. Use of the wrong grade of wire and extending lobes beyond qualified lengths will cause constant or intermittent transmission errors. Additionally, installation problems like stray voltage, electrical or communication crosstalk interference, and ever-present static electricity can span network segments, causing unanticipated and unreasonable havoc. Such limitations are resolved and hidden from an organization by good vendor installation teams or good administrative management and a large network budget. Unfortunately, networks do grow, equipment does age and fail, and random events do unfold that can break a network. Repair times range from minutes to months.

Most of these problems plague the inexperienced manager, while the seasoned network manager can forecast with ease the problems that will arise, and will know how to dispatch them quickly. The experienced network manager will have acquired the necessary tools and hired competent people who understand how to operate these special network tools, interpret findings, and apply expedient solutions. The problems of Token-

Ring are not insurmountable with knowledge and experience; a good book guides the inexperienced along the path to learning.

Most mechanical problems, once understood, are quickly recognized by symptoms. Mechanical problems are also categorized by frequency and likelihood of occurring. Since Token-Ring is a ring where each node must repeat every signal, the failure of a single node can defeat the ring.

A partially failed network, single malfunctioning nodes, and long waiting time rates, all, for example, point to high traffic loads, electrical shorts, or breaks. Continuous shutdowns of the network suggest failed transmitting gear or improper component installation. High traffic loads and slow service rates suggest improperly installed wiring, a network overloaded with traffic or nodes, or faulty software. Cabling connections can be checked to solve such problems, and if the problem is an overburdened network, various options exist to first verify this theory and then reduce load or provide alternative communication routes. More rings can be installed to match capacity, or bridges and smart repeaters can isolate and partition large rings into manageable groupings. Software problems are resolved by system restarts, programming repairs, or replacement of corrupted file systems.

The common network problems masquerade as either hardware or software failures. Without guidelines, it is often impossible to distinguish one from another. Network testing and monitoring provide the means to identify the root causes of Token-Ring problems, the understanding of how to isolate or remove the problem, and the experience to repair it. The *Token-Ring Management Guide* addresses these issues and provides a practical approach to Token-Ring network problem-solving.

Chapter

# 4

# Network Health Risks

Computer professionals increasingly express concern about the possible health consequences of networks. Overt and acute dangers include contact with electrical current used to power computer equipment and the risks from climbing ladders to reach lofty ceiling cables. Frequently, computer professionals lift heavy laser printers, servers, or furniture which results in hernias, lower back pain, or pulled muscles. However, there is also a growing concern about the circumstantial but unsubstantiated long-term health consequences from exposure to radio-frequency and magnetic field pollution emanating from computer equipment. This chapter will cover the obvious health issues and discuss the more insidious danger from energy pollution.

## Acute Dangers

The danger of electrocution or a fall from a ladder are the more likely physical dangers facing network support people. In most organizations, people are relocated an average of once every six months. Computer equipment and the associated networking access must be changed to accommodate the dynamics of the organization. This exposes the network team to various acute hazards like exposure to the computer power supplies, electrical connections, and the common ceiling-mounted cabling.

## Electrical Safety

Occasionally in the networking industry someone does get burned or badly shocked. In general, the danger from electrocution is minimal. Internal computer circuitry voltages utilize 12V direct current, and are for the most part harmless. Power supplies, transformers, and direct power connections transport more dangerous US 120V alternating current or European 230 V. The shock risk is minor because Underwriters Laboratories and other private testing groups have checked for electrical hazards in consumer products; these standards and safety concerns have been incorporated in many commercial and exempted products like personal computers, workstations, and peripheral devices. The frequency of access to the internal power transformers, connectors, and cables, however, exposes the networking team members to a better chance of doing something wrong or finding a defect. Mainframe environments with large peripheral devices like reel-to-reel tape backup and removable "washtub" disk drives frequently have more significant power demands of 240V. There is a corresponding increase in risk of course, although this technology is rapidly becoming specialized and obscured by microcomputers. For most personal computers or engineering workstations only the 120V power supply itself presents a real danger. Video monitors do, however, have very high internal voltages—on the order of 10,000V.

The best precautions to minimize the risk of electrical burns and shocks is common sense. Do not open cases unless you have sufficient knowledge to repair or diagnose the contents. Check the integrity of power cords, plug equipment into properly wired wall-, floor-, or desk-mounted electrical sockets, verify grounds and plug computer equipment in grounded receptacles, and repair damaged equipment to minimize this risk. Power off equipment before moving it or making physical configuration changes. Figure 4.1 outlines a robust electrical safety policy.

Most Token-Ring network cable carries only 4.5V with a small current, as per the IEEE specifications. There is virtually no danger from those voltages. There are secondary electrical dangers. Twisted-pair bundles frequently share the same wiring conduit as phone lines and electrical power cables.

"Stray" electricity leaks from substantially overloaded or ancient wiring onto the nearest and largest ground. This does include network wires. Network wiring also can acquire an induced current with simple proximity to nearby power lines that could be significant. It is important that the Token-Ring shield/ground bleed off these unwanted currents for safety reasons (and also for communications reliability and network equipment integrity). The standard IBM Type 6 STP contains two pairs

- Turn equipment off before moving
- Turn equipment off before installing or reconfiguring options
- Check the integrity of power cords
- Replace or repair defective or damaged equipment
- Do not open the cases of computers
- Do not open the cases of video monitors
- Minimize the use of power extension cords
- Verify electrical grounds
- Do not defeat 3-wire plug grounds

**Figure 4.1** Electrical hazard precautions.

of wires plus a foil shield and a woven signal jacket. This could carry a substantial electrical potential. Since many Token-Ring networks are built to conform with modular phone wiring specifications, it is possible that some network lines could be crossed with 48V phone circuits. Phone ringing voltages approach 100V DC. Although this does not pose a substantial hazard to people because the amperage is minimal, network equipment (such as NICs, hubs, and routers) is liable to assault network equipment.

It is also possible that breaks in an electrical power cable leak electricity to the STP ground because this shield provides the path of least resistance. Mistakes can happen when electricians or other mechanical installers make changes to the building wiring. Computer room air conditioning units lacking an unobstructed water discharge could create an immediate shock hazard or a slow corrosive problem eventually exposing power cables. Installations may not be complete or safe. Never hold two sections of a network in separate hands until you are certain of their safety, as Figure 4.2 shows. First touch connectors together (and watch for a spark) or check connections with a multitester.

Additionally, Token-Ring wiring is often installed into a building as a retrofit rather than as a planned part of the new construction process. As a result, it is rarely installed in a special conduit or wiring ladder. Instead, the wiring is rigged through the air-return or forced-air ceiling plenums. Air, particularly when very dry, blowing over the length of the shielded wiring also can induce a current. This static charge is highly unlikely to be dangerous; yet a static shock can surprise the unwary and dislodge a person atop a tall ladder. This raises another serious risk, that of a fall.

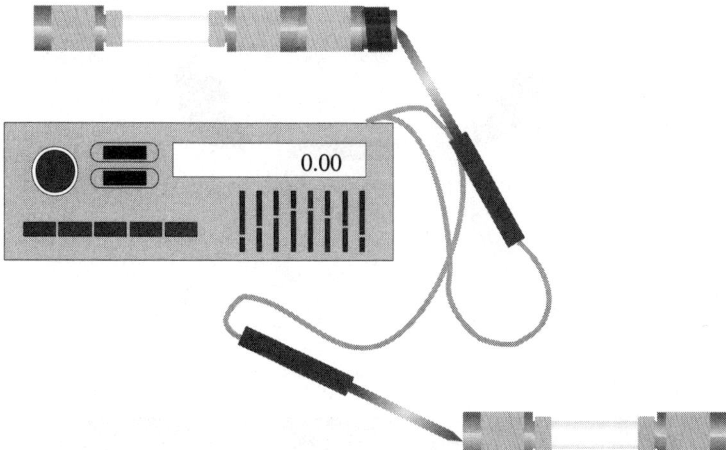


**Figure 4.2** Electrician's safety precautions.

## Ladder Safety

Falls from ladders are an occupational risk for network staff. Unfortunately, a fall from a ladder is not considered preventable until you or a member of your staff falls and breaks an ankle, shatters a pelvis, or lands in the hospital with a concussion. Take this risk very seriously. A fall could cause grave personal injury, damage to network installations, and subsequent downtime. There is the additional loss of productivity while the person heals. There are also financial consequences to the organization such as sick time salary, workman's compensation, and perhaps Occupational Safety and Health Administration (OSHA: see Appendix A) inspections and fines. Workman's compensation does not compensate the person injured for pain and suffering, or any lifelong problems as a result from that fall. Acquire safe ladder skills. Insist on ladder safety.

The art of climbing ladders is not taught to most people nowadays; it is a skill from yesteryear. Furthermore, network management is often a white-collar profession and there is a blinding perception that computer-related jobs are safe. Learn to climb ladders properly. Park the ladder on level ground, lock the ladder's folding supports, and never reach out so that your center of gravity is off the ladder. Never overextend your reach. Avoid the top step of folding A-shaped stepladders. The T-bar in the ceiling you think will help you balance or support your weight will probably give way. If you cannot reach, step down. Move the ladder. Remount the ladder and continue your work. Install tool caddies or hooks to keep important tools within reach, or use belt-mounted or vest tool carriers. Avoid painter's extension-type ladders since they do not provide stability. Add a "bear hug" gripper to the top of your ladder for additional stability, as Figure 4.3 shows.

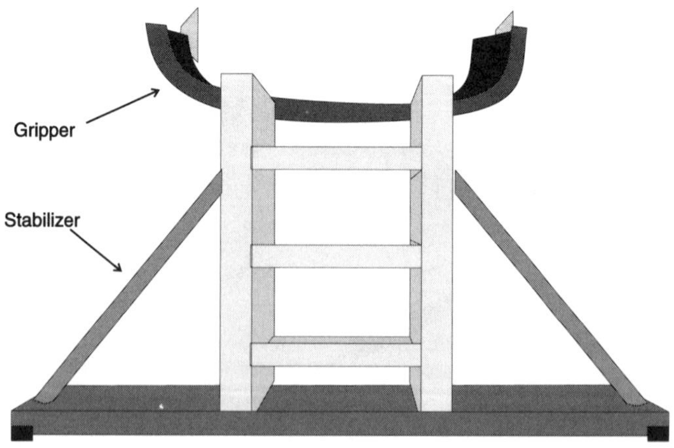


**Figure 4.3** Ladder safety extension (or stabilizer) attaches to standard ladders.

Consider the condition and utility of your ladders. Maintain ladders in safe condition. Tighten bolts. Replace rickety ladders. Since network management often begins as an ad hoc process, that old maintenance ladder is often the only available ladder. Do not chance it. Purchase a new ladder. Wooden rather than aluminum stepladders are inherently safer since they do not conduct electricity. Fiberglass is stronger and is another good choice since it is electrically non-conductive. Beware of carbon fiber laminates since they do conduct. Multijoint ladders which can assume a variety of articulated shapes tend to be more stable, utilitarian, and safe although they are usually made from aluminum. Additionally, ladders vary in quality and strength as well as composition. They are graded as Class I, Class IA, Class II, and Class III. Class III ladders are inexpensive. They are generally intended for intermittent household use and for persons under 200 lb. Class I and Class IA are industrial strength reinforced ladders for constant use. Consider the legal and moral liability of an insufficient ladder.

Ladders are not the only tools to extend your reach. Library-style rolling stairs are a practical acquisition and inherently safer than ladders because of their larger silhouette and side railings. If the ceilings are unusually high, acquire scaffolding. Hydraulic lifts, sometimes called "cherry pickers," have safety cages. For industrial complexes, factory manufacturing floors, and space buildings with extended ceilings, obtain a rolling platform (perhaps even motorized) to reach those heights. Platforms are inherently safer than long ladders and provide immediate tool access. Some people attach safety lines with quick release clips to roof trestles for added precaution. Remember that falling tools can injure bystanders below. Remember, too, that extension cords to power your tools are a risk atop the ladder both for the electrical potential and their chance of snaring you with a dangling cord. Figure 4.4 summarizes practical ladder precautions. These precautions are equally valid for all networking protocols since the cabling is often run from stations, upwards through ceiling plenums, and finally to a terminating wiring closet.

## Indoor Pollution

Most people would laugh aloud that the major health risk from a computer career would comprise lumbago, paper cuts, and overweight from a sedentary lifestyle. Whatever the reality of that view of the on-call lifestyle of a user and network support person, computer equipment does create substantial indoor pollution. Laser printers (and photocopiers) create ozone, a highly active form of oxygen (natural in our environment in low concentrations) that is corrosive to eyes and lungs. Ozone exposure is known to induce asthma and other respiratory disorders. It is thought to muddle thoughts and make people tired and lethargic. Long-term risks from elevated ozone exposure are unknown. Most people do not realize that laser printers and

- Set up the ladder on level ground
- Lock the ladder's folding supports
- Maintain center of gravity over ladder silhouette
- Never overextend your reach
- Do not move suddenly—move deliberately and carefully
- Do not balance on ceiling components
- Move the ladder directly beneath your work area
- Avoid the top step of folding A-shaped ladders
- Select a ladder tall enough to safely reach your work area
- Carry tools on a belt or vest
- Avoid extension-type ladders
- Add a bear hug gripper to the top of the ladder
- Maintain ladders in safe condition
- Replace rickety ladders
- Select wooden or fiberglass rather than aluminum ladders

**Figure 4.4** Checklist for safe ladder use.

photocopiers have ozone filters. Replace the filters at the recommended intervals. Although, in reality, computer equipment cases, the paint on the case, the fiberglass substrate used for computer circuitry, and other plastic materials may leach volatile resin solvents into the air, this is a minimal concern. Computers do create substantial energy pollution; the risk and extent of this energy pollution are the topics for the next several sections.

## Dangers From Electromagnetic Pollution

All electrical equipment, including computers, emit electromagnetic pollution as a waste by-product of extracting energy from electricity. Such pollution is suspected to cause a variety of serious illnesses. Concern is warranted because the empirical evidence is mounting. Networks that connect computer systems also generate radiation and their risks should not be overlooked, either. In fact, that risk may be greater because the network wiring is invisible and therefore forgotten. Moreover, wireless network NICs and hubs broadcast not only radio signals to transport the Token-Ring packets but also a constant carrier signal. Cables and wireless networks discharge radiation over a more disperse physical area than a singular personal computer. As such, people usually not considered at risk are exposed to this hazard.

Fear over the dangers of the computer and network environment is derived from a higher incidence of serious and unusual illnesses for people living near other known sources of electromagnetic pollution. Illnesses and disorders include leukemia and other cancers, miscarriages, headaches, eyestrains, immune system problems, and juvenile growth disorders. Additionally, an observed increase in cataracts (deterioration and discoloration of the eye's lens) for mainframe data entry operators raises the direct suspicion that computers are not as safe as first perceived.

Suspected sources include the massive electrical power lines linking power generating plants with substations, radio stations, power stations, airports, and electric train lines. Even residential power lines and electric blankets are suspect. The problems are attributed to radiation generated by the flowing electricity itself. The force of electricity at very high voltages forcing its way through and over the high tension wires creates radio noise and localized but powerful magnetic fields. As computer operators have *attributed* similar health problems to long-term exposure to video display terminals (VDTs), concern grows over the health consequences of working near the ever-growing legions of personal computers and engineering workstations. Even at the lower voltages associated with computers, electricity can create pollution, too, albeit at lesser levels than caused by power lines. Electricity passing through the silicon paths on a computer chip or a wire (or coiled wire as found in a power transformer or electron beams within a video display terminal) creates an emanating energy field, as Figure 4.5 shows. Personal exposure even to this lower-level pollution is higher within the typically confined work areas of offices and cubicles.

It is important to realize that all forms of electromagnetic pollution are suspected to induce human illness. There are two basic types of electromagnetic pollution, either radio-frequency (RF) emissions or magnetic fields. RF emissions like $x$-rays, infrared signals, microwave emissions, radio and television signals, even sunlight, are all forms of light with different wavelengths, as Figure 4.6 denotes. Light is partly unseen particles, called *photons,* and partly wave energy. The spectrum varies with the energy context. $X$-rays are very short, intense signals that pass through most materials, whereas infrared is a very long and less powerful energy source that tends to bounce off things like air,

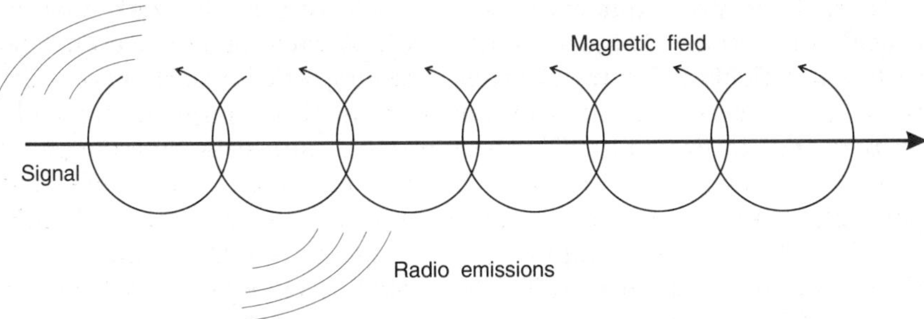


**Figure 4.5** Flowing electricity creates electromagnetic interference (EMI) and magnetic field pollution.

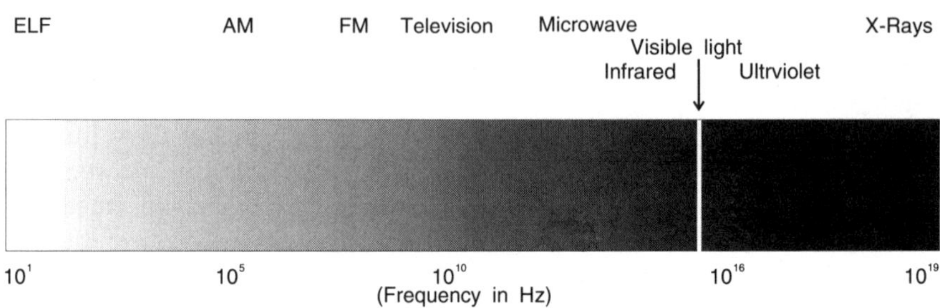


**Figure 4.6** The electromagnetic spectrum.

people, and walls. Magnetic fields are not forms of light but rather are unseen rivers of electrons, a particle much larger than the photon. In general, RF pollution can be shielded with enough material to reflect or absorb the energy. On the other hand, magnetic energy is not easily shielded with solid materials, although it can be dampened by creating new magnetic fields to counteract it.

Dr. Carol Weingrod, faculty member at Boston University School of Medicine, explains the reputed risk factors from exposure to radio-frequency pollution. The energies of the electromagnetic spectrum are propagated waveforms with particle properties. This energy is inversely proportional to the wavelength; the longer the wavelength, the less energy associated. Nonionizing, or lower-level radiant energy (including microwave and radio-frequency), generally is thought to produce biologic hyperthermia. (In other words, cells get cooked.) The effects of radiant energy on biologic systems depend on the degree to which the energy particles penetrate the system and the chemical changes undergone by the molecules of the system once exposed to the energy. At issue is the seriousness of these biological changes and the ramifications of long-term, low-level exposure to energy pollution. Prudence clearly dictates an attempt to limit penetration of this energy into the biologic system.

There is no proof that magnetic fields have a health risk, merely causal connections. Magnetic energy is not wave or particle energy; rather, it is fields of flowing electrons and magnetic force. However, like radio-frequency emissions, the danger from this energy is inversely proportional to proximity. The best research suggests that magnetic energy is thought to accelerate chemical reactions within cells and perhaps create ozone, a triple-molecule form of oxygen that is highly reactive. This speeds the aging process, damages the DNA, and defeats the cell's ability to repair itself. Such biological changes are believed to cause cell failure or promote rampant cellular growth such as leukemia and other cancers. Prudence clearly dictates an attempt to limit exposure of this energy.

## Inconclusive Evidence

Results to date on the dangers of energy pollution remain inconclusive despite the government agencies, insurance companies, and private organizations that have commissioned studies. Simple reasons for the lack of hard evidence include the difficulty in excluding other environmental factors like lifestyle, diet, family background, the long periods required for illness to manifest itself, and other risk factors. Additionally, most hot sites that have been investigated are not "statistically significant;" although many residents alongside major power grids have experienced serious illness, the mathematical variances from what are considered the normal incidences of these maladies are too small to prove a definitive cause.

Furthermore, many of the studies are funded by groups with a vested interest in the study results. Computer manufacturers see increased product costs for equipment radiating less energy. Power companies do not want to be inundated with wrongful-injury lawsuits. Insurance companies certainly want to absorb fewer medical and liability claims. Radio stations broadcasting from within metropolitan districts atop the tall buildings and within residential neighborhoods have few other alternatives. Cable TV is a new and expanding industry that wants to maintain its profitable status. Airports and airplanes use powerful forward and downward viewing radar to provide passenger safety. The U.S. government as well has large military grids for broadcasting radar and special extremely long frequency (ELF) communication signals.

## FCC Emission Ratings

The Federal Communications Commission (FCC) rates computer equipment for its potential to create RF pollution. All equipment designs are supposedly tested prior to commercial or consumer sale. Computer equipment is rated as Class A or Class B. Class B is suitable for use in a residential neighborhood, while Class A is for industrial zones only. This classification refers to the computer's ability to interfere with neighboring radio and television reception. Class B emits less RF pollution. Do not be fooled by the incorrect assumption that Class A equipment must be better than equipment with a Class B rating. There is no merit to the letter designations. These ratings detail nothing about the levels and signatures of magnetic fields; they explicitly state only that the magnitude of the radio signal emitted by these machines must fall within acceptable broadcasting noninterference standards. In other words, the FCC warrants that a certified item will not create "snow" on a nearby TV set. There is nothing stated about the health risks of sitting directly in front of a radio transmitter for hours each day over many years. Although RF pollution is assumed to be an unsubstantiated health risk, it is not within the jurisdiction of the FCC to qualify health risks; it merely manages use of the radio-frequency spectrum. Additionally, the FCC ratings provide no information about the magnitude or danger of emanating magnetic fields.

It is important to note that the power of these fields, both RF and magnetic, are proportional to the size of the electrical load. Basically, RF and magnetic pollution are direct by-products of the amount of electricity consumed. The more electricity consumed, the more energy pollution. The less electricity consumed, the less energy pollution. RF and EMI are also proportional to the force, or voltage, of the electricity. The higher the voltage, the more energy pollution. The lower the voltage, the less energy pollution. Practically, this means that video displays and power transformers create more hazard than the actual computer circuitry.

Exposure is inversely proportional to distance and therefore dissipates rapidly with distance from its source. In other words, the smaller the power supply and the further from the equipment, the safer a person will be. This is true for both RF and magnetic field pollution. For example, a video monitor tends to have a larger envelope reaching out behind it because of its higher internal voltages than, say, a personal computer. Larger monitors have larger envelopes and color monitors with three or four electric beams broadcast to a larger area than do monochrome monitors with single beams. Monitors with higher scan rates have larger fields in general because they consume more electricity. Monitors that can display super video graphics array (SVGA), multisynch, and multiscan signals with resolutions greater than 1024 × 768 pixels are more powerful than monitors supporting the video graphics array (VGA) 800 × 600 standard. The VGA display monitor emits more energy than enhanced graphics array (EGA) with resolutions of approximately 480 × 320. The EGA-compatible monitor in turn broadcasts more extensive energy than color graphics arrays (CGA) with resolution of 320 × 240 pixels. Early monochrome character-based monitors vary widely in their technology and safety. (Some even may emit more powerful and dangerous *x*-rays. It is wise to check older equipment carefully.) Under US Federal law, detectable levels of ionizing (*x*-ray) radiation from VDTs have not been allowed since 1970.

## Prudent Precautions

Despite a lack of conclusive proof for these health risks, sufficient circumstantial evidence exists for the prudent network manager to take precautions. (Although cigarette smoking was known to have health consequences, only recently have scientific studies actually proven and defined this risk for the primary smokers and those who breath the secondary smoke. Only recently, has this evident been sufficient to cause restrictions in tobacco advertising, public consumption. Yet, risk-conscious people stopped smoking long ago.) Automobiles in metropolitan areas are the leading cause of ozone pollution and this should be balanced against the minimal levels produced by laser printers. Note, however, that most modern energy-efficient buildings are inadequately ventilated so that ozone does accumulate to levels exceeding regulations. It is equally important to place the risk of these radiation dangers into appropriate perspective, because ambient background energy pollution from all other sources is greater than that from computers and networks. However, realize that the risk from radiation created by computers is based on a constant exposure and the user's proximity to emitting computer equipment.

Although the Token-Ring signal is high frequency [8 or 32 megahertz (Mhz)], the voltage and hence the electromagnetic emission levels are relatively low. The shield on the standard *shielded* twisted-pair is also designed to minimize RF emission (to improve reliability but to the detriment of signal impedance). Although RF radiation from wireless networks is less powerful than the ambient radiation from radio and television signals, these wireless signals are designed to penetrate walls and reflect around corners—and pass without distortion through people, too. Infrared is a relatively weak light signal unless transmitted as a coherent laser beam; its major danger is causing immediate retinal burns and not biological cell changes. Additionally, magnetic radiation or magnetically induced electrical fields surround us from fluorescent light fixtures and high-voltage, high-frequency lighting (halogen and the like). Moreover, the amount of energy pollution is in proportion to the amount of electricity consumed by the electrical equipment and its proximity. The real danger of these energy fields is that we normally position ourselves close to the sources when we sit in front of a computer workstation. This magnetic radiation is insidious because it is most pervasive, invasive, and continuous because we sit within two feet of a computer screen. These fields radiate outward in various circular patterns from computer equipment and cabling, as Figure 4.7 illustrates. Although the patterns are consistent and maintain their shapes (they may surge outward when you first turn on the equipment), every piece of equipment will have its own signature.

## Safety Recommendations

There are four basic safety provisions. Figure 4.8 lists some possible solutions. First, isolate laser printers (and photocopiers) in a well-ventilated area. This will minimize exposure to ozone by distancing the source of this gas from people and secondarily will provide a cost-effective and energy-conservation means to ventilate a major source of indoor pollution. (The other major source of indoor ozone pollution is smoking.)

Second, shield people from radio energy by buying Class B equipment and position it as far from people as possible. That lessens exposure to

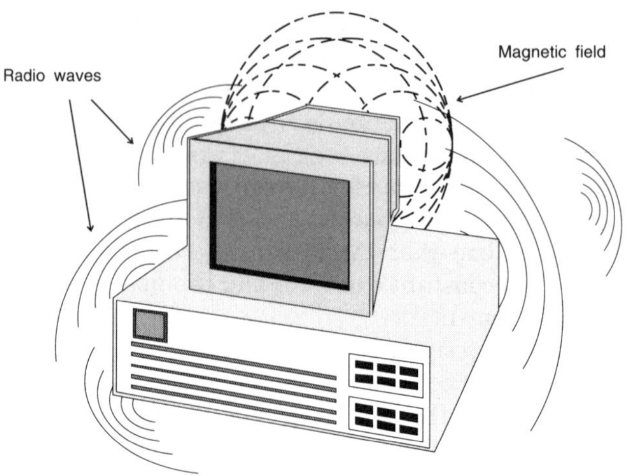


**Figure 4.7** Computer equipment energy emission signatures.

- Ventilate laser printers
- Power off equipment when not in use
- Minimize the use of power extension cords
- Concentrate remote equipment away from people
- Provide file servers
- Provide limited access to computer rooms
- Run cables as far from people as possible
- Provide adequate electrical power cords
- Route network cables away from people
- Choose workstations with internally mounted options
- Position equipment as far as physically possible from user
- Select low-energy consumption equipment
- Install diskless workstations
- Choose equipment with lower capacity power supplies
- Limit installation of options:
  - Modems
  - Tape drives
  - Extra memory
- Choose FCC Class B equipment
- Choose newer equipment with reduced magnetic emissions
- Verify FCC ratings compliance
- Avoid use of serial port NICs
- Assess the emission levels of RF networks
- Replace electrical networks with optical fiber

**Figure 4.8** Network safety precautions.

RF (and magnetic energy to a lesser degree by proxy). Do not assemble or upgrade PC motherboards or power supply components within a computer since these components may not be FCC-certified and may not be certified within your particular hardware configuration. Also, since obstructions like metal-clad walls effectively reduce the energy dispersion, consider concentrating remote computing equipment in limited-access computer rooms and placing computer workstations in a computer work area away from desks, meeting rooms, and common areas. Consider replacing copper-wired networks with optical fiber networks. In many cases, such actions are impractical or costly. Since Token-Ring is a low-voltage medium, it is less of a risk than most other network-related computer equipment. The only risk, and also an unsubstantiated one, is the chance that the cabling itself will provide a conduit for energy and "beam" it, if you will, to users. Route cabling, both electrical and network twisted-pair, away from users. For the most part, the real risk is the high voltage components like display monitors, and to a lesser degree, the computer circuitry, including the Token-Ring network interface controllers which should be considered the real health risks. For these reasons, position workstations and the video monitors as far physically from users as they will tolerate.

Third, because magnetic field pollution is a direct function of energy usage, select computer equipment with lower energy requirements. Do not rely merely on the FCC Class B rating and assume that the equipment is safe. Ratings could be wrong and, furthermore, are significantly increased by installation of option cards (e.g., NICs, hard disk controllers, and memory boards). While radio signals can be shielded by design and by thicker equipment cases, magnetic fields are impervious to normal shielding techniques and can be diverted only by other magnetic fields. Since health consequences of magnetic pollution are a new phenomena and still unproven, effective designs and safer products are not yet available. Instead use your discretion. (Select equipment with smaller power supplies and fewer options. Although this produces less powerful magnetic fields, it also provides less margin for voltage fluctuations; in some rural areas this may be a serious shortcoming to this approach.)

Video monitors are the primary cause of magnetic field pollution because of their high internal voltages. Install black-and-white (B&W) monitors with its single electron beam rather than color monitors with multiple beams. Do not assume that single beam color grid-masked color monitors are safer; the electron beam scan rate may be 300 percent faster and thus require a higher internal voltage. Choose equipment promising lower magnetic pollution. It is possible to counteract the magnetic field pollution by creating an equal and opposite magnetic field. Video monitors are available with countercyclical windings (cancellation yolk) designed to decrease this pollution (the NEC 4FG is one such monitor). Liquid crystal display (LCD) or gas plasma provide no radiation other than the minimal amounts generated from the computers chips.

Alternately, select smaller monitors with lower energy consumption. Where possible, install equipment as far from people as practical; since the strengths of magnetic fields decay rapidly with distance, the purported biological risk will also decrease with distance. Consider the video monitor carefully. SVGA monitors and other high-resolution displays cause an increased dosage of energy exposure. Not only do these devices emit more energy pollution, they also increase exposure to energy pollution because the type size and image size itself is smaller, thereby forcing the user to sit closer to the monitor to read the type. The dosage is increased exponentially by sitting closer. Microsoft Windows, for example, supports various screen resolutions including VGA, and EGA. X-Windows also supports workstations higher resolutions and monitors with scan rates for 1640 × 1320. Icons and text at set point sizes will appear progressively smaller at the higher resolutions. The higher resolution is a mixed health blessing since you need to be closer to the screen to discern the small letters.

Fourth, carefully weigh technology that is new or untested for its safety aspect. Manufacturers of radio-frequency networks say that the signal is 1000 times less powerful than a radio station. Transmitters emit up to 4 watts of power by FCC limitations. Recall, however, that exposure is an issue of proximity, and it may be undesirable to bathe your work environment with a constant low-level signal. Practical matters may outweigh this concern; the simplicity of adding wireless Token-Ring may be safer than adding cabling to a building already wired-bound. Or, wireless may in fact pose a less serious health risk than installing twisted- pair wire in an asbestos-clad ceiling.

## Safety Testing Tools

Few formal safety tools are available. Those that are available include Gauss meters, radio-frequency analyzers, gas chromatography equipment, spectrum analyzers, *x*-ray detectors, and ozone detectors. Not only are these sensitive laboratory instruments; they are also prohibitively expensive for most network sites. If you foresee the concern for employees becoming a company ethic and formal policy, acquire these tools *and* learn how to use them. Test for magnetic fields, radio-frequency pollution, *x*-rays from monitors, and indoor air pollution. If you suspect a substantial health risk hire a consultant to test your facilities. This will be cost-effective and it is more practical.

There are also cheaper routes and ones more likely to get approval from upper management. Buy instant film. Buy an AM radio. Get a compass. Film fogs in the present of hard radiation like *x*-rays (however, computer equipment including VDTs is highly unlikely to produce

$x$-rays). The radio will not tune in clear radio stations near to radio emitting equipment. The compass will indicate magnetic fields and their relative strengths by deflecting the needle from pointing northward.

A portable radio is a good and inexpensive tool for measuring radio emission from computer equipment. Noise that drowns out bona fide radio stations indicates poor shielding. The static will decrease with distance from the radio source. You may choose to replace such equipment. Some manufacturers took shortcuts and sold equipment lacking thorough certification. Not only is this a health risk; it also has consequences for network functionality. As stated later in this book, Token-Ring network performance can also be adversely affected by unshielded radio sources, including a renegade personal computer (non-FCC-compliant).

A compass is a useful tool for evaluating the power of magnetic fields. Use it to plot the size, shape, placement, and intensity of the fields emanating from the computer equipment and cabling. This tool could suggest which equipment is better not purchased. The plot will show how to position a workstation, for example, to minimize the risk for a user. Figure 4.9 illustrates a typical plot and how to position a personal computer and the Token-Ring lobe cable to minimize the risk to the computer user. Note the placement of the video monitor against the walls with the backside positioned so as not to expose people.

Note that the computer chassis containing the motherboard, hard disk, Token-Ring NIC, and other accessories is placed as far from the

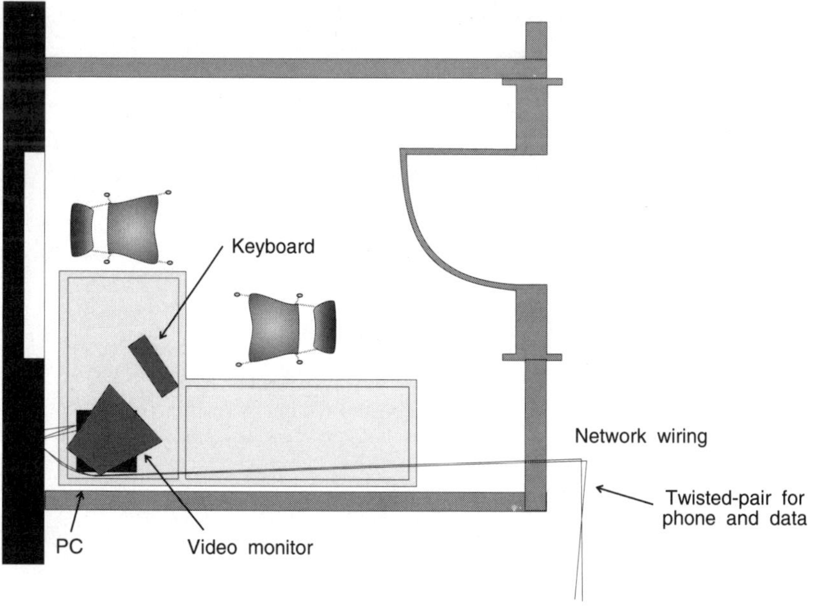


**Figure 4.9** Optimal safe workstation placement.

body as possible. The keyboard obviously requires a convenient location; this should be of lesser concern since it has a very low quotient of energy pollution produced *only* when a key is pressed. In this example, a large display monitor was placed on a higher platform, pitched forward, and moved as far from the user as tolerable. The limitation to video monitor placement is often the size of the office (or cubicle) and the user's visual acuity.

# Part 2
## Software and Hardware

This section describes the mechanical processes of Token-Ring networking, the hardware, the software, the installation and expansion process. It builds a basis of understanding for the operations and management of a Token-Ring network. Chapter 5 presents the standard Open Systems Interconnection reference model and the variations in Token-Ring. It describes standard twisted-pair variations, transmission speed options, and other protocol enhancements.

Chapter 6 describes the hardware and the mechanical process of Token-Ring. The components of a Token-Ring network are described and illustrated to help the reader understand the ingenious simplicity of a Token-Ring network. Chapter 7 explains the Token-Ring process. This includes the transmission methodology and characteristic features of network-level software. Chapter 8 details the planning procedures for the mechanical components of Token-Ring networks, completing what vendors' spartan instructions omit. This chapter outlines those issues that an experienced network manager considers before building or expanding a Token-Ring network. Chapter 9 explains the installation procedures for the mechanical components of Token-Ring networks, supplementing vendors' incomplete instructions. This chapter suggests what steps an experienced network manager can take for testing and benchmarking a newly installed network. Chapter 10 explains why bridges, gateways, and repeaters are necessary on a large Token-Ring, and how these units are installed. Since organizational growth is likely to outstrip the capacity of any original network, bridges, gateways, and repeaters are also presented as solutions to overloaded networks.

Chapter 11 addresses the concept of the enterprise-wide network. Internetworking and network software issues are gaining importance as crucial LAN issues. Client-server computing is displacing downsized mainframe data processing, and local area networks are becoming integrated into distributed computing and enterprise-wide environments. Although local area networks may preoccupy the efforts and attentions of many network managers, linking multiple LANs and host computers at distant sites is becoming an important topic.

Chapter

# 5

# Token-Ring Standards

Conformity to a network standard represents important progress. Standards promote reliability, product growth, compatibility, and interconnectivity for local area networking. Standards are of prime importance for interconnectivity of heterogeneous local area networks, as well as necessary for development of effective network management tools. Although Token-Ring is standardized, there are at least four major physical permutations, and two software-based options. Token-Ring exists in two transmission speed variants, 4 Mbits/s and 16 Mbits/s. Transmission media can utilize either shielded twisted-pair or unshielded twisted-pair wiring with media filters, as explained in the prior chapter. Furthermore, Token-Ring is supported on optical fiber, although this is intended for special-purposes. The software options include *early token release* (ETR) and a *packet burst mode* (PBM) for increased throughput. Chapters 16 and 17 will discuss the statistical and performance effects from these enhancements.

The Token-Ring standards are based upon IEEE 802.2 (transmission protocol codified by the Institute for Electrical and Electronic Engineers) and IEEE 802.5 (topology). This chapter uses the ISO OSI model as a reference to describe the functions of Token-Ring. This model is gathering widespread international acceptance, while Token-Ring hardware vendors recognize that conformity to these standards supplies an important selling point. This chapter also describes four types of transmission media: shielded twisted-pair wiring, unshielded twisted-pair wiring, wireless, and optical fiber. Token-Ring network configurations conclude this presentation.

## The ISO OSI Model

Token-Ring was proposed by IBM in early 1983 to contest the Xerox, Intel, and DEC proposal of Ethernet as the LAN data communication coaxial-based standard. In response, the IEEE 802 committee was divided into subcommittees to consider media (802.1), protocols (802.2), the two bus-based architectures [Ethernet (802.3) and token bus (802.4)], and a ring-based architecture (802.5). Token-Ring (802.5) was incorporated into commercial products in 1984. While this design preceded the development of the Open System Interconnect (OSI) model by a few years, nonetheless, it partially conforms to this layered architecture model of networking. The OSI model was developed by the International Standards Organization (ISO) as a generic model for data communication.[1]

Because modularity of communication functions is a key design criterion in the OSI model, vendors who adhere to the standards and guidelines of this model can supply Token-Ring-compatible devices, alternative Token-Ring media, higher-performance Token-Ring networks, and bridging protocols that easily and reliably interconnect other types of data networks to Token-Ring. Additionally, conformance to the ISO OSI model means that the latest software monitoring and management software will simplify network management. Conformance to the OSI model offers remote management that will work even across bridges and other devices usually not viewed as Token-Ring compatible.

The OSI model specifies seven layers of functionality as shown in Figure 5.1. It defines the layers but does not define the protocols that implement the functions at each layer. That is important for compatibility, protocol independence, and the future growth of network technology. Layer 1 is the physical layer (electrical, mechanical, optical). Layer 2

| Layer | | |
|---|---|---|
| Layer: 7 | **Application** | User application process and management functions |
| 6 | **Presentation** | Data interpretation, format, and code transformation |
| 5 | **Session** | Administration and control of sessions between nodes |
| 4 | **Transport** | Transparent data transfer and transmission control |
| 3 | **Network** | Routing, switching, and flow control |
| 2 | **Data link** | Maintain and release data; link, error, and flow control |
| 1 | **Physical** | Control of data circuits; physical media definition |

**Figure 5.1** The International Standards Organization (ISO) Open Systems Interconnect (OSI) model.

1 *Datapro Network Reports* includes information on the OSI plenary groups and frequently prints the membership lists.

is the data link layer (flow, standards, connections). Layer 3 is the network layer (routing and switching of the actual transmission). Layer 4 is the transport layer (transmission and transfer of data). Layer 5 is the session layer (administrative control of transmissions and transfers). Layer 6 is the presentation layer (interpretation and data transformation). Layer 7 is the application layer (system computing and user applications).

Implementations of the OSI model provide for a protocol for communication at each layer on two processors (that is, session to session) and an interface for communication between layers on one processor (that is, presentation to session). Physical communication occurs only at layer 1 (the protocol for electrical transmission on the transmission medium, bit by bit). The protocols for the other layers define virtual connections in the software. In other words, only layer 1 physically connects to layer 1. All communication, even from upper layers, transpires through a chain of layered control. Peer-layer communication is not possible in this model. MAUs, repeaters, bridges, routers, and gateways all must conform to this, too. All other layers communicate downward to lower levels in steps, or in the OSI terminology, communicate through *protocol stacks*. The following paragraphs describe the functions of each layer. Noncompliance causes compatibility problems and complications with network management software.

Layer 1, the *physical layer*, specifies the electrical and mechanical control of the actual data circuits. This function is managed by the Token-Ring NICs and MAUs (or hubs), and the cabling between them. While the transmission medium is formally defined by the IEEE standards, it is generally included in the OSI definition, and it can be thought of as the underlying layer of the OSI model. The model does not specify (and limit) the media, only the operative functionality for a standardized communication protocol. It is not directly specified as part of the layer 1 architecture; this is an important factor since many vendors do not provide UTP support. For example, vendors are considering implementations of FDDI on twisted-pair (CDDI) while other vendors are substituting plastic optical fiber for glass. In fact, this margin has led to the formal codification and commercial acceptance of unshielded twisted-pair Token-Ring by IBM.

The transmission media layer specifies the physical medium used in constructing the network, including size, thickness, and other characteristics of the actual medium. The electrical, mechanical, wireless infrared or radio frequency, or optical pulses travel along a transmission medium, which may be twisted-pair telephone line (which Token-Ring currently uses), wireless, optical fiber, or microwave.

Layer 2, the *data link layer*, describes the software that manages transmissions, error acknowledgment, and recovery. The mechanical devices, such as NICs, are mapped data units to data units, to provide physical error detection and notification, and link activation and deactivation of a logical communication connection. This is the *media access control* (MAC) 3 layer, and the NICs maintain a local station Token-Ring address at this level.

Layer 3, the *network layer*, is the borderline between hardware and software. At the network layer, the protocol mechanisms activate the data routing by providing network address resolution and flow control in terms of segmentation and blocking. The network layer also provides service selection, connection resets, and expedited data transfers. The *NetBIOS Protocol*, a common Token-Ring software, runs at this layer.

Layer 4, the *transport layer*, controls data transfer and transmission. This software program is called *NetBEUI* or *IPX*, depending upon the network operating system.

Layers 5, 6, and 7 are generally supplied as vendor-specific software and are not part of Token-Ring. Layer 5 recognizes the nodes on the LAN and sets up the tables of source and destination addresses. It also establishes, quite literally, a handshaking for each session between different nodes. Technically, services at layer 5 are called *session connection, exception reporting, coordination of send / receive modes*, and, of course, the actual *data exchange*.

Layer 6, the *presentation layer*, transfers information from the application software to the network session layer to the operating system. The interface at this layer performs data transformations, data formatting, syntax selection [including American Standard Code for Information Interchange (ASCII), Extended Binary Code Decimal Interchange Code (EBCDIC), Tagged Image Format (TIF), and other numeric or graphic formats], device selection and control, and finally, data compression or encryption.

Layer 7, the *network application layer*, supports identification of communicating partners, establishes the authority to communicate, transfers information, and applies privacy mechanisms and cost allocations. It may be a complex layer. The application layer supports file services, print services, and electronic mail. These "applications" are not to be confused with user applications. The application layer is the network system software that supports user-layer applications, like word or data processing, CAD/CAM, and image scanning. Figure 5.2 lists specific examples of standard protocols for each layer of the OSI model.

RS-232 and RS-449 are twisted-pair network standards. DDCMP is Digital Data Communications Message Protocol. LAP-B is Link Access Control-Balanced. SDLC is an acronym for Synchronous Data Link Control, whereas HDLC is an acronym for High-Level Data Link Control. UDP is User Datagram Protocol. ARP is Address Resolution Protocol. IPX is Internet Packet Exchange. SPX is System Packet Exchange. IPX and SPX are Novell NetWare layers 3 and 4. TCP is *Transaction Control Protocol*. IP is *Internet Protocol*, an early and important wide area communication

| ISO | Example Architecture |
|---|---|
| Layer 7 | X.400, LAN Manager, NFS, NetWare, PC LAN, SNA, vendor-specific |
| Layer 6 | NAPLPS, MAP, vendor-specific |
| Layer 5 | Vendor-specific |
| Layer 4 | IPX, TCP (as in TCP/IP), vendor-specific |
| Layer 3 | X.25, IP (as In TCP/IP), DECnet, SPX, vendor-specific |
| Layer 2 | IEEE 802.2, DDCMP, LAP-B, NetBIOS, SDLC, HDLC |
| Layer 1 | IEEE 802.5, RS-232, RS-449, Token-Ring, V.22, V.32, V.42 bis |

**Figure 5.2** Examples of standard protocols in the ISO architecture.

language borrowed for Token-Ring-related software. XNS represents Xerox Network System. DECnet is a Transaction Control Program/ Internet Protocol (TCP/ IP) implementation from Digital Equipment Corporation. MAP is Manufacturing Automation Protocol. NFS represents Sun Microcomputers *Network File System*, NetWare is a Novell software, Vines is a Banyan product, and Microsoft and IBM are responsible for PC LAN, LAN Server, OS/2 LAN, LAN Manager, and the AS/400 Token-Ring LAN software. SNA is IBM's *System Network Architecture* used for linking host mainframes to dumb terminals or personal computers running terminal emulation software. Interoperability is an important consideration. While many of these protocols conform to the TCP/ IP datagram or OSI standards, connecting networks with the different protocols will remain a thorny problem for some time.

The ISO standards also specify how repeaters, bridges, routers, and gateways are established to extend the topology of a network. The simplest of these OSI definitions is the LAN repeater, which receives, regenerates, and amplifies the transmission signal from one network segment onto another network segment.

### OSI Repeaters

*Repeaters* extend signal. They represent active devices, though they are usually not network nodes, per se. On Token-Ring, a repeater allows a single network segment to exceed the maximum drive limitations of 770 m and 346 m and nodes to exceed the lobe limitations of 200 m and 100 m for 4 Mbits/s and 16 Mbits/s signal speed variations. See Figure 5.3 for the ISO repeater model. Signals are amplified to reach nodes or hubs beyond the normal lobe or trunk length. "Smart" repeaters, devices (actually OSI bridges or routers) which provide special performance improvements, communicate at other layers, including the data link, network, transport, and session layers. MAC-layer routers filter Token-Ring packets for higher traffic rates by maintaining a MAC-level or ring address routing table.

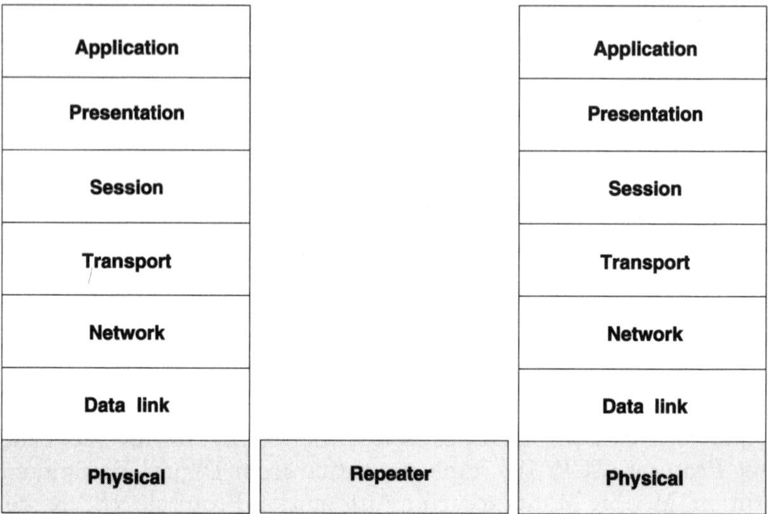


**Figure 5.3** The OSI repeater model.

### OSI Bridges

The *bridge*, as shown in Figure 5.4, interconnects network rings. A simple bridge, for example, might connect a Token-Ring 4 Mbits/s with a Token-Ring 16 Mbits/s or optical fiber network. A bridge can convert a digital signal into a frequency-modulated electrical signal or a laser

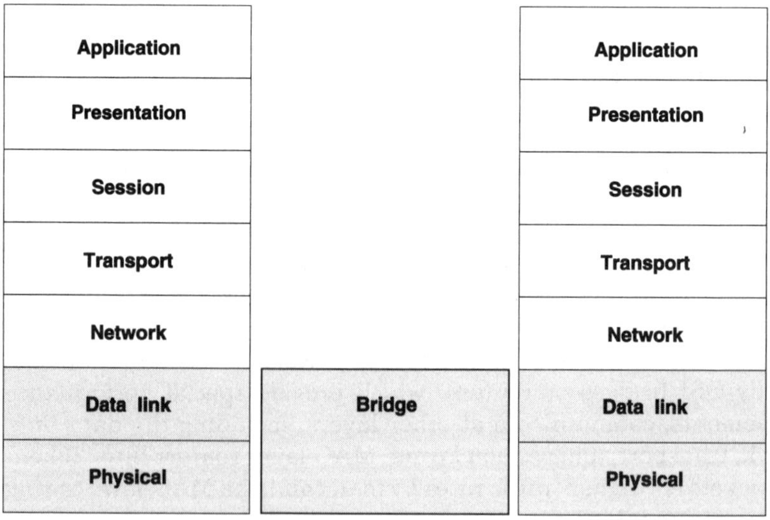

**Figure 5.4** The OSI bridge model.

signal. Network, transport, session, presentation, and application layers are not affected by the bridge, so the bridge is totally transparent to the user. A bridge does not examine the protocol header above OSI layer 2. The protocol, per se, is not bridged, only the transmission medium itself. A bridge can interconnect two Token-Ring-based rings with a third Ethernet segment in the middle that cannot understand the packets traveling through it. The bridges see only the middle segment as a routing path, important when FDDI is applied to link multiple rings in a distributed campus setting or within the vertical structure of a high-rise corporate building.

There are also intelligent bridges that limit traffic between network segments. These bridges learn addresses, filter packets, and forward a subset of packets based on the contents of a routing table. Dual-port bridges isolate segments in just this manner and only forward packets addressed to devices on the other segments. Multiport bridges provide an effective solution to interconnect LANs and WANs, replacing a trunk backbone. It can function as a packet switch to eliminate multiple hops between segments with similar characteristics. They provide better performance and more flexibility in network design.

### OSI Routers

The *router*, as shown in Figure 5.5, interconnects network segments at OSI layer 3, the network layer. It is protocol-dependent. In fact, the major failure in connecting networks is that NetBIOS, UDP, and NFS protocols are not routable. Routers read the protocol header and forward packets to other segments which request forwarding to those

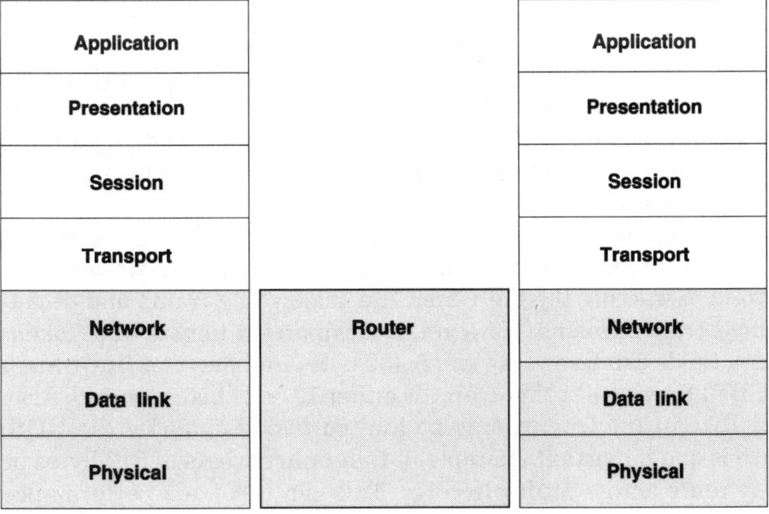


**Figure 5.5** The OSI router model.

other segments. Routers often support multiple protocols. They can interconnect network rings with different physical or data link protocols. Transport, session, presentation, and application layers are not affected by the router.

There is some confusion between the definition of the bridge and a router. A router is a device that spans the media, data link, and transport layers of the OSI model. It receives only those packets addressed to it by a transmitting node or another router. It does not forward packets transparently as the bridge does; instead, the router requires other routers for this task. Additionally, spanning-tree routers determine the best transmission path when there are active loops. This functionality requires extensive routing tables and preferences to determine the best route.

Multiprotocol routers provide an effective solution to interconnect LANs, optical fiber, FDDI, and long distance connections where there are multiple network protocols such as Ethernet, Token-Ring, FDDI, and T-1. They provide more flexibility for network design but are difficult to configure and complex to maintain. Multiport routers connect multiple rings at a single point in concept much the same way as a three-way plug.

### OSI Gateway

A *gateway* in the OSI model interconnects networks and equipment with different characteristics. Information, presentation (ASCII to EBCDIC for example), source and destination addressing, and physical connections are translated by the gateway. A gateway might, for example, translate a file into a stream to be directed over an RS-232 phone link or translate that same file into an IBM file format and X.400 interconnection. Gateways frequently *decouple* communication from the application.

See Figure 5.6 for an example of this translation. The gateway is a strict definition within the context of the OSI model and differs from the common connotation of a "software" repeater, which is a workstation interconnected to two different network rings. In some cases, a gateway may encapsulate or translate one protocol within another for transport as with FDDI backbone.

It is becoming more common to encapsulate Token-Ring packets into the 4478-byte (8956 symbols) FDDI frame because it is simpler and faster than extracting the data from the Token-Ring frame and decoupling those transmissions. However, it is important to note that Token-Ring data fields can be as long as 18,432 bytes and may not fit within a single FDDI frame (the other frame is either 13 or 21 bytes longer). Also, bridged Token-Ring frames may be limited to 512 bytes by the NOS; NetWare is one important example in that only packets of 512 bytes or less may route across multiple rings. This can become a performance bottleneck. As such, substantial overhead would be wasted encapsulating the frame with FDDI. Additionally, this same technique can be

| Application | Gateway | Application |
|---|---|---|
| Presentation | | Presentation |
| Session | | Session |
| Transport | | Transport |
| Network | | Network |
| Data link | | Data link |
| Physical | | Physical |

**Figure 5.6** The OSI gateway model.

modified for Novell, Vines, Ethernet, PC LAN, LAN Manager, and the myriad of proprietary, network operation system protocols. Compare this with packing thousands of individual postal letters into containerized crates for ocean shipping.

## The Definition of Token-Ring

*Token-Ring* comprises layers 1 and 2 of the OSI model. Layers 3 through 7 are not part of Token-Ring. Token-Ring is represented only by hardware and media access protocols, transmissions, error acknowledgment, and recovery. The mechanical devices, like NICs, are mapped data units to data units, to provide physical error detection and notification, and link activation and deactivation of a logical communication connection. This is the media access control layer (MAC), and the NICs maintain a local station Token-Ring address at this level. The operating system components that provide the communications functions at each node build upon the Token-Ring controller function. This is where Token-Ring-related software diverges significantly and incompatibilities, if any, emerge. However, foreign languages are easily transmitted, or even secret code. Token-Ring, like a telephone, will handle different application software. Just as with any phone that accesses a network of other phones, it must adhere to certain standards. These standards are the software protocols described in Chapter 6.

Figure 5.7 translates the ISO OSI model into the comparable IEEE 802 model, of which Token-Ring 802.5 is one example. Token-Ring is

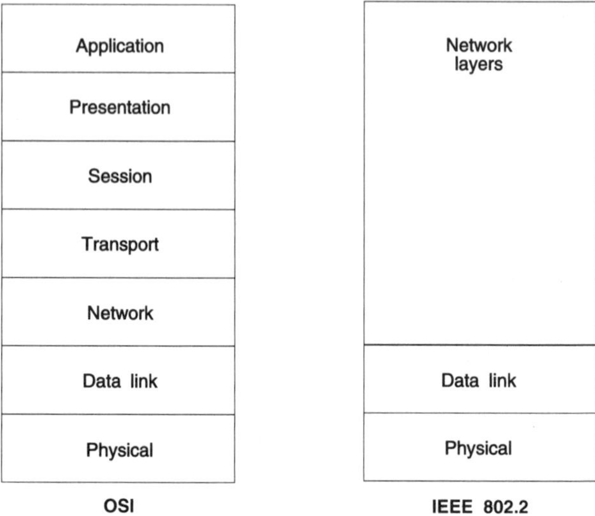


**Figure 5.7** Comparison of the OSI model to the IEEE 802 standard.

specified solely by the physical layer (802.5), the media access control layers, and the logical link control (802.2). The most common application for ISO layers 1 through 4 in a Token-Ring environment is Novell NetWare, followed by Microsoft LAN Manager and IBM OS/2 LAN Server or OS/2 LAN. The network layers are not defined by the IEEE standards, although Token-Ring generally runs "standard versions" of the NetBIOS protocols. The distinction to convey is that "Token-Ring" is physical, although popularly a Token-Ring network includes a network software like Novell NetWare. This disparity between the OSI model and Token-Ring is likely to fade as multinational communications increase the premium on interoperability.

The next illustration in Figure 5.8 expands the IEEE 802 networking model into the Token-Ring representation. The physical layer is called a *ring* in the Token-Ring nomenclature, and the data link layer is represented by the software. This differentiation is important to understand why incompatibilities exist between Token-Ring and OSI and why implementation of network management protocols is delayed.

## Token-Ring Variations

This section defines the Token-Ring hardware, variants, and the physical differences among them. It also describes mechanical standards for the various transmission media, shielded and unshielded twisted-pair, radio frequency and infrared, and optical fiber.

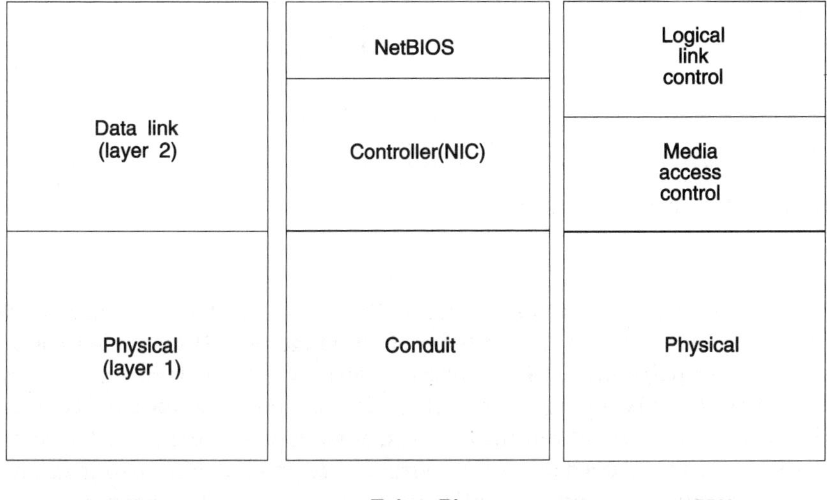


**Figure 5.8** Expansion of the IEEE 802 protocol model into the Token-Ring and NetBIOS representation.

Since shielded twisted-pair (STP) is the prevalent medium, most of this chapter addresses this standard. Because many buildings are wired for telephones and mainframe terminal data lines using voice-grade unshielded twisted-pair (UTP), this option will be discussed as well. Many corporate downsizing strategies begin with a transition based upon the suitability of UTP as the LAN medium. The hazards for this transition will be discussed in Chapter 7. It is important to note that the Token-Ring protocol is the same for all media; the actual signaling method does not vary. Figure 5.9 presents the Token-Ring family tree. Figure 5.10 lists the formal conventions for Token-Ring transmissions.

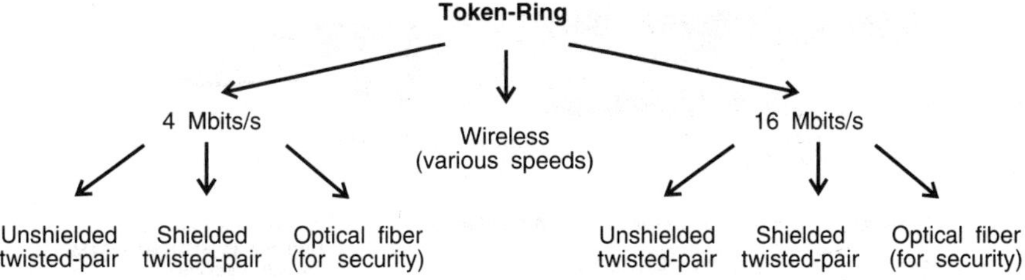


**Figure 5.9** The Token-Ring media and transmission speed family.

| Medium: | Twisted-pair wires (2 or 4 pairs) |
|---|---|
| Electrical: | 3.0 to 4.5 V DC Manchester encoded signal |
| Signal technique: | Digital |
| Protocol: | Token-Ring IEEE 802.5 |
| Conventions: | Token passing |

**Figure 5.10** The Token-Ring standards.

Shielded twisted-pair Token-Ring is the 802.5 standard. Physically, the Type 1 cabling consists of two pairs of 22 gauge (AWG) vinyl-clad copper wire. These pairs indeed twist about themselves three times per foot to minimize the affects of signal crosstalk. It is called "twisted-pair" because the bundles of wires containing four, six, or eight direct current (DC) wiring pairs twist around each other. The wires are twisted to minimize crosstalk, signal attenuation, and susceptibility to stray noise. The pairs are color coded. One pair of wires supports *receive* (RX) signals (input to the NIC), while the other pair supports *transmit* (TX) signals (output to the MAU or hub). These two pair of wires are surrounded by a metal foil that is the ground (negative potential). The foil in turn is surrounded by a braided wire tube that is called the shield, and serves to both contain internal signals and exclude external false signals. This is surrounded by an extruded vinyl jacket. Building or fire code may mandate that the fluorinated ethylene propylene (FEP, trade name, Teflon) be used in place of vinyl for plenum and wall installations. Figure 5.11 illustrates the composition of IBM Type 1 shielded twisted-pair. STP jumpers (Type 6) have a similar composition but the wires are smaller and not as frequently twisted. This wire should not be applied for trunks or lobe runs longer than 30 m. There is a special STP product called Type 2 that also includes four unshielded twisted-pairs for voice (telephone) communication.

Unshielded twisted-pair is comprised of a very different medium. The wire is vinyl clad 24- or 26-gauge copper wire. Four pairs are twisted

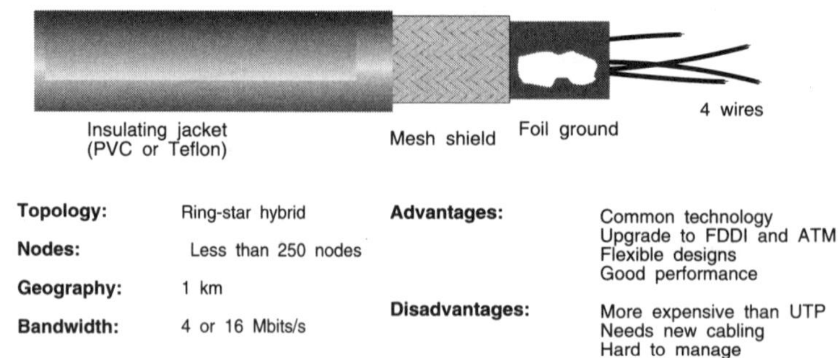


**Figure 5.11** IBM Type 1 shielded twisted-pair wire.

four or five times per foot. The four pairs are color-coded with candy stripes. A gray vinyl insulating jacket surrounds this group in turn. Generally, 25 pairs are bundled into a larger bundle and vinyl clad as well. Building or fire code may mandate that Teflon be used in place of vinyl for plenum and wall installations. Figure 5.12 illustrates the composition of a typical unshielded twisted-pair.

The major differences between these media variations are the trunk and lobe lengths supported. The same NIC and MAU units usually support both STP and UTP media, although newer active devices automatically sense (or are manually set for) the different media characteristics and boost signal strength and signal receive gain for UTP installations. Optical fiber technology is newer and provides greater bandwidth and higher transmission speeds than either STP or UTP, although it remains a more expensive and difficult technology. Fiber cable 2 is difficult to extend, comparatively difficult to splice and repair, severely tests those expecting to add new nodes and rearrange locations of existing nodes, and suffers transmission degradation over time through exposure. Expansion and contraction, and extremes from heat and cold fracture the cable. Heat and cold and particle radiation discolor the optical qualities and gradually decrease the bandwidth. Managers at several sites with very large installations have discovered this first-hand. Furthermore, optical cable requires a different and specific set of connectors, polishing equipment, cutting tools, and diagnostic tools. The infant technology to bridge Token-Ring to fiber networks (including FDDI) is ill-defined and not standardized, although dedicated FDDI multiprotocol routers are changing this.

## Token-Ring Compatibility

Token-Ring is consistent with the IEEE 802.5 standard for the physical interconnection of nodes on a network. Signaling characteristics are all the same for the various options. Figure 5.13 lists the Token-Ring signaling characteristics. In effect, all 4 Mbits/s Token-Ring LANs conform to the original 802.5 specification unless the physical medium

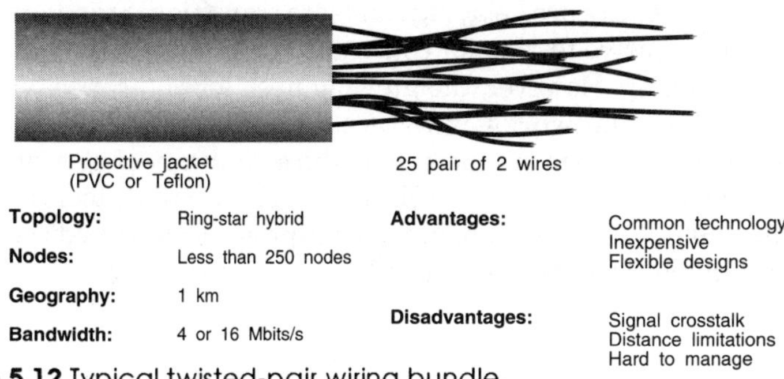


**Figure 5.12** Typical twisted-pair wiring bundle.

- DC to upper frequency limit
- One channel per pair of twisted-pair
- Token and ring poll provides "carrier"
- Manchester encoding scheme; non-return-to-zero
- Digital transmission (no modem translations)

**Figure 5.13** Token-Ring signaling characteristics.

is not the standard STP medium. 16 Mbits/s is a later refinement. Also, UTP refinements, which are included to revisions in 802.5, are more susceptible to noise and wiring resistance loss. There are at least five major IEEE subcommittees on LANs; one to define a standard for media (802.1), the logical link (802.2), Ethernet (802.3), token bus (802.4), Token-Ring (802.5), and the Metropolitan Area Network (802.6).

Network compatibility is also a function of network length and length of individual node connections. Token-Ring transmission is based upon a statistical signal and ranges of signal acceptance. Violation of those specifications does not per se mean that a network will not work; it merely means that the network could function, albeit poorly. Exceeding trunk lengths or lobe lengths, or inserting shielded twisted-pair connections and unshielded twisted-pairs stresses the network. Compatibility should be viewed in these terms as well. Chapter 6 illustrates these limitations.

Note that while NetBIOS and IPX/SPX are supposed to provide a consistent application-layer function, these definitions leave enough gray area for different vendors to define inconsistent software standards. This is rapidly changing as vendors see a reason to agree with competitors on compatibility. However, Token-Ring and TCP/ IP do provide a migration path to the ISO protocol.

The OSI model has become generally accepted by industry due to the globalization of telecommunications and data communications; it is a *de facto* standard. Despite the many vendors' claims that OSI architecture and compatibility are priorities for new products, implementation shortfalls plus the massive weight of the existing installed base of noncompliant hardware and software are delaying complete transition. Standardization implies comprehensive testing for conformity to OSI, and this is a monumental undertaking. However, the growing need for enterprise-wide networks, corporate networks with access to most employees, and multiple-site installations are increasing the complexity of network management. The desire for new network tracking and control tools as promised by the OSI CMIP network management protocol will speed transition to the OSI standards and encourage full vendor compliance.

## Operational Comparisons

Wireless networks are based upon infrared or radio frequency signal transmissions. Token-Ring functions exactly the same by transmitting signals through the air and through the walls. Even *spread-spectrum technology* (SST), which uses multiple frequencies, carries a single Token-Ring channel. The only differences between the more traditional STP network and a wireless network are the lack of media and the higher cost for wireless. No connecting wires are required.

This technology is useful for environments where equipment is frequently relocated, although the same results could be achieved simply by constructing a modular wiring plant. It is also useful for new or small networks where it would not be necessary for anyone to learn how to wire a network. It is superb for buildings where adding wiring would be a prohibitive process; this includes old buildings without conduits, hollow walls, or false ceilings, or buildings with an asbestos problem.

Infrared technology is not advisable for dusty, dirty, or smoky environments because particles degrade signals. Infrared technology is also limited by line-of-sight installations and potential conflicts with other infrared transmitters. In other words, transmitters and receivers must see each other. Radio-frequency is useful for small installations since it is a single channel network. Transmission frequency is usually a single channel which limits installation to about 32 nodes. See Chapter 11 for more information about sideband, spread-spectrum transmission, and multiple-frequency units. Figure 5.14 shows a wireless transmitter-receiver unit.

### Token-Ring Reliability

Token-Ring is generally a reliable medium when it is designed, installed, and maintained according to specification. When a node fails electrically, the MAU or hub will try to isolate that lobe by switching relays. When a MAU fails, other MAU units automatically try to ring wrap by isolating it from the ring. This "fail-safe" operation is not perfect and

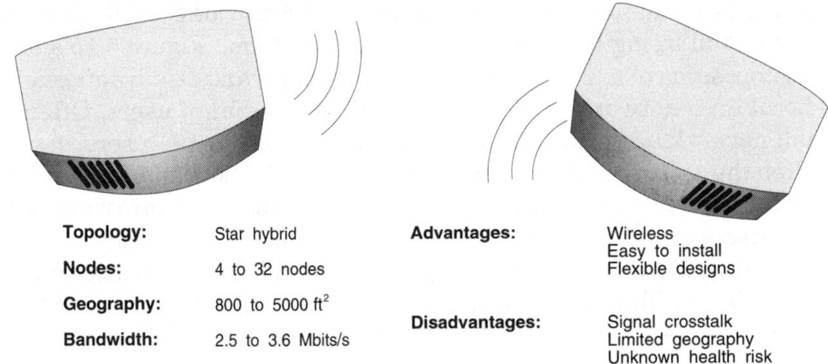


**Figure 5.14** Baseband wireless units.

sometimes nodes and MAUs will be incorrectly disconnected. The passive nature of all Token-Ring connections excludes devices from the ring until they send out the phantom voltage; this tends to preserve the integrity of the ring. Similarly, the genderless (hermaphroditic) connectors mail fail over time or use. They normally create a closed ring when a jumper is removed from a MAU or node, or when a node is physically detached from a wall plate. Nonetheless, these genderless media connectors may not detach properly—the fingers do not electrically short as intended. As a result, the ring breaks because a lobe is stuck in a open state. Metal fatigue, improper force at installation, or dirt can cause the metal fingers in the connectors to remain open. This open link will defeat the ring. However, nodes that beacon may require active intervention.

Review new installations or upgrades that are not working for improper installation techniques, connector and connection failures, bad components, as well as configuration settings for nodes. Typically, a Token-Ring node set for the wrong speed at the NIC will disable the entire LAN since that node must repeat every other node's signal. Similarly, different buffer sizes, packet sizes, or memory mapping for buffers could disable one node, and thus the entire network.

### Token-Ring on Optical Fiber

Optical fiber Token-Ring is defined for a special connection to repeat signals between two distant segments and, increasingly, for high-performance Token-Ring. Token-Ring is not normally transported by optical fiber, although a small group of vendors are providing PC adapter boards for optical fiber Token-Ring, encapsulating transport mechanisms to bridge networks and connections to standard STP Token-Ring. Optical fiber is a transitional method for building enterprise-wide networks.

Optical fiber networks are more expensive and more difficult to debug, maintain, and expand than an electrical network but it provides greater reliability, faster transmission speeds, and a larger geographic reach for the LAN; is not susceptible to electronic noise or signal crosstalk; and provides excellent security. Optical networks also provide 4- to 10-km rings, although full lasing FDDI links can extend to 36 km. Figure 5.15 shows the composition of a fiber cable and its advantages and disadvantages.

Local area networks rarely service just a handful of users. Often, a small network has grown rapidly to encompass 50 or 100 users, and as is often the case with Token-Ring, becomes a traffic bottleneck. The most common and effective solution is to partition the network into rings with fewer users and connect the segments to a Token-Ring bridgeiBridge, router, or packet switch. However, the demand for backbones with a greater bandwidth is encouraging many users to install optical fiber backbones like Fiber Data Distributed Interchange (FDDI). Not only does optical fiber (FDDI) provide a greater bandwidth at faster speeds than STP 16 Mbits/s; it also promises a precocious upgrade path and

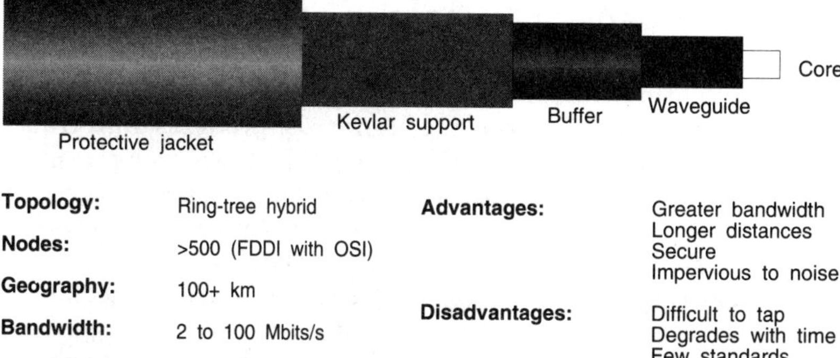


| | | | |
|---|---|---|---|
| **Topology:** | Ring-tree hybrid | **Advantages:** | Greater bandwidth<br>Longer distances<br>Secure<br>Impervious to noise |
| **Nodes:** | >500 (FDDI with OSI) | | |
| **Geography:** | 100+ km | **Disadvantages:** | Difficult to tap<br>Degrades with time<br>Few standards |
| **Bandwidth:** | 2 to 100 Mbits/s | | |

**Figure 5.15** Optical fiber cable.

priority traffic support. However, FDDI integration is not a simple process. While some vendors provide plug and play functionality for copper (CDDI), you must assess the level of service that each vendor's technology supports. Remember that internetworking, distributed processing, and network computing require advanced bridging and routing, as well as gateway applications that can decouple communications so that faster 16 Mbits/s segments are not slowed to accommodate the slower, standard 4 Mbits/s Token-Ring.

The physical layer (PHY) is a standard consisting of a 100 Mbits/s token ring using 62.5 and 125 micron twin optical fibers. The modal bandwidth at 850 nanometers should be 160 MHz/km. Cable attenuation at that distance should be -3.5 to 5.0 decimals/km. The FDDI connector is a polarized duplex connector housing two ferrules within a single shell. One connector transmits; the other receives. The connector polarization prevents mismatching. An FDDI network has a ring topology with concentrators providing branches to achieve a physical star configuration with special node attachment requirements, as Figure 5.16 lists. Transmission is via a single or dual fiber (or four-wire copper) counterrotating ring. The ring itself is self-healing and will link itself together to bypass a failed station when a fault is detected.

- DAS—dual-attachment station (workstations)
- SAS—single-attachment station (secondary networks)
- Wiring concentrators—DAS devices to connect multiple SAS devices

**Figure 5.16** FDDI ring topology. FDDI supports three devices that attach to the dual ring to form a ring and star configuration.

## Network Management Protocols

Management and control functions are perceived as a major requirement for the continued success, increased complexity, and advanced technical development of networking standards, protocols, and transmission media. This is particularly relevant to the development of heterogeneous networks, enterprise-wide installations, and distributed networks. Since the Token-Ring protocol actually defines very few network management functions other than token passing, ring poll, beaconing, and ring-wrap, network management is usually seen as a feature of the network software. Two important network management protocols are currently defined but only partially available to service these needs. The acronyms are SNMP and CMIP. There is also a transitional implementation of CMIP over TCP (CMOT). CMOT is an interim solution since TCP/IP stacks do not mesh with the OSI protocol when applying a UDP protocol.

### SNMP

*Simple Network Management Protocol* (SNMP) is an network management protocol released in a 1988 Request for Comment by the Internet Activities Board. This *de facto* protocol was constructed to address the long lead times facing review and acceptance of more formal standards drafted by either ANSI or ISO. SNMP is implemented by many network hardware and software vendors. Clearly, vendors are trying to address the complex and increasing user need for managing and maintaining networks and communicate to customers that they do understand the need for conforming to network standards.

SNMP definition is one of simplicity, flexibility, and current availability. This has made it attractive. It is consistent with TCP/IP networks (almost all Token-Ring sites), which make sense since it was defined by Internet. Some proponents tout this standard as realistic as well. It consists of three parts. This includes the structure of management information (SMI), the management information base (the MIB database), and the SNMP protocol itself, as Figure 5.17 indicates.

The SMI and MIB specify the information database structures and network alert conditions, and actually store this data. The SNMP protocol transports the information to and from SNMP agents at the MAC datagram level; a logical link does not even have to be established. This implies that data capture is simple and passive. SNMP agents are any network devices that capture, maintain, and forward MIB data to a management station. Agents include MAUs, intelligent hubs, bridges, routers, gateways, specialized remote monitors, and computers at any legal node location. Agents have also included household toasters, mechanized toy animals, and other gadgets automated by vendors to demonstrate the flexibility of their own extensions to the SNMP function-call library. Since these extensions are by no means standardized,

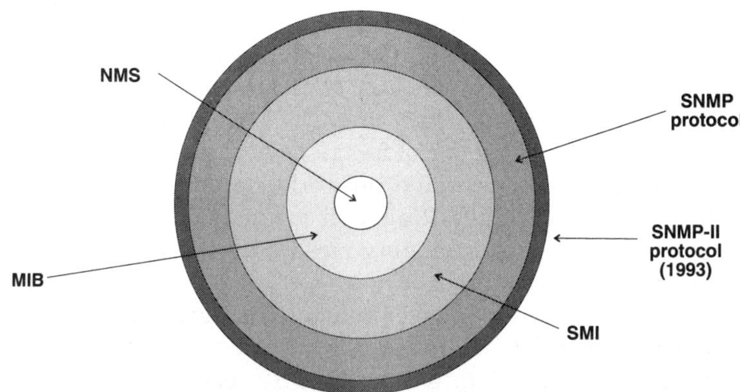


**Figure 5.17** The Simple Network Management Protocol (SNMP).

there is substantial risk of nonconformity, noncompatibility, and selection of the wrong network management software. The SNMP database and the delivery of its data can provide global network management or control of selected subsections.

A centralized network management station (NMS) is the master repository for all managed agents and the MIBs. It controls network agents via commands issued and transported at the datagram level. No logical connections are maintained between the NMS and any agents; this lowers network overhead. SNMP can trigger alarms on the basis of captured agent information and unsolicited alert information from a network agent. However, the implementation of SNMP does not detract from the more rigorous goal of a comprehensive network management tool to provide management information on complex networks. Ordinarily, SNMP does not provide information across bridges and gateways since it is a TCP/ IP derivative and not OSI- compliant. Novell IPX/SPX is also a derivative protocol and is not fully OSI-compliant. To meet this limitation, vendors are providing remote management tools (hardware and software), or transitional CMOT as an interim compromise. These tools collect and transport network performance data over various communications channels to bypass bridge or gateway limitations.

### CMIP

The *Common Management Information Protocol* (CMIP) is a model formally accepted by the International Standards Organization (ISO) for network management in 1990. The obstacle to acceptance and implementation is that CMIP requires the network hardware and software including upper-level protocols to provide complete compliance to the Open Systems Interconnect seven-layer network model. Many networks do not adhere to segmentation of the OSI model and allow layers to bypass the chain of layered control and communicated directly with other layers. Additionally, due to its increased power and complexity, the storage requirements for the CMIP database are least 3 times larger and code is 2.5 times larger.

The CMIP management protocol functions at the highest layer of the OSI model. Many widely accepted networks do not comply with this standard. This includes Token-Ring as it is functionally implemented. TCP/ IP does provide an overlapping mesh with these standards, but lacks clear demarcations within or between OSI layers 2 and 3. It does not maintain a clear chain of layer control. This structure for CMIP, CMOT, and SNMP are illustrated in Figure 5.18.

Additionally, developers state that the OSI network model requires code segmentation and "bloat." While SNMP requires only 8.7K for protocol and 63K of computer memory for message code/decode instructions, in comparison, CMOT instead requires 127K for protocol and 182K for code/decode. This results in extensive code, even duplicate code for each layer, and severe performance degradation on most network nodes. Few personal computers yet have the necessary CPU capacity to be OSI-compliant. This is an even more serious concern where smart repeaters, bridges, and gateways must reprocess frames in real time for retransmission. Note that FDDI networks frequently provide management from the hub with FDDI's station management protocol in lieu of SNMP or CMIP.

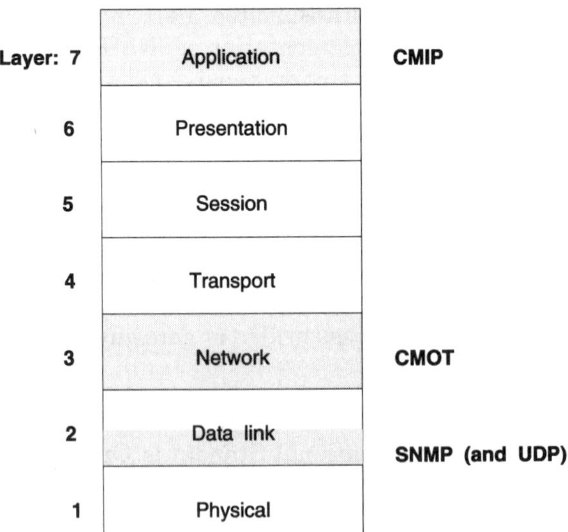


**Figure 5.18** CMIP is activated at the application layer, whereas SNMP functions only partially at the data link level as datagrams. CMOT is a network-level compromise that allows User Datagram Protocol (UDP) frame inclusions within 802.5 packets.

Because both IPX/SPX and TCP/ IP and SNMP derived from the Internet organization, there is a realistic symbiosis for this new management tool. However, vendors promise to supply SNMP and add the more rigorous CMIP functionality in transitional steps. Furthermore, many vendors will likely provide both within the same software to manage traditional NetBios networks bridged from OSI networks. Old protocols endure for many years and must be somehow integrated with advancing technology.

The OSI and CMIP model provide four aspects of network management. This model is mapped in Figure 5.19. These are network security, naming, addressing, and actual network management functions. The network manager interacts with the Management Application Process (MAP), or simply the *Network Manager AP*. This software application are the *Management Specific Application Service Elements* (MSASEs) and the *Common Management Information Service Element* (CMISE). The MSASE are global-application functions, while the CMISE interacts with a set of *Local Management Application Entities* (LMAEs). LMAEs are peer-to-peer objects that are managed. The bulk of the information is contained in the MSASEs and the CMISE. LMAEs only allow the means to obtain or control operational parameters used within each OSI protocol layer. Note that not every layer must have a LMAE, but LMAEs must respond to commands from the MSASEs.

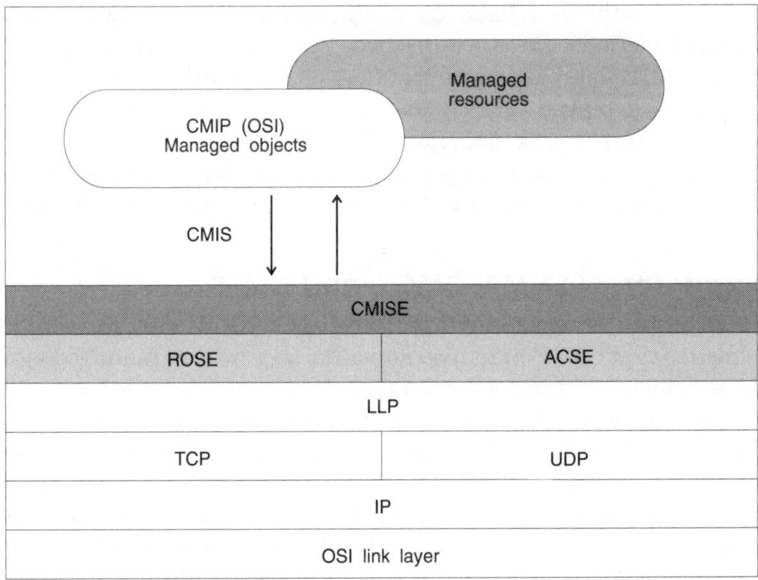


**Figure 5.19** The CMIP layer representation.

There are five MSASEs residing on top of the CMISE. These include *Account Management* (AM), *Configuration and Name Management* (CM), *Fault Management* (FM), *Performance Management* (PM), and *Security Management* (SM). These tools must respond to commands from a MSASE component. The *Association Control Service Element* (ACSE) is a software application entity programmed with sufficient information to access an appropriate LMAE. The ACSE also obtains and transfers information to the *Remote Operation Service Elements* (ROSEs). Remote objects include repeaters, routers, bridges, gateways, nodes, and other devices that have been recognized as OSI management agents. These agents are known as *OSI resources*. Remote-object control and management is particularly relevant for extended networks of networks including enterprise-wide networks. Essentially, CMIP is useful when there are linked sets of LANs which are called *domains* in the OSI CMIP terminology.

Once an association has been established between the CMISE and any LMAE (using the services of the ACSE), network data can begin to flow. This information provides event reporting, information transfer, and control. *Event reporting* is used to initiate transfer of information from an agent (LMAE) to the CMISE. In other words, the managed agents send their information back to the network management database. *Information transfer* is the operation where the network management software requests specifically statistical data from the managed agents. *Control* is the terminology used where the CMISE initiates selected actions by the LMAE agent. Figure 5.20 lists the CMIP MSASE and their functions. Response to these commands are actions, entries into the CMIP database (once the flow of information is initiated), or information displayed directly to the network manager's console. The MSASE is the network manager's interface to the MAP. It is either interactive or embedded in operations that can occur as automatically required. Information that can be captured is included in Chapters 16.

## Comparison of SNMP, CMOT, and CMIP

CMIP is a connection-oriented protocol, while SNMP is connectionless. This means that CMIP-managed networks require that managed agents must establish communication links and maintain these conversations. This requires network resources in the form of packet transmissions. On the other hand, SNMP also requires network resources in the form of UDP/ IP frame transmissions. The difference is that CMIP management is assured that messages, alarms, and data will be delivered unless there is a break in the network, while the comparable SNMP protocols are not guaranteed. SNMP alarms, messages, collision, and packet counts are like junk mail; they may or may not arrive, and if the management station is offline even if they arrive, that transmitted

| CMIP MSASE | MSASE Actions |
|---|---|
| AM | Initialize request |
| | Abort request |
| CM | Manage primitives |
| | Reset |
| | Load |
| | Time |
| | System print |
| FM | TCP |
| | Event |
| | Confirm event |
| | Linked |
| | Confirm get |
| | Set |
| | Confirm set |
| | Action |
| | Confirm action |
| | Terminate action |
| | Quit |
| PM | Get information |
| | Put information |
| SM | Username |
| | Password |

**Figure 5.20** MSASE Commands to CMISE Services.

information is lost. SNMP has a limited trap capability to catch unsolicited error messages and sends out only six types of unconfirmed asynchronous messages. SNMP is statistically efficient much as CMSA/CD is more efficient than Token-Ring but not as reliable. CMIP requires much more overhead. However, SNMP alarms and traps of network failure may go unacknowledged, nor can it provide authentication. SNMP requires approximately 300 bytes per managed device and network management host structure. CMOT implementations require about 500 bytes.[2]

CMIP can synchronize operations and perform multiple requests with a single transaction. CMIP operations can be linked for the same performance and efficiency effect. It can also browse MIB (managed devices) databases, whether the devices are newly installed or under prior management. While SNMP cannot review multiple objects at a time, CMIP can do wildcard searches. Since CMIP must poll to get data, there could be a maximum of 4500 managed devices against the 180,000 or so that SNMP could invisibly track. CMIP might be able to poll only

2 *Communications of IEEE*, Networking Management of TCP/IP, July 1990.

750 devices on a WAN because of the slower transmission speeds. SNMP cannot perform actions. CMIP does allow for the direct and imperative management of devices. In conclusion, SNMP is more useful as a protocol analyzer for monitoring network performance than as an active network management tool. While CMIP is the better solution, to date it has not been implemented sufficiently.

## Network Economies

The economies-of-scale for STP, UTP, and optical fiber networks are significantly changing as technology develops and matures. STP provides a moderate-cost LAN. Initial cost is moderately high, although each additional node is inexpensive. It is highly flexible. UTP is almost identical, although the media cost runs about two-thirds the cost of STP. All other component costs are the same. UTP is also marginally feasible in some sites with existing phone wiring. Tread carefully, because subsequent installation and management costs often make UTP more expense than STP. However, the TIA/EIA-586 premise wiring standards provide a means to apply UTP with minimal risk. Fiber networks provide higher speeds and even multiple-channel capacity, although the greater bandwidth is available at very high initial costs. There are also very high costs for additional nodes, for repairs, and for configuration changes. It is highly inflexible. STP Token-Ring is more common than UTP Token-Ring or optical fiber networks. STP- and UTP-based networks are likely for new Token-Ring installations because of cost, availability, existing cabling options, performance, and compatibility considerations. Consider UTP category 5 as an option since this provides a ready path for upgrade to 100 Mbits/s. Furthermore, the application of a standard wiring methodology provides a means to interchange Token-Ring, FDDI, telephones, Ethernet, serial terminals, or other data communications equipment (DCE) without recabling a site. Economizing with unshielded twisted-pair is clearly effective, although distance and performance limitations are apt to create reliability problems without careful attention to installation, specification, and network maintenance.

Chapter

# 6

# Token-Ring Hardware

This chapter describes the hardware commonly employed to construct Token-Ring networks, and the physical channel limitations inherent in Token-Ring. Token-Ring is often selected because the hardware is simple and operating software is readily available in multiple alternatives (Novell, LAN Server, LAN Manager, AS/400 LAN, and OS/2 LAN). The protocol is defined by IEEE standards. Furthermore, hardware is interchangeable to some extent among vendors. This provides compatibility between the equipment of different manufacturers. Token-Ring is often selected because it can bridge operating systems and ignore some inherent differences in data and file structures (Unix, DOS, OS/2, AS/400, and IBM 30XX). This basic simplicity promotes reliable interconnections. Relative to other network building blocks, the hardware for Token-Ring is simple, reliable, and uniform, and varying very little from vendor to vendor.

## Hardware

The hardware required for the actual Token-Ring network is elementary. The most minimal configuration is made up of *node-based* wireless transmitters, which eliminate the need for any network wiring. The more usual configuration is a *star-based* wiring scheme with a central focal point. It is important to recognize that while Token-Ring is logically configured as a ring or loop with computer nodes—hence the "ring" nomenclature—the actual physical wiring configuration is a star. Although some token-based networks are wired exactly as physical rings, the predominate IBM Token-Ring is always physically wired as a star. This configuration comprises a *multiple access unit* (MAU) or *multiple station access unit* (MSAU) and spoke wires, called *lobes*, to interconnect all nodes. The MAU is a central hub, passive wiring concentrator, or intelligent device which provides star-configured wiring to *multiple* nodes. A MAU usually supports eight nodes; some support 16 or 24 nodes, while intelligent hubs provide bus slots for up to 16 boards supporting eight nodes apiece. The connecting wire consists of twisted-pair wire bundles, genderless (hermaphroditic) connectors, and telephone modular jumpers. [Optical fiber (IBM Type 5, dual 100/140 mm) supports Token-Ring, although this is rarely implemented except where NSD A1 level security is sought; see Chapter 17.] Shielded twisted-pair (STP), and to a lesser degree unshielded twisted-pair (UTP), are most commonly used because of their performance characteristics, extensive vendor experience and product support, and pricing.

STP consists of dual pairs of wire twisted about themselves three to six times per foot; this twisting minimizes crosstalk. It is then surrounded by a foil and woven strand shield. It is often designated as as IBM Type 1, IBM Type 2, IBM Type 3, IBM Type 6, and IBM Type 9. Type 1 is the most prevalent grade. Type 6 is used for jumpers, and Type 2 is identical to Type 1 but with the addition of four UTP pairs for voice communications. Alternatively, the *Electronics Industries Associations / Telecommunications Industries Association* (EIA/TIA) has ratified a premise wiring standard called EIA/TIA-568 provides precise guidelines defining communications wiring (data, image, and voice). It formalizes category 3 100-ohm unshielded twisted-pair wire with four copper pairs as suitable for transmission speeds to 10 Mbits/s, category 4 100-ohm unshielded twisted-pair wire, also with four copper pairs as suitable for transmission speeds to 16 Mbits/s, and category 5 100-ohm unshielded twisted-pair wire with four copper pairs as suitable for transmission speeds to 100 Mbits/s. STP with 150-ohm dual pairs is rated up 155 Mbits/s and thus suitable for the low-end ATM cell relay. STP-3 is comparable to Type 9, but is often used for Ethernet 10Base-T; STP-3 is adequate for Token-Ring subject to some significant length limitations.

It is important to recognize that IBM STP Type 3 represents a different designation system from category 3 wire. The wire itself is typically 24-gauge copper wire with a PVC or Teflon coating. A better grade of UTP-3 performs 100 percent better than a low-quality version. UTP-4 is more expensive and recommended by many twisted-pair suppliers. There is a quality difference between voice-grade and data-grade UTP. Qualify the one you install. STP performs better than UTP because it has better insulation against insertion capacitance and resistance to low-frequency electromagnetic noise—which means that it shields the signal and is rarely affected by external interference or internal crosstalk for the intended applications. The EIA/TIA specifications are intended to circumvent the market confusion and spurious claims for the many different types of wiring.

Rigorous manufacturing specifications and true adherence to EIA/TIA wiring and connector ratings will help ensure a reliable network and ensure a generally-accepted conformity among different lots of cable and different manufacturers. Shielded wire provides dramatically improved service and longer run lengths than unshielded wire bundles because crosstalk is minimized, signal disruption is less, and signal attenuation is decreased. The transmitting characteristics for an STP or UTP wiring bundle are comparable but notably different. However, they can be bridged easily with a device called an unshielded media *lobe attachment module* (LAM) or a Type 3 media filter. The IBM LAM retimes and amplifies Token-Ring signals for UTP (categories 3, 4, and 5). The LAM supports distances to 90 meters at 16 Mbits/s on UTP category 3.

The signals on twisted-pair are DC current fluctuations. Twisted-pair is actually two pairs; one for transmission and the other for reception. These pairs cross over so that a transmitter circuitry operating on DC current connects to the receiver circuitry and the receiver connects to a transmitter for each node pair to form the ring architecture. Although this may appear as a two-lane, two-way highway, the transmit pair is really only a continuation of the receive pair to complete the ring structure. Transmission is uni-directional. One of the reasons shielding is so important is that the Token-Ring NIC functions as a repeater and while it is still receiving a signal on the *receive* (RX) wire pair it will be retransmitting that signal on the *transmit* (TX) wire pair with an electronics-based delay of only a few milliseconds. The stronger and more stable outgoing signal has a tendency to distort the weaker incoming signal, as Figure 6.1 indicates.

This explanation is pertinent to the understanding of why STP performs better than UTP. Token-Ring was designed to be a modulated DC current closely corresponding to a digital waveform. The differences between media and quality of media are reflected in the overall achievable network lengths and lengths between nodes. Shielded is better than unshielded twisted-pair because it provides less signal distortion, timing irregularities, and strength loss.

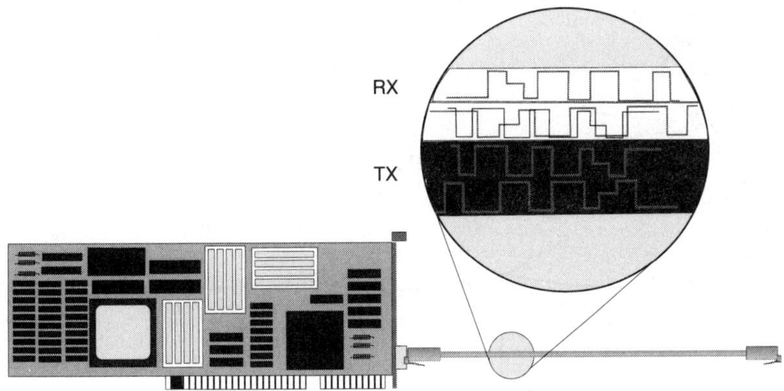


**Figure 6.1** Incoming signals tend to be distorted.

As explained above, Token-Ring specifies a logical ring design, but a star cluster design for the actual twisted-pair wiring. The MAU or other hub device is at the center of the star. Nodes connect independently to the twisted-pair hub. Independent wires or composite bundles traverse a facility, and special bridging hardware interconnects stand-alone segments and other twisted-pair hubs, and extends the geographic reach of the network. Figure 6.2 shows a typical network configuration with a simplified representation of the Token-Ring hardware.

A Token-Ring network consists of wire; connectors, including modular connectors and jacks; the MAU; and the individual node network interface controllers. Often, the wiring is connected through a central wiring closet with a patch panel and jumpers.

The network has electronic components, limited to MAUs or hubs, and controllers at each node location. The difference between MAUs and hubs are that MAUs tend to be passive devices (not powered by external AC) switched by a sudden *phantom voltage*. Hubs are active (powered by AC) and sometimes intelligent devices that monitor the nodes for activity and conformance to specification. Phantom voltage is important since it activates relays when a node wants to insert itself into a ring and maintains that node within the ring. When a node does not conform to specification, those relays maintaining the connection for that node may drop it from the ring to protect the integrity of the ring. Similarly, when a MAU or hub is perceived to be failing, other MAUs of hubs will deactivate relays and drop that device. This event is called a *ring wrap*, and it automatically reconfigures the LAN to exclude potentially disrupted devices.

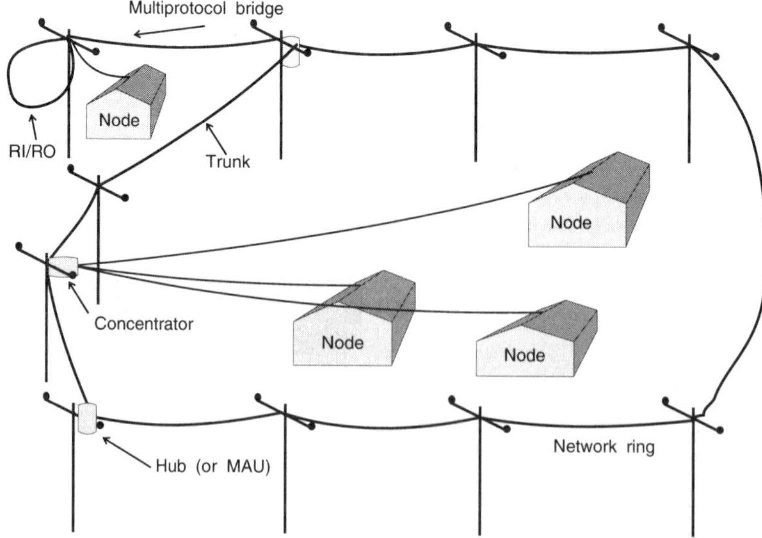


**Figure 6.2** Representation of a Token-Ring network.

## Token-Ring Operations

Conceptually, Token-Ring is simple. The wireless or twisted-pair provide one-way channel connectivity between communicating parties (computer nodes) like daisy-chained Christmas tree lights; the ends of the chain connect together, however, to form a closed ring. The channel is the data communications pathway. A packet or Token-Ring frame is the transmission vehicle. While Token-Ring is a line waiting for a single phone booth (only a single transmission can proceed at a time), the transmission token protocols, which are rules of privacy or silence, accomplish an orderly transition for deciding who can transmit. Figure 6.3 pictures this analogy.

Each node has transmission and reception hardware, telephone handsets, if you will. This hardware controls access to the communications channel twisted-pair wire or wireless, and monitors traffic. Additionally, each node has hardware that builds the messages to match the required Token-Ring frame format. The transmission-reception hardware is called a *network interface controller* (NIC) or *network adapter*. This is analogous to the earphone and microphone. There is no traffic control hardware. Traffic control is handled totally by software; packet destination information—analogous to the box and dialing mechanisms of a phone system—is provided by a variable address within each packet. The adapter for each node connects into the ring through the MAU or hub just as a telephone cable stretches to the overhead wire from each house. At the other end, the Token-Ring controller connects to the workstation hardware via the computer bus, and interfaces with system software. The single component raises reliability and lowers hardware cost.

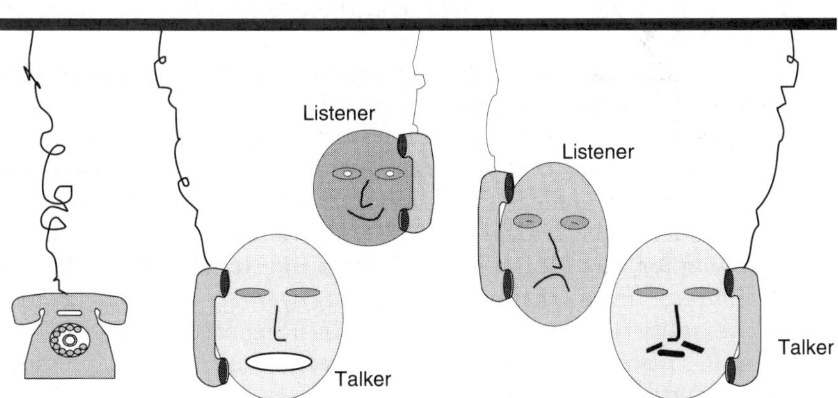


**Figure 6.3** The party-line telephone analogy.

## Controller Functionality

Continuing the telephone analogy, the adapter (and network software described in Chapter 5) limit access to the telephone to one caller at a time and direct the transition from one transmission direction to another. The adapter waits for a token. A *token* is a fixed sequence of digital bits. It is also a Token-Ring frame without source address, destination address, or any data. "Capture" of this token provides the permission for a node to send data. A packet, which is assembled by the controller either in workstation memory or in special buffer memory on the controller board itself, is then broadcast on the outgoing transmission line. This packet is a series of digital electrical pulses (within a range -3.0V to +4.5V DC) called a *signal.* This signal is transmitted at a fraction (approximately 48 to 67 percent) of the speed of light ($3 \times 10^2$ meters per second). This packet signal travels through the lobe wires to the MAU or hub where it is switched to the next downstream node. This node in turn receives, retimes, and repeats the signal to the next downstream node. This sequence is replicated until the signal returns to the originating node where only the token (e.g. an empty packet) is then transmitted to the network. Packets addressed to intermediate nodes will be copied into packet buffer memory by those nodes.

Despite this enormous signal propagation velocity, the *token rotation time* (TRT) is measurable in milliseconds. In fact, the protocol requires that the TRT must be at least 7.9 ms for 4 Mbits/s LANs and 4.8 ms for 16 Mbits/s LANs. This corresponds to the time required for a 24-bit token packet to propagate around the shortest possible ring and accommodate the electronic signal repeater delay inherent in active nodes. Nodes on LANs which are too short (about three nodes, one MAU, and minimal trunk of lobe wiring) will hold the token so that the minimal TRT is achieved.

The Token-Ring adapter dials the number and builds the metaphorical phone call that is actually transmitted. This packet, or *frame* as it is also termed, must conform to a rigorous format that ensures that party calls are minimal and that the transmitted packet is addressed to a designated node; by analogy the caller dials the number assigned to the person intended to receive the call. The *network interface card* (NIC), or network adapter, also disassembles packets and transfers this information to the receiving workstation's operating system. Figure 6.4 charts the functionality flow provided by the Token-Ring adapter.

This NIC, also be called a *network access unit* (NAU), provides additional services to increase reliability. First, the NAU shuts down when it senses that the twisted-pair wire is connected to a live telephone circuit. Second, it tests that the wire crosses over so that the transmitter ends of the two pairs connect to a receiver. Third, NAU circuitry on the *wiring concentrators*, which are also called *hubs,* actually boost signal

- Receive signal
- Transmit signal
- Test for reception
- Test for transmission
- Generate beacon signal
- Convert serial-parallel and parallel-serial
- Transmit and receive buffering
- Frame packets
- Encode and decode broadcast signals
- Recognize addresses
- Detect errors and collisions
- Generate and parse preamble
- Provide ring poll sense and deference
- Generate and verify frame check sequences
- Filter signal noise and lack of signal differentiation
- Filter alignment errors and overruns
- Limit data rate to prevent overruns

**Figure 6.4** Token-Ring controller (NIC) functionality.

strength and gain (the difference between the signal highs and lows) to accommodate the lower quality of the unshielded network wiring.

Token-Ring adapter functionality is specified by the OSI model and by the IEEE 802 specification as layers 1 and 2. Some vendors provide "Token-Ring" that is only marginally compatible with other vendor equipment and network software. Equipment from several different vendors will access a Token-Ring and communicate with other equipment from the same vendor and coexist, but will not communicate with any other vendors. The usual causes for such incompatibilites are wiring violations or installation flaws, transmission speed differences, packet and buffer size inconsistencies, or application software differences. Only rarely will vendor implementation of software, NIC drivers, or hardware design errors be at fault. Where network data and voice lines are intertwined, investigate the possibility that telephone ringing voltages (48V) may have damaged hubs or NICs. Because Token-Ring is a universal standard, such specification integrity adds to the desirability of Token-Ring.

## Gateway Functionality

The Token-Ring *gateway*, as presented by the OSI model in Chapter 5, provides network expansion capabilities for network connectivity and packet repetition. The gateway unit provides multiple-segment access, signal retransmission, and medium or software presentation conversions among networks with differing protocols. This mechanism is not normally added unless a network has grown complex or exceeded the basic topology. By analogy, the gateway is either a long-distance switchboard or a telephone call to Western Union Telegram Services which translates format for retransmission to another medium.

## Token-Ring Physical Channel Limitations

Token protocols place certain limitations on the physical channel. These limitations specify maximum signal propagation times and node counts, and as a consequence, maximum lobe lengths, since lobe lengths and propagation time affect the slot time, or TRT. While the precise ring specifications are provided in Table 6.1 at the conclusion of this chapter, these same physical configurations are presented below. These commonly stated limits were derived from the actual electrical specifications of the IEEE 802.5 Token-Ring model.

These limitations are determined by the clock rates, the speed of electrical transmissions, and lobe and adjusted ring lengths, although throughput is limited by node counts, electrical signal delays, and packet overhead. These limitations are explored in greater depth in Chapters 16 and 17.

The ring is composed of two types of wire paths, trunks, and lobes. Trunks connect MAUs or wiring concentrators (hubs). These wires connect into the *Ring in* (RI) and *Ring out* (RO) ports on a MAU. Note that even a single MAU requires a genderless RI/RO patch cable to complete the logical ring for Token-Ring. When a LAN consists of more than a single MAU, RO from the first MAU connects to RI on the next MAU, and so on, until the last MAU. The RO port on the last MAU connects to the RI on the first MAU, thus completing the logical ring structure. Lobes connect nodes to the MAU. This lobe wire may consist of many spliced sections or jumpers, the smallest unit of wire. One or many jumpers, lobes, and trunks with MAUs constitutes a ring, which is a stand-alone network.

The overall *drive distance* is the limit of reliable signal transmission without the aid of repeaters. This distance comprises the combined length of all trunk cables plus twice the length of the longest lobe cable. The drive distance represents the distance an active node must force that signal through a lobe cable, through a MAU, through trunk cables, and through another lobe cable until it reaches the next active node, as Figure 6.5 details. The maximum shielded twisted-pair (IBM Types 1 and 2) drive distance is 770 m at 4 Mbits/s and 346 m at 16 Mbits/s. This decreases to about half for unshielded twisted-pair. The overall ring, called *trunk length*, generally may not exceed 570 m (770 m less maximum 200 m lobe length) at 4 Mbits/s or 246 m at 16 Mbits/s. This is a calculated item and is a combination of the trunk RI/RO cable lengths connecting MAUs and is a factor of the internal wiring within each MAU (about 3 m).

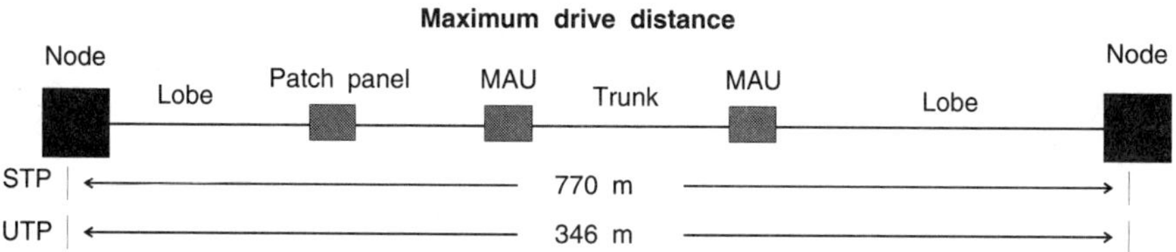


**Figure 6.5** Maximum Token-Ring signal drive lengths.

The *adjusted ring length* (ARL) is the longest potential drive distance that would exist after recovery from the failure of the shortest trunk. The passive relays in the MAUs will close to isolate the failed trunks or MAUs; they automatically reroute the signal around the ring in an alternate path. Node failures do not "ring wrap" unless a segment supported by a MAU fails. As a result, the maximum total coaxial ARL along the longest possible path between any two adapters is twice the longest lobe length plus the total trunk lengths. The propagation velocity is assumed to be 50 percent light speed (300,000 m/s in a vacuum), in the worst case. In this case, the failing MAU will be extracted from the ring, as Figure 6.6 illustrates.

In fact, the ring cannot be composed of a single length of wire. The MAU or hub, and each node forms an arc (or spoke) of the ring. This arc or spoke is generally called a *lobe*. Very often wiring patch panels and multiple jumpers constitute each lobe. Figure 6.7 illustrates this architecture. Many jumpers can be spliced to construct a Token-Ring lobe. These, in fact, ease the burden of debugging most types of network hardware faults. However, in contrast, too many splices will increase

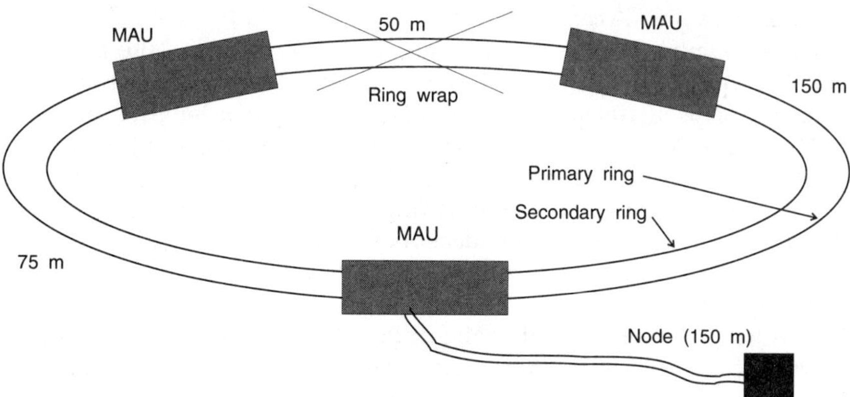


**Figure 6.6** Maximum Token-Ring adjusted ring length. Basic ring is 275 meters. When a ring wraps, the drive distance should not exceed 750 meters.

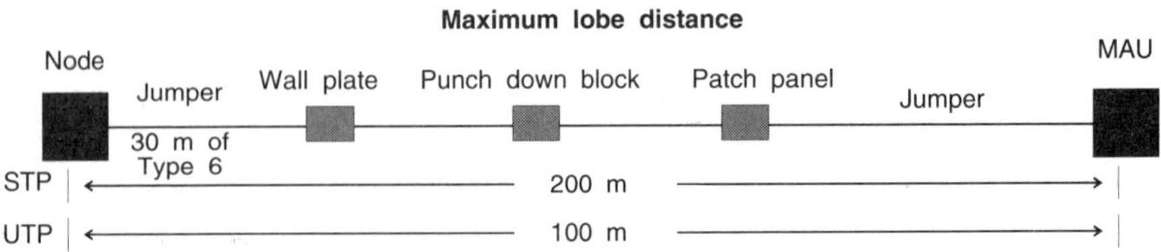


**Figure 6.7** Maximum Token-Ring lobe cable lengths.

the signal distortion and degrade signal quality. Token-Ring connectors are either hermaphroditic media connectors typically used with STP, or 6 pin RJ-11J-11 or 8 pin RJ-45 with UTP. While Token-Ring requires only four pins just like a standard telephone, the different design prevents cross-wiring phones and network equipment. The hermaphoditic plugs provide a self-connecting capability so that jumpers can form their own extension cords without the need for a gender changer. UTP connectors, jacks and plugs are male or female. Moreover, networks utilizing UTP wiring will require a media filter to retime and adjust the distortions caused by unshielded wiring.

There may be repeaters in the path between any two stations. Repeaters can be used to extend the length of the lobe or to extend the one-dimensional ring topology into three-dimensional configurations encompassing different groups, floors, and buildings. Repeaters occupy port positions on each ring and count toward the maximum number of nodes on a ring; this is 250 units for 4 Mbits/s and 136 for 16 Mbits/s STP rings. UTP node capacity is further reduced to 72 nodes. Cabletron Systems recommends a maximum of 66 nodes for rings mixing STP and UTP. The total worst-case round trip delay for all wiring in a single ring system is 366μs for 4 Mbits/s and 296μs for 16 Mbits/s. Figure 6.8 illustrates this node count limitation.

The maximum lobe length is a function of the speed of the network and the type of wiring installed. In no case should it be longer than 200 m for 4 Mbits/s or 100 m for 16 Mbits/s. Maximum lobe length decreases to 100 meters for 4 Mbits/s and 60 meters for 16 Mbits/s. This distance is reduced by about half for unshielded twisted-pair, although this can be sometimes extended with media filters, active nodes, or special hubs that retime, resync, and rebroadcast signal. As such, active nodes may be able to drive signals at 16 Mbits/s the full 100 m at 16 Mbits/s, as Figure 6.8 illustrates.

This length is an optimal configuration. Superb hub and NAU units provide strong and well-differentiated signals, while quality wiring will carry the Token-Ring signal within acceptable distortion and crosstalk limits. In practice, keep this length to practical minimums less than 200 and 100 m for 4 Mbits/s and 16 Mbits/s transmission speed variants. There

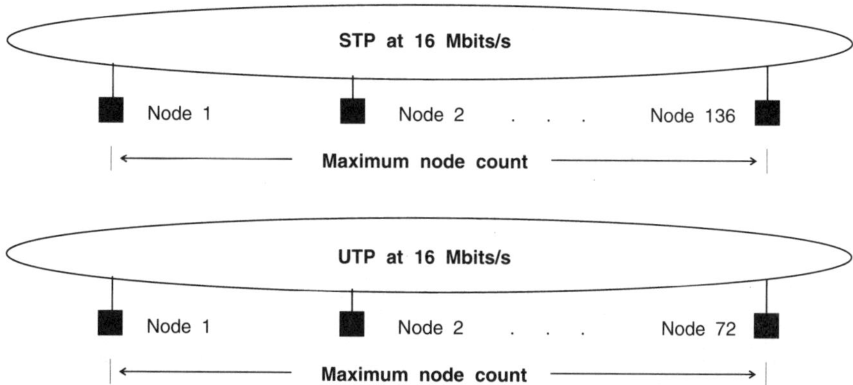


**Figure 6.8** Maximum Token-Ring twisted-pair node counts.

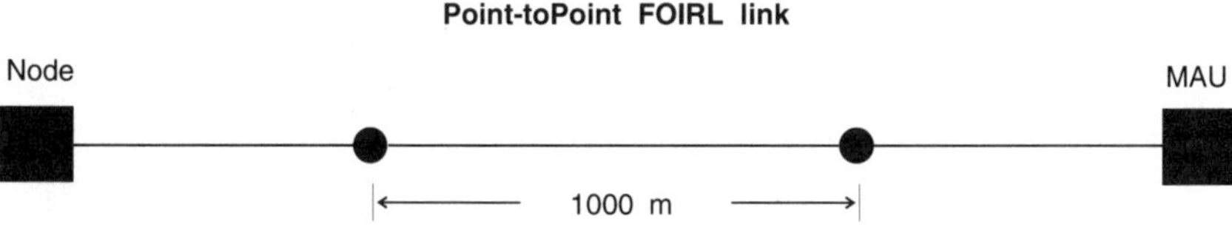


**Figure 6.9** Maximum Token-Ring FOIRL point-to-point link.

may be a maximum of 1000 m of point-to-point fiber optic interconnect repeater link (FOIRL) optical fiber link anywhere in the system, as illustrated in Figure 6.9. This will typically be used to link separate segments in distant buildings. The propagation velocity is assumed to be 78 percent light speed, in the worst case.

Packet size is a maximum of 4621 bytes at 4 Mbits/s and 18,021 bytes at 16 Mbits/s. Packet burst mode and early token release do not affect these limitations. Upper-level protocols, encapsulations, and protocol translations will affect packet (or frame) sizes. Since ARCnet limits frames to 507 bytes and Ethernet to 1518 bytes, interconnected Token-Ring networks will need to adapt to these shorter packets. Because 16 Mbits/s frames can be as long as 18,453 bytes (18,432 bytes of data), FDDI limits its data contents to 4478 bytes (8956 encoded symbols) and the Token-Ring will need to adjust accordingly. Of note, IBM LAN Server and MS LAN Manager create full frame lengths. Novell limits bridged hops to 512 bytes, although it can enable the burst mode protocol. Novell IPX frames are always 4202 bytes or less. Since Novell NetWare is the predominate Token-Ring NOS, the frame limit is a pertinent limitation.

| Twisted-pair specifications | Shielded | | Unshielded | |
|---|---|---|---|---|
| All lengths in meters | 4 Mbits/s | 16 Mbits/s | 4 Mbits/s | 16 Mbits/s |
| Maximum drive distance | 770 | 346 | 346 | 346 |
| Maximum ARL | 570 | 246 | 246 | 246 |
| Maximum trunk segment | 200 | 200 | 100 | 100 |
| Maximum number of nodes | 250 | 136 | 72 | 72 |
| Maximum lobe length | 200 | 100 | 100 | 60 |
| Maximum packet size (in bytes) | 6221 | 18453 | 6221 | 18453 |
| Minimum TRT (in μs) | 7.4 | 4.5 | 7.4 | 4.5 |
| Maximum TRT (in μs) | 510 | 330 | 260 | 280 |
| Signal progagtion speed (c) | 0.58 | 0.58 | 0.54 | 0.54 |

**Table 6.1** Important Token-Ring specifications .

Chapter

# 7

# Token-Ring Software and Process

This chapter explains the Token-Ring data communications process in terms of the operational mechanics. First, data transmission process and structures are outlined. Second, the transmission and reception procedures are presented. Third, transmission deficiencies are described. Last, layer protocols are described.

## Transmission Process

Token-Ring transmits a single digital channel. Transmission is digital because the information is shipped in a cyclic representation, the cornerstone of digital representations. Analog transmission, on the other hand, would convert each digital bit into a voltage representation that parodies the analog value. For example, 0 might require 10 nanoseconds (ns) of no voltage, whereas 1 might require 20 ns of positive voltage. Alternatively, sound could be employed to represent data, whereas gaps might represent lack of data.

Token-Ring, or IEEE 802.5, the standard representation, generates a base voltage level of 0V. When transmitting, a NIC or MAU unit alters the voltage level from a low-end range of -3.0 to -4.5V to the high-end range of +3.0 to +4.5V. By modulating this voltage level, the transmitting node propagates a digital signal wave outward in both directions down the twisted-pair wire. Figure 7.1 demonstrates this signal process.

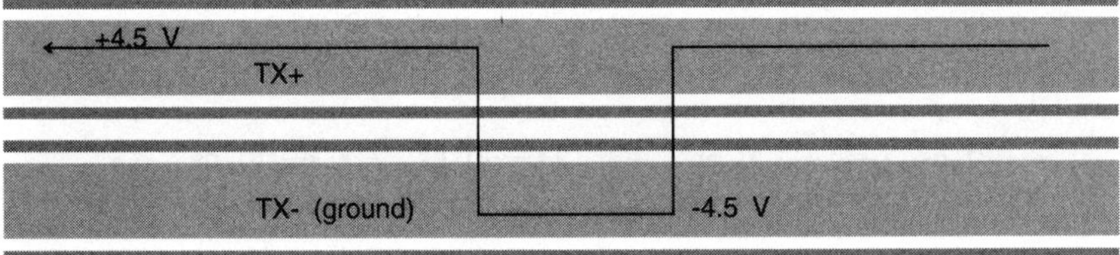


**Figure 7.1** Voltage-modulated signal wave transmission.

In the differential Manchester encoding scheme, the digital signal represents the 0 as a high voltage with a transition to a low voltage, and 1 as a low voltage with a transition to a high voltage. Twisted-pair transmission is accomplished by transmitting the digital voltage modulation to the receiving electronics of the wiring hub concentrator. The cycle time for each partial transmission is 31 ns, thus the time to send each individual bit is 62 nanoseconds; 62 ns translates into 1|16 of a millisecond or into 1/16000000 s, thus yielding the 16,000,000-bit-per-second transmission capacity of Token-Ring. The method is comparable for 4 Mbits/s transmission, although cycle times are four times longer. Figure 7.2 illustrates the Manchester encoding scheme, and shows how Token-Ring achieves these high transmission rates. Note that data coding and compression, a method of packing data into a smaller space, and signal interphasing, a method of transmitting multiple signals simultaneously, conceivably will increase the effective speed above this raw transmission capacity. Also, because Token-Ring employs a differential transition on the electrical signal for each bit, it may be possible to nearly double transmission speed by altering the signal formats. In fact, FDDI encodes four bits into five bits.

It is important that the highs and lows of either the signal wave or DC voltage modulation be well differentiated, as Figure 7.3 shows. Signal interference, signal crosstalk, signal attenuation, or the length of the drive distance itself will degrade the signal and smooth the shape of the signal. This leads to transmission errors. Every active node is a twisted-pair repeater which interprets and regenerates signals for retransmission to the next downstream node on the logical ring (usually

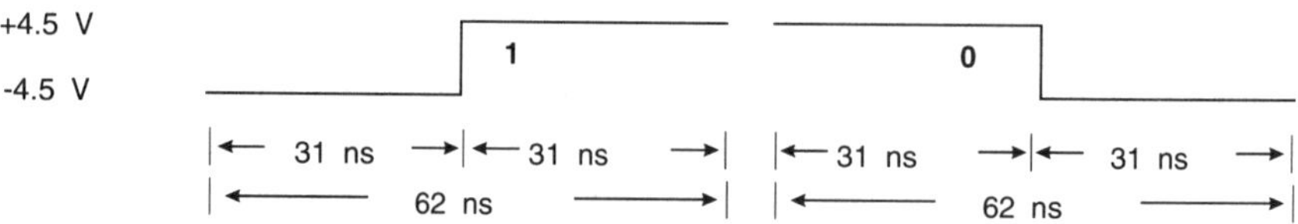


**Figure 7.2** The Manchester encoding method.

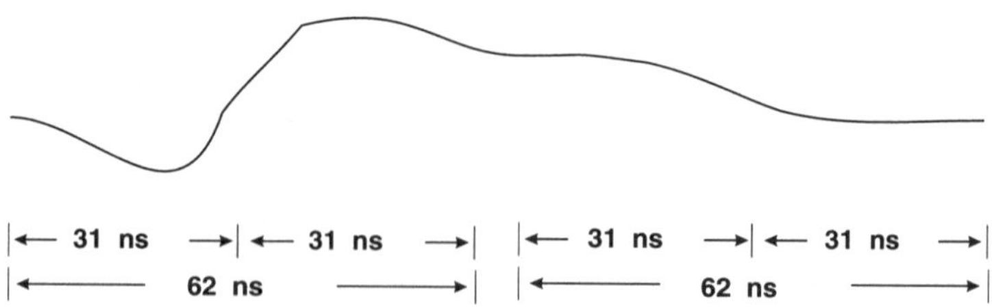


**Figure 7.3** Signal shape must be well-differentiated.

MAU port number + 1). Bad signals only get worse and are less likely to be interpreted correctly. Note that twisted-pair concentrators provide an integrity check; the phantom voltage maintained between transmit-receive pairs ensures that any break, short circuit, stray voltage, static shock, or other electrical malfunction will cause the twisted-pair wiring hub to remove that failed node.

## Packet and Frame Components

Token-Ring transmits information in a "packaged" format. This means that individual bits are not transferred from location to location without preamble or explanation as they are in a dedicated link between mainframe and terminal or between modem-connected DTEs. The information to be transferred, however small or large, must be packaged, weighed, mailed, and checked upon receipt for proper delivery. This packaged format is called an information *packet* or *frame*. Like any postal letter, this packet or frame contains a destination (the destination address), a return address (source address), a delivery weight (control field), the letter contents (actual data field), and a registered receipt (frame check sequence field) as pictured in Figure 7.4. Encapsulation of Token-Ring packets for transport over bridges or gateways requires a secondary format that also must retain the internal characteristics of the Token-Ring packet.

Since Token-Ring is an electronic letter carrier, and letter transits can occur simultaneously, an agreed-upon handshaking between transmitting and receiving nodes prevents letters from crashing into each other and being scrambled (the token passing protocol). When the network is not busy, the token circulates the ring endlessly. The token is a 24-bit signal. It can also be visualized as a packet without address information or data. A token is not informationless, however. It provides information that the ring is functional, and it conveys permission to transmit. The packet and token are represented in Figure 7.5.

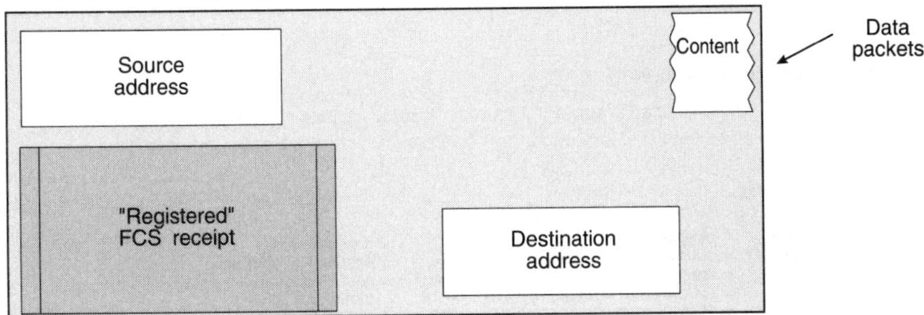


**Figure 7.4** The Token-Ring packet (or frame).

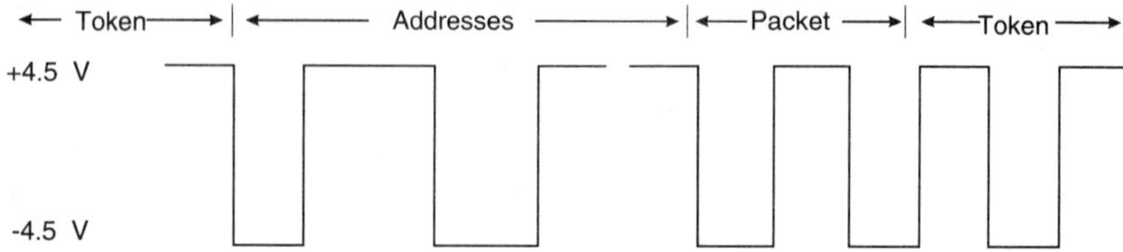


**Figure 7.5** The digital Token-Ring signal.

This voltage information will be referenced in later chapters, specifically for cable testing and troubleshooting. More specific information is contained in Chapters 13 and 14, and again in Chapters 21, 22, and 23, which detail the troubleshooting techniques required by a network management team. Rather than concentrate on voltage-level representations of data, the frame format is presented pictorially in Figure 7.6. The voltage transmissions are handled by the transmission media and the lower layers of the OSI model: media, physical, and data link layers. Above these layers, data are handled within the structure of the frame format. The frame consists of four components: address, type, data, and error detection fields.

## Token and Data Components

Token-Ring has two types of frames. The *token frame* consists of three components: a starting delimiter, access control field, and the ending delimiter. The token frame is basically an empty information field. It serves an important purpose by providing the permission to transmit information when it is held by a node. The *information frame* has the same fields as the token frame plus a few other fields. Specifically, the information frame has frame control field, destination and source address fields, the information field, a frame check sequence, and the frame status.

## Address Components

The *address fields* of an information frame consist of source and destination. No Token-Ring-compatible device has an address until it is assigned

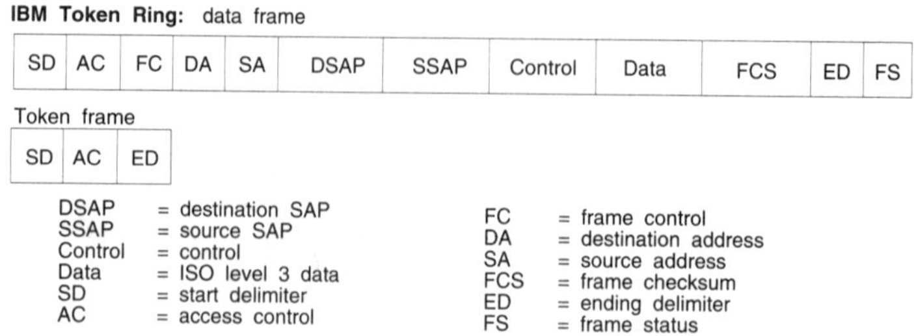


**Figure 7.6** The Token-Ring frame, delimeters, and control fields.

by the active monitor (AM). Depending upon configuration, the address field is 6 bytes. The smaller 2-byte address option has been discontinued. When a LAN is small and is not interconnected because the extra 4 bytes are necessary when there are more than 250 nodes. The potential 4-byte savings became irrelevant and unwarranted to support. The Token-Ring transmission software directly accesses this address. IPX and TCP/ IP, for example, use a 2-byte Internet address, IPX/SPX uses a similar scheme, while OSI employs a 64-byte address. Upper-layer protocols build symbol tables to reference this address and may include *media acces control* (MAC) or *logicaL link control* (LLC) addresses within the actual information field. When a packet is transmitted, these logical addresses are resolved to the actual source and destination Token-Ring addresses.

Addresses are important for all Token-Ring communications. The source node will recognize its own token and remove it from the ring. Destination node(s) will recognize packets as directed to them, copy the information field data, and reset the frame status field. Routers, bridges, and gateways broadcast requests for information in order to build and maintain their routing address tables. Of note, many routers and bridges create a substantial amount of network traffic that can be a bottleneck. The multicast addressing scheme is useful for maintaining router tables. It is also of particular relevance for distributed processing applications. For example, a user might request a specific data item but the application might not know which database on which file server has it. Asingle multicast request packet to all likely file servers is an efficient use of the Token-Ring channel.

### The Data Field

The *data fields* contain up to the maximum 4600 bytes for 4 Mbits/s and 18,432 bytes for 16 Mbits/s. This size is part of the 802.5 specifications and conforms to the "reasonable" *token hold timer* (THT) delay. Although the physical token ring specifications provide these maximum sizes, Token-Ring as implemented by many NOS vendors limits frames to 4202 bytes or 512 bytes when the LAN is bridged (the data field itself is 21 less due to the bytes allocated for ring addresses). The minimum data field size holds 0 bytes. A byte may be referred to as an *octet* to confirm that it is an 8-bit byte. Transmissions of data streams longer than maximum data field size, as in a file transfer, a bit-mapped screen display, or document printing, require multiple packets. Since many nodes contend for channel time, a large transmission might not be a contiguous signal. The upper levels of Token-Ring protocol understand this. In fact, many less powerful computers cannot accept a full 4 Mbits/s because these slower machines need time between frames to disassemble and process received data. The upper-layer protocols on a receiving machine accept such block data communications and modify the rate of frame transmissions to prevent overload.

### The Frame Check

The *Frame Check Sequence (FCS)* is an error detection scheme designed to indicate transmission problems. FCS is sometimes referred to as a *Cyclic Redundancy Check (CRC)*, or simply as a checksum, since the FCS field contains a CRC checksum value. The encoding is defined by a standard generating polynomial, where $x$ is packet length:

$$G(x) = X^{32} + X^{26} + X^{23} + X^{22} + X^{16} + X^{12} + X^{11} + X^{10} + X^{8} + X^{7} + X^{5} + X^{4} + X^{2} + 1.$$

### Frame Status

The frame status provides an accessible update as to the disposition of the frame. This field usually shows whether the destination node has received the data and whether the packet is a valid packet. It is a single byte field.

## Packet Preamble and Overhead Components

There are two more related frame items. The starting delimiter and ending delimiters are 8-bit (1-byte) fields. The starting field serves to synchronize clocks and base transmission timings for the receiving node. The active monitor uses this field to reset the TRT time counter. After unreasonable delays with data or token frames, the active would send out a request to reinitialize the network. This starting delimiter also serves to forewarn NICs that a packet is headed in their direction. The ending delimiter resets the THT.

The first 4 bytes of the data field are reserved for the 802.2 logical link control (LLC) table. The DSAP is the destination service address port while SSAP is the source service address port. The LLC field contains the packet field control information. The rest of the data field contains the actual information transferred by level 3 of the ISO model.

## Token-Ring Protocol Control Fields

The data field is not strictly application-oriented data. Data link layers require control information to initiate, maintain, and conclude any conversation. TCP/ IP and IPX/SPX requires a logical link control. This field often contains additional source and destination addresses and status codes. These status codes are called *service address points*. Figure 7.7 maps these service address points. Two addresses define the link level source and destination, and monitor the framing and synchronization of network transmissions.

**Figure 7.7** 802.2 service address ports of the logical link control field.

## Logical Link Fields

The *logical link control field* specifically provides framing and synchronization, error control and recovery, message acknowledgment, link initialization and disconnection, and addressing. Additionally, this field varies in format depending upon its function. When the data field contains instructional information, this field is called a *supervisory frame*. As stated previously, some receiving stations cannot accept data at the sustained Token-Ring rate of 4 or 16 Mbits/s; one of these supervisory control field functions synchronizes packet transfer rates. When the data field contains acknowledgments and control information, this field is called an *information frame*. Otherwise, when the Token-Ring frame contains only user application data, this field is called an *unnumbered frame*. All logical link control fields contain 16 bits.

## Usage-Specific LLC Frames

Logical link control is also represented by the IEEE 802.2 standards. It is important for transparent packet connectivity and network interconnectivity. The supervisory frame differs in format from both the information frame and the unnumbered frame. It contains a 4-bit reserved field, a 2-bit supervisory command code, and 2 bits indicating the control field format. Seven bits define the transmitter and receiver sequence numbers, and 1 bit serves as both a poll and a final bit. The control field for an unnumbered frame is only 8 bits, and the data field contains an extra byte of application-level data. Five modifier bits define the function code. This information is mapped in Figure 7.8.

Depending upon the Token-Ring physical implementation and network operating system software chosen, the data link layer may do the initial address recognition. Other connection-oriented communications functions may be provided at this level, including message acknowledgment, link initialization, and disconnection. An important feature is the Simple Network Management Protocol, which functions at this datagram level to collect packet information for network management services. The upper layers provide additional link control, to be discussed in the next section.

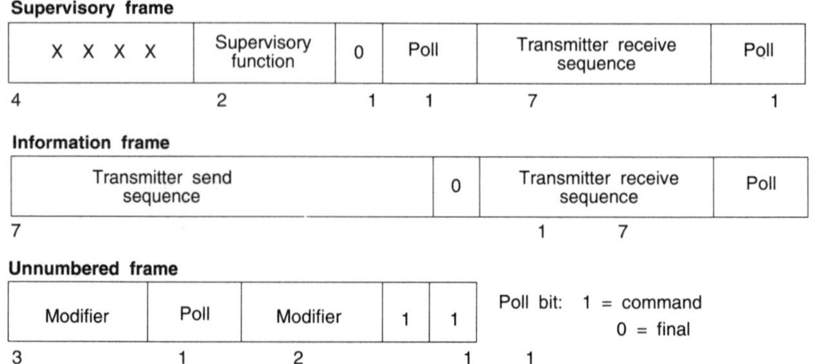


**Figure 7.8** The 802.2 control field format.

## How Token-Ring Transmits

The data and other frame components are built into a special buffer on the Token-Ring controller. This buffer is a critical component of the controller. In fact, the Token-Ring controller should have several buffers for better performance, one for building packets to be transmitted and at least two buffers for packets received. The IBM PS/2 controllers map buffer to a high memory range, usually hex C0000 or CD000, so that the data field is available to drivers and software applications. Bus mastering controllers contain a secondary CPU to offload and bypass the main CPU. They can thus move data faster and more efficiently given sufficient bus capacity.

Often the 16-Mbits/s transmission far outstrips the node processing speed. As an example, most personal computers process information at only 1.3 to 3.8 million instructions per second. If the PC processor were exposed to the Token-Ring transfer rate and not buffered by means of the control field within each information packet, it would soon be swamped with packets. Figure 7.9 represents the importance of the NIC controller buffer in a PC.

Once the data set is packaged into a frame, the Token-Ring controller awaits a token. Upon capture of a token, the NIC then transmits the information packet. The packet signal propagates to the next downstream neighbor over the twisted-pair wire. Each node, in turn, hears the transmission, synchronizes its clock, and repeats the packet. This clock synchronization is important to delineate the beginning and the end of the packet, as illustrated by Figure 7.10; the starting delimiter provides this frame alignment, as shown. If the frame were misaligned the FCS checksum would show an alignment error indicated by the power line. Nodes which see a frame error modify the status field, but still repeat the signal with the error. Some minor corrections are sometimes made if the error is

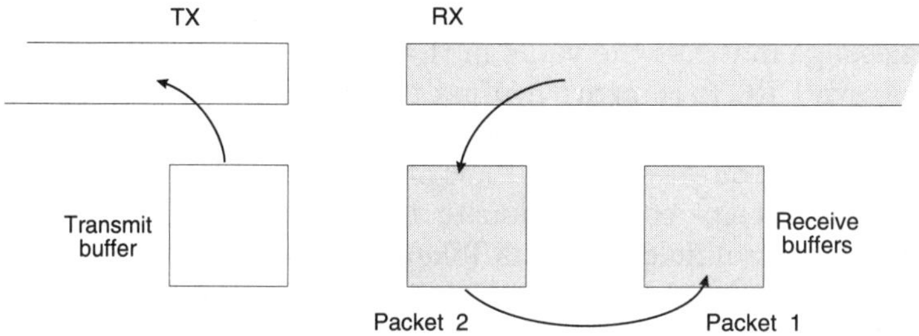


**Figure 7.9** Token-Ring controllers require packet buffer space.

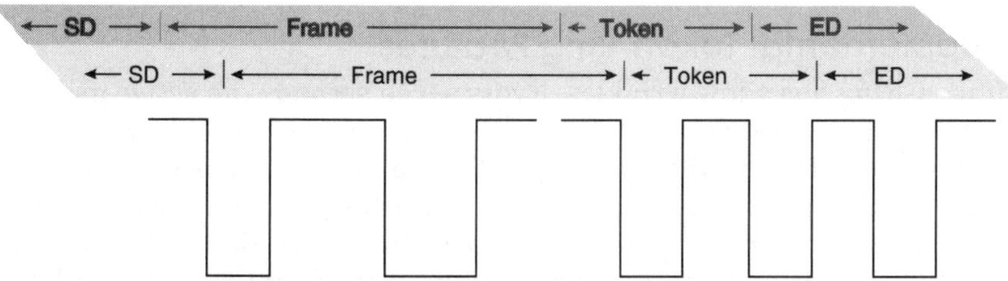


**Figure 7.10** Synchronization prevents mistiming transmissions.

nothing more than the preamble overshooting the NIC. The packet would be discarded by the destination node(s) and depending upon the network system software, the source node might retransmit the frame.

Every node on the network reads the address information. When a packet destination address matches the Token-Ring address of a node, the NIC for that destination node transfers the Token-Ring signal into the receive buffers on its Token-Ring controller. The signal is repeated by every station. The source station will recognize the source address as its own address; it does not repeat the signal. It returns the token to the ring upon passage of the token holding time or upon completed transmission, whichever comes first. This process is displayed in Figure 7.11.

The received packet is disassembled by the Token-Ring controller into three major components: the information frame, the data frame control,

**Figure 7.11** Token-Ring receives a signal.

and the CRC checksum. The controller verifies that the length of the data message matches the value in the frame control field, and generates its own CRC to compare against the transmitted CRC value. Any discrepancies are passed to the software protocols. IPX and TCP/ IP, for example, will request a rebroadcast of the damaged packet. IPX/SPX also reports receipt confirmation to the transmitting node via that logical link control field, whereas Token-Ring does not do so directly. If the transmission has been successful, the data field contents are passed to the software protocols and eventually transferred to the application level for its ultimate use.

## Supplemental Token-Ring Features

Token-Ring has a few wrinkles. Every seven seconds the active monitor sends out a broadcast request for all active nodes to reply with their addresses. This is called a *ring poll.* The ring poll ensures that the network is still active and configured with the same number of nodes. The active monitor signal serves to retime all nodes, establish the functional status of the network, and keep track of the next available station address. The active monitor is established by the Token-Ring hardware and is the first active node established on the network. This usually corresponds to a server or an intelligent hub, but this is wholly random. There is minimal overhead to this feature.

The active monitor usually initiates ring recoveries. When a node is removed from the ring or the ring wraps and the token is lost, the active monitor will issue a demand for the token. Other nodes can issue a request for the token. Upon acknowledgment of ring recovery—this means the ring is functionally complete though perhaps smaller with fewer nodes—a new token is issued.

Downstream nodes waiting for a token that never arrives, receiving a signal that is clearly incomplete, sensing two or more overlapping transmissions, or sensing some physical error on the ring will issue a *beacon* signal. This transmission overrides all other events. Usually the beacon is indicative of a node insertion. It could indicate more serious problems such a failed lobe or trunk, a cut in the wiring, or power lost to a hub and other critical active components. The beacon usually indicates to nodes and the active monitor that the ring is broken or that a node is not generating or repeating signals properly. This beacon initiates a sequence called the *ring recovery*. A failed node may be removed from the ring or a hub may wrap and seclude other hubs that seem to be failing. This is a function of the MAU or intelligent hub units.

A packet is almost certainly corrupted when a new node inserts itself into the ring. The noise cause by the phantom voltage opening relays and the brief loss of the ring structure with near certainty will corrupt a token or information frame. This is normal. As a result, a ring with 120 nodes should show approximately 120 errors related to "node insertion." Every time a PC is rebooted, power cycled, or the NOS reloaded, that node will reinsert itself into the ring. This is a normal process and to be expected.

*Soft errors* are ring failures that do not generate a beacon. This may include corrupted packets, lost tokens, overlapping signals, nodes that run on beyond the THT limit, or a signal that is not stable. A *jabber* is a signal cause by a node that exceeds the allotted THT limit. A *jitter* is signal degradation or a non-stable signal. It is indicative of lobe wires that exceed specification length, of NICs that are not performing properly, missing media filters, or extensive crosstalk in UTP. Abundant soft errors are indicative of installation or software flaws in the LAN. They degrade performance, waste channel capacity, and increase the average waiting times.

Token-Ring can be likened to a one-line phone system. You wait in line to make the call. When you are first in the line (grab the token), you ask for the operator to connect the call (transmit). The call is placed and the phone line is now busy. Only the person receiving the call is supposed to listen. The call has a time limit that is preset and a function of the transmission speed. No priority is enforced to get the line after a transmission; it is on the sequential basis of the token circulating about the ring. Token- Ring, like the party-line, is public, and all nodes can listen to every call as it is repeated around the ring; hence, the "party-line" moniker. Token-Ring is, however, very fair and even with the highest levels of traffic, every node will get a change to hold the token and transmit data.

## Network-Level Software

The last sections of this chapter describe the network layer software corresponding to OSI layers 3 through 7. For the purposes of this book, the functionality of these layers will be compressed into administrative and content layers. The administrative layer directs the packets and deals with traffic problems independently from packet content; whereas the content layer controls content, decides what should be transmitted, and processes the transmitted information.

The administrative layer software provides the functionality to know what nodes exist. Some systems map network workstation names into logical Internet addresses, which are in turn matched with physical Token-Ring addresses. The network software also provides the interface between the Token-Ring process and the network software processes. This interface, additionally, maps user data into the packets. In other words, failed transfers are indicated for retry.

A node is considered "dead" if retransmissions continue to fail or if a twisted-pair node continuously transmits (jitters). Some network software has blind spots to failed transmissions, and this software will continue to load the network in error. Compare the role of this administrative layer to that of the telephone operator. The operator provides connections, distributes telephone numbers and verifies wrong numbers, retries the connection after a "busy" signal, switches connections onto other networks when the main network fails, troubleshoots the mechanical connection, and informs the calling party of network problems. Figure 7.12 demonstrates the operator role in terms of Token-Ring.

This network content software can be likened to the language and the grammar, and any cultural standards applied to phone conversations. The role that the calling party assumes is presented in Figure 7.13. Just as the telephone transmits language transparently, the Token-Ring administrative software transmits packets without inquiring into packet content. Content depends on the two parties communicating.

The network software builds, accepts, and interprets the packets, and applies the information. The range for Token-Ring data application is as large as that of the telephone. Not only can many languages be spoken over a telephone, but each can be encrypted. The language could convey news about the weather, be a sales call, contain a request for help, or provide

- Resolve data location into a NetBIOS address
- Resolve LLC address into a NetBIOS address
- Resolve "domain" address to node address
- Accept data set
- Build protocol frame:
  - Include addresses (source and destination)
  - Insert data
  - Calculate packet length
  - Calculate checksum
- Send frame to controller
- Wait until "circuits" are not busy; hold token
- Await successful transmission
- Inform calling party of network problems

**Figure 7.12** The "operator" role.

- Request a connection
- Initiate a connection
- Await the connection
- Handshake ("say hello")
- Build the data for insertion into data frame
- Pass data to administrative level software
- Await results
- Process responses
- Process errors

**Figure 7.13** The "party" role.

an explanation or the solution to a problem. In just such a manner, the content and logical composition of Token-Ring packets can vary.

## Network and Transport Services

Protocols also initiate system and network operations. Just as a phone call to the fire station precipitates a frantic rush to save a burning building, an Token-Ring packet can contain information that initiates events. Network software, consequently, will provide such functionality as system boot, network initialization, electronic mail and bulletin boards, transfer file data, simple message routing, file services and print services, and system monitoring. Figure 7.14 shows this upper-layer network functionality.

## IPX/SPX

Simple networks build upon IPX, which is derivative of the TCP/IP protocol. Internet packet exchange (IPX) and NetBIOS protocols are the predominant Token-Ring software due to the success of Novell NetWare. These protocols provide intercommunication between nodes for messages, cumbersome file exchange, and terminal services. Such a network configuration would appear to be a mainframe computer serving dependent terminals, although the hardware wiring scheme has been simplified through the application of Token-Ring. More complicated networks simplify the file transfer operations, provide electronic mail instead of message capabilities, network fax services, and add bulletin board operations. Improvements to this include block file transfers, remote workstation operations, system kernel services (that is, the "remote boot"), file interchange capabilities, multiple-node access, multiple-file sourcing, single sourcing of network-wide software (for example, word processing, databases, and engineering programs), and remote device access and services, such as printing.

- Remote workstation boot
- Network software initialization
- Internode addressing
- Electronic mail and network Facsimile
- Computer bulletin boards
- File services
- Print services
- System monitoring
- Network performance monitoring

**Figure 7.14** Upper-layer network services.

These user-layer applications are represented by such vendor offerings as LAN Manager, LAN Server, NetWare, OS/2 LAN, and other proprietary and nonproprietary network systems. Perhaps more of a manager's time will be devoted to network software problems such as interoperability than hardware issues. As a consequence, manuals describing specific vendor networks need to be reviewed for the specific details of upper-level software. While hardware problems are easily diagnosed (see Chapters 12 through 14), network software problems can be narrowed to specific nodes with software tools and protocol analyzers, as explained in Chapter 16. However, many specific software failures often need to be resolved with vendors' own technical support people, because the additions to the basic TCP/ IP are extensive and complicated. Figure 7.15 illustrates the relation between the Token-Ring packet, IP, and TCP.

The *Internet protocol* had its roots in communications addressing scheme known as *Address Resolution Protocol* (ARP). This formed the basis of the Department of Defense's Advanced Research Project (DARPA) four-node network called Arpanet. Arpanet evolved into Internet during the 1970s as TCP/IP was adapted for LANs. This now forms the major connectivity effort for interchanging data between Ethernet, Token-Ring, WANs, and many other network protocols. A serious limitation of TCP/IP is that the Internet address is limited to 32 bits (while OSI provides 16 to 160 bits). This is simply insufficient space to provide unique addresses for growing numbers of network nodes. The IP address contains a network and host address divided into parts; the first two components of "145.150.102.10" represent a network, and the rightmost two entries designate the host node. The *Domain Name System* (DNS) maps hosts names for nodes (such as "mickey," "donald," "field com," "T1F99S56," or "Marty@SST") into the IP and node addresses.

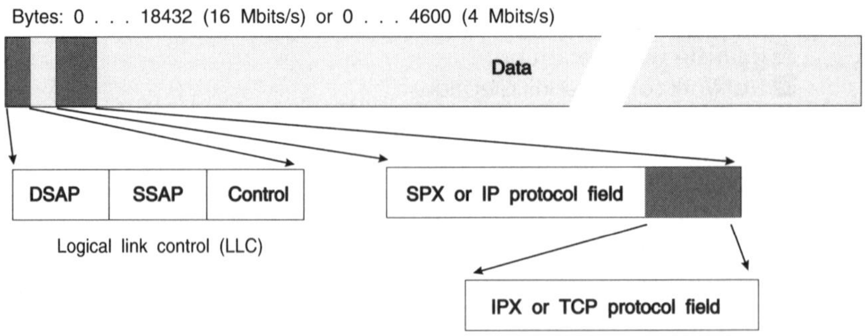


**Figure 7.15** TCP/IP mapping from the Token-Ring frame data field.

### LLC Protocol

Internet protocol provides the lowest level of software access and interface to the Token-Ring environment. This protocol provides the link initialization and termination, node recognition, and packet control operations. The Internet control field, part of the LLC unit, resides within the first few bits of the Token-Ring packet data field. Figure 7.16 maps its components. This datagram is sometimes called the *MAC-level format* and is the primary information field for SNMP network management. It is important to note that system software utilizing the UDP implementation under TCP/IP will not be routable, and this will severely limit attempts to interoperate TCP/IP networks. Although TCP/IP supposedly conforms to the OSI model, there are gray areas. Also, this UDP implementation confounds CMOT network management tools.

### TCP Protocol

*Transmission Control Protocol* (TCP) is a higher level communication protocol. This protocol sequences data transfers and the actual packet transmissions. It exists within the IP data field. In fact, TCP resides at the OSI layer 4, whereas IP is OSI layer 3. Figure 7.17 illustrates the components of this control field.

## Protocol Comparison

Token-Ring running at either 4-Mbits/s or 16-Mbits/s has an extensive share of the personal computer networking market (40 percent share), and is particularly prevalent within the corporate world. Ethernet, the other major LAN protocol, has a 46 percent share of the PC market, but

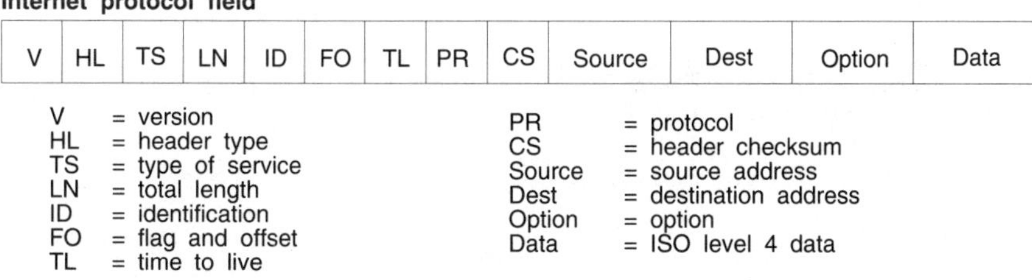


**Figure 7.16** Internet protocol.

**TCP protocol field**

| SP | DP | SN | AN | OF | W | CS | UP | Option | Data |
|---|---|---|---|---|---|---|---|---|---|

SP = source port
DP = destination port
SN = sequence number
AN = ACK number
OF = flag and offset
W = window
CS = checksum
UP = urgent pointer
Option = option
Data = ISO level 5 data

**Figure 7.17** Transmission control protocol.

an 80 percent share of the workstation and scientific market. Thus, Token-Ring and Ethernet frequently need to interoperate. Many vendors provide bridging hardware or internetworking software solutions to connect these two important network standards. At a minimum, networks must intercommunicate. The Ethernet datagram, mapped in Figure 7.18, indicates why protocol interoperability remains a thorny problem. The data field could contain 0 to 1500 bytes of information. At the high end this is certainly less than even a single Token-Ring packet, although Token-Ring to Ethernet encapsulation or translation could pose a problem. The additional overhead required by IP, TCP, and the LLC or any other MAC-level addresses will profoundly slow the transition from an Ethernet frame to complete Token-Ring delivery. Also note that Token-Ring has two types of frames, the token and the data frame to Ethernet's single frame format. This duality must be represented within the multiprotocol environment.

Another serious network concern is that the IBM LAN Server or MS LAN Manager program could require almost 600K from the 640K of DOS server memory. Since DOS itself can require 40 to 80K, fitting the network software into memory is a significant and sometimes a lengthy task. Unix or OS/2 can provide multiple concurrent sessions; this allows for a gateway function. Special extended or expanded memory management software, including HIMEM.SYS, EMM.SYS, and proprietary memory software, may allow network software to load. This memory shortage can be more pronounced when multiple protocols are loaded simultaneously to provide gateway services, as Chapter 11 describes. Of note, Novell NetWare translates between Token-Ring and Ethernet almost transparently. It is easy to run both of these protocols from the same server. The server only needs at least one NIC for each protocol.

| Frame element | Byte location |
|---|---|
| Destination address | 1 to 6 |
| Source address | 7 to 12 |
| Type or length field | 13 to 14 |
| Data field | 15 to 1515 (variable) |
| FCS (CRC) | Last 4 bytes |

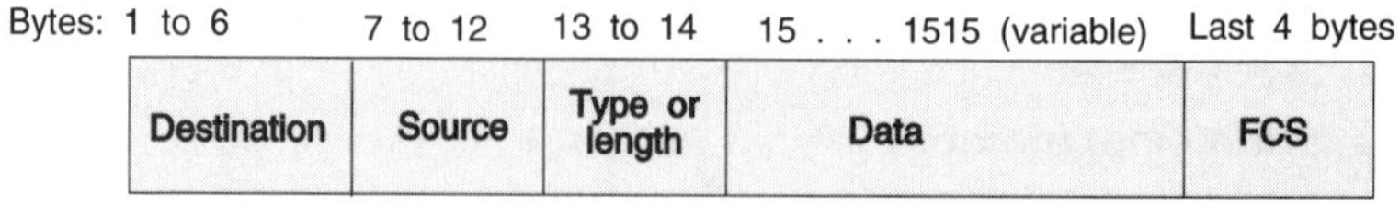

| Bytes: 1 to 6 | 7 to 12 | 13 to 14 | 15 . . . 1515 (variable) | Last 4 bytes |
|---|---|---|---|---|
| Destination | Source | Type or length | Data | FCS |

**Figure 7.18** Ethernet frame and token map.

Chapter

# 8

# Planning a Token-Ring Network

Token-Ring installation encompasses both planning and physically connecting the media-level hardware. This chapter describes the planning process and the components that must be included in the plan. The components include twisted-pair wire bundles; wire fittings like modular connectors, hermaphroditic media connectors, jacks and plugs; hub concentrators, wiring patch panels, jumpers and trunk cables, and bus boards. This discussion addresses cable hangers and cable tie mechanisms. It also addresses a valid concern about the physical and dimensional stability of the wire itself. An experienced network manager understands the value of blueprinting the installation, and this chapter describes how and when to blueprint. This presentation serves to augment vendor-supplied technical documentation. Figure 8.1 illustrates Token-Ring components described within this chapter.

The first step in planning any installation is to analyze the user requirements and understand the network technology. The network plan should address both current and future needs by allowing for expansion at a later date. If at all possible, it is wise to begin with a small network and expand over time. A small network will simplify the learning process and minimize the complexity of problem-solving.

- Blueprints
- Cable ladders or wiring conduits
- Wiring concentrators (MAUs and hubs)
- Controllers
- Twisted-pair wire (STP or UTP)
- Flat twisted-pair jumper wires
- Media filters
- Packet switches
- Modular jacks and connectors
- Punchdown (path) panel

**Figure 8.1** Typical items required in Token-Ring network installation.

Designing and planning the network configuration builds the foundation for long-term success of that network. Both under- and over- design constitute network management failings. An overdesigned network—one built to accomodate more traffic, more network nodes, and more users than foreseeably possible—constitutes a costly network. An underdesigned network constitutes the more serious flaw; a network that does not match minimal traffic volume need is unreliable, and provides negligible room for expansion. Instead, improper estimation of network loading and user requirements at this stage will lead to poor network management by overloading the staff with problems. Consider this fundamental reality; poor network performance is the key issue that forms the basis for a negative operational evaluation of the network administrator. However, performance is dependent upon the foundation of network design and many networks are inherited or built ad hoc. While operation and implementation issues addressed in Chapter 10 ultimately make or break a manager, design and planning concerns addressed in this chapter ultimately define the complexity of daily network implementation and operation. These basic items are expanded in Figure 8.2.

## Design Criteria

The design of a network is a complex problem, with far-reaching ramifications. Insufficient capacity, incorrect media, and inadequate loading characteristics frequently cause performance lags. These design shortcomings are avoided by understanding organizational needs and network performance issues before contemplating a network. Break the analysis into small pieces. Understand who will use the network, what load each user will place upon the network, what access to devices each user requires, and how growth or organizational change might strain resources. See how competitors or other LAN customers are applying networking technology and what loads are transported by these networks. Compare this to your organization's needs.

- Network design configurations
- Network user needs
- Physical plant limitations
- Power protection
- Network installation
- Compatibility
- ANSI, CCITT, IEEE, and OSI standards
- Connector integrity
- Network profiling

**Figure 8.2** Practical network design concerns.

Lease versus purchase decisions hinge upon financial concerns as well as the lease vendor's attentiveness to customer support. This matter is not addressed here, although the reader might consider lease or rent as a viable alternative to outright purchase. Additionally, turnkey systems and professional installation save time, money, and personnel without the need to hire people normally associated with a network. Also consider the availability of spare parts and outside expertise to solve internal network problems. Figure 8.3 shows these network design and maintenance questions.

Construct the network from small, separable building blocks. Twisted-pair concentrators, wireless transmitters, MAUs, and wiring panels are just some of several mechanisms to segment the network. Complement these devices with gateways, repeaters, and subnetworks to divide the size and complexity of the network into comprehensible units. Such segmentation adds reliability, durability, and design simplicity, and may, in extreme cases, provide the only means to trace Token-Ring problems to their source.

When designing a network, insist that all classes of components come from the same manufacturer. Slight interpretative differences in ISO or Token-Ring specifications could mean that parts are not compatible. This issue is expanded within a following section. When it is not feasible to select uniform network components, segregate the parts that differ. Avoid mixing network interface cards, MAUs, and workstations of different purpose and manufacture. If node equipment includes personal computers and engineering workstations or different network operating systems, place these units on separate rings. PCs paging MS Windows may create problems for client-server accounting workstations while masking the true source. Thus, segmentation is an appropriate design criterion.

Last, do not overstate the capacity of a single Token-Ring channel, or of the Token-Ring system as a whole. Capacity saturates eventually at 100 percent of theoretical rated capacity (see Chapter 17), although performance grows slower with more network stations and higher traffic

- Who will use the network?
- What load will each user place upon the network?
- What access to devices should each user have?
- What individual growth is anticipated?
- What centralized resources are needed?
- What load or peak loads can the network sustain?
- What spare parts are needed?
- What outside expertise is available?
- What other networks must connect to Token-Ring?
- How will a network conform to physical plant limitations?

**Figure 8.3** Network design and maintenance questions.

loads; waiting time increases and slows network performance. Unlike Ethernet, Token-Ring does not fail with too much traffic. It simply gets slower.

Select a transmission speed compatible with existing equipment. Install capacity sufficient to match predicted needs. Be certain that vendors have provided the necessary references to verify not only their implementations of Token-Ring but also the expected quality of after-sale support. Token-Ring is at its best for occasional file transfers, electronic mail, and communication. It will function under high loads of distributed client-server databases. It may not be appropriate for massive file backups, data transfers, or single-keystroke remote terminal support. Understand the limitations of this medium and the organizational needs. Where one medium is insufficient, research the benefits of another. Understand how expansion can be effected to support user and traffic growth, and technological change.

## Design Subject to User Needs

When designing a network, it is important to envision the purpose of the network, the type of traffic it will accommodate, the distances between areas that need to be serviced, and the total load to be placed upon the network. Realize that Token-Ring specifications may inhibit or hinder your design; consider distance limitations and node counts, as well as repeater placements. Figure 8.4 outlines issues to consider when designing a network, some of which are considered in this chapter. Because Token-Ring is a token-passing medium, it will handle a maximum of 100 percent of its rated transmission speed under ideal conditions, minus tokens, minor active monitor polls, ring inserts, beacons, jitter and misalignment, minus the results of all suboptimal hardware and software, minus a random error rate. Application-level protocols, semaphores indicating receipt and acceptance of transmissions, packet

- Network purpose
- Traffic volume
- Peak traffic volume and traffic composition
- Network size and configuration
- Network user community size
- User workload
- Network functionality
- Security
- Reliability
- "Mission-critical" requirements
- Suitability
- Alternatives
- Installation, maintenance, and upgrade costs

**Figure 8.4** Network design issues.

overhead, and interpacket spacing delays also lower the true throughput. Effective usage may yield 45 percent of the rated capacity.

Consider the very suitability of Token-Ring. A bus configuration network with a random access scheme may be better suited than the token-based Token-Ring for various reasons. For example, an engineering shop may get improved customer support with TCP/IP than with IBM LAN Server for the simple reason that the technical support staff is familiar with that software.

From a technical standpoint, a network with consistently low peak loads, centralized file access, and centralized computer processing may benefit from the bus wiring scheme and a single corporate network. Token-Ring may be precisely the proper medium, in cases like client-server mission-critical accounting or data entry, small LANs, IRMA connectivity to mainframes, or LANs supporting a downsizing transition from a mainframe environment. Networks of few users or minimal requirements might better be served by ARCNET or a "zero-slot" LAN such as LANtastic or a peer-to-peer network such as MS Windows for Workgroups, both low-end networks.

Many factors increase the cost of Token-Ring; these should be established prior to the actual installation process. The shielded cable itself is an expensive proposition at several dollars per foot installed, possibly more if local building codes specify special "fire-safe" cable which ignites at a higher temperature and will not release toxic gas when it does burn. This may suggest installing UTP twisted-pair wiring bundles or using the already available and unused wires in the telephone bundles. Match these needs against node-to-node lengths, and growth requirements. The NICs, MAUs, and other related Token-Ring hardware also present expenses. While Token-Ring hardware is an expense to consider, installation and maintenance are other cost factors, usually ten times larger than the initial installation costs. Large Token-Ring configurations are difficult to maintain, and therefore costly. The interaction of large networks, disparate hardware, and disparate loading are prime considerations in defining costs, because problems increase rapidly as a network grows in complexity and load.

For lower-volume serial lines, cheaper and lower-capacity networks are options worth consideration. This encompasses T-1, RS-232 connections with CCITT V.32 data compression modems, LANtastic, direct serial connection, or repeated parallel lines, as well as proprietary PC networks. Note that Token-Ring volumes can become sizable and require the organizational resources of a dozen full-time staff. RS-232 networks are a very mature technology, both in terms of the hardware and management techniques. An IBM mainframe computer network may support 40 users each on 100 separate channels. This means that a single network will support 4000 terminals. That is, by the numbers, a very large management problem, because there would be at least 4000 users, maybe as many as 12,000 with channel multiplexing and multiple users sharing each terminal. Each user requires a login, accounts, and file storage space. Often, each account must be billed, and this creates a need for an accounting organization.

A Token-Ring network can be as complex, although not in the same terms. Token-Ring is far more difficult to manage because it is relatively newer, has a shorter track record, and has not demanded the vendor support applied to the more developed serial line technologies. Token-Ring can be just as demanding if it supports terminal servers (Token-Ring stations fanning out to multiple RS-232 lines) and IRMA links to a host mainframe. Not only is the hardware still developing; management tools are less developed than in the mainframe environment. Additionally, Token-Ring supports a traffic load at least equivalent to an RS-232 network. At 9600 baud (about 900 bytes or characters per second), 4000 users on an RS-232 network account for a maximum of 3,640,000 bytes/s, which is similar in volume to an average Token-Ring channel. While the physical and administrative demand is numerically greater, the frame in an RS-232 environment is also transmitted from the mainframe to the terminal. Characters are returned only to the mainframe. A Token-Ring environment is a true interconnected network, not a tree of decreasing importance. The topology is very different and loads distribute differently as illustrated in Figure 8.5. The mainframe network provides link-to-link access from the dumb terminals to the mainframe. A user at one such "node" seeking access to another "node" must connect through the mainframe, and the interconnecting power is more limiting than in Token-Ring. On the other hand, every packet broadcast on Token-Ring is repeated by every node. Although this does not require station CPU effort (or very minor activity), it does subtract from available network bandwidth and decreases the overall network response time.

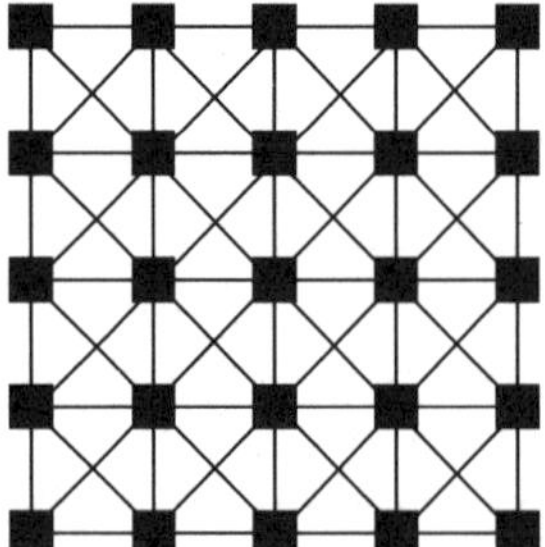

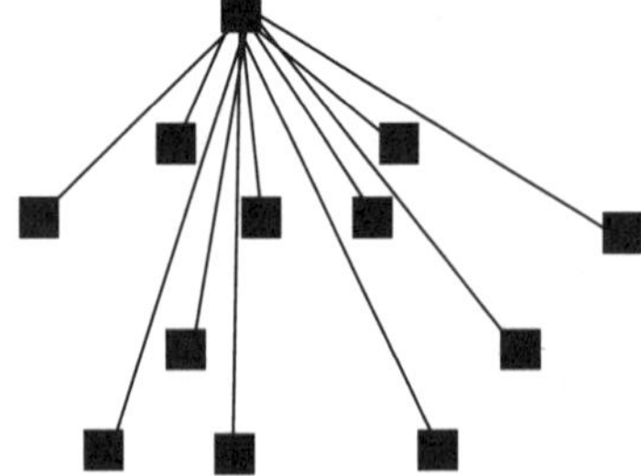

**Figure 8.5** Token-Ring (left), although a star-wired network, is an interconnected network unlike a host star topology.

## Physical Plant Limitations

Sharing computer resources and exchanging electronic mail through a built-in computer network is not reserved for well-funded start-up ventures in newly built industrial parks. Older buildings, unplanned sprawling complexes, and high-rise buildings can have networks, too. No building, no matter how old or how busy, will prohibit the installation of the type of equipment your organization wants. While it is possible that the layout of the building may constrain the wiring efficiency, neither the building design nor the lack of space will limit the kind of network that you can install. If your building is of an older design, examine the premises more carefully because there may be additional cost for installing network wiring because the ceiling is inaccessible. Hanging ceilings or return-air plenums may be small or nonexistent. Existing pathways between floors or buildings may be unsuitable for new wire, or filled with old installations. In such cases, new conduits or cable trays may provide part of the answer. PVC cable produces a toxic gas when it burns, and is often banned from return-air plenums, the space above the hung grid ceiling. Teflon wire, although more expensive than PVC, exceeds most building codes without any restrictions.

Twisted-pair, the cable most often existing in old buildings and now in new installations, may provide a ready means to network a new or expanded LAN. Qualify the wiring for its ability to aquately convey Token-Ring traffic at 16 Mbits/s. Even if 4 Mbits/s is originally proposed, it is likely that network will be enhanced to the faster transmission rate. If growth, large numbers of far-linked machines in different directions, or video imaging are required, it may not be economical to reroute, add, or maintain twisted-pair. Rather, line-of-sight wireless infrared networks or the technology of radio-frequency (through the walls and floors) Token-Ring networks may be a good accommodation.

Both STP and UTP have distinct disadvantages. STP must be run from central wiring hubs to each station. It does not provide flexibility. When a contractor has to drill holes through walls, ceilings, and beams, in order to route single cables through narrow plenums, it often makes more sense to pull a single Ethernet coaxial cable through a facility from floor to floor or provide standard twisted-pair wiring bundles from office to office. ANSI and other standard-setting organizations are endorsing the concept of a modular and centralized wiring plant based upon UTP. Notwithstanding, UTP does not provide as suitable transmission characteristics for LAN data communications as STP. Node lengths are shortened. Signal quality is decreased.

Locations of computer rooms may be suboptimal but possible in many locations. Select the location with the best cable access and most stable climatic environment, and one that will provide security to meet design requirements. Computer facilities are best if locked and if the temperature remains constant. Overheating and low humidity, which increases static, cause component failures. Climate-control equipment generally solves these problems. However, these concerns are best addressed during the planning stages rather than as retrofitted necessities.

Consider how best to schedule installation. If cabling conduits and STP are installed as part of new construction, the work is just one more item for the building contractors. Cabling an existing facility may require working around physical limitations and the office hours. If your organization cannot be closed during the network installation, the contractor may have to coexist with employees and customers. Additionally, scrap, dirt, and constant traffic may create a need for frequent cleanings. Acquire a good vacuum cleaner with extension hoses. A vacuum is a good tool for removing dust from circuit boards, and grime from workstation air filters and inlet cooling ports on all electronic network components.

Remember one last point. Wire is often installed within a ceiling plenum that is about 8 ft above the network connection for most nodes. When planning wire runs from blueprints add the necessary height drop or you will find that estimates are significantly short—and the network may be longer than planned. While 8 ft (or 16 ft, representing up and down) may not mean much in terms of buying more wire, accumulations of such extra lengths could push the ARL or lobes beyond specification.

## Power Protection

Most network managers are aware of the danger of lightning striking outside wiring and sending a jolt down the line to damage anything unfortunate enough to be plugged into the outlet. Most managers are also aware of power surges and spikes that can cause premature failure of computer chips and magnetic media. Network wiring can also acquire induced or live voltages from proximity to power lines, not to mention the possibility that network wiring can be accidentally switched into live power. Some have experienced the slow degradation that occurs during a power brownout when voltage levels decay. Everyone knows the effects of a power blackout. The problem for the network manager is what can be done about these disabling situations.

Wiring errors are particularly revelant as data and voice lines are routed in pairs to offices. The higher telephone ringing voltages, although not fatal to people, are often damaging to LAN equipment. Figure 8.6 lists the typical problems that can create network havoc. Also, *radio-frequency interference* (RFI) and *electromagnetic interference* (EMI) can travel through the power lines with disastrous results to sensitive computer equipment. The damage from such events is not limited just to damaged computer equipment, data loss or corruption, and downtime. There are also lost opportunity costs, aggravation from frequent crashes, and additionally, the certainty that other damage will

- Power surges
- Power spikes
- Power sags
- Brownout
- Blackout
- Lightning strikes
- Stray voltage
- Static electricity

**Figure 8.6** Electrical problems that threaten networks.

be spawned. A crash can destabilize a chemical reaction or a long clinical test, damage patient records and lose critical allergy information, or ruin a part in a computer-controlled manufacturing process.

It is important to weigh the importance of uninterrupted service and the cost of downtime. Frequent downtime affecting order entry, order processing, or accounts payable may be of little consequence, but it may represent the germinal stages of a bad customer-relations problem. The cost of the computer equipment is apt to exceed significantly the cost of protection, although the purchasing decision rests on the risk that the organization is willing to assume.

There are solutions to these problems. Specifically, filters screen out electrical noise from the incoming power, while suppressers level out the wave crests of power surges. Isolation equipment provides capacitance to level out the wave troughs of low power. Voltage regulators filter the electrical power so that the voltage is stable. Standby battery supplies and uninterruptible systems provide the same emergency power function. *Uninterruptible power systems* (UPS) (usually) provide electricity automatically when the sensing apparatus detects power problems. Since UPS provides temporary emergency power only, most network managers allocate UPS capacity for an orderly and rapid server shutdown; monitoring software can track the performance of a UPS and initiate an orderly file server shutdown when power reserves are depleted. If UPS should support continuous operations, acquire a generator that will handle capacity including the starting surges of several machines. Blueprinting AC wiring and routing of network wiring, and careful labeling of twisted-pair bundle use can minimize errors. One important note to realize is that most surge suppressor technology is based upon on a metallic oxide capacitor which degrades with each voltage spike. These should be replaced—at least tested—annually before they fail to provide equipment. Most UPS systems include surge suppression; these suppresion components may lose effectiveness and need replacement too. Figure 8.7 lists commonly available electrical computer protection devices.

- RF and EMI filters
- Surge suppressers
- Isolation transformers
- Voltage regulators
- Hot standby battery backups
- Uninterruptible power systems

**Figure 8.7** Power protection devices.

## Token-Ring Compatibility

Token-Ring provides some measure of compatibility. Not only does it offer a certain mechanical consistency, but many vendors sell products to interface disparate "Token-Ring" components. Compatibility is often used as a selling point. However, this doesn't always mean that Token-Ring-compatible equipment will transmit to other Token-Ring-compatible equipment; different speed equipment or different NOS protocols on the same network can blindly share the network with each other. There is a potential for interfacing problems. While the physical media and the transmission standards may be the same or similar, software discrepancies (at the NOS level) may make the Token-Ring versions listed in Figure 8.8 functionally incompatible. The major Token-Ring versions all share media and transmission standards. They differ in packet signal speed and in the impedance of the media.

*Token-Ring* is defined as a medium and an electrical configuration, as well as the media access method (e.g. token passing). These versions maybe "Token-Ring-compatible," but not Token-Ring-comparable with-

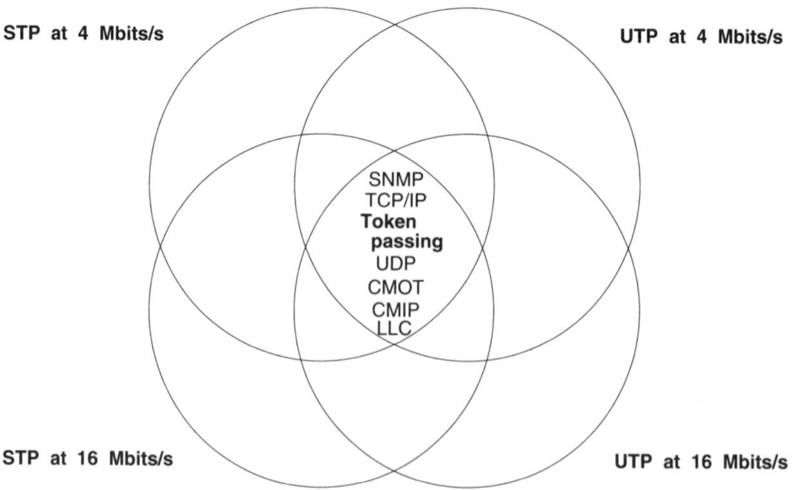


**Figure 8.8** Token-Ring version compatibility.

out a special bridge. This means that these versions will communicate to a standard network through a specified mechanism; it does not mean that these alternative networks are electrically-compatible, or software-compatible with standard Token-Ring. An ISO bridging or gateway mechanism, sometimes called a *linkage product*, connects totally separate networks for enterprise-wide communications.

In order for any third-party vendor products to function correctly with the existing network, all transmission and reception hardware must synchronize timing; NIC crystal clocks are not always accurate. Subtle differences will become more apparent as the network grows in size and loading factors; these differences should be understood and the ramifications explored prior to actual purchase or installation. Likewise, secondary sourcing of so-called commodity items may breed incompatibilities later when a network is upgraded. Controllers without 16 Mbits/s capability are a prime example. Be aware that prime vendors may substantially alter their equipment or software over time for any number of reasons, including bug fixes, better performance, a new sales strategy, or an attempt to undermine other vendors. As a consequence, third-party solutions may no longer be ideal.

In any event, get verified customer references from *both* happy and unhappy customers. Assess compatibility and the eventual upgrade and customer support policies. Vendors must support not only their own products, but also other network items that will interface with them.

Compatibility must be supported on the first three ISO layers for machines to share the same physical transmission highway. Compatibility must be supported on layers 3 and 4 for differing hardware to even acknowledge another protocol. Layers 5 and 6 must be identical for machines to interconnect. Layer 7 is only the application layer, and compatibility at this level is necessary only insofar as different machines need to share code, mail, network software, and other user-level application software.

A network ideally requires hardware and software components that match a single specification. Where components deviate from a single design criterion, isolate those unique components with subnetworks, bridges, routers, or gateways, as Figure 8.9 suggests. The backbone (trunk network) performing as subnet bridges, multiport bridges, or high-speed packet switching bridges interconnect LANs which are thus isolated.

Since Token-Ring is a physical specification for a communication network, this network design only specifies the media and the electrical transmission standards; it does not define file transfer, mail systems, or other upper-layer protocols. These processes are supplied by NetBIOS, IPX, or TCP/ IP, and other such ISO layer 3 definitions; differences in the programmer's implementation of IPX cause one major incompatibility. Figure 8.10 outlines possible Token-Ring discrepancies.

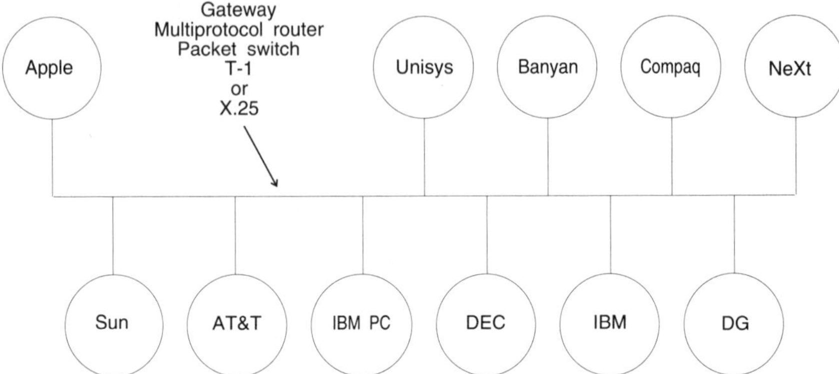


**Figure 8.9** Isolate different equipment on separate rings .

- Transmission speed dissimilarities
- Transmission media dissimilarities
- Electrical timing differences
- Controller buffering limitations
- Packet incompatibilities
- Logical link control differences (as in IPX or UDP)
- Error handling discrepancies (at NOS level)
- Acknowledgment differences (at NOS level)

**Figure 8.10** Possible Token-Ring incompatibilities.

Different vendors supply their own interpretations of Token-Ring and especially NetBIOS. While Token-Ring should be robust enough to provide access to all devices, in practice, slight differences are indeed likely to create transmission problems. Such incompatibilities are more prone on saturated networks. Different networks should isolate different types of equipment.

Not only are there two Token-Ring transmission speed variations and two minor wiring versions, and an erratic migration to OSI stacks, but each equipment and component vendor can redesign the functionality to minimize costs or maximize features. Small details, such as controller buffer parameters, NIC drivers, or how upper-layer software device drivers will access physical devices, can make difficult-to-trace problems. Furthermore, vendor-supplied components can vary in small ways. While these minor deviations may not disrupt communications, incompatibilities may mean machines from different vendors can share a network without the ability to talk to each other. More ominously, such small differences can cause serious application-level shortfalls. For example, application software might not recognize the network printers, could crash suddenly and sporadically, corrupt data files, or fail to load within the PC or workstation memory.

## Network Limitations

The Token-Ring specifications outline the requirements for a functioning network. Most of these specifications present maximum configurations for the following: length of lobe segments, ARL size, wire conductivity, number of nodes, length of trunk cables, and numbers of protocols running concurrently on the network. As previously mentioned, Token-Ring never fails except for physical flaws; it will always transmit data although at increasingly slower rates. Therefore, these specifications are more suggestive than absolute. It is wise to plan a network with enough capacity for growth and *not* assume that the specifications can be stretched to accommodate that growth. Therefore, Figure 8.11 reiterates the Token-Ring configuration parameters.

## Token-Ring Network Components

Because planning requires an understanding of the Token-Ring components, this chapter continues with a discussion of the options available for basic network components. Figure 8.12 outlines items of importance when planning a network. Components required for even the simplest installation include wiring, connectors, cable ties, NICs, and MAUs or hubs.

### Token-Ring Trunks

Crucial items in any Token-Ring are the MAUs and trunk connections. Figure 8.13 shows these devices and their wiring structure. Older MAUs provide Ring in/Ring out ports on opposite ends of the box. New models (such as the AMP unit) place these ports side-by-side. As simple as this change is, it provides a major improvement in minimizing the wiring "spagetti" typical in wiring closets.

MAUs are available in two major variations that are best categorized as active or passive wiring hubs. Passive devices are boxes stuffed with mechanical relays. These devices simply function as a computerized switching yard to reconfigure and selectively include lobes and trunks. They do not regenerate signals. Most have eight attachment ports for lobe cables and a Ring in and a Ring out port. When no lobe cables are connected, the box forms a no node ring with a ring length of about 6 meters. As each lobe wire is connected to the box, the ring ARL is expanded potentially by twice the length of the lobe cable. This is only a potential ring ARL increase because the ARL is the sum of the *longest* lobe cable and all trunk measurements. Additionally, the lobe is not actually inserted into the ring

| Parameter | STP | UTP |
|---|---|---|
| Data rate | 4 or 16 Mbits/s | 4 or 16 Mbits/s |
| Max trunk length | 570 | 260 |
| Max network span | 2500 | 1200 |
| Max nodes/ring | 132 or 250 | 72 |
| Trunk wire: | | |
| Type | Type 1 or 2 | UTP-3 or UTP-4 |
| | | Datagrade UTP |
| Connectors | Genderless | Modular |
| | Modular | Modular |
| | Patch panel | Patch panel |
| Impedance | 8 ohms | 12 ohms |
| Lobe wire: | | |
| Type | Type 1 or 2 | UTP-3 or UTP-4 |
| | | Datagrade UTP |
| Connectors | Genderless | Modular |
| | Modular | Modular |
| | Patch panel | Patch panel |
| Impedance | 8 ohms | 12 ohms |
| Jumper wire: | | |
| Type | Type 1 or 2 | UTP-3 or UTP-4 |
| | Type 6 | Datagrade UTP |
| Connectors | Genderless | Modular |
| | Modular | Modular |
| | Patch panel | Patch panel |
| Impedance | 8 ohms | 12 ohms |
| Hubs: | | |
| Ports | 8, 12, 16 | 4, 8, 12, 16,24, 48 |
| Ring wrap | Yes | Yes |

**Figure 8.11** Token-Ring network parameters.

until a NIC sends a phantom voltage to activate the relays in the MAU and reconfigure the ring to include the lobe.

Active hub devices provide the same services as passive MAUs. Additionally, they retime and regenerate signals. This feature increases the maximum possible distance between the hub and nodes at the end of the lobes, and is pertinent for increasing the coverage and reliability of UTP-based networks. Some active wiring hubs are "intelligent" in that they monitor the transmission signal, collect network traffic and performance statistics, and automatically reconfigure the ring based upon error conditions.

- Network cable sectioning
- Multiple access units (MAU)
- MAU racks
- Patch panels
- Punchdown blocks
- Trunk cables
- Lobe cables
- Jumper cables (patch panel and wall)
- Twisted-pair wire
    - Network interface cards (NIC)
    - Modular connectors
- Token-Ring cable routing
    - Avoidance of water, high-voltage, and temperature extremes
    - Cable ladders and cable supporting logical routes
- Inventory necessary components
- Wireless networks
- Selection of components
- Blueprints

**Figure 8.12** Planning considerations addressed in this chapter.

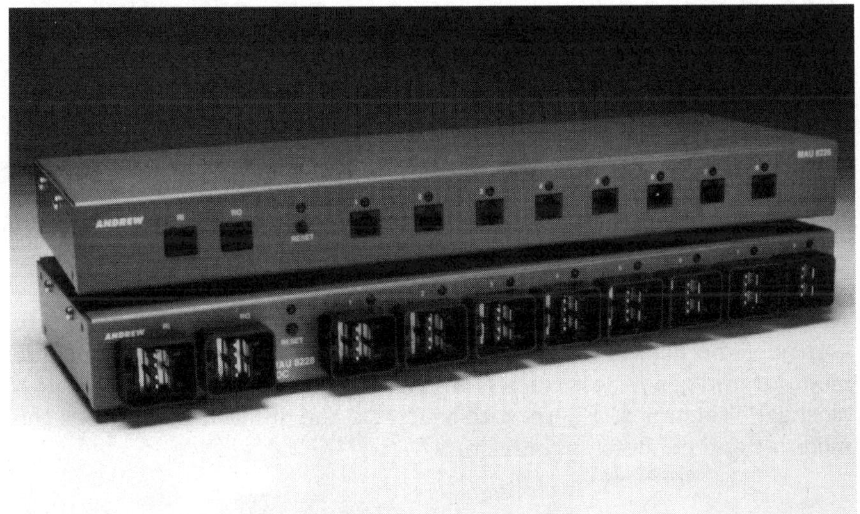


**Figure 8.13** Typical passive MAU. (Andrew Corporation)

## Network Cable Sections

A network does not require a single continuous length of twisted-pair wire for trunk or lobe cables. The network will work adequately if it is sectioned into convenient lengths and jumpered at central patch panels. There will be almost no detectable degradation if all the connections are properly installed. In fact, it is common practice for twisted-pair networks to route the wire bundles through several patch panels for configuration convenience. Many network managers might assume that such construction of a network hodgepodge with segments is in poor form. However, installation of shorter segments will not only prove easier, but installation costs will probably be less, installation time will be faster, and verification of the new network will proceed smoothly.

In fact, such segmentation demonstrates good planning. Token-Ring does experience transmission problems. Problems become more prevalent on longer and busier networks. Larger rings often span rooms, run vertically through ceilings and walls, and traverse floors and even buildings. There is limited practical benefit to installing long runs of twisted-pair without patch panels. It is awkward to string a bulky, inflexible cable through tight bends, and pull long lengths through the ceiling. The weight of the cable makes such practice difficult, and the friction along its length makes it virtually impossible. It is likely that the weight of the unsupported cable will break some pairs.

Another important reason for segmenting the ring is that certain test instruments, such as a time domain reflectometer (see Chapter 12), work poorly if the network segments are sectioned in lengths exceeding 100 m. (Note: lobes longer than 100 m violate Token-Ring specifications.) This tool sends a radar-like signal down the network cable and illustrates blockages or breaks. This signal dissipates over distance, thereby providing less accurate information.

Ideally, a manager would section lengths of runs, and conveniently section these at patch panels and areas with many nodes. Too many connections and segments increase signal reflection. This reflection is often referred to as *cable impedance.*

## Connectors

Token-Ring has standardized parts that simplify and improve the reliability of the network, and ease problem-solving. These parts include modular and genderless connectors and type 66 or type 110 punchdown blocks. For instance, Figure 8.14 contrasts the differences between the modular and genderless connectors.

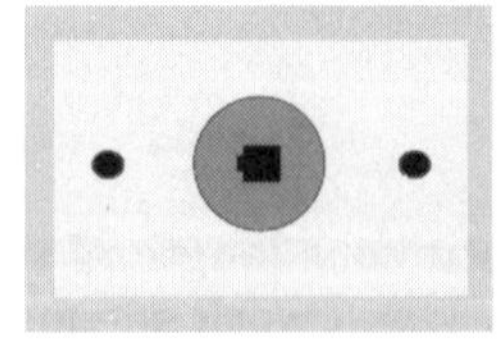
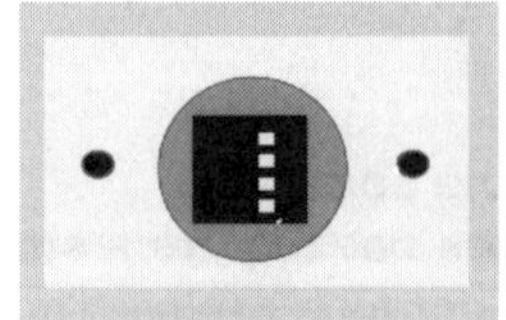
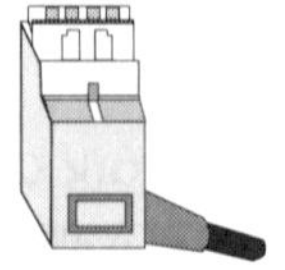

**Figure 8.14** Modular and genderless connectors.

Modular phone UTP wiring is a very simple installation medium and is finding favor for installation in new buildings and for many network extensions and retrofits. While more difficult to install correctly and maintain conformance to the rigid Token-Ring specifications, twisted-pair is effective. Twisted-pair bundles usually contain 25 "pairs" of wires, six or eight wires per pair. Token-Ring utilizes only four wires. The wires within each set are twisted around each other for the entire length to minimize signal interference and crosstalk from the other pairs. Wire is routed from a patch panel through walls or wiring conduits to modular jacks in walls or modular office furniture. RJ-11 and RJ-45 connectors crimp onto ribbon-like jumper cables (also called "twisted-pair" for convenience) that are not wiring bundles nor even twisted. They are flat ribbon cables. Minimize jumper cable usage since it does not conform to the twisted noise-cancelling specification. Note that the modular connectors are not easily installed on eithet STP or UTP; the bundle and each wire must be stripped individually. These four, six, or eight wire cords connect the wiring concentrator hubs or the NIC to the modular jacks as Figure 8.15 illustrates. The actual wiring connections are "straight through" as is standard with phone connections. Where the wires cross should be carefully controlled since you do not want to cross an odd number of times, or twist the standard phone connections and confuse the telephone system, either. (Some phone systems will "work" but not ring.)

### STP and UTP

Twisted-pair wiring is not only a simpler technology because it uses wire rather than coaxial cable, and it is also a packaging advance. A four-wire assembly connects the cards directly to a comparable assembly in the wiring hub. This is a star configuration. The one important element to remember is that the connecting cable should not cross-over; although transmitting electronics send signals to the receiving electronics, the physical wiring transition is furnished internally. Some NIC interface boards either indicate a *polarity* error or perhaps even correct for the irregular wiring cross-over. The NIC and each port on the hub or multiport (8 on average) has separate transmitter and receiver circuitry. Figure 8.16 lists the wiring scheme for the 6-pin RJ-11 and 8-pin RJ-45 Token-Ring modular connectors. Figure 8.17 lists the wiring scheme for genderless connectors. Note that twisted-pair installations that make

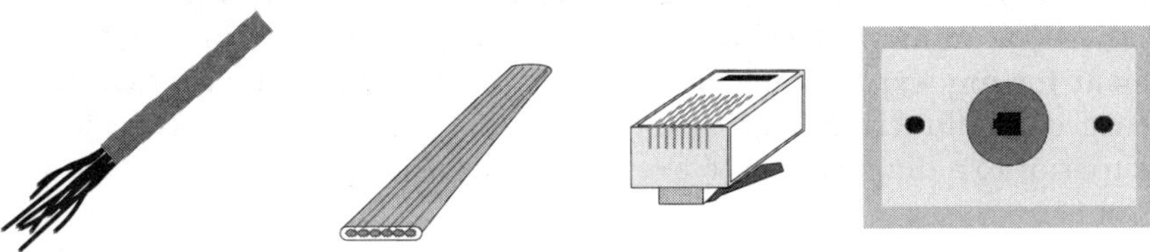

**Figure 8.15** STP and UTP is stripped first for modular connector installation.

| RJ-45 Pin Number | Function | Function |
|---|---|---|
| 1 | Unconnected | Unconnected |
| 2 | Unconnected | Unconnected |
| 3 | Transmit- | Receive+ |
| 4 | Receive+ | Transmit+ |
| 5 | Receive- | Transmit- |
| 6 | Transmit+ | Receive- |
| 7 | Unconnected | Unconnected |

| RJ-11 Pin Number | Function | Function |
|---|---|---|
| 1 | Unconnected | Unconnected |
| 2 | Transmit- | Receive+ |
| 3 | Receive+ | Transmit+ |
| 4 | Receive- | Transmit- |
| 5 | Transmit+ | Receive- |
| 6 | Unconnected | Unconnected |

**Figure 8.16** Modular connector wiring scheme

| **Genderless pin position** | **Genderless** | **DB-9** |
|---|---|---|
| Black | Transmit+ | Receive- |
| Orange | Transmit- | Receive+ |
| Green | Receive+ | Transmit+ |
| Red | Receive- | Transmit- |
| Shield | Ground | Ground |

**Figure 8.17** Genderless connectors wiring scheme.

full use of the wiring bundle for long runs, or intermix its use with RS-232 serial lines, are apt to increase crosstalk problems and expose pairs to excessive noise. Limit bundle utilization to 50 to 75 percent.

### Cable Routing

The next planning step is to define the route that the cable will take through the building. This route should provide ready accessibility to all workstations to minimize lobe lengths or twisted-pair lengths. This route should also provide adequate expansion capability. Specifically, a route that minimizes cable for the current installation may be insufficient for any expansion. The cable should also be easily accessible in case of malfunction. For example, a path that follows a corridor is superior to a diagonal route over cubicles.

### Avoid Water, High-Voltage, Temperature Extremes

Twisted-pair is inert. However, it is prudent to keep it away from water sources since these can short the electrical transmissions if water seeps along the cable and into a connector or tap, and from high-voltage electrical sources which can interfere with and disrupt the signal.

Electrical or magnetic fields may conflict with the Token-Ring transmission and introduce high error counts. High-frequency radio sources disrupt communications. High-frequency lighting—vapor lighting—lab or medical apparatus that transmits—can disrupt network traffic. If possible, route main cables away from the sources shown in Figure 8.18. Continual expansion and contraction from a heat source such as the air conditioning ductwork near the cabling plenum will cause micro-fractures in the copper cores and accelerate metal fatigue. These invisible fractures alter the electrical properties of a network. The fractures will slow the speed of transmission; increase electrical impedance, causing high jitter rates; or completely disrupt communications. Slowing the transmission speed is not necessarily a problem unless the network is generally heavily accessed, in which case even a 10 percent transmission speed degradation can disrupt the NIC timing and cause transmission to fail.

### Installation Routing Options

Standard practice suggests that wire is best installed in cable ladders or wiring conduits. A cable ladder is a metal open-rung ladder for securing cables and wiring. Wiring conduits are sometimes called cable trays and are metal U-formed channels for concealing wire. Both items are best installed at the time a building is initially built since false

**Figure 8.18** Sources of EMI.

ceilings and ductwork usually preclude retrofitting ladders or trays. J-hooks provide adequate support for retrofitted cable. J-hooks bolt to a stud shot into steel or concrete support beams. See Figure 8.19 for samples of hooks, ladders, and the plastic cable tie.

Cable routing depends in great part on the building design, the available financial resources, and networking goals. Wire can be routed through underfloor ducts, through cellular floors with trench headers, or beneath raised plenum floors as found in the standard computer room. The cable tie is an important item to ensure that wire, once installed, stays where intended.

Other options include conduit systems in modular office furniture (so long as bend radii are not exceeded), surface raceways, or installation within a ceiling plenum. PVC cabling has a minimum bend radius of 3 in—a circle diameter of 6 in, while Teflon cabling requires double that. Newer technology allows high-velocity transmission on existing telephone wiring as in UTP applications and this cable can be pulled through common modular office partitions and furniture with few problems. The routing should address the need for growth and change, equipment relocation, and expansion of basic network services. A good design is patterned on the voice networks which have confronted and solved most of the same issues now affecting data networks. This analogy explains the explosive acceptance of UTP twisted-pair wiring; it does *nominally* coexist and use the same wiring as the telephone voice networks. Nonetheless, twisted-pair for networking is a better grade than generally installed for telephone lines. Two reasons that some organizations denounce the UTP technology are their own failure to install the specified quality of twisted-pair wiring bundles (category 3 or better) and their failure to adhere to rigorous length limitations. Substitution of "satin" wire, or the flat ribbon-like patch cord designed for telephone jumpers, defeats the noise cancelling property of true twisted-pair wire. These failures represent installation errors.

### Install Wire in Straight Runs

In general, it is better planning to avoid distance-minimizing wire routing. Stair-step patterns, wave or sawtooth zigzag are brilliant ideas whose time has passed, as shown in Figure 8.20. Odd routing patterns

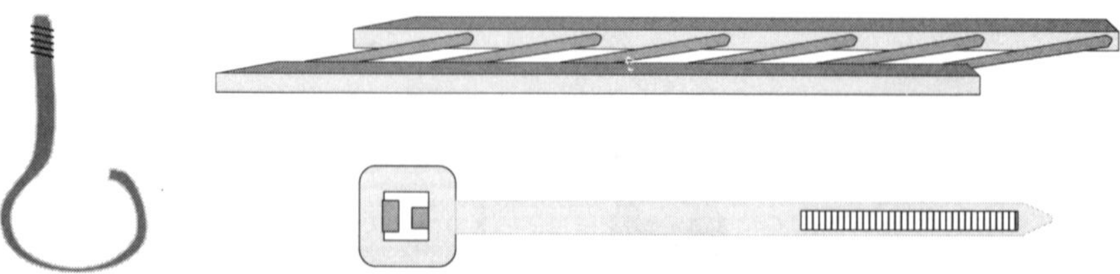

**Figure 8.19** Hook, cable tie, and cable ladder.

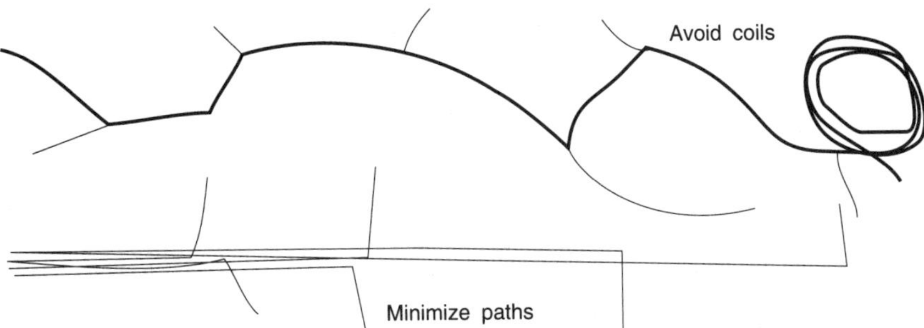


**Figure 8.20** Avoid zigzag cable runs or coiling excess UTP.

create a problem with pursuant wiring malfunctions and more at operational time; simple, straight runs are better. Wiring hubs, concentrators, and standard multiple access units provide high-density service while reducing cabling.

Often the lobe cable will run to a standard modular (or genderless) wall plate. The cable can be segmented at a wall plate, although this shortens maximum lobe length slightly as a result of signal impedance. A separate cable, possibly with a media filter, will connect from the wall plate to the computer device. Shorter cables can be used like extension cords and plugged together for longer lengths up to approximately the maximum specified length. Both UTP and STP are available in PVC or Teflon.

While twisted-pair could be threaded over pipes, ductwork, lighting, and electrical lines, and physically tied to any of these items for support, it is best practice to install it in straight runs supported by hooks, ladders, or conduits. Simple paths endure longer.

## Inventory Necessary Components

Once the route the cable will take is defined, it is appropriate to select the type and quantity of the components. Use the discussion of components presented earlier in the chapter as a guide. Refer to Figure 8.21 for the component quantities required for building a network. Additionally, this chart lists some simple rules for component selection. Some commercial tools provide automated methods to create the parts, materials, and time requirements for successful installation. LANBuild from Network Performance Institute is one such product.

## Wireless Networks

Planning cabling for wireless networks is simple; there is no network ring and no wiring star. There is a wiring connection requirement between the transmitter-receiver units and the node workstations that may need to run

**A LANBuild Design and Planning Tool Report**
**Network Installation Bill of Materials**
**for an Token-Ring 16 MB**

| Unit | Description | Quantity | Notes | |
|---|---|---|---|---|
| network | KW electricity | 391.40 | | |
| network | Dedicated Circuits | 55 | | |
| network | Tons BTU A/C cooling capacity | 696.07 | | |
| network | patch panel | 1 | | |
| network | patch panel blocks | 8 | 6 | |
| network | patch panel hydra bundle | 28 | 6 | |
| network | wiring rack | 2 | | |
| network | patch panel jumpers | 267 | 2 | |
| network | MAU or hubs w/8 ports | 12 | | |
| network | trunk cables | 13 | 2 | (Average likely length is: 5.00 |
| network | hubs w/8 ports | 11 | 2 | |
| node | node workstation | 80 | | |
| node | support workstation | 6 | | |
| node | NIC | 86 | 2, 9 | |
| node | STP lobe wire in meters | 86 | 2, 9 | |
| node | STP lobe wire footage in meters | 17747 | 2, 9 | (The longest likely length is: 288.00) (Average likely length is: 105.70) |
| node | Conditioned AC power | 17 | 2, 7 | |
| node | cable ties | 313 | | |
| node | network user software license | 89 | | |
| node | network software drivers | 89 | | |
| node | NIC device drivers | 89 | | |
| **Optional:** | | | | |
| node | wall conduit | 89 | | |
| node | wall wiring box | 89 | | |
| node | wall box plate cover | 89 | | |
| node | wall plate to NIC jumpers | 89 | 2 | |
| node | UPS Power Supply | 9 | 7 | |
| node | Surge protectors | 89 | 7 | |
| **Structural Components:** | | | | |
| network | ceiling conduit-- meters | 2294 | | *guess* |
| network | installation J-hooks or studs | 8724 | | *guess* |

Note 1: Hub and node dispersion will affect hub, MAU, and node count.

Note 2: Most hub nodes require AC electrical power for operation. Very few local nodes operate from workstation DC power. Although transmitter power requirements are fairly low, plan for adequate conditioned power in the desired locations. The same is true for servers, support nodes, and other critical powered components.

Note 6: A hydra connects easily into most standard patch panels and simplifies installation while increasing operating reliability.

Note 7: Uninterruptable power supplies (UPS) are battery-backup devices to provide needed service in case of power failures or spikes. Also, it is best to install isolated/grounded circuits for all critical computer equipment, active hubs, routers, and gateways.

Note 9: The NIC PROM chip contains the Token-Ring address. This is usually unique. Node addresses are usually established when the station is inserted into the ring (on a first-come, first-served basis), although some IBM equipment and many NOS permit the boot files to establish variable station addresses or domain names. Note that duplicate addresses, names, or ring numbers create problems. The NIC speed and buffer must be configured for 4 Mbits/s or 16 Mbits/s transmission speed. However, the packet buffer size is further restricted by NOS and bridge/router configurations. Match these parameters for best utilization of stations speed and resources.

Note 10: Failure to plan for adequate wiring conduit capacity generally represents the beginnings of a wiring problem that increases with success of the LAN or with organizational growth.

Note 11: LAN to LAN connectivity via modem lines, T-1, dedicated lines, SMDS, frame relay, or even serial lines often requires common carrier phone lines. Assess this need and plan for installation accordingly.

**Figure 8.21** Component quantities required for the basic network. (LANBuild bill of materials report courtesy of Network Performance Institute.)

within a wiring conduit, walls, or modular furniture to meet local fire codes. However, installation of wireless networks is not as simple as placing the transmitters and connecting them to PCs unless you opt for the NCR NIC with an external adjustable antenna. Pairs of infrared units must adhere to a line of sight installation and also be placed within the specified distances. There are also paired units that provide access to a limited number of other stations. Although most Token-Ring wireless sets transmit at speeds less than than 4 Mbits/s, nonetheless, the limited areas that they reach (approximately 800 square feet) conform to an acceptable TRT, as previously shown in Table 6.1.

Radio-frequency units do not require as stringent placement since they can broadcast around corners, through walls, and between floors of a building. In fact, they can even provide links between buildings. For unresolved health reasons, it is reasonable to install these transmitter units as far above and far from people as possible. As with the infrared units, there is also a wiring connection requirement between the transmitter-receiver units and the node workstations that may need to run within a wiring conduit, walls, or modular furniture to meet local fire codes. Figure 8.22 illustrates proper placement of wireless units. When wireless units require a central hub, strategically placing this unit in the center of the circle of nodes increases the wireless coverage area. For example, a central unit with a reach of 40 feet can cover 40 feet in four opposing directions to reach approximately 1600 square feet. Of course, when the immediate aim of wireless (RF or infrared) transmitter-receiver pair is to bridge separate buildings, a comparable strategy should be applied to maximize reception between these buildings.

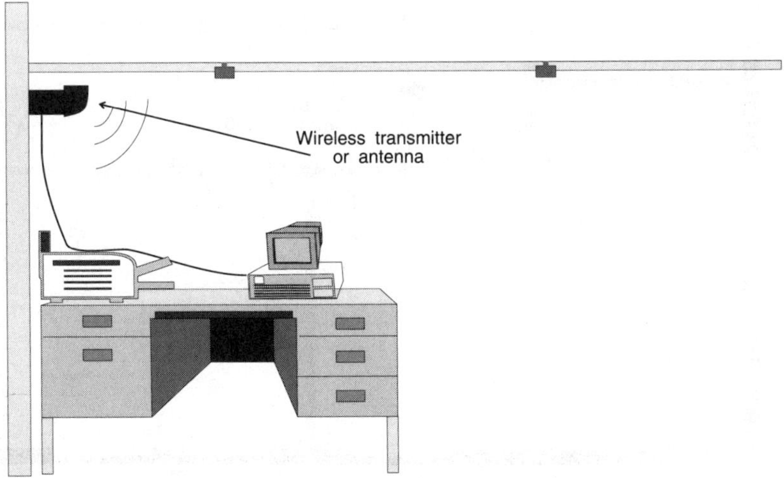


**Figure 8.22** Placement of wireless network units.

## Blueprint the Planned Network

A wiring installation should be precisely blueprinted. Wire placement is one of the most critical items. Location can be lost in the false ceiling plenum, thus making shorts and breaks difficult to find and fix.

There are several methods for blueprinting. Important items to document are changes in wire direction, endpoints, and places where the cable is jumpered. This is important in order to locate the places where failures are likely to occur and where a time domain reflectometer or ring scanner might connect to the network wiring. Another method for above-ceiling installations is to photograph the ceiling with the tiles removed and wiring exposed. A photograph can show the position and orientation of twisted-pair wiring cable trays.

Installations that have CAD/CAM systems can computerize illustration; computerization improves the access to copies and allows for the construction of overlays. For example, one level might show only the main trunk cables, while other layers may show subnetted rings, paths of lobe cables, and location of MAUs, bridges, or repeaters. See Figure 8.23 for a sample of blueprinting that illustrates wiring, MAUs, and lobe-cable routing, as well as twisted-pair connections.

Pictures of the internal wire dynamics (compiled in reports generated by serial downlinking from a ring scanner, such as the the Microtest Ring Scanner and Pair Scanner) can be compared against views when malfunctions are disrupting network communications. Discrepancies

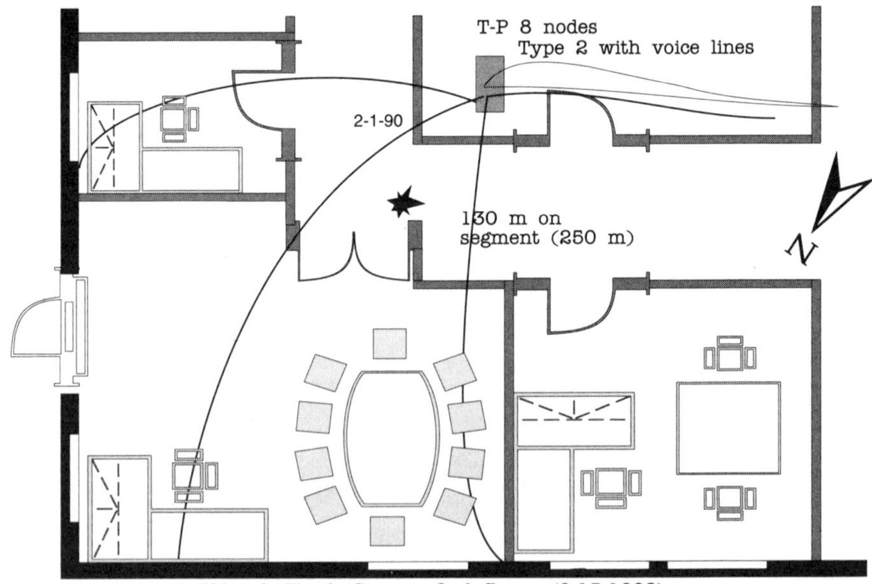


**Figure 8.23** Architect's style for network blueprint.

between the photographs and the current view indicate malfunction location. At a minimum, the wire length should be measured. It is folly to underestimate the network length and later discover that network wiring expansion has extended the network length beyond maximum length specifications. Networks are certain to fail sometimes; information about where the wires are located and repeaters are installed, while expensive to generate initially, will be more expensive to gather later when there are problems.

Chapter

# 9

# Installing a Token-Ring Network

A network design blueprint, a capacity and performance report, and a list of the required components are sufficient precursors to the installation process. This chapter describes the steps you must take and the tools you will need to put a Token-Ring network together.

## Planning for Installation

Installation requires a qualified design and a good plan. Network blueprints should be detailed enough to represent all the network hardware components required for a complete installation. This should comprise the actual physical components for the LAN and *also* ancillary factors such as electrical power requirements, cooling needs, and software. There are an increasing number of products that provide network design, capacity planning, and time and material estimates for LANs. While such tools are not absolutely required, they will minimize the chances for designing and building a flawed network. Examples include Bones or Planet, both from Comdisco, and LAN·CAD, LANModel and LANbuild, all from Network Performance Institute.

If the vendor does not supply full plans or provide complete network parts and installation services, it is vital to coordinate the arrival of all the network components. The network will not work without MAUs, wiring concentrators, or hubs, station lobe cables, or any number of other components, not the least of which is functioning network software. Insufficient electrical power or inadequate cooling resources for 100 workstations drawing 720 watts at 4 amps per unit could easily stress a standard office environment. Any problems arising may not become apparent immediately. The installation can certainly be staged, since many installation procedures can be completed concurrently. Just about any missing part can, no matter what its simplicity or general insignificance, become a critically needed component.

Therefore, plan your installation timetable with an eye to the steps in network installation and coordinate delivery of components to ensure a smooth process. Figure 9.1 illustrates critical steps and a logical progression for network installation. Each step encompasses several individual stages not included in the figure. STP, or wiring bundles, for example, requires cutting to length, applying media connectors or jacks and attaching the ends into MAUs or patch panels; and installing the actual wiring media in its final location. Installation is a mechanically simple process but a challenging experience if the technology is new to the organization. Sufficient skills may not have been developed to adequately identify and repair network problems.

Therefore, consider the benefits in hiring the vendor or an experienced contractor to string the network cabling. Gather as much outside experience and expertise as possible to augment the internal network administrative team. The installation procedure requires a shakedown period. Premature acceptance of a new installation is unwise, and making or disseminating promises of network availability before most of the problems have been resolved will devalue the reputation of the network administration team. Budget sufficient time for overruns, problems, and missing components. Be certain to negotiate preconditions for any final acceptance with the vendors. An installation may provide marginally acceptable operations, but fail to perform the level of service desired. To forestall any future problems, define clearly what your expectations are. This is critical for successful vendor relations and achieving your organization's network goals.

## Preparing for the Physical Installation

Installation of a new network goes smoothly if you gather the preliminary blueprints and all the equipment and components before beginning, and if you proceed in the order listed in Figure 9.2.

## Installation Tool Kit

Installation requires a sizable tool kit. The contents are enumerated here solely to provoke some ideas. This kit should contain screwdrivers;

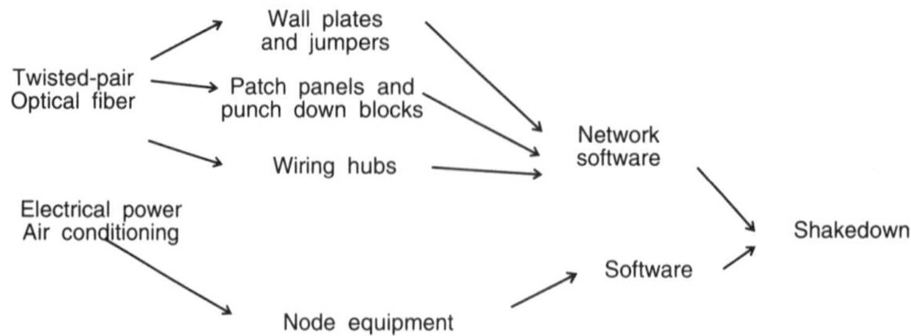


**Figure 9.1** Critical paths for network installation.

| # | Steps | Equipment |
|---|---|---|
| 1 | Inspect cable visually | Cable |
| 2 | Test wire | Wire and test equipment |
| 3 | String wire and label | Wire, tool kit, blueprint, tape |
| 4 | Secure wire | Cable ties |
| 5 | Install connectors | Tool kit, connectors, insulation |
| 6 | Test connectors | Test equipment |
| 7 | Install hubs and patch panels | Tool kit, ladder |
| 8 | Wire punchdown blocks | Jumpers and punchdown tool |
| 9 | Install and test other components | Tool kit, ladder, test equipment |
| 10 | Secure network components | Cable ties, velcro |
| 11 | Update blueprint | Preliminary blueprint |

**Figure 9.2** Steps and equipment required for installation.

pliers (including needle-nosed); diagonal cutters; a cable cutter; a wire stripper; a bright flashlight, preferably rechargeable; crimping tools; a soldering iron and silver solder; desoldering device; asbestos (or heat resistant) pad; a small mirror on a flexible handle; a shorting plug (a connector with a wire soldered to short the core conductor); and various spare parts like modular connectors, probe tips, junction boxes, and wall plates. Include specialty tools such as a manual or electric (vibrating) punchdown tool for modular patch panels.

Less obvious tools include a rechargeable vacuum cleaner, ladders, a stud finder, walkie-talkies, and a radio. A powerful vacuum cleaner is invaluable for retrieving screws dropped inside a computer chassis, for clearing shards from a tap core that might short the coaxial cable, and for clearing accumulating dust that shortens the life of all electronic components. Avoid magnets for this purpose since they destroy integrated circuits and erase magnetic media. In a clever application of a standard carpenter's tool, the electric stud finder or electrical power proximity checker (much like the stud finder) also locates active cables and wires. This can be useful to find AC lines so as not to route network cable too close to the electrical power lines.

A portable AM/FM radio not only serves to relax hard-working installers but also provides cheap testing of any audible EMI sources that might disrupt network communications. Given the location of most cabling, a ladder or scaffold is suggested; a special multiple jointed ladder that acts like a scaffold fills both needs. A floor tile lifter for extracting raised floor panels may be another choice. Walkie-talkies or similar mobile communication devices provide a simple way to keep the installation or repair team in touch. Include a standard No. 2 pencil, or an abrasive block eraser; it cleans edge connectors of circuit boards, chips, and Molex connectors, which corrode with time to cause intermittent problems. Add a spray can of an electrical contact cleaner and lubricant. Some sprays chemically improve electrical contacts. A multitester, a ring scanner, and various other test equipment are suggested. Figure 9.3 illustrates a robust tool kit. Chapters 12 through 16 describe these network-specific tools in more detail.

Another highly useful tool is the electronic tape measure. This device sends out an infrared signal (beware since it has the same wavelength as wireless infrared) to measure distances within an accuracy of centimeters (or inches). It is particularly useful as a planning tool to estimate wiring requirements very accurately. When measuring cable runs, do not overlook the vertical heights between nodes, wiring hubs, and other devices, and the possibly circuitous channels where the wire or cables will actually be installed.

## Installing Twisted-Pair Wiring

Twisted-pair wiring is available in at least two major variations for Token-Ring; shielded twisted-pair and unshielded twisted-pair. The standard and recommended medium is shielded twisted-pair, or IBM Type 1. This consists of two pairs of wires (four color-coded wires), a foil ground, a braided signal shield. A variant, IBM Type 2, wire has identical characteristics, but also contains four pairs of voice grade twisted-pair. IBM Type 6 is not as heavily built, shielded, or twisted. It is useful for jumpers only.

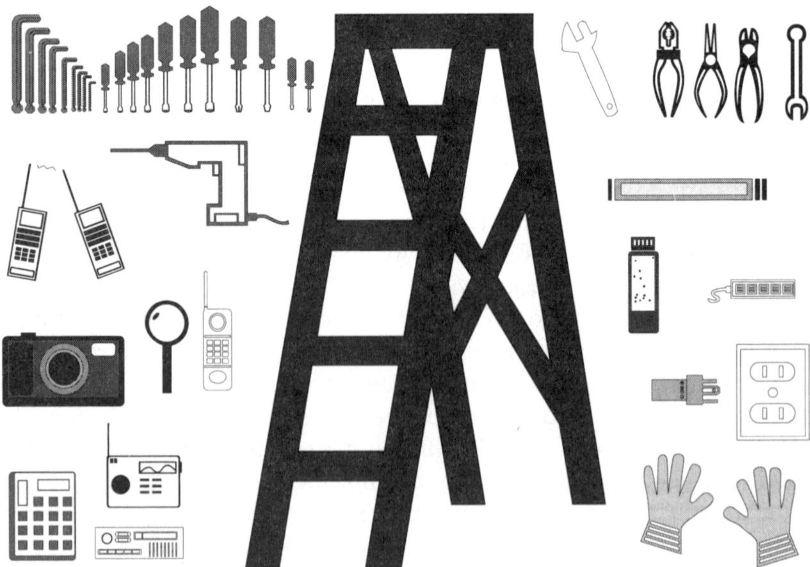

**Figure 9.3** Typical installation tools.

These shielded twisted-pair variants are wired from a central wiring hub to individual offices or cubicles. The data communications wires are pressed into a hermaphoditic media connector at the hub end and either a female 9-pin D-socket, a female RJ-11 jack, or a female RJ-45 jack at the station end. Voice lines, if any, are either crimped into standard RJ-11 or RJ-45 plugs, or punched down into a patch panel at the wiring closet and crimped into a female RJ-11 or RJ-45 jack at the office. A jumper cable with accommodating connectors will interconnect with the phone equipment and the NIC. Figure 9.4 illustrates the various modular connectors.

Unshielded twisted-pair is usually installed as a 25-pair bundle. Since each data or voice line usually requires two pairs, the bundle is sufficient for a mix of 12 voice and data lines. Do not mix a spare pair from one bundle with a spare pair from another bundle; it is too difficult to document correctly. Save the spares in case lines fail. Unshielded twisted-pair is also available as a set of two pairs. Grade, quality, and wire diameter is important for data communication reliability. Token-Ring performs better with a bigger gauge. Note that 22-gauge wire is actually larger than 26-gauge wire; the gauge numbering system is inverted so that smaller numbers represent wires with thicker copper cores.

Most UTP networks require a media filter to retime, filter, and passively correct distorted signals. In older networks, these devices are often incorporated into the wall jack. Media filters that connect between NIC and a wall jack are a better alterative since they do not specify how a particular wire run from the wiring closet will be used. This provides more flexibility in that a dual jack could conceivably support two phone lines, two network nodes, a fax line and a serial line, CDDI and a phone, or any combination thereof. A media filter incorporated as part of the jumper cable provides a more modular approach to UTP wiring. Some intelligent hubs or UTP-compatible NICs include active media filter circuitry. IBM sells a *concentrated access unit* (CAU)—their updated version of a passive MAU and media filter—with active media filtering circuitry. This approach works better than the passive filters, and provides better reliability with high signal jitter, too. Beware of upgrading or expanding an existing UTP network and using more than one media filter on each lobe; the resulting signal loss can create a very difficult-to-

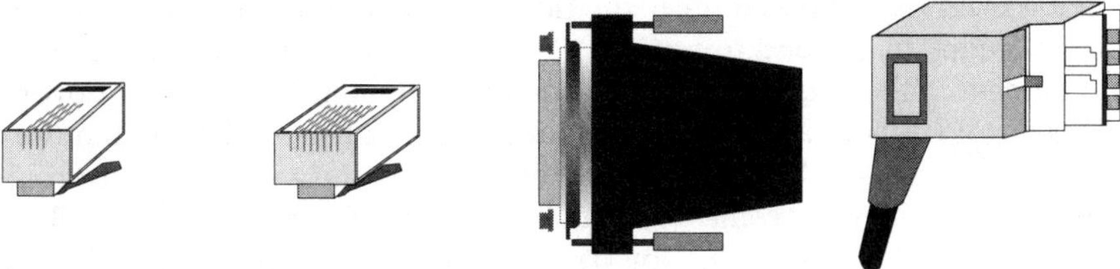

**Figure 9.4** Modular, DB-9, and genderless connectors.

debug failure. While one media filter is good and necessary for some UTP installations, more than one filter is *not* better.

Generally, twisted-pair is not a satin ribbon cable (often used to patch a phone to a wall jack) that can be stripped, inserted within a connector, and crimped tight in one simple step. Installation is usually more labor intensive. First, the outer skin on the bundle is slit. This reveals from 2 to 25 five pairs. The many individual pairs are then separated from the clump. Each pair of wires is then individually stripped for about 40 mm. Carefully—according to the color-coded wiring scheme—the bare ends are inserted into modular connectors, jacks, or hermaphroditic plugs. This process is described in detail later in the chapter.

### Wiring Installation

Before installing any new, repaired, or additional twisted-pair wiring, the wiring bundles should be inspected for visual defects. Twisted-pair is rarely installed as single wires. Instead, a *wiring bundle* containing multiple sets—often 25 pairs—is pulled through wiring conduits or the ceiling plenum. Two wire pairs are connected to a data set or combination phone and data set jack. IBM Type 1 STP is four wires (two pairs not bundled as pairs); one such cable must be pulled separately for each node. This conforms to the established norms for installing phone systems. However, do not make the mistake and assume that data communications wiring is identical to that used for phone systems. The grade must be of a higher quality. The modular connectors must match the exact gauge of the twisted-pair wire. Otherwise, modular connectors work loose from the wires over time to cause hard-to-trace intermittent network failures.

The wiring bundle should have no obvious physical defects like cuts, tears, or bulges in the outer jacket. Electrically, the individual wires in the bundle should conduct electricity without discontinuities. Each should be electrically isolated and not short out to each other. Techniques for testing with a multitester, time domain reflectometer, and the twisted-pair scanner are presented in Chapters 13 and 14. To install the twisted-pair wiring bundle you will need the tool kit, the preliminary blueprint, the cable, cable ties, and colored electrical tap for labeling the bundle.

Begin installation by extending the wire along the route mapped out in the blueprint, although it is wise to label the wire first. Any deviation made from this planned path should be noted on the blueprint. Deviations might be needed to avoid a ceiling light, an air conditioner, or a steel beam. There are several details that the installer must not overlook. Avoid bundle jacket abrasion and excessively bending the bundle. Avoid cable jacket abrasion, excessively bending the wire, and installing the wire with too extreme a radius (the minimum approximates a 3-in radius for PVC, and 6-in for Teflon. Wire with cracked insulation becomes brittle sooner, which causes electrical short circuits. In general, prudent concern and attention to these details will yield a successful Token-Ring installation. An AM/FM pocket radio, a simple and cheap, as well as readily-available tool, can locate radio interference that would affect twisted-pair transmissions.

Each IBM Type 1 cable is usually shielded enough so that cross-interference will not create a problem. However, since standard unshielded twisted-pair wiring for voice is not shielded, it is affected by both external and internal interference. Note, however, that high traffic situations actually generate enough traffic that bundled cable may experience inductance problems. Voice grade bundles lack any shielding whatsoever and are susceptible to electromagnetic interference from nearby devices. Therefore, space the bundles and do not create a compact bunch. Buildings with radio transmitters on the roof or nearby may necessitate special insulation or substitution of STP for UTP; the extra shielding may be required. When actually wiring the individual pairs, maintain polarity and do not cross the pairs over; the wires should at all times be "straight through" from plug to plug. This is true for all phone lines (or the bell will not ring), RS-232 serial, Token-Ring on UTP, Ethernet 10BASE-T, and the STP twisted-pair standard. The twisted-pair wire is used to connect the actual nodes to the wiring concentrator.

## Unshielded Twisted-Pair

UTP Token-ring cable segments use four unshielded wires that connect to ports 1, 2, 3, and 6 of an ISO standard physical interface. This is typically made up of an RJ-11 or RJ-45 telephone-type plug and jack. The plug and jack are not normally compatible with phone equipment. They are similar, but different enough to protect the network and baffle the unwary installer. The wires are typically 22- to 26-gauge copper wire. Wires 1 (red) and 2 (green) correspond to tip and ring receive, while wires 3 (yellow) and 6 (black) correspond to tip and ring transmit. While the formal Token-Ring specifications do not actually limit networks connections to 100 m—they say that lobes lengths are "normally limited to 100 m." In other words, a higher grade of wiring—shielded wiring is one possibility—could support greater segment lengths as the specifications indicate in Chapter 5.

### Labeling Bundles

As you string the wire, label it with some identifying marks. Although the unshielded twisted-pair jacket is color-coded—each pair contains some combination of two colors—red, green, yellow, and black, red and white, or blue and yellow—in candy cane spirals. Each of the jackets for these pairs has a different color and hash mark to identify the individual "pair" at each end of the bundle; multiple bundles are confusing and should be labeled. Shielded twisted-pair is usually a black cable with an extruded groove pattern. One cable is indistinquishable from the next. Color-coded electrical tape at 15 ft intervals helps sort out the spaghetti. Do not obscure any printed markings on the cable. Medical supply houses also carry alphabetic labels useful to indicate more specific information. Fluorescent marking tapes provide exceptionally effective identification above false ceilings when you are perched on a ladder 3 m high; visibility is often impaired by ductwork, supports, and wiring.

### Securing the Wiring Bundles

Once the wire is properly routed and installed in the cable trays, ladders, and J-hooks, or draped over the suspended ceiling supports, the cable should be tied with plastic ties to prevent damage. See Figure 9.5. Velcro is also effective for securing cable bundles, individual wire, and MAUs.

### Installing Connectors

To install connectors, you must have already installed the cable (or at least measured and tested the cable). Sometimes, it is expedient to cut the trunk cable and jumpers to length and install connectors on a bench before stringing it. Generally, this is pertinent only for short runs under 30 m that are not pulled through the ceiling, conduits, or modular tracks. Avoid stressing the installed connectors if they are pulled through the ceiling. You will need the blueprint and tool kit to complete this step. The tools required to install the connectors include cutters, a wire stripper, and crimping tools.

There are five basic types of Token-Ring connections: modular jacks, modular plugs, genderless (hermaphroditic) connectors, D-plugs, and wire ends that connect into the clips in a punchdown rack. The next sections detail these items and how they are installed.

### Modular Plugs

Modular plugs were developed by AT&T to streamline the installation, maintenance, and repair of phone systems. This technology has been adapted for use with LAN data communications as well. In the simplest terms, an *unstripped* ribbon cable is inserted into a plug blank. A crimping tool forces a plastic tab into the jacket securing the cord. At the same time, four, six, or eight brass contacts pierce this outer jacket and the insulation on the inner conductors. Figure 9.6 shows the crimping tool attaching a jack. This procedure is almost impossible to perform without a tool specially designed for the job. A screwdriver and

**Figure 9.5** The cable tie provides extra support for bundles and connectors.

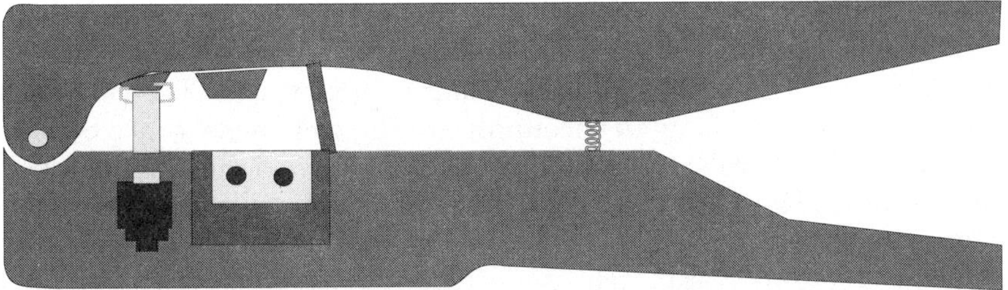

**Figure 9.6** The crimping tool attaches a modular plug to STP and UTP.

hammer do not work reliably. Recycling used plugs is a guarantee of future problems. Furthermore, plugs are available in many sizes and keyed shapes (RJ-3, RJ-11, RJ-22, and RJ-45, for example) and wire gauges. They are not compatible or interchangeable, although some may fit the same jacks. Verify the exact part designation.

Modular plugs also fit onto the wire with two orientations, up and down. The springy latches on both ends of the wire should always face the same direction. On long lengths of wire, the wire may coil, twist, and make it impossible to tell if the plug is installed correctly. The wires should run straight through and not twist. Instead, orient the color-coded wires such that the colors line up in the plugs as Figure 9.7 illustrates.

Shielded twisted-pair does not install as easily into modular connectors as the unshielded wire. Individual wires usually must be stripped individually and each wire of the two pairs must then be inserted into the modular plug. The gauge is thicker and the wires do not line up like the ribbon cable. As such, there are at least 15 ways (more with six or eight wires and with plugs with six or eight positions) to incorrectly insert them. Once all the wires (four, six, or eight) are inserted, crimp tight. Some phone systems require more than four wires for voice mail, paging, intercom, and other special functions. Therefore, the wiring may be designed for interchangability and quick setup from a central patch panel. Consider creating a color chart to show where each wire belongs and memorize it.

**Figure 9.7** Line up plugs to prevent twisted-pair crossover.

### Modular Jacks

Modular jacks are the female counterpart to the plugs. NICs, MAUs, patch panels, and wall sockets are usually female jacks. The only ones a network team is likely to encounter are the wall jacks. Since STP or bundles of UTP are strung to these jacks, the wires must be stripped individually. The most expedient jacks are identical in concept to the plugs; wires are held in place by crimping. The most common jack requires a screwdriver to tighten the individual screws which hold hold each stripped wire in place. Since the four wires carrying the RX/TX lines may be buried with a total of eight wires, know the color code. Telephone lines usually apply the red, green, yellow, and black wires. Normally, use these lines for RX and TX for consistency in use with fax, data, phone, serial lines, or CDDI as needed in the future. The candy-striped pairs are auxiliary lines; in a pinch or mixed for voice and data applications, use all eight wires.

### Hermaphoditic Connectors

These *genderless media interfaces* connectors were defined by IBM. A major source is AMP. They are the STP standard. The STP wire contains four and only four wires. These outer cable jacket is stripped exposing about 1.5 cm (1/2 in) of wire. Slide the plastic ring that is part of the housing over the STP cable. The shield is then cut and wrapped back along the outside of the cable jacket and a metal band is wrapped on top of this shield. The band is slid into place. This provides the ground and a fair method to protect the pairs from lateral force. The inner wires do not need to be individually stripped. They should merely be placed into the clear plastic retaining cover. Note the red, green, orange, and black color codes on this clip. The twisted-pairs should correspond to this color scheme. When the twisted-pairs do not conform—they might be yellow, gray, green and pink—but nonetheless maintain a uniform pattern and document it. When all four wires are placed into the cover, force the cover over the c-shaped wire retainers. The design is such that the metal retainers slit the insulation on the individual pairs and make a good electrical contact. The wires should not be stripped. Verify that no stray pieces such as foil, shield, or little wire chaff remain in the housing; these could move about and short the connector. Slide the plastic ring into the connector shell housing and snap the cover into place. This process is partially detailed by Figure 9.8. Avoid recycling these components since the metal fingers tend to wear and deform with usage.

### Male and Female D-plugs

Nine pin plugs usually connect into a corresponding socket on the PC. Some networks are designed for nine pin plugs on wall plate. This connection is the end that the user usually sees, as Figure 9.9 shows.

**Figure 9.8** Installation of genderless STP connectors (cover removed).

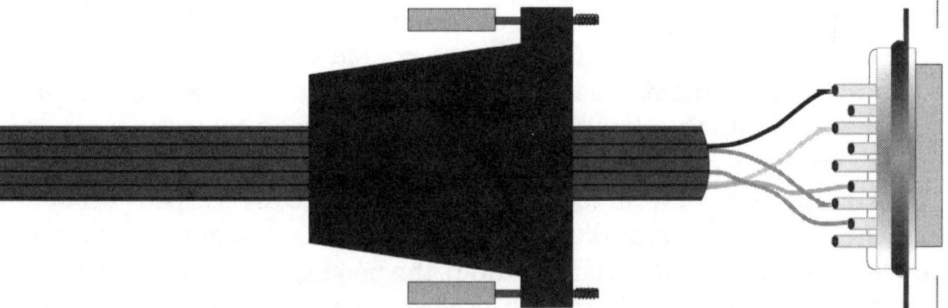

**Figure 9.9** Installation of DB-9 connectors..

Strip 2 cm (3/4 in) from the end of the STP cable. Crimp or screw the retaining ring to the end of the outer jacket of the cable. This protects the cable from lateral force. The shield must be soldered or crimped to the connector shell ground. This ground is important for safety, signal integrity, and minimizing crosstalk. The black wire goes to pin 5, the red wire to pin 1, the orange wire to pin 8, and the green wire to pin 6. This is true for both male and female connectors. Soldered connections are usually more reliable and durable than crimped ones (since lead solder resists corrosion better than the zinc crimping material). Adjust for color code differences, but do so consistently. Document any such variances. Place the two retaining screws into their channels. These screws ensure that the male plug is not easily dislodged from the NIC socket in an accessible slot in the PC or from the wall. The outer connector shell snaps or screws together.

### Punchdown Blocks

Wiring pairs, shielded or unshielded, can be connected into a modular punchdown block. Since the components are modular, failed components are easily bypassed or replaced. A punchdown block snaps into punchdown panel. A typical block (type 66) contains 50 rows of four claw connectors or eight claw connectors. Some block designs feature five rows of *dual* sets of ten claws. The horizontal type 110 block is usually installed for small sites. However, choose a punchdown block that has been certified for data communications usage. Units with gold-plated contacts tend to be more reliable over time. Avoid installing voice-grade components and recycling available parts.

The four connector block is wired into four *hydra* or *50-pin champ* connectors on each side of the block, as Figure 9.10 details. When wiring bundles are connected to a hydra on each side of the block, there are no individual wires. In the more usual format, each set of two pairs is held in the punchdown claws across a row. Wires individually attach to the claw connectors. Without a punchdown tool, wires must be stripped and forced into the teeth with a small screwdriver. This is labor-intensive and is best employed only for emergency field fixes.

Manual attachment is as follows. The pairs are stripped individually and inserted into the claws. Maintain the color code, which is commonly black, yellow, green, and then red. Twenty-five-pair bundles rarely contain single colors; instead, there are candy cane-striped jackets. A punchdown tool, hand-powered or battery-powered, separates the claws and forces the wire into place without the need to strip wires. The claws notch the insulation to establish a good electrical contact. Punchdown tools are inexpensive and improve the accuracy and speed of installation dramatically. Realistically, this tool is a necessity for installation.

### Grounding the Network

At all steps during installation of both wire and connectors, be aware that all metallic outer casings, shields, and fittings that connect to an STP shield should be insulated with a nonconducting sleeve—a potential source of ground-induced noise. Avoid any possible accidental

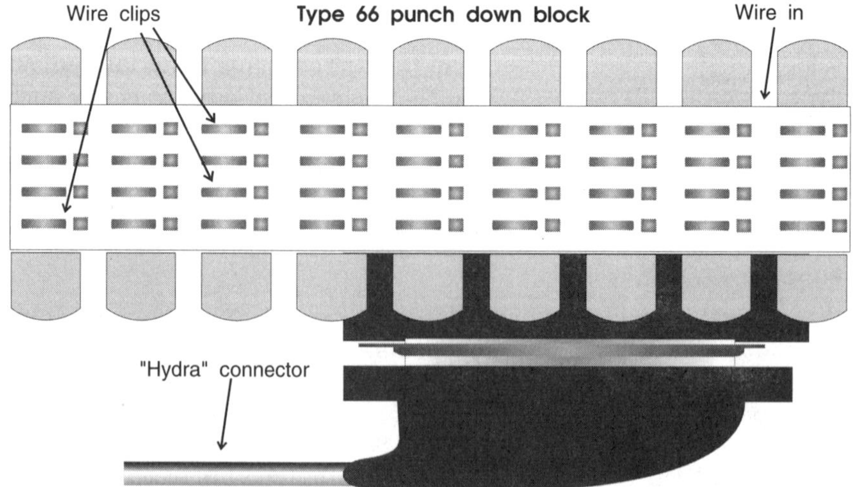


**Figure 9.10** Punchdown block shown with 50-pin champ, or hydra, connector.

grounding. Figure 9.11 shows these critical points. Installation of rubber sleeves—if necessary—prevents random grounding. Differential grounding—when there is an electrical potential difference between grounds on the network—creates both static and surge problems. Typically, equipment should be attached to a common ground within the same building and isolated between buildings. All exposed conductive fittings should be insulated with a rubber boot or wound with insulating electrical tape to prevent a random ground. The MAU or the workstation provides the necessary ground. Since STP and UTP are protected by vinyl or Teflon jackets, accidental groundings to cable trays, ductwork, and steel support beams are rare. One simple and inexpensive solution is to purchase a rubber coating dip (often sold at hardware stores) and brush or dip abrasions.

### Testing Connectors

A quick check with a multitester as explained in Chapter 13 or a ring scanner as explained in Chapter 14 will verify that the end connectors are not shorting and have a sufficiently good contact with the wire to actually carry the electrical signal. Modular wire is best tested with a phone line tester and a ring or pair scanner. Since these tests work only when there is something at the other end—live telephone line or network MAU—test with the appropriate tool. Vendors will usually verify installation as part of the process. Insist on that.

As with any installation, a check that the connectors are properly installed is good policy. Verification with a multitester and a wire scanner should be standard practice, as outlined in Chapters 13 and 14.

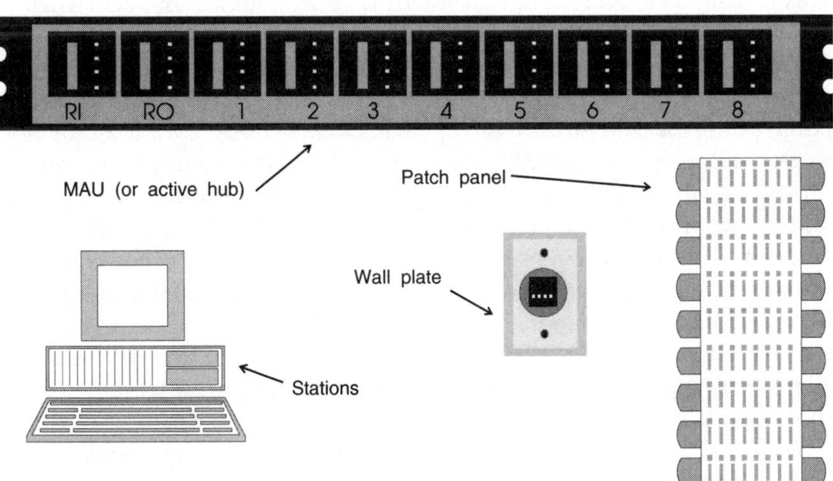


**Figure 9.11** Avoid random (or differential) grounding of network components.

### Observe Distance Limitations

IEEE 802.5 specifications for twisted-pair allow a maximum of 200 m between the wiring closet (where the wiring concentrator is placed) and the actual node devices for STP at 4 Mbits/s; this falls to 100 m for 16 Mbits/s or UTP. This length is actually for perfect conditions. Perfect conditions are rarely obtainable. Twisted-pair is apt to be routed alongside AC electrical lines, near to radio-frequency emitters, and other wiring bundles which will distort the signal. Transformers and other energy sources can alter the impedance of the wire. Minimize the wiring bundle lengths, and do not leave tails of wire (coils of extra wire) above the wiring closet; cut the wiring bundle to the shortest possible length but leave sufficient slack for temperature-induced expansion and contraction as well as for the possibility that wiring punchdown panel or office partitions may get moved a few feet.

If you anticipate that the distance limitations or external interference may cause transmission problems, select the highest quality of UTP. Do not overlook vertical heights in estimating all cable or wiring measurements. As an alternative, select a higher grade. The normal grade is UTP-3. Substitute UTP-4; this corresponds to UTP category 4. Shielded 25-pair twisted-pair is available at a substantial premium since it is not as widely used or as common. STP-4 will perform better for all network applications since crosstalk, signal degradation, and insertion to capacitance are improved. Synoptics and UTP substitutions for Token-Ring STP may have different wiring grade requirements. In all cases, check with the NIC, MAU, or hub vendor for recommendations, or verify wire utility with a pair scanner that measures attenuation, impedance, and crosstalk.

### Patch Panels

Token-Ring STP is modular, although UTP is modular and centralized. The installation differences are distance limitations and that one STP cable is required per node while each UTP bundle provides service for at least eight nodes. The star configuration encourages installation of a patch panel for centralized wiring. Additionally, since twisted-pair networks and telephone circuits often share the same wiring, the common telephone wiring schemes are used. Punchdown patch panels separate and differentiate the 25 pairs of wires from each UTP bundle. The wires within the bundles are usually differentiated with two striped colors for the insulating jacket as opposed to solid vinyl insulation for single phone lines and modular jumpers.

Since Token-Ring (also, Ethernet 10Base-T, and TPDDI) requires four wires, each bundle yields 12 connections; you might want to use no more than eight to minimize crosstalk and keep some wires as spares. Transmission is most reliable when each bundle is used for only eight connections. The patch panel is marked (which is highly recommended) with the locations of the other ends of each pair, and each individual wire is snapped into a retaining clamp, generally with a punchdown tool. Acquire a specialized punchdown tool which will speed installation of pairs in the panel and increase the chance that the connection is true. When actually wiring the individual pairs, maintain polarity and do not cross the pairs over; the wires should at all times be "straight through" from plug to plug. The NICs and MAUs handle the RX-to-TX crossover. Note that for network applications it is best not to overutilize the wiring bundle; many vendors suggest leaving at least 25 percent of the pairs unused to lower the crosstalk that will occur on the higher voltage, higher frequency employed even by 4 Mbits/s Token-Ring than by normal telephonic circuitry. Also, beware of mixing Token-Ring and serial lines within the same bundle. This may happen where terminal servers, Token-Ring, 10BASE-T, and serial printer connections coexist. Signal crosstalk *may* distort these four types of communication channels. Figure 9.12 illustrates a common punchdown or patch panel with modular wall jacks and jumpers. Jumpers are constructed to connect each pair on the panel into the wiring concentrator. Figure 9.13 illustrates a common punchdown or patch panel with DB-9 and genderless connectors typical for IBM type 1 STP installations.

A few problems need to be solved for Token-Ring to work on UTP. The cabling must not be too susceptible to electromagnetic noise (from transmitting devices, fluorescent lights, etc.); other devices transmitting similar frequencies; crosstalk between twisted-pair sets; or jitter, which occurs when preamble or packet signals are out of phase. Performance is a function of the signal-to-noise ratio. Higher-quality cable, better cable installation, shielded cable, low utilization of cabling bundles, superior wiring connections, shorter wiring runs, and superior

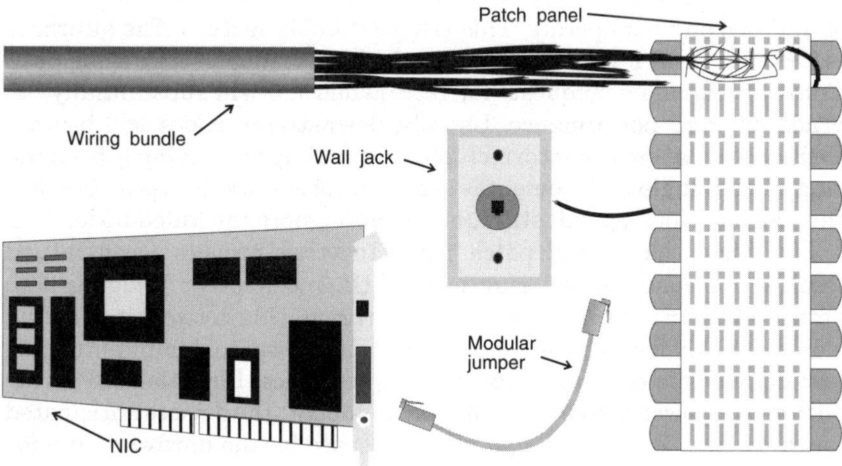


**Figure 9.12** Twisted-pair patch panel and modular components.

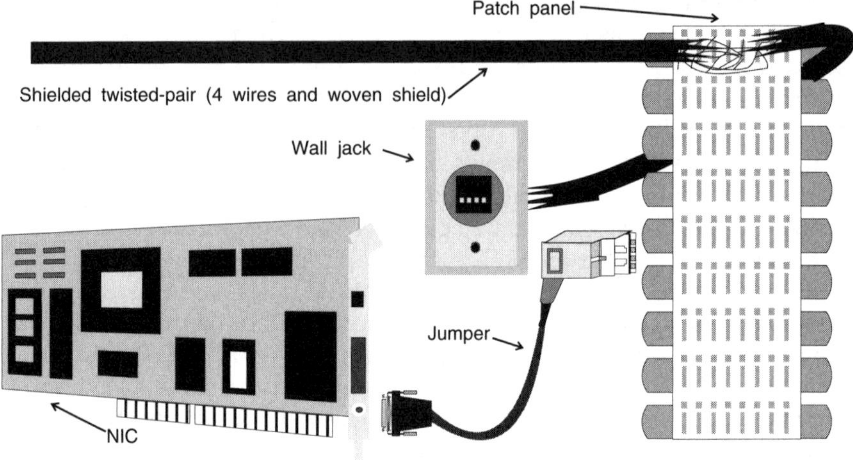


**Figure 9.13** Patch panel with standard STP components.

hardware including hub concentrators and the controller cards improves the chance that the signal will reach its destination. It is important to remember that Token-Ring is a sequential delivery since every node repeats the transmission signal; the management game is to improve that chance for consistent transmission.

It is important to label all the connections carefully and maintain up-to-date records for each wiring pair. Neatness counts for time saved when later adding new lines, debugging problem lines, and resolving interconnected phone and data lines. If you interconnect a hub or network node with a telephone circuit, the network device *usually* will shut down and not operate. This is a good safety feature. The alternate is for the node or hub to assume that the high voltage is a jittering peer. Constant signals or requests for retransmission will substantially degrade network performance. Usually, downstream nodes will beacon, thereby indicating the incorrect lobe and perhaps removing it from the ring. If the single bad element is taken out of service, it is possible that the twisted-pair hub will still function and ignore the failed node.

The wiring closet and patch panel together provide a centralized location for connecting a ring into FDDI, modems, or bridging it to optical fiber. In organizations with enterprise-wide networking, wiring closets quickly develop into phone maintenance space, computer rooms, and multimedia concentrators and adapter space. Plan ahead. Provide enough AC power and cooling capacity to support the devices anticipated for this space. Provide enough physical space for the hardware and for people to work. Route cables directly to this wiring closet, or provide enough slack in cables and optical fiber to later loop them into the room.

### Twisted-Pair Wiring Tips

Twisted-pair wiring is ubiquitous in office buildings. Twisted-pair is a cheap and an old technology. Twisted-pair fits the concept of the star topology for ease of installation and network maintenance. Rarely is the existing telephone cabling suitable for data networks. Shielding is nonexistent, routing is suspect and not documented, and the telephone cable probably does meet the more rigorous specifications required by data connections (category 3, 4, or 5). If you want your network to be reliable, the road to twisted-pair networking should begin with a new cable job. Of note, there are specialty tools available for qualifying the utility of existing UTP cable. The Next Scanner and Token-Ring pair scanners from Microtest are handheld devices which measure signal decay, crosstalk, capacitance, and attenuation. This information is necessary to determine whether existing UTP wiring will support a stable LAN, and also how long the trunk and lobe cables can be. It is important to differentiate unshielded twisted-pair from shielded twisted-pair wiring bundles. A pair scanner will perform the assessment directly. Poor wire could increase jitter, jabber, and chatter. See Figure 9.14 for twisted-pair wiring installation tips.

You can estimate lengths of existing wire by measuring DC resistance with a multimeter. For example, 1000 ft of 24-gauge wire will measure 16 Ω. It is important to note that RJ-11 plugs and jacks are interchangeable with the RJ-45 counterparts. However, the wires will not match up correctly. There are also variations on RJ-45 connectors to account for

- Ensure that straight-through polarity is maintained
- Use cabling that meets operating specifications
- Use cabling that meets fire code specifications
- Maintain uniform color code
- Maintain 9-Ω/100 m impedance
- Limit use of flat cable to under 5 ft on any connection
- Install UTP matched to media filters or active hubs
- Avoid the use of standard punchdown panels
- Route twisted-pair away from RF and electromagnetic radiation
  6 in from standard power lines
  12 in from fluorescent lighting
  36 in from transformers
- Do not overallocate the twisted-pairs in a wire bundle for carrying data signals to minimize signal crosstalk
- Check for loose connections
- Use RJ-45 (not RJ-11) connectors matched to the wire gauge
- Observe pair polarity
- Apply a conductive spray to connections when installed
- Hire a qualified data cable installer

**Figure 9.14** Twisted-pair wiring tips.

shielded and unshielded twisted-pair sets and flat ribbon cables. Most STP installations require that the connectors are installed manually since each wire must be stripped individually, although a power punch-down tool speeds insertion of wires at the patch panel.

When installing Token-Ring, be certain that the cable installer recognizes that there are indeed differences and installs the correct RJ-45 connectors for data communications lines. Consider acquiring a large supply of RJ-45 components in a nonstandard color to provide immediate and effective visual differentiation from standard telephone connectors. Also, for the same reasons, avoid intermixing standard telephone punchdown panels and data communications punchdown panels for three reasons. They are not always reliable for data connections and they encourage incorrect wiring and possible cross connections with active telephone circuitry. Also, telephone ringing voltages, which range from a minimum of 48V to more than 100V, can cause considerable crosstalk effects on 4.5V data lines. This causes hubs to shift into a *link failure mode* and not transmit on the faulty lines.

## Checkpoint Testing

After the transceivers or wiring and hubs have been installed, test the installation. It's a good checkpoint in the installation process because the network is now functionally complete. The tools required and how to use them are explained in Chapters 12 through 16.

If the network is broken, disassemble it, and restart the process. Assuming the network is still functioning and there is no indication of an electrical short, measure resistance between the pairs. A multitester should read approximately 16-Ω resistance per 100 m on a completed network. A ring scanner as outlined in Chapter 12 is better tool to use. Readings should not fluctuate if pressure, twisting, and hard knocks are applied to connections. Twisted-pair should be tested for correct polarity and no crossover of the pairs. While many NIC and wiring concentrators do switch contacts automatically in instances of polarity exchanges for pairs, they cannot handle miswiring of the both pairs. Check genderless connectors for mechanical functionality.

## Token-Ring Addressing

There is no formal Token-Ring hardware addressing scheme. A NIC does have a vendor number. Usually, the NetWare active monitor will assign a sequential node number when a node inserts into the ring. LAN Server and LAN Manager expect valid station ID numbers when a node inserts into the ring. These ID numbers are established by the system administrator in boot files. Session addressing is a function of the LLC (IPX, TCP, and NetBEUI), upper-level connections, and applications.

In all cases, make certain that there are no duplicate addresses, a situation which could immobilize the network or confuse stations that capture misaddressed packets. Furthermore, some NOSs will ignore packets even though addressed to them when the receive flag has been set.

## Shakedown New Installations

New installations, retrofits, additions, and any changes to the network all require a shakedown period. It is foolhardy and unprofessional to assume that any new installation will, from the start, work as promised. This is particularly the case for extensions and retrofits with new, upgraded, or untried components. There are always surprises, like a loose connection, vibration from an elevator shaft, overheating, marginal components, vendor incompatibilities, lot incompatibilities, and overloading. Premature assurances sap credibility. Certainly, basic testing of those items listed in Figure 9.15 is, at a minimum, appropriate.

A shakedown period should be initiated when additions, major network configuration changes, and physical relocations are effected. This requires that additional material and time resources be allocated. Allow half a day for each node of a network for new installations, and an hour for each node when a network is segmented, rerouted, or extended. Figure 9.16 represents a core network that has ballooned to support new groups, multiple protocols, and wide area services.

## Securing the Components

Once twisted-pair wiring is properly installed in the cable trays, ladders, and J-hooks, or fitted to the suspended ceiling supports, all connecting wire should be tied with plastic ties. This ensures that the wire will not get damaged, and that connections will not be unplugged accidentally. The cable tie, as illustrated previously in Figure 9.4 is useful to attach lobe cables to the MAU, hubs, or workstations. This also relieves connector strain.

- Twisted-pair wiring and connectors
- Controller installation
- Controller electronics
- MAU or hub units
- Patch panels and punchdown blocks
- Node equipment
- File servers
- Network software
- User network access
- Peak load operations

**Figure 9.15** Shakedown network components.

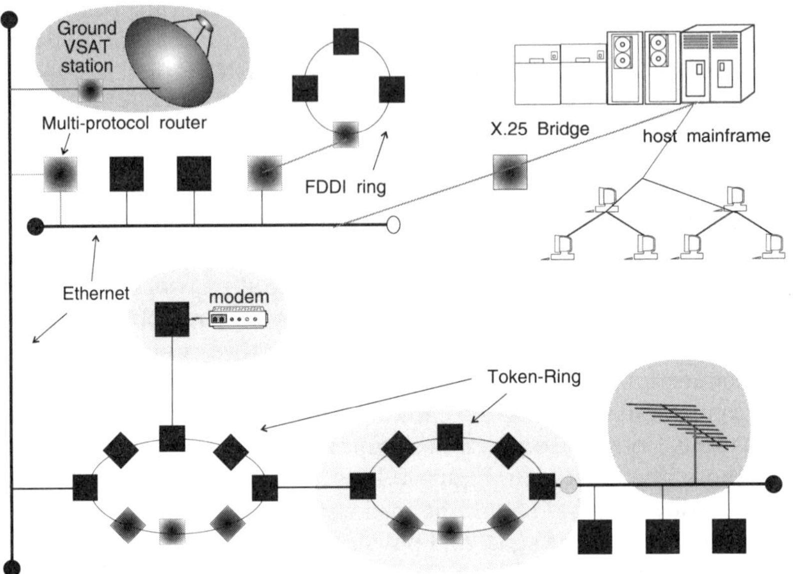


**Figure 9.16** Shakedown additions, changes, and retrofits. This gradual network growth provides for focused testing of network additions.

## Blueprinting: Confirming the Design

Once a network is measured and tested, and connectors installed, it is good policy to benchmark it. The pair scanner with serial data downlink capability or a time domain reflectometer and an instant film camera or oscilloscope recorder provide extraordinary blueprinting. This is an important benchmark against which to compare at later times when network problems occur. While the wire is accessible, it can be purposely shorted at the connectors for benchmark photography. An instant camera also can blueprint physical wiring and deviations from the original plans. Any subsequent changes should also be added to the network blueprint to maintain an accurate view of the network.

## Common Installation Failures

Slipshod work will complicate the installation and subsequent network management problems. Cable jacket abrasion can cause excessive impedance. Overbending or installing cable with an excessively tight radius will often fracture and break or short out the pairs.

An RJ-11, RJ-45, D-plug, or hydra connector may not make a good contact. Frequently RJ-11 jacks and modular plugs are often mistakenly substituted for RJ-45 when installation is performed by telephone people. Although each connector is physically interchangeable, RJ-11 has only four contacts instead of six. While MAUs, hubs, and NICs often handle pair polarity errors, only *some* components may accommodate this wiring flaw while others do not. Complete crossover of the twisted-pair is usually a fatal defect for network functions (telephones will work although the ringer will not).

Wires and connectors fail in a limited number of ways. The cable or the NIC electronics can be bad, or can fail over time. The likeliest reason for error is poor installation. Either the individual wires don't make good contact with the connector contacts, internally cross, or stray wires in the connectors short the network. Twisted-pair wiring presents a myriad of hazards. The most likely problems include connections between the hub and nodes that exceed specified length. The cable from the wiring closet may be looped or coiled. Not only does this lengthen the segment, it also has the potential to induce significant crosstalk. Poor-quality (or the wrong cable and wire types) cable attenuates the signal too rapidly to cause signal distortion, loss in signal strength, or insufficient voltage spread between the highs and lows. Also, the modular connectors could be improperly installed, the transmit-receive pairs may cross over, or individual pairs may switch polarity at either end. Since Token-Ring frequently shares the wiring bundle with live telephone circuits, other likely failings include connection of a Token-Ring line into a live telephone circuit, or overuse of the pairs in the wiring bundle. The last point of installation failure is the D-plug. Half a connection is worse than a completely severed connection because the NIC might receive signal correctly but transmit a continuous signal onto the network or no signal whatsoever, thus, jamming the network completely.

In this chapter, installation procedures for shielded and unshielded twisted-pair, connectors, punchdown blocks and modular components have been examined. Chapters 10 and 11 discuss devices and methodologies that expand Token-Ring service from a minimal linear configuration to a multidimensional topology.

Chapter

# 10

# Expanding a Token-Ring Network

The Token-Ring specifications limit STP drive distance in a single network ring to 770 m and 250 nodes at 4 Mbits/s, 346 m and 136 nodes at 16 Mbits/s. This drive distance is reduced by UTP cabling to 300 m with 72 nodes at 4 Mbits/s, and 117 m with 72 nodes at 16 Mbits/s. Rings with mixed wire (STP and UTP) are limited to 66 nodes.

Token-Ring limits placement of nodes to within an absolute of 200 m from a wiring hub for 4 Mbits/s operation, 100 meters for 16 Mbits/s, and about 70 for UTP wiring. These node count, ARL, and lobe length limitations may be restrictive limitations for some organizations—doubly so when the desired medium is UTP. IBM states that its LAM UTP filters support UTP lobe lengths to 90 m. These limitations can be circumvented by special design or by installing expansion devices, such as the repeater, the bridge, and the gateway.

## Inspire Design Simplicity

One network management generality to consider meticulously when building, enhancing, and expanding LANs is to avoid the novel and unusual enhancement products. This includes all expansion devices, MAUs, NICs, wiring concentrators or hubs, specialty bridges and gateways, and enterprise-wide linkage hardware and software. This is particularly relevant when networks are essential to internal application or production and manufacturing operations. Complexity and fragility in any component decreases the overall reliability of the LAN. This rule is strengthened by the realization that Token-Ring is a logical ring where the failure of any node in the series may cause the whole ring to fail. Assess the reliability and integrity of intelligent hubs to handle failures.

The logic for this assertion is the premise that maintaining reliable network operations takes precedent over all over other concerns including cost, ultimate performance, upgrades, user satisfaction, efficiency, austerity measures, personnel reductions, and ego gratification. While these other concerns frequently arise in the political structures of most corporations, the absolute need to keep the network reliable is tantamount. When the LAN is crucial to business and functionally replaces traditional mainframe DP operations, such mission-critical applications require absolute reliability. All other LAN issues should be subordinated.

As such, the simplest configuration for the network (that meets requirements) will by nature have the fewest parts to fail, be simple, and easily replaced in part or repaired in whole when inevitable failures occur. Specialty hardware that improves cost, performance, and the myriad of other facets comes with a price of oddity, complexity, and increased failure rates. In time, odd parts may not be serviceable.

Even spanning trees, redundancy, redundant disk storage, fault-tolerance or mirroring components do not necessarily decrease the statistical chance for downtime—that is a complex calculation requiring expert consultation. Also, more complex solutions require more elaborate management, or perhaps tax the abilities of any person or team to maintain large local and enterprise-wide networks that support critical DP activities. Instead, keep it simple and retain skilled people *always available* to resolve catastrophes.

Recognize, too, that anything that binds small, unique pieces together to form the whole is critically dependent upon each of those pieces being available, operable, and correct. Local networks, distributed computing, client-server networks, file component linkages, and other binding computer events become more fragile as they become more complex. Duplication, redundancy, and application mirroring is frequently unattainable. Keep it simple.

## Speeding up LANs

While most network bottlenecks are not caused by channel usage or speed limitations, those 20 percent that are can be upgraded by increasing the LAN transmission speed. Four Mbits/s Token-Ring may be increased to 16 Mbits/s for about a true doubling in channel-bound performance. Packet sizes may also increase for an additional performance gain, this depending upon the NOS. The next step for 16 Mbits/s Token-Ring is 100 Mbits/s CDDI. In fact, some vendors provide controllers that are plug and cable compatible with existing STP LANs for a true two- to three- fold performance improvement; fewer vendors as yet provide UTP CDDI.

The transition from 4 Mbits/s to 16 Mbits/s requires suitable trunk and lobe wiring and NICs that can support the higher speed. Some controllers are dual speed. If existing controllers do not support or do not have sufficient RAM for the higher speed, they will need replacement. Similarly, the shift to CDDI requires replacement of the controllers. While the drivers for Token-Ring at both speeds are the same, the CDDI will require new drivers since it is an OSI-compliant technology.

## Expanding LANs

An extensive network can be constructed with a complex, nonlinear geometry to serve high concentrations of users, longer distances, and the global OSI network maximum of $2^{64}$ Token-Ring nodes. Wiring hubs provide dense service immediately from 66 to 250 nodes per ring. Multiple MAUs and racks with MAUs in one wiring closet can connect an arbitrary number of nodes (and hence rings), subject to the aforementioned ring count limits. By interconnecting rings, the full OSI limit is conceivable. The *bridge* interconnects different networks into Token-Ring. The *gateway* interconnects separate Token-Ring rings or segments with other protocols to one Token-Ring network. The *repeater* boosts signals for longer lobes on a single ring or connects trunks of two rings.

There are also other devices including the *network switch* (packet or matrix switch hub) and the *spanning-tree bridge* which are useful for creating mission-critical and fault-tolerant networks since they provide alternate channels and multiple point-to-point routes.

## The Wiring Concentrator or Hub

Although the *wiring concentrator* provides base-level service for a Token-Ring network, the hub also serves as an effective expansion unit. These devices usually support from 4 to 16 nodes each. The standard multiple access unit supports eight lobes. Twisted-pair jumpers and lobe cables connect individual-node workstations to the hub. Figure 10.1 illustrates a typical twisted-pair wiring concentrator.

If you recall, twisted-pair IBM Token-Ring is not a true ring-configured network. It is a star topology, and as such, all signals are transmitted from each node to the hub, which then passively switches (or actively repeats) the signal to the other nodes. Smart hubs check the destination address, presence of errors, and defective packets before repeating the Token-Ring packet. Since the electrical signals on twisted-pair must be regenerated by all NICs, signal errors do arise. Also, defective packets are repeated to the nodes for obvious reasons.

Packets destined for nodes beyond the immediate ring would be transmitted through the standard MAU device to bridge, router, spanning tree, or gateway providing the multihop services.

The easiest solution to high-concentration nodes is placing a MAU or multiple units on location subject to limitations of the ARL. This multiport unit provides more than single-station access for a lobe from the central wiring hub. This placement is subject to all lobe length limitations and the ARL calculation. Transformation of a lobe cable with a significant length into a trunk cable could easily breach the specification limits. The use of such "outboard" hubs yields other economic and reliability benefits. Not only is the connecting wire from the node to the hub minimized, the reliability of the local connections are superior. The

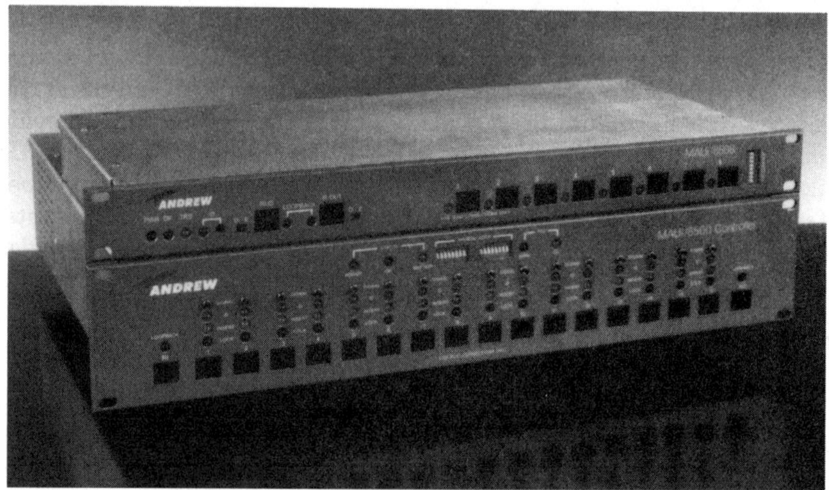


**Figure 10.1** Typical twisted-pair wiring concentrator (Andrew Corporation).

disadvantage is that the concept of the centralized wiring closet is defeated, simple reconfiguration from the wiring closet is made complicated, and the possibility for similar additional expansions is remote. These problems can all be overcome by wiring all concentrated nodes to a local wiring closet are creating a local ring. Bridge that new ring to the existing LAN.

Some newer products include multiport NIC and access ports contained within a single PC expansion board. This component is essentially both a NIC and a MAU for an additional number of ports. In such an architecture, this board fits within a personal computer. A lobe cable from the MAU connects to this machine. Four other PCs with special client expansion boards attach locally to the expansion board with twisted-pair ribbon cable. Since the the first PC is merely functioning as a repeater, total node and lobe count must include the client PCs in the total ring count limitation. Similarly, overall lobe length must include the length of the longest client connection cable. However, this design is conducive to minimizing expensive STP cable runs or adding lobes after the fact. Expansion and growth within a concentrated area is easily met by establishing a local ring, or, subject to the limitations of the ARL and drive distance, just installing a local MAU.

## Network Repeaters

A *repeater* unit boosts the transmission signal for wiring runs which are longer than specification. A common unit is represented by Figure 10.2. Token-Ring is limited to a maximum drive length of 500 m (or 200 m,

**Figure 10.2** Typical repeater unit (Andrew Corporation).

depending upon the cabling variation), and the repeater can augment this length to 2500 m. Many repeaters can be used on a network, although it is important that no node be separated from any other node by more than two repeaters. There are three variations on repeaters: the simple repeater, the smart repeater, and the half repeater.

The *simple repeater* just extends the signal, as shown in Figure 10.3. Note that the repeater unit connects into a trunk or lobe cable. If these are node devices, the repeater uses a node location and subtracts from the maximum network configuration. Repeaters will increase the TRT and ring latency.

The *smart repeater,* or *learning repeater,* filters packets by destination. This hybrid device is actually an ISO bridge because this functionality is supported at the OSI data link layer. If a packet were destined for another ring, the repeater captures and transmits the packet when that other network is free. A common error for such bridges connecting saturated rings or Ethernet segments is to create a performance bottleneck. Other packets are ignored. This smart repeater reduces the probability for decreased performance since a fraction of packets are filtered and not forwarded. Figure 10.4 illustrates these two principles.

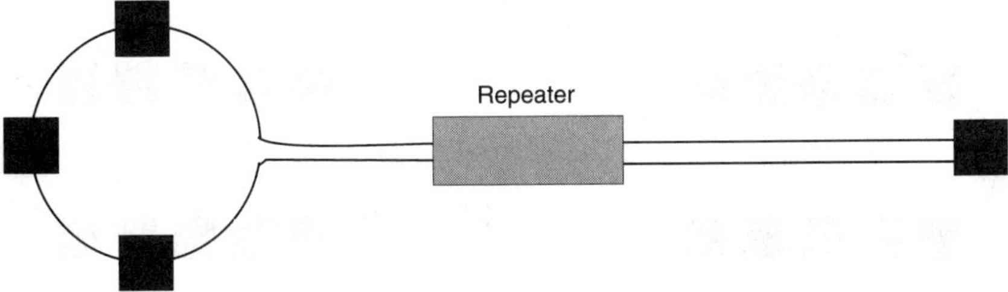

**Figure 10.3** Nodes linked with a repeater.

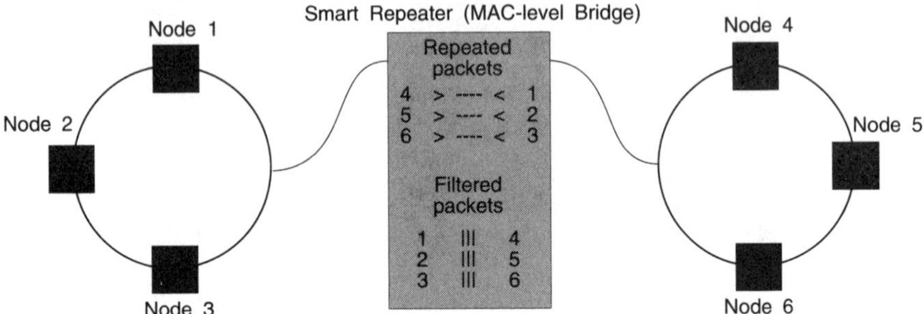


**Figure 10.4** Two rings linked with a smart repeater.

Only packets sourced from node 4, 5, or 6 destined for node 1, 2, or 3 are repeated across this gateway. Likewise, only packets sourced from node 1, 2, or 3 destined for node 4, 5, or 6 are repeated. Internetwork traffic is thereby reduced for an effective performance gain.

*Half repeaters* transmit signals from one building to another. A half repeater might utilize a Token-Ring baseband or broadband coax, fiber optics, PBX network, infrared or microwave, or satellite transmission medium. The half repeater is often a long-haul link between distant networks. Specialized hardware filters, decouples, and synchronizes transmission and reception in order to eliminate increased TRT. *Decoupling* is the intertwined process of informing the sender that transmission has been logically and properly delayed to allow that sending process to continue processing. When transmission is finally completed, the sender receives a confirmation message within the scope of the *proper* network protocol. A half repeater, as illustrated in Figure 10.5, effectively joins two distinct networks.

Microwave interface units often include a store-and-forward buffer to decouple the microwave transmission. The buffer must prevent packets from colliding, or both coupled networks could exhibit a constant state of collision and saturation. Extra software is required to belatedly indicate transmission completion.

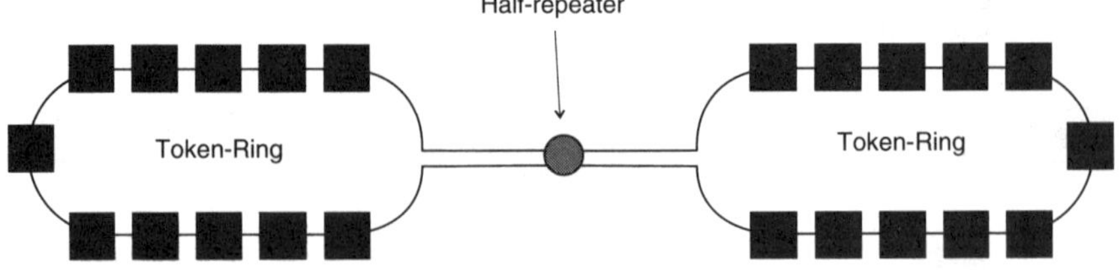


**Figure 10.5** Half repeater connects rings.

## Multipurpose Devices

Multipurpose devices economically expand Token-Ring. These units are frequently called *concentrators*, *wiring hubs*, *bridges*, *routers*, and *gateways*. Multipurpose devices interconnect multiple networks and handle incompatible media. Multipurpose devices like concentrators are critical for building enterprise-wide networks since the network media is likely to include baseband twisted-pair Token-Ring, RS-232, T-1, Ethernet, SNA, proprietary optical fiber, and FDDI. Concentrators provide a single focus for connecting these disparate media and protocols. In addition to the physical connectivity and the centralized focus, these devices also include management tools such as CMIP or SNMP for managing these complex interconnected networks.

Synernectics, Shiva, Racal Interlan, BICC, and Cabletron are among the many vendors providing these complex connections. Most vendors now produce so-called hub devices that integrate disparate Token-Ring networks into a central wiring closet, and then provide twisted-pair service from a star configuration—with the same physical architecture as Token-Ring. These products provide a focal point for controlling a network and asynchronous and synchronous networking services. Additionally, some concentrators provide multiple-channel routing and bridging that locates the fastest, shortest, or only available route between nodes. This technology is complex, difficult to install and maintain, but invaluable for networks suffering from overloading. It is presented later in this chapter. Cabletron and Synernectics, among a growing field, produce such units. They provide local area connectivity for asynchronous and synchronous networks, terminals, and peripherals. Specifically, these devices provide access to a modem pool, printer support, terminal concentration, host computer concentration, synchronous protocol conversion, Ethernet, FDDI, and Token-Ring access. In many cases, these units contain multiple power supplies, hot swap capability, and fail-safe operation. This is unusual in that repairs and configurations can be performed while the hub remains in operation.

Another important multipurpose device is the *terminal server* which services 20 RS-232 lines for data entry terminals, serial printers, or modems. The terminal server looks very much like a Token-Ring hub; output, however, does not propagate Token-Ring signals, but separate RS-232 serial lines. Frequently, these servers are employed where client-server distributed processing is not required for all users since less expensive dumb terminals can provide appropriate user access to host databases, mail services, network fax, network optical storage and retrieval of scanned documents, and typical desktop applications.

In general, bridges, routers, and gateways do not simplify networks or network management. They tend to add to the topological and managerial complexity. As such, they should be applied only when performance improvements or expansion requirements demand them.

More esoteric hardware includes advanced *rings-in-box* technology. Hubs eliminate the requirement for trunk networks while hubs with *switched backplanes* and *cross-point switches* provide intermediate methods to reconfigure networks in real time for fault-tolerant operation. These uncommon devices for Token-Ring—most are designed to overcome saturation problems with Ethernet—are designed for high-volume and critical networks. While networks constructed with trunk service provided by a hub frequently experience capacity bottlenecks at the hub, these newer technologies endeavor to bypass the bottlenecks. Of relevance, too, vendors are producing more multipurpose, multiprotocol bridge and hub devices that utilize Reduced Instruction Set Computing (RISC) chips, Complex Instruction Set Computing (CISC) chips, and Application Specific Integrated Circuits (ASIC). These are important in terms of providing adequate network performance for routing and gateway operations since each routing operation can require between 50 and 250 instructions to route a packet.

Despite this complexity and uniqueness, specialty products may provide the only solution for saturated large LANs and enterprise-wide networks. For example, the faster processing time becomes important when real-time protocol translation rather than frame encapsulation is required so that client-server distributed processing can occur with heterogeneous protocols. Protocol translation often requires multiple outgoing frames for each incoming one and perhaps complex address conversions, in addition to any simpler routing decisions.

## Network Bridges

The simple *bridge* connects different types of networks together and promotes interconnectivity between multivendor networks. Figure 10.6 shows a node that bridges two networks. A bridge is either a specialized type of hardware that converts transmissions from one type of network into a medium required by another, or a computer computer device that is compatible with two communication device that interfaces with two communications networks. A bridge is totally transparent to the devices on the network. A bridge is also protocol independent. *Protocol independence* means that packet signals are converted for transmission on another medium and the data format is invisible to the bridging device. The two media may be the identical or different. The most common bridging mechanism is a modem that converts digital baseband signals into a broadband format for long-haul or multiple-channel transmission. Figure 10.7 illustrates this bridging technology.

As larger organizations require enterprise-wide networks and integrate microcomputer technology and microcomputer networks like To-

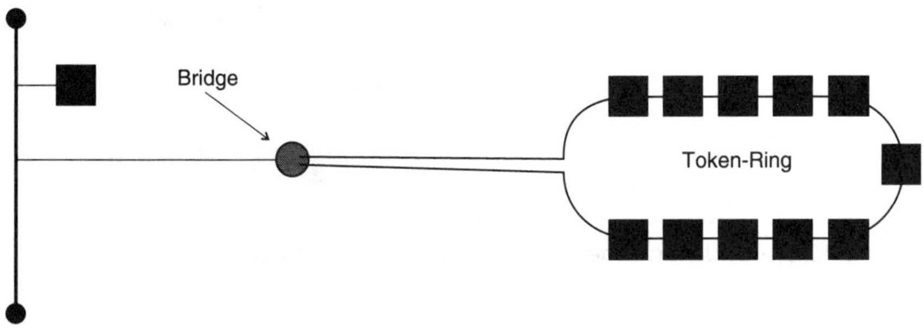


**Figure 10.6** An Ethernet bridge to a Token-Ring network node.

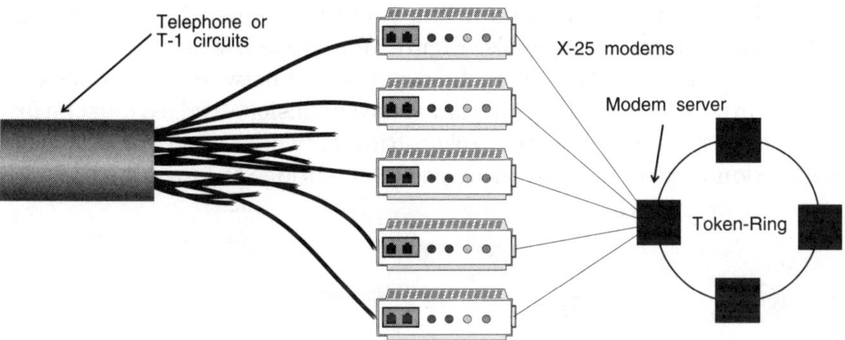


**Figure 10.7** Modems bridge Token-Ring to long-haul nodes.

ken-Ring, the importance of the microcomputer grows. Users find the microcomputer less restrictive than mainframes, and more available. It provides software unavailable on mainframes. File server networks present a viable downsizing opportunity, as Chapter 11 details. Uploading and downloading of information between mainframe and microcomputer is a growing requirement, and bridges establish a common link, common transmission formats, and increasingly, common data formats. The mainframe to microcomputer bridge is explained by Figure 10.8.

Bridges provide access to T-1 and networks like Tymnet and Telenet, which are public data networks (PDNs), or private branch exchanges (PBXs), which are no-dialing-required lease lines. However, transmission protocols must decouple the packet transmission since transit time will exceed the expected Token-Ring roundtrip delay of 51.20 ms. Devices such as *frame relays* or protocols including *network block transfer protocol*

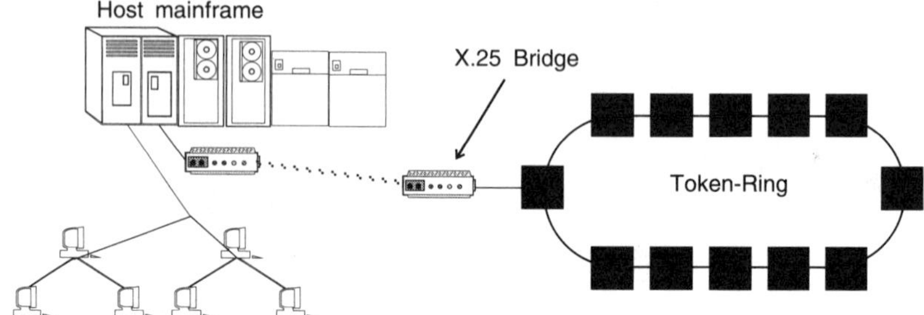


**Figure 10.8** A bridge connecting a mainframe to Token-Ring.

(NETBLT) encapsulate or interpret the frame for the linkage. The encapsulation technique is protocol independent. Note that while a mainframe can be a node on Token-Ring, mainframe communication protocols typically differ from the Token-Ring protocol, and a router or gateway (something above the OSI data link level) is required to translate and interface incongruous protocols. Figure 10.9 shows a large network.

Although bridges do support the expansion of networks into a network of networks, they can also limit that same expansion. Bridges must be fast since they read every packet. Token-Ring networks approaching packet saturation may overwhelm the capacity of a bridge to forward packets. If

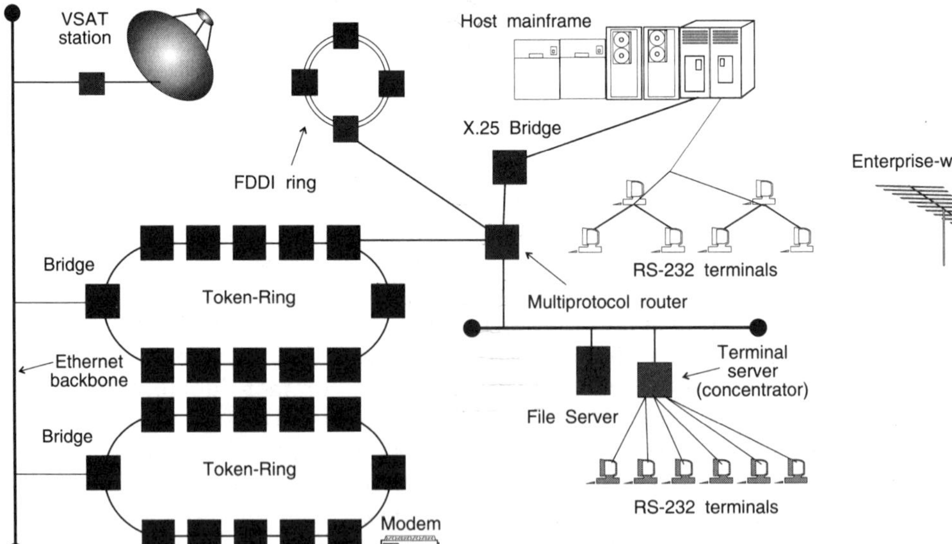


**Figure 10.9** An expanded network topology.

a bridge cannot accommodate the network load, it will lose packets. Not only will performance suffer directly; the lost packets will have to be retransmitted as an added load. Although bridges are transparent to network devices, the same is not always true for software applications. Bridges are not the solution for every network expansion. In fact, *intelligent bridges* also create traffic when they poll devices to maintain routing tables and unleash a *broadcast storm* when they cannot accommodate a lower-level protocol. This happens when some broadcast LAN protocols cause packets to be passed through to each port. In the event of a malfunction or an improperly set parameter, this traffic can create a bottleneck on the entire network and render it inoperable.

Hybrid devices such as intelligent bridges provide a destination-filtering component to improve network performance. This overlaps the definition of the smart repeater and the router, and performs an identical function while also bridging different media types. Just as some smart repeaters often build their own routing tables, intelligent bridges learn addresses of devices on the network. This means that a new device can be added to the network without any special configuration. Intelligent bridges offer the added capability to selectively filter traffic. Security for a network segment can be enforced by establishing a set of nodes that cannot traverse the bridge or be reached from the other side of the bridge. *Source explicit forwarding* (SEP) allows the establishment of privileges by defining addresses in the routing table as either accessible or inaccessible for sets of users and node devices. Other routing algorithms do exist; they tend to be proprietary, or in a state of definitional transition. Not that the use of multiple routing algorithms will create a performance bottleneck on most hybrid networks.

### Bridging Media

Bridges frequently interconnect different networks. A bridge could interconnect multiple networks. These networks are

often Token-Ring or Ethernet. The bridges merely duplicate all signals originating from all source networks to the other networks for NetBIOS, NetBEUI, or LLC (802.2) protocols; otherwise, protocol routers are required. This holds true for all simple bridges. Packets are not filtered before retransmission. The primary benefit of this process is that the junction bridges maintain throughput with minimal packet loss. Another benefit is that bridges extend the maximum network configuration beyond the specified ARL length or lobe limitations. The most substantial disadvantage is that all the interconnected networks experience a traffic level that is the sum of all interconnected networks. This is likely to yield severe network jams. For this reason, vendors have developed and enhanced hybrid devices including smart repeaters, intelligent bridges, complex routers, brouters, and packet switches. Packets switches effectively share the operating characteristics of multiport routers. Reduced instruction set computing chips (RISC), recently engineered for network routing, have resulted in the construction of switched backplane and cross-point switches that are not only more reliable but also perform faster so that packet routing can be optimized for reduced network loading.

Bridges also couple different media sharing the same protocols. A bridging device shuttles packets between the different media. For example, a bridge converts 4 Mbits/s Token-Ring to 16 Mbits/s Token-Ring. Some wiring hubs perform transmission speed conversions. Although the token protocol is identical for each, packet sizes may be larger within the faster environment. When these devices bridge media, for example from FDDI to Token-Ring, the protocol is not transformed in any way. Bridges are protocol independent. The LLC protocol must be the same at each end of the bridge for a bridge to be the proper connectivity device.

### Spanning Tree Algorithm

Most Token-Ring networks, in fact most networks, are configured such that there is only a single path between any two devices. Even Token-Ring networks provide only a single path between devices since the signal is unidirectional. (FDDI provides multiple paths in event of cable failure because it is a dual ring.) Common network failures therefore can disable the entire network. Intelligent bridges can partition the internetwork into still functioning segments. However, this does not maintain network functionality for critical operations that might retain that functionality if other paths were available. Token-Ring does not normally allow two segments to be connected with more than a single device, repeater, bridge, router, or gateway. However, multiple bridges could be installed if they support the IEEE 802.1 Spanning-Tree Algorithm (STA). A *spanning tree* is any unique device-to-device path within the network, as Figure 10.10 illustrates. Several could exist. STA negotiates the optimum path (least time for transmission) and establishes one path as the forwarding path; all other paths are blocked. This guarantees a single active path between all node pair combinations so that there will be no active loops. Additionally, STA tracks for path failures and automatically establishes an alternative path in the event of failure. STA provides redundancy for critical operations.

Frequently, the alternate paths lack the bandwidth for normal throughput. The alternate paths guarantee only that a connection (such as RS-232 or X.25) is available within a specified interval (ranging from milliseconds to minutes). The spanning trees are frequently fail-safe alternatives for priority data communications and mission-critical DP.

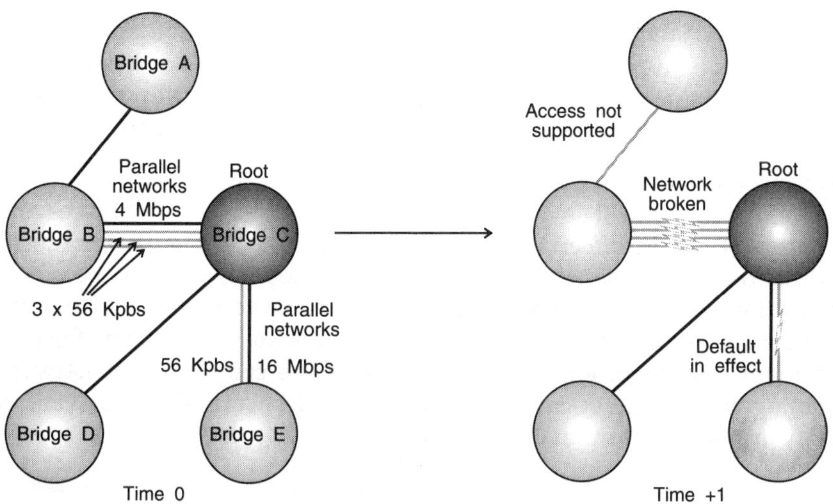


**Figure 10.10** Spanning trees provide redundancy without active loops.

## Network Routers

A *router* is a bridge that is not protocol transparent. It must be addressed directly by a device on the network. Routers require routing tables that contain device addresses to identify network segments, the paths to these segments, and the relative efficiency of these paths. A router does not use the tables to locate specific devices on the network; rather, it relies on other routers. A router uses this information to determine the optimum route for each Token-Ring packet. *Static* routers require explicit routing table maintenance when devices are added, subtracted, or relocated on an internetwork, whereas *dynamic* routers automatically configure the tables. Dynamic routers usually require less maintenance although they are inadvisable for large networks. Nonetheless, routers are difficult to install and require specialized knowledge and a high level of network knowledge for performance optimization. Routers increase the complexity of network management dramatically, and make troubleshooting in the event of network failure that much more difficult. There is less control, and the process of automatically maintaining the routing tables increases the network traffic. Routers are not the solution for every network expansion. In fact, they also create traffic when they poll devices with a broadcast storm to maintain their automatic routing tables or check the operational status of the extended network.

Routers are one of the prime devices included within SNMP or CMIP management protocols. They are good agents for assessing traffic, TRT, latency, and timing errors. Some routers include priority network management software and display SNMP statistics directly. An intelligent router can improve network performance with various methods. They perform the functions of a smart repeater. They store, save, and forward packets at a later time. Intelligent routers also prioritize packet transmission by device address or inform a device that it will not transmit packets from a device *(source quench)* until the network traffic is lower.

### Hybrid Bridges and Routers

*Brouters* are hybrid devices combining the functionality of bridges and routers. They are effective for complex, compound, or busy networks, or where an enterprise-wide network is warranted. They are devices best installed by the vendor since they are difficult to install and require specialized knowledge and a high level of network knowledge for performance optimization. Brouters increase the complexity of network management dramatically, and make troubleshooting in the event of network failure that much more difficult.

## Network Gateways

Specialized *gateways* interface between different Token-Ring protocols and translate the transmission before retransmitting, as per the ISO definition. The gateway also has a software connotation, which is not to be confused with the ISO hardware definition. A software gateway performs the same function as a repeater, although it usually provides a routing mechanism that transmits only those packets clearly destined for that segment in the same way as a smart repeater routes packets. It relays traffic to the proper destination. More typically, a gateway is a software tool that provides interoperability functions at the OSI application and presentation layers. Such functionality includes data conversions, data presentations, protocol conversions and translations, encapsulation, and actual user file transfers.

A typical gateway has two or more controllers to connect separate networks. The most usual form of a gateway is a workstation or computer processor with two Token-Ring controllers. Each controller connects into separate networks. This is not a bridge, although the node performs a bridging function. This is a true gateway because data interpretation occurs at all levels of the OSI model. The gateway unit supports two Token-Ring addresses, but one, two, or more Internet or IPX addresses. Most computer workstations support multiple controllers but require specialized software to function as a gateway. See Figure 10.11. Network gateways and foresighted network planning can localize groups and functional units on different networks for significant performance gains.

This subnetting isolates problems to each ring and allows loads, demand, and storage requirements on file servers and print servers to be controlled by the people who use those services, averting the possibility of developing a politically tense situation. Subnetting isolates a

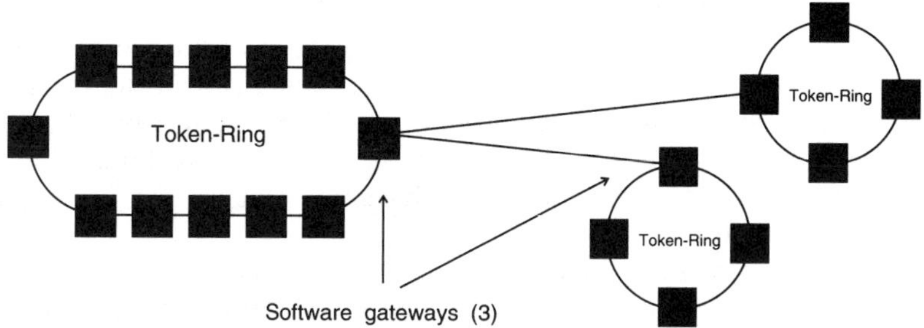


**Figure 10.11** Node serving as gateway to interconnect three rings.

group to a subnet while lowering overall network traffic. It is one solution to overloading problems induced by cascaded networks.

This is a manageable approach to controlling resources by group and division, as well as by individual subnets throughout the institution. As an example, a backplane network would provide interconnection through multiple hops to all local rings and supply network-wide access to expensive and low-usage specialized peripheral devices such as typesetters, image scanners, video entry cameras, pen plotters, coprocessors, and tape storage or disk storage devices. Subnets would concentrate each group onto a single Token-Ring, so that excessive demand for services could be controlled, analyzed, and prevented from interfering with processing and traffic on other rings.

## Gateways Integrate Networks Protocols

Gateways frequently form the primary prerequisite for building enterprise-wide networks. Existing ad hoc networks often represent multiple media and protocols and the gateway is required solely to interconnect these disparate parts into a cohesive whole. Replacing incompatible networks with the organization-sanctioned standard is often an unsatisfying and expensive alternative. Replacing functional networks with another type is one of those projects upper management is likely to quickly veto. Furthermore, suggesting such an inclination may make your stable network management positions suddenly tenuous. That is a tough battle to win, best accomplished in slow, concealed, and incremental steps.

While a growing number of vendors offer multiprotocol bridges, routers, and packet switches, nonetheless these network connectivity tools often yield insufficient utility. They might seem too difficult to install and manage. They might appear too expensive. They also function only at the lower protocol levels (OSI layers 2 and 3). Protocol translation at OSI level 7 is typically required to interconnect networks with incompatible protocols. Frankly, where possible, a single-purpose stand-alone gateway will perform better. It will actually be less costly overall than improvised solutions using a computer as a gateway (due to administration and maintenance costs). At the present time, Novell NetWare will support Ethernet, ARCnet, Token-Ring, FDDI media, Macintosh, OS/2, DOS, Unix, and connections to other client operating systems. When a commercial gateway does not exist, the only solution is a homemade software gateway.

The *software gateway* is a computer that runs two or more network protocols simultaneously. This is rarely a peer Token-Ring-to-Token-Ring connection since either a bridge or router can reroute and redirect Token-Ring packets at a low protocol level. When LLC protocols do not mesh—examples include UDP, NetBIOS, NetBEUI, and OSI—the software gateway is appropriate. Sometimes, multiple low-level protocols (such as TCP/IP, UDP, IPX/SPX, NetBIOS, and NetBEUI) will coexist within the same Token-Ring, but these must be translated and rerouted across a gateway for protocol and presentation conversion. Figure 10.12 lists typical translations.

In addition to bidirectionally translating Token-Ring, it is also relevant to bidirectionally translate other protocols as well. For a classic Fortune 100 consider this situation: several departments need to interconnect Token-Ring LAN Server to LAN Manager. Research and development environments might translate FTP to NFS or to Ethernet and Novell. A database server running on Novell IPX/SPX might need to communicate with an Ethernet client. Although the larger network software vendors seek to establish standards for high level interoper-

- Token-Ring 802.5<--- | |--->Banyan
- Token-Ring 802.5<--- | |--->Ethernet
- Token-Ring 802.5<--- | |--->FDDI
- Token-Ring 802.5<--- | |--->Frame relay
- Token-Ring 802.5<--- | |--->GOSIP
- Token-Ring 802.5<--- | |--->MAPS
- Token-Ring 802.5<--- | |--->Novell IPX/SPX
- Token-Ring 802.5<--- | |--->OSI
- Token-Ring 802.5<--- | |--->Proteon Token Ring
- Token-Ring 802.5<--- | |--->TCP/IP
- Token-Ring 802.5<--- | |--->TCP/IP with UDP
- Token-Ring 802.5<--- | |--->Token-Ring with LAN Manager
- Token-Ring 802.5<--- | |--->Token-Ring with LAN Server
- Token-Ring 802.5<--- | |--->Token-Ring with Novell NetWare
- Token-Ring 802.5<--- | |--->Token-Ring with OS/2 Comm MGR
- Token-Ring 802.5<--- | |--->X.25
- TCP/IP with UDP<--- | |--->NFS

**Figure 10.12** Typical gateway protocol translations.

ability and interconnectivity, these "standards" are just proliferating this translation problem. There are both commercial and technical reasons why vendors do not adhere to a full OSI network implementation and rely upon interoperability at the datagram level. Frequently, establishing an improvised gateway remains the only viable solution.

### Configuration of the Software Gateway

The software gateway is a computer, typically a PC or engineering workstation, running two (or more) protocols and containing two (or more) network interface cards. Multiprotocol routing is certainly feasible. Notwithstanding, it is typically a complex installation. Each network protocol software requires memory-resident device drivers with controlling software. Each set of device drivers activates a single type of network interface card. The controlling software codes and decodes information, builds the protocol, and often provides application-level services like remote file access, print services, and electronic mail. The network software may set *hooks* into the underlying operating system to intercept interrupts and service requests (for redirecting directory requests, port outputs, and the like).

The number of possible ways of providing a protocol gateway with just the 19 options listed in Figure 10.12 is 17! combinations, a number too large to print here. While some network vendors may provide some direction for successfully building a gateway or providing connectivity to selected competing products, it is often an unsupported task. Technical support services might say, "Good luck! Let us know how it works out."

### Memory Competition

When both sides of a protocol link do not support homogeneous protocol, the unorthodox loading of two very similar applications into computer memory simultaneously can create significant obstacles. Each driver and protocol set may exceed 100K of system memory. Difficulties arises when multiple network operating system programs fill memory or overlap the same memory addresses. This produces ruinous results. A solution may entail repeated time-consuming, trial-and-error reinstallation to determine the correct combination of installation sequences, device drivers required, bus and NIC IRQ interrupt settings, as well as memory allocations. It is likely that certain network software functionality (including print services, disk and file redirection, security, and even the network menu system) must be disabled to free needed memory. Note that if you must disable password and user login security—one of the least liked network features—do so only with full recognition of possible consequences.

PC-DOS or MS-DOS, currently limited by 640K of addressable memory space, often yields a marginal gateway. Furthermore, DOS establishes discontiguous segments of memory. Low memory is the space from

0K to 640K where the MS-DOS or PC-DOS operating system and MS-DOS application software is loaded. High memory represents the space from 640K to 1024K (1MB). High memory is also some composite of *expanded* and/or 16K selectable blocks of *extended* optional memory above 1024K. Memory discontinuities slow paging performance, complicate conflict resolution, and seriously hamper successful establishment of a functional dual- or multiprotocol gateway.

Note that even a paired-down MS-DOS with the requisite network drivers takes the first 50K, leaving 590K of free operating system memory. Now consider as an example, two network drivers and two network operating systems such as Banyan and TCP/IP can easily consume at least 200K of that 590K available memory leaving only a meager 390K of free memory. Whereas, IBM LAN Server might require up to 590K all to itself. This leaves nothing for another protocol without disabling some LAN Server features such as the redirector, print services, and security.

Assuming that multiple network protocols will load and not conflict, the PC can access both networks sequentially. However, automatic translation and rerouting applications must fit within the remaining operating system memory area. Still, insufficient memory may frustrate even loading simple user-level applications accommodating the manual transfer of files (or bits and bytes) and mail. LAN Server or LAN Manager in conjunction with a Token-Ring-compatible protocol (such as TCP/IP, Novell, or NFS) might not even load concurrently within memory as implied above. When they do fit, it is likely that the DOS BIOS device calls will overlap and so entangle DOS as to disable one or both network protocols since they are so much alike. Together, they may even destabilize DOS causing it to "hang." Furthermore, both softwares with DOS overlapping interrupt vectors may create a conflicting NETBEUI or NETBIOS function thereby disabling the network NICs at a hardware level.

Memory management tools including QEMM, 386MAX, and QRAM remap DOS memory and enhance expanded and extended memory ranges (from 640K to 64M) for greater utility. While this often permits relocating operating system code, hardware drivers, and network software into high memory, this does not always provide for the concurrent usage of two or more network protocols. Each protocol may still demand absolute overlapping of DOS low memory locations. If the network operating system can be relocated to different memory addresses, either one protocol or another can run selectively. This may prevent a gateway from working concurrently as intended. A network operating system is much like a DOS *terminate and stay resident* (TSR) program. It stays in memory and fills memory although it may require less when deactivated. A network, analogously to a TSR, takes full control of the computer and temporarily disables all other operations or TSRs. Similarly, it frequently destabilizes the underlying operating system.

Just as third party memory managers do, MS-DOS 5.0 provides a more robust operating system with the ability to load drivers into high memory ranges. Network operating systems may fail with this (or other) progressive operating system due to compatibility problems. In fact, Novell had to effect substantial changes to NetWare for it to coexist within MS-DOS 5.0. Add one or more additional network protocols and problems are compounded. This does not mean that MS-DOS cannot support a gateway. It only means seek commercial solutions first before committing to undertaking a complex and by no means certain path.

When a concurrent MS-DOS gateway is not possible, consider a momentary gateway to gain connectivity for an application or for file transfers. Commercial and shareware programs such as CONFIG.EXE, REBOOT.COM, and REBOOT.EXE provide a simple method to select from various boot configurations. Alternative copies of the operating system boot files CONFIG.SYS and AUTOEXEC.BAT files (from a *backed up* subdirectory) replace these two files while the system is powered cycled or merely rebooted with a DOS call to memory address 03. These alternative configuration files can activate ARCnet, Token-Ring, or FDDI and install a zero-slot LAN, Token-Ring, LAN Manager, LAN Server, NetWare, or Vines. It is only necessary that the NICs are installed in the computer; generally, they are always physically installed in the machine. They do not conflict when their system drivers are not installed at boot time. Additionally, these files might establish different \ETC\HOST listings, a variant Internet address, X.400 and X.500 global naming services, different exportable disk partition names, or even a different workstation or server name.

The primary advantage of this method is that it always can be accomplished. While possibly difficult to establish initially, once the alternate boot files are built, they can be invoked at will. It is easier than struggling to get network stacks to be co-resident within a single gateway host or user node. First, files are copied from one network. Second, the PC is reconfigured and rebooted. Third, the files are then available to another network. This is relevant for mail access, availability to specialty printers compatible with one network protocol only, and connection to mainframes, host servers, and source code control systems. The disadvantages are that this represents no true gateway, solely momentary linkages. It is unwieldy; configurations must be backed up and sometimes all must be changed to reflect a new hardware driver or the peccadilloes of a newly installed obstinate software such as MS Windows. Because the linkage is only temporary, it is not reliable nor always available to other network users. This may mean that they cannot send mail, annotate files, or access files or another network resource. It is also costly in terms of the idle process time needed to shut down the applications, reconfigure the boot files, halt the system, and finally reinitialize it for each momentary need.

### Unix and OS/2 Gateway Solutions

Unix and OS/2, unlike MS-DOS, map memory within single contiguous blocks. They also provide concurrent multiple software applications. This is called *multiprocessing* on Unix and *threading* on OS/2. Multiple drivers and multiple sessions share the processor and coexist without conflict. In fact, it is possible under these operating systems to load multiple copies of even a single network protocol and associated device drivers to provide automatic routing services. Since the multitasking and concurrent operations are better managed by Unix and OS/2, these platforms are a better choice for gateways. Additionally, many client-server network protocols are only fully functional under Unix or OS/2. This includes Sun Microsystems NFS and LAN Manager.

Notwithstanding, each protocol needs a separate NIC card to run concurrently. Do not overlay duplicated or different protocols on the same NIC memory space unless this connection is momentary. Although the gateway may provide peer-to-peer Token-Ring-to-Token-Ring bridging, separate memory stacks must be built for the gateway to function. Note that the gateway could provide a four-way Token-Ring-to-Ethernet connection and Token-Ring-to-token ring simultaneously. As each Token-Ring packet is captured on one side of the gateway, it must be rebuilt for retransmission to the other side. In fact, the gateway may receive a packet from one network while simultaneously sending a packet to the other network(s). A card and the protocol stacks therefore cannot be shared. Peer-to-peer examples include translating NFS to Novell on Token-Ring, Token-Ring LAN Server to Token-Ring LAN Manager, and Novell IPX/SPX datagram packets to TCP/IP.

Although boot configurations can be altered for OS/2 and Unix using a similar method as that for MS-DOS, the time requirements to safely shutdown and restart these more complex disk file systems may make this less practical. It is very unwise to terminate OS/2 or Unix file services by stopping the machine. Multitasking and threading expose many temporary and permanent files to unstable states. Failure to flush database records or sectors of files that reside in cache memory and close these files may unchain (damage) them. These operating systems may require a more complex approach to establishing multiple protocol connectivity.

Installation of multiple protocols, while easier under Unix and OS/2, may still retain the same trial-and-error approach required for an MS-DOS-based gateway. Configurations such as device addresses, setting priorities for Unix multitasking, or OS/2 LIB, PATH, and DPATH might require careful tuning to get multiple protocols to install on the hard disk, much less even load. Executable code files could require hexadecimal editing so that addresses, paths, or file names are altered to prevent conflicts. Installation sequences and selected subdirectory names might need alteration. You might need duplicate driver files with different gateway node names or addresses so that each network will see the gateway server under a different node name; this prevents circular routing errors where a packet would never be captured and thus not be retransmitted or terminated.

### Gateway Duality and Automation

Sometimes, multiprotocol translation is an either/or proposition, particularly the case under MS-DOS. The PC is configured to install NFS over Token-Ring to capture a file. Then, the PC is reconfigured (booted with alternate AUTOEXEC.BAT and CONFIG.SYS files) to move that file to another network such as Token-Ring, Banyan, or FTP TCP/IP. When multiple protocols load and function concurrently under Unix or OS/2, the mechanism for moving mail files or data files from one network to another may also require a similar sequenced manual transfer. The process would proceed like this: access one network and fetch the file, access the other network and transfer the file. This might represent a remote copy or a capture of a mail message. The resulting file might require character conversion or new mail header information to be useful on the destination network. There might even be a need to route that packet through translation on a second gateway. For example, Unix line endings differ from the MS-DOS counterpart, because of backspaces, linefeeds, new line characters (ASCII 8, 10, and 13), and because host mainframe EBCDIC differs from PC ASCII. Also, few mail message formats conform to the X.400 standards.

A medium akin to a routing mechanism is required to translate and route information across the gateway, whether manually or automatically. Sometimes a low-level protocol like TCP/IP or NETBEUI is available on both sides of the gateway. Then, the Internet address or another type of native address is sufficient to speed the information to the ultimate destination. Otherwise, a process must capture the packet and analyze the contents to determine what to do with it. The IPX/SPX client-server process is one example of a gateway translation process. Internet address routing is another. Although this routing function occurs due to OSI level 3 and 4 datagram functionality, the transfer must be achieved at OSI level 7. The translation is an application-level job because the datagram must be converted within the context of the application to which it is directed. For example, the transfer of a Lotus 1-2-3 data file is straightforward unless it gets to its destination blocked out of sequence. The file will not load into the spreadsheet program, and is unusable with any amount of effort. The only solution is to acquire a better copy. Basically, an automated process replicates what a user would do by remotely copying bytes from one network and then remotely copying them to another network within a new mail message or duplicating file structure.

## Gateway Performance

The interoperability and interconnection provided by gateways comes with a steep price. A gateway is either a specialized device that is expensive, or it is a computer that serves that singular gateway purpose and was installed, configured, and optimized over a lengthy period. Gateways rarely are fast. This is a serious performance limitation. While repeaters tend to retransmit everything with only several milliseconds delay, bridges might rebroadcast only 11,000 of the 13,000 packets received with several hundred milliseconds of delay. Nothing is filtered, merely rebroadcasted.

Routers are even slower. A router first must capture all arriving packets (or create a LAN bottleneck). It decodes it for the destination address. If this address is contained in a routing table, the packet is retransmitted to a new network segment. Otherwise, the packets are discarded. The router may assign new addresses from the routing table (since routers only recognize other routers or packets addressed to addresses in the routing table or even reformats the information to the same or an alternate frame format. Finally, the router broadcasts it to another router or the ultimate destination node. The routing delay may approach a half second with 9,000 of 18,000 packets received and 5000 rejected. Newer algorithms based upon hardware solutions rather than software may decrease the transit time and increase packet throughput.

The discrepancy between packets received and packets transmitted represents failed delivery. This is an important statistic. Failed delivery is about 2000 packets for a bridge and 4000 packets for a router on a busy network. Generally, successful transmission for each packet requires that the receiver return a message to the sender. After the specified delay, lost packets are retransmitted until the sending process responds to them or the sender "times out" concluding that there is a network failure or that the recipient node is unavailable.

Gateways are slower yet since they embody the repeater, bridge, and routing functions with potentially more complicated translation and rebroadcast functions. Frequently the gateway is not expected to work in real time and transmission is decoupled, as previously defined for routing operations. In other words, a Token-Ring node does not expect an extended delay from a node across a gateway. For example, Token-Ring does not expect a gateway to translate a packet into VSAT format, transmit the packet to a station 9 seconds distant, and receive a reply within 500 milliseconds (twice the Token-Ring round-trip delay plus interpacket spacing delays and the typical network-configured retransmission delay). Transmission must be decoupled. A gateway might process 2000 packets of 18,000 received, while rejecting the 14,000 not directed to it. The 2000-packet overflow creates a serious network problem. As another example, this is very obvious to users of distributed client-server databases. Applications that query a remote database intensively stress a gateway by requesting complex SQL SELECT statements which often are not processed at the remote database server. Massive numbers of data records are transmitted to the users' local nodes for local processing. If the network demand on the gateway exceeds its ability to translate and route that massive amount of information, it creates a bottleneck. Chapter 19 provides more detail on improving performance with gateways.

### Gateway Traffic Jams

Lost packets are normally retransmitted within a few hundred milliseconds. If they collide with new packets, the sending network exhibits a traffic jam. Because most networks provide two-way transmission with a single channel only (dual ring FDDI is the one exception), the receiving network across the gateway sees the traffic jam as well. It cannot reply to packets received because it cannot get them through the traffic blockage. As a result, outgoing receipt messages on that recipient network collide with incoming packets. The sending network doesn't realize that packets have actually transversed the gateway because the transmission wasn't yet acknowledged, and it tries to send them again. This gridlock escalates into network channel saturation; recovery requires that all processes must be halted and restarted with reduced demand. That traffic level must be restrained or the obstruction will perpetually reoccur.

### Gateway Routing Tables

Furthermore, a gateway requires routing information for true efficiency. It is unproductive for a gateway to replicate packets across a gateway unless they are destined for a device there. That would degrade the performance of the gateway and add an unnecessary load to the other networks. If those other networks were rings, the gateway could conceivably translate multiple copies of the original packets back to the originating network. This could escalate traffic to a virtual standstill.

A routing table is essential. It is nothing more than a list of nodes with network locations relative to the router or gateway. A gateway can be manually provided with a routing table or build its own dynamically. Refer to Figure 10.4 again for a simplified illustration of a routing table.

Manually supplied tables tend to accumulate errors. Nodes and devices get moved (as expressed previously, about 50 percent of all workstations and PCs are moved annually at corporations). Consequently, many addresses or node names are changed. The Internet address once 123.45.678 might become 123.44.678, or a workstation called "Spooky" might be relabeled as "Marty." Old entries accumulate and bloat the table dimming performance. New entries get added when users complain about lack of enterprise-wide network access. On the other hand, dynamic tables require that the multiport or multiprotocol gateways poll the separate networks for node names, addresses, and locations. As an aside, this is as equally true for simpler multiport and multiprotocol routers. The routing table building process is achieved by broadcasting a request to all devices to identify themselves and their addresses. Routing table entries resolve to actual network locations. This broadcast storm often collides with normal network traffic causing a performance hit. This broadcast request for active nodes and node addresses must be repeated at intervals to see if machines have been turned on, and therefore connected to a network or physically relocated. In the likely event of a glitch, manual power cycle, power failure, software error, or some other random occurrence, the routing table must be rebuilt from scratch. Also, when multiple paths through the network exist, the operational or optimal path often changes as a result of which nodes are active, which paths are active, which internetwork linkages are active, and the traffic levels on subnetworks and linkages. Various algorithms are available for optimizing these linkages; they vary by vendor and LAN or NOS configuration. Traditionally, the complexity of maintaining multiple paths leads most network managers merely to choose whichever protocol works reliably rather than optimize performance; even IEEE 802.1 spanning bridges are slow and not always reliable.

## Essential Connections

Internetworking and interoperability are frequently difficult to achieve. Commercial gateways are too costly to acquire while the improvised variety may require too much hardware, too many resources, and perform unreliably. It may be impossible even to establish a functional peer-level gateway at all. Additionally, the gateway may not be practical because transferring mail and files may require a convoluted effort. The format of mail messages may necessitate a program to route the mail message to the gateway, another program to translate the header information, and another process to remail the message on the new network segment. Similarly, files may require text conversion to reflect the differences in system storage formats, as previously conveyed.

Nonetheless, access to files on other networks are frequently imperative. Under these conditions, while peer-level gateways are not practical, another, simpler type of linkage is feasible. This type of gateway requires no bus slots, minimal software, minimal system memory, and frequently coexists with network operating systems. Examples include an IRMA Token-Ring to twinax AS/400 linkage, terminal emulation software with text capture performed via a dial-up modem, serial or parallel links, or a zero-slot LAN. Public domain products include Xmodem and Kermit. Complete MS-DOS commercial products also are readily available. IRMAtrac or IRMA WorkStation for Windows from DCA supplies host access for a PC whereas LYNX 3270/X provides a 3270 emulation with a host computer for X Windows workstations and terminals. Crosstalk captures text and files via modem and a serial port. Brooklyn Bridge, LapLink, and WinLink connect communication ports on two PCs for file transfer and some remote control features. Zero-slot LAN requires only a communication port that is built into virtually every PC.

When it is not possible to link an IBM 30XX host into a LAN using TCP/IP for Token-Ring compatibility, an IRMAtrac communication board provides a narrow access into the network. This is one option presented here that requires an interface board. The IRMA WorkStation for Windows otherwise can connect with an asynchronous connection, DFT, Token-Ring, and SDLC. Similar mainframe connectivity may be implemented through gateway software on a LAN connectivity host either on a NetBIOS Token-Ring, a separate X.25 connection, or by installing Token-Ring adapters in the mainframe. Many networks, since they are not PC-based, cannot receive an IRMA linkage board since most such cards are built for IBM AT, *Micro-Channel Architecture* (MCA), or *Extended Industry Standard Architecture* (EISA) bus slots. Some do exist for multibus. Nor do they support 3270 or 5250 terminal emulation for data capture. Although these network nodes cannot match mainframe protocol, they can host a client IBM-compatible PC connected to the mainframe. A single PC, when running suitable MS-DOS or MS Windows software, can capture text screens, select single database records, and obtain entire files. Files then can be distributed by the local network to needy users.

Shareware and public domain software, such as the Clarkson TCP/IP drivers provide Internet and Unix-to-Unix system copy (UUCP) mail connections for any platform supporting a C-language compiler. Once Internet is supported, the common *remote copy protocol* (RCP) and mail with attached files provide rudimentary interconnectivity for that platform. Internet mail is widely supported and generally available in most cities worldwide through a central mail facility. Stanford University in Stanford, California assigns Internet Class A, B, or C Internet addresses when requested. These addresses provide unique identifications for Internet users, and consequently all TCP/IP and most Token-Ring users.

Other options are simpler and more commonplace. These options require only a serial or parallel connection. Conflicts over IRQ interrupts or memory addresses are rare since both PC- and MS- DOS, OS/2, Unix, and most network operating systems recognize the serial or parallel ports as vital for printed output. These programs sometimes conflict with mouse-input devices, graphics tablets, and unusual input or output devices. Supporting multiple ports, or conflicts over whether the print spooler, the modem, a null modem, or the printer ports represent the likely conflicts. Just note that A-B switch selector boxes for multiple connections generally defeat communication links; the printers may work, yet the send-receive signals for data transfer are defeated.

A modem with a text capture and file transfer capability provides linkage independent from distance, independent from machine protocol, and independent from platform. A PC can talk to another PC, an engineering workstation, a second-hand minicomputer, and most mainframe RS-232 serial ports. Only the transfer speed is limited to the modem's baud rate, of course, as stated previously. Speed limitations and transmission reliability faults can be partially resolved with X.25 data protocols, MNP modems, CCITT V.32 and V.42 bis data compression, and error checking modems. Where nodes on different networks share a common area, a null modem cable (wires 1 and the ground connect, wires 2 and 3 cross over) can link these two computers. A parallel port connection is also supported. File transfer and remote control software easily copy files from one computer to the other. These MS-DOS programs, though simpler than network operating systems, infrequently conflict with configurations and systems drivers. When they do, the solution could require minimizing the CONFIG.SYS or AUTOEXEC.BAT files or rebooting with alternate versions. WinLink was designed to overcome the inherent MS Windows memory problems by relocating itself anywhere in memory. It works within the MS Windows environment.

Although MS-DOS communication software rarely works in the OS/2 compatibility box due to conflicts over multithreading and access to ports, OS/2 and Unix versions are frequently available rewritten specifically for these operating systems. Modem text and file capture programs are also available for these operating systems, as well as for AS/400, VMS, and IBM OS. Some are available from the public domain, thereby providing wide accessibility; examples include Xmodem and Kermit.

In all cases, transfer speed is limited since the parallel or serial channel capacity peaks around 125,000 bits/s. Such solutions are not true gateways, merely narrow conduits for getting bits and bytes across the gulf of incompatible protocols. Serial, parallel, RS-232, and X.25 connections bridge these protocol differences when it is essential to provide something less tedious than media conversions and "sneakernets."

## VSAT

Satellite networks utilizing *very-small-aperture terminal* transmission (VSAT) connect host mainframes and LANs into an enterprise-wide network. This is a practical and effective technology to link multiple sites (more than 100) across long distances, or for a small number of sites when a local carrier can provide an inexpensive "piggyback" service on its existing network. While it is about the same cost as a comparable dedicated T-1 10-mi phone link, it is also a third of the price of a 1000-mi phone link. The cost of a satellite link is independent of distance, unlike a phone line. (Note that phone costs are becoming less price sensitive to distance because the public carriers also utilize VSAT.) Initial costs for the ground hub, antennas, and remote stations can run $1 million, but with a lease operating costs can average $500 per month. Also, a satellite user might provide incentives for others to piggyback on that preexisting capacity. This is available in most major metropolitan areas. Additionally, VSAT provides about 10 times the bandwidth (hence 10 times the data throughput) as a T-1 line, with increased reliability.

A ground-based hub transmits either a *time-division multiplexing access* (TDMA) or *frequency-division multiplexing access* (FDMA) radio-frequency signal to a satellite in geosynchronous orbit around the earth. FDMA combines and splits the channel into multiple TDMA channels for data, voice, and video conferences. The C-band uplink frequency (to the satellite) is around 4 GHz, while the downlink (from the satellite) is around 6 GHz. These bandwidths are shared with terrestrial microwave systems. Signal interference is a serious problem. Alternately, the Ku-band uplink frequency (to the satellite) is around 14 GHz, while the downlink (from the satellite) is around 16 GHz. This bandwidth is allocated *only* for satellite transmissions. For both bands, though, VSAT in the neighborhood can cause a conflict. In either case, the FCC regulates both bands and limits antenna size, performance, transmission characteristics, and satellite separation. The satellite repeats the signal to star-configured, remote earth stations, or to mesh configured stations. A *mesh* design allows peer-to-peer access without communicating to the central hub on the star configuration and is appropriate when all sites regularly talk to each other. The hub controls the protocol, network management, and channel rerouting.

A risk when relying upon a satellite link is that the satellite could fail. Quick repair or replacement is unlikely, although simple circuit failures are solved by shifting the failed channel to other spare circuits. There is a good deal of spare capacity because there are alternatives for satellite channels and there are many competing organizations with satellite communication capacity. For critical links, research how the satellite channel vendor handles downtime. Consider installing land-based fiber or traditional T-1 connections with spanning-tree bridges to automatically reroute transmission in case the main link fails.

## SMDS

Wide area linkages are generally slow or expensive. T-1, T-3, PBX, PDN, and VSAT fall within those two categories. *Switched Multimegabit Data*

*Services* (SMDS) is a high-speed digital link that provides shared service to cheaply connect remote sites. AT&T is beginning to introduce this service, as are other vendors. The key problem for this LAN to WAN to LAN connectivity is that the protocol is split for multiple users and shared uses. As such, there are interface inconsistencies and vendor inconsistencies. In other words, while sites can be connected physically with this service, the data must be framed with a recognizable format for translation or encapsulation.

The current protocol is called *SMDS interface protocol (SIP)* and it is a mix of OSI levels 1, 2, and 3. SMDS provides concurrent T-1 (1.544 Mbits/s) and T-3 (50 Mbits/s). The physical protocol is either *High Speed Serial Interface* (HSSI), HDLC encapsulation, V.35, or RS-449. Because the interfaces and communication protocols can coexist, transmission of critical data can be prioritized, something seriously lacking within Token-Ring.

## FDDI

*Fiber data distributed interchange (FDDI)* is a network protocol designed for implementation on optical fiber for transmission speeds of 100 Mbits/s. CDDI (*copper-based FDDI*) runs on UTP and STP at 100 Mbits/s. TP-DDI, or *twisted-pair FDDI*, and ST-DDI, *shielded twisted-pair FDDI*, represent various vendor alternatives to fiber-based FDDI. While comparable, these varieties of copper-based FDDI are not fully compatible with each other. Note that CDDI may not conform to FCC operating requirements for sites bordering residential areas. Information delivery is provided by a Token-Ring protocol capable of transmitting from 0 to 4478 8-bit bytes of information. The network configuration can be more complex than a typical ring as this network design also incorporates trees and branches. FDDI serves two types of traffic, synchronous and asynchronous. Synchronous transmission must be preallocated for priority service to an FDDI station for access within two token rotations, while the asynchronous service is shared by all FDDI stations in a fair and deterministic manner by applying a token passing protocol.

It is important to recognize that the ANSI X3T9.5 standards committee drafting the FDDI definition in 1982 separated the physical layer into two subcomponents. This corresponds to the physical layer (layer 1) of the OSI model. These two components are the *physical-medium-dependent* sublayer protocol *(PMD)* and the *physical sublayer protocol (PHY)*. For reference, the PHY component is logically positioned above the PMD component. Since it is necessary only that the PHY and PMD components know how to communicate between themselves, it is possible to separate the hardware component (the PHY physical sublayer) and redefine it to function on another medium. This allowed cabling developers to develop and test twisted-pair wiring to transport the CDDI signal. Although twisted-pair has a large installed base, shielded twisted pair is a rarity. The 100-m limitation for shielded cable and 50 m for unshielded cable could constrict effective network design. Furthermore, the electrical noise and RF pollution at 100 Mbits/s imparts a serious limitation. Nonetheless, vendors see an attractive market potential and perhaps technical solutions to these current limitations.

There are several fundamental applications for the faster 100 Mbits/s FDDI Token-Ring technology to bridge or internetwork 10 Mbits/s Token-Rings. First, FDDI can serve as a simple backbone conduit between Token-Ring networks, or it can also provide network and file server support and also provide a more complex bridging function to interconnected Token-Ring networks. When FDDI is used as a long distance repeater for a Token-Ring segment, its use must accurately match the Token-Ring timing specifications, or excessive delays will compromise the network. This is a fairly simple application for optical fiber.

FDDI-II is an upward-compatible (and perhaps backward-compatible) enhancement for FDDI. This is best grasped as a bandwidth allocation mechanism. While prearranged synchronous expects a channel within two standard revolutions of the token, FDDI-II allocates bandwidth based upon the cycle clock, typically set at a 125 ms frequency. Subdivision of the delivery channel is the primary benefit of this refinement. T-1, video, voice, images, and network traffic can coexist. While connection to Token-Ring is available, the Token-Ring packet is transported as a "payload" without full FDDI station-to-Token-Ring station interoperability. Additionally, FDDI-II, like SMDS, will support priority transmissions with isochronous (non-packetized) data for simultaneous data and full-motion video transmission, and prioritized transmission of critical data.

FDDI and FDDI-II are not the only optical fiber standards. *Synchronous optical network* (SONET) is a standard designed by the long-distance carrier community (for example, AT&T, MCI, and Sprint) and uses the previously mentioned TDMA protocol. SONET conforms to the IEEE 802.6 metropolitan area network (MAN) specification and provides bandwidths from 50 Mbits/s up to 18 billion bits per second when multiplexed. Furthermore, SONET is designed to be a "survivable" network by mixed bandwidths and channels. Selecting SONET may be relevant when planning enterprise-wide networks since the optical fiber LAN and VSAT connection should be compatible. Bridging is possible, but the address and packet must be encapsulated for the "payload," as a VSAT packet is termed.

## ATM

*Asynchronous transmission mode* (ATM) transmits streams of 56 byte packets through a PBX-like switching system at speeds greater than

150 Mbits/s. The paths for each packet may vary, but arrival is guaranteed. This is a copper-based protocol using equipment with much in common to a central telephone switch. Not only will this protocol provide data communications and LAN-to-LAN connectivity, it will also integrate voice, full-motion video, and other data that can be packetized. The technology is expected to be prohibitively expensive when initially offered during the next two years. However, costs should drop with competition and competition fromthe other high-speed WAN options.

## Wireless Networks

Wireless Token-Ring minimizes the need for wiring. A wireless network does not require twisted-pair hubs and the wire, or patch panels and MAUs. Sudden growth in users or a requirement for a special taskforce suggests this type of solution. One of the big benefits of this technology is that the wireless hardware can be literally taken along when groups and their equipment are moved. The cabling portion for traditional networks is usually abandoned in the ceiling when the network is moved since it is expensive to retrieve and unwise to recycle UTP or even more durable STP. That part of the network investment is eliminated with wireless networks. As stated previously in this book, computer shows are good places for these networks, assuming that others are not using the same frequencies.

A wireless network is not totally wireless, however, in that it does require a connection from the transmitter-receiver units to be physically wired into the each workstation node. Some NIC cards provide external antennas that protrude from the PC card. Infrared networks work on the principle of modulating a light beam. The transceiver and receiving units must be in line of sight. Although the light beam diverges and brightness decays over distance, alignment is not critical but distance is. The WaveLan networking system is one example of a modular wireless network. This system is effective in areas under 800 square feet, a coverage similar to the NCR WaveLAN product. Note that vendors including NCR are also producing a directional antenna for bridging distances up to five miles.

The distance limitation is not only a function of signal strength and antenna efficiency, it also derives from the slower transmission speeds of RF or infrared networks. Token-Ring wireless networks typically accommodate between 1 Mbits/s and 2 Mbits/s transmission speeds. Protocol specifications are based upon maximum signal transit times and not necessarily distance per se. Slower bit transmission speeds (not signal transmission speed) therefore shorten the overall length of a wireless Token-Ring segment.

Radio-frequency units are best installed as high above people as possible. Until the evidence on health risks is finalized, assuming extra precautions is humane and legally advisable. Also these units should be installed with as few obstructions as possible. Although RF does penetrate objects, the effort does weaken and distort the signal. Note that users may require FCC licenses to install RF units since they do broadcast within the bandwidth, power levels, and extended periods of time specified for jurisdiction by the FCC. Vendors usually complete the licenses and submit them for each installed site as part of the sales process. Many vendors also have joined the IEEE plenary committee to generate a standard. This active IEEE committee, designated 802.11, is seeking to codify transmission for data and real-time voice using isochronous RF signals.

Wireless networks are infrequently installed at new network sites. Without actual installation experience, most managers reject the extra hardware expense and rue the slower transmission throughputs. Since most wireless networks are installed at sites with existing network investments, interconnection of wireless with the hard-wired networks requires a bridging mechanism. Typically, a wireless server would have a secondary Token-Ring controller and standard transceiver. This represents a routing configuration. Since configuration of home-made routers and gateways tends to be complex and unreliable, vendors like NCR Corporation and Persoft, Inc. provide specialized concentrators.

A very serious limitation to RF networks is that they can be tapped, jammed, or transmission altered unless encoded or multiple frequencies are applied. Wireless RF shares the same frequencies as garage door openers, cordless phones, and baby monitors. Although the 1986 Electronics Communications Privacy Act makes it illegal to intercept or jam wireless signals, this security can be breached with almost legal impunity. This is a ripe opportunity for industrial spying. If your organization services privileged information, recognize this limitation. Ordinary frequency scanners can listen to wireless broadcasts. Although it is difficult to decipher these signals, an astute spy can establish a wireless receiver and funnel the signal into a protocol analyzer. If your organization provides financial transaction processing, there may be SEC rules governing the security and integrity of data.

Another serious limitation to wireless networks is that they rarely support SNMP, CMIP, or CMOT network management protocols. Vendors providing low throughput transmission networks hardly want to further impede that performance with the overheads associated with management protocols. If customers are unhappy that some Token-Ring devices are not managed while most other devices are, vendors in time will update the software and hardware with the required agents. Note, however, that tuning performance on partially managed wired and wireless networks may represent an herculean task. Proceed cautiously before committing to mixed networks.

### Sideband and Multifrequency Wireless

Most wireless units broadcast on a single wavelength. This is called *narrow-channel transmission,* and it provides the possibility for multiple networks to coexist with different channel frequencies within the same envelope. However, many vendors have discovered that there may be clashes over the channel. Instead, there is a technology called *spread-spectrum technology* (SST) which is applied to increase reliability, boost transmission speeds, lower power requirements, and bypass the need for a user license. No FCC license is required because the signal strength on any channel is below regulation limits.

SST broadcasts multiple copies of the data signal over a broad frequency range. In fact, NCR's WaveLAN broadcasts uses spread spectrum. This technology has been around since the 1940s in military applications to minimize enemy jamming, eavesdropping, or even interference from natural sources. It may be appropriate for secure networks.

Another cellular technology, called *code-division multiple access* (CDMA), is an SST broadcast for transmission of multiple channels at the same time. This is even more secure than a single channel and less susceptible to deliberate jamming or environmental noise. Operations where remote data entry, point-of-sales (POS) inventory activities, or shipping and receiving are required might benefit with hand-held network-connected nodes. This is an available technology for hand scanning and similar activities. There are some concerns that the nonlicensing of SST may cause crowding of the airwaves, a low limit to the number of user services within a cell area, and network performance degradation with increasingly heavy traffic.

## Extended Token-Ring Network Configurations

Figure 10.13 shows the simple ring structure. Figure 10.14 expands this design with the inclusion of multiple rings to provide clusters which isolate traffic for workgroups. Figure 10.15 contrasts those simple networks with a network expanded by multiprotocol routers.

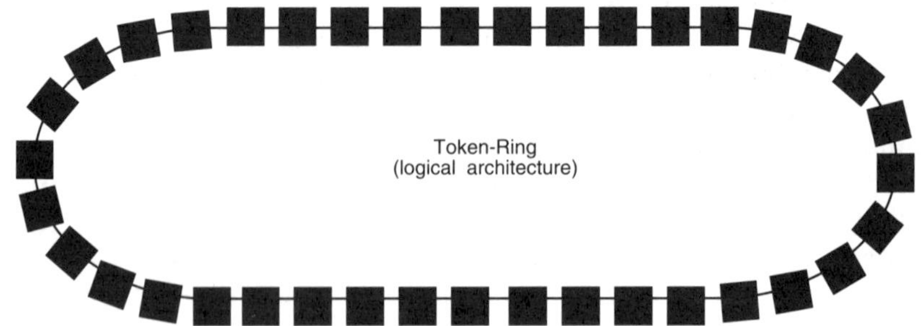


**Figure 10.13** The simple ring structure.

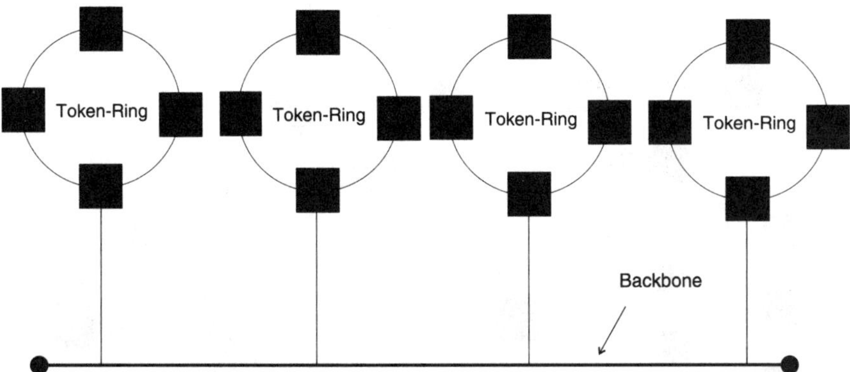


**Figure 10.14** A ring structure expanded with bridged backbone.

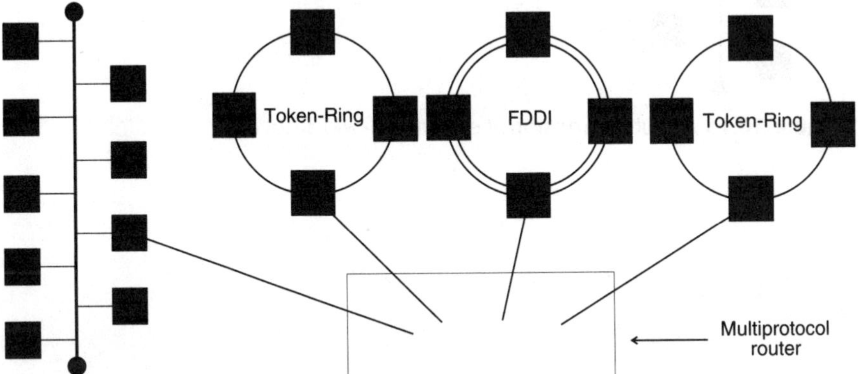


**Figure 10.15** The ring structure with multiprotocol routers.

Figure 10.16 presents a configuration that might provide service to an entire building, with a backplane FDDI segment serving as the connecting link between all ring subnets. This last illustration suggests the communications power inherent within the Token-Ring network.

Multiple channels provide an easily implemented method of expansion for overloaded networks. A segregated network also isolates the effects and interruptions inherent in a network. Furthermore, subnetworks ease accountability, while providing a measure of increased data security. Few alternatives exist to subnets; the most readily available is, of course, broadband cabling. Optical fiber provides the most security.

The listings in Figure 10.17 summarize the differences among the alternative devices, and suggests their uses. Now that the details for Token-Ring process, installation, and network expansion methodologies have been explained, the next chapters apply this information to practical day-to-day management.

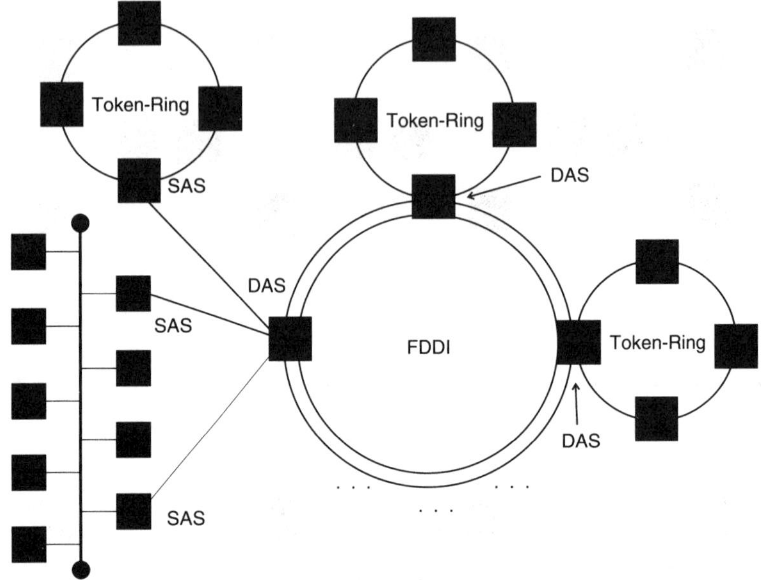


**Figure 10.16** A multidimensional enterprise-wide network.

### Twisted-Pair Networking

**Advantages:**
Is less expensive than Ethernet coaxial cable
Is easier to install than coaxial cable
Makes node relocation simple
**Disadvantages:**
Serves a smaller geographic area
Has less tolerance to crosstalk
Has less tolerance to interference
Makes fault isolation more difficult

### STP Networking

**Advantages:**
Has better tolerance to crosstalk than UTP
Has better tolerance to interference than UTP
Is more durable and reliable than UTP
**Disadvantages:**
Is harder to install than with UTP
Is more expensive than UTP

### UTP Networking

**Advantages:**
Is cheaper than STP
Is easier to install than STP
May be able to use preexisting phone wiring
**Disadvantages:**
Is less reliable than STP
Is harder to maintain and debug

### Networking with CDDI/FDDI Trunk Backbones

**Advantages:**
Provide better performance than cascades
Provide simple expansion possibilities
Provide the means to segment failed networks
Are easier to troubleshoot
**Disadvantages:**
Simplify chance of exceeding length specifications
Are hard to trace and blueprint

### Wireless Networking

**Advantages:**
Is simple to install
Makes node relocation simple
Can be taken completely from site to site
**Disadvantages:**
Is expensive
Has a realistically limited distance
May provide slower transmission speeds
May have health consequences
Is susceptible to eavesdropping
Has poor tolerance to interference

**Figure 10.17** Comparison between network expansion devices.

**FDDI (optical fiber) Networking**

**Advantages:**
Has exceptional tolerance to crosstalk
Has exceptional tolerance to interference
Is durable
Is light
Is reliable
Provides security from eavesdropping

**Disadvantages:**
Is harder to install
Is more expensive than other media
Is difficult to internetwork with Token-Ring

**CDDI Networking**

**Advantages:**
Provides 2 to 3 times the throughout of Token-Ring
Can run on existing STP Token-Ring wiring
Is reliable

**Disadvantages:**
Is harder to install
Is difficult to internetwork with Token-Ring

**MAU Networking**

**Advantages:**
Provide high-density service
Are easily installed
Do not require AC power
Can increase the size of a network
Are transparent to network devices

**Disadvantages:**
Extend ARL lengths beyond limitations
Do not offer good fault isolation
Increase the complexity of network management
Concentrators do not offer good fault isolation
Do not offer distributed management capabilities

**Concentrator (Wiring Hub) Networking**

**Advantages:**
Isolate errors better than MAUs
Are easily installed
Can increase the size of a network
Are transparent to network devices

**Disadvantages:**
Increase the complexity of network management
Require AC power
Do not offer distributed management capabilities

**Figure 10.17** Comparison between network expansion devices. (*continued*)

**Modems, PBXs), and PDNs(RS-232, V.32, X.25, etc) for Internetworking**

**Advantages:**
Are easily installed
Can provide LAN to WAN connections
Support several common protocols
Provide interconnectivity
Provide interoperability
Can support error checking and correction
**Disadvantages:**
Are slow
Are prone to signal interference
Do not provide security from eavesdropping

**Frame Relay for Internetworking**

**Advantages:**
Is faster than X.25
Can provide LAN to WAN connections
Supports several common protocols
**Disadvantages:**
Is slow; reserve bandwidth is unreliable
Does have frame error checking
Protocol interfaces are not standardized
Provide delayed transmissions
Does not provide security from eavesdropping

**SMDS for Internetworking**

**Advantages:**
Has adjustable bandwidth
Can provide FDDI WAN connections
Has good tolerance to interference
Supports priority transmission
Supports several common protocols
**Disadvantages:**
Media interfaces are not standardized
Protocol interfaces are not standardized
Provide delayed transmissions
Does not provide security from eavesdropping

**VSAT Internetworking**

**Advantages:**
Is distance independent
Has good tolerance to interference
Is durable
Is rarely effected by disasters
Is reliable
**Disadvantages:**
Networks are harder to install
Provide delayed transmissions
Is expensive
Is difficult to internetwork with Token-Ring
Does not provide security from eavesdropping

**Figure 10.17** Comparison between network expansion devices. (*continued*)

**Intelligent Hubs for Internetworking**

**Advantages:**
Can integrate incompatible media
Can integrate incompatible protocols
Provide high density service
Provide localized management
Can increase the size of a network
Are transparent to network devices
Might provide protocol translation
Might provide fault-tolerant networking

**Disadvantages:**
Are complex to manage
Increase the complexity of network management
Do not offer good localized fault isolation
Increase the chances for complete centralized network failure

**Repeaters for Internetworking**

**Advantages:**
Are simple to install
Require no configuration
Are transparent to network devices
Can increase the size of a network

**Disadvantages:**
Do not provide significant fault isolation
Do not offer distributed management capabilities
Might constrain performance of the entire internetwork
Increase the complexity of network management
Make networks more difficult to troubleshoot

**Bridges for Internetworking**

**Advantages:**
Are simple to install
Require no configuration
Are transparent to network devices
Adapt automatically to the environment
Can connect networks running different high-level protocols
Are flexible and adaptable
Connect networks of any speed if they conform to the timing constraints imposed by the fastest segment
Can provide network management functionality

**Disadvantages:**
Cannot take advantage of multiple paths to a network
Can constrain the topology of the internetwork
Create transmission delays
Can limit the size of a bridge-based internetwork
Do not provide significant fault isolation
Do not offer distributed management capabilities
Might disable software applications
Might constrain performance of the entire internetwork
Increase the complexity of network management
Make networks more difficult to troubleshoot

**Figure 10.17** Comparison between network expansion devices. (*continued*)

Routers for Internetworking

**Advantages:**

Are configurable
Can be fine-tuned to improve internetwork performance
Are simpler if they automatically update routing tables
Provide security protection
Are easier to maintain than bridge-based equivalents
Provide protection between segments
Are not susceptible to the time delay constraints
Do not limit network topology
Permit more complex networks
Permit active loops
Offer distributed management capabilities

**Disadvantages:**

Require a considerable configuration
Are more difficult than bridges to install
Are protocol-independent
Cannot route low-level protocols
Are complex
Cannot interconnect different high-level protocols
Are more expensive than bridges
Create transmission delays
Might disable software applications
May limit performance of the entire internetwork
Increase the complexity of network management
Make networks more difficult to troubleshoot

**Brouters for Internetworking**

**Advantages:**

Offer all the advantages of bridges and routers
Provide flexibility of bridging, routing, or both concurrently

**Disadvantages:**

Offer all the disadvantages of bridges and routers
Are more complex to install and maintain

**Figure 10.17** Comparison between network expansion device. (*continued*)

### Gateways for Internetworking

**Advantages:**
Are configurable
Can be fine-tuned to improve internetwork performance
Provide security protection
Provide protection between segments
Do not limit network topology
Permit more complex networks
Can connect networks running different high-level protocols
Can route low-level protocols
Permit active loops
Offer distributed management capabilities

**Disadvantages:**
Require considerable configuration
Are difficult to install
Create transmission delays
Are susceptible to the time-delay constraints
Are protocol-independent
Are complex
Are more expensive than bridges
Might disable software applications
Might constrain performance of the entire internetwork
Increase the complexity of network management
Make networks more difficult to troubleshoot

**Figure 10.17** Comparison between network expansion device. (*continued*)

Chapter

# 11

# Enterprise-Wide Networks

The complexity of enterprise-wide networks, interoperating applications, and network management overshadows the relative triviality of physically connecting the components into a larger whole. Often disparate local area networks, grown through hodgepodge efforts, appear as a serious organization constraint. The common vision that construction of an enterprise-wide network will reduce the chaos is mistaken unless firm controls and directed network management are provided. Comprehensive networking management is crucial for success of expanded networks.

The issues of enterprise-wide networks often encompass downsizing host mainframes; substituting PC- and network-based client-server processing; supporting distributed processing, interconnectivity, and interoperability; and performing information and network management. In fact, enterprise-wide networks frequently underlie any efforts to downsize data processing (DP) operations, create enterprise-wide E-mail and network fascimile (FAX) services, and build mission-critical networks. This chapter addresses such topics while the final section lists the components essential to forge enterprise-wide networks. For a review of the strategic issues relating to corporate-wide networks, refer to Chapter 1.

## Network Communication Growth

The interconnection of many networks into a single entity has become a critical issue for many organizations. Networks of networks and the replacement of host mainframes with local area networks have warranted the construction of large networks. Connectivity for multiple platform product development, software application porting (rebuilding and optimizing software built for one operating system for usage within another), *executive information systems* (EIS), optical storage and retrieval systems, organization-wide electronic mail and computerized fascimile services, and operational consolidation (including personnel reduction) drive this strategy. Extended networks sustain transactions in the event of an emergency when primary sites have failed. There is also a visible shift for responsibility and control of information more in line with the usage and source of that information—to the end user. This impetus drives the installation of enterprise-wide networks. The realization that information is one of the strategic assets has increased the demand that these networks function together. This appetite for global access to corporate information and the desire to prevent corporate information from fragmenting into small, useless pieces has propelled the enterprise-wide network into the forefront of local area networking. Large organizations cannot thrive with LANs as islands, isolated and unreachable.

The concepts and the jargon of enterprise-wide networks mask the complexity and confuse the underlying issues. Many consider an enterprise-wide network to be nothing more than terminals and modems linking a mainframe for data access; this is a misuse of that term for what is really a collection of host connections, or even possibly a wide area network (WAN). While is is possible to debate that definition, it misses the issue that enterprise-wide networking remains a complex and confusing current topic.

For the purposes of this book, an *enterprise-wide network* is a network that interconnects LANs at multiple sites and could provide, *in addition,* other types of communication services throughout the distributed sites of the organization. It could also include the live interconnection of customers and suppliers into the corporate network. This type of facility is also termed a *premises network* or simply an *enterprise network*. Figure 11.1 illustrates the possibilities for an enterprise-wide network.

Enterprise-wide networks frequently must interconnect and interoperate. *Interconnectivity* embodies the physical attachment of local area

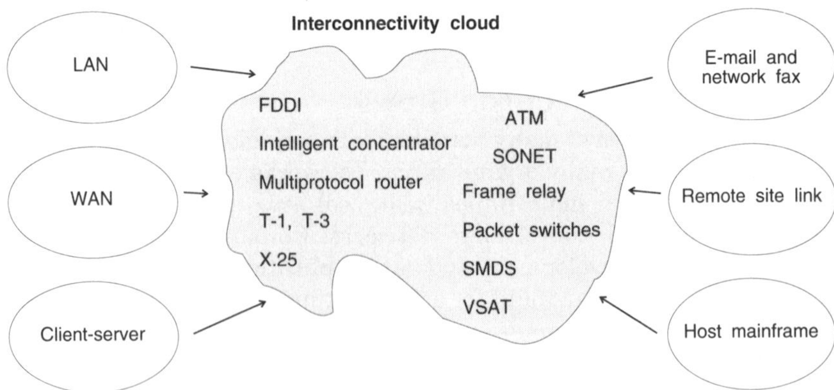


**Figure 11.1** The enterprise-wide network.

networks, devices, and processes that are not necessarily peers, not necessarily compatible, and do not necessarily conform to the same standards or methods of functionality. *Interoperability* means that despite the physical, logical, or functional differences, networks, devices, and processes can share network services, data, and processing power. Interconnection remains relatively easy to obtain with bridging hardware. OSI bridges, simple modems, and long-haul transmission techniques provide physical network interconnection. Interoperability, however, is more elusive. Terminal emulation software, screen capture routines, data conversion programs, and shared media (as in a "sneakernet") facilitate the logical sharing of network resources. When networks, devices, or processes are homogeneous peers (in that they use the same protocols), interoperability is immediately available through physical bridging. While network management, resource access (through passwords, establishment of user password accounts, or share rights), and security are valid concerns, operability is straightforward. Networks frequently incorporate heterogeneous protocols such as those listed in Figure 11.2 and maintain data and software code in incompatible formats. With heterogeneous protocols, data formats, and incompatible software code, interoperability necessitates complex gateways and translation software so that multiple processes can share data. This may well entail different databases which can read the storage formats, or require complex custom software which controls and commands different softwares to process parts of a solution.

For example, a mainframe database should be readable and possibly changeable from a networked PC. IRMA links over Token-Ring are effective for providing a simple terminal emulation from a PC, or from

| Connection | Protocol or Communication Technology | | | | |
|---|---|---|---|---|---|
| Host | SNA | IDSN | HLLAPI | APPC | CPIC |
| LAN | Token-Ring | Ethernet | FDDI | Zero-slot | ARCnet |
| | NFS | TCP/IP | | | |
| Network Operating Systems (NOS) | LAN Server | LAN Manager | Novell NetWare | Banyan | U-B Access1 |
| | StarLan | XNS | OSI | OS/2 LAN (Comm MGR) | |
| Interop Solutions | OSI | HLLAPI | TCP/IP | NDIS | ODLI |
| | IPX/SPX | Serial | Parallel | Etherlink | RS-232 |
| Translation | FTP | SPX | NFS | X.400 | X.500 |
| | Banyan | | | | |

**Figure 11.2** Typical organizational networking protocols and software.

within a GUI window. Within an advanced environment, the mainframe database should be completely available for processing on a PC; in actuality, database products, including Oracle, Progress, and Ingres, do provide data file portability. These and other tools function within certain heterogeneous network constructions by specific design only.

Interoperability does convey the notion that software application code will be portable across platforms and networks as well. In other words, code written for one platform should work on others. Additionally, interoperability implies that data distributed across multiple platforms, formats, and processes can be globally manipulated. Interoperability has been termed *code portability, portable applications, code migration, transportability, platform transparency, open systems,* or *architecture-neutral distributed format* (ANDF) by the Open Systems Foundation (OSF). Unix and most high-level computer languages have thrived because of this interoperability vision, albeit more promise than premise. Each revision and upgrade of Novell NetWare includes a connection for a new operating system as a client: DOS, OS/2, Macintosh, Unix, RISC, to name but a few. Interoperability also represents the solution for a serious training problem.

The enterprise-wide network can include and embody other features as well. It can include distributed processing with a host computer servicing end-user computers. It can incorporate networked computing where idled devices are accessed for their capacity either to speed completion of a process or to add sufficient parallel computing capacity to solve the problem. It can also include downsizing host mainframes—replacing them with desktop machines—and the addition of global network management controls.

The enterprise-wide network concept is such a new threshold that the literature includes minted terminology and concepts to define the technology and add precision where little exists. For example, *cooperative processing*[1] and network computing concepts recognize the increasing distribution of locations where the user physically interacts with the computer, where the processing power is supplied, where files reside, where data resides, where output devices reside. This concept can be presented as a sharing of networked resources. Trends for sharing resources across a network show a clear need for faster networks, more complicated network management tools, and correspondingly more experienced network managers. This network is no simple LAN; it is an extended topology of interconnected and interoperating LANs forming the enterprise-wide network.

1 John Gantz, "Cooperative Processing and the Enterprise Network," January 1991, a *Networking Management* White Paper.

## Enterprise-Wide Potential

Enterprise-wide networks are an outgrowth of many separate LAN installations. The application of extended networks also reveals the need to communicate between dispersed and multiple sites with some immediacy and with a complexity exceeding that of wide area networking. Enterprise-wide networks represent a means to prosper by cutting DP costs through downsized operations or to provide a competitive advantage achieved with rapid and comprehensive information access and connectivity. Organizations link distributed sites together for the basic reasons listed in Figure 11.3.

Enterprise-wide networks are not merely data communication pathways. They may also transport voice and continuous motion video, too. The disparate technologies of information are converging together. Indeed, most networks can transport data, image, video, and voice using the same mechanisms; it is only necessary to packetize the information representation within a transmission protocol. Data processing, communications, networking, and information management are slowly becoming consolidated into a new concept. This centralization is reflected in the management and authority of these functions. The enterprise-wide network is a new rubric to bind functions together, as Figure 11.4 denotes.

- Downsizing opportunities
- DP operational consolidation
- Better control and management of subsidiaries
- Distributed client-server computing
- Mission-critical computing
- Consolidation of information management
- Preventing fragmentation of organizational information
- Integration of voice, data, and image carrier services
- Interconnectivity for LANs
- Electronic mail (E-mail) and network fascimile (FAX)
- Remote procedure calls (RPC)
- Remote processing
- Remote file transfer
- Terminal services and remote terminal emulation
- Source code control
- Online document (image) storage and retrieval
- Object-oriented tools
- Work-group computing
- Name services
- Executive information systems (EIS)
- Strategic vision

**Figure 11.3** Reasons for enterprise-wide networks.

- Data communication
- Voice communication
- Facsimile (simple and broadcast) transmission
- Multimedia
- Telecommunications
- Office automation
- Production automation
- Data processing
- Image processing
- Motion video
- Video conferencing
- Information storage and retrieval
- Command and control

**Figure 11.4** Enterprise-wide information management.

## Downsizing to LANs

The technology and the cost-benefit ratio of host mainframe-based computing have been superseded by microprocessors, client-server environments, and network-based computers. The data processing economics favor downsizing and networking for all but the most specialized applications. Various research reports conclude that organizations save 40 to 60 percent with microcomputer and LAN-based applications over the cost of mainframe-based operations. This cost savings derives from the fierce margin competition in PC hardware and software and the open systems available on engineering workstations and desktop microcomputers. Nearly every computer manufacturer has developed a line of desktop computers and these prices are pressured by clone makers. It also accrues from the quicker software development times typical of PC or Unix environments. Debuggers, graphical user interface (GUI) tools, interactive third generation language (3GL) and fourth generation language (4GL) databases, spreadsheets, screen painters, and code generators halve development, maintenance, and upgrade time. Most of the ancillary "savings" above 40 percent are amassed from pushing as much of the cost as possible to the end users. This shifts budgets and manpower from centralized DP departments to operational groups.

Literally, the cost basis favors networks of client-server processing over mainframe applications for all but very specialized or very entrenched data processing activities. While microcomputers have matched the raw processing speed of mainframes for years, accessibility, interconnectivity, and interoperability have limited most organizations from downsizing DP operations. While downsizing is an extraordinary difficult undertaking—one full of risks and problems—the risk of not considering and trying downsizing is that competitors will try it, and will succeed. Even entrenched DP activities should be reviewed for potential and significant changes. Such consideration is particularly relevant to organizations creating computer applications; they should worry that more cost-efficient competitors will erode their markets.

Microprocessors assembled as minicomputers represent direct and immediate replacements for mainframes. Digital Equipment Corporation (DEC) MiniVAXes and MicroVAXes replace the VAX mainframes. Midrange IBM AS/400 series machines replace 30XX mainframes. Microcomputer-based "superservers" and disk-based high-performance subsystems challenge the outdated notion that thousand transaction-per-second mission-critical applications are the domain of $3 million mainframes. Although the central processing unit (CPU) box may change, tape, disk, and other peripheral devices may not. Computer room requirements or space needs rarely shrink; cost savings are within reach because expansion can be planned to utilize a more cost-effective technology. When there is need to expand existing entrenched mainframe services, substitutions with downsized platforms provide significant cost savings. However, the real benefit in downsizing occurs when mainframe environments are replaced with client-server networks, microcomputers, and the superservers. Ethernet and Token-Ring are the major client-server networks, with Ethernet leading, given its interconnectivity and interoperability components, as well as its large entrenched base. However, the corporate culture embodied by IBM and long-ingrained buying habits provide an enormous market share for Token-Ring. With the advent of faster microcomputer bus structures such as *extended industry standard architecture* (EISA) and *microchannel architecture* (MCA), personal computers have overcome a significant bottleneck. EISA provides 32-bit pathways whereas the *industry standard architecture* (ISA) found on most IBM AT-compatible PCs supports a more limited 16-bit channel. Wider pathways for data transfer and data communications mean that personal computers performing as file servers can match the storage performance of the mainframe for a fraction of the cost. Superservers and "disk farms," a concentration of storage disks, address the data storage, input/output, and data bus bottlenecks inherent even in the MCA or EISA architecture. This has created a distinct and viable opportunity for many organizations to rethink their data processing policies. This does not mean that the mainframe is dead, altogether replaceable by PCs. Mainframes too are getting more powerful and faster with emphasis toward specialized processing. This trend for installing PCs in place of mainframes only points to restructuring and a new emphasis toward end-user and *ad hoc* activities.

Bottlenecks and extraordinary expenses required to build the new mainframe applications—those perceived as providing a strategic advantage for an organization—have compelled many within the organization to try new approaches in desperation. Users of information want control and responsibility for it; they do not want it held by a technical department divorced from their needs. Personal computers with electronic spreadsheets, fully functional databases, and ingenious and effective user interfaces have seemed a simple and possible alternative. Indeed, this technology has thrived not merely because of the wide distribution and lower entry costs. The organization-wide distribution of identical tools enhances productivity and the value of any computer work. Better tools speed development. Implementation times for critical but simple projects are hours or days instead of months or years. Intermediate concepts can be tested as a spreadsheet or a database. Later, they can be fully programmed, data entry and validation routines can be overlaid, and the implementation can be extended for multiple users. Intermediate results (rarely seen in mainframe applications) encourage management and bolster this shift to microcomputer solutions.

The actual differentiation among the computing power of PCs, client-server workstations, and mainframes is not really at issue. The proposition is shaped more by perception than any true differentiation. This mentality is driven by MIS managers, computer organizations, and vendors. While most platforms, in addition to host mainframes, can support extensive disk farms with gigabytes of storage, implementation risks and the perceptual "ideal" architecture are encouraging the notion that mainframes are best as the host repositories for corporate data; network channels merely convey it to the workhorse PC platforms.

In part, this notion is driven by an outdated mentality and the inertia of elaborate organizations supporting mainframe activities. In part, it is also driven by the reality that time-sharing mainframes provide exceptional security, stability, reliability, and honed backup procedures whereas networks in practical observance do not. Most organizations *do* have insecure *ad hoc* networks lacking disciplined password policies and off-site file backup procedures. While not universally true, it usually is. Perhaps, this differentiation is best until the majority of organizations attract and promote communication managers, network managers, and information specialists to the same executive levels as that attained by mainstream MIS managers. Then, downsizing will not represent such a technical and collective risk to an organization.

One important point is that downsizing should not be undertaken merely to upgrade technology. Consider the disparagement one might make to defeat the proposal for replacement of terminals with networked PCs: "You are going to spend thousands of dollars per person to make an intelligent microcomputer into a dumb terminal?" *High-level language application program interface* (HLLAPI) is only a front-end mask to give a PC terminal connectivity to a host mainframe; it may not be cost-effective to replace or expand an installed base. A fundamental benefit must drive the shift from host mainframe DP operations to a distributed network environment. For example, PC-based data entry and data retrieval may benefit from reduced transaction processing times; when data filtering and verification can occur locally the time lag from a remote host is reduced. Building a network of PCs for terminal emulation so that a few users can get data from the mainframe is a misuse of the technology. Data conversions and "sneakernet" is cost-effective for minor applications. While it is not as convenient to ask the mainframe group to prepare a floppy disk when you want it, it is certainly more convenient than maintaining a network. Instead, consider replacement of failed star-configured wiring to the host with networked PCs and terminal emulation; this augments basic data access and file manipulation with superior PC-based tools. Keep the need for enterprise-wide networks within perspective; new technologies are no panacea.

It takes time for any technical knowledge and its ramifications to be fully realized. While personal computer advertisements and press reports initially touted that the power of these then newly-introduced microcomputers matched that of many mainframes, the concept that they could replace a mainframe was not immediately perceived. Certainly, a PC cannot replace a mainframe application directly. As a result of this oversimplification and mindless promotion, the potential for the PC was actually disbelieved. *Customer information computing system* (CICS), *system network architecture* (SNA) applications, and *virtual sequential access method* (VSAM) are just not transportable to or as easily interoperable on a PC, although OS/2 CICS without rollback functionality, VSAM record structure with PC COBOL, and SNA attachments are available for personal computers.

The structure, the perception of the task, expectations of outcomes, responsibilities for control, the methodology—all these must be modified for the personal computer environment. Software development tools for personal computers have also superseded the power, complexity, effectiveness, and efficiency of the mainframe counterparts. This, too, has shifted the perception that downsizing is a strategic endeavor since it provides not only a cost reduction but also significant technological advances.

## Client-Server Computing

*Client-server* computing represents the establishment of a host computer to provide services, including data storage and retrieval, software application file storage, printing, and mail delivery to end users. The host is the *server*. An end user is the *client*. Typically, a server is a file server, a database server, a mail server, or a print server. Generically, a PC-based file server performs all these functions concurrently within a multiuser format.

The benefit of client-server computing is that typical mainframe applications can be redeployed within a distributed database environment with *structured query language* (SQL). SQL is the PC-based successor to CICS, Cullinet, COBOL, and most other typical mainframe data processing development tools. Do not infer that SQL is the only or brightest option for a distributed database connectivity tool; many others exist, too. Many applications developed for NetWare utilize a b-tree *indexed sequential access method* (ISAM) developed by Novell called Btrieve. In fact, many SQL front ends form a shell for Btrieve including Novell's XQL. While the cost of the client-server hardware with the required local area network connections is far less than the mainframe and the software is also cheaper to buy (build or customize), the client-server environment provides ancillary services with minor additional investment. These include word processing, animation and multimedia presentations, desktop publishing, spreadsheets, databases, graphical charting, illustration, time and billing, accounts receivable (A/R), accounts payable (A/P), payroll, project management and task scheduling, and other PC applications. The important perception is that you get extra performance and functions without (or for a relatively small additional) cost.

Mainframe connectivity implies a large distributed geographic network—only a limited number of users physically sit in the computer room and the information the mainframe contains has a generic and universal value throughout the organization—adding a new user (node) often is as easy as adding a modem and terminal. On the other hand, a LAN is geographically limited to within a few thousand meters. Client-server computers within LAN environments encourage the growth of networks, which become enterprise-wide and raise the thorny specter of interconnectivity and interoperability conflicts. Downsizing computing facilities to interconnected LANs do not guarantee interconnectivity or interoperability. Downsizing is best planned with foresight.

## Interconnectivity and Interoperability

Software integration and the physical and logical management of networks are critical networking issues because people "interoperate" and share information. There is a gap between what is viewed as necessary and what is available. There is a gap between what technology promises and can be achieved. There is also a gap between what technology can provide and what value can be understood for actual usage. While the concept of linking local area networks into a single enterprise-wide network is paramount, the difficulty in logically connecting them is extraordinary. Not only do transmission media vary, data link protocols, transport methods, and data presentation limit interconnectivity; but also software application disparities complicate the task. Additionally, local networks may be managed through *ad hoc* management efforts. Each individual network may be controlled as a fiefdom with total independence from MIS operations or even other peer groups. It is unprofitable for this chaos to spill over to the enterprise-wide network. Duplicate node names, file partitions, user logons, and different levels of security or electronic mail protocols can limit interconnectivity and interoperability. For these reasons, standards such as *open data interface* (ODI), *network device independent specification* (NDIS), X.400, X.500, and the complete OSI communications model are so important. Even when different LANs conform to the OSI model, there is no guarantee that these LANs can even interconnect, let alone interoperate. The gray area in interpreting standards and implementing hardware and software creates disfunctionality.

Interconnectivity has become a sought-after service. The ensuing network complexity has made many networks nearly unmanageable. Networks with multiple servers or backbones with multiple subnets represent complex managerial tasks. This vacuum has attracted vendors to provide complex internetworking products and management tools to link different types of networks and provide file services independent from the underlying platform or network protocol.

The selection of competing vendor products has widened and diverged. Corporate users have opted for STP or UTP Token-Ring for its simpler wiring demands while software developers have selected Ethernet for its interconnectivity. These choices were often predicated by software requirements or simple preferences. While Token-Ring networks and Windows applications have provided effective access to mainframe processes and data, high-end workstations (like Sun-, HP-, and Unix-based systems) providing specialized turn-key solutions are now manufactured with integrated Ethernet connections. This has created a stalemate. Neither network controls the market. However, the convergence of many protocols to a single multimedia transport protocol—that is, IPX—shows that the users want to simplify internetworking.

In fact, as previously mentioned, many common PC-based network operating systems will work atop either Token-Ring or Ethernet. This relatively new development indicates network integrators' interest in supporting a large number of products. Indeed, vendors are responding both to their support limitations and the customers needs for network interconnectivity and interoperability through the introduction of *hybridware*. Hybrid devices include intelligent hubs, multimedia and multiprotocol routers, network concentrators, and multiprotocol management software. For example, 3Com Corporation now provides irregular drivers for their Ethernet boards and 10BASE2 hardware. EtherDisk transports protocols, which are typically run on Token-Ring, atop Ethernet. These popular Token-Ring protocols include NetBEUI, NetBIOS, LAN Manager and OS/2 LAN (Communication Manager).

Although the network software might be successfully transported on either standard medium, getting the different softwares to route and gateway through to each other is a serious problem, as Chapter 10 established. LAN Manager packets on Ethernet will not necessarily provide the TCP/IP interchange desired; Ethernet is merely the transport mechanism. Additionally, the economics and apparent ease of unshielded twisted-pair cabling has created extensions to the Token-Ring family while higher-performance optical networks such as FDDI are increasing the complexity of network integration and management.

Bridges, multiprotocol and multiport bridges, more advanced multiprotocol and multiport bridges, and complex gateways are only the physical links. Software and management control tools are frequently required at a minimum to link mainframes, heterogeneous networks, and the actual workstations to accomplish file transfers and data sharing. On the other hand, TCP/IP is media-independent. TCP/IP runs on Ethernet, NetWare, RS-232, serial or parallel wiring links, X.25, and other common media and connections. In many cases, activating reliable and functional interconnections with TCP/IP drivers is impossible. The memory requirements for multiple protocol stacks saps so much system memory that ordinary software applications cannot fit into active memory. This is prevalent for MS-DOS, less so for OS/2 and Unix. When multiple stacks fit within system memory, name or memory range conflicts frequently disable all network links; the protocols do not coexist.

For example, it is a feat of system integration and installation for LAN Server and Novell to coexist. Nonetheless, NDIS drivers are believed to be efficient with PC- and MS-DOS memory (requires about 80K) and are only 20 percent slower while providing generic access to media and protocols. Because NDIS supports multiple protocol stacks simultaneously, this new protocol is gaining support for LAN interconnectivity. Many hardware vendors will provide an NDIS vendor for their network interface cards upon request; this is a good place to start when linking diverse LANs.

Usually though, remote access, file transfers, and mail forwarding simply will not work. In such cases, X.25 modem links provide slow but reliable TCP/IP file transfers and Internet mail connections, as Chapter 10 explained. When mail services work, files can be transferred as part of the mail message or attachments to the mail message. The lowest common denominator, the one interconnection method available for every computer system and hardware configuration, is the RS-232 modem controlled by terminal emulation software. Terminal emulation software (public domain software such as Xmodem and Kermit, or commercial products such as Attachmate or Crosstalk) includes text and file send and capture features. Mail and files are thus transferred at speeds ranging from 300 to 9600 characters per second (chars/s), and even higher—to 38,000 chars/s, with special CCITT V.32 data compression methods.

Furthermore, terminal emulation provides some powerful remote control functions and remote processing capabilities. PC Anywhere and similar remote network support tools provide terminal emulation with the processing at the remote site with only screen updates and keystrokes transmitted to local PCs. With terminal emulation running within MS Windows, *object linking and embedding* (OLE) and *dynamic data exchange* (DDE) hot links are feasible; minimally, MS Windows provides a textual or graphical cut-and-paste facility. Other operating system extensions, including the graphically-based X Windows and the character-based Desqview (also available with X Window supplements) support cut-and-paste capability for any character-based application. This means that any PC- or MS-DOS-based terminal emulation can be enhanced for a basic remote interconnection.

Although terminal emulation does not provide true LAN interconnection, it is a slow but functional WAN interconnection. The bandwidth is, of course, limited by the modem transmission speed and common carrier line clarity. While modem connections affected within a single building might represent a continuation of an internal LAN, modem connections are actually independent of distance. As such, they therefore represent a WAN configuration. At any rate, enterprise-wide networks built around RS-232, T-1, T-3, or X.25 "pipes" are apt to exhibit severe traffic bottlenecks at those pipes. When the bandwidth of these links inhibit effective operations, frame relay, SMDS, and SONET provide nearly unlimited and both incrementally and constantly adjustable connectivity for remote LANs. Note that Token-Ring and NetBIOS packets require complex protocol translation or encapsulation within the format of the frame relay of SONET protocols.

Interconnectivity is only the forefront of the problem. Interoperability is more complex and functionally important. *Interoperability* is a NATO term expressing the concept that military forces could standardize and share ammunition. Within the computer and network environment, the computer system is the weapon, data is the ammunition, and the structures and manipulations must be standardized. Although OS/2 supports DDE, the stunning success of Windows 3.1 is due in part to its advancing facilities to share information through the DDE and OLE interfaces. Second party suppliers provide robust network DDE. Note well that while any such creation of compound documents, processes, and objects radically promotes interoperability, it *also* increases the inherent fragility of the very specific linkages. DDE and OLE require an application name, topic name, and specific item name. This represents a one-way linkage from the client program to the server application. The server knows nothing about the client program and retains no information that any such linkage is in effect or has been established. Removal of a file linked through OLE or an insertion of rows and columns into a spreadsheet cell linked through DDE can potentially break the chain. Failure of any single cell, OLE object, or networked

DDE cells and objects could undermine the very intent of the enterprise-wide network. When such a network provides mission-critical operations, consider *not* establishing and depending upon linkages that are one-way. Any loss of the DDE or OLE information (type of link, location for insertion, availability, or means to grab the cells) is not easily restored. Moreover, such linkages are not easily restored or repaired from backups since the linkages are time-critical; effective restoration assumes that backup has been performed within the *same* time periods on *all* LANs, servers, remote hosts, export disk partitions, and local user disks. The essential risk is that simultaneous backup is a highly unlikely proposition and a very management problem.

Recognition that fragility is a management problem is not new; it has been studied. Products do exist to address it. For example, Hewlett-Packard's New Wave interface for MS Windows in part addresses the limitations of the DDE and OLE linkages by maintaining cross-tabulated lists to prevent such likely errors. Not only does the client program link to the server application or file, but a server or file retains information describing these secondary uses. As another example, while simple database languages provide data dictionaries to show how fields are used, named, and linked, distributed databases also maintain details about location and state.

The essential risk for any distributed processing or client-server operation is, in fact, reliance upon resources not directly managed or controlled with the framework of the network setting. This is particularly prevalent with peer-to-peer networks, such as MS Windows for Workgroups, where data and application file storage is distributed across many computers; this data is not always uniformly backed up. Despite the risks inherent in distributed processing, interoperability is only gaining in importance. Establishment of a file transfer path does not guarantee effective utilization of the network. For example, consider the problem of a Lotus 1-2-3 spreadsheet containing important data that should be uploaded to a mainframe or another PC database. While the interconnection for copying the file is established and functional, what is the format for that file? Should it be a 1-2-3 version 2, 2.2, 3.0, or 3.1 file? Assuming that you could determine an appropriate application file format, even that is not necessarily useful. Transfer of data between applications may require a comma-delimited or *stream data format* (SDF) file. Although these are common formats for transferring the actual data between different application software, the construction of such a file loses the logical interrelationships (that is, the cell formulas) between rows, columns, and cells within the worksheet to cause a significant loss of interoperability.

In spite of this divergence and complexity, the demand for internetworking increases. Organizations performing multiple platform software development require connectivity. This becomes increasingly important when a development source code control system must be reliable and available. Consequently, solutions which integrate and manage heterogeneous networks have extraordinary value. For example, Banyan provides peer-to-peer file access for a variety of machines including MS-DOS-based PCs and Macintosh computers through a file server based upon their proprietary Streettalk software.

Public domain (free or nearly free, copyrighted) software, such as the Clarkson drivers, provide TCP/IP interconnection for a variety of mainframe, Unix, and workstation platforms, as well as the ability to support multiple communication stacks for concurrent connectivity to multiple LANs. Commercial products such as Atlantix Axxess provide multiuser file servers which simultaneously handle MS-DOS, Macintosh, Unix, Xenix, LAN Manager on Token-Ring, ARCnet, and OS/2 with little regard for the underlying network. Although files are stored and named differently under each operating system, both Banyan Streettalk and Atlantix provide a transparent interface consistent with the expected norm for each operating system. Novell NetWare not only supports homogeneous clients operating its own *network operating system* (NOS), it also provides client access for OS/2 and DOS stations. Increasingly, other NOSs will support such hooks into heterogeneous systems to integrate the diverse LAN and WAN world.

LAN and WAN linkage is only part of the interconnectivity issue. It is also relevant to reach mainframes and other traditional host computing environments. *High-level language application programming interface* (HLLAPI) turns PCs into "smart" terminals running over *synchronous data link control protocols* (SDLC). HLLAPI with SDLC illustrates an old and limited connectivity tool. LAN gateways, including Rumba, AS/400, and other host-based gateways, tend to be both more effective and cost-efficient since the host mainframe attachment is just one more device on the network. The alternative is for *each* PC to support an IRMA card or modem for terminal connectivity with limited interoperability; Goldengate, IRMALAN, and Attachmate are among the many PC-based terminal emulation softwares which provide interconnectivity to host mainframes. These tools do not merely allow a modem-connected or networked PC to access mainframe data in the manner of a terminal, additional tools capture, transform, upload and download, and interactively and interoperatively manipulate application information.

Other tools such as IBM's advanced *program-to-program communication (APPC)* running on LU 6.2 is frequently advanced as IBM's strategic interconnection for host-to-PC networking. It is *system administration architecture* (SAA) compliant with the *common program interface communication* (CPIC) protocol. CPIC is an application programming interface (API) designed so that applications can multitask and interoperate without regard for the underlying computing platform, much like DDE and OLE link disparate objects. Standards do promote interconnectivity; slowly, the interoperability need is being reviewed and addressed. Manufacturers, vendors, and interested users can and do establish consistent standards. The IEEE committees, ECMA, CCITT, OSI, and NTSC set and establish standards for interoperability. For example, CCITT has defined X.400 for universal mail delivery via unique and differentiable addresses akin to international telephone numbers. CCITT, similarly, is considering an X.500 proposal for a universal file directory structure. This would promote accessing, viewing, and modifying files across networks and heterogeneous computing platforms.

Although manufacturers and buyers want to buy into standard computing solutions, there is little hope that stable long-term solutions will emerge and endure any time soon. Technology and its applications change dramatically and suddenly. TCP/IP has a protocol called *user datagram protocol* (UDP), which does not route well and defeats even networks that appear homogeneous. Novell and IBM have subscribed to the NDIS data-level protocol that is likewise not fully OSI compliant. Operating systems such as Unix, OS/2, and MS-DOS, while "standardized," show disruptive variety. There are multiple flavors of Unix including BSD, AT&T, X Windows, OSF, OpenLook, Xenix, and each hardware manufacturer bundles a slightly divergent version with the hardware. OS/2 exists as 1.1, 1.2, 1.3, and 2.0, along with base and extended editions and special file server versions. OS/2 even provides a LAN Server-like software for AS/400 interconnection not directly functional with IBM's own LAN Server. Even MS-DOS, the single most widely distributed software product, exists as a multivendor, multitiered product. There are intermediate numbered versions from 1.0 through 5.0, as well separate IBM PC-DOS and MS-DOS versions to support hardware BIOS differences.

Significant competition for these products exists with DR. DOS, Multiuser DOS, and 4DOS. Even MS Windows 3.1 provides another substantial API for networking development. Since networking is not an integral aspect of MS-DOS, it is extended with network software such as NFS, PC LAN, Novell NetWare, Banyan Vines, software and hardware drivers to support network attachment, and application software including network-smart Microsoft Windows. Microsoft is promoting Windows NT, even more than Windows 3.1, as a product that will transparently provide a network interface. Both Banyan and Novell provide a DOS-derivative network operating system that is not MS-DOS, Unix, nor OS/2. These are NOSs geared for server support of the client architecture networks. Drivers, boot configurations, memory management software such as QEMM.SYS and memory resident TSR software alter performance and compatibility to create a jungle of problems that infringe upon network operations and integrity.

Performance and response time is another quasi-compatibility issue of pertinence to client-server and host connectivity. Frequently, now, large data agencies install PC-based front ends to improve performance of host mainframe data collection and retrieval operations. Data validation and data entry are performed on a client PC without assistance from the host. When the record is validated, it is then shipped to the mainframe. Better performance in terms of response time for retrieval of a record means that the single data record only is fetched for viewing on the PC. Some systems that are designed to optimize processing may transmit blocks of master records with many unnecessary detail records. This clogs the network and creates bottlenecks at the host. This is particularly true for such new products as network fax, client-server database products, and any server-based software. This client-server technology is relatively new and not optimized to the same degree as host mainframe-based applications. Also, organizations spend considerable time and money to unify the data formats. Data is then transmitted using *electronic data interchange* (EDI).

## Consolidation of Information Management

Network management has become information management, a prevalent and critical concern for enterprise-wide networking. Network management encompasses data processing, management information systems, imaging (as in image storage and retrieval, multimedia, and image processing), telecommunications, data communications, networking, and information management as well. Information management will subsume all these functions and is increasingly being perceived as a critical function that cuts across business lines, management levels, physical locations, and organizational structure. Management is a distributed process with participants spread throughout the organization. What makes information management so difficult is that it represents so broad an area with no functional paradigms.

Even where organizations have installed integrated information systems (including enterprise-wide networks), the sheer complexity and difficulty in explaining the benefits and training users how to achieve organizational goals limit the very success of large network projects. Maintaining enterprise-wide networks is significantly more complex than running a small Token-Ring. One of the biggest hurdles is the assumption that when local networks are effectively maintained at the local level, the interconnections will function smoothly. Unfortunately, traffic spills onto local networks. Maintaining reliable internetwork links may persist as a substantial ongoing challenge. Files shared or applications distributed on an enterprise-wide network may not be available or may effect internetwork performance . Additionally, internetwork maintenance falls into the category of a patching activity rather than a proactive discipline.

Such comprehensive networks tend to represent critical elements for an organization. In the literature, important networks are ostentatiously called *mission-critical networks*. Any failure, however time-limited, represents a serious threat and financial loss to the organization. Enterprise-wide networks perform more than the transmission of computer data from point to point; the changing perception that voice, video, and data require different networks is underscoring the importance of consolidating networks into a single paradigm. As such, network management is important, essential, and critical.

Additionally, the technologies and choices made for mission-critical networks are profound. Any interconnection or interoperation increases operational fragmentation; success depends upon the weakest links. Internetworking links themselves are distributed, but only because the data, the processes, the people, and the locations where results are required themselves are distributed and fragmented. Although it seems feasible to create standby, redundant, or fault-tolerant backup arrangements for both these weakest and even the strongest links, it is still a ruse. The enterprise-wide network is a complex organism. Some connections may seem cheaper, faster, or more reliable; the cost is bought in terms of complexity. A lack of skilled management and operational personnel quickly can unravel any gains. Mission-critical networks are not necessarily improved by redundant components, fail-safe links offered by multiple spanning-tree bridges, or fault-tolerant computers. Redundancy is a reliability "red herring." Statistical reliability and enterprise-wide networks represent complex analytical problems requiring experts.

Many problems can easily undermine enterprise-wide networks. These include the lack of skilled management and crisis teams. Operations may be disrupted by reliance upon a singular and overlooked DDE, network DDE, or OLE linkage. Even nonredundant network monitoring and control systems or malfunctioning fault switching components may cause widespread network failure. The best policy is to build networks with common components (Token-Ring, Ethernet, NetBIOS, TCP/IP, Novel LAN Workplace, T-1, and *simple* routers and gateways) and simplify operations wherever possible. Retain bright, resourceful, and competent network managers.

Although network management paradigms are becoming available as real products, vendor variety, entrenched mentality, and a lack of *management information database* (MIB) agency limit SNMP or CMIP utility. Protocol analyzers remain the generic tool of choice because they capture and count packets with minimal error. The analyzer forms the basis for more complex internetworking management tools. Again, information—primarily traffic volumes, transmission delay and transit times, and error conditions—is the most basic requirement for network management. This is useful for locating faulty workstations, workstations which are saturating the network and perhaps best segregated to subnets, and optimizing work output and network performance. In fact, analyzers, which have traditionally been sold as hardware, are now software products. These tools form the basis for minimal distributed network management and pass captured information to mapping and statistical software that runs on generic MS Windows PC platforms. This is paramount to any consideration to implement a campus network or an enterprise-wide network.

New management tools include blueprinting tools, PC-resident information gathering packages like protocol analyzers and net usage software (specifically, SNMP and CMIP), as well as new invasive tools which allow an authorized person to remotely control a networked PC (Control Room or Carbon Copy, for example). Such tools are merely the vanguard. Network managers require more complex tools to simplify enterprise network management.

## Enterprise-Wide Linkage Products

Interconnecting local area networks should be a planned process. It is no quick fix or the solution to file access limitations. It is likely to create as many or more problems than solved, particularly when unmanaged or unmanageable local area networks are included in the grand plan. For example, see Chapter 10 for a discussion about gateway complexities. LANs that are out of control, overloaded, badly installed, or failing to achieve objectives can be integrated successfully into enterprise-wide networks under certain conditions. First, local networks must be controlled and local problems resolved prior to providing connectivity. Second, poor LAN performance issues must be understand before large storms of broadcast traffic are passed to the larger network. Spanning-tree bridges and multiprotocol routers which filter traffic can actually improve LAN performance, if properly tuned. Third, standards for the enterprise-wide network must be pushed down to the LANs and rigorously enforced; naming conventions (for users, nodes, and addresses) are a key reason more complex networks fail. Fourth and last, management must be convinced of the concept and provide sufficient motivation, encouragement, strategy, and funding to insure that the new linkage networks will have a fair chance to succeed; users must understand the strategy, too, and not feel alienated by this technological overhaul.

Given this favorable environment, nonetheless, maintenance, consistency, reliability, user access, and security will be more difficult issues with enterprise-wide networks. However, once the decision is cast to construct network linkages, software and hardware will be required. The hardware frequently provides a plug-and-play capability, whereas software and hardware or software-only products require complex installation and tuning. The true test remains in the intangibles such as determining strategy, matching user stated needs with objects and rationality, and maintaining a reliable and consistent network environment. Figure 11.5 shows a tabular consolidation of enterprise-wide linkage products. For additional information regarding the utility, performance, and limitations of these enterprise-wide network building blocks, refer to Figure 10.17.

| Device | Attribute | Interop | Internet | MGT notes |
|---|---|---|---|---|
| Repeater | Expand net | None | Lobes | Adds load |
| Bridge | | | | |
| Multiport | Expand net | None | Rings | Adds load |
| Multiprotocol | Expand net | Protocols | Rings | Adds load |
| Router | | | | |
| Multiport | Expand net | None | Rings | Adds load |
| Protocol | Expand net | Protocols | Rings | Complicated |
| Spanning trees | Fault tolerant | Minimal | Networks | Better reliability |
| Packet switch | Net trunk | None | Networks | Improves performance |
| Gateway | Software | Applications | Networks | Unreliable |
| FT protocol | Transfer files | Minimal | None | Improved sneaker net |
| MS Windows | GUI | Concurrency | None | Useful front end |
| Terminal emulator | Software | Cut-and-paste | Cut-and-paste | Useful within MS Windows |
| T-1 | WAN | None | LAN/WAN | Decouple net |
| X.25 | WAN | None | LAN/WAN | Decouple net |
| Frame relay | WAN | Adequate | LAN/WAN | Faster than X.25 |
| X.400 | Common files | None | LAN/WAN | Uniform fileand path names |
| X.500 | E-mail | None | LAN/WAN | Basic need |
| VSAT | WAN | None | Global | Faster than T-1 |
| SNMP | Local Mgt | Minimal | Marginal | Connectionless |

**Figure 11.5** Enterprise-wide linkage products.

# Part 3

## Practical Management of Token-Ring

This section presents rules of thumb and suggestions for successfully applying Token-Ring. The formal CCITT, IEEE, and ISO specifications do little to explain the hows and whys of success and failure with Token-Ring. Therefore, this part presents the design, planning, implementation, operational, and strategic issues. Emphasis is placed upon the practical issues that are often overlooked; therefore Chapter 12 concentrates on operational management.

Chapter

# 12

# Managing a Token-Ring Network

For most situations, Token-Ring has been selected because it is the networking medium with a "Big Blue" label. In other situations, Token-Ring has been selected for its long-standing acceptance, its relative simplicity, its growing site installation, or its compatibility with many host computing platforms and software applications. In all cases, management becomes a critical and necessary task. Figure 12.1 lists the categories of network management from the simplest survival mentality to the most complex, forward-thinking processes.

## Rules of Thumb

Token-Ring is not necessarily a simple conglomeration of parts, nor is it easily upgraded or maintained; it is often a critical and necessary organizational component. However, some simple steps and foresight can ease the burden of those who maintain that network. Building on an understanding how Token-Ring works and how it is physically assembled, as presented in Chapters 1 through 10, this chapter addresses the practical and realistic expectations of an experienced network manager in the

| | |
|---|---|
| **Survival** | At this level, the emphasis is to maintain a functioning network andkeep critical applications working. |
| **Response** | At this level, network usage, performance, and future requirements are collected and analyzed. |
| **Added value** | At this level, network management seeks to improve the organizational benefits that accrue from the network and networked data and software. |
| **Strategic value** | At this level, network management is integrated into how the organization evolves to meet changing business competition. |

**Figure 12.1** Levels of network management.

design and installation stages. Figure 12.2 outlines the organizational and implementational items detailed in this chapter.

Sisyphus would have made the ultimate network manager. The job is never-ending, and each improvement—when finally accomplished— begs additional upgrades, changes, and fixes; uncovers oversights; and encourages new user requests. Moreover, as is the case for any service organization, major work and excellent improvements yield no recognition.

All LANs require a great deal of babying. An irascible LAN requires extraordinary craft. Good work habits, good network documentation, and good technicians can keep any network functioning. With sufficient funds and an astute eye for applying those resources, a network will provide growth capability and reliability to yield significant advantages for the organization.

## Network Administration

Network management is a subservient role, and the players must be responsive in a timely manner to the network user community and to

- Network administration
- Understanding user needs
- Resource allocation
- Financial planning and assessing budgetary allocations
- Evaluating resource allocation decisions
- Setting priorities
- Security
- Environmental problems
- Failures and repairs
- Downtime
- Crashes
- Planning for catastrophes
- Staging upgrades
- Upgrade policies
- Locating potential failure points
- Pilot projects
- Long lead times
- Replacement parts
- Ethernet monitoring
- Backup
- Coordinating network disruptions
- Moving equipment
- Tape backup and storage
- Questions to ask prospective vendors
- Squeaky wheel versus problem resolution
- Short-term versus long-term planning

**Figure 12.2** Implementational and operational issues.

network problems. The manager must determine the acceptable level of services required to meet the community needs, the level of resources available to fulfill them, and the effort required to sustain them. Until these parameters are defined—often through consensus of many quarters—network administration will be a hodgepodge geared to crisis-level maintenance, instead of a controlled, foresighted team.

Network administration is a supportive activity just like data processing. As a consequence, network management is very much a vendor in a vendor-buyer relationship, the buyer in this case being the network user community. The audience is captive; the network may be the only game in town, like any monopolistic utility, because alternatives are difficult to implement when substitutes don't exist in the short term. Consider the breakdown in Figure 12.3 of the typical activities required for effective network management.

Because a network intertwines hardware, software, and procedural and labor components, resources must be available to assess and repair each of these layers. Not only does a network include these layers, but the network interacts with almost every layer within the organization. Figure 12.4 illustrates the matrix organization often confronted by network managers. Frequently, the network manager and the support team are the most visible persons (other than mail room clerks or front desk guards) within an organization. With this visibility comes responsibility. The support team is not a secret organization. The support team does not directly bring revenue to the company; in fact, it is a cost center, which is a euphemistic way to say that network administration is a large and difficult-to-manage overhead expense. Also, the network is a support function that rarely creates a discernible value to the organization.

| Core Services | Operations | Management |
|---|---|---|
| Cable laying | Network management | Network design |
| Hardware installation | Performance analysis | Network planning |
| Additions | Network optimization | Network analysis |
| Changes | Cost analysis | Network selection |
| Moves | Configuration | Network implementation |
| Updates | Network expansion | Network configuration |
| Repairs | Network installation | |
| | Education | |
| | Training | |
| | Diagnostics | |
| | Network testing | |
| | Fault isolation | |

**Figure 12.3** Categorization of network management.

| | Network Management | Deparments | Junior | Senior |
|---|---|---|---|---|
| Network Management | ⊗ | ⊗ | ⊗ | ⊗ |
| Departments | ⊗ | | | ⊗ |
| Junior personnel | ⊗ | ⊗ | | ⊗ |
| Senior level | ⊗ | | | |

**Figure 12.4** Matrix management.

Like a telephone switchboard, the network provides a basic support service that defies easy quantification.

The network, like a telephone switchboard, is noticeable only when it doesn't function correctly. When it works well, users assume that they have a right to its resources; when it fails, then and only then do users take notice of the (bungling) efforts of the network administration team. The job is a service-related task: fix and repair, replace and maintain. Planning and implementation for the future are not perceived to be as critical as the immediate functionality; the team must maintain the fragile service. This breeds a reaction to crisis mentality and an emotional bent to avoid any change that could upset the fragile equilibrium. This breeds management conservatism.

## Understand Network User Desires

A flattened, decentralized organization fits well with a network strategy because the network provides service to a wide range of people. Some will have computer experience, whereas others will not. Also, users will have expectations brought from other experiences and organizations, or will generate expectations from analogous situations. One example is the data processing (DP) department. The services of a network are somewhat similar to those of the DP department, and users may expect the same respect, response, or results. Understand the user community, respond to those needs, and if necessary, educate that community to the benefits, processes, and limitations of the newer networking technology. Nail down specifications for users and your vendors. Ask them the important questions first—not later. Communicate policies to all affected by the network. This will build credibility and respect, and alleviate some of the inherent work overload.

## Resource Allocation

Because network management is a service organization catering almost exclusively to internal needs, it is a money hole. As suggested above, the network is a cost center, unless the network is large enough to service many departments within a sizable organization or provides enterprise-wide services and support activities to suppliers, allied field offices, and customers. In that case, it may be feasible to assess each department for the cost of network services rendered and establish a suitable charge-out policy for customer activities. Such a strategy generates an income for the network administration team, and thus a clearly defined market. Increases in service to a particular department can generate valid requests for a larger allocation for networking operating costs.

Many Fortune 1000 firms encourage profit center orientation for computer centers, in order to control and contain the rampant growth of a support group. In past years, computer service organizations have sought continuous improvement to the basic installation, adding to cost with new equipment and people. Benefits from such growth never coincide with the addition of equipment and people. This accentuates the cost to the organization of any new resources.

The "black art" of data processing management, the difficulty in attracting qualified people, and the leverage held by such experts provided enough intimidation in the past to increase DP budgets at rates inconsistent with company growth. Eventually, this problem can be resolved by assigning administrative responsibility for budget issues to the DP manager, vice president, or director, and basing the performance evaluation of such a manager on budget and profit issues. As a consequence, mainframe software and services usually support user accounts and charges, and a fee-chargeback policy can be directly implemented. Because networks are geographically distributed and network services tend to be more nebulous and intangible, there is no directly applicable fee structure. However, there are clear, concise, and fair methods for assessing network uses and assigning user or departmental costs.

## Financial Planning

Three major factors affect the implementation and usage of a Token-Ring network: reliability, organizational growth, and technological change. These three items determine the level of service achieved and the success of the network administration group. The solution used by many companies for any network constraint is the addition of more resources. Unfortunately, unlimited DP budgets no longer exist, and networks are usually derived from a different mentality than host services.

Networks are new resources to most organizations, and despite the many similarities, neither appear as glamorous nor are held in as high esteem as the DP groups were in the 1950s, 1960s, or 1970s. In the 1980s, personal computers often supplemented overloaded DP departments. Even now, distributed data processing and improved user-layer software have achieved a higher user sophistication, greater user expectations, and less reliance on a DP department. Also, distributed processing power with superservers allows the addition of less costly computers incrementally rather than a single, indivisible mainframe to cope with trickle growth; this better coordinates needs with resources. As the new networking technology unfolds, communication networks complement the desktop "toys." As a result of this perception, network budgets are modest and more tightly controlled than DP budgets are.

Good network management requires self-imposed financial controls. External controls devalue the esteem of network administration. It is vitally important to justify the expense of every aspect of a network. You cannot add up the numbers and ask management to sign a blank check. Intangible benefits of a network do not carry much weight when money can be spent on something else. Check signers want sophisticated cost-benefit analyses. Demonstrate the project payback. Calculate the net present value of the network over time. Show how downsizing DP operations will actually generate money in the present year. Show how the return on the networking project exceeds the organization's cost of capital.

For these reasons, a planning mechanism is necessary to address the existing network and to acquire additional resources to match organizational growth and technological change. Financial planning can be *ad hoc* in an environment in which there is a cost-plus mentality, or zero-based budgeting. Either method is better than none. Zero-based is better politically than *ad hoc* because every expense has been justified.

*Ad hoc* planning devalues the decision-making process, because needs are addressed sporadically and without clear controls. Each newly identified need becomes a battle for budget. Zero-based budgeting schemes are difficult to implement, since they require more management time. All hardware, software, and labor costs are addressed up front, and organizational change becomes a detailed, preplanned financial issue. Growth in head count becomes a known quantity, and technological advancement is no longer an unknown quantity with nebulous ramifications, but rather a clearly stated and clearly controlled financial cost. Figure 12.5 contrasts the advantages and pitfalls of each financial tracking method.

| | Ad hoc | Zero-Based |
|---|---|---|
| **Advantages** | Specific goal orientation | Nonspecific |
| | Easy | Concise |
| | Fast | Informative |
| | Accurate | Prestigious |
| **Disadvantages** | Devalues management | Inaccurate (assumptive) |
| | Creates surprises | Time-consuming |

**Figure 12.5** Network budgeting choices.

## Resource Allocation

Financial planning encompasses the entire network. Very often, resources are allocated to many individuals and groups within the framework of the network. When the network is a "free" resource, like telephone, secretarial services, desk space, or other utilities, the network is devalued. After all, it is free. Financial planning provides that first step for understanding the resources applied to intercommunication. A budgetary methodology builds that first stage for inventorying network uses. The second step is to gain an understanding of user needs. A network supplies easily discernible services, some of which are listed in Figure 12.6.

Understanding the consumption and depletion of these resources completes the picture of network management. Additional resources certainly will be procured to alleviate network overloads. What types of resources, to which sets of problems these resources will be targeted, and how much will be allocated are, in part, within the purview of the network manager.

## Setting Priorities

Resource allocation decisions hinge upon the size of the network budget and user demands for services. Unilateral decisions are inappropriate, since the user community mirrors a vendor-buyer relationship. Ignoring the needs of the user is tantamount to a service failure. Applying technical skills without responding to the full measure of user questions, requests, and complaints is certain to breed resentment and distrust. Only two-way dialogue can simplify the resource allocation process.

Users must feel that their issues are recognized and understood. Silent and unpublicized repairs (as though accomplished by the proverbial "elves") may solve network problems per se, but create a public relations nightmare. Therefore, all users must be able to voice their concerns and pet interests and see how this information adjusts the priorities of the network administration group.

While network managers may technically and politically understand the problems on hand, these problems must be clearly presented to the user community as well. The prioritized list of network administration goals and charters must logically match the perception of the identified and acknowledged network problems so that the community "buys into" any plan.

- Communication
- Electronic mail and network fascimile
- File and print service
- Centralized coordination
- Centralized maintenance
- Automation

**Figure 12.6** Network services.

This inclusion in the problem identification and resolution process and in task prioritization will yield a better perception of the network group and a more satisfied community. The priorities should be delineated clearly to avoid possible misunderstanding.

## Assessing Budgetary Allocations

If it is preferable to establish a profit center mentality, network costs can be allocated in several ways. All methods require determining a cost basis for equipment, software, labor, and repairs. Additionally, a basis should be established for a matching service level. Figure 12.7 lists some common network costs that form a cost basis.

Fixed costs include overhead such as inadequate and insufficient space, heat, power, and management salaries. This includes semivariable, fixed-cost items, like the initial cable, transceivers, and node equipment. Consumable materials include file space, paper and other media, and replacement and repair parts. Labor includes a portion of overhead, all network administration labor, and consultants. It also includes the fair cost of training sessions, shows, and documentation purchased. A cost basis should reconcile growth or shrinkage, since new users within a department require additional resources, place additional loads, and often request new types of services not previously provided.

The service level is the yardstick for prorating the network costs listed. Fee application schemes for allocating costs of the services are difficult because network service is the pie that all users and groups share. The costs for providing network services are black and white, whereas the value of the services rendered is not as clear. It is usually unreasonable to charge for each individual event because the accounting system will grow large and cumbersome, and will itself affect the level of network service. Complex schemes will win no friends, either.

Therefore, the cost charge-out system should be simple. Some possibilities include assigning costs by head count. This is immediately simple, but may shortchange the demands some groups place upon network load or network administration services. Another method

- Overhead
- Equipment
- Depreciation
- Labor
- Maintenance
- Media
- Consumables
- Training

**Figure 12.7** Network costs.

might apply node counts as an appropriate measure. Either file space or paper output could form a prorated basis. Another basis could be built from the network traffic level. In fact, Chapter 14 includes an example in which Token-Ring packets are counted and used as a measure by which to assign costs. Figure 12.8 represents these and other possibilities.

Carefully weigh which measure is to be used as the fee basis since each user will adjust network usage so as to minimize statistics in that area. Users will optimize their usage and play against the system. This can, however, be applied to advantage. If it is important to minimize the growth or utilization of certain resources, the fee basis can be changed to encourage conservation. If a network is too busy and it is important to decrease load until upgrades are installed, arbitrary increases in the fee basis will compel users to conserve. Frequency of reassessing the fee basis is also an important consideration, since users will shift usage during the measurement period. Secret measurements that cannot be validated will infuriate everyone. The system must be open and honest, in addition to being simple. It will be necessary to defend the internal pricing strategy.

## Licensing and Warranty Issues

Many organizations assume that the purchase of a software product guarantees the right to use that product in any manner, including multiple-site installation. This is rarely the intent of the software vendor. Personal computer software is particularly vulnerable to this type of pirating; a single master copy gets installed on all the computers. Most organizations today, however, are too mature for this behavior.

Because networks are often installed as an organization grows, there is usually an installed base of existing tools and products. Software is often sold under a precondition that it is to be used on a single machine. It may not be supported within the context of a distributed network or multiuser environment, not because of legal issues, but rather from technical limitations and complexities in the networking environment. Therefore, it is important to consider whether a software package your

- Head count
- Node count
- File space usage
- User connect time
- CPU time
- Prorated traffic level
- Service requests
- Individually negotiated
- Replacement part costs

**Figure 12.8** Basis for prorating network costs.

organization depends upon is guaranteed to work within a networked environment, will be supported within that environment, or even, whether the product can be legally licensed for your use within a networked environment.

## Security

Security is a factor that needs to be built into the initial network design. Security encompasses many aspects, including limits to physical equipment, such as access to the coaxial cable and network communication hardware, and software access to machines, file storage media, and information replicating devices like tape drives, floppy disks, and cartridge tape units.

As a rule of thumb where security is desirable, the physical network as a whole should be as inaccessible as possible. Additionally, as many software keys as possible should be applied to the network. The role of network administrator is a conservative role, and such conservative security measures are best instituted. Therefore, all media backup devices should be locked up to prevent theft of information on portable media. Network servers that provide global services should also be removed from public access in order to curtail marginally qualified network users from trying to fix server problems. Access to power service, fuses, circuit breakers, and any other network transformers should be secured. Building managers regularly lock access to such building power panels; it is a safe and reasonable procedure. Figure 12.9 illustrates these simple and wise steps. Details and rationale for these policies are examined in Chapter 18.

## Environmental Problems

Token-Ring is mostly inert media, although certain environmental factors will disrupt communication and network data processing. As stated in Chapter 6, electrical or magnetic interference in proximity to the twisted-pair can adversely affect network impedance or color packets with random noise. Additionally, many wires side by side may cause

- Limit access to physical network equipment and wiring
- Limit access to physical equipment
- Limit access to physical network servers
- Limit access to physical backup media devices
- Limit network access to servers and nodes
- Limit access with password protection
- Limit access to backup media and store it off-site

**Figure 12.9** Rule-of-thumb security steps.

mutual interference despite internal shielding; this is not a proven assumption for minimum networks, but has been verified by independent sources for long parallel runs of cable. It may cause problems when voice, serial, and other data lines share UTP bundles.

Users may unconsciously force a workstation against a wall to create more desktop space and place pressure on modular or hermaphroditic connectors. Also, extremes of temperature can distort magnetic disk alignment, thus rendering a disk useless. High temperatures can overheat computer chips and cause premature node equipment failure. Likewise, temperature extremes can damage transceiver electronics. Low humidity will cause static electricity to build up, static being a likely candidate as the cause for chip failure (particularly PROM chips) and a contributing factor to momentary power surges.

Figure 12.10 illustrates these environmental concerns. Solutions include installing climate control, securely installing cable to building structures or installing wiring conduits, and selecting a site carefully. Also, many facilities install monitoring devices that track deviations from acceptable operating conditions. It is reasonable to track temperature, humidity, smoke levels, security and facility access, system failures, and network failures.

## Standards

American National Standards Institute (ANSI) generates a list of acceptable standards for computer languages, character sets, connection compatibility, and many other aspects of the computer industry. Adherence to a standard in network design may ease maintenance, spare parts, and upgrade problems. Non-ANSI components should be viewed with a healthy skepticism, but not necessarily ignored. However, some standards exist only because they were accepted as *de facto* before better or more rational solutions existed. Similarly, nonconformity to EIA/TIA-568 wiring standards may preclude simple protocol upgrades in the foreseeable future. Plan accordingly amd build networks to standards.

- Excessive temperature or temperature fluctuations
- Low or excessive humidity
- Vibration
- Stray and static electricity
- Fire, smoke, steam, and water
- Crosstalk and radio-frequency (RF) interference
- Electromagnetic interference (EMI)
- Security

**Figure 12.10** Environmental concerns.

## Wiring Mechanical Integrity

Rules-of-thumb encompass those soft issues that a practiced manager discusses with peers over lunch. These include hard-learned solutions, as evidenced by this next item. As presented in Chapter 3, the hardware is specified by rigorous IEEE 802.5 descriptions. However, some mechanical features of that specification should be improved. Specify wire from recently manufactured and not recycled stock. Qualify recycled or existing wiring with a scanner prior to use. Furthermore, wiring should be installed far from electrical signals and tied to a firm support or installed within a cable tray.

## Maintenance and Repairs

All networks require maintenance and repairs. *Maintenance* is defined as repairs performed before a problem exists; they are often preventive measures. Repairs are effected when the network fails. While maintenance often saves repairs, some maintenance causes problems which will require unexpected repairs. Understand the consequences of maintenance and that the consequences can be far-reaching, possibly including network downtime. Mechanical and software components require repair work. Parts fail, software malfunctions, and power surges or failures corrupt both hardware and software. Likewise, network configurations change in subtle ways, requiring hardware and software work-arounds, DIP switch resets, and component changes. Failures in these components create downtime.

## Downtime

Network downtime is costly. Local area networks tend to limit the effects of the downtime, while enterprise-wide networks often globalize the effects of downtime. Although it is possible to install RF switches, self-healing circuits, and bridges and routers that isolate failing segments, effects are nonetheless likely to ripple throughout the organization. Various consulting organizations have calculated that downtime costs the average networked organization at least $15,000 per year in lost revenue, and $200,000 in productivity costs. Larger organizations can see these values in $1 million and $15 million ranges.

Problems are endemic even in the best of networks. At the first symptom of trouble, clear the network of users and determine the problem. Determine if the problem is localized or system-wide. Network downtime is part of the "excitement" of managing any network. Token-Ring is no exception. There are many reasons for a network to fail; some of these have been explicitly stated in prior chapters, while other reasons will follow in concise detail.

Network problems can, in part, be avoided with good initial design, compatible equipment, installation according to specification, and appropriate vendor post-sale support. Additionally, network segmentation and planned preventive maintenance may forestall such events from incapacitating the entire network. Preplanned downtime for upgrades and maintenance is preferable to system crashes. Users do not like surprises or the drama that accompanies a forced network halt. Connections, filters, software, device drivers, and the devices themselves can be checked for functionality on a periodic basis. While unplanned crashes are unpredictable, a stated policy for resolving crises and answering user questions can lessen the severity of a crash's impact as well as build confidence in the network team.

## Crash Policy

Crashes are inevitable. Hardware and software will malfunction, and many known or totally new problems will incapacitate network sections, segments, or the entire network installation. Since these cannot be prevented with complete success, it is best is to have a crash policy. The network management team must know what to do to solve the problem, and they must also know what to say. Users who depend on the network for completing their jobs might prefer to leave for the day if the problem will not be resolved in a reasonable amount of time. Groups may seek to hold meetings during this dead spot of activity.

While Token-Ring network crashes are certain to occur, far-reaching ramifications can be diverted with clear and concise explanations and open answers. The user community has few alternatives to the network administration group, and while the network team may feel pressured and overworked, they should also realize that the user community depends on them. The network team should answer the questions in Figure 12.11 for each user.

- How long will service be unavailable?
- Why am I affected?
- Who else is affected?
- Will I be able to work?
- When will service be restored?
- What causes the downtime?
- What solutions exist?
- Will the solution be stable?
- Will the problems reoccur?
- What can users do to help?
- What should a user expect?
- What alternatives exist to complete my work?

**Figure 12.11** Typical user questions during downtime.

## Planning for Catastrophe

The network manager is responsible for the security and continuing operation of the network. When the network crashes or when node equipment that is under network administration management malfunctions, the manager is pressed to restore service with rapidity. Minor software or hardware fixes are the grist for daily operations, but network disaster could make or break careers, the livelihoods of many people, and the very continuation of the organization. Catastrophe could be the result of a natural disaster, arson, accident, or sabotage. While any one of these is a rare event, the disruption is too massive to ignore.

Information backups, alternative emergency sites, redundant sites, and spare parts are the basics for restoring service after a disaster. Additionally, skilled and prepared people, a plan of action, an understanding of the critical needs, and a staged implementation are necessary components for network restoration. Figure 12.12 outlines these factors.

Most organizations prefer for business reasons not to make public disclosures of disasters or interruptions of operations. Likewise, recovery plans are kept secret. Whatever the recovery plan, the procedures should be pretested to ensure the completeness of the plan and to uncover any existing weaknesses, as well as those operations most critical to the business. Some commercial corporations provide "hot sites" and staff and support services for a fee. While this may be advisable for some organizations, others may prefer to plan their own disaster recovery procedures. At a minimum, keep an up-to-date list of the phone numbers of key personnel for users to contact in cases of network emergencies. This is a no-cost solution to many problems, and it generates goodwill as well.

## Staging Upgrades

Planned downtime can include fixes and improvements to the network. Although these are often noncritical, they may be far from trivial to network operations. Because such changes are usually tested and verified prior to their application, these changes can be applied off-hours or

- Information backups
- Alternative emergency sites
- Redundant sites
- Spare parts
- Strike team
- Plan of action for recovery
- Understanding of critical services
- Stated implementation plan

**Figure 12.12** Data recovery components.

concurrently with the repair of an unplanned crash. Notification to the users of planned changes is good public relations because it forewarns users of possible negative side effects, as well as service improvements. It also serves to remind users of the events that happen behind the scenes, to their benefit. Common courtesy and savvy management dictate that you give users as much lead time as possible before implementing changes.

## Upgrade Policies

The time for staging upgrades must be carefully orchestrated, and the user community must be made to understand and accept the inherent risks beforehand. Additionally, there should be an upgrade policy coordinated with all vendors. Fixes, improvements, and changes in technology should be applied where optimally beneficial, although technological changes at times may obsolete network components. Vendors should stand by their sales, and they should be willing to support all network equipment. There should be a policy on handling minor upgrades that would not unnecessarily outdate components. Also, it may be that secondary sourcing of so-called commodity items may breed incompatibilities later when a network is upgraded. Be aware that prime vendors may alter their equipment or software, and third-party solutions may no longer be ideal. Some upgrades and installations might require a year of planning and several years of gradual implementation (while the old hardware and software are phased out). This is particularly true when critical operations are transferred from a mainframe to a LAN, or from a nonessential LAN to a mission-critical client-server operation.

## Locate Failure Points

The last four chapters expressed a need for network blueprinting. Possible network failure points should be located. While the maintenance logs suggested later in this chapter document what has gone wrong in the past, it is also appropriate to consider what might go wrong in the future. This preparation might encompass listing failures theorized but not actually experienced; it may be mentioned in trade journals or books. When a failure occurs that defies the usual solutions and is not listed in the troubleshooting section of this book pertinent to your network, peer table talk and theorized solutions are invaluable.

The normally recurring trouble spots might also be added to such a list. If the user community has access to such information, it can lend its diagnostic skills when failures do occur. Often, users have more information readily available than any member of the network administration team and can narrow the possible problem set, thus saving time.

## Pilot Projects

It is anathema to test on unwilling and unknowing users. Few users want to be guinea pigs, and certainly no one should ever be an unknowing test subject. Major network changes, cable rerouting, or upgrades are best pretested and not indiscriminately applied with only a vendor's guarantees. As a consequence, it is is often difficult to test changes. Pilot projects are an appropriate solution. They certainly lower the risk of failure and localize the test to an observable network subset.

Pilot projects remove the effect of changes from the daily operational or manufacturing environment of the larger network. Isolated tests concentrate problems in a select and willing group and lessen the risk all will face when such changes are later applied to the complete network. Try changes using spare machines. Build a small network and test on that. Find willing users who want to feel that they are in the thick of things and like to talk about what they do and what the network team is doing. Locate a subnet that provides less critical services. Select a time when a segment is unused, perhaps after hours. Weekends or after hours may be the best time to effect global changes so that, should unforeseen side effects surface, all changes can be reversed without affecting the user base. Figure 12.13 illustrates when it is best to implement changes with test pilots.

## Long Lead Times

Most projects on the network have long lead times. Either the parts are difficult to obtain, senior-level management is slow to understand and respond, or manpower is in short supply to complete the workload. Projects with long lead times are best launched immediately so that crises and constraints will not deteriorate network performance. Such projects might include installation of parallel networks, gateways, faster machines, and optical fiber. The continued employment of network management may not only be at risk; a competitive advantage might be at stake as well.

- Network extensions
- Gateway Installations
- Network bridges
- Repeater installation
- Subnetworks
- Superservers
- RAID and disk farms
- New types of node equipment
- New network configurations

**Figure 12.13** Pilot projects.

## Replacement Parts

In the normal course of network operations, components will fail. There are two policies for restoring service. The first is to swap parts from other working equipment to restore service. The second is to have an inventory of spare parts. Either method is reasonable, although in actual operation, some combination of the two will actually be applied sooner or later. Most managers prefer to maintain a parts inventory because repairs are simpler, do not affect functioning network users, and do not require duplicate efforts, that is, repairing the defective components as well as later repairing the unit that was the source of the problem. When a network uses old, antiquated, or unusual equipment, a spare-parts policy is recommended, because parts can be very difficult to obtain. If the equipment is more common and parts are nonetheless difficult to obtain from the manufacturer, a spare-parts inventory is critical.

Most upper-management teams seek to trim expenses. Replacement parts are nonfunctioning items, usually expensive in the quantities sought, and therefore rarely stocked. Convincing upper management that a spare-parts policy is absolutely necessary requires a mathematical analysis. Compare the costs of inventory against the costs of downtime, both partial and complete. Determine through consensus how often this might occur. Figure 12.14 presents the mathematics for such an analysis.

Audit the replacement-part inventory as the network evolves, new equipment is purchased, and other equipment is sold or antiquated. A spare-parts inventory must reflect the current network, and not the network as it was months ago. Turn over the inventory with regularity, and replace all parts in the inventory that are defective. Bad inventory will fail not only to solve a network failure, it will seriously degrade network management's credibility.

The inventory should cover the expected loss of network downtime in the event that spare parts are unavailable. The spare-parts inventory does not need to equal the suggested inventory valuation if the organi-

+ Hourly network costs
+ Hourly network user costs
+ Loss of goodwill
+ Loss of network access

=Total hourly network costs

. Spare inventory valuation
÷ Lifespan and turnover rate

= Depreciated cost of spares

**Network failure rate**
(number chosen by consensus or the past failure history)

Total hourly network costs × network failure rate =
Spare inventory valuation ≤ depreciated cost of spares

**Figure 12.14** Spare-parts inventory justification.

zation is willing to accept some risk of downtime. Note also that an inventory does not guarantee that the necessary part is always in stock.

Consider acquiring used parts for the spare inventory. It is also possible to build new networks with used parts. As organizations replace 4 Mbits/s Token-Ring components with 16 Mbits/s or with FDDI, old NICs, workstations, servers, and MAUs are often sold as scrap. Buy these parts. They are likely to be cost-effective. Needless to say, test these components carefully. Refer to Chapters 12 through 16 for testing methods.

However, avoid recycling the wiring. It will have a significant number of bends and scrapes, and may have sustained injury in the removal process. However, recycling NICs, PCs, and workstations as routers and gateways may be unwise and represent a false economy. Four Mbits/s NICs provide the same upgrade path for you as for the original owner. Routers and gateways are critical and nonredundant network components. While it may be possible within the Token-Ring-based LAN Manager to establish primary and backup *domain controllers*, which provide services such as file services, exported disk partitions, electronic mail, and print support, duplicate servers and spanning trees actually providing intelligent (hot) redundancy are very difficult to establish. Also, recycled components tend to represent last generation equipment with lower levels of performance. Because routers and gateways often become traffic bottlenecks, these nodes often require the highest performance of all network components.

## Token-Ring Monitoring

Network monitoring is good policy. The network management should know how the network is performing and should see problems before users are aware of them. While this is often impossible, traffic monitoring and performance analysis can yield information about the state of the network that will aid in design, planning, implementation, and control over network operations. User complaints can be answered with an informed response such as that the network is overloaded, that certain nodes have failed, or that a network server has malfunctioned. Answers like those breed trust, respect, and a happy user community. Channel load and TRT time are basic requirements. Token-Ring monitoring is possible with node software or special network monitoring equipment. This equipment is the subject of Chapters 13 through 15.

## Maintain a Network Profile

Every organization requires a good inventory system. This holds true for network management as well. Not only must spare-parts inventories be maintained so that component failures do not hamper network access, but network node component inventories should be maintained.

Many vendors provide automated inventory programs that capture PC node information, such as total disk space, free disk space, CPU type, memory configuration, boot file configurations, and monitor resolution and type. Since these tools do not provide database fields or even capture machine types, serial numbers, performance statistics, and user names, the manual method is still necessary until vendors provide more robust software. These high-profile items are partially outlined in Figure 12.15.

A network manager finds a complete hardware-software profile invaluable. Network failures can often be traced to incompatible equipment, mismatched revisions, outdated standards, or any number of other configuration differences. Furthermore, when a component is suspect and there are no replacement units, swapping such a part with a comparable item from another node is an efficacious method of verification.

It is worthwhile to track network equipment and node locations. Include in the node profile such information as part revision codes, versions, dates of installation and repairs, plus any maintenance information. Additionally, it is sound procedure to track software versions, installation dates, and dates when patches of test code were applied, since "tests" that work become permanent. Furthermore, certain networks allow nodal interlinking with ease, and this accessibility should be tracked at least for performance evaluation, if not for security reasons. Some of these items are documented with blueprints and notebooks, as the next sections discuss.

## Blueprint the Network

A complete network profile includes a schematic rendition of the network, with cable, electronics, node equipment, repeaters, and any other device which might need to be located at a later time. Several styles of physical blueprinting were presented in Chapter 7 and are repeated elsewhere, and Figure 12.16 lists common network items that are tracked and managed.

## Managing Change

Although some organizations actually relish change, new technology, and constant shifts in priorities, most organizations, in fact, do not.

- Distributed files and databases
- Users
- Spare parts
- Network support equipment (printers, faxes, backup units)
- Node equipment
- Hubs, central wiring, and interconnectivity devices
- Software variations

**Figure 12.15** Maintain a network profile.

- Location of wiring
- Connection points
- Location of patch panels
- Paths and lengths of lobe cables
- Location of node equipment
- Location of MAUs
- Location of repeaters, bridges, routers, and gateways
- Lengths of all wiring, sections, and segments
- Cable stress points and repair points
- All completed physical plant alterations

**Figure 12.16** Common items to blueprint.

Deviation from the status quo is perceived as a threat to the power structures, to the patterns of group interaction and interpersonal behavior, and a risk to successful results. Change is usually perceived as a threat by higher-level supervisors and the top executives since it threatens their power base and the flow of information which they have developed. Most others within the organization see change as a challenge to their abilities and the comfortable knowledge of how things work. Some see change as a means to further their power base, their indispensability, and a chance to advance.

Networks are especially disruptive since they alter access to information. Networks—LANs, WANs, and enterprise endeavers—as well as software applications represent a pattern of accomplishing results. View this as a complex production process, much like any assembly line, where the end product is information. Changes to this production structure tend to produce precipitous results. Changes foisted suddenly create explosive responses. It is a political and process problem, that once created, is nearly impossible to rectify.

Without support from users, network management authority is likely to be severely undermined and challenged. At the very least, trust and support will be broken. As such, communicate the reasons for considering changes *in advance* to all users and supervisors. Integrate responses and suggestions. Acknowledge concerns, fears, and needs. This insures that users in the network community feel that their needs are being understood and addressed, not ignored. While it may be necessary frequently to reject and deny user requests since resources are bounded and technology has its limits, still it is courteous and important to recognize the users. The network is, after all, for the benefit of the users and not for aggrandizement of the network manager and the network team. Chapter 21 elaborates on these issues and addresses some of the political ramifications as well.

## The Problems of New Networks

The installation of a network changes the nature an organization in unanticipated ways. While it provides substantial benefits in terms of providing interconnection for mail, application and file access, and workgroup flow, a network is also an extraordinary investment in time, effort, and money. It is easy to see the benefits; frequently, new network managers and work groups fail to see the required effort until problems arise. A typical network is installed to provide uniform application access to a work group.

For example, a publishing group wants to use the same word processor and page composition program and so purchases site licenses. This software is installed on a single centralized server for automatic distribution by the network to the clients. The server is now an application server for its user group clients. Since it is also useful to streamline the writing and editing process in order to share files, all work is stored on the same server for shared access. The server is a file server, too. A database coordinates production schedules, stores name and address information, and provides a consistent source of scanned photographs (maintained as binary database field data). Since information is stored in a multiuser database on the server as well, it is also a database server. This server also has a postscript printer attached since it is cheaper to buy one printer for everyone's use. As such, the server is also a print server. This machine is a critical and multifunctional component.

This network works as envisioned for a while. Software must be added. Changes to system configuration files are required. A motherboard in the server must be replaced because the printer port has failed. Each of these events requires that the server be removed temporarily from network service. When that occurs, the client-server network is not functional. If the clients are personal computers, they could be run in stand-alone mode to perform other work. However, when the network server or (the network cabling) is unavailable, then all access to the printer, the database, the site-licensed application software, or any of the files residing on this machine are lost. Simple changes to the server that were supposed to take five minutes require several reboot cycles, several editing changes to configurations files, and the five minutes is now easily an hour. The work group members go to a hastily planned meeting after 30 minutes in order to salvage the morning while the server administrator fixes the network.

Suddenly, the critical nature of the network and the network components because apparent. Off-hours and lunch become important time slots for server administration and file backup. The server cannot be disabled for changes without informing users. A sudden loss of the server may leave work in progress in an unstable state or damaged. It may leave the user with little means to detached himself from the network to use the PC as a stand-alone. This depends upon configuration. PC-DOS CONFIG.SYS and AUTOEXEC.BAT files should provide selective access to the network. OS/2 supports similar files as well as a STARTUP.CMD. Consider establishing client network access as an option rather than as a certainty.

Server backup is an important function. It is no longer a matter of backing up single-user machines; the work and success of an entire department resides on the server. Data distributed throughout apeer-to-peer network is only as safe as the latest complete *network-wide* backup. Configuration files, database files, scanned photographs, and page makeup files should be duplicated to another medium on a regular basis and relocated to a physically remote and protected site. Rare as it might be, consider what would happen if the hard disk crashed with all that work?

It is important to recognize that a new network rapidly becomes a key cog. As such, the *ad hoc* approach to managing a dozen personal computers will not work so well with a network and server. It becomes a critical and central focus of operations. A network is a system, and creates its own work routing. A successful new network should be consistent in its behavior, available during work hours, functional in what it provides, and reliable, as Figure 12.17 illustrates.

## Log Work Requests and Network Changes

An organized network manager keeps a network notebook. The organized manager tracks all wiring, network communication hardware, and node hardware, and logs many other aspects of the physical network. These include wiring closet changes, work currently in progress, a wish list of major or minor network improvements, and both a problem log and a problem resolution log. The network notebook is represented in Figure 12.18.

### Databases and MIS

Often all these lists can be maintained across the network on a database for rapid access from any node. The database also coordinates information and simplifies the data entry and data tracking requirements, and concise reports can be generated to provide otherwise unavailable insight into local or global causes of network problems. Figure 12.19 shows the interrelationship among several tracked components and suggests the power inherent in database tracking.

- Reliable
- Consistent
- Available
- Functional

**Figure 12.17** Attributes of a successful network.

- Work completed on twisted-pair
- Work completed on hubs and central wiring
- Work in progress
- Wish list
- Problem log
- Problem resolution log
- Network traffic level log
- Network TRT log
- Symptom—solution workbook
- Version—compatibility workbook

**Figure 12.18** Network administration notebook.

Management information systems (MIS) yield flexibility to deal with change and uncertainty through information technology. They foster creative thinking and innovation, because information can improve both performance of the organization and the manager's ability to solve operational problems. "What if?" becomes easily tested when the data have been collected over time. Tools and the experience to use them are also already in place. MIS can also reduce the need for other problem-solving activities, because the tools and methodologies are already in place. It also requires additional resources not necessarily available.

However, the basic MIS technologies can be bootstrapped with networking technology to provide new opportunities otherwise not available within the narrow context of the network team. Figure 12.20 lists

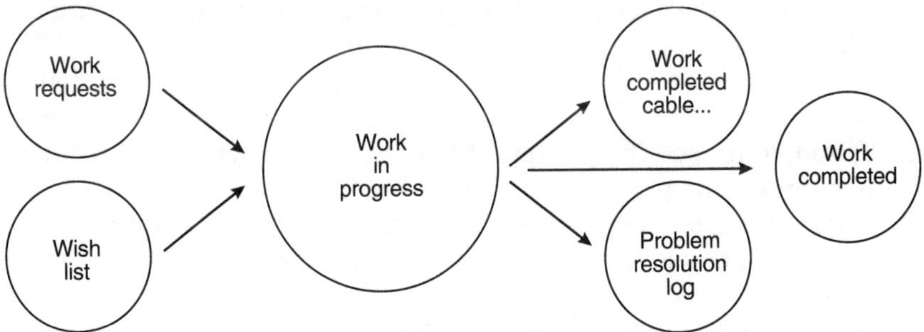


**Figure 12.19** Database interrelationships between work logs.

- Define the implications of network technology
- Construct relevant business scenarios
- Evaluate alternative network architectures
- Select a technical direction
- Establish a review process
- Uncover otherwise unknown relationships

**Figure 12.20** MIS and networking benefits.

these possibilities, while the next several illustrations represent database output or typed pages that a network manager might maintain. Changes to the network coax (Figure 12.21) and node-site transceiver drop cables (Figure 12.22) are logged on separate files or pages. Work in progress (Figure 12.23) provides a managerially inspired progress check on the status of all user- or management-initiated requests. A wish list (Figure 12.24) compiles those nonessential repairs or changes that should be completed. A problem log (Figure 12.25) tracks all network failures, and the problem resolution log (Figure 12.26) reflects the work actually completed.

Recurrent problems and users that seem prone to destroy equipment or software may regularly appear within the database reports. A database pays off by providing comparisons among network traffic statistics not otherwise noted. Correlations between collisions, volume, peak volumes, particular equipment manifestation, and cross-linked malfunctions are more easily recognized. Figure 12.27 maps this relationship.

Figures 12.28 and 12.29 illustrate two important traffic reports that can be generated from an on-line database. Other pertinent statistical information and formulae to generate such information are presented in Chapter 16.

## Backup

Backup of information, services, hardware, and labor, and sometimes even backup processing are important functions of network management. No network is fail-safe; malfunctions and invasions happen. In order to protect the organization, a backup policy is suggested. Chapter 18 details backups and redundancy issues at length.

A good portion of any network is resident in unique files that define the relationship of nodes on the network, the operations of the network itself, and, quite possibly, scripts that have been programmed to automate many arcane processes that have become complicated over time. This information usually has value to the organization. Network backup is, therefore, a crucial procedure to ensure network integrity and security. Chapter 18 details network backup, including data, equipment, and software, as critical operational concerns.

## Coordinating Network Disruptions

Network disruptions happen mostly by surprise, although some are planned. Those few times when downtime is actually planned, it is a good policy to inform the user community. It is a common courtesy. Users do not like surprises. If the user work schedule is disrupted by the network management team when advance notification was possible, users have every right to shout their displeasure. Also, the power the

*Work Completion Log: cable and wire*

| # | Date | Location | Repair | Tested |
|---|---|---|---|---|
| 34 | 4/6/91 | 30 m from PC | replaced lobe | good |

**Figure 12.21** Work completion: coaxial cables.

*Work Completion Log: MAUs and NICs*

| # | Date | Location | Repair | Tested |
|---|---|---|---|---|
| ~~107~~ | ~~4/6/91~~ | ~~@ soft lab~~ | ~~beacons~~ | ~~marginal~~ |
| 108 | 4/6/91 | no transmit | | not yet |
| 109 | 4/7/91 | @ soft lab | beacon? | still off |
| 110 | 4/8/91 | @ soft lab | hub 2, jitter? | |

**Figure 12.22** Work completion: taps and transceivers.

*Work in Progress*

| # | Date | Location | Repair | Status |
|---|---|---|---|---|
| 34 | 4/6/91 | 30 m from PC | new lobe | good |
| 108 | 4/6/91 | no transmit | | not yet |
| 109 | 4/7/91 | @ soft lab | beacons | still off |
| 110 | 4/8/91 | @ soft lab | bad jumper? | |

**Figure 12.23** Work in progress.

**Wish List**

| # | Date | Location | Repair | Due Date |
|---|---|---|---|---|
| 35 | 4/6/91 | node 32 | defragment disk | 4/11/91 |
| 36 | 4/6/91 | node 48 | defragment disk | 4/11/91 |
| 37 | 4/6/91 | node 48 | upgrade sftwr | 4/11/91 |
| 38 | 4/6/91 | node 48 | test perf...poor | 4/14/91 |

**Figure 12.24** Wish list.

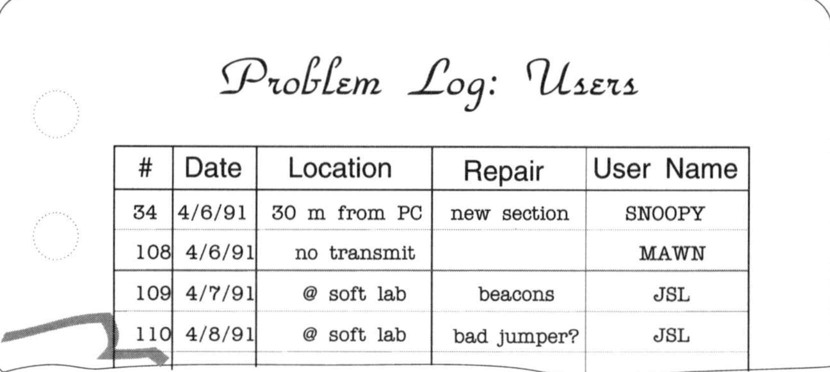

**Problem Log: Users**

| # | Date | Location | Repair | User Name |
|---|---|---|---|---|
| 34 | 4/6/91 | 30 m from PC | new section | SNOOPY |
| 108 | 4/6/91 | no transmit | | MAWN |
| 109 | 4/7/91 | @ soft lab | beacons | JSL |
| 110 | 4/8/91 | @ soft lab | bad jumper? | JSL |

**Figure 12.25** Problem log

**Problem Log Resolution**

| # | Date | Location | Resolution | Date |
|---|---|---|---|---|
| 34 | 4/6/91 | 30 m from PC | user happy w/fix | 4/6/91 |
| 108 | 4/6/91 | no transmit | OK | 4/24/91 |
| 109 | 4/7/91 | @ soft lab | user on net | 4/7/91 |
| 110 | 4/8/91 | @ soft lab | OK | 4/11/91 |

**Figure 12.26** Problem resolution log.

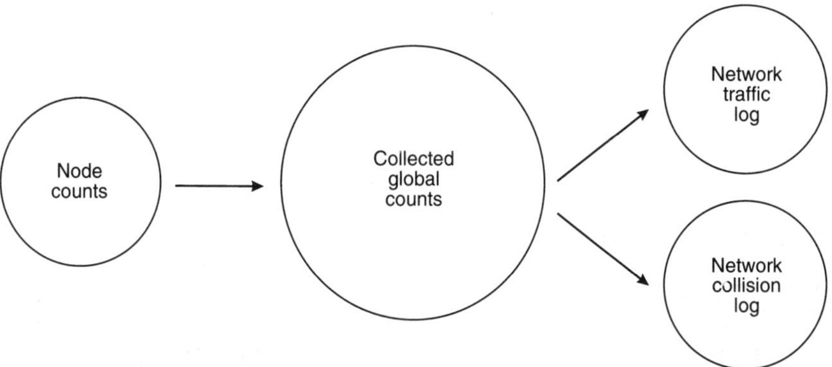


**Figure 12.27** Databases provide insight into network traffic problems.

*Network TRT Log*

| Date | Time | TRT | Notes |
|---|---|---|---|
| 4/6/91 | 8:12 | 15 | hub jitter... |
| | 11:30 | 35 | before lunch rush...normal |
| | 14:30 | 35 | Normal, despite user ? |
| 4/7/91 | 7:52 | 8 | No problems... normal |

**Figure 12.28** Network TRT log.

*Network Traffic Log*

| Node | Date | Packets | Percent | Notes |
|---|---|---|---|---|
| 34 | 4/6/91 | 525,678 | 0.110 | hub problem? |
| 108 | 4/6/91 | 34,580 | 0.005 | |
| | | | | |
| TOTAL | 4/6/91 | 4,457,820 | 1.000 | What a busy day! |

**Figure 12.29** Network traffic log.

user community wields in part affects the courtesy that the network administration group shows. If the user community has control over operations common to many DP departments, almost no courtesy will be shown. Whatever policy is applied, remember to be consistent. Users will assume that each change is a permanent improvement. A downtime schedule should include the actual period of downtime, warnings beforehand, and notification if the duration of downtime will exceed the initial schedule. Courtesy wins respect. Consistency breeds trust.

### Moving Equipment

Physical equipment moves can be planned events and, like scheduled downtime, should be coordinated with the user community for minimal disruptive effect. Few other events can erode valuable network management credibility more than bungled prearranged events. Problems are apt to occur and simple transitions are rare.

Inform those affected in the user community how much time is required for the actual change, what can go wrong, and what will happen if such problems arise. In order to achieve successful equipment relocation, set up parallel installations. Figure 12.30 illustrates one example in which a node connection can be installed and tested in advance of the actual node move. Other events, too, can be performed with such foresight. Also, moves may require extra parts, software tapes, extra hands. Plan for all exigencies, any surprises. Be aware that equipment or network configuration changes may have small but significant side effects. A little forethought will preserve that hard-earned respect.

## Vendor Support

Network installation and management is by nature becoming less of an *ad hoc* activity. Hardware and software components are rarely acquired from the same sources, and frequently do not coexist well together. Advanced network devices such as bridges, routers, and hybrid brouters require complex installation and continual monitoring and configura-

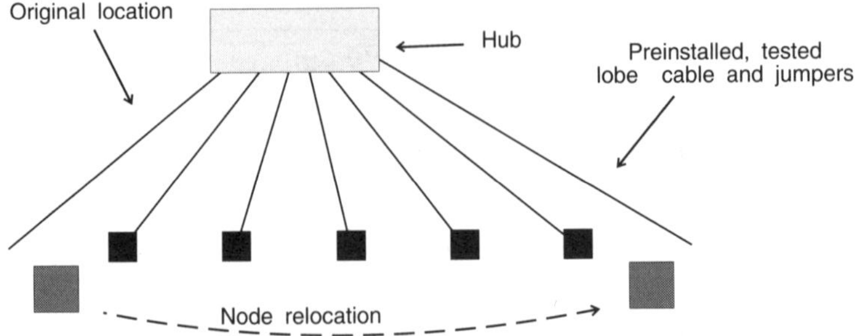


**Figure 12.30** Preplanned equipment relocation and parallel setups.

- How often are preventive (maintenance) services, such as new software releases, delivered, and how often are problems with these services reported?
- How long does it take to correct problems?
- How important is customer service for your company? Where does customer support fit in your organization's hierarchy?
- How many people provide support?
- How is the support function structured?
- Is support provided from many locations or a central site?
- Are product developers available for consultation?
- Do barriers to direct communication with developers exist?
- During what hours is support available?
- Can you talk to support personnel immediately? Do you have to make an appointment? Do you have to leave a message and wait for a return call?
- How are support calls passed along? For example, do you speak to an administrative person for customer identification, talk with first-level support, and then wait for a return call from second-level support?
- How is support handled during off-hours and holidays?
- What are the vendor's standards and goals for support? Areas to look for are the times for returning calls, code repairs, and successful completion of calls.
- What procedures are followed if the product doesn't work?
- Do support members have online access to notes made from prior conversations with other support members?
- Are reference numbers provided for verified program problems?
- Does the vendor provide a support brochure?
- Does the vendor follow up on all calls?
- Are there differences between pre- and postsale support? Ask current customers as well as the vendor.
- Is training offered? If it is, request a copy of training policies, schedule of classes, and an overview of course content. Check out references (past attendees) as to the quality, focus, and suitability for the courses.
- If the need arises, will the vendor work with other vendors?
- What procedures will be followed if the vendor must work with other vendors?
- What information must users have in hand before calling for support?
- Does the vendor supply a list of common questions typically asked to prepare the caller to answer questions and perhaps solve the problem with the typical answers?
- What ways, in addition to the telephone, can you communicate with the support department? By fax? Telex?
- Does the support staff have the ability to mirror a sequence of steps while they talk on the phone with you? Can they dial into your system and provide remote diagnostics?
- Is there a technician experienced in enhancing performance?
- Are they authorized to sell and repair the equipment and software for which your organization foresees a future need?

**Figure 12.31** Questions to ask your vendors.

tion. Vendor support is all too critical, and before building or expanding networks with a hodgepodge of components, consider the questions listed in Figure 12.31. Additionally, if you are considering leasing equipment or hiring a vendor to install and maintain your local area networks and enterprise-wide networks, give full weight to each of these questions. Poor vendor selection creates lasting conflict.[1]

## "Squeaky Wheel" versus Problem Resolution

As the squeaky wheel gets the grease, so, too, the loudest voice often gets the most response. In many situations, responding to the loudest voice lowers tension, cools tempers, and makes more people happier. As a side effect, however, such attention side-tracks normal planning and problem resolution. It diverts attention from fixing critical failures, performing preventative maintenance, and attending to a controlled agenda. Responding to the squeaky wheel may undermine management initiative, degrade the credibility of network administration, and ultimately strip decision-making responsibility from the network administration team. Therefore, the better policy is to plan network needs, assess network resources, determine both short-term and long-term network direction, and last, reach a detailed agreement with users as to network problem prioritization and resolution.

## Short-Term versus Long-Term Planning

Attention to the squeaky wheel underscores an attention to crisis-level response. While management of a new network or changeovers in management of a problem network may require crisis resolution, long-term success requires a long-term outlook. A manager should seek to maintain his or her job long term, seek to retain the management people on a long-term basis, and plan for long-term network growth, service growth, and technological change. Short-term planning resolves only immediate issues. Long-term planning attends to the configuration of network services over years. Figure 12.32 illustrates why neither of the areas covered by short-term and long-term planning can be overlooked for long.

## Easier Said than Done. . .

Network management is a difficult task. Matrix management impedes easy control of people and resources. It also raises the specter of squeaky wheel problem resolution, a policy apt to undermine network manage-

1 Modified from *Information Center Quarterly*, winter 1991.

| Short-term Planning | Long-term Planning |
| --- | --- |
| Repairs | Preventative maintenance |
| Upgrades | Performance problems |
| Equipment relocation | New technology |
| Labor problems | Strategic application of networking |

**Figure 12.32** Network short-term and long-term planning issues.

ment and divert attention from more pressing problems. The complexity of a network, the sheer size of a network, the number of possible failures and malfunctions, the overloading, and the technical complexity of not only the network but also the devices accessing that network, create a difficult job. Stress is often the norm. Furthermore, senior management usually is unwilling to allocate sufficient resources to resolve even the most pressing network problems; resource scarcity is likely.

For these reasons, network management is a difficult task. Respect is won grudgingly and lost easily. Radical changes, unless always successful, will undermine the network manager's authority; management conservatism will erode any authority to fix, change, or improve the network, the communication channels within the organization, or the satisfaction and status due the management team. Work hard for credibility. Maintain that credibility with carefully chosen words, respect, understanding, and accuracy. Promises are easy to make, but they are easier made than kept.

## Dos and Don'ts

Figure 12.33 concludes this chapter with a general-purpose list of management dos and don'ts. Add to this list as your experience dictates. Copy it and affix it to your wall, if you are so inclined. However, don't regard these few items as all there is to network management; "feel," experience, and other intangibles are learned with time.

| Do | Don't |
|---|---|
| Design a segmentable network | Overdesign |
| Adhere to specifications | iolate specifications |
| Pretest new components | Assume component functionality |
| Define an overall strategy | Mix standards |
| Define a user pricing policy | Forget to create LAN usage policies |
| Define a repair policy | Scrimp on technical labor |
| Install extra wiring | Install "just enough" wiring |
| Identify potential failure points | Mix untested equipment |
| Experiment before implementing | Ignore user requests |
| Gain experience | Assume that users understand |
| Search for trouble spots | Look for complicated solutions when simple ones may suffice |
| Promote preventative repairs | Overlook the organization's culture |
| Build credibility | Confuse management objectives |

**Figure 12.33** Network dos and don'ts.

# Part 4

## Network Troubleshooting

When the network fails there are various techniques to identify, locate, and repair problems. Many techniques are time-consuming without specialized tools like a multitester, a Token-Ring scanner, a transceiver tester, and a network analyzer. Because each of these tools is indispensable on a large, busy, or very critical network, the knowledge needed to use them and interpret their results is presented in separate chapters complete with photographs, illustrations, and tables.

Chapter 13 suggests practical tools that test, monitor, and analyze network status. When the network fails there are various techniques to identify, locate, and repair problems. Some techniques require specialized tools like a multimeter, a twisted-pair wiring scanner or time domain reflectometer, and a network analyzer.

Chapter 14 details the usage of a time domain reflectometer and twisted-pair scanner and the practical steps to check the usability of network hardware, and to verify correct installation. These tools also provide a highly desirable method to benchmark a network.

Chapter 15 describes the necessity for network management software, the network protocol analyzer, and how to identify, locate, and isolate suspected network problems.

Chapter

# 13

# Network Monitoring Tools

A network manager who administers a large or growing network is certain to experience slowdowns, bottlenecks, or downtime. In order to combat these common problems, a network manager should have network monitoring tools. Chapter 8 mentioned the need for certain installation equipment including cable cutters, pliers, screwdrivers, tap set, crimp set, soldering iron, integrated circuit (IC) extractor, flashlight, hammer, cable ties, and other such tools. Because the network is both a mechanical and software entity, complex analytical tools are needed to evaluate that installation. This network-monitoring tool kit which supplements the normal installation tools should include a cable tester, a time domain reflectometer, and network traffic-analysis software or a protocol analyzer. Not only are tools needed, but an understanding of how to use these tools and interpret their results is critical for effective network installation and maintenance. Token-Ring, unlike other "pipes," transmits invisible contents. While a plumber can see current water leaks and the results of past problems and see that a pipe is plugged up or running slowly, Token-Ring carries signals invisible to the eye without special viewing tools. Tools make signal leaks and bottlenecks visible.

## Wiring Tester

A wiring tester is a generic name referring to a multitester, continuity tester, a telephone line tester, or a scanner. Figure 13.1 illustrates a typical multitester. The multitester measures ohms, volts, and thus shows the basic condition of the wiring in terms of shorts, breaks, and other bad connections. This is a useful tool to check continuity of patch cord or panel connections. The continuity tester is even simpler and measures whether the two probes contacting metal form a complete circuit. The telephone line tester is a specialized tool for verifying that a modular plug is a live telephone circuit with a dial tone and that all pairs are connected in the proper places. Although a multitester or continuity tester is useful in jam, it does not compare to the utility of a

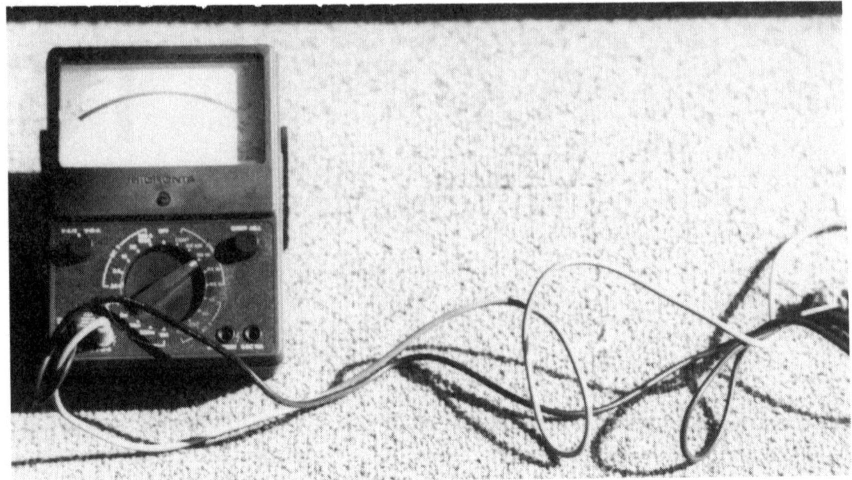

**Figure 13.1** A multitester (Radio Shack, Tandy Corporation).

scanner. The pair scanner is the most useful of these tools. It is basically a handheld time domain reflectometer and is outlined in the next section and subsequent chapter.

## Time Domain Reflectometer

The time domain reflectometer (TDR) uncovers breaks, shorts, and similar cabling anomalies. Figure 13.2 shows a typical bench-type unit with a built-in oscilloscope. The more common units for Token-Ring are the hand-help units, as shown by Figure 13.3. *Time delay* refers to the radar-like process employed to display the properties of wiring and location of any cable breaks. This technology is a significant refinement over continuity checkers and multimeters.

For example, the scanner or TDR will indicate whether a lobe cable is correctly wired, is attached to an active ring, and how long that lobe can be and still provide adequate network support. Chapter 14 specifies procedures for using this tool.

## Network Protocol Analyzer

The protocol analyzer verifies correct operation of a LAN based upon capture and parsing tokens and packets. A network manager is blind to network performance, capacity levels, and software transmission problems without such traffic monitoring capability. These tools can be either hardware-based or software applications which run on a standard node platform.

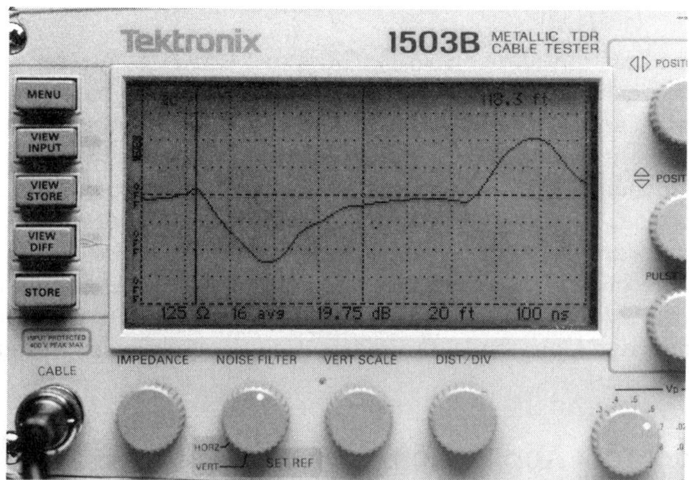


**Figure 13.2** A time domain reflectometer with oscilloscope. (Tektronix)

**Figure 13.3** A handheld Token-Ring scanner. (Microtest)

The analyzer performs the following functions. It computes *token rotation time* (TRT), channel utilization as a percentage of the transmission capacity, packet sizes, defective packets, packets with bad *cyclic redundancy check* (CRC), duplicate packets, and packets with user-defined parameters. Some decipher beacons to indicate a likely source of the ring failure. Most such tools can collect statistics around the clock to trace intermittent problems that are suspected but difficult to localize without constant supervision. Chapter 15 details the many additional features of a protocol analyzer and explains how to use this tool.

## CMIP and SNMP

Since the functionality of SNMP, CMIP, and CMOT somewhat overlap the functionality of a protocol analyzer, these software-based protocols are also discussed in Chapter 15. Although SNMP is a protocol monitoring and traffic-analysis tool, it is an effective database that is in effect a protocol analyzer. CMIP and transition CMOT also provide the ability to set alarms, establish automatic events, and initiate activities. Since most hardware-based analyzers can perform these tasks, CMIP represents more intelligent network monitoring and analysis software with the associated cost of a hardware-based analyzer. Refer to Chapter 5 for definitions and Chapter 16 for information on applying captured LAN statistics.

## Network Tool Application

Token-Ring is simple in design and increasingly complex in terms of daily operation. The network manager faces hardware, software, and traffic problems. As of yet, no network has been free from installation, operational, and mechanical problems. Without these problems, there would be no justification for a network manager. The complexity of these problems and the ability of the network manager to solve them justify the existence of that job. Some problems will be camouflaged. It takes an astute manager and network team to trace these problems and maintain a functioning network. A good tool is surely indispensable.

A multitester or continuity tester is a necessity given its insignificant cost and versatility. A full-featured TDR with video display screen and Polaroid camera is expensive and, as such, best employed by specialists who frequently install networks. The time spent learning how to use this tool well is usually unwarranted for most small corporate LANs. Instead, a pair or ring scanner is cost-effective and utilitarian for small LANs (10 to 50 nodes). This tool provides the most value when first installing a new LAN, expanding an existing network, or when debugging a LAN that is not reliable. This use of this tool is best learned before actually installing the LAN; in reality, it will probably be learned within two or three hours in crisis mode.

The protocol analyzer is a tool best ignored on small LANs, particularly Token-Ring. The beacon is a sufficient message to indicate ring hardware failure and provide some insight as to the location of the lobe or node failure. MAU, CAU, or hub indicator lights are more effective for debugging wiring failures. If necessary, the pair or ring scanner is sufficient to expedite isolation of wiring failures. Since training time and costs for learning the analyzer will easily equal or exceed the cost of the protocol analyzer, this tool is best suited for large LANs with internetwork hops or LANs supporting multiple protocols, or for an organization with multiple LANs and LANs of more than 70 nodes.

This should not to suggest that a protocol analyzer is useless on small LANs. The tool is designed to disassemble the protocol information from Token-Ring packets. Rather, the comprehensive tools—the suitcase-sized, full-featured $15,000 tools—are complex and generally unwarranted. A low-end model, generally under $2000, is sufficient for occasional use on the small LANs. A protocol analyzer is a good instrument for optimizing performance, uncovering LAN deficiencies, and for stressing the network.

These tools have overlapping functions. This section provides some insight into the overlapping functionality and limitations of each tool, as Figure 13.4 indicates. The multitester or continuity tester is a quick tool to demonstrate that a problem exists, while the scanner also indicates the exact position of that problem. The protocol analyzer provides strictly software information based upon information contained in Token-Ring frames. This reveals software problems, channel overloading, configuration errors, or software flaws. It can in some cases pinpoint the source of a beacon or failed node—if the ring is still physically complete. Since there are many conditions that will break a ring, the scanner is an important tool to locate those failures. A protocol analyzer for Token-Ring will not work on a broken ring. Figure 13.5 shows how each tool is best utilized.

| | Multi-tester | TDR | OTDR | Tester | Analyzer | SNMP | CMIP |
|---|---|---|---|---|---|---|---|
| Coaxial cable | ⊗ | ⊗ | . | . | . | . | . |
| Drop cable | ⊗ | ⊗ | . | ⊗ | . | . | . |
| Twisted-pair | ⊗ | ⊗ | . | ⊗ | . | . | . |
| Optical fiber | . | . | ⊗ | . | . | . | . |
| Wiring hub | ⊗ | ⊗ | . | . | . | . | . |
| Trans. Installation | o | ⊗ | . | ⊗ | . | . | . |
| Transceiver | o | ⊗ | . | ⊗ | o | o | o |
| Controller | . | . | . | . | ⊗ | ⊗ | ⊗ |
| NIC | . | . | . | . | ⊗ | ⊗ | ⊗ |
| Repeater | . | . | . | . | ⊗ | ⊗ | ⊗ |
| Bridge | . | . | . | . | ⊗ | ⊗ | ⊗ |
| Router | . | . | . | . | ⊗ | ⊗ | ⊗ |
| Gateway | . | . | . | . | ⊗ | ⊗ | ⊗ |
| Node level config. | . | . | . | . | ⊗ | ⊗ | ⊗ |
| Network config. | . | . | . | . | ⊗ | ⊗ | ⊗ |

**Figure 13.4** The overlapping functionality of network test equipment. The small solid bullets indicate a primary testing function, whereas the large hollow bullets indicate that the unit can provide minimal testing functions.

Token-Ring can fail to perform for a variety of reasons, as shown by Figure 13.6. Any of these conditions can severely affect the overall network response time. Some may cause a node or several nodes to fail, even when nodes are on different rings. An overloaded file server and a network fax saturating the network with images could defeat a LAN. The next two chapters show how to decipher such common problems using the scanner and the protocol analyzer.

| | Hardware | Software |
|---|---|---|
| **Physical level** | Multitester | TDR |
| | TDR | CMIP |
| | OTDR | |
| **Transmission level** | Tester | Protocol analyzer |
| | | SNMP |
| | | CMIP |

**Figure 13.5** Network test equipment utilization.

- Poor cable connections
- Faulty MAUs and hubs
- Faulty Token-Ring controllers
- Improperly configured network
- Excessive network traffic
- Overloaded node devices
- Overloaded servers
- Improperly configured software
- Defective software
- Overlapping network addresses

**Figure 13.6** Network failures uncovered by network test equipment.

Chapter

# 14

# Debugging with the Scanner

This chapter describes the pair scanner, the ring scanner, and time domain reflectometer, all three of which are variations on wire scanning tools based upon time domain reflectometry. This chapter shows the history, the functionality, usage, and alternatives to this technology. The time domain reflectometer (TDR) supersedes the multitester and continuity tester because it can provide the same electrical feedback as the multitester. Of note, the TDR is not a time *delay* reflectomer, as some people suggest. The ring scanners and pair scanners are just TDRs in a small, handheld format. The electronics and complex display capabilities are replaced by simpler LED displays; in some products, the display features are available through a downlink to a standard PC.

In addition to basic wiring continuity tests, the TDR will precisely locate a wiring short, open, or break relative to a wire endpoint. Furthermore, this test instrument, when used in conjunction with a camera, or serial port attachment to a PC, can blueprint a network. This aids in debugging the all-too-common network failure. The TDR locates twisted-pair wire perforations and twisted-pair wire shorts, and can identify an electrically defective modular or genderless connection. For Token-Ring networks, a *short* circuit means the TX- wire is somehow connecting or touching the TX+ wire, the RX- wire is somehow connected to the RX+ wire, or the TX wires are in contact to the RX wires. Signal is therefore diverted from its proper node. An *open* circuit means that there is a cut through one of the four wires or that one of the four Token-Ring signal wires is not attached correctly to a connector. A *break* means that all four of the Token-Ring signal wires are open, and thus not conducting signal. The break is usually indicative of a patch panel or connector failure, or damage to the twisted-pair wire. Figure 14.1 illustrates these three common wiring failures.

The pair scanner also can categorize the signal clarity of STP and UTP, the signal strengths, and wavelengths in use and any NIC transmitter on the fringes of those ranges. Since Token-Ring networks are rather

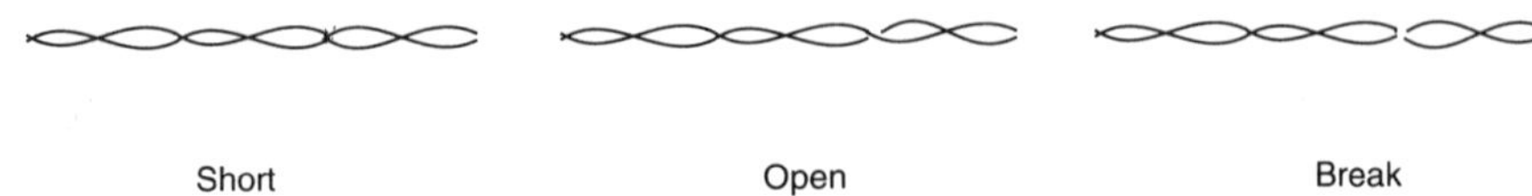


**Figure 14.1** Twisted-pair wiring circuit short, open, and break.

star-configurations, the scanner can verify that each node can accurately repeat and relay signals.

## Time Domain Reflectometer

Refer to Figure 13.2 for a photograph of a typical bench-type time domain reflectometer unit. This unit contains an oscilloscope display, a TV-like screen which displays a trace curve on a grid. The technique applied by this tool was developed in the early 1950s for locating cabling breaks in high-tension wires. The TDR was further refined specifically for use in tracing cable television broadband problems. It was used to locate shorts, breaks, cable impedance variances, and overloads on city-wide installations, but has been modified for use in baseband and broadband computer communication environments; the problems encountered are identical. Figure 14.2 shows several handheld scanners.

The TDR unit connects onto the network in place of a node. The standard TDR or pair scanner will not send out phantom voltage and will not repeat signals. It will just view the lobe wire (or a trunk wire). It thus can remain connected onto the network at all times. Some ring scanner units (configured for IBM Token-Ring) will send out the phantom voltage to activate the MAU relays, but they will not repeat token or packet signals. As such, the scanner will disable the network; downstream nodes should institute beacons to indicate a failed upstream node. It is an important tool in a crisis when a network fails completely. At such times few other tools, especially network software tools which depend on a functioning network, can operate; only noncomputer, nonsoftware tools operate when a network is broken.

The TDR operates somewhat like radar. It sends a voltage signal pulse from the attachment point (typically at the MAU or NIC connector) down the network media, as illustrated in Figure 14.3.

Note well, however, that this pulse is not compatible with most network protocols. The pulse may match normal network voltage levels or use a different voltage and wavelength. In any event, it will disrupt normal network traffic if the MAU or hub is enabled. In other words, testing a live network is apt to spawn continuous beacons. Reiterating,

**Figure 14.2** Typical handheld scanners. (Microtest)

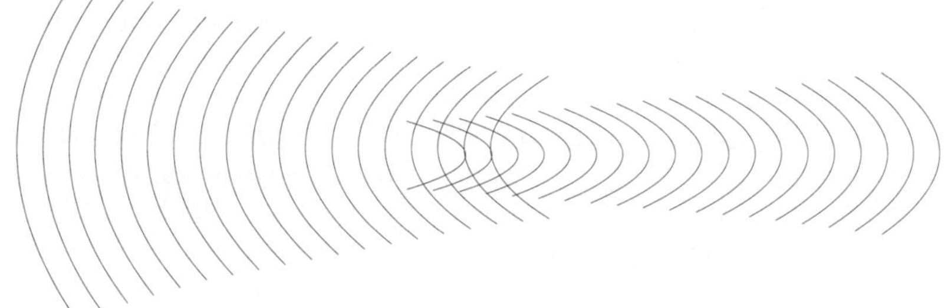

**Figure 14.3** The TDR sends a signal which reflects from anomolies.

many Token-Ring testers will emulate the phantom voltage to test the performance of the MAU relays. Because the TDR knows nothing about network protocols, for example in the case of Token-Ring, the TDR signal will override token and data traffic. Any node that is transmitting a valid packet will soon see that the packet was corrupted. As a consideration to network users, before attaching these devices to a network, inform them that network performance may degrade due to the testing. On the other hand, an individual lobe can be tested without network repercussions if the line is bypassed from the MAU or hub.

## Propagation Velocity

The TDR must be set for signal propagation velocity, wire ohms and voltage, and signal degradation over distance. Some pair scanner units will sense the impedance and signal speed and assess whether the cable is of sufficient quality for use in Token-Ring. Some units will assess whether a lobe is qualified for 4 Mbits/s or 16 Mbits/s operation, and if not, why not, or determine the maximum qualified length for that lobe. Be sure to set the correct propagation velocity for the wire that you are testing. Pulses travel at different rates on different media, on different ages of wire, and on networks with excellent connectors and installation. Note that STP increases signal attenuation (signal strength decay and dispersion), but minimizes the crosstalk inherent on UTP. Measurements displayed by the TDR will be inaccurate if this information is not correctly set.

## Interpreting Results

All obstructions reflect the signal with various signatures which are read from an oscilloscope or numerical display. These signatures must be learned as their interpretation is an art. Patch panels, splices, connectors, different grades and ages of cable, and, of course, breaks and shorts in the wire are visible in the oscilloscope display. The same is analogous for optical networks. Connectors, media attachment units, media breaks or shorts, excessive bends, and segments that are too long are visible in the display. On a digital TDR unit (typically the hand-held scanner) lacking a visual display, these anomalies are visible as deviations from the normal numerical display or by a red indicator light.

See Figures 14.4 through 14.6 for samples of TDR oscilloscope results. The reticule grid—vertical and horizontal lines that run through the middle of the oscilloscope display—is set at 000 or 085 m. Each horizontal grid line is about a meter. The large spikes represent the 6-m (20-ft) test lead.

Figure 14.4 shows a break in a cable. Breaks caused by overextending the bending radius of twisted-pair wire or cuts through a wire pair, or radio-frequency interference from powerful sources (such as transformers, high-intensity lamps, and other electrical cables) show as large bends, spikes, and kinks in the display. Faulty NICs or MAUs show up as a waveform different from that of a functioning unit—it usually lacks a large spike. If nonstandard or old wire is inserted to replace a defective or damaged section of twisted-pair, the TDR will show this with a large pulse deflection. The test pulse wave will reflect with a dramatic difference in height, and with sufficient art one can interpret these deviations. The handheld scanners will indicate these anomalies with indicator lights or by reports downloaded to a PC.

The oscilloscope CRT also shows distance to the anomaly which is overlaid in the photographic samples. If the Token-Ring wire is measured at installation time and properly blueprinted, any anomaly such as that shown in Figure 14.5 illustrates an unconnected lobe cable. For example, if the TDR

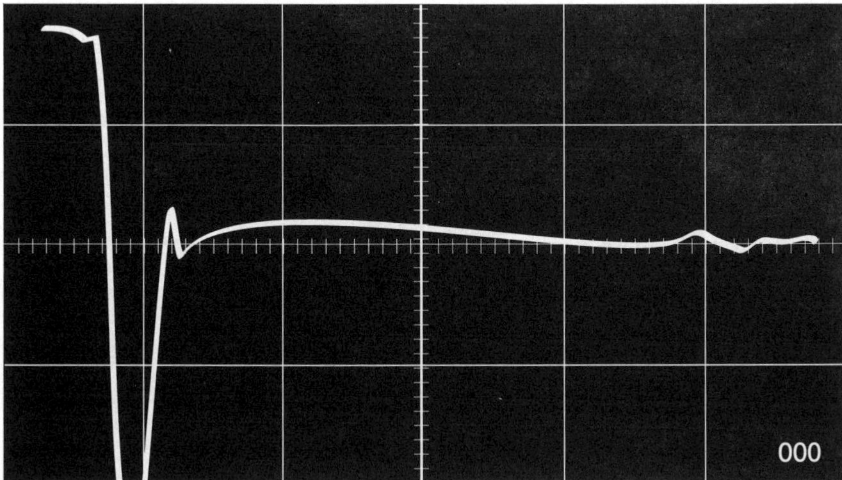


**Figure 14.4** TDR display of a break in the cable. The break shows as the "u-shaped" line that runs off the display. Shorts are identical in shape, but appear inverted as "n-shaped" lines.

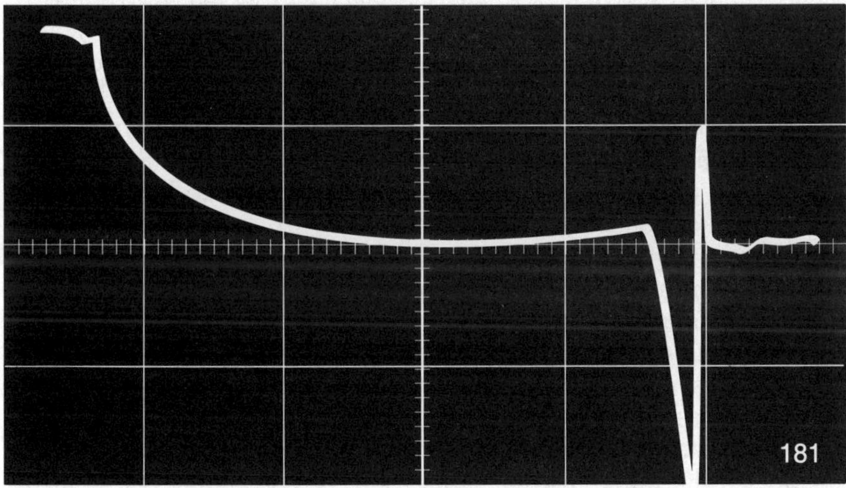


**Figure 14.5** TDR display of unconnected lobe cable. The spike at the far right is a false reflection caused by the TDR signal striking air. The display would show a flat line to the right of the center scale if the air offered no impedance.

showed a similar problem at 200 m on a blueprinted 200-m twisted-pair lobe, this would be an open circuit clue that the distant connector was installed incorrectly, or that the fingers on the genderless connector have failed. Figure 14.6 pictures this common installation problem.

As another example, if the display indicates the network length is longer than specified, the genderless connectors may be stuck open.

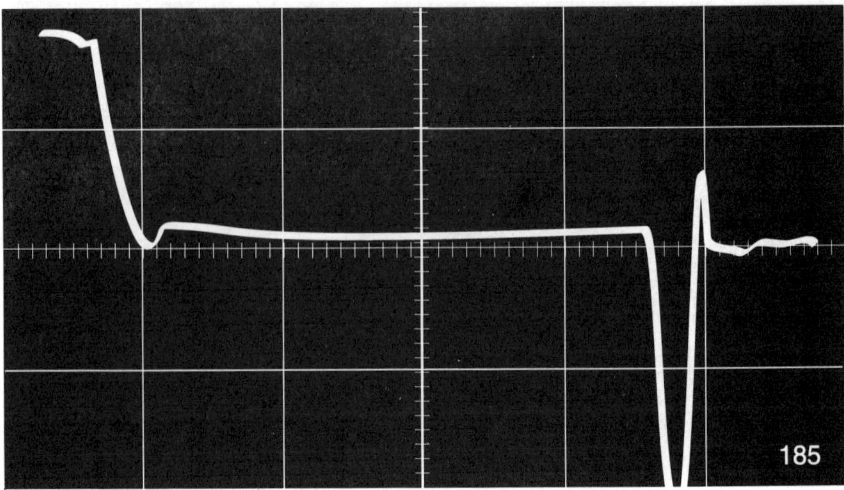


**Figure 14.6** TDR display of a missing genderless connector (pins could be improperly aligned, bent, broken, or missing). Note that this may not be observable via the TDR directly. Instead, a missing or unattached connector would show without a full spike or as a deviation from the expected wave pattern.

Similarly, a network MAU without a proper RI/RO patch cable or terminator (that is, actually, a logical ring completion) will fail to operate properly and disable the network; this situation will not normally pose a problem for a TDR unless the network is measured for ARL or trunk length. The open ring will fail the length test. A second indication of missing ring closure or improperly installed connectors is a display that is mirrored beyond the blueprinted network length, as Figure 14.7 indicates. This happens because the wave strikes the end of the wire, finds a medium with a different transmission quality, and reflects back down the cable inversely as shown. This is similar to the transmission characteristics of light when it passes from one medium, like air, through another medium, like glass, and back into air. Depending on the reflective angle of incidence, the image will be deflected. A mirror image occurs at the $90^{\circ}$ deflection of an improperly terminated end; the image will cease at hubs or MAUs. Handheld scanners usually will indicate a lobe flaw on a loopback test. The loopback test requires that a special genderless connector is attached at the opposite end of the lobe wire to *loopback* signal originating from the scanner back to the scanner.

Series inductance (evident as a scrape or break through the STP wire shield) shows as a positive pulse followed by a negative pulse. The last common wave form shows that the network cable impedance is out of specification, as would happen when improper cable is installed. This is typical when voice-grade UTP of insufficient quality is applied for

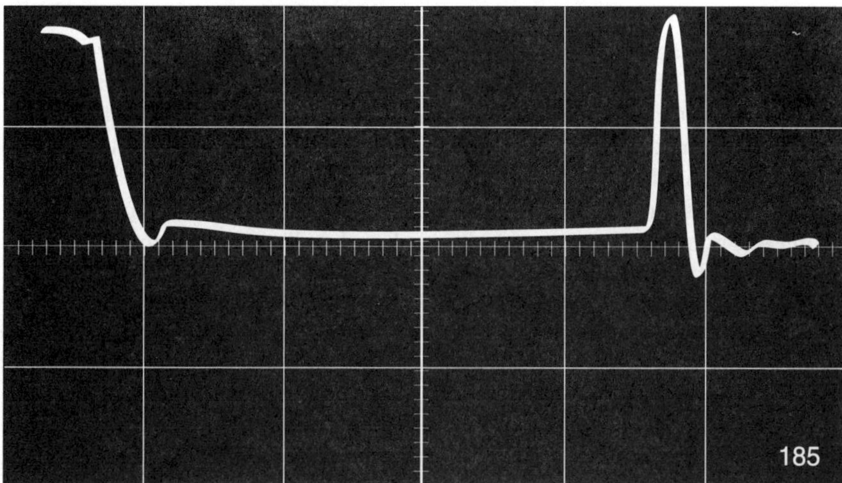


**Figure 14.7** TDR display of a short in the vicinity of the distant connector (at 185 m). As in Figure 14.5, the spike at the far right is a false reflection and has the same structure as the image in the photograph in this figure. The display would show a flat line to the right of the center reticule, if the air offered no impedance.

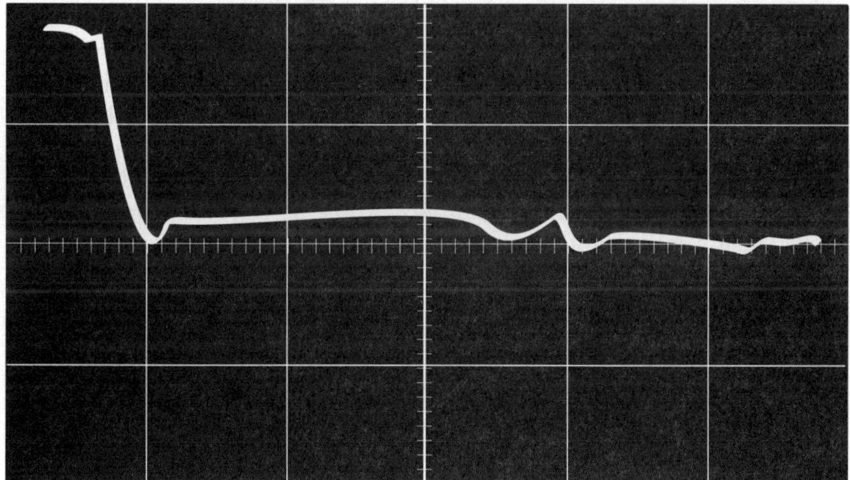

**Figure 14.8** Twisted-pair signal reflection caused by different types of wire.

Token-Ring lobes for runs longer than 30 to 50 meters. A series of alternating pulses would suggest this problem. Figure 14.8 details a TDR image caused by spliced twisted-pair wire with different transmission characteristics.

It is important to realize that since Token-Ring is logically a ring, any break or short in the ring will halt all network operations. This does include failure to properly attach RI/RO cables to a single MAU or to improperly connect them when there are many MAUs. Breaks are more common than shorts. Pairs that crossover will break the network, a live telephone circuit in place of the proper LAN lobe certainly breaks the circle, and partial media connections or failed punchdown ties will halt the network. While node beacons may provide general indications where the break is, the scanner or TDR is the superior tool for actually locating and fixing short circuits, open circuits, or breaks. These tools supersede the multitester because they accurately position the problem. There are also certain problems that cannot be diagnosed by just a multitester with any immediacy. These include bad wire, wrong grade of wire, radio- frequency interference, internal flaws, and mismatched sections. While a multitester will identify that one of these problems exists, it will not pinpoint the problem so that it can be categorized or localized, and diagnosed.

Without a TDR, the course of action would be to segment the ring progressively until the problem is localized sufficiently. Since Token-Ring is a star, each lobe or trunk is accessible and can be individual removed from the ring. Power-off workstations and they will be logically removed from the ring. Disconnect lobe cables or remove jumpers at the patch panel to physically remove workstations from the ring.

Visual inspections are time-consuming and often fruitless. The time requirement for such a search is excessive and demonstrates why the scanner is the tool of choice. A full-featured TDR will also send pulses continuously down the network twisted-pair wire. While jabber and signal jitter can be diagnosed with the TDR, there is no ingenious means to locate a NIC with the TDR other than as an endpoint on a lobe cable. As with a multitester, more complex problems require more complex tools. In this case, a software or hardware problem requires more than a hardware solution. This is best solved with a protocol analyzer.

## Blueprinting

The time domain reflectometer and handheld scanner with serial downlink capability are the best available instruments to effect physical network blueprinting. The TDR, in conjunction with a film recorder or screen camera, can illustrate the internal workings of the network wiring. These photographs or data downlinks (from scanner to PC) form a record against which future problems can be compared. It is a map of permanence. Figure 14.9 demonstrates the type of information that could be logically included in a careful ring scanner analysis. Figure 14.10 shows a representative cabling blueprint with notations.

Last, note that many integrated and specialized communications chips may incorporate TDR functionality within the chip themselves. Examples include several chip sets from Intel and National Semiconductor. Although software to utilize this function is not yet available,

| Lobe | Length | Status |
|---|---|---|
| RI | 6.0 | Ok |
| RO | 6.1 | Ok |
| 1 | 70.4 | Ok |
| 2 | 66.2 | Ok |
| 3 | 56.0 | Ok |
| 4 | 56.0 | Ok |
| 5 | 56.0 | Ok |
| 6 | 56.0 | Ok |
| 7 | 46.8 | Ok |
| 8 | 98.2 | Atten. |

**Figure 14.9** Ring scanner data downloaded to PC.

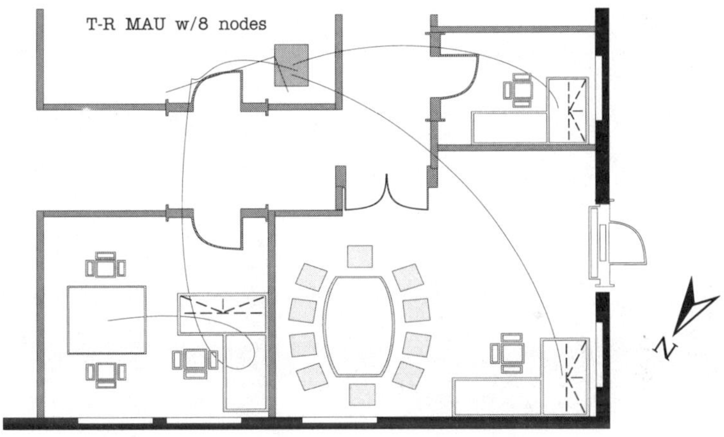


Bldg. 4, North Corner, 2nd floor (4-15-1991)

**Figure 14.10** This annotated instant photograph shows network documentation appropriate for a careful blueprinting.

expect that it will become an important selling feature because it can simplify network management. Specifically, when the TDR function is combined with protocol analysis, building true topological (although linear) maps representing the network is simple. Reflectometry provides distances to wiring anomalies for each node lobe that can be matched against sent and return protocol packets. The packets provide node names (OSI or Internet addresses) that are matched to physical locations for network nodes. Some anomalies will be connectors, minor flaws, or true faults. Not only is the combination of information provided by these two tools useful for intelligently blueprinting the network; but also it is useful for indicating potential failure points as well.

In actual practice a network manager and an assistant might use two TDRs to analyze the network and move them around from location to location. A centralized wiring closet simplifies this type of analysis because the units can be plugged into different locations at the patch pane. The TDR locates breaks and shorts, and indicates the occasional chattering or jittering NIC. Bad packets, duplicated addresses, and loss of tokens or packets require a protocol analyzer.

The next chapter details the use of this tool, and how it works. For more precise verification of network software errors, the protocol analyzer is the tool of choice. The workings of this instrument are described fully in Chapter 15.

Chapter

# 15

# Debugging with the Protocol Analyzer

The last chapter explained how to test the mechanical layers of Token-Ring. The handheld pair scanner and larger TDR test wire for proper functioning. These simple tools are limited to resolving hardware problems on single-ring Token-Ring networks; few tools provide real insight into malfunctions across multiple ring networks because bridges, routers, and gateways are effective "firewalls" to isolate network activities. The protocol analyzer is one tool that transcends these limitations.

However, the protocol analyzer is not an essential Token-Ring debugging tool. The protocol analyzer will not solve all critical Token-Ring problems. It will not resolve many hardware problems. It is required only for large LANs, multiple ring LANs, LANs with hops or WAN segments, newly installed or expanded LANs, or LANs with many problems. While the protocol analyzer is useful for performance analysis, balance its high cost, difficulty in learning how to use it, and the infrequent need to use it against the possibility of borrowing or renting the tool for brief periods or paying an expert with an analyzer for a few days. Since the Token-Ring protocol is deterministic in that a token circulates around the ring with some consistency, a protocol analyzer is necessary *only* in special cases; most Token- Ring failures are hardware-based or wiring-induced. When LANs or enterprise networks support multiple protocols—examples include NetWare, IPX, TCP/IP, 802.3, and OSI—the need for protocol analysis increases. Large and multiple segment Token-Ring LANs may benefit from the exclusive use of a specialized hardware-based protocol analyzer.

In fact, the firewall is seen as increasingly representative of the operational mentality applied when interconnecting multiple LANs. Although the firewall is effective for isolating individual LANs from the effects and failures in other segments, the firewall may also, as a result, limit the scope of protocol analysis. To some degree CMIP overcomes the firewall. Some vendors provide *remote probes* for incorporation in the rings or segments of interconnected LANs.

Many network failures can be traced to software that transcends the physical layers of Token-Ring, network loading characteristics, and firmware, which is software loaded into a specialized hardware processor. This type of failure requires network management software and protocol analysis. The management process is based upon the collection of relevant network operating statistics like throughput rates, errors, beacons, ring recoveries, source and destination addresses, and overhead. Protocol analysis is a process where you view the transmission protocols, most likely IEEE 802.2 LLC or 802.5 Token-Ring frames, IPX or NetBIOS data layer elements like MAC-level frames and datagrams.

The tools available consist of network communication protocol-based "software" such as Simple Network Management Protocol (SNMP), Common Management Information Protocol (CMIP), and the CMOT implementation, workstation-based tools, including Sun Microsystem's NFS-based *NETSTAT, PERFMON*, TCP/IP-based *PING*, or a protocol analyzer, which is a stand-alone computer, network interface card, and data collection and analysis software. Increasingly, as the sophistication of networks and software improves, expect to see more protocol analysis software, including tools such as the Protolyzer. They empower the network communication hardware to perform loop-back tests, add scanner and TDR functionality, and correlate this information with performance metrics.

The process of locating intermittent transmission failures with hardware testers is a random proposition. Such failures require more analytical techniques and a different network monitoring tool. A generic network monitor, also called a *protocol analyzer*, is the right tool for locating such software-based failures. It provides information to solve network problems. The protocol analyzer collects network traffic data, reports the LAN status, and many different variables, and converts that data into statistics, while some analyzers with sophisticated statistical packages can chart numerical results for visual analysis. The protocol analyzer confirms perceived performance degradation with hard evidence. This is a very important tool to verify bridge, router, and gateway functionalities, particularly now that they are so complex.

## Network Management Protocols

Hardware protocol analyzers may become antiquated as network management protocols are incorporated into networks and as Token-Ring hubs become more sophisticated in debugging media- and performance-level errors. Protocols such as SNMP, CMIP, and the CMOT overlap many of the features provided by stand-alone analyzers; in some cases they provide even more powerful features. Chapter 5 described these important three protocols. All these tools, including the protocol analyzer, collect and retain network performance statistics. Such information is important to assess reliability, work throughput, and functionality of any network, whether simple or enterprise-wide. Nonetheless, network management protocols often have blind spots, fail to route across bridges, routers, and gateways, or ignore Token-Ring hardware and software variants. Additionally, older networks and mixed networks with wired and wireless components likely lack the required network management protocol *agents* required for complete data capture and performance analysis. This comprises the major difference between hardware analyzers and software counterparts. Networks with components in excess of 20 percent unmanaged are best monitored with external protocol analysis tools; do not rely upon SNMP-or CMIP-derivative protocols with an agency requirement.

## Network Management Software

Network management software represents a new application area. These utilitarian tools automatically map the network matching node numbers with the corresponding addresses. They also determine the physical layout of the network by using the built-in TDR functions found in most network access chip sets (such as are found in the Intel or National Semiconductor integrated network chips). Network blueprints are otherwise very time-consuming to construct. Perhaps the most important feature provided by network management software is an ability to interpret captured network statistics. These assessments and suggestions are valuable for tuning networks, recognizing physical limitations, and uncovering any violations of the network specifications. Additionally, some network management software can intelligently act upon alarms to segment the network, reroute network traffic to underutilized alternate paths, and perhaps even disable malfunctioning (chattering or jittering) network devices.

## Protocol Analysis

The protocol analyzer is a computer workstation (or specialized software running on a standard network node) that is a network node. It requires access through one connection of a multiport access unit or hub. The analyzer can send and receive Token-Ring packets just as any other workstation does. Figure 15.1 shows one such unit. The analyzer watches the network for all Token-Ring packets, not just for signals directed to its node. The protocol analyzer is said to be "promiscuous" because it "eavesdrops" on all nodes in the network and potentially can capture any packet. It is a complicated tool in order to match the full network bandwidth and compile relevant statistics in real-time.

Commensurate with this complexity, it provides detailed information to trace complicated problems. A protocol analyzer listens to the signal on the local area network and finds a packet with known source and

**Figure 15.1** A protocol analyzer (Network General Corp.).

node destination, a multicast, or a broadcast destination. Packets with improper addresses, logical addresses for other rings or subnets, and non-responsive addresses represent network errors and inefficiencies. The analyzer must also listen and identify jitter, beacons, ring recoveries, and misaligned signals on the local network. Furthermore, this tool must be able to identify packets derived from and destined for remote gateways. Anonymous packets must be filtered and captured for analysis and eventual problem resolution.

A Token-Ring network carries traffic for many different purposes, as outlined in Figure 15.2. The consistency of traffic varies by load rate, by source and destination, and by peak characteristics. Control of the network and proper management require an understanding of the flow of packets. Since hardware testers only indicate the status of the physical plant, another tool like the protocol analyzer provides input for network use, load, consistency, resources distribution, and implied resource allocation decisions.

Thus, the protocol analyzer is an important tool for network management. Although software tools, such as PERFMON or NETVIEW, are invaluable for network analysis, a full-function protocol analyzer is a safe investment for a network of significant size or complexity; generally, this means multiple rings, or networks with multiple protocols (e.g. ARCnet, Token-Ring, Ethernet, and FDDI). This tool is useful for collating error

- Virtual terminal support
- File transfer
- Electronic mall
- Network file services
- Network print services
- Network node data backup
- Network file system support
- Database client-server
- Network utilities
- Network programs
- Network output services
- Network facsimile
- Distributed processing applications
- Phone integration
- Voice mail
- Online conferences
- Workgroup meeting scheduling and calendar functions
- Image storage and retrieval

**Figure 15.2** Typical Token-Ring traffic activities.

rates, performance levels, and internode traffic. Such statistics, when above normal ranges, provide direct correlations to network problems.

For example, a high rate for CRC errors for a specific source node might indicate a faulty Token-Ring controller, whereas a high jitter rate may indicate that its NIC is not sensitive enough or that the lobe wire is too long. In general, rates as captured with the protocol analyzer correlate to specific problems that are easily matched to their sources for quick diagnosis.

However, the protocol analyzer does have its limitations. It does not provide a model for understanding network performance loading, give specific indications of why a network is performing badly, or offer suggestions about how to improve the performance of bottlenecked segment within the context of a larger enterprise- wide network. The protocol analyzer frequently is unable to track networks supporting multiple protocols, such as IPX/SPX, TCP/IP, XNS, NetBIOS, and NetBEUI, although they are all much alike. It often ignores useful information from networks with multiple segments or extensions provided by routers and gateways. Although some vendors are adding expert systems to their protocol analyzers to address some of these shortfalls, true network analysis requires a performance queueing model, as described in Chapter 16. This network performance model, however, requires extensive network information as gathered by a protocol analyzer. Despite the protocol analyzer's limitations, for all of these other reasons, it is a critical tool for network management on large rings.

## Network Information

Network management software or a stand-alone protocol analyzer dedicated only to the task of watching the network is an important tool for network maintenance and evaluation. Token-Ring communication is a deterministic process. Basically, the token goes around the ring. A node that wants to transmit must get that token. If the token does not circulate once during the *target token rotation time* (TTRT), it is a certainty that something is wrong. Most problems on Token-Ring are obvious. Downstream nodes *beacon* when an upstream neighbor does not function correctly. MAUs *wrap* when trunks fail. An intelligent hub will drop misbehaving nodes and nodes that it thinks are misbehaving. Even when network traffic increases to extraordinary levels, it is still impossible to break the ring. The TRT will be longer and users will be unhappy with ring latency. Nonetheless, the network will still provide communications, albeit at a reduced speed.

## Network Performance Questions

In order to resolve higher-level network bottlenecks and Token-Ring traffic failures, the network administrator must view the network as a highway carrying data traffic. The network administrator seeks to answer operational questions as outlined in Figure 15.3 in order to evaluate the operational efficiency of any network. Understanding why these questions are relevant is the subject of the next section.

- What stations transmit on the network?
- Do stations correctly transmit?
- Do stations respond correctly to transmissions?
- Do stations defer to the busy network?
- What is the traffic volume?
- What is the traffic consistency?
- What is the length of messages?
- What is average peak loading?
- What is full capacity?
- What is the average intermessage timing (latency)?
- What is the average wait delay (response time)?
- Which stations talk to each other?
- Do messages have frame errors?
- Can some stations not reach other stations?
- Which nodes cause problems?
- Which rings or segments are overloaded?
- Do all stations comply to Token-Ring specification?
- Are gateways and repeaters performing to specification?

**Figure 15.3** Questions answered by the protocol analyzer.

## Heisenberg Uncertainty Principle

If the monitoring equipment actively requests and captures information, the process itself skews the results. Since every node on Token-Ring must capture, regenerate, and rebroadcast the packet signal, and since a protocol monitoring node is an active device, the inserted monitoring node will add between 2 and 32 ms delay to the TRT. It is also quite likely that file service requests, information probes, and process swap requests performed in the pursuit of network status data will generate network loading in addition to that of the base-level network traffic. The essence of the Heisenberg Uncertainty Principle is that the active process of observing an event alters the outcome of that event. Passive monitoring, on the other hand, watches each broadcast packet without accessing or affecting the network. This eliminates performance losses and potentially obviates any speed limitations that the monitoring actually seeks to chronicle. Unlike most vendor-supplied software tools, most protocol analyzers provide passive monitoring.

## Vendor-Specific Limitations

Most vendors of network workstations provide resident software tools to track network access and usage for individual workstations. Some vendors even provide software that will measure network usage. Choose software and hardware that conforms to the SNMP or CMIP standards. This provides an agency address for SNMP or CMIP data collection. Hardware and software lacking in this regard are effectively invisible to the management protocols. If these software tools are accurate and not approximate, an analyzer may be unnecessary.

However, vendor-supplied network monitoring software tools will exhibit the same flaws and faults as their workstations and overlook some types of problems. Therefore, a specialized device is required to capture and parse all types of network packets. This is particularly pertinent for mixed protocol and multiple hop networks. The protocol analyzer fills this function because it is protocol-independent. The analyzer can view all IEEE 802.3 (Ethernet) and Token-Ring packets that conform to TCP/IP, HPnet, XNS, DECnet, OSI, OSI (FDDI), NetBIOS, NetBEUI, SPX, or any other "standards." The tool passively captures a burst signal containing a Token-Ring frame, then parses this packet to whatever the upper- or lower-level protocols dictate. Within this framework, SPX information and IPX control information, for example, can be viewed without reliance on questionable network-level software.

Some workstation vendors build analyzers as part of their product line. In general, it is a good management practice not to rely on single solutions in this specific case; it is desirable generally to install networks with components from a single vendor. Test equipment is sometimes better acquired from a competitor. These backup and alternative methods are reasonable. Therefore, consider purchasing a protocol analyzer from an independent vendor so that any vendor-specific problems or incompatibilities to "standard" Token-Ring can be uncovered.

## The Role of Network Monitoring

Although Token-Ring can be viewed as analogous to a party-line telephone network, at other times a highway analogy is more appropriate. Since Token-Ring is a deterministic medium, certain traffic models represent Token-Ring's capacity, throughput, and timing attributes with a high degree of accuracy. These statistical models are presented in Chapter 16, but in this chapter the emphasis is placed upon the methodology for analytically tracing network problems by deciphering transmission packets, counts, and rates. The mathematical details underpinning Token-Ring follow later.

## Understanding Network Performance

Token-Ring is a purely deterministic transmission medium. Network node stations transmit when they capture a token, transmit for a duration not to exceed the token hold timer, and finally release that token when the transmitted packet circulates the ring and returns to that source node. Burst mode and early token release add a random feature to Token-Ring; to date, these have been rarely implemented. [Should you foresee a need to improve multiple hop performance by adding burst mode, or maintain a large ring populated with very small acknowledgment packets (under 200 bytes), specify a protocol analysis tool that supports these protocol enhancements.] Since Token-Ring (versions in common usage) assumes a minimum TRT, there can be no "tailgating." Additionally, traffic speed is enforced at 16 Mbits/s. Overloads and traffic problems tend to occur at the nodes themselves, barring wiring or hardware problems. Network problems can be grouped in a hierarchical progression. It is usually worthwhile to check for node hardware problems before searching for network hardware failures. Likewise, it is usually best to search for node software problems before searching for more global network bottlenecks, incompatibilities, or failures.

In order to monitor network performance, it is important to know how many nodes there are on the network, and which actually transmit. The first order of network problems occurs when nodes do not transmit correctly. This is usually indicative of improperly specified hardware or network software, or defective components. Likewise, nodes may not respond to transmissions (including beacons). The analyzer gathers measurements to pinpoint these problems.

Once the deterministic network hardware problems are resolved, the second order is to compute the actual traffic load. Each and every piece of equipment may function correctly. Systems may be reliable. Nevertheless, a network may perform slowly and erratically. This is usually indicative of an overloaded transmission channel.

The most significant network measurement is the packet count, which tells how many packets, good or bad, have been transmitted on the network. This count can be subdivided into good packets and bad packets, by source and destination, by characteristics of packet length, type, frequency, or by error condition. Figure 15.4 groups these items in a matrix framework with practical implications.

Basic network monitoring is the process of capturing packets during a known time frame since problems occur within an interval of time, or can be pegged to a certain event in time. Therefore, packet volume (or throughput) is an important measurement. The consistency of volume is another important unit because inconsistency creates traffic bottlenecks that frequently do not clear; traffic consistency will be discussed in the next chapter. If network problems occur and the assumption is that the network is overloaded, volumes and peak volume statistics may validate this theory. However, it is important to compare observed volume to a theoretical capacity.

Other areas of network transmission problems are the degenerative transmission situations that occur when packets are defective, long, short, misaligned, wrongly addressed, or incompatible with the network standard. The search for the cause of these problems transcends statistical measurements because bad packets have to be repeated until they are received correctly. Bad packets can flood a network and halt its effectiveness. In order to expose any sources for bad packets, defective packets must be examined for content, and the packet fields should be parsed and viewed, as Figure 15.5 illustrates.

In fact, protocol variances usually show in address discrepancies, length or type of field variations, or the LLC and upper-level protocol fields contained within the actual Token-Ring data field. If underlying causes for

| Good packets | Bad packets |
|---|---|
| Length | Beacons |
| Type | Short |
| Frequency | Long |
| | Misaligned |
| | Frame errors |
| | FCS errors |
| | Protocol errors |
| | Stray signals |

**Figure 15.4** Network packet measurements. These measurements are also useful when subgrouped by packet source and destination.

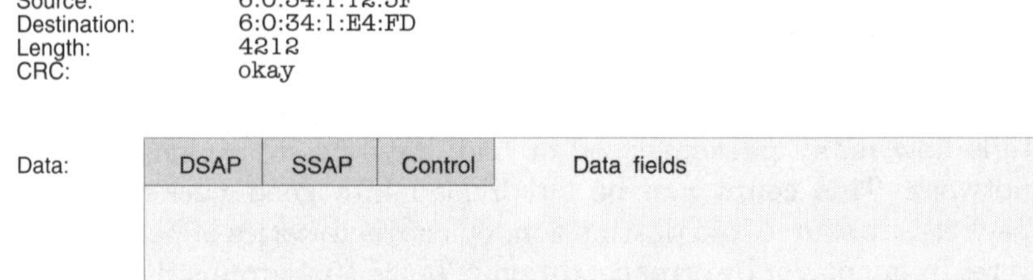


**Figure 15.5** View of the decoded packet, data only.

corrupted packets, address discrepancies, or mismatched upper-layer protocols are to be exposed, packets must be captured and dissected.

## Corrupted Packets

Comparisons of rates for short, long, and corrupted packets are important statistics, also. Damaged packets imply a hub, MAU, or lobe wire problem, a defective Token-Ring NIC, late acquisition of the frame or lack of synchronization, problems with signal regeneration or crosstalk, or outside noise. A damaged packet usually has a bad checksum, or *cyclic redundancy check* (CRC). Short, long, or damaged packets imply faulty software or hardware at a workstation. Statistics on corrupted packets should focus attention on the root causes of problems rather than on some ephemeral "global" problem. Excessive numbers of short, long, or defective packets could imply that transmission from a NIC was interrupted or that the transmitting workstation did not have the token but still transmitted. These corrupted packets could also indicate that the ring is supporting a NIC configured at the incorrect transmission speed or a NIC with a bad clock crystal.

A protocol analyzer with a robust software package (such as the Protolyzer) eases the difficulty in calculating these items because it will automatically tally packet counts, calculate percentage rates, and graph trends. Graphic display of these items lends more meaning and can show trends not otherwise noticeable. However, even with a less satisfactory software package, the basic information can be collected and downloaded or rekeyed to a spreadsheet program for the same results.

## Packet Counts

At a minimum, some metrics are required to compare network performance over different time frames. Another network status indicator, in addition to the TRT and the error rate, is a packet count. This number can be compared against a count from another day to see if unusually heavy traffic is the reason for perceived performance problems. For example, if there were 15,000,000 packets today versus 12,000,000 packets yesterday—a 20 percent increase—the magnitude of this difference would explain why performance has suffered, assuming no significant change in the TRT. It all depends on the "burstiness"—a general term describing the sudden requirement to transmit large numbers of packets on a network with an otherwise predictable load—and time of day distribution of that extra workload. Sometimes, although less frequently, burstiness can also refer to a network load with great variance in packet sizes. An even more useful statistic would be a packet transmission rate per time period, called a *traffic rate.* While a packets-per-day rate is useful for comparison, more immediate packet counts are better. Counts per second, per minute, or per hour constitute a traffic rate. These counts allow comparisons during the shorter intervals within which most Token-Ring problems occur.

## Statistics for Network Planning

The number of good packets is irrelevant until correlated with other information. By combining the number of good packets transmitted (rather than the total packet count) with either the lengths of each packet or average length of transmitted packets, a transmission-level count is generated. This is a *bits-per-second* (bits/s) figure. Other literature uses a "bps" acronym. Every manager needs an indication of how much work is actually accomplished for planning growth, managing new tasks, and maintaining a functioning network. The TRT is practical since it increases linearly as a function of packet size and number of stations, and is a linear proxy for network latency. Latency is a better measure, but is usually too difficult to calculate. Usage rates aid planning by providing a nearly independent statistic. It is nearly independent because as the network grows and the load increases, response time decreases and less work can be completed within any interval. Consequently, usage rates are apt to be lower per node on a saturated network than on a nonsaturated network. Usage rates are more consistent.

The usage rates also show type and quantity of work by node. They provide the necessary data to make informed network planning decisions. Chapter 18 presents many options to tune network performance. The problem remains identifying what should be tuned.

## Network Traffic Composition

A subset of nodes will have higher rates of usage than other nodes as a consequence of the work performed, or as a result of those nodes' need to access network resources. Different users work different hours, perform various duties that load a network differently, and generate different consistencies of Token-Ring packets. Also, too many users and nodes clearly can overload a network and create bottlenecks and slow network response. Indicators of node-specific overloads are outlined in Figure 15.6. Figure 15.7 lists symptoms of a LAN-wide traffic performance problems. To understand the root cause of uneven traffic problems, it is important to understand the composition of that network traffic. The pie chart in Figure 15.8 summarizes data from captured packets. Of 3300 packets, 500 were mail messages, 300 were follow-on packets for mail messages, and 2400 were applied to other uses. Only 100 packets were identified as collision fragments. The graphs imply that 25 percent of all network traffic in this sample is mail. Because there were follow-on mail packets, 60 percent of all mail messages average longer than a kilobyte. Note that 40 percent of all messages are brief. It is possible that one message is 0.3 megabyte (Mbyte) in length (and requires all 300 follow-on packets). This would skew the statistics and is one hypothesis to investigate.

The analysis does show that most mail messages are fairly brief, and 500 messages are a fairly significant number. If they come from a single node, it may imply that one user is broadcasting globally, and this may be unacceptable. Perhaps this type of transmission should be restricted to certain hours. If most messages are transmitted to a single node, perhaps this transmission level may imply the need for a bulletin board system rather than a mail broadcast. These are courses of action that packet content may suggest. Packet header information could be correlated with each mail message to indicate the actual length since the packet header does contain the length of the actual information it contains.

- Overloaded network
- Too many nodes (exceeding specification)
- Too many workstations
- Too many lengthy transmissions
- Chattering, jittering, or jabbering NICs
- NICs set to wrong transmission speed
- Mismatched hardware
- Defective application or network software
- Nonspec equipment

**Figure 15.6** Typical causes for node-specific overloads.

- High density of packets (high-level load)
- Lengthy transmissions (high peak demand)
- Maximum token rotation time
- Slow user response (overloads)
- Slow server response

**Figure 15.7** Indicators of network-wide traffic problems.

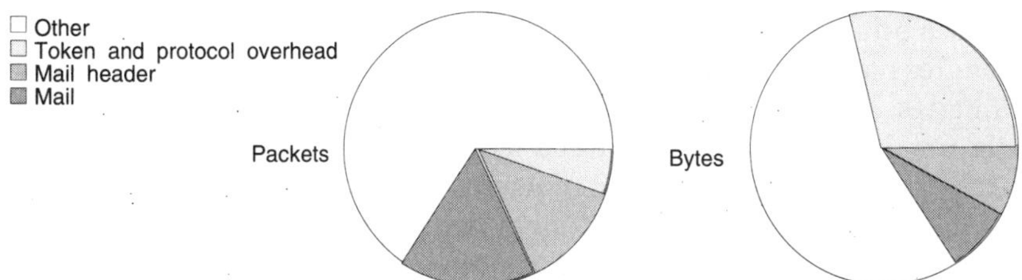


**Figure 15.8** Indicators of network traffic composition problems. The pie charts detail the percentage of network traffic allocated to a particular function. In this example, most of the packets are small, but a few large mail packets correspond to most of the network utilization.

Some processes may demand a significant portion of network traffic. Electronic mail, for example, may be a hidden use of network resources. The implication in this example is that mail is disproportionately overloading the network; while packet counts for mail are not large, the effect of actual traffic is skewed toward servicing mail requests. Likewise, data file uploading and downloading may be a significant load; this can be verified by examining the contents of the long trains of packets sent between specific pairs of nodes. Time-stamping of packets would aid in this type of investigation. Perhaps, like mail, this type of transmission should be restricted to certain hours, too.

A solution, if usage-specific traffic is deemed a problem, may be to identify the need for electronic mail. Another similar source of network traffic is graphic paging, sometimes known as "screen refresh." This condition may imply that large blocks of high-density graphic information are being transferred with frequency from one machine to another. Several solutions to these types of problems are possible. First, transfer could be accomplished by tape or floppy disk rather than by the network. Second, a special link might be constructed to remove the burden from the main network, for example, another Token-Ring cable or RS-232 line, solely to support this transfer channel. Third, mail could be posted on a passive bulletin board rather than broadcast or multicast across the network. This last option not only reduces the load on the network, it also reduces disk storage space for multiple copies of identical messages. Furthermore, there is a double performance hit when mail is stored on and accessed from a file server since mail access requires network resources.

## Global and Node-Specific Data Collection

Network software tools are sometimes available on the workstations, network servers, or PCs that are connected to the Token-Ring network. Network software tools may count packets, TRT, and sometimes identify sources and destinations with packet counts. Most often this software provides only single-node information and not global information about all nodes. Both node-specific and global information is required for the best results in network maintenance. This information must be accurately acquired and displayed in useful formats. Figure 15.9 presents the minimum functionality for monitoring transmission-level network operations required to answer the network manager's questions.

Unless single-node statistics can be captured inexpensively and analyzed globally, network software tools are only transient indicators of network problems. Single-node statistics may pinpoint a problem with a particular node without indicating a specific node as the source of problems. Global counts may indicate a local or global problem, but rarely will pinpoint the cause. Unless global information with node-specific corroboration is available, problems cannot be isolated to a specific node. Even a problem as common as a jittering NIC cannot be resolved without such corroboration. Without the specific node information correlated to the global information, excessive transmissions of meaningless packets cannot be traced to their hardware sources except by trial and error or a binary search with physical test equipment.

The network statistics in Figure 15.10 show a high TRT. This global statistic would lead one to believe a problem exists everywhere. Node analysis from simple node-specific software would suggest that both nodes 1 and 3 are faulty, whereas in fact only a single node may be causing problems, since a doubling in the TRT is significant. One node may be demonstrating that it is having difficulty communicating with the other node. The discrepancy of 400 packets could be associated with "runt" or oversized frames (bad packets) that would occur if node 1 had a faulty NIC and could not rebroadcast the frame as it had received it.

- Count packets: all packets—short packets, long packets, corrupted packets, good packets
- Display length of each packet
- Display average size of packets on network
- TRT and TTRT
- Store packets to memory (and/or disk)
- Monitor traffic levels

**Figure 15.9** Statistical information and functions required for network analysis.

| | Node 1 | Node 2 | Node 3 | Network |
|---|---|---|---|---|
| Output packets | 12400 | 15000 | 15000 | 42400 |
| Input packets | 6000 | 22000 | 900 | 37000 |
| TRT | | | | 39.4 μs |

**Figure 15.10** Node-specific data bring global analysis into perspective.

If usage rates seem localized to certain groups of nodes, or localized to a certain manufacturer's parts, or certain types of users, then it might be desirable to localize those groups on subnets, or allocate special resources to the groups. Often, those groups may not warrant the extra costs associated with the additional resources, or it may be politically unfeasible. It is important to note that Token-Ring is a public resource without locks or accounting statistics. The added resources may be applied to improve the global performance incidentally in the attempt to improve performance for a selected group of nodes and users. Capacity is a global constraint, not a controlled resource.

## General-Purpose Network Flow Information

Figure 15.11 lists some typical questions and corresponding important network statistics by name. The listing, by no means complete, is representative of the most expedient manner to answer each question posed.

Figure 15.12 lists some important counts, rates, and calculated statistics by name. This is not by any means a complete listing, just representative of that network monitoring information generally provided by protocol analyzers. The equations for these, or the methodology to generate them, are explained in detail in the next chapter. This list is included here in order to annotate several of the next charts and detail the applicable uses for the individual counts and rates.

| Typical Network Questions | Statistics of Relevance |
|---|---|
| What stations transmit on the network? | Source and destination costs |
| Do stations correctly transmit? | Eliminate packets with error and analyze |
| Do stations repeat transmissions? | Simulation; utilization rate |
| Do stations acquire tokens correctly? | TRT |
| What is the traffic volume? | Counts, rates and utilization rate |
| What is the traffic consistency? | Capture packets; source and destination |
| What is the length of messages? | Size distribution |
| What is average peak loading? | Utilization rate; capacity rate |
| What is full capacity? | Packet counts or rates ; packet sizes |
| What is the intermessage timing? | Interarrival times |
| What is the average wait delay? | Latency distribution |
| Which nodes talk to each other? | Source/destination matrix |
| Do messages have frame errors? | Analyze and sort packet errors |
| Can some stations not reach other stations? | Analyze pattern of lost packets; simulation |
| Which nodes cause problems? | Packet counts, error counts |
| Which rings are overloaded? | Rates, TRT, interarrival times |
| Are gateways and repeaters to spec? | Rates, TRT, interarrival times |

**Figure 15.11** Typical management questions and corresponding statistics.

**Packet Counts:**

All packets on networks
Packets transmitted
Packets received
Packets deferred
Packets per node
By source
By destination
By source to destination
Size distribution in bytes (-, 13, 64, 128, 256, 512, 1024, 4024, 6200, 18432, +)
Network period peaks node period peaks

**Packet Errors:**

All packet/frame errors
Alignment errors
CRC errors
Short packets
Long packets
Invisible packets
Incompatible packets
Misaddressed packets

**Channel Utilization:**

TRT
Throughput
Peak rate
Utilization as a percent of capacity

**Capture:**

All packets
Packets during an interval
Packets with errors
Packets with specific errors
Packets with certain data types
Packets from specific source node(s)
Packets directed to a specific destination
Node(s) packets with specific source/destination
Packets with a certain size
Packets without a protocol
Packets with a specific protocol
Rerouted, switched, and encapsulated packets
Packets under UDP
Packet fragments
Packets with SNMP information
Packets with CMOT information
Packets with CMIP information
Broadcast packets from routers and gateways (storms)
Alarms

**Figure 15.12** The protocol analyzer collects these common counts and rates, filters packets for specialized content, and calculates statistics useful for network analysis.

**Statistics:**

Network usage as a percent of capacity
Interarrival times (0 to 100 ms)
Latency distribution
Packet size distribution
Node usage as a percent of capacity
Node usage as a percent of network utilization packet
Rate per second
Bits/s
Bytes/s
TRT
Retransmission rate
Delivery error rate

**Figure 15.12** The protocol analyzer collects these common counts and rates, filters packets for specialized content, and calculates statistics useful for network analysis. *(continued)*

## Network Performance Data

Having identified statistics of interest, a measurement methodology needs to be developed. Although the troubleshooting chapter at the conclusion of this *Token-Ring Management Guide* outlines some ranges for common network indicators, the worksheet in Figure 15.13 includes sample data for a large, complicated network, and the necessary steps to convert the collected data into applicable information. In this sample, the users experienced a network that was slow and unresponsive; they have complained to the network manager, who must validate or discount the users' claims. As a consequence of a thorough analysis with a protocol analyzer several unrelated problems were uncovered.

In this example, information has been captured during a 24-hour period on a network with 26 nodes. The column headings represent each node, the number of packets input (i.e., received), the number of errors at the transport layer for these input packets, the number of packets output (that is, transmitted), the number of errors at the transport layer for these output packets, and four columns for rates. The first column shows input errors as a percentage of packets received. The second column shows output errors as a percentage of packets transmitted. The last two columns cannot be calculated until all the other information has been completed since these rates require network totals. These two right-hand columns show a method to compare node usage against network usage: "%tot" entries calculate packets transmitted from each node as a factor of all packets transmitted on the network.

The following seven graphs and one table (Figures 15.14 through 15.20, and the table in Figure 15.21) compress a large number of network statistics into a clear picture. The network represented is a complex network with one main segment interconnecting four lesser segments; it has 172 nodes in total.

| Node | Input | Error | Output | Error | %input | %output |
|---|---|---|---|---|---|---|
| A | 89897 | 261 | 37307 | 5 | 0.29 | 0.01 |
| B | 2492034 | 0 | 6116816 | 5 | 0.00 | 0.00 |
| C | 192212 | 251 | 129838 | 11 | 0.13 | 0.01 |
| D | 561151 | 0 | 415580 | 10 | 0.00 | 0.00 |
| E | 15987246 | 0 | 10022484169 | 362252 | 0.00 | 48.39 |
| F | 812002 | 446 | 747493 | 25 | 0.06 | 0.00 |
| G | 42862 | 0 | 44130 | 2 | 0.00 | 0.00 |
| H | 611480 | 1923 | 42840 | 14 | 0.31 | 0.03 |
| I | 115363 | 38 | 64289 | 1 | 0.03 | 0.00 |
| J | 103 | 0 | 84478 | 867 | 0.00 | 1.03 |
| K | 82097 | 234 | 40996 | 14 | 0.29 | 0.03 |
| L | 65316 | 346 | 10880 | 2 | 0.53 | 0.02 |
| M | 153256 | 0 | 120172 | 94 | 0.00 | 0.08 |
| N | 618 | 452 | 3140 | 3 | 73.14 | 0.10 |
| O | 1040322 | 1824 | 604794 | 48 | 0.18 | 0.01 |
| P | 1334398 | 347 | 1315634 | 9 | 0.03 | 0.00 |
| Q | 44748 | 0 | 53752 | 0 | 0.00 | 0.00 |
| R | 91380 | 0 | 32778 | 4 | 0.00 | 0.01 |
| S | 476121 | 266 | 483599 | 59 | 0.06 | 0.01 |
| T | 80594 | 0 | 72483 | 4 | 0.00 | 0.01 |
| U | 79780 | 0 | 71956 | 4 | 0.00 | 0.01 |
| V | 92126 | 0 | 21619 | 1 | 0.00 | 0.00 |
| W | 141428 | 0 | 108958 | 0 | 0.00 | 0.00 |
| X | 6018 | 0 | 501 | 3 | 0.00 | 0.60 |
| Y | 116901 | 150 | 66893 | 9 | 0.13 | 0.01 |
| Z | 33 | 2 | 59 | 7 | 6.06 | 11.86 |
| NET | 24709488 | 6540 | 20713472 | 1370 | 0.03 | 0.01 |

| Indicator | Nodes | Solution |
|---|---|---|
| Busy nodes: | B, E | Sub-net or filter |
| Bad hardware | N, Z | Check out the hardware |

**Figure 15.13** Statistical network worksheet.

The rate of utilization reaches saturation levels so that typical problems are presented to the reader. Figure 15.14 subdivides the network load by source machine type. In this sample, a conclusion to be drawn is that the Xerox equipment is providing a baseline activity during the course of the day, perhaps data backup, coprocessing, global modem, or mail services. The load on the IBM equipment is countercyclic to the normal workday, suggesting some planned off-peak process, whereas the Sun and DEC equipment appear to be servicing users during the normal workday. Such assumptions could be verified by packet capture techniques or learning about the specific processes on the network.

This same information is displayed in a different format by network service usage in Figure 15.15. Most of the peak load is created by user demands during the normal work hours.

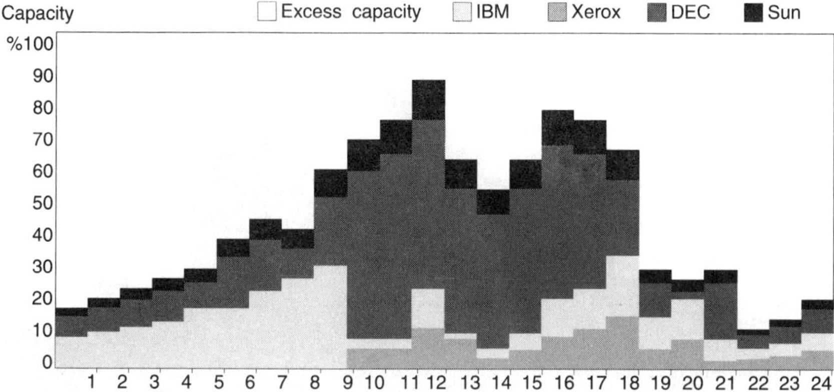


**Figure 15.14** Peak load by source computer during a 24-hour period.

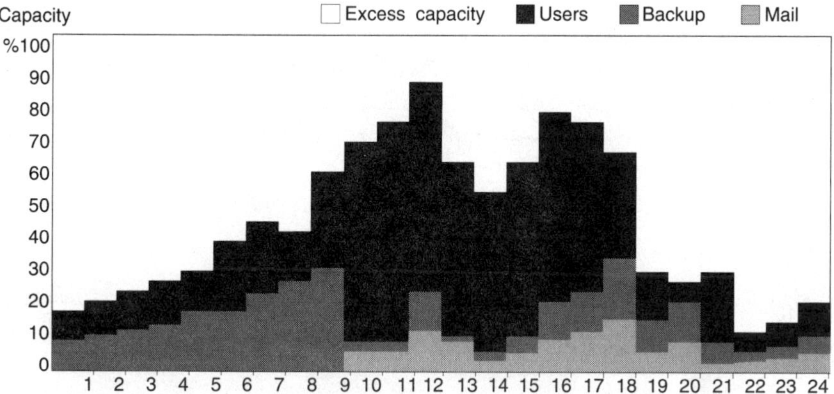


**Figure 15.15** Peak load capacity by usage during a 24-hour period.

The graph in Figure 15.16 presents loading on the main network segment that interconnects with four other segments. This traffic is identical to that represented in the above figure, as the overlay implies, although some of the load is localized on the subnets and therefore does not appear on the main net.

The data used to construct the graph in Figure 15.16 are repeated by the histogram in Figure 15.17, which displays traffic by packet size. Several upper-level protocols and errors are overlaid to indicate the common packet sizes. In this sample, Novell NetWare at 16 Mbits/s with IPX is the upper-layer protocol. Errors are represented by packets that are less than the 13 bytes minimum that represent tokens, or those packets that exceed 4204 bytes that represent NIC jabber.

Each different size represents a different type of purpose. The high loading is obvious during peak business hours, and drops off during lunch and afternoon slack times, as Figure 15.18 illustrates. Interarri-

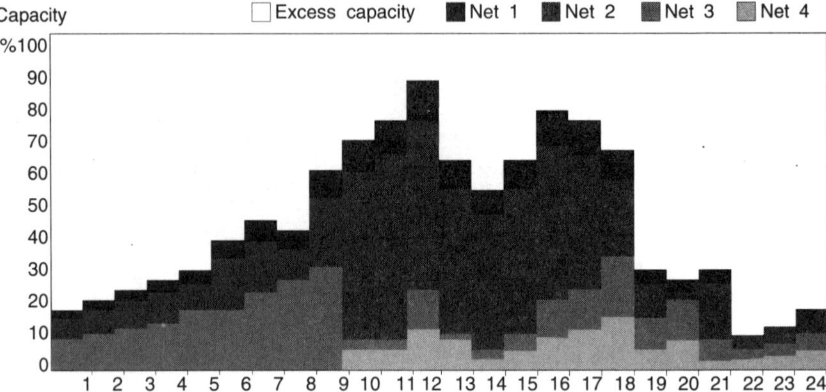


**Figure 15.16** Peak load by network source during a 24-hour period.

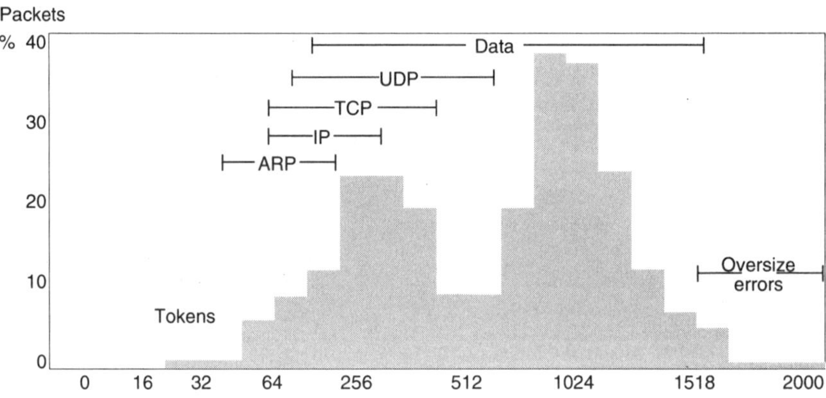


**Figure 15.17** Distribution of packets by size, and packet protocol or usage.

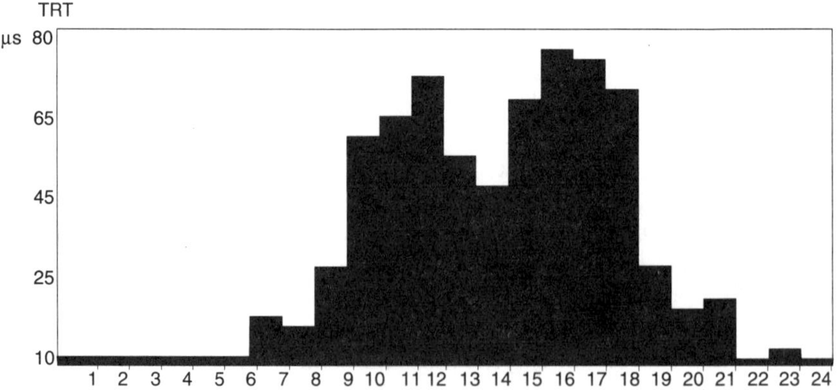


**Figure 15.18** TRT during a 24-hour period.

val times should be a minimum of the TRT at 45 ms. Interpacket spacing of less than that represents signs of hardware defects. The network interarrival time in Figure 15.19 implies a TRT of 45 ms rate, thus duplicating information in Figure 15.18 converted to another format.

Network access latency, as shown in Figure 15.20, is the time required for a request to be filled. The information is superimposed on the interarrival time for comparison. Latency times provide less important information than do collision rates or error rates, although they can confirm whether the problem is overload or hardware. In this case, since the latency shows a bell curve, the implication is that the network functions correctly except when the traffic load is too high, and latency shifts outward.

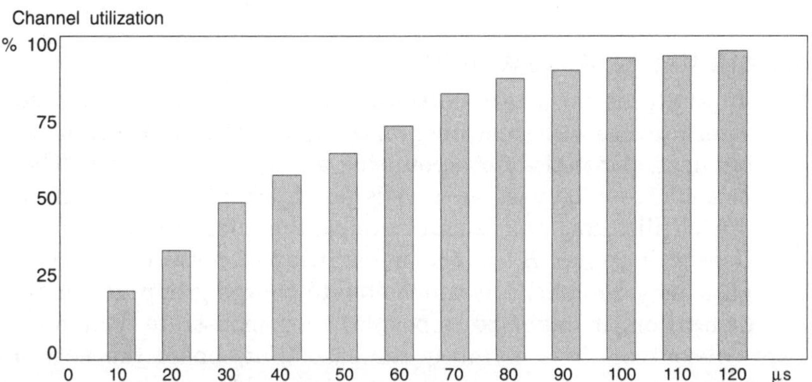


**Figure 15.19** Histogram of interarrival times in ms.

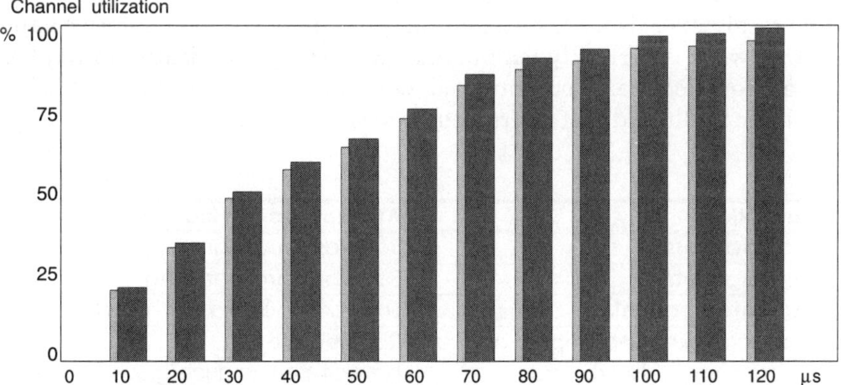


**Figure 15.20** Histogram of network access latency.

## Node Simulation

When statistics fail to identify network problems, node simulation on a protocol analyzer is a powerful methodology. Specialized software constructs packets of any length and content. A packet could thus contain any combination of errors, sources and destinations, and actual data content. Furthermore, network loading could be artificially increased to saturation levels to exercise the node software or develop statistics otherwise unavailable within a specific network situation. This is useful, for example, to test network conditions with the addition of 25 nodes. Figure 15.21 suggests the types of packets that can be built and the types of tests possible with node simulation. The delay and utilization characteristics of a network under various load conditions is an important consideration in design and planning stages.

## Network Usage Assessments

While an analyzer can chart network performance, it also performs other esoteric duties with some imagination. Its functions might include preparing usage statistics for accounting and billing purposes. These statistics could then be used as a basis for charging users and groups for network utilization. Take as an example the information in Figure 15.22. User *f* in group *B* is the major user of network resources. Although it may be politically unfeasible to charge group *B* for that user's utilization, it might be important to demonstrate demand for network resources. It is certainly the case that should the network become saturated and unable to meet the demand for services, network access for user *f* may need to be changed. Group *C* might, for example, be the accounting department that provides the paychecks, payables, and receivables. Network utilization is minimal; however, relative value of this work is certainly maximum. This example indicates an implicit resource allocation decision, and perhaps the means to establish a realistic audit and cost charge-out system as well.

| Simulation | Anticipated Test Indications |
|---|---|
| Short packets | Software error handling |
| Long packets | Software error handling |
| Corrupted packets | Software and hardware error handling |
| Duplicate tokens, non-repeat of tokens | Ring recovery |
| Percentage network loading | Network performance/growth capacity |
| Misaligned packets | Controller hardware |
| Specified sources | Node functionality |
| Specified destinations | Node functionality |

**Figure 15.21** Network simulation for preconceived theories.

| Group | User | Daily Average Packets | Utilization | Network Utilization | Network Share |
|---|---|---|---|---|---|
| A | a | 10000 | 10 | 0.47 | |
| | b | 40000 | 40 | 1.88 | |
| | c | 50000 | 50 | 2.35 | |
| | | 100000 | | | **4.7%** |
| B | d | 400000 | 20 | 18.94 | |
| | e | 700000 | 35 | 33.15 | |
| | f | 900000 | 45 | 42.62 | |
| | | 2000000 | | | **94.7%** |
| C | g | 1000 | 10 | 0.05 | |
| | h | 2000 | 20 | 0.09 | |
| | i | 7000 | 70 | 0.32 | |
| | | 1000 | | | **0.47%** |

**Figure 15.22** Budgetary allocation by prorated network usage. Packets were captured and collected by source address in order to generate the utilization percentages. These percentages can be used to allocate network overhead to the appropriate groups or even individual users.

## Capture and Store

Another key feature of a network analyzer is the tool's ability to intercept and retain packets. It should be able to capture every packet, although on a busy network available buffer space may prevent more than seconds or minutes of data to be stored. Some analyzers are too slow to capture every packet; they may capture one in five packets. This is statistically sound if the tool is capable of identifying and tracking each and every packet without storing the packet's contents. Some analyzers are too slow to recognize all packets. This means that packet counts do not accurately represent traffic; this is not sufficient. At a minimum, the statistics must be collected accurately. Node workstations often provide resident software to track this information for the node. Some node workstations provide software for global tracking. If this information is accurate and not just approximate, a protocol analyzer may be unnecessary. The ability to filter selected packets or extract only header information is a powerful tool for statistical compilation, usually available only with a protocol analyzer. Also, time stamping of packets is a desirable feature for matching individual packets with function as demonstrated in the mail example. Time-stamping also provides latency and interarrival statistics and a reality check on the accuracy of these statistics.

Several analyzers store from 0.5 Mbyte to 4 Mbytes of packets. They take a photograph of the network activity. On a saturated network, 4 Mbytes may represent only 3 s of activity. Captured packets can be stored on disk and analyzed later with word processing tools. For example, 4 megabytes of network traffic could be stored to disk. A quick view might indicate many mail packets as in the earlier example. Electronic mail and network fax seems to require considerable disk space (confirmed by other tools) and now it seems to require a large portion of the network. How large is a matter for estimate unless the 4 Mbytes can be analyzed and measured by content. If the file can be edited and parsed, an accurate percentage figure can be compiled. Unix tools like GREP, WC, and AWK are especially competent for this analysis; otherwise edits and sorts with line counts are appropriate.

## Snooping with the Analyzer

A protocol analyzer allows anyone who understands the use of this tool to monitor transparently and unobtrusively. By capturing and parsing packets, it is possible to decipher what users are doing on the network, particularly who is doing things illegally, unethically, or against policy. One use is to see who is using what resources on the network. While this seems Machiavellian, it can prevent unwarranted use of organization resources. It can uncover thefts, breaches in security, or hidden intrusions via unauthorized MAUs replacing a single station access. Another use of the protocol analyzer, if it has the ability to build specified packets at the bit or byte level, is to falsify packet designs and break whatever security is in place. If this tool can break security, this would indicate that others could undermine the security systems as well. Chapter 18 details these and other security issues.

The ability to capture and view packets adds a level of sophistication to network performance tuning. It also promotes spying. TRT, packet counts, defective packet counts, and any counts by source nodes are information of value and useful to tuning a network. However, at higher levels of sophistication—when all other problems have been identified and resolved—it becomes important to understand the mix of information actually transmitted. Informed guesses may indicate a particular set of nodes are used for long-haul uploading and downloading of large files. Other nodes with heavy but sporadic network loads may indicate large electronic mail requirements. By visually inspecting selected packets, it is possible to confirm these hypotheses.

This chapter explained the workings of a protocol analyzer, the types of information it can collect, and how to analyze and apply those data. The next chapter derives the mathematical underpinnings for traffic analysis with an emphasis on degenerate network performances. Chapter 17 will apply this practical understanding to the logic of tuning networks.

# Part 5
## Network Management

This section explores the management and strategic issues of Token-Ring networking. Performance tuning, security, backup, and human aspects are covered since these are critical management concerns. As network technology evolves, competition and the usage of networks for strategic advantage is increasingly an organizational concern. This section provides the reader with an understanding of Token-Ring technology and operations.

Chapter 16 calculates the statistics of Token-Ring transmission protocols and the deterministic characteristics of token passing protocols. This information is useful in order to understand why bottlenecks and slowdowns occur and why performance becomes suboptimal. Chapter 17 builds upon the information in preceding chapter, and shows how to tune network performance. This chapter builds upon the knowledge from the chapters on installation, configurations, network traffic, and statistics for the same purpose. It also discusses optimal planning, network loads, and alternative solutions for overloaded rings. This single chapter can be invaluable when network trouble occurs, when no solutions are self-evident, and when there appear to be no options for locating network failures. Chapter 18 discusses security issues, explains why the networking model contains no references to either data or physical security, why Token-Ring is not secure, and what precautions can be taken to protect a network from outside prying and unauthorized access. It also discusses what specialized hardware and judicious management procedures help maintain security. Chapter 19 explains backup procedures and suggests what hardware, software, or operational procedures can be implemented to produce a nearly fault-tolerant network. Issues and redundancy for the important network services—file storage, printing, tape backup of network data, shutdown of failed segments—are discussed in this chapter. Chapter 20 illustrates why trained and qualified people are an important resource for network administration. Token-Ring depends on people with expertise and experience. Without knowledgeable people, the network will perform below capacity, cause severe operational problems, constrain organization growth, and in extreme cases, even fail to function.

# Chapter 16

# Statistics for a Token-Ring Network

The last chapter detailed the workings of the protocol analyzer. This chapter derives the mathematics behind it and reveals further insights into Token-Ring mechanics by confirming rules-of-thumb with statistics. The assumptions are that Token-Ring networks perform well until the TRT degrades. The TRT is a proxy indicator for poor performance, and suggests that these problems can somehow be solved. The statistics show that a large TRT does impair efficiency, but that Token-Ring is efficient when understood and tuned.

## Network Traffic

Token-Ring relies on a deterministic transmission process with token-passing priority enforcement. One 802.5 enhancement, *early token release* (ETR), is non-deterministic, but its utility is marginal except for very large LANs with very small packets. Packets are transmitted only when a node holds a token, which is a 24-byte packet that gives one and only one node permission to transmit. Packets from the sending node are broadcast downstream to the next node, which in turn, repeats the packet to its own downstream neighbor. When the packet completes a circuit of the logical ring, the original sending node does not repeat that packet. Rather, it sends just the token component to its downstream neighbor. ETR allows for immediate release of the token after the packet is transmitted; the transmitting node does not wait for the packet to circumnavigate the ring. Hence, there may be many packets on the ETR-protocol ring, but still only one token at any time. Since Token-Ring transmission is unidirectional on the logical ring, always in the same logical direction on the ring, and packets are repeated by each node to the next logical node, nodes are represented as *upstreamand* downstream nodes. An upstream node always transmits to the next active downstream node. Many disabled (unpowered or bypassed) nodes may physically separate the upstream and downstream nodes. Phantom voltage at a MAU activates and determines the upstream and downstream nodes. If a node wants to transmit, it captures a token and sends a packet. Otherwise, it sends just the token to its immediate downstream neighbor. It is the responsibility of the receiving node to accept, acknowledge, and reply to those transmissions. Co-resident transmission is actually allowed only when *early token release* (ETR) is implemented, and then special conditions must exist. The first packet must be short, in fact, shorter in bit than the ring TRT.

This token-passing method is efficient and fair for high traffic loads, as Figure 16.1 illustrates. It is inefficient for low network loads, more inefficient than Ethernet. However, Token-Ring capacity and performance is predictable for all loading levels. It is virtually impossible to saturate the channel or overwhelm Token-Ring. Data delivery becomes slow, although consistently slow for all nodes. There is no priority enforcement. Nonetheless, performance does become unacceptable when the node count increases toward the maximum and all nodes have data to transmit. Utilization grows with load, but it also grows merely with an increase in network node count. It is almost impossible to fully utilize the Token-Ring bandwidth unless every node wants to broadcast all the time and the network node count meets or exceeds protocol limitations.

## Token-Ring Blind Spots

In some implementations of Token-Ring the NIC and software often exhibit blind spots. These software or hardware design bugs perpetuate certain types of network problems, such as sporadic network saturation, abnormal preambles, or inability to see certain Token-Ring addresses or packet types. This is most prevalent when different types of hardware

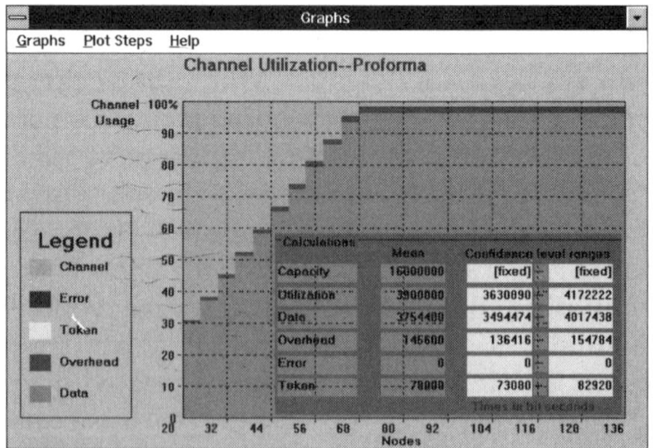


**Figure 16.1** Token-Ring network model plotting efficiency as a function of traffic load. The best application is in the range of 10 to 45 percent channel utilization, although this protocol does not fail or saturate with increased traffic levels. (Network Performance Institute)

and software utilize the same network bus, such as FTP, NetWare, LAN Server, and AS/400 token ring.

For example, some high-level network processes do not know how to respond to multicast packets addressed to a subset of network nodes, or broadcast messages addressed to no specific node. Such a situation creates a lot of network "noise," increased traffic levels, and some sending nodes frustrated for lack of a reply. A typical blind spot many network managers will need to understand is the router- or gateway-induced broadcast storm. Multicast and broadcast messages are propagated by routing or gateway devices to update the routing tables. Devices lacking compatibility with a routing subprotocol—and many different routing protocols do exist—and lacking SNMP or CMIP agency will not respond to the broadcasts.

## Rate Statistics

Some simple statistics decode the operating efficiency and generalized status of a Token-Ring LAN. This information is generally collected from application-layer software, SNMP, CMIP, or the protocol analyzer. The most applicable is rate information. *Rates* are the counts of a specific type of event during a fixed time interval. Rates are useful statistics for determining efficiency. For example, three types of rates to look for are the *packet rate,* sometimes called a *transmission rate* or *traffic rate,* a *token rotation time rate,* and *error rates.* Figure 16.2 lists some operation tracking formulas. *Error rates* represent transmission errors as a percentage of total packets transmitted, and these rates should be calculated in this way for uniformity. Most network managers make decisions based upon these simple rates.

It is important to note that rate statistics are most useful for diagnosing specific types of network bottlenecks and problems, plus both logical and physical locations for active network breakdowns. Additionally, rate statistics are good predictors of network performance when nodes are added or

| Transmission rate | Traffic |
|---|---|
| | # of packets sent / time period |
| Transmision rate/sec | # of packets sent / second |
| Transmision rate/min | # of packets sent / minute |
| Transmision rate/hour | # of packets sent / hour |
| Beacon rate | # of beacons / # of packets sent |
| Oversize frame rate | # of oversized packets / # of packets sent |
| CRC error rate | # of CRC errors / # of packets sent |
| TRT | [Provides ring length, latency, network load] |

**Figure 16.2 Formulas for basic network statistical calculations.**

traffic rates are increased. Rates are good for analyzing specific performance conditions subject to existing network configurations. When analysis is limited within this context, there is a one-for-one utility for solving network problems with rates. However, planning network growth or configuration changes requires a more complex model based upon nondeterministic mathematics. Such a model is defined and developed later in this chapter. This model is particularly effective for mixed protocol networks, networks of LANs, and enterprise-wide networks.

The count for packets transmitted generally matches the count for packets received. Any disparity between these two numbers—number of packets output and the number of packets received—indicates a network hardware problem. If the difference substantially varies from this, some packets are under- or oversized, or have faulty addresses. This is indicative of a software problem.

More complex network performance and traffic bottleneck problems do not necessary require more complex information. In fact, the data required for a queueing model (described later in this chapter) is nothing more than the times when packets are transmitted and those packet sizes. The relevant information usually requires the capture of information about *all* packets; this would require collection and collation of packet sizes, source and destination addresses, errors, and a time and date stamp. The packets themselves are rarely captured—just details about them to calculate accurate interarrival and service time statistics, network loading, and performance metrics. Additionally, expanded LANs and enterprise-wide networks may require service levels and throughputs for repeaters, bridges, routers, packet switches, gateways, and any other special pipes including ATM, FDDI, SMDS, SONET, T-1, X.25, and VSAT.

## Definition of Abnormal States

Token-Ring statistics are not necessary on a network where all works well. Compulsive managers may collect such information just as a matter of course. As such, that information pays dividends when a problem does occur, and benchmarks, just like cable blueprinting, are valuable as measuring sticks. The equations in Figure 16.3 will provide useful results in suboptimal networks. There are also other situations indicative of malfunctioning hardware that can be tracked through statistics.

Transmission errors are classified as cyclic redundancy check (CRC) errors, alignment errors, under- or oversized packets. A *CRC error* is a checksum error on the Token-Ring frame and is usually discovered in conjunction with other types of errors. An *alignment error* occurs when a packet is not a multiple of 8 bits and is usually indicative of a framing error, NIC clock error, or jitter and crosstalk on the ring.

*Jitter* or the *jitter budget*, though principally indigenous to Token-Ring, affects all protocols. It represents variance from the acceptable

| **Packet Counts:** | **Process** |
|---|---|
| Packets transmitted per node | Count outgoing packets |
| Packets received per node | Count incoming packets |
| TRT | Time for token to pass a node twice |
| Packets deterred | Requires special node-resident software |
| Packets per node: | Count outgoing and incoming packets by source |
| By source | Count incoming packets and filter by source |
| By destination | Count all packets and filter by destination |
| By source and destinations | Count into matrix |
| Size distribution | Extract length and plot |
| Network period peaks | Track highest transient network loads |
| Node period peaks | Track highest transient node load |
| **Packet Errors:** | **Process** |
| Alignment errors | Filter and count |
| CRC errors | Filter and count |
| Short packets | Filter and count |
| Long packets | Filter and count |
| Invisible packets | Capture packets and sort |
| Incompatible packets | Capture packets and sort |
| Misaddressed packets | Capture packets and sort |
| **Channel Utilization:** | **Process** |
| Throughput | Summation of packets by packet size |
| Peak rate | Highest transient load |
| Utilization as a % of capacity | Throughput (Mbits/s)/ transmission speed |
| **Capture:** | **Process** |
| All packets | Filter by specific parameters |
| Packets during an interval | Filter by specific parameters |
| Packets with errors | Filter by specific parameters |
| Packets with specific errors | Filter by specific parameters |
| Packets with certain data types | Filter by specific parameters |
| Packets from selected node(s) | Filter by specific parameters |
| Packets to selected node(s) | Filter by specific parameters |
| Packets with selected source/destination pairs | Filter by specific parameters |
| Packets with a certain size | Filter by specific parameters |
| **Statistics:** | **Process** |
| Interarrival times (0-100 ms) | Subtraction between clock times of arrivals |
| Latency distribution | Average waiting time to transmit |
| Packet size distribution | Sort sizes and count |
| Node usage as % of capacity | Packets/node/transmission speed x average packet size |
| Node usage of channel | Packets/node/throughput |
| Packet rate per second | Packets transmitted/second (exclude fragments) |
| Bit rate per second | Packet rate x average size x 8 (bits) |

**Figure 16.3** Common statistics applied to network analysis.

signal characteristics. Signal frequency variability, strength, stability, deficiency in the square form signal, and a lack of differentiation between "0" and "1" are all characteristic of jitter. Jitter is most pronounced with 16 Mbits/s Token-Ring transmission speeds. It is important to note that although all computer logic is based upon discrete values, ultimately all network traffic is based upon analog waves. Figure 16.4 shows how signals lacking differentiation decay to become unstable.

This instability is important when signals are regenerated and repeated at each Token-Ring station or regenerated by repeaters, bridges, routers, and gateways. Since the repeating stations cannot interpret the meaning of the signal, only the CRC checksum bits can decay. This may force frequent retransmissions. When jitter errors occur, the obvious test is to capture and compare the same frames at different parts of the network. When there are obvious differences, tighten the gap between protocol analyzers until the offending repeating device is localized. Although this is not an infrastucture error per se, it is a hardware error that should be resolved. Of note, newer Token-Ring cards may contain a chip designed and produced by Texas Instruments and IBM with a "ringing tank," which is designed to filter signal instability.

A *short packet* contains less than 24 bytes (the frame size for a token, and thus, the minimum packet size). Long packets result when a NIC *jabbers* or *jitters* beyond the end of the packet or ignores protocol limitations. They could also result from software protocol errors, multiple ring hops, multiprotocol routing flaws, or retransmission problems. A network should experience no beacons and no abnormal preambles. A *beacon* means that a downstream node thinks that there is a break in the cable after the immediate upstream node. When a packet is improperly repeated, it is received at the next downstream node with either a CRC or an alignment error, if it is received at all. Long delays may also generate a beacon, although they are more likely to initiate a *ring recovery,* which is a request to generate a new token and restablish the network access protocol. An *abnormal preamble* occurs when the first few bytes of a frame do not match the expected Token- Ring starting delimiter synchronization pattern. The normal Token-Ring network experiences a negligible number of CRC, alignment, or packet size

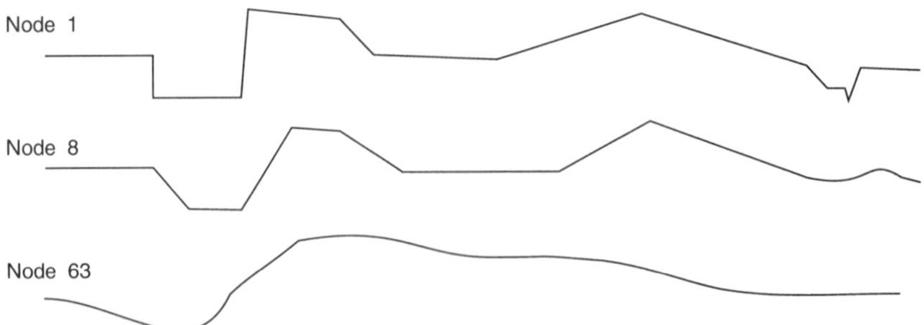


**Figure 16.4** Crosstalk, EMI, RFI, and excessive cable lengths cause signals to decay; this causes signal jitter.

errors. Errors for these items should be insignificant; significant error rates imply malfunctioning hardware, software, or network overloads.

## Theoretical and Obtainable Capacity

Another useful statistic measures obtainable (or realistically achievable) performance against a rated capacity. See Figure 16.5 for theoretical and attainable transmission rates. The difference relates to server and node performance; a superserver could conceivably obtain the theoretical rate. The theoretical capacity of Token-Ring is 4 Mbits/s or 16 Mbits/s. This corresponds to 500 Mbytes/s and 2 Mbytes, since a byte contains 8 bits. Sustained traffic rates on Token-Ring, really an attainable rate as determined empirically, is about approximately 312,000 bytes/s, and this can be represented as a rate. This yields a difference between the theoretical rate and actual throughput. Calculated and plotted graphs detail this later in the chapter.

Note that in most computer nomenclature megabits (Mbits) and megabytes (Mbytes) are usually octal numbers and are rounded for convenience. A megabit is actually 1,048,576 bits ($2^{21}$), and a kilobit is 1024 bits ($2^{10}$), but these numbers are not pertinent here. Token-Ring is an exception to this generic computer nomenclature as all of its numerical calculations are based on a decimal count; transmission rates are based upon 8 or 32 MHz, or 1,000,000 clock cycles per second. Since this clock timing drives a Manchester encoding scheme, as outlined in Chapter 5, this cycle yields 4,000,000 bits/s and 16,000,000 bits/s in communications terms.

## Token Rotational Time

The token rotational time (TRT) is the time it takes for the token to make a complete circuit of the LAN. This is true for a true physical circuit or for a logical circuit of a star-configured structure such as IBM Token-Ring. This statistic is difficult to acquire without special equip-

| Rate of Transmission | Bits | Bytes | Packets |
|---|---|---|---|
| Specified rate/sec | 16 Mbps | 2 Mbps | 0;108;66,667 |
| Attainable rate/sec | 2.5 Mbps | 312 Kbps | 0;16;10,416 |
| Specified rate/min | 960 Mbps | 120 Mbps | |
| Attainable rate/min | 150 Mbps | 19.25 Mbps | |
| Specified rate/hour | 36,000 Mbps | 7200 Mbps | |
| Attainable rate/hour | 9000 Mbps | 1125 Mbps | |
| Specified rate/8-hour shift | 288,000 Mbps | 57,500 Mbps | |
| Attainable rate/8-hour shift | 72,000 Mbps | 9,000 Mbps | |

**Figure 16.5** Token-Ring transmission rates for two-node networks.

ment since a ring without stations inserted means that there are no tokens on the loop; it can be estimated fairly accurately with a simple formula. Generally, this value represents the time for a signal to propagate around the LAN and is solely a function of the MAU switching delays, NIC electronic delays, trunk distances, lobe lengths, and arrival frequency and size of packets.

As stations are actually activated and inserted into the LAN, TRT slows by the delay imposed by the electronics in each NIC unit. This also explains (one reason) why some networks perform well with nodes activated and badly with fewer live nodes. The token signal decays with distance and it is being routed through a MAU and extensive ring wiring. Realistically, this represents the minimum TRT most network managers will ever see. When all stations are quiet and the token circulates, TRT is signal propagation time plus approximately 2 μs (20 bit times) electronics delay at each station's NIC unit. The absolute minimum TRT represents the time it takes for the token to complete a rotation on the LAN with no stations inserted. It must exceed 4.5 μs by specification for 16 Mbits/s operation, or 9.6 for 4 Mbits/s LANs. The active monitor or the node holding a token will artificially increase the TRT to that level if the network is too short or poses no load.

Under an ultimate load—when every station wants to transmit full-sized packets and exercises that right when it acquires the token—TRT degrades to signal propagation time, approximately 4 to 5 μs electronics delay at each station, plus the bit times for the data in the packet, with preamble and delay. For example, a 16 Mbits/s Token-Ring with 250 stations (the maximum) will show a minimum TRT of about 7 μs (7x16 bit times), and a realistic maximum TRT of about 253 μs, although this would increase if every node transmits full 18,432 byte packets.

Token-Ring networks are controlled by the token passing protocol. Token errors include a lost token and duplicate tokens. While it is functionally difficult to see these problems, the proximate method is to count claim tokens. The *claim token* is a station's attempt to claim access to the network in lieu of a token passing within two average TRT units, or the average TTRT. The claim token is generated after a satisfactory response to a station's ring recovery request. The protocol for *asserting* authority—based upon the claim token—is to issue a new token. This may require four or five average TTRT units. When stations insert into the network (usually when they are powered on and the passive bypass in the network NIC becomes active and now repeats signals), the sudden signal noise or disruption may corrupt a few packets or tokens during that brief interval. An excessive number and continuing incidence of purge and claim tokens usually indicates protocol errors, faulty NIC units, or other basic hardware problems.

When collecting and evaluating Token-Ring data, recognize that the token rotational time remains useful even when the network employs early token release (ETR) effectively. The TRT should be less with ETR enabled. A good performance measurement is to capture the TRT with ETR enabled and disabled. ETR usually yields a 1 to 2 percent improvement, rarely more. ETR is useful only when a LAN is physically large (that is, has many nodes and lots of wiring) and most packets can be delivered and the token released before the start of the packet returns to the source node. This means the bit time for delivery is less than the TRT. What was an important value for evaluating Token-Ring performance and stability retains validity under ETR. However, under ETR the protocol is no longer deterministic; multiple packets could circulate the network. Hence packets per period, average packet size, channel utilization, and latency form important statistics.

TRT remains one of the most useful Token-Ring statistics, and one generally not understood. Specifically, the TRT comprises the time for the token to complete a revolution on the network during which time all nodes may capture the token and transmit bits for the duration of *token capture timer*. The token capture timer, or *token hold timer* is determined by the transmission speed or overridden by the NOS. Specifically, the token hold time permits a node to transmits a 6200-byte packet at 4 Mbits/s, 18,432 bytes at 16 Mbits/s, but this is reduced by NetWare to a full frame size of 4202 bytes (or less for multiple hops). As such, this TRT is a total of all NIC electronic delays for all network nodes, the time for the transmission signals to complete a ring circuit, and the time to transmit a packet or the token itself. In other words, channel utilization, node counts, the network wiring length, and the TRT are parameters in a single equation that can be solved.

The TRT consists of the six components. These include transmission time and signal propagation time. Figure 16.6 lists the six components. The actual TRT times vary by protocol, media, and network length. The example in this section is based upon calculations on the fixed-sized IBM Token-Ring token of 24 bits. Furthermore, the *target TRT* (TTRT) varies by network load. Therefore, it is useful as input for utilization and

- Network transmission speed (and enhancement protocols)
- Number of network nodes (stations)
- Network wiring lengths
- NIC electronic delays
- Packet size and protocol-based size limitations
- Frequency of node requests to transmit

**Figure 16.6** The six components of the token rotational time (TRT).

network length calculations.[1] Specifically, the TRT can be extrapolated to network load and channel bandwidth utilization, as well as *total* network cabling lengths, as the following equations detail:

Utilization = Number tokens /second

Maximum number of tokens /second

Since each token indicates a token revolution:

Number tokens/second = 1 /Token Rotation Time (TRT)

These two equations reduce to the following useful formula:

Utilization = 1 - Ring latency /TRT

Additionally, the basic latency and utilization equations can be rewritten in another format to solve for the overall network length (when latency, TRT, and utilization values are available):

Ring delay = TRT (1 - Utilization)

where

Ring delay = latency + number of stations × (jitter and electronic delay)
+ network sections × 5$\mu$s/k

or

L = 8(TRT)(1-U)-7-5/8N) × 82′

where

L = Length of the network wiring

U = Network utilization

N = Number of network ring nodes

The ring latency represents the minimum time for the token and all data packets to go around the ring. Think of this value as the waiting time for station that wants to transmit. For Token-Ring running at 4 Mbits/s, the minimum latency is the TRT for an unloaded network. Thus, the minimum latency is sum of all token rotation components. Figure 16.7 charts these values.

These basic formulae were modeled in Lotus 1-2-3 to generate graphs contrasting TRT with channel utilization. Figure 16.8 shows 4 Mbits/s IBM Token-Ring, and Figure 16.9 plots the 16 Mbits/s IBM Token-Ring. Both plots were generated with the Lotus graph option.

1 Novell Inc. LANalyzer Support Group.

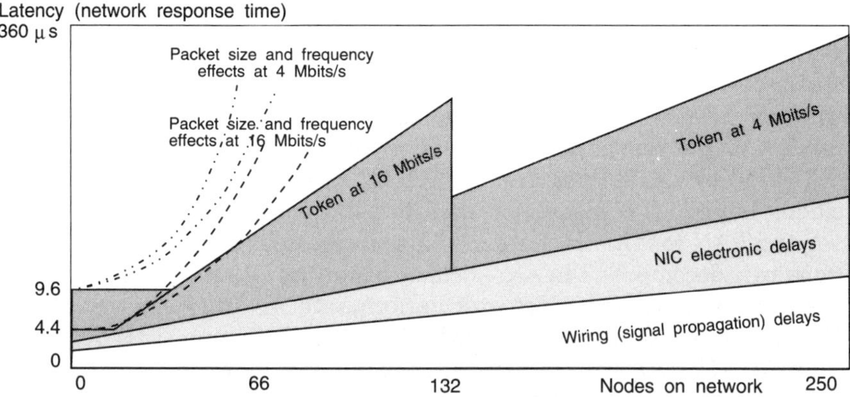


**Figure 16.7** The minimum latency components for Token-Ring.

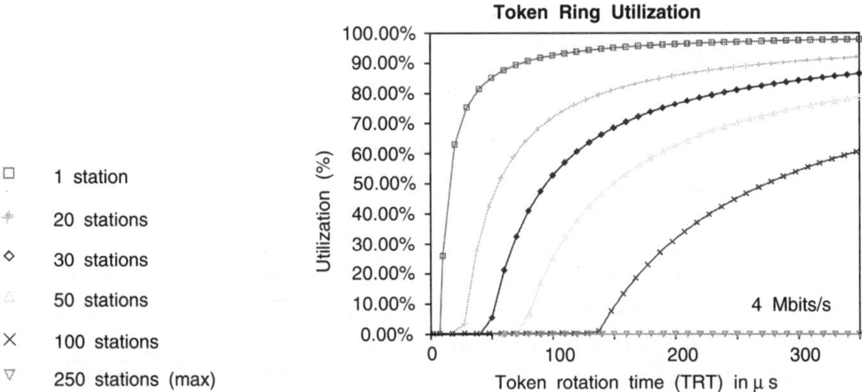


**Figure 16.8** 4 Mbits/s Token-Ring traffic load as a function of TRT.

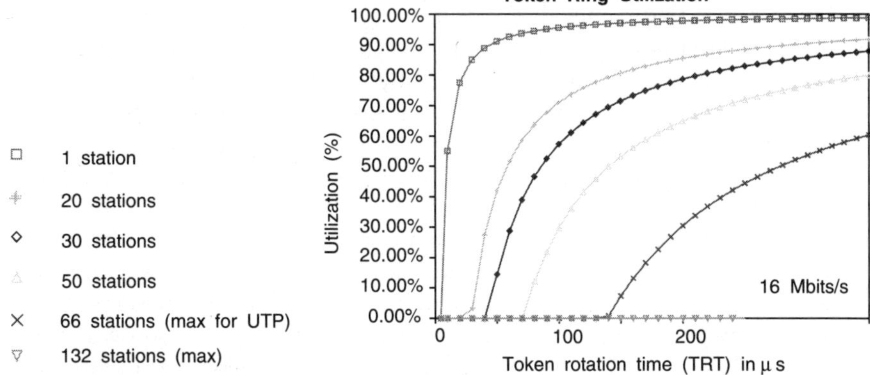


**Figure 16.9** 16 Mbits/s Token-Ring traffic load as a function of TRT.

These two graphs illuminate two important points. First, Token-Ring very rarely saturates at either 4 Mbits/s or 16 Mbits/s. Any free bandwidth is filled by token rotation. Second, additional stations increase the base latency time by adding to the jitter loss and electronic signal repetition, but do not necessarily affect the average latency time.

The McGraw-Hill/Windcrest book, *LAN Performance Optimization,* includes Lotus 1-2-3 models on disk to show performance levels under varying LAN conditions. Anyone who is interested in the complete equations can decompose the spreadsheet equations. Alternatively, a small freeware program from Network Performance Institute is available on CompuServe and other electronic bulletin board services. This program, called *RINGSTAT,* will calculate either the complete wiring length, channel utilization, or the TRT when provided with two of the three other parameters. It is based upon the equations on the previous page.

## Transmission Efficiency

Packet size is inversely proportional to packet rates, as Figure 16.10 illustrates. The false implication is that Token-Ring is more efficient with smaller packets. However, each packet requires a fixed-cost overhead that detracts from "efficiency" and the TRT is wasted channel time. The TRT, packet delimiters, and addressing and checksum overhead represent the least overhead for the largest packets.

While gross transmission efficiency is a linear function of packet size as Figure 16.11 displays, other events alter efficiency. For example, transmissions that exceed maximum packet length are parsed and broadcast in multiple packets with the overhead toll of multiple packets. While the gross evaluation suggests reasonable efficiency, the internal and external control information often demanded by IPX/SPX, NetBIOS, or NetBEUI lowers these figures. If the reader recalls, the IPX protocol requires a confirmation.

Transmission *efficiency* is defined as the percentage of data actually transmitted to the effort applied. Token-Ring packet sizes vary from the 24-byte token minimum to the 6200-byte maximum at 4 Mbits/s to 18,432-byte maximum at 16 Mbits/s. While physically feasible according to the Token-Ring protocol, these packets sizes are not achievable under NetWare IPX. If you recall, maximum packet size is limited to 4202 bytes. While the packet does contain data, anywhere from 1 byte to about 4178 bytes, each packet also contains a minimum of 24 bytes of address and accounting information. Additionally, upper-level protocols such as TCP/IP or IPX demand control information fields. These reserve the first few positions of the Token-Ring data field. Because overhead items are fixed sizes for each packet transmitted, efficiency is higher for larger packets, as Figure 16.12 charts.

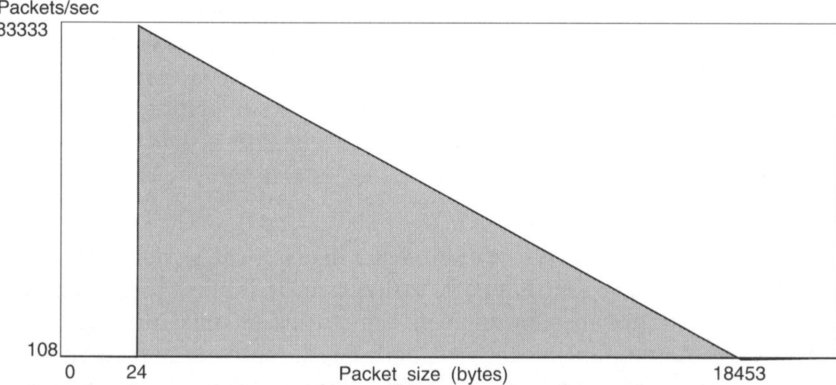


**Figure 16.10** Token-Ring throughput as a function of packet size.

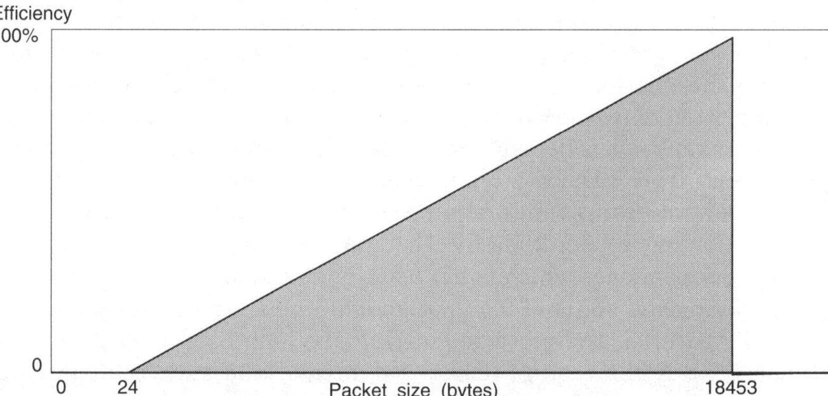


**Figure 16.11** Token-Ring channel efficiency as a function of packet size.

| | Minimum Packet Size | Maximum Packet Size |
|---|---:|---:|
| Address | 8 bytes | 8 bytes |
| Overhead | 16 bytes | 16 bytes |
| Data frame | 0 bytes | 18,432 bytes |
| TRT | 4.5 μs | 261 μs |
| **Total frame** | 24 bytes | 18,453 bytes |
| Tokens-packets/second | 83,333 | 108 |
| TRT time | Ring minimum | 38 μs |
| Overhead | 1,999,992 | 2,592 |
| Data frame | 0 | 1,990,656 |
| TRT delay | 450,000 | 1,882,071 |
| **Efficiency** | 0.00% | 99.00% |

**Figure 16.12** Token-Ring transmission efficiency by packet size. The data frame is the variable-sized element with a minimum of 0 bytes to a maximum of 18,432 bytes, for 16 Mbits/s LAN Server or LAN Manager operation.

Obviously, this information represents theoretical capacity. In actual usage, average packet size and the distribution of packet sizes affect network performance, data throughput, and data transmission efficiency. The capacity and the detrimental effects of errors and beacons must be developed with a completely different type of mathematics.

## Token-Ring Modeling

Since Token-Ring node count and packet size are the major limitations to channel capacity and network utilization, it is important to model this. Because transmission requests are statistical and interdependent with many factors like packet size, node count, or average transmission rate, nonlinear methods are required to understand the transmission mechanics. The probability of a node actually transmitting is difficult to determine. First, a load level must be determined for each and every node. Second, that load must be applied independently for each node despite the possible correlation between events and the non-uniform loading often experienced on a network. This is often impossible since node transmission is dependent on what the network or other nodes are doing, and transmission often synchronizes due to the packet waiting times and processing times required for each transmitted packet at the destination node. Additionally, the mathematics assumes node and traffic independence which is not usually provided. For example, users work during the hours of 9 a.m. through 5 p.m., attend meetings, and work in parallel, therefore requesting the same services. Also most Token-Ring NOSs require acknowledgments, and such confirmations are not processed independently.

## Operations Research and Token-Ring Modeling

More complex branches of mathematics are required in order to accurately describe Token-Ring. This includes *Operations Research,* which encompasses probability theory, simplex reduction techniques, and heuristic modeling. These models have been developed and amplified since the 1950s as an outgrowth of formalized Operations Research. This is a fertile field for new findings, further research, and new applications. The mathematics are, however, practical enough to apply to Token-Ring network service modeling. In fact, the graphs in this chapter were prepared using operations research models and equations.[2] From this

2 MS Windows-based queueing models and performance analysis tools for Token-Ring and other protocols are readily available from Network Performance Institute (NPI) and Comdisco. All graphs were generated by *LANModel* from NPI.

science, two mathematical models accurately represent the transmission operations of Token-Ring. The first is called a *queueing model*, and the other is called a *Markov chain*.

### The Queueing Model

The *queueing* (or, variously, "queuing") *model* describes waiting lines (hence queues), service response times, and throughput. It is an appropriate Token-Ring model because nodes wait in line for slot time to transmit. Queueing theory provides a large number of alternative mathematical models for predicting different real-world events such as airplane arrivals, gas station servicing time, and metropolitan traffic jams. The traffic jam analogy is appropriate here. The queueing model defines process steps, waiting times, service times, service fulfillments, and service request denials (e.g., errors and beacons).

The three features of the Token-Ring mechanism are the arrival process, the waiting queue, and the service mechanism, as shown by Figure 16.13. This waiting line design illustrates the major mathematical groupings, which include the source distribution, the waiting queue, and throughput as represented by serviced requests. Because interconnection of LANs is an important data communications issue, expansion of this model is particular effective for mixed protocol networks, networks of LANs, and enterprise-wide networks.

### The Markov Model

The Markov chain defines transition states for an environment. In the case of Token-Ring, a transition is the change from a quiet network to a network in error, or from a network in the state of transmission to a network in the state of idle. There are many more transition states. Markov modeling, sometimes used as part of Monte Carlo calculations, is particularly effective at representing games of chance. In fact, most

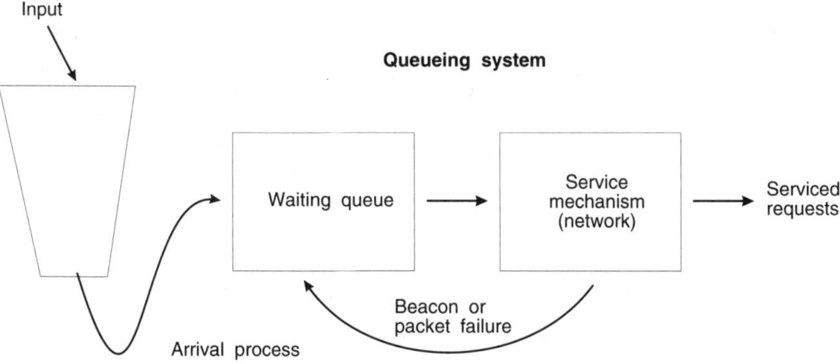


**Figure 16.13** The queue service model.

of these algorithms were developed to increase the personal odds at the card tables of Europe in the eighteenth and nineteenth centuries as the Monte Carlo designation implies. Gambling provided the major impetus to the development of mathematics and calculus as we know it. Markovian models are appropriate tools to describe the behavior of LANs because part of the Token-Ring transmittal process includes the random arrival of transmission service requests.

The state transitions described by the Markov model are presented by the flow diagram in Figure 16.14. The three states in Token-Ring are *idle, error,* and *successful transmission.* This yields nine transitional phases that include the change from idle to transmission, from idle to error, and from error to idle. These nine factors can be solved in the steady-state equilibrium.

## The Token-Ring Model

Figure 16.15 shows the single-server mechanisms of Token-Ring transmission fulfillment. Token-Ring is a single server—one mechanism

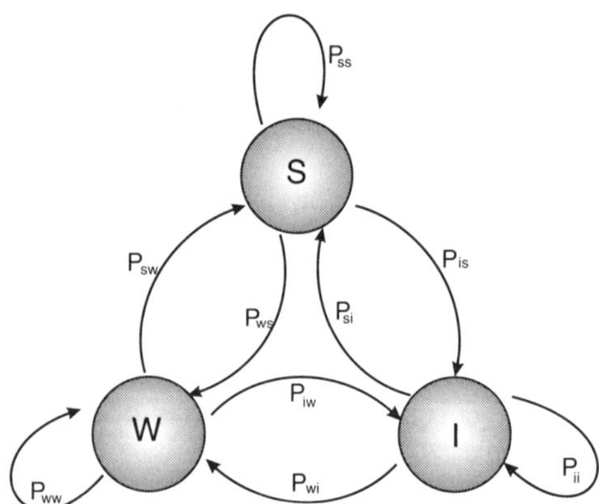


**Figure 16.14** The classic Markovian state transition model as illustrated for Token-Ring. The nodes represent event states which are transmission, token request, and channel idle (token rotation). The arrows illustrate transitions between states.

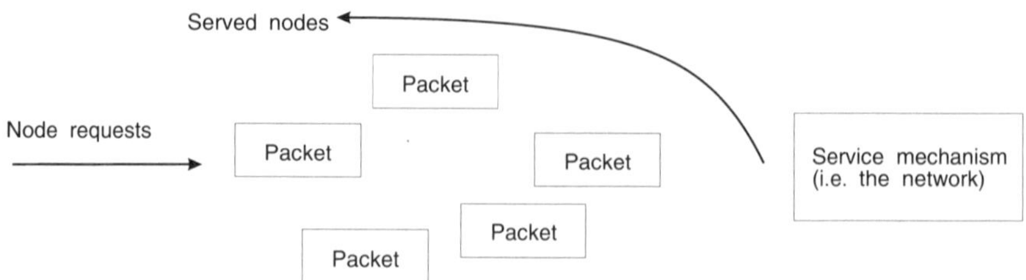


**Figure 16.15** The classic Markovian model for Token-Ring.

services all requests for transmission throughout a network—and this designation is independent of the node or machine count, or the actual network configuration. Only one packet request can be serviced at a time (unless ETR is activated). There is no other alternative. This illustration is a Markovian model because it represents the process rather than the waiting times, lines, and throughput as in Figure 16.13.

The next representation, in Figure 16.16, condenses the many nodes into an organized and elegant model with a single server. This design simplifies the mathematical rendering into a queueing model architecture where the three basic statistics are introduced: successful throughput, error, and traffic, which is the sum of tokens, throughput, and errors.

### The Poisson Model

The classic queueing model assumes an infinite number of nodes and a fixed arrival time. This needs to be modified to model the mechanisms of Token-Ring. Because each Token-Ring has a finite number of nodes (maximum 250), transmission request arrivals can be estimated with the Poisson process.

The *Poisson process*, which defines the mean arrival time, is described in Figure 16.17. The Poisson process models the inter-arrival time, the time between consecutive requests, and describes a phenomenon involving events which occur "rarely" in small time intervals. It is frequently applied when event distributions are studied, as in the case of Token-Ring transmissions service requests. Transmission requests are fulfilled based upon a *birth-and-death process* in queueing theory. *Births* refer to requests for network service, and *deaths* refer to the fulfillment of the communication request. Births and deaths occur randomly where the rates depend only upon the current state of the system. The crucial

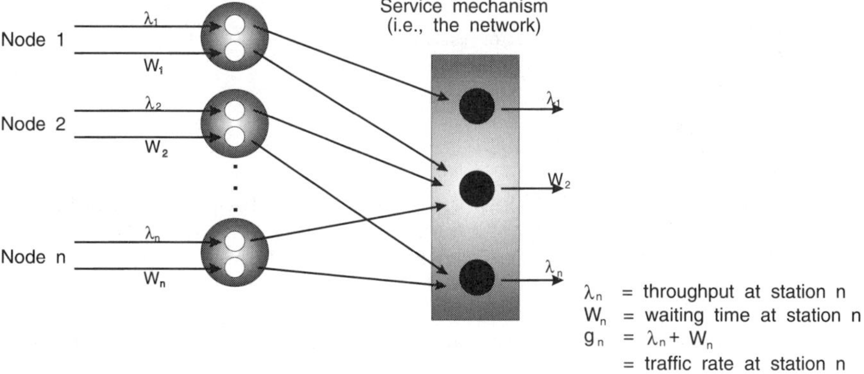


**Figure 16.16** The classical queueing model architecture for Token-Ring.

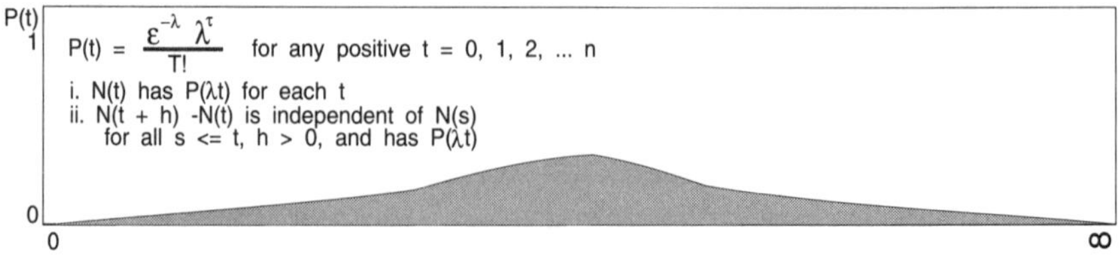

P(t)
1
$$P(t) = \frac{\varepsilon^{-\lambda}\lambda^{\tau}}{T!}$$ for any positive t = 0, 1, 2, ... n

i. N(t) has P(λt) for each t
ii. N(t + h) -N(t) is independent of N(s) for all s <= t, h > 0, and has P(λt)

0
0 ∞

**Figure 16.17** The Poisson model for random transmission requests.

assumption for a Poisson distribution is that only one birth or death can occur at a time. Token-Ring is a special case that is called a *limited source model* because the calling population is finite.

With these arrival (birth) and service (death) times assumptions, the mathematical architecture can be reduced to a set of queueing equations. In fact, the equations are necessary to answer questions posed at the beginning of this chapter; as a by-product, other important statistics can be derived. The waiting queue itself is a quasi-random process that is not useful to model independently since the queue is determined by the Token-Ring controller. Standard queuing equations[3] are listed in Figure 16.18.

For example, if packets arrive every 16,000 ms and contain 1024 bytes (or 8192 bits), the utilization level will approximate 50 percent by equation (1). Likewise, the length of the queue will be 0.25 packet requests by equation (3) and (4), and wait time will average 16,000 ms by equation (5);

| | | |
|---|---|---|
| $\rho = \lambda/\mu$ | network utilization factor | 1 |
| $P_0 = 1 - \rho$ | network initial state | 2 |
| $L_n = \frac{\rho^2}{2(1-\rho)}$ | expected transmission queue length | 3 |
| $L = \frac{\rho}{1-\rho} = \frac{\lambda}{\mu-\lambda}$ | number of requests in queue | 4 |
| $W_n = \frac{L_n}{\lambda}$ | waiting time in transmission queue | 5 |
| $W = W_n + 1/\mu$ | waiting time in total system | 6 |

$\lambda_n$ = mean packet arrival time
$\mu_n$ = mean transmission service rate
$P_n(t)$= probability of N transmissions at time t

**Figure 16.18** The Pollaczek-Khintchne equations for steady-state solution of the Token-Ring model. Many solutions are available because of the large number of mathematical interrelationships.

3 Frederich S. Hiller and Gerald J. Lieberman, *Operations Research,* Holden Day, San Francisco, CA., 1974.

this is solved by plugging the resulting values of .25 and 16,000 ms into the formula. The total system time will logically include the 16,000 ms wait time plus the transmission time of 8192 ms by equation (6). Despite the appearance of simplicity and linearity (and some very logical equations) many nonlinear assumptions support these estimates.

It is interesting that as service times increase, all waiting times increase. Therefore, the key conclusion is that consistency of node service and the number of nodes in the ring has as important a bearing on network performance as average service speed. In other words, if the network is erratic, performance will be that much worse. A key result of these equations shows that as arrival times approach service times, the users' waiting time (latency) increases as expected.

Logically, the probabilities for all nine transitional stages must sum to unity since only one stage can occur during a given interval. The times associated with each stage can be solved as a series of linear equations as shown by Figure 16.19.

Each state change probability is reduced to simplest form in Figure 16.20, and these entities are substituted into the four preceding linear equations and reduced. The results also yield utilization and throughput factors based upon these same equilibrium values. The equations from Novell are simple, thus useful.

$$\begin{bmatrix} P_s * P_{ss} + P_w * P_{ws} + P_i * P_{is} = P_s \\ P_s * P_{ss} + P_w * P_{ww} + P_i * P_{iw} = P_w \\ P_s * P_{si} + P_w * P_{wi} + P_i * P_{ii} = P_i \\ P_s * 1 + P_w * 1 + P_i * 1 = 1 \end{bmatrix}$$

simultaneous linear equations

$$s = P_s / (P_s * L_s + P_w * L_w + P_i * L_i) \quad \text{throughput} \qquad 1$$

$$u = s * L_s \quad \text{channel utilization} \qquad 2$$

**Figure 16.19** Equilibrium probabilities for the Markov state transition model.

| **Transition** | **Representation** | **Reduction** |
|---|---|---|
| $P_{ii}$ | $P_0^{(\infty)}$ | $0$ |
| $P_{is}$ | $P_0^{(a)}$ | $e^{-ag}$ |
| $P_{iw}$ | $1 - P_{is}$ | $1 - e^{-ag}$ |
| $P_{si}$ | $P_0^{(1)}$ | $e^{-g}$ |
| $P_{ss}$ | $P_1^{(0)} P_0^{(a)}$ | $e^{-g-(1+a)g}$ |
| $P_{sw}$ | $1 - P_{si} - P_{ss}$ | $1 - e^{-g} - ge^{-(1+a)g}$ |
| $P_{wi}$ | $P_0^{(\bar{y})}$ | $\bar{e}^{-Yg}$ |
| $P_{ws}$ | $P_1^{(\bar{y})} P_0^{(a)}$ | $ge^{-(\bar{Y}+a)g}$ |
| $P_{ww}$ | $1 - P_{wi} - P_{ws}$ | $1 - e^{-\bar{Y}g} - ge^{-(\bar{Y}+a)g}$ |

**Figure 16.20** Reduction of the steady-state transition probabilities.

**Dissimilar Arrivals**

A Markovian model modified to handle a finite number of nodes can explain how peak load periods generate dissimilar arrival rates. "Random" has a special meaning in probability mathematics. It refers to a process with a predictable outcome but stochastic events. Randomness does not mean "erratic." There is rarely a microscale pattern to network loading, and thus networks display a very "random" and erratic transmission arrival process. In keeping with the practical bent of this book, the reader will be spared the tediousness of this mathematical expansion. However, the preceding solutions assumed a Poisson arrival rate of uniform distribution. In point of fact, arrival rates are not mathematically random but erratic and, because of the coordinated nature of most transaction processing, arrival rates correlate. Figure 16.21 lists the reasons.

Two major Poisson distribution assumptions fail with Token-Ring because there are variations in service times and requests are not random. Packets clearly have different lengths and require varying transmission service times. Furthermore, the token is presumed to pass any particular point with the average TRT. Protocols remove the randomness of transmissions from the system by providing resolution of transmission contentions and failures. *Interarrival time* is the transmission slot time, or the time between consecutive transmissions. This interarrival time represents one and a half x the TRT time and the ring node count x the average packet size, as might be expected. Poisson's limited source distribution is not heuristically matched for actual Token-Ring as observed on live networks. For these reasons an Erhlang distribution is sometimes used to approximate network statistics, despite its assumption of random interarrival times. The Erhlang distribution is useful because it approximates empirical observations more readily. Figure 16.22 illustrates utilization rates for different skew values of the Erhlang distribution. Notice that it shows the same traffic features that were first presented in Figure 16.1; this completes the mathematical modeling.

These statistics show that higher utilization rates will not actually saturate Token-Ring, but in the end, larger numbers of nodes will halt efficient use of the network as the sheer number of transmitting nodes raises the probability (and actuality) of waiting time to unacceptable

- Process coordination
- A standard workday
- Transmission and receipt
- Nonstochastic load demands
- Queue pressure from incompleted transactions

**Figure 16.21** Reasons for nonrandom service request distribution.

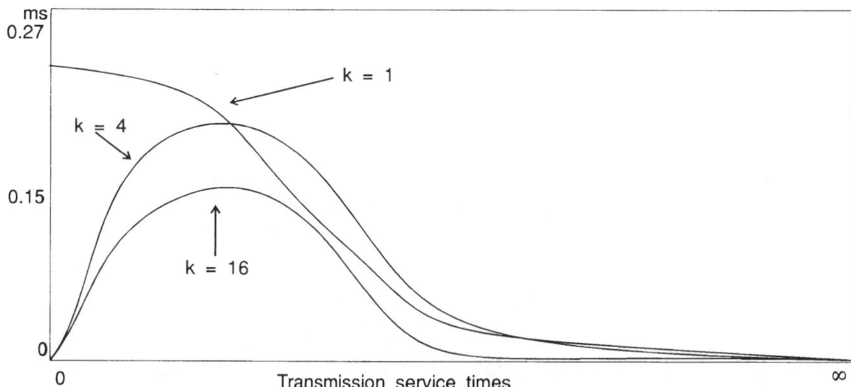


**Figure 16.22** The family of Erhlang probability density functions. Service times are presented along the horizontal axis. The variable *k* is proxy for packet lengths and frequency of transmissions.

levels. Performance degrades as the channel saturates, either through larger numbers of nodes, more frequent transmission requests, or larger packets. Despite the fact that the channel is a single server and the multiple node requests from a single node appear to correspond to single requests from multiple nodes, multiple nodes more readily degrade performance. This is akin to the familiar highway crawl not merely because too many cars use the highway during the day, but because there is too much traffic during selected intervals and the bottleneck never clears; every automobile is different and can't be likened to a bus even though a bus logically provides a similar distribution service. Mathematically, the reason for this observable phenomenon is that the standard deviation for transmissions (or, packet arrivals) increases as the number of nodes increase. Additionally, more nodes generally provide a proxy for a longer physical network or larger packet size. There is no proxy for greater variability in packet arrivals or with packet sizes. Variability tends to increase latency for users very dramatically, as the statistics support.

## Conclusion

In conclusion, when all is said and calculated, it is clear that Token-Ring is a very predictable medium. Protocols such as Token-Ring, which are deterministic, provide a uniform utilization based upon node counts and packet sizes. As it is overloaded, the LAN will merely get slower until performance is unacceptable. But, it will not break and saturate without any throughput, as Ethernet does. The realization is interesting when considering other protocol alternatives such as ARCnet, SMDS, SONET, and FDDI. Additionally, the statistics and modeling confirm the practical limits that network designers and managers have learned by trial and error. Plan for a maximum of 50 nodes per Token-Ring channel when most of these nodes are diskless and require client-server support. Limit single rings to a maximum of 60 nodes, and try to avoid sub-rings with more than 30 nodes, particularly where nodes utilize remote file service or frequent file transfers. The subdivision of the network not only provides better localized performance; also, it provides for "firewalls" in the event of network failure. A fully populated Token-Ring with 255 nodes is fine if the network is sparsely used, or provides only minimal functionality. However, realize that the longer token rotational time will reflect the longer physical ring wiring and the electronics delay from the many nodes which must repeat each signal. For practical application, the original graphs in this chapter provide a measuring stick against which to measure a network's performance, health, and load. Should you desire better information of the performance and functionality of a data communications network, acquire and apply protocol analysis software and a hardware analyzer; feed these statistics into an *appropriate* network queueing model. The next chapter applies this information to network performance repairs.

Chapter

# 17

# Tuning Performance

While the last chapter detailed the mathematics of Token-Ring in terms of queueing models, state transitions, and the expanded algebra of performance models, this chapter explores methods to rechannel overloaded networks, improve throughput, increase network speed, and improve network reliability. Most network managers eventually experience network performance degradation as network software functionality decreases or workload increases. Improving performance usually implies providing a faster server, faster server disks, or better input/output (I/O) performance. I/O is the culprit in LAN performance bottlenecks 40 percent of the time. Violation of specifications and poor network design, installation, and management account for another 40 percent. Rarely is LAN performance so dependent upon packet throughput and the consistency of the transmission rate. Performance also encompasses network reliability and efficiency.

## Performance Solutions

There are several ways to solve network problems, including adhering to specification, rechanneling, installing routers and gateways, as well as implementing more exotic technologies. A very sophisticated software solution requires establishing priority enforcement. Unfortunately, no Token-Ring NOS supports priority transmissions, although FDDI-II does. Best solutions are usually based on a clear understanding of the network problems and the available, simple, and relevant technologies.

This chapter details the techniques necessary to tune a Token-Ring network. These techniques include monitoring system performance, analyzing network statistics, and understanding the condition of that network. Figure 17.1 outlines performance tuning methods in a time-saving list.

- Monitor network load
- Monitor network performance
- Analyze network statistics
- Apply a queueing model
- Verify that the network matches Token-Ring specifications
- Ensure component consistency
- Install alternative channels for specialized needs
- Install multiple channels to balance loads
- Isolate segments with gateways
- Remove network repeaters
- Install "smart" repeaters and routers
- Provide fan-out units to improve configuration
- Buffer messages with store-and-forward devices
- Disable active SNMP or CMIP software

**Figure 17.1** Performance tuning methodology.

## Network Performance and Bottlenecks

Token-Ring networks exhibit poor performance for many reasons. Saturation of transmission channel capacity, while the most obvious and frequently blamed for a failing Token-Ring, is only one of many. In fact, authentic Token-Ring channel saturation is rare except in cases where there is a flaw. It is impossible to saturate Token-Ring; the latency just becomes longer and longer. Usually performance problems result from other component failures or overloading, hardware performance bottlenecks, or installation flaws. Component failures including chattering, jabbering, and jittering, as well as poor wiring, faulty installation, signal interference, and networks breaching specification. Performance is also a function of the speed of service for each individual component. Slow network cards, overworked file or application servers, disk-bound file servers, excessively large databases, queries to a distributed database that are not optimized locally, and slow computer memory also create bottlenecks that impair not only network performance but also the performance of individual network nodes.

Repeating an important point, Token-Ring networks never become saturated with too much traffic. They simply become slower. Too many users, too many file transfers, too many requests for data from a remote or distributed database, and too much reliance upon slow client-server processing are the most common causes for poor network performance.

Other more likely causes for poor network performance exist in addition to channel saturation. The transmission channel is only one component of the network. Most Token-Ring controllers provide average transmission throughput of about 1 Mbits/s, which is either 25 percent or 6 percent of the channel capacity depending upon signal transmission speed. Very few Token-Ring controllers provide 3+ Mbits/s (or more) data throughout to the network channel. (Note that the Token-Ring NIC always sends signals at 4 Mbits/s or 16 Mbits/s as per Token-Ring specification, but few PCs or even engineering workstations can sustain that transmission rate for more than a few seconds per minute. A time delay exists for gathering the data, assembling it into packets, transmitting frames, and verifying acceptance by the recipient.) Additionally, few file servers have hard disks that can transfer 1.2 Mbytes of information from disk into memory per second, let alone buffer a significant portion of that full image in memory at any one time while waiting for the controller to construct packets at its capacity. Most PCs (with ISA disk controllers) can achieve the slow disk transfer speed of 256K (or 0.25 Mbyte) per second. Even if the file server with an SCSI-2 disk drive and controller were to sustain the data transfer speed of 4.4 Mbytes/s, the receiving PC may not be able to handle more than 256Kbytes/s. Similarly, although "superservers" or specialty I/O backplanes may provide outstanding rates of I/O, the recipients may be overwhelmed. Although this per se may seem like a bottleneck, this data transfer rate is faster than most Token-Ring controllers. Floppy drives create bottlenecks due to their slower transfer speeds.

Consider the following example. Transfer of a 10-Mbyte graphics file on a two-node network nominally requires 8.165 s across the communications channel. [The time is derived by dividing 10,000,000 by 4181 (maximum NetWare data frame size) to find the number of packets required. This figure is then multiplied by 8 (bits per byte) and divided by the channel speed.] This assumes Token-Ring packets with the maximum data field size of 4181 bytes while ignoring stack or protocol overheads. The fractional seconds indicate frame address overhead and the TRT delay. Additionally, higher-level protocols expect a one-for-one acknowledgment of each packet sent. This could increase the transmission time by 0.40 s assuming an additional 2391 minimum-sized Token-Ring frames (and the interpacket delay). Recall, however, that the local Token-Ring controller can sustain only 10 percent of channel capacity. This will suggest a transfer time around 90 s.

In fact, in reality upper-layer protocols are not that efficient. This is particularly true when OSI stacks (say, for an FDDI link) are layered on top of Token-Ring to provide multiplatform routing and multiprocol connectivity. The application software will need to monitor transmission if only to count packets received and administer the sequence of data parsing and transmission. The graphic image in this example is a complex delivery, and the packets must be reassembled like a puzzle. Failure to reassemble the graphics data in sequence at this application level will result in a processing problem, as illustrated in Figure 17.2.

Furthermore, recall that the IPX, MAC, and LLC protocols require space within the data buffer of each packet. This is easily overlooked since these bits and meager bytes are hidden at the lowest levels. Since

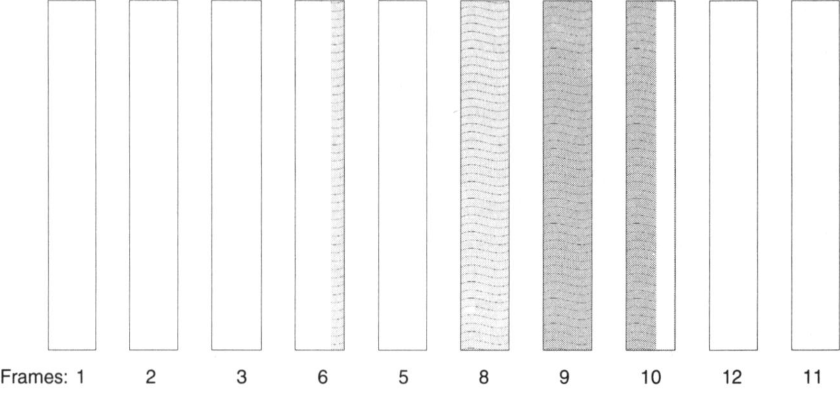


**Figure 17.2** Sequence error for block image transmission.

they are encoded as bit information, decoding the MAC and LLC parameters requires some effort. However, the point is that each OSI or NOS protocol layers add control blocks and bytes to the actual Token-Ring frame, thus decreasing throughput efficiency. Transmission of the 10-Mbyte image may require 120 s.[1] A Token-Ring under normal load (45% channel load, 38 μs TRT) will actually require more than 18 minutes to transfer the image. A 24-bit color TIFF image for a two-page magazine spread or a typical medical imaging CAT scan (that is illegal to compress) comprises about 55 Mbytes. Under such conditions, image transfer times could easily exceed 2 hours.

Few networks consist of a mere two nodes; most have many nodes. Nonetheless, the controller transfer limitation implies that about 16 nodes (ignoring collisions) could probably transmit at constant capacity to 16 other receiving nodes before approaching the 16 Mbits/s Token-Ring channel capacity. A bottleneck at the server level may masquerade as poor Token-Ring channel performance. Bottlenecks will occur when multiple nodes send to or request information from a single node at once. The single node becomes a bottleneck despite excess channel capacity. This occurs not because this node simultaneously receives 16 packets at once. In fact, it cannot. If you recall, only one packet can exist on Token-Ring at a single time by definition. (Even with ETR, sufficient time would exist for a node to cope with multiple packets because these packets must be under 200 bytes and are still sequentially transmitted packets. They do not overlap.) The bottleneck occurs because this node must process the requests associated with each transmission.

1 *The Seybold Report on Publishing Systems*, Vol. 20, No. 10/11, Autumn 1990.

For example, a file server handles user (or application) requests for data from files while an application server overlays sequential or program overlays for client users. Each request requires the server to interpret and process this. A client requesting an SQL view wants the server to extract specific information from a database and formulate that view for transmission to the client. That processing is not simple and is usually CPU-intensive. Similar multiple requests from clients will cause a performance bottleneck at the server. This contrasts the issue of maximum network performance against maximum server performance. While these requests may necessitate some higher-level protocol transmission, network load may reach only 15 percent of capacity. By comparison, the file or application server has reached 100 percent of CPU, controller transmission, disk access, or bus capacity.

One solution for poor client-server LAN performance is to replace existing servers with faster units. Often, this means that a standard high-end PC is replaced by a so-called "superserver" from a company such as Netframe, Parallan, and Tricord. These machines are designed with wider bus channels than standard MCA, EISA, or ISA PCs. For example, while MCA supports a 50 MHz bus and EISA supports a 33 MHz bus, Tricord provides at least 135 MHz. Because all data I/O, *direct memory access* (DMA), and control signals are passed across the bus, widening the bus usually improves performance dramatically. When disk access is the performance limitation on the network, high performance "disk farms" from a company such as Core International or Sanyo-Icon may relieve the bottleneck. Note that when these I/O bottlenecks are resolved, performance will improve. The next performance problem that surfaces after such I/O bottlenecks are resolved is the CPU or the LAN channel. Bottlenecks tend to move to new places as the network is optimized.

Client-server network performance also is adversely affected by full disks. Traditionally, Unix-based Token-Ring networks require file servers to have a minimum of 10 percent free disk space. In fact, a Unix disk is not actually "full" until it is 110 percent full. This extra 10 percent freedom provides room to maneuver large files while confusing novice system administrators with this new math. DOS-based, NetWare, and OS/2 systems also require the same disk freedom, particularly when providing database file service. As files grow under most disk operating systems, the file is rewritten over the old disk tracks while additions are chained and stored wherever free disk space is available. This is more efficient than creating a new file without extents. It is particularly relevent for database record reads, creation, and updates. This is efficient when writing data on a mostly empty disk, but inefficient when this data is reread multiple times. The chains must be followed to termination and this requires multiple reads and repositions of the hard-drive heads, as Figure 17.3 indicates.

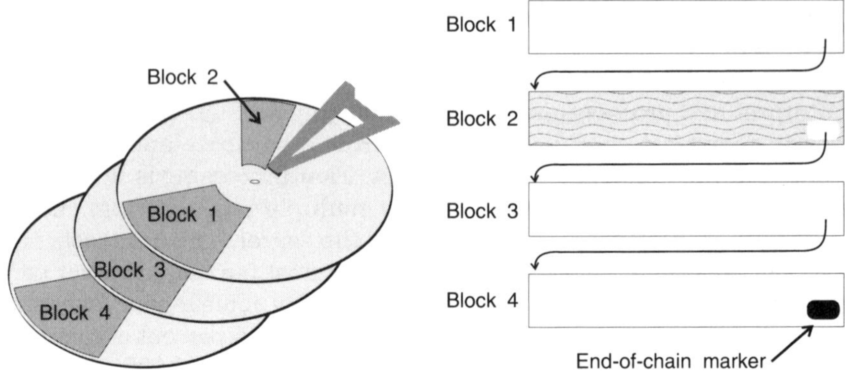


**Figure 17.3** Chained files are inefficient to read.

When a disk becomes very full, finding free disk space becomes a slow process as well. This is true for most operating and network systems. The free chains of space must be traced. Additionally, when large blocks of free space are required, minimum 4-K blocks may be chained together to provide it. This makes for a slow writing process. While it would be prudent to provide a disk with at least 10 percent free space (and 30 percent would be even better), it is also important to realize that the fragmented files and free space waste disk access time and create bottlenecks. Tools including Norton Utilities, Mace, and PC Tools provide disk defragmenters that gather all the files together into efficient contiguous segments. These tools also gather all the free space together into contiguous spaces as well. This dramatically improves disk performance for operations where files are continuously read, such as application software, system code, and database files, as Figure 17.4 indicates. The net result is faster server performance and potentially a better functioning network.

## Network Load and Performance Monitoring

Network management is responsible for knowing what happens on the network. Ideally, the management will see the load approach unacceptable levels and take the necessary precautions to maintain high-quality service before users are aware of traffic overloads. Few tools other than a protocol analyzer or specialized packet-counting software tools provide sufficient services to monitor network performance with any accuracy. Small networks supporting limited file transfers and mainframe to personal computer downloading and uploading, usually avoid capacity problems. Larger or more utilized networks often demonstrate a creeping traffic growth, and eventual and sudden network capacity constraints. While it

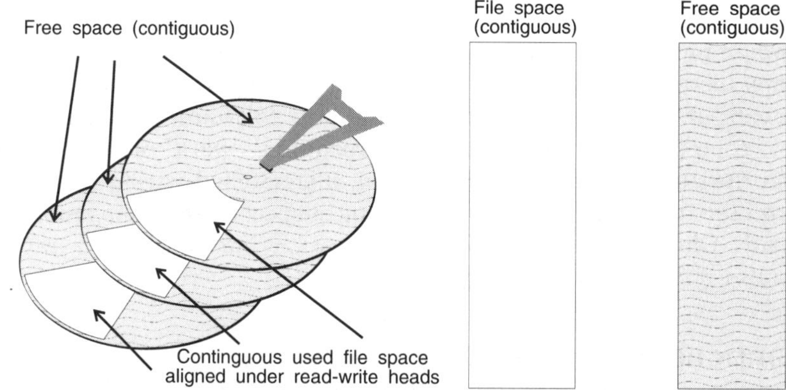


**Figure 17.4** Defragmented files provide faster disk access.

is possible to localize and resolve network overloads without understanding the composition of the network traffic, network load and performance monitoring pinpoint locations of problems and provide the network manager with information necessary to correctly implement repairs.

## Network Statistical Analysis

The mathematics are a curiosity unless understood and applied. Proper network load and performance analysis is most efficient with an understanding of the basic equations. Traffic rates (relative and absolute), collision rates, and request resolution time (interpacket timing) are based upon some of these important equations. Any rates that exceed a "normal" load imply a possible problem situation. If all rates vary, but do not vary logically, this, too, can be a clue to performance problems. Chapter 21 includes statistical evaluations for different states of network performance to aid in comprehension and troubleshooting.

## Verify Configuration to Token-Ring Specification

On small networks, the prevalent causes of network performance problems are misspecification problems. The network limitations were detailed in Chapter 4. Trunk and lobe length violations, node count excesses, and subnetted rings with too many hops are frequently causes for performance problems. It is important to realize that lobes that are 300 m will not necessarily cause a performance problem but rather are *likely* to create signal bit decay, mistimings, and crosstalk. Similarly, a 16 Mbits/s network utilizing UTP wiring that supports 130 nodes might still function. Violations of specifications are not clear indicators for performance problems, but they certainly suggest it. Furthermore, installation flaws may exist if violations exist. Figure 17.5 reviews common network misspecification problems. Other root causes include sloppy installation that results from faulty wiring, loose connections at jumpers or patch panels, poorly configured software, or mismatched cable components. Lobe and trunk wires often "work" on Token-Ring until the network becomes overloaded; mismatched wiring raises the impedance above acceptable levels. If you suspect one of these problems, consult Chapters 4 and 5 for configuration information, or review Chapter 8 for installation suggestions.

## Component Consistency

Another common cause for degraded network performance is noncompliance with a single Token-Ring standard. Token-Ring 4 Mbits/s does not work well in conjunction with Token-Ring 16 Mbits/s because of the signal timing difference. None will work efficiently across a bridge if the bridge packet limitation is 512 bytes.

All Token-Ring LANs are similar. Timing differences are the primary cause of traffic inconsistency. The same argument can be made with NetBIOS, NetBEUI, Novell IPX, and TCP/IP derivatives. When multiple system software architectures must interface on the same network, the different systems can be isolated on separate network segments, as Chapter 8 suggested. At a minimum, monitor mixed networks specifically for transmission deficiencies. Other specialized interfacing equipment such as routers, gateways, or bridges can adequately protect network users from performance degradation due to mismatched standards and minor operational or component variations.

Token-Ring components, too, can create intractable problems. Different vendors may supply NICs with transmission rate clocks with subtle timing differences, or marginal signal quality. This equipment, while tuned for single-vendor usage, may communicate with other vendors' equipment unpredictably. A vendor may not subscribe to NITS testing to ensure standard compatibility. Therefore, maintain consistent network node configurations for best performance.

- Maximum trunk length exceeded
- Maximum node count exceeded
- Maximum lobe length exceeded
- Lobe grounding incomplete
- Poor electrical connections
- Low-quality components
- Mismatched components
- Sloppy installation

**Figure 17.5** Critical parameter violations.

## Network Slowdown Solutions

Most Token-Ring networks experience performance degradation when the traffic level is too high. The last chapter developed the mathematics and explored the methods to track and confirm this problem. If the traffic level is too high, and it cannot be reduced through user incentives (like peak time toll charges), there are several other methods to divert traffic for better performance including off-loading, installation of "local disks," additional or alternative channel installation, and specialized routers. Load, traffic consistency, peak volumes, capacity, node location, recabling, and network extension techniques are a few of the issues covered within the next few sections to aid in resolving performance problems.

## Distribute Load

The most economically available method to lower network usage is to charge for network service at graduated rates and offer users incentives to avoid prime-time network access. This is what a telephone utility does to reduce daytime traffic and encourage off-peak usage. Since any network is built to handle a peak load, and since a peak load may be several times larger than off-hour usage, there is a built-in network excess capacity. Unfortunately, any extra capacity is generally useless during nonprime workinghours. Figure 17.6 illustrates this principle by graphing network load during the progress of a normal day. Harried users often implicitly understand this principle and reorient their work schedules to reduce the impact on the overloaded network. Publish a graph of daily network loads to encourage off-peak usage if financial incentives are impractical.

When this last option is unavailable, the next-easiest method to reduce traffic levels is to filter the traffic and not allow certain vehicles on the network during peak usage. The network administration group,

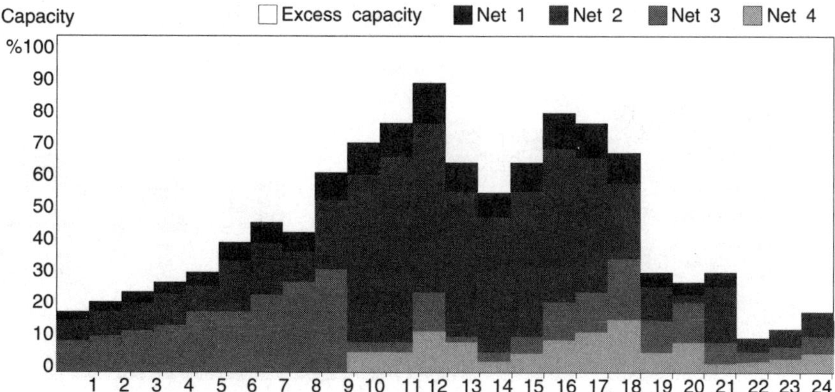


**Figure 17.6** Peak network load capacity.

for example, doesn't need to perform data backups when the network is overloaded. Electronic mail can be stored and forwarded when the network shows a lull, or else saved for distribution during nonpeak hours. Other processes may be hogs of network resources. Curtail such processes. Figure 17.7 illustrates a typical distribution of network traffic. Note that this display represents volume percentages each hour of the typical day. Collision traffic parallels the peaks of the last figure, but most traffic is disk access. Mail and graphics paging is a minor component in this sample.

Electronic mail often starts as a 10-line memo containing 1000 characters, but then is directed to 150 users. Since each user receives a separate copy, 150,000 characters plus the mail addressing information and Token-Ring packet information must be included. That simple mail message therefore requires upward of 300,000 characters of network transmission. A bulletin board with a single posting reduces this "junk mail" load almost fully. Side benefits include a reduction of "temporary" mail disk storage, temporary because each day's new mail will require that old space.

Data backup could be banned from the network and performed exclusively from the node bus. Such a policy may entail additional backup devices; it shifts financial costs from network communication channel improvements (infrastructure) to node-specific upgrades (depreciable usage-specific equipment).

## Provide Local Resources

Since network traffic often consists of paging information, graphics display, or mail transmissions throughout a facility, a solution is to install local resources. Network printing can be relegated to local nodes, as can file storage. Determine the composition of the network traffic and rebuild the network to optimize for local solutions. Local disks and

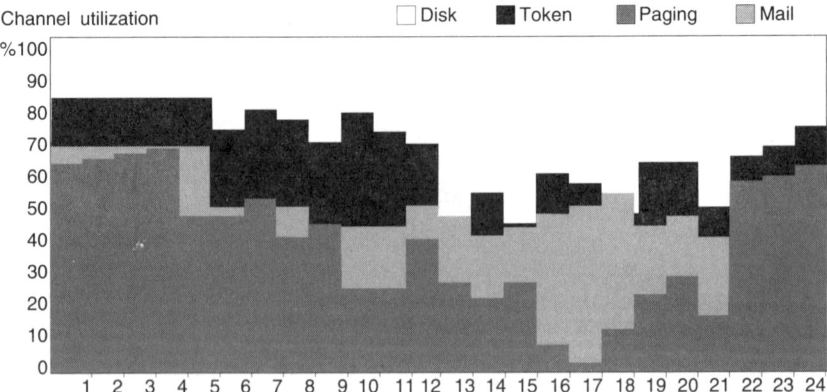


**Figure 17.7** Traffic composition.

segregated backup channels might be an appropriate step to improve the performance of the sample networks illustrated in Figures 17.8 and 17.9. This type of analysis is ideal before embarking on any network reconfiguration. The down side to partitioning a network into clusters of local resources is that the concentration of resources originally available through networking is reversed and shifts financial costs. Management load increases, and costs increase, with the addition of local resources because local units are generally more expensive than the public "bulk" versions. This reverses the economies of scale available through network resources. While this alternative may be more expensive, or take too long a time to install, it is an option.

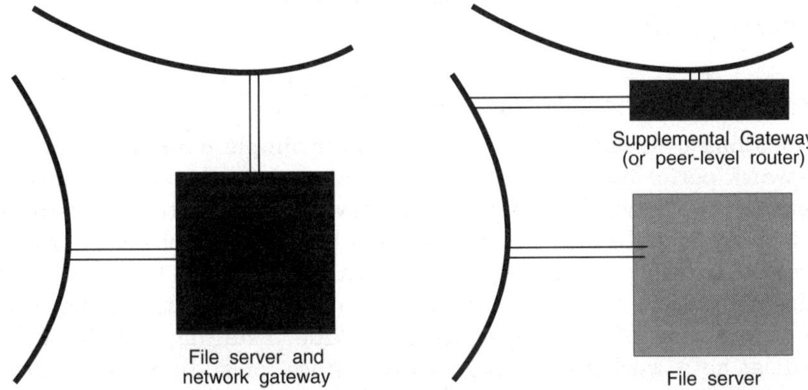


**Figure 17.8** Gateway provides dedicated service to reduce a bottleneck.

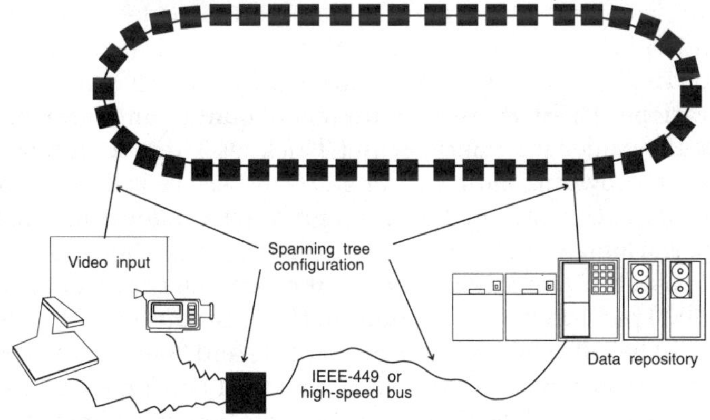


**Figure 17.9** Alternative channel (as in an IEEE 802.1 spanning-tree bridge) provides dedicated service to reduce a bottleneck.

## Specialty Controller Hardware

There are more sophisticated and expensive methods to resolve Token-Ring bottlenecks. It is possible—but unlikely for most network users—to modify TCP/IP or build a new operating system to provide for priority transmissions. There are also specialized hardware implementations that can improve Token-Ring performance. Controllers with more buffer space increase throughput for slow workstations by caching large transmissions. Specifically, Token-Ring controllers are a growing tuning option. As an example, the *bus mastering controller* provides better node performance by offloading disk and network activity from the CPU to local processors on the expansion board. Other controllers that compress data achieve more efficient network utilization, while some vendors are designing hardware that will provide optimized protocol translations faster than software.

## Optimize Node Bottlenecks

Unloading overburdened nodes is another simple method to improve network performance. A common example is a workstation connected between two networks that provides gateway service. If this workstation is heavily used for processing, it will not have enough power to provide protocol translation and data rebroadcasting. Note, too, that the Token-Ring controllers are usually bound to the node workstation's bus speed or to the disk I/O speed. Solutions include installing a faster CPU, dedicating a workstation to gateway service, or adding a specialized gateway to supplement the workstation.

There are three possible performance gains from substituting specialty gateway or bridge units for dual-ported nodes. First, there is better individual node performance. Second, there is faster throughput by off-loading suspect node controller hardware or constrained bus configurations. Third, there is better signal quality and interconnectivity for multivendor installations and Thicknet-Thinnet crossovers; the workstation providing multivendor gateway service is likely to perform better for its native information than for other vendors' information.

One performance bottleneck may actually be a bridge, gateway, or smart repeater. If a unit is rated at 12,000 packets per second, it should handle 6000 packets *per side* under optimal conditions. This does not mean it will handle 9000 packets on one side and 3000 packets from the other side. Do not overlook this as a potential bottleneck on extended topologies. Also, consider that the interpretation of a higher-level protocol can slow the repeating process. As a consequence, a fan-out unit is faster than a repeater. A simple repeater in turn is faster than a bridge. Bridges are faster than routers. Routers are faster than gateways.

## Provide Alternative Channels

When a Token-Ring network carries a traffic volume at design capacity, performance deteriorates proportionately with more load, as illustrated mathematically in Chapter 15. This is true for Token-Ring, since Token-Ring is a deterministic process, but not true for Ethernet networks, which are random. Alternative channels provide additional communication paths, much as local side roads and highway "shoulders" relieve a highway bottleneck after a traffic accident. Alternative channels lower the demand on the network in much the same way that local devices lessen the number of requests for network access. An alternative channel might provide specialized high-speed disk-to-disk file transfers, imaging information transfer, or terminal services. Performance improvements are, however, limited by a node's ability to support multiple channels. Tests with a server that supports one, two, and more network controllers show a modest gain (5 percent)[2] when a second controller is added to the server for average server loads. This gain decays totally as the load increases. Subsequent controllers create a performance *deficit* of about 10 percent each.

Terminals (DTE) or IRMA links require full packet transmission for each key stroke and are an overlooked Token-Ring resource hog. Terminal equipment transmissions reveal efficiencies of less than 2 percent when most network traffic may experience 60 percent efficiencies or higher. RS-232 lines—twisted-pair serial connections, for example—yield a better match than Token-Ring for such low-speed transmission. Conversely, an imaging camera or scanner often digitizes upward of a megabyte of information from a single picture. At Token-Ring speeds, 1000 or more packets will need to be built and transmitted. Such a load could jam an unloaded network completely for 4 s, or a network at capacity for several minutes while the involved nodes wait for tokens. Direct device-to-node bus connection improves transfer rates and transfer success rates. Many managers recommend hybrid networks and tune performance in just this manner.

## Remove Repeaters and Bridges

Repeaters and Bridges generally create performance problems by extending the token rotation time since they represent a network node awaiting tokens. This increases the waiting for all network nodes. A repeater simply increases the potential for too large, too busy network configurations by extending the network architecture to the breaking point. In situations where a network is grossly overloaded, disconnec-

2 *LAN Magazine,* June 1992.

tion of repeater units may solve the traffic bottleneck by decreasing the electronics delay. In situations where a network is grossly overloaded, disconnection of repeater units may solve the traffic bottleneck, as shown in Figure 17.10. This obviously defeats the purpose of the network by cutting intercommunication channels. There are other alternatives, but this iconoclastic solution can be quickly implemented to solve short-term overloading until more reasonable (and expensive) options can be implemented. A router with a filtering technology, a high-speed packet switch, or a backbone in a bus are superior alternatives.

## Substitute Routers for Bridges

The simple bridge, as described above, just repeats a transmission signal onto another network segment. Useless packets circulate the ring, stealing valuable token slots. The other category of repeater, the smart repeater (OSI level 3 router), filters packets for retransmission. The smart repeater can isolate and section a network for better performance. The router transmits only those packets with a destination on another ring segment. Figure 17.11 illustrates the function of a smart repeater or OSI level 3 router.

While a ring of 100 nodes may generate, for example, 100 units of global traffic, a network segmented in three smaller rings connected with two bridges or routers will generate the same volume of traffic because the bridges or routers will be forwarding the complete 100 units of traffic. If the network is correctly designed, the load originating on each ring is perhaps as low as 33 units (the average). If smart repeaters are installed instead, the result is a possible reduction in network load of 66 percent, although a more reasonable expectation would be about

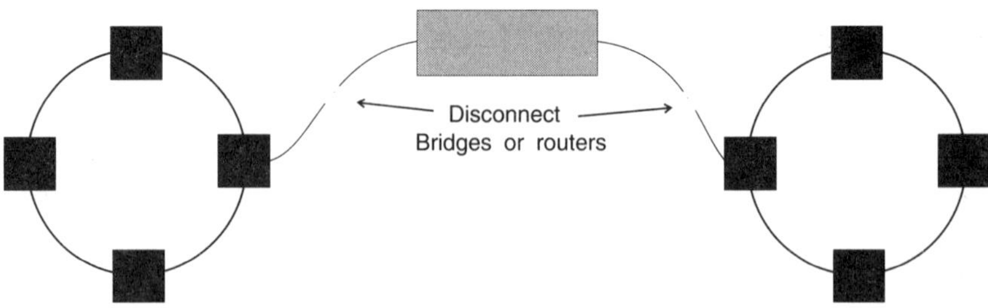


**Figure 17.10** Unlink rings on an overloaded network.

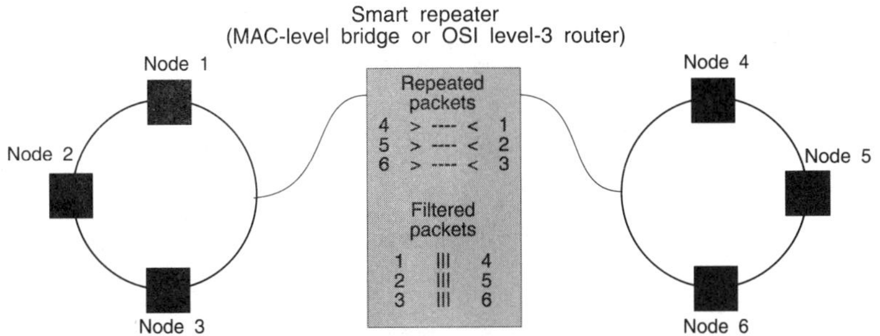


**Figure 17.11** Install smart repeaters (routers) on an overloaded network. Only packets sourced from node 4, 5, or 6 destined for node 1, 2, or 3 are repeated across this gateway. Only packets sourced from node 1, 2, or 3 destined for node 4, 5, or 6 are repeated. Traffic is thus reduced.

50 percent. In point of fact, this separation may yield even better gains since protocol and packet overhead affects actual throughput. End rings (sections on the figure) will experience a lower traffic level, while the middle ring will often be forced to repeat traffic bound for the other end ring. This economy is illustrated in Figure 17.12.

One other approach for improving Token-Ring network performance is to subdivide the ring with multiple network controllers in the server or merely add additional network controllers to the server, as Figure 17.13 illustrates. The extra packet buffer space and multiple controllers level the load, thereby improving performance. This is an effective approach only when the server bus is not at its capacity. Typically, a second controller card improves performance about 5 percent for client-

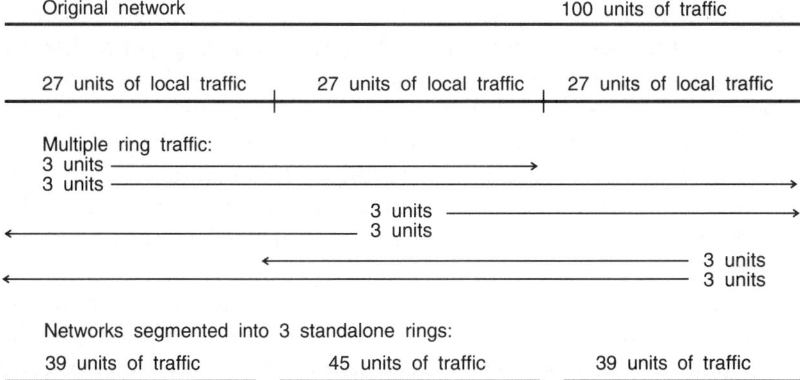


**Figure 17.12** Routers reduce network load by isolating traffic to the necessary sections. Three sections of a single segment have an average of 33 units of traffic, of which 27 are local and 6 are destined for other segments. When these segments are subdivided with smart repeaters, traffic volume decreases by 55 to 61 percent.

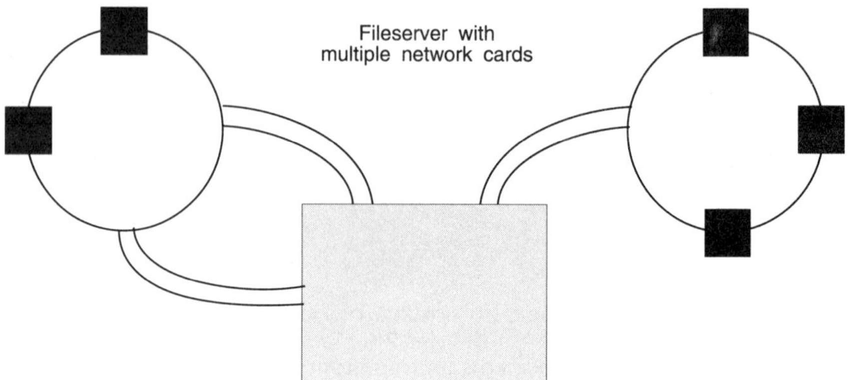


**Figure 17.13** Multiple controllers can improve LAN performance.

server networks, from 7 nodes to about 35 nodes; there is no improvement outside that range. There is a mere 0.5 percent improvement for the third card and some performance degradation for subsequent cards due to DMA and bus waiting time conflicts.

## Buffer Networks with Store-and-Forward Gateways

The store-and-forward mechanism duplicates some of the filtration functionality of the router. It also understands the concept of waiting for a token and will store a message packet for an unlimited amount of time until network slot time is available; it might save the message packet until off-peak hours. This store-and-forward technology is used for long-haul optical fiber networks and microwave links to overcome the inherent weaknesses of the collision detection technology, because long-haul connections cannot function efficiently in real time at Token-Ring speeds. In effect, the token packet is converted to another protocol and medium, as outlined by Figure 17.14. Recall that store-and-forward mechanisms require that network protocols be decoupled from a return receipt message.

This is an expensive technology usually installed as an ISO gateway. It is, however, suitable for low-volume, low-priority transmission. It is dependent upon the robustness of the network software and effective protocol conversion or encapsulation. In fact, receipt confirmation may not be supported except at the mechanical level of the store-and-forward gateway. The concept is akin to a receptionist taking a message when the telephoned party is already busy; no message receipt confirmation is provided to the caller and the intended recipient of the call never knows he or she was wanted until a message is received, or until a follow-up call is accepted.

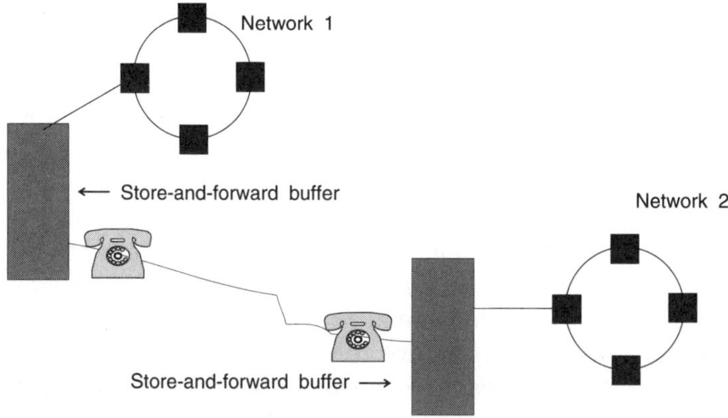


**Figure 17.14** Store-and-foreward buffering relieves bottlenecks by holding nonessential packets until the network is less loaded.

## Rechannel with Additional Rings

When network bottlenecks are endemic, the best solution is additional Token-Ring rings. This implies that new cable and additional Token-Ring access hardware will have to be installed. This option is costly, and the decision-making process must contrast the financial costs, maintenance issues, and the risk of acquiring a new technology. It is important to realize that multichanneling is no panacea; sufficient capacity must exist on each channel to provide transmission for local traffic and the detoured traffic.

## Expand Conservatively

When other expansion options have been applied as deemed appropriate, the actual recabling should be planned in stages to minimize downtime and disruption. For example, the overloaded original network is left intact *until* a new channel is designed, built, and tested. Changes proceed in simple stages until successful operation is assured. If subtle problems arise in the early stages of the transformation, the changeover can be reversed until resolved. This philosophy is useful for new installations, and also for revisions and repairs of existing networks.

## Tuning Performance

There are two basic conditions requiring tuning. These are an extended network bus topology and network overloading, conditions which are encountered by the network manager on all but the simplest networks. Even a network with five personal computer nodes could create performance issues. For example, all five units might be within the same office and require a 250 m lobes to a wiring closet. As another example, these five personal computers could be sited 1500 m apart, requiring special repeater hardware. While such design problems are possible on the minimal network, traffic overloading is a more common network constraint. Network extension options for Token-Ring include adding bridges and routers, installing repeater hardware to yield a maximum contiguous lobe or trunk length of 1500 m, or installing gateways which can arbitrarily extend the length and width of the network topology. Longer networks tend to increase the loading and strain on Token-Ring, and therefore any extensions require careful analysis as part of the design phase. This is particularly prevalent with routers and other devices that create broadcast storms or forward SNMP data to a centralized repository.

## Expand Reach with Wider Area Networks

As technology advances, most organizations discover that information becomes a critical component to their success. Information gathered from distant and occasional sources assumes a transmission technology different from local area networking. Modem, satellite, infrared or microwave transmission, T-1, ATM, and PBX are viable options to service those wide area networks. These technologies connect into Token-Ring LANs via ISO bridging.

## FDDI

FDDI performance for Token-Ring backbones and links is complex when it serves a multipurpose internetworking role. Consider the following complications. When FDDI is installed to bridge Token-Ring networks, Token-Ring packets are translated for optical fiber transport into the FDDI *subnet access protocol-service access point* (SNAP-SAP) packets. Major complications of this process arise in that the data translation must be performed in real time to keep up with the 100 Mbits/s FDDI speed, but also maintain the timing requirements of all interconnected local Token-Ring LANs. Encapsulating bridges operating at less than 4 (or 16) Mbits/s will cause bottlenecks. Additionally, traffic jams caused by saturated segments on either end of the FDDI link will create an FDDI bottleneck.

Token-Ring packets often are encapsulated for transport over the FDDI bridge. Encapsulation is necessary to handle Token-Ring's addressing scheme and ensure the Token-Ring packet integrity. However, there is apt to be a loss of compatibility since the encapsulation scheme is proprietary to each FDDI vendor. It also limits the ability of a workstation on Token-Ring from directly addressing any file server or workstation residing on the FDDI network, or the reverse. In such cases,

FDDI is merely a faster piggyback carrier of the Token-Ring signal and provides no internetworking access. Internetworking requires a translating and addressing processor to correctly route these more complex service demands. Translation becomes necessary and becomes more complex when FDDI is used to "bridge" (e.g., multiprotocol route) Token-Ring to Ethernet and ARCnet, or any other LAN and WAN protocols, including X.25 and T-1. True protocol translation requires RISC and other optimized hardware to minimize this routing bottleneck. Since FDDI becomes the high-speed backbone, it must be a bridging and rerouting server. Hodgepodge bridging (actually, OSI-level routing) would only increase the data delivery times, increase the odds of delivery failure, create a wide variety of performance and traffic bottlenecks, and leverage the chance for incompatibilities.

Performance is complicated further by differences in packet sizes. Encapsulation works well for Token-Ring packets shorter than the 4478-byte FDDI data frame maximum. It can be a problem for 18,456-byte Token-Ring packets. Although there is a loss in efficiency since each FDDI packet carries a single Token-Ring frame, the greater channel speed mitigates this problem. The distribution of Token-Ring packets is not uniformly maximum-sized packets; it regularly includes collision signals, return receipts, and even fragments. It is advantageous to filter extraneous packets before encapsulating them to avoid performance degradation on the FDDI link. Despite its high throughput, FDDI could be swamped with meaningless and empty Token-Ring noise. Routers (or hybrid bridges) filtering source and destination addresses minimize this problem, assuming that they can process the packets in real time. Segmenting Token-Ring packets into multiple FDDI packets also creates the potential for several performance hits. Potentially, each Token-Ring packet could be disassembled into three or more FDDI packets, a large burst of FDDI information could oversaturate the translation speed of the bridge, overwhelm the slower Token-Ring transport mechanism, and saturate Token-Ring with fragmentary packets. This two-way process must occur in real time with expert tuning to prevent a traffic bottleneck.

However, CDDI (FDDI on copper) provides a direct method to upgrade an STP Token-Ring network that does not meet performance requirements. The wiring is the same. The NOS is the same. The NICs and NIC drivers need to be upgraded. The MAUs are replaced with a junction box. Although this may be an expensive undertaking, CDDI bypasses the requirement to install FDDI optical fiber and more expensive NICs.

## Solve Traffic Overloading Problems

On a overloaded network, the immediate problem is to lower network demands, or rechannel that load. Figure 17.15 outlines the steps necessary to alleviate this problem.

## Tuning Recommendations

Network tuning encompasses more than remedial repairs. Token-Ring should be designed to service current loads with expansion points for future growth. Chapters 8, 9, and 10 detailed many of the planning and operational concerns. Another of those concerns is building a network with enough foresight to meet the user community's future communication needs. The last figure in this chapter, Figure 17.16, lists tuning recommendations.

- Reschedule peak loads
- Remove repeaters
- Remove bridge
- Segment network with router
- Install alternative channels
- Gateway busy sections
- Install more channels
- Install a high-speed backbone
- Install faster controllers or bus-mastering units
- Localize remote tasks
- Replace dual-purpose nodes with gateways

**Figure 17.15** Steps to relieve a saturated network.

- Plan for capacity
- Plan for overloads
- Set options to resolve in short term
- Set options to resolve in long term
- Provide the network with automatic "firewall" mechanisms
- Provide local access only when the network is saturating
- Disable all active SNMP or CMIP routines
- Educate users

**Figure 17.16** Tuning recommendations.

Chapter

# 18

# Network Security

This chapter confronts the issues of physical and data network security. Approaches that combat threats, strengthen vulnerabilities, and lessen risk are exposed to the reader. It is critical to differentiate computer system security from network security because computer security is possible without network security. LANs in general complicate security issues by extending the computer architecture to a physically distributed area and undermining the basic textbook data security procedures. There is a basic fundamental contradiction between the need to provide distributed access to information and, at the same time, to provide controlled and restricted access to information.

As a consequence, the need for networks should be carefully investigated in light of security concerns. For any network installation, the ramifications of open network architecture should be understood, and the many alternatives to network security should be learned. The chapter outlines security vulnerabilities, and offers security measures for the reader's evaluation.

## Security Overview

Attitudes about computer security are changing, not because theft and abuse are so common, but because the stakes have become so high. Computer processing and networking technology are no longer simply business tools; they are the lifeblood of many organizations. For these reasons, a concerted effort is required to divert attacks on networks.

Literature and movies have long had a special fascination with computer crime and abuse. Reports of yet another clever intrusion or massive "white collar" theft is the grist of good reading. Like everyday burglaries, breaks in security are something that happen to someone else. In general, only minimum protection measures are applied, although such steps provide a false sense of security.

"Security" is hard to define. What one software or hardware designer invents, another can crack given enough incentive. Computer system and network users invent new problems because they hit upon novel methods to attack the protection mechanisms, just as viruses adapt to new protection measures. Hardware security has been the traditional route for control because it has been possible to limit physical access to equipment. Yet, with the increasing distribution of equipment onto the factory floor, or into individual offices, and with remote links via networks and enterprise-wide communication systems, the cost and difficulty of applying security has increased significantly. Traditional security is a secluded room; but that is no longer possible with networks. The acceptance of networks raises the organizational cost and significance of a careless, dishonest, or disgruntled employee damaging the machinery and information, or stealing information. Figure 18.1 cites common reasons for security breaches.

## Token-Ring Lacks Inherent Security

Token-Ring itself provides no security, neither network security nor data security. Token-Ring is designed as a simple and open physical medium for data transmission. Furthermore, Token-Ring is not immune to snooping and spying, nor diversion of information. Figure 18.2 outlines these basic vulnerabilities. This startling limitation may surprise some; how could a network exist and succeed where security is either virtually impossible, or comes at very high cost? However, Token-Ring transmission protocols are straightforward, and thus allow for transparent transmission of encrypted data.

Token-Ring, like Unix, has prospered because of its simple elegance and wide range of uses. While some specialized networks succeed solely

- Inadequate physical security
- Inadequate indication of "sensitive" material
- Lack of locks on workstations
- Lack of organizational security policy
- Inadequate password systems
- No access logs or journals
- No records kept of efforts to penetrate security
- Lack of end-user security education

**Figure 18.1** Common security breaches.

- Open architecture
- Repeated (thus "broadcast" ) communication
- Easily spliced and "tapped"
- No hardware security measures
- Easily jammed transmissions

**Figure 18.2** Token-Ring security vulnerabilities.

because they meet strict government security criteria, or enforced contract bidding specifications, other networks have succeeded because they are simple enough to promote equipment interconnection and a generic platform. Token-Ring fills this description admirably. Token-Ring is simple and consequently, robust. It does, however, face security threats.

## Threats to the Network

There are four categories of network security threats: internal and external vulnerabilities, and physical- and data-related risks. Externally, an organization is at risk from events that might compromise the physical integrity of the network. An organization is at risk from external threats posed by modems, network and microwave, or PBX telephone tapping performed by computer "hackers," the occasional career crook, and motivated competitors.

Internally, the organization is vulnerable to profiteering employees and contractors, disgruntled employees, and the random disaster. Unless the network is perceived as a toy, and data never have value, and all users perceive that work accomplished on the network is totally exposed and expendable and agree to this, then and only then is security an unnecessary constituent of network design and administration. Figure 18.3 illustrates those items at risk in a simple matrix.

### External Threats

A network is exposed to external threats from physical attacks, and to a significantly greater degree, from data tapping. Most local area networks are contained within a single building, and as a result are usually secure from physical affronts. A saboteur cannot cut network wire or cable if it is locked away, nor disrupt power if power lines are underground and similar in appearance to many other lines. While this issue is often overlooked by many organizations, computers, in particular mainframes,

| | External | Internal |
|---|---|---|
| **Physical** | Power lines | Power supplies |
| | Data lines | Data lines and coax |
| | Network facilities | Network facilities |
| | | Access units |
| **Data** | RF signals | RF signals |
| | Dial-up lines | Network nodes |
| | Microwave links | File server data |
| | Line links | Output devices |
| | Wastepaper | Wastepaper |

**Figure 18.3** Network items at risk and vulnerable to attack.

have been attacked by terrorists and competitors. A destroyed mainframe or severed network is not only an expensive item to repair or replace; the data or time lost can bankrupt a business, especially when data are the lifeblood of the business. Last, do not discount the possibility of catastrophe: computer damage from chance events such as fire, flood, hurricane and tornado, explosion, lightning and power surges or power deficits, or a collapsed building, could set the organization back more than need be under such extreme circumstances.

While extrinsic damage to a network might occur (it is best not overlooked), dial-up modem and remote connections are the more frequent avenues of assault on a network. Most networks, even Token-Ring, often see the external world through telephone connections. There is no reason to prohibit such contact, although there are many reasons to control it. Most organizations have local offices and satellite facilities, and communicate professionally and academically with others off-site. The problem is to prevent unauthorized entry onto the network that would allow a "user" to delete files, modify files, power down the network, access privileged information, copy information for profit, or disseminate information to the public to discredit or supplant the organization. Figure 18.4 lists the potential dangers that must be guarded against.

### Computer Viruses

Of relevance to many Token-Ring network managers is the Internet virus propagated by a computer science graduate student. This virus replicated itself without causing real damage other than filling disk space and memory with its copies. It also propagated by reading the Internet address tables and reached out across Token-Ring to infest all the other machines on the LANs. Some network managers may rightfully argue that the Internet virus did damage. Not only did it halt networks, it also caused the attached machines to attend to the high-priority processing of the virus itself. PC networks are more prone to destructive viruses like "PC is stoned," the Jerusalem virus, Michaelangelo, "Ping Pong," the "disk killer," and the disk boot sector virus from Pakistan called "Joshi." While these personal computer viruses are

| Physical | Data |
|---|---|
| Catastrophe | Network jamming |
| Power disruption | Network tapping |
| Terrorism | Theft of information |
| Network jamming | Data "diddling" |
| | Data tampering |
| | Misappropriation of data |

**Figure 18.4** External network threats in need of protection.

disruptive, a network expands the damage by providing an easy path for infection. A new virus infects Postscript-PDL printers and damages the CMOS setup configuration. To date, no one has died as a result of a virus. It is easy to imagine a situation where a computer is monitoring a patient, controlling aircraft, a nuclear power plant, or chemical additions on an assembly line. A virus could unwittingly and unintentionally halt the computer with devastating effect.

### Internal Threats

A network is under scrutiny from the inside. Once the basic physical security of the network is breached, as often is the case, the network equipment is at risk. Unauthorized access to information is simplified, and prevention and detection are progressively more difficult to achieve when there is an amorphous "intrusion." The simplest security flaw is caused by users not logging off their machines. This is akin to leaving a door ajar, so that anyone can enter. While remote network links can be tapped between buildings if they are radio or microwave signals, internally the network can be physically tapped like a common telephone eavesdrop. Token-Ring, as explained above, expands the horizon for eavesdropping since Token-Ring repeats the transmission packet globally to all network nodes. An intruder with a means to promiscuously read packets can intercept information without anyone being much the wiser.

A highly sophisticated user can override any software protection by directing falsified Token-Ring packets to a target node; this scheme progressively modifies those software protection schemes for an eventual intrusion. The source and destination addresses could both indicate the target node, and few protection schemes are designed to protect a user from harm. This level of power is possible because Token-Ring is open, and most operating systems key upon packet address information. As a consequence, protection stops far short of top security.

While eavesdropping has its many risks—breach of organizational secrets and theft of information—modification of data can be more devastating because it can remain hidden indefinitely, or be propagated and disseminated before errors are detected. Money can be siphoned from a payroll and redirected to other pockets, trade secrets can be tampered with, private files can be read, development efforts can be hindered, and "ironclad" results can be scrambled, discrediting the innocent. Figure 18.5 lists ways that security can be breached internally.

Physical access to the network equipment raises the possibility of sabotage from a disgruntled employee or an authorized visitor. The physical network, the node equipment, and the data residing thereon are at risk. Most organizations assume no need to protect the equipment from employees. This is often an expensive assumption.

| Physical | Data |
|---|---|
| Power disruption | Network jamming |
| Network sabotage | Networktapping |
| Equipment damage | Theft of information |
| Network jamming | Data "diddling" |
| Network tapping | Data tampering |
| | Misappropriation of data |

**Figure 18.5** Internal network threats in need of protection.

## Protection Countermeasures

There are some straightforward measures which will protect the network. These include physical network isolation, standard password protection, limits applied to outside access, occasional changeovers in network operating policies, data encryption, and last, the monitoring of access channels, both physical and logical. Loss-limiting measures include fall-back provisions and a good network backup policy. Figure 18.6 indicates these progressive countermeasures.

## Physical Network Isolation

The most effective network protection is simply to lock up the network and make it unavailable. Obviously, this severely curtails its usefulness. However, when more emphasis is placed upon physical security, and when access to the network is controlled, the network is more secure. This holds true for both physical and logical devices. Therefore, the best medicine is to limit access to the network where feasible. Unfortunately, most networks provide necessary communication channels for business, usually as electronic mail, change notices, meeting announcements, and other normal messages; and thus such draconian measures are inappropriate.

- Physical network isolation
- Identification *and* password protection
- Limited external access and internal subnetwork isolation
- Occasional policy changeovers
- Spread-spectrum technology (for wireless)
- Access control for network monitoring devices
- Vandal detection and incorrect password logs
- Application access and usage limitation
- Hierarchy of access (user, group, and limited file access)
- Fall-back countermeasures
- Network backup

**Figure 18.6** Security measures applicable to Token-Ring.

However, the concept of physical security through access limitation can be extended as far as necessary to meet requirements. The rule is to lock up as much as possible. Mainframe and network file servers should have limited and controlled access. If printed or drafted output (fighter plane plans, for example) is confidential, then certainly lock up the printers and delegate one person to burst, collate, and distribute all network output. For additional confidence, bond that person and shred paper and magnetic trash. Since data storage mechanisms often use removable media-like tapes, disks, punched output, or removable magnetic or optical platters, a cautious approach is to restrict access to these classes of devices and their active media. Log all mountings, and catalog all purchases, uses, disposals, and distributions of storage media.

If more security is required, lock up the coaxial cables and other transmission channels. Place cables beyond reach, in a plenum, in locked corridors, or, restricted areas. Position multiplexing fan-out units beyond occasional reach and protect the Token-Ring transceiver and transceiver drop-cable connection. If this is unfeasible or impractical, then at the minimum, restrict access to as much of the physical network as possible. The node equipment is always vulnerable, although on a broadcast transmission medium like Token-Ring, each node provides a window of vulnerability to all other network node equipment, including file servers.

Multiports not fully populated because some ports are not utilized offer a ripe invitation. The lobe is already in place, and the additional repeater or other multiport hub is invisible to the network monitoring tools. Therefore, it is wise to disable the extra unused ports where security is an issue, and periodically inspect all lobes for unauthorized tinkering. A lobe cable could be diverted from a single station node via a concentrator without anyone being wiser unless a periodic physical inspection is actually performed. Figure 18.7 illustrates a common node with an added hub. This illustration also demonstrates how a cable can be intercepted with the hub unit, subject to lobe and ARL length limits.

## Password Protection

At the software level, password authentication protection is the most effective mechanism for network protection. Passwords prevent unauthorized access to files and network devices, and protect information

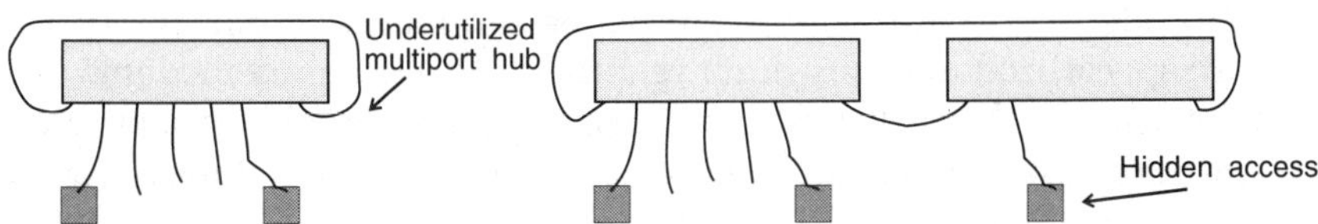


**Figure 18.7** Hubs and multiports provide a hidden opportunity to spy.

from "diddling" and tampering. Unix is one of many operating systems where security can be breached when physical access is granted to the equipment. However, for most novice users, passwords keep prying eyes out. Most serious data thefts have been perpetrated by novices who exploit a hole in the system. Password protection limits software access to a node, thus limiting access to the network. Additionally, contingent upon the network operating system and support services, password protection may lock individual files. In situations where security is of utmost concern, tools that analyze files at the bit and byte levels can be entirely removed from the system or locked away from the casual user. Such tools can invalidate bit-level protection mechanisms.

Password protection is only as strong as the weakest link. User logon names and passwords that are freely disseminated ease access to the system. Common passwords that everybody knows breach the security. Hired consultants with external dial-in privileges can be a serious security problem. Prudent management of security requires that passwords be changed regularly, and that when an intrusion is indicated, passwords be deleted from the log until ownership of a logon is requested again by a user. Good policy also requires that when people leave a company, their passwords be removed from the log, especially when a person has left under questionable circumstances.

Password protection is the most readily available network protection. Most networks provide password protection as a minimum security measure. It is also the most easily applied countermeasure, although it requires vigilance.

## External Access

Most published security breaches have occurred through phone access modems. The most often perpetrated breaches occur through trusted employees or careless procedure and password controls. A phone line is a doorway into the network, the modem is a lock, and the password is the final key. Therefore, the best protection is not to have any protection, but also not to have any external phone access to the network. When phone lines are necessary, several precautions are relevant. Do not publish the phone number. Change the phone number frequently. Use modems that wait for a tone from the caller. This has the advantage of not accidentally informing a dialer that a computer exists at the number dialed. Install call-back modems that do not accept calls without verifying the identity of the caller, the phone number, and the password. Install specialized modems that are difficult to use (many modems talk only to others identical to themselves), or that scramble transmission. While data encryption usually adds a dramatic overhead, it may provide assurance for external links. Additionally, where feasible and available, install Caller-ID technology to verify the actual number of the calling

- Avoid dial-up connections
- Don't publish the dial-up phone numbers
- Change the phone numbers frequently
- Use modems that don't supply a carrier tone
- Install call-back equipment and/or Caller-ID
- Control distribution of logons and passwords
- Change passwords frequently
- Install specialty modems

**Figure 18.8** Limit dial-up access.

party at the time of the call. Note that is some concern that Caller-ID can be defeated so that no identifying telephone number is provided, or that a phony phone number is supplied. Until these concerns are resolved, Caller-ID should be installed in conjunction with other security measures. Figure 18.8 outlines these crucial procedures.. Figure 18.8 outlines these crucial procedures.

Where a network runs between buildings, lock up the cable, or install optical fiber which, at least for the present, is difficult and expensive to tap. If these possibilities are unfeasible, inspect the connections daily for signs of possible intrusion. If microwave or a radio frequency is used, scramble those transmissions. There are few legal remedies once an eavesdropper is detected spying on RF signals. Select sideband or multiband transmitters rather than single frequencies. Be aware of the possible security leakages at time of installation, understand the need for organizational security, and weigh the benefits of applying the necessary security countermeasures. Figure 18.9 outlines these items.

Networks isolated by bridges, gateways, or smart repeaters provide additional security. Every step taken to isolate a network from public access increases the inherent security. While internetwork access is frequently required, subnets add a buffer. All transmissions destined for nodes on the originating network are not globally broadcast beyond that originating network. A router or gateway filters only that

- Lock up access to wiring closets and hubs
- Check for intrusions
- Install optical fiber
- Alter transmission frequencies
- Apply SST and sideband transmission methods
- Scramble or encode transmissions
- Root out anomalies
- Remain vigilant
- Maintain network blueprints

**Figure 18.9** Limit physical access.

traffic which must be transferred to the other networks; source or destination address-explicit forwarding effectively retains sensitive material. As noted previously, this does not preclude the conveyance of "doctored" packets unless transmission is a one-way process. In this way, a network could be constructed with a centralized and rigorously secured network facility. This secured network would lock out all remote links and dial-up access. On the other hand, the central secured network could reach out and remotely access the other networks and their resources, including dial-out telephone communication lines. Many such secured subnets could be constructed with access to a general-purpose network backbone. Once one-way transmission is established from the core area, a vulnerability is nevertheless established.

## Occasional Policy Changeovers

The best security relies upon sudden change. The most complete physical security systems, the best password and encryption systems depend upon new people, new passwords, new keys. You cannot bribe someone who is new and cannot break what you do not know; any security system is improved by constant and unpredictable variety.

Computer network security can implement such changeovers. Access codes, passwords, sign-in procedures, and front desk guards can be rotated with frequency. Change upsets best laid plans, and improves the odds that a trail of evidence will remain if an intruder actually breaches the network. Figure 18.10 outlines security measures that should be changed frequently.

## Data Encryption

Token-Ring transmits anything placed in the data fields. Token-Ring easily supports data encryption. As stated in Chapter 4, Token-Ring, like the party-line telephone system, is blind to the nature of the conversations. Anyone who wants to listen to a party-line conversation is welcome, but unless the listener understands the key, the conversa-

- Sign-in procedures
- Access process
- Guard personnel
- Location of computer
- Door keys
- IDs and passwords
- Codes
- Network links
- Remote access
- Locations and names of files

**Figure 18.10** Security measures that should be changed frequently.

tion is privileged. Just as a telephone will handle foreign languages, Token-Ring will transmit "foreign" data. Even promiscuous capture of packets will prove valueless if the data are properly encrypted. Data encryption is the most easily implemented security measure. It is, however, expensive in terms of computer time to encrypt and decrypt data, and should be applied judiciously. Furthermore, a motivated intruder could break almost any encryption scheme. Therefore, in those situations requiring encoded data transmissions and encoded data storage, other security measures should also be applied.

Wireless networks pose a serious transmission risk. While infrared signals rarely function through even clear glass windows, radio-frequency signals pass through just about everything. SST signals make interception that much more difficult. In fact, SST and randomly shifting frequencies represent the transmission technology of choice for secure communications.

## Access Control for Network Monitoring Devices

Certain monitoring devices like the protocol analyzer allow promiscuous access to all Token-Ring traffic. With such a device, mail, file transfers, in fact all network traffic, can be passively, selectively, and silently captured. All mail, all data, all files can be cracked, read, and understood (unless encrypted). While the traffic may provide only a glimpse into the full information desired by an intruder, such a device can clearly unlock private secrets. Hidden connections that are not authorized are more difficult to spot, but once noticed are obvious for what they are. Not only is such a monitoring device highly effective at uncovering secrets, its presence is easy to hide. It is a suitable piece of network equipment, and it belongs.

An analyzer, or network software like SNMP, CMOT, or CMIP with certain packet capture features, will allow anyone with enough skill to capture and analyze Token-Ring packets transparently and unobtrusively. This promiscuous data capture technique raises a first-line security issue. Additionally, many protocol analyzers will allow a sophisticated intruder to build falsified packets that could crack security locks by forging valid keys. However, if a network administration removes, limits, or monitors usage of all such tools, a minimal measure of security can be achieved. Other measures are required for more certain protection.

A protocol analyzer's inherent danger is so obvious that it can be overlooked. While there is a clear need for it, unauthorized usage constitutes an invasion of privacy and breach of network security. Therefore, lock up such devices, and when they are in use, monitor their usage.

## Application of Monitoring Devices to Detect Intrusions

While the protocol analyzer can actually intrude on private communications, it can uncover unauthorized network access. Nodes that shouldn't be on the network will appear as unknown Token-Ring addresses, or will transmit at unusual or unauthorized times. Furthermore, access to unauthorized devices, supposedly prevented but actually achieved, can indicate vandalism, and so be disclosed.

If transmission facilities on the analyzer were disabled to prevent such inadvertent data diddling, the snooper would still seek network access. This access is most often provided through an unauthorized connection or secondary MAU. The TDR would show that the network is longer than it should be. When security is an issue, precise network blueprinting becomes critical. Furthermore, a detailed impedance chart should indicate any present or past unauthorized tapping. The vampire clamps leave marks and increase the parallel impedance, and end connectors or cuts into the network coaxial cable are impossible to hide, becoming clues to tampering if detailed blueprinting is maintained.

Although data encryption will foil some vandals, time works against data encryption. The key can be lost, passed around the office as passwords often are, broken with enough time and poor key recycling procedures, or broken by a clever person. There are additional techniques to thwart data theft. While the network monitor allows a sophisticated user to capture and read packets, it also can indicate who is utilizing network resources and thus indicate the possible presence of a spy. While the promiscuous mode of data capture is invisible to the network because the Token-Ring signal is a global broadcast, certain clues can correlate excessive CPU load with limited network access. Sooner or later, an unauthorized node is bound to request a retransmission. This, however, requires good detective skills to uncover.

## Vandal Detection

A crook does not play by the rules. This is the prime danger, of course. In order to counter such danger it is important to understand the value of the data on the network and the damage that can be perpetrated; knowing this will point to the possible danger and to the people who will benefit from such intrusion or damage. The information resident on a network has no value except to certain parties. There are usually warning signs in security breaches. Train the network operators to spot anomalies since they often monitor all network traffic and could uncover problems as they happen.

Most of the administrative emphasis should be applied to prevent vandalism. The original network design should factor in security as a basic configuration constraint. Daily operations should be altered occasionally to disrupt the norm. Such strategies protect the network in anticipation of vandalism and snooping, but in no way completely preclude them. After most intrusions, there are traces that can be analyzed to prevent further access. These traces include log files, packet traces, time stamps, improper network impedances, unusual network interference, computer server problems, and missing or changed data files. The traces are outlined in Figure 18.11. The TDR in conjunction with network blueprints, administrative information, and good detective work can reveal electrical improprieties, while the network analyzer can indicate other software and traffic disparities as explained above.

## Hierarchy of Access

There are several categories of security access created to clarify and evaluate the growing number of protection methods and escalating "secure" operating systems. To address this problem, the National Security Decisions Directive lists a framework for security evaluation.[1] This framework is outlined in Figure 18.12. The highest level is the verified subcategory under the verified protection level. To date, these exotic systems are merely in the design stages. Previous attempts at complete security failed either through excessively slow response time or under the concerted efforts of expert system crackers. Unix and MS

- Network logon times
- Network logon names
- Packet traces
- Node impedance differences
- Network transmission interference
- Unusual entries on log and error files
- Missing output
- Missing or altered data files
- Unusual network activity

**Figure 18.11** Clues to network intrusion.

- A: Verified protection
  - $A_1$: Verified design
- B Mandatory protection
  - $B_1$: Labeled protection
  - $B_2$: Structured protection
  - $B_3$: Security domain
- C Discretionary protection
  - $C_1$: Discretionary security protection
  - $C_2$: Controlled access
- D: Minimal protection

**Figure 18.12** Hierarchy of access.

1 National Security Decisions Directive (issued September 17, 1784, no. 14).

Windows NT, for example, are both C2, although with a little effort can meet C. Multics, CMS, VMS, and other like systems also fail at C2. CP/M and PC-DOS are clearly minimally protected and are classified as D.

## Fall-Back Countermeasures

Network access audit trails and network security audits are standard procedures when security is an important network concern. Often, the logs will indicate an anomaly suggesting an intrusion. If an intrusion has been detected, it is necessary to act. If the intruder is known and the access point revealed, the problem is solved, although damage may already have been done. If the intruder is unknown, there are two courses of action. The first is to watch and wait, and trap the intruder. The second is to lock up the network without hope of catching the intruder. Which course of action appears best depends upon the costs of continued damage, repair of that damage, and the vindictiveness of the affected organization.

There are clear detective methods for trapping an intruder. The TDR, OTDR, and network analyzer provide one method of electronically locating snooping. Sherlock Holmes' style of observation is likely to reveal more cautious intruders. However, when the danger is clear and acute, and the identity of the intruder is less important than protecting the network, a staged shutdown of network doors is the best course of action.

There are elements of both hardware and software that can be shut down. These steps are outlined in Figure 18.13. From the hardware viewpoint, change as much as possible and disconnect as much as possible while retaining the required minimum functionality.

The procedure is as follows: disconnect all dial-in lines and change the access numbers to prevent future intrusions. Power down all remote transmitters and alter the transmitter frequencies. Inspect all coaxial cables, optical fiber cables, and wire connections for signs of tampering, splicing, and all other indications of line tapping. If you suspect that the intruder may have discovered information derived from wastepaper, or from stolen printed material, make rapid plans to alter paper disposal methods and output distribution. Lock up the printers and hand-deliver printed output. Shred wastepaper. Certainly, data storage media hold the entirety of the organization's secrets. Lock up those media, both online and on backup tapes. Furthermore, log the disposition of the data storage media. Change keys, codes, and access procedures.

Many steps can be taken in software to locate signs of tampering. They may appear as missing or altered data files, or unusual log entries. Restore whatever damage is discovered. Additionally, change the password access. Purge outdated password entries. Limit remote access to other network nodes and network devices. Change the access to network software that might allow data tampering and data snooping. This

- Disconnect modems
- Change dial-in telephone numbers
- Shut down remote transmitters
- Alter radio or microwave frequencies
- Inspect cables and links for tapping or intrusion
- Inspect network software and files for tampering
- Change ID and password file and purge outdated entries
- Alter executive code file ownerships
- Relocate and/or rename critical data files
- Disconnect bridges and gateways
- Cut hard-wired connections
- Change wireless frequencies
- Lock up printed output and storage media
- Reduce network user access
- Restore physical or data damage
- Limit access to remote devices
- Change door keys
- Alter entrance codes
- Change guards

**Figure 18.13** Security roll-back countermeasures.

includes programs that read "protected" disks or files at the bit and byte levels and programs that override disk- or file-level protection schemes. Restricted access is possible to security-sensitive materials by moving them or changing their names.

Access to any machine in the network where sensitive data reside might require a magnetic access card like an automatic teller machine or credit card. Additionally, keyboards might have software locks to deter casual use. In any event, physical cases of networked machines should be locked securely to prevent replacement, removal, or temporary installation of hardware components, including floppy disk drives, tape archival units, hard disks, security components, serial or parallel ports (used to link to a laptop computer for downloading data), or nonsecured output printer.

These are generic techniques and work equally well when initially installing a network or at any time the organization suspects a problem. If the network is insecure, it is prudent not to tarry and wait until a problem is revealed before applying such countermeasures. Security entails a cost in time, materials, labor, and aggravation.

It is important to have adequate protection mechanisms; tight security could mean that it will be forever unnecessary to repair damage or prevent damage from happening again. Security is a series of applied techniques that are disruptive, inconvenient, and rarely transparent.

The hope is that such techniques will never be required, but they are instituted purely on a prophylactic basis.

## Network Backup

The network is hardware, software, and the data. If the hardware were damaged, it could be replaced more easily than the information it contained. Despite this relative ease of restoring hardware, do not overlook the need to have spare parts on hand. File servers and key-board-level components are good candidates for the spare inventory. Assess the damage if a key component failed and were irreplaceable for a period of time. Keep spares of those units that could create a crisis if broken. Do not limit backup procedures solely to the data and software.

Many organizations are critically dependent upon data. Either they are the organization's product, or they provide records of funds payable and receivable. Data also can explain critical production or operational techniques. Network backup procedures provide a means to repair software and data damage. If a catastrophe occurs, backup media may change a catastrophe to merely a major inconvenience. As trite as that sounds, backups are a standard policy for most organizations with mainframe computer facilities. "Mainframe computer facilities" is referenced here mainly as an example of the attitudes and policies that have developed from the experiences now affecting the new network technologies. Many networks, however, developed from small components and therefore the organization and its managers lack the realization of the network's crucial importance. As a result, backups are nonexistent, infrequent, or applied to that minimum of personally owned files deemed important. A critical portion of any network is resident in unique files that define the relationship of nodes on the network, the network operations itself, and scripts automating arcane processes that have become complicated over time.

In the final statement, braggarts will often reveal their activities and indicate problems and a security breach. Listen well, be vigilant, and evaluate the level of security required. Cleverness will undermine all security systems, and ruthlessness will sway the most secure. Note well that the strongest security program will fail if the network operators and network users who are assigned to protect the resources are compromised.

This chapter has presented the issues surrounding network security. Threats and real dangers have been outlined, and practical and effective countermeasures have been proposed. Additionally, fall-back measures including backup procedures were prescribed when the preventive measures failed. These backup measures are detailed in Chapter 19.

Chapter

# 19

# Backup and Redundancy

The last chapter introduced the subject of file backup and network component redundancy within the context of network security. Backup and redundancy are also operational concerns since users' work, organizational information, or products may reside on network equipment. Prophylactic concern is warranted; only in those situations where the network is a toy, simply a communications backbone, or where network users are responsible for their own work will such backup concerns be moot. Therefore, most network managers will discover that backup and redundancy are crucial aspects to their success and continued employment, and thus are best disclosed in a concise and clearly communicated policy.

## Network Backup

The Token-Ring network is an amalgamation of hardware, software, and network data. The hardware is more easily replaced than the information contained within. Despite the relative ease of restoring hardware, do not overlook the need to have backup spare parts on hand. Assess damage to the organization should a key component fail and remain unavailable for an indefinite period; hubs units, file servers, and keyboard-level components are good candidates for the spare inventory. Superservers often provide a level of redundancy with paralleled power supplies, busses, CPUs, NICs, and *redundant arrays of inexpensive disks* (RAID). Do not limit backup procedures solely to the data and software aspects; also, consider the human aspect.

As explained in the preceding chapter, data diddling—the act of adjusting information from outside the normal systems and protections—and tampering can disrupt operations and cause manifold problems. Examples of data diddling include editing accounting files with a bit editor, adjusting school grades by changing exam scores, or recreating and altering a backup tape which is then used to restore a file "error." Backups and the network redundancy procedures explained in this chapter provide a time limit for the propagation of damage. If an intruder deletes or alters a file and this is discovered, backups provide recovery. Very few problems can be created that cannot be repaired from backup. Backups have value for the data they contain.

Since backup media are very portable, they should be tightly controlled and protected; damaged media may prevent restoration. Because catastrophe may strike a site, or an entire region, or sabotage may be very extensive and thoughtfully planned, backups should be removed off-site for additional security.

Backup and redundancy are necessary processes to ensure continued and consistent network operations. Backup and redundancy encompass more than tape or disk duplication of critical files; they imply duplication of critical data files, configuration files, software, password keys and access codes, physical wiring cables, hubs and MAUs, node equipment, and network servers. When a network provides the unique infrastructure to link different departments and functions within an organization, the network assumes an importance far in excess of its real value. The network's ability to disrupt the normal ebb and flow when it breaks justifies expensive procedures to maintain that network. A network may be indispensable; for those short periods of time when it cannot be used, it must be preserved. To this end, backup and redundant procedures are the corrective action.

Backup and redundancy exceed duplication of data. Any component with the power to disrupt operation should be duplicated. This includes software, hardware, data, and human labor. Figure 19.1 illustrates the elements warranting this attention.

## The Value of Information

Many organizations depend upon electronic filing. It is either the organization's product, or it provides records of funds payable and receivable. Data in the form of lists of detailed instruction sets (CAD/CAM programs) may direct production or operational process. Network backup provides one of the few available and certain means to repair software and data damage. Should disaster strike, the backup may change a catastrophe to merely an inconvenience, as trite as that phrase may seem. Backups are a

| Hardware | Software | Data | Labor |
|---|---|---|---|
| Gateways | System software | User data | Administration |
| Connectors | User-level software | Configurations | Planning/analysis |
| Backup devices | Network software | Procedural scripts | Software repair |
| MAUs and hubs | Utility programs | Network data | Debugging |
| File devices | | Backup scripts | Repair |
| Wiring plant | | | |

**Figure 19.1** Network components that require periodic backup.

standard policy for most organizations with mainframe computer facilities. Many networks, however, are outgrowths of the free-form and independent personal computer environments, and therefore the organization and its managers lack experience with the cost of a network shutdown. As a result, backups are nonexistent, infrequent, or personally performed without clear or detailed instructions and without a fixed interval between backups. Network backup is a crucial procedure to ensure the continued operations of the network.

## Media Backup

Most networking organizations create, modify, or disseminate software or data. The network provides the conduit for information. Since this information is easily damaged or lost, and not easily recovered if lost, much attention is given to preserving its integrity. Media backup is the usual form for duplicating and saving data. Magnetic media—floppy disks, cartridge tapes, cassette tapes, disk packs, reel tape, videotape or video cassettes—and paper copies or punch cards are the usual format for backups. The data and software are copied from the source hierarchy to this archival media for long-term storage. Figure 19.2 presents a sampling of stable data storage media.

There are many issues to address about media backup. Figure 19.3 outlines some of these. Questions often asked include what data should be saved, and on what media should they be saved. It is also common to weigh how frequently data should be backed up, and during what time of the day, or before and after what operations should information be duplicated. Because there are security concerns, where the information is stored is a pressing issue. Since backup media are both expensive and eventually bulky, media are often recycled. How media are reused could have long term ramifications if they are prematurely recycled.

Not infrequently, customer commitments, venture-capital development agreements, and other legal agreements require media backup, including storage of software releases, and research data sets to be

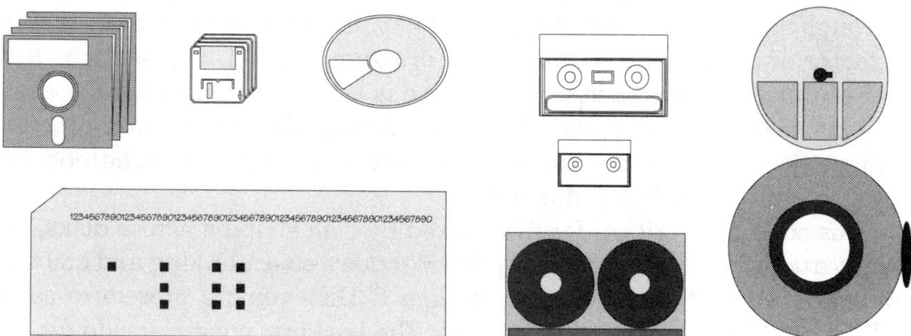

**Figure 19.2** Data storage media.

- What should be saved?
- How often should data be saved?
- Where should the media be used?
- How should the media be stored?
- Where should the media be stored?
- What access precautions should be applied?
- How should data recoveries be instituted?
- What happens when the media are incompatible?
- How often should data be saved?
- How long should backup data be kept?
- What legal requirements must be fulfilled?

**Figure 19.3** Data storage questions.

stored in escrow and financially insured. The IRS requires that financial records be retained for a number of years. Backups that fail to restore damaged or lost information are obviously worthless. This raises the issue of verifying backup media for content and accuracy.

In fact, many NetWare-based LAN backup programs do not function adequately. Many bugs have been reported where the backup procedure has required literally hours but only a handful of files would have been successfully copied. Errors or software bugs in the backup software prevented a complete procedure. Furthermore, the errors uncovered or generated were not reported during or at the conclusion of the backup process. Other failings include backup up servers and other critical data sets, but backing up the files peer-to-peer clients, the system configurations, or process files, such as batch files, macros, or command sets. Another backup disaster includes a full file-level backup lacking directory path names, security rights, or owenership information; such a backup is almost useless when files with similar names overwrite each other.

Special consideration should be given to any distributed databases, distributed processing, peer-to-peer networks (such as LANtastic or MS Windows for Workgroups), or extended or linked file structures. When operations are so intermeshed, the data integrity is not only ensured through sporadic or carefully planned physical backups, integrity is also a factor of timing and sequencing. For example, SQL transactions are not *committed* until such time as there is assurance that all databases can be accessed and updated. Failure during the transaction process otherwise results in a *transaction rollback*, a procedure whereby all intermediate results are flushed.

This concept is critical for files linked by disk striping across disks, by applications across a network, by MS Windows object linking and embedding (OLE) or dynamic data exchange (DDE), remote procedure calls (RPC), and for distributed databases. The backups must coincide for all these elements; otherwise, data integrity is breached. For example, consider the failure of a distributed database. Timely backup was available for the master server, but was outdated for the slave servers. Consider that the database was corrupted for an unspecified reason. Restoration was performed only for the master because it was available. This results in an addition of a master record to a distributed database on one machine without comparable supporting detail records that were distributed to the slave servers. Such disparities create reporting errors, patient record oversights, products delivered but never billed, and other costly problems.

It may be far-sighted to consider the ramifications for linkage and coprocessing techniques and the absolute requirement for them. Perhaps—until the management technology for distributed data has evolved more—consider dissuading organizational implementation of OLE, DDE, networked DDE, distributed databases, and object files linked across networks.

## What to Save

The simple answer is to back up all information that the organization cannot afford to lose. Software and network information that can't be replaced easily, or is expensive to replace, should be duplicated. Data and financial records should be saved. System software rarely changes and can be saved infrequently. Purchased software is often provided on media that are suitable as the backup in their own right, and a working copy should be made from the original while the vendor's master becomes the backup.

A backup procedure has costs, too. Media are expensive. The labor required to duplicate the information on a periodic basis is expensive. The backup process itself requires computer time, and often increases the level of network traffic, slowing other operations. These costs, which would be incurred for each and every backup, can be quantified as Figure 19.4 demonstrates. One way to determine how much should be saved is to calculate the costs of a backup strategy against the replacement value of what could be lost. Lost data can be recreated at some cost in time. This cost can be calculated. The work lost while the data are reconstructed can be assigned cost. These costs, which would be averted by a backup, can be aggregated and valued.

| Tangible | Intangible | Long Term |
|---|---|---|
| Media | Network time | Storage costs |
| Labor | Network traffic load | Security risk |
| Storage costs | Network downtime | Media degradation |

**Figure 19.4** Network backup costs.

A direct comparison between averted costs and periodic backup costs is not necessarily correct. The backup procedure is an insurance policy. Direct comparison between averted costs and incurred costs implies a need for 100 percent coverage; however, an organization must determine an appropriate level of risk (of potential data loss) which it is willing to assume. This risk may be 0 percent (no risk) or 100 percent (all the risk). Generally speaking, daily, semiweekly, or weekly backups are adequate. Even a daily backup does not avert all risk since there is a window of risk. A daily backup might imply a 5 percent risk, whereas a weekly backup may imply a 10 percent risk. Risk is difficult to assess because it factors in such items as the probability of a data storage device failing and a data loss, and also the probability that recovery will take a certain amount of time. Since any backup scheme can fail—backup tapes could be corrupt, for example—risk is always inherent. Even "fault-tolerant" networks still exhibit a likelihood of failure.

Last, how much risk the organization is willing to assume must be considered. Some organizations will bet that the computers and the network will never fail, whereas others recognize that the business livelihood could be jeopardized by data loss. This simple mathematical relationship will determine the frequency of backup and the type of information to back up.

## Who Provides Backup Services

Once a backup policy is determined—how often and how much—it is necessary to determine who actually provides the backup service. The network manager or network administration group provides these services if global network resources exist for network backup, if few other events disrupt the routine of the administration group, and if time is not an issue.

Personal information could be saved globally, or saved by the individuals to whom it has value. Most mainframe environments perform global data backups since the data are stored in a single, concentrated location. This may be the case on a network which has centralized file servers. Where a network is distributed, as in the example of a personal computer network, and few facilities exist for global data backup, individuals are responsible for personal backup. Where users provide their own network service, users often are exhorted to provide their own backups. Impress upon users that doing their own housekeeping is in their best interests, but the network administration group will help as needed.

## What Media

The media that are regularly available to the network machines should be the backup media of choice. PC networks generally have floppy-disk drives. This is adequate. Where storage of local fixed disks exceeds the size of the floppy disks, cartridge disks or streamer tapes are suitable devices for data redundancy. Also, data can be easily copied to another machine. It is less probable that both fixed disks will fail at the same time. (Probabilities of dual failures are generally factors of individual failures plus any correlated risks such as power surges, overheating, or sabotage.)

When data backup is a frequent and disruptive event floppy disks or streamer tapes may have insufficient capacity and speed. Reel units with 8-in or 11-in reels provide higher density and larger storage capacities. *Digital audio tape* (DAT) provides 5 gigabytes (or more) in a micro-cassette format. Cache space for backups also moves the process off line. Convenience and capacity are usually the most important criteria for selecting backup media.

The media should also be long-lived. When the computer is powered off, the information should not be lost. Therefore, electronic memory is not appropriate. Cartridge or reel tape, floppy or cartridge drives, punch tape or cards, and disk packs are common backup media. Furthermore, the medium chosen should be stable in the environment in which it will be stored. Do not choose paper or cards if they are liable to be eaten by insects or mold. A sealed disk pack is more secure for such a hostile environment. In addition, if electrical or magnetic interference is apt to erase data, paper stock is more appropriate as a medium. Most media will endure if care is exercised.

The media should be selected for compatibility with other machines. If a catastrophe does occur, destroying the entire facility, overspecialized media may complicate data and network recovery, or force network hardware replacement decisions that are not completely forward-thinking. Technology does change; do not allow a disaster to have ramifications for the network restoration. Also, make sure that if a backup unit fails for any reason, the organization will not be exposed to unnecessary risk. For example, if a tape drive fails, another unit should provide continued backup procedures and lost data recovery.

Last, obscure media provide both benefits and potential problems as suggested above. Although obscure media add a level of security to the network, they make external data recovery more difficult; unusual disk or tape formats raise the cost of information theft. Likewise, the selection of a large tape reel or a disk pack instead of a disk or tape cartridge makes it less likely that information will be removed from the building. However, obscure formats may increase the risk of losing information should equipment fail and be difficult to repair.

## How Often and When to Back Up

A frequent question is how often should backups be made. The answer is twofold. First, back up as frequently as necessary to protect the work and data you are unwilling to lose. Vendor software may not need backup since it is available on the original installation media, although site specific installation information does. Network configurations change infrequently and can be duplicated whenever a change is made. Data files that change with regularity such as personal workspaces and account information might be backed up once a week, once a day, or even two or three times a day. Networks that provide commercial transactions, such as air-traffic control, real-time manufacturing control, or financial transfers might need support in parallel with an entire duplicated network and file spaces. Again, the cost of loss must be balanced against the cost of providing protection. Backup frequency depends on an organization's view of risk.

Second, perform a cost-benefit analysis. Determine the cost of providing the backups: include media (which can be recycled after a time), time, network degradation and downtime, labor, and storage costs. Compare those costs against the value of the lost work, or the value of recreating the lost work. Include the social, publicity, and aggravation damage wrought by loss. Choose whichever is least. Note that backup is an insurance cost, and the comparison between backup costs and possible material loss should be a fractional factor. In other words, if the possible loss is $X$, it is appropriate to apply only $X \times n$ where $n > 1$ reflects only the probability of loss. It is too expensive to insure the actuality of loss except when deemed necessary. If you think that data loss costs customers, respect, and other intangibles, and that it is necessary to completely insure against the loss, consider that the value of $X$ should include the value of such soft costs. Figure 19.5 outlines the mathematics for such a calculation.

## Where to Store

Backup media should be stored in a "safe" place. This means that the media should not deteriorate from elements, nor should it be subject to theft, misuse, or loss; it would be a serious management concern if backups were missing or corrupted. Backups should also be conveniently located. To insure security in the event of a far-reaching disaster such as a fire, flood, Hurricane, or theft, backups might also be stored off-site. Consider as a possibility a bank vault or a warehouse that specializes in storage of computer media. Generally, a locked off-site room with restricted access and an entry log provides an adequate location. Note that precautions for safe media storage should be followed. Figure 19.6 lists these precautions.

## Recycling Policy

Generally, backup media are recycled after a time. Backup media are expensive and when information has been superseded, the media can be used again. Also, the media are bulky, and require adequate storage

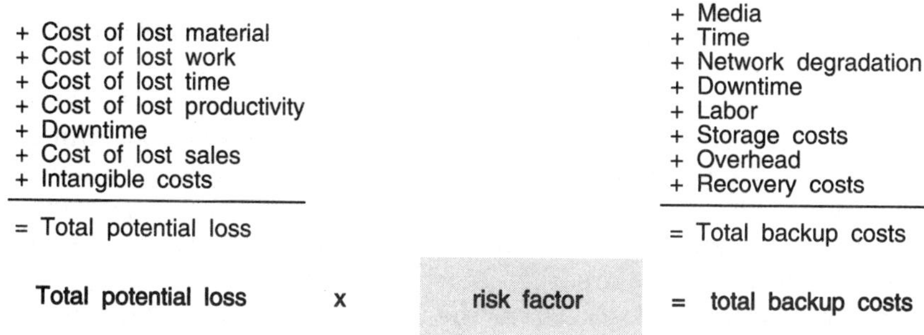


**Figure 19.5** Network backup insurance analysis.

**Figure 19.6** Precautions for safe media storage.

space. Over time, this can be expensive and can precipitate a decision to recycle. Figure 19.7 depicts a recycling policy where media storing monthly backups are recycled after 2 months and media storing daily backups are recycled after each month. Note that quarterly media storing backups are not recycled until a year has passed.

## Value of Stored Information

Stored data have value to the organization and potentially to others, such as competitors. Thus, it may be important to take all measures necessary to insure their safety and usability. Many organizations cover the value of their data with an insurance policy. While many media

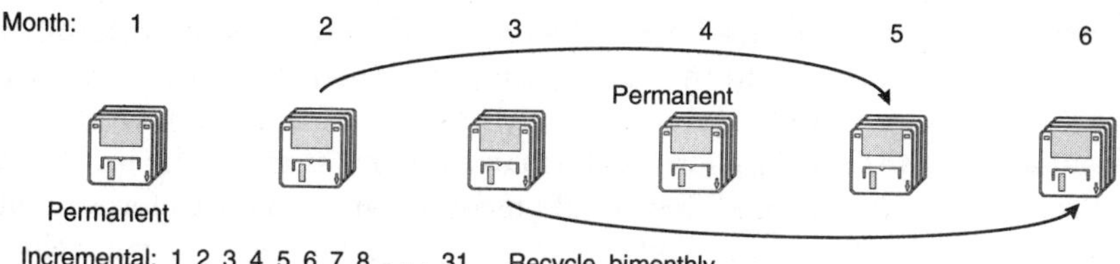


**Figure 19.7** "Leap-frog" media recycling policy.

storage service companies do insure readability and safety of the physical media, they may not insure the data on the tapes. In fact, without reading the tapes to verify that information actually exists, the service company could not know what exists on the tapes it stores. It guarantees the physical safety of the media only, not the logical content. Therefore, when information is a key constituent of a business it is important to evaluate and insure the monetary worth of that information. As elsewhere, insurance costs are high. Most organizations insure only what they cannot afford to lose. Assess the level of risk your organization is willing to assume and insure the remainder. Decrease risk with insurance on the media.

The caveat is that media dependability may fade over time as the media are used again. This can be checked, but note that wear on the media and the equipment tends to degrade performance and longevity.

## Verification of Backup

Once a data backup and media recycling policy is implemented, the process should be tested occasionally to verify that it is effective and working as anticipated. It is appropriate to audit the library and ensure that the inventory of backups matches expectations. Sometimes, a backup will complete on an unformatted tape with no indication of errors, but nonetheless be invalid and incomplete. It is prudent to verify that the policy governing access to the information is actually enforced so that backups are not lost, corrupted, or stolen. Those who should have access should know how to locate pertinent media and perform the necessary tasks. Those without access privileges should be denied access to the media. The data backup should be usable. A crisis could be compounded unnecessarily if lost information was discovered after the fact to be irretrievable. A lot of trust rides upon the network management when the team establishes a disaster recovery plan. A periodic audit of the backup media and their accuracy is a simple but effective measure to ensure that implementation matches planning, a crucial step for any manager.

## Hardware

Duplicate data backup devices in case a backup or data restoration unit fails, forcing extensive work-arounds. The choice of the backup hardware should be predicated upon the choice of media, media reliability, media compatibility, and interchangeability. If disaster strikes and the backup media are unreadable, not only has a lot of time and effort been wasted, but the organization has been unduly put at risk. The hardware selected for backup procedures should meet certain standards for reliability, speed, ease of use, and ability to be repaired. Other concerns include storage density and dropout, recycling, and compatibility.

Certainly, a medium that is specific to a single unit has marginal worth; should that unit ever fail, the medium is useless. Therefore, media should be interchangeable from one machine to another. Also, consider that should a network catastrophe occur, it may be critical for the continuation of the organization that the data backups be accessible by another organization or another network site. Data backup compatibility, in media format, media density, track alignment, and physical accessibility, is an underlying criterion. Likewise, data density has some bearing. The higher the density at which information is stored, the higher the risk that it will erode, be damaged by time, or experience dropout. *Dropout* is when information on media degrades from usage and time. Dropout is often seen on much-used videotape; it occurs with all magnetic media. Laser-burned media are usually immune from such problems while also serving to meet the Securities and Exchange Commission (SEC) regulations for permanent retention of security transactions.

However, whatever the media actually selected, the speed raises secondary concerns. As the density of storage is increased, the media are more prone to dropout and media failure. At the same time, storage space is reduced, labor and media handling costs are reduced, and potentially, backup time is saved. Additionally, higher densities often place a higher transmission load on the network because the storage device services a faster rate of data transfer. The media transport mechanism is usually the limiting factor on speed. Thus, by increasing the media density, higher speeds and efficiencies are achieved. Common reel tape densities include 800, 1600, 3200, and 6250 bits/in. The media for each density are identical, although total information storage increases by nearly a factor of 4 from the lowest to the highest density. Cartridge tapes often store from 1.2 to 6.0 Gbytes (gigabytes) on a small format cassette. This is a distinct improvement over the larger format magnetic storage supporting from 20 to 40 Mbytes by a factor of 100. Not only are they more reliable; they also minimize operator time jockeying tapes since one tape replaces 100.

Also, contemplate redundancy in communication channels. Consider what might happen should a phone line wiring bundle be cut within the organization by a careless contractor or damaged under the street by an errant backhoe or broken water main. These unexpected events do happen and thus need to be anticipated. Likewise, wide area X.25, PBX, PDN, microwave, and VSAT links do fail. AT&T data lines could be brought down by a storm 2,000 mi away, while a satellite battery system could go dead or the satellite could drop into the atmosphere. Where is the redundancy?

The IEEE 802.1 spanning tree configuration provides automated switching of data communications pathways to alternate routes in the event of a channel failure. Note, however, that the time required for the spanning tree bridge—100 ms or more— to recognize a channel failure and establish a remote dial-up phone link—120 s—may be insufficient to maintain real-time operations. Add firewalls between networks, local or otherwise, so that security or network failures do not undermine an enterprise-wide network. This is especially relevant for mission-critical networks, too, when the financial basis of entire organization depends on one or more file servers. Spare servers may seem expensive—until they are actually needed.

Lack of expertise is a risk. When personnel is untrained, processes will be inefficient, slow, or poorly administered. Problems that might be simple for trained personnel attain an air of catastrophe and confusion when handled by a staff that is too inexperienced. Expertise, both technical and managerial, mitigates rough edges inherent in any network. Expertise is expensive. It gravitates to the most interesting jobs, the ones with the most salary or enjoyment. As elsewhere, assess the level of risk an organization is willing to assume uninsured.

## Labor

A network administration team is generally employed where a network is large and distributed, where the problems are many and complex, and where the network fulfills a critical role within the organization. In critical situations it is important to have backup for all key components. Not only does this mean software, data, and node and network hardware, it also includes the people that maintain the network. Sickness, vacations, consistently long work days, job dissatisfaction, and other factors can mean that labor is not always available. If 24-hour network response and problem coverage are required, then extra resources must be available for around-the-clock coverage. If only one person knows the answers, the crisis-level discomfort is increased, breeding mutual distrust. Adequate resources resolve such issues.

## Disasters

Man-made and natural disasters verifiably do occur. Redundancy and secondary sites are important considerations when operations depend upon having a working LAN. Hurricane Andrew hit south Florida in August 1992 and caused at least $65 billion in damage mostly in rural and suburban areas. It missed most of the Miami-metropolitan area by a mere ten miles, and did little damage to the central city and office towers. Nonetheless, several major corporations were severely affected. Many suspended operations since they were without basic facilities and services. Others relocated in desperation to survive. Most—at the least—were inconvenienced for more than three weeks due to lack of power, phones, water, and people who could not commute because of roadblocks, downed power lines and trees, or concern over their own wrecked homes.

For example, the Burger King corporate headquarters sustained heavy structural damage. LANs were literally washed away and PCs were blown through the windows and up to several miles away by storm-induced secondary tornadoes. Backup media stored on site in filing cabinets or inside plastic desktop storage boxes became inundated with seawater and rendered unreadable, thus lost. Backup paper copies also suffered water damage and mildew before they could be salvaged. Original software, manuals, and ownership licenses suffered similar fates. The site itself was rendered unusable for nearly nine months. Since the extent of the storm covered a wide geographic area and many vacant offices were destroyed as well, alternate sites were not readily available either. Replacement PCs (without software or hardware) were unavailable locally and had to be ordered from out-of-state mail-order operations for two-day delivery. Although the manufacturers of engineering workstations outdid themselves and diverted units from other customers, this specialty hardware and unusual software required nearly two months to restore to operation.

Homes were destroyed and people were dispersed to new living situations. As a result, computer operations were lost for an extended period. Operations were suspended without the necessary electrical power, critical people were lost by attrition as they became unable to cope with extended commutes from new housing locations, and efficient procedures that had developed over time atrophied. The organization required emergency sites. Although multiple emergency sites were established within days, new phone lines for T-1 or modem connections did not represent a priority for the Southern Bell. The disaster was just so widespread that Southern Bell did not have sufficient resources to immediately repair existing lines and install any new circuits at the same time. Although this hurricane was an unusually powerful one, the message should be clear to many organizations: backup and redundancy is absolutely critical to the continued operation of an organization.

If this last example seems too singular, consider a more common accident like the flood that halted activity in parts of Chicago during February 1992. (The Chicago flood occurred when a maintenance diver broke through a wall between an old underground passageway and Lake Michigan. This inundated subterranean passageways throughout much of the old city and flooded out sub-basements, electrical systems, and underground mass transportation.) This example is similar to the previous one; but more likely to occur: New construction on a nearby building is proceeding without prior incident when a bulldozer strikes an area underground water main. While the accident does not straightaway affect business operations in nearby office towers and office complexes, it ultimately does halt business at those sites for an extended time. First, building sprinkler systems and local fire hydrants are crippled. This renders the nearby buildings unsafe. Second, lack of functioning sanitary facilities renders the buildings functionally uninhabitable. Third, concern about the safety of underground power lines renders the now flooded street areas unsafe until the power is shut off. This lack of electrical power now halts elevators, and computer and LAN operations. Since most new energy-efficient buildings do not have windows that open, this subsequent lack of ventilation prevents any usage whatsoever of the office space. Businesses in the buildings can not even inform calling customers by phone that the system is shutdown; they have been ordered from the building by concerned city safety officials.

Tape backups are useless—they are not really needed. What is needed is a secondary site with water, electricity, phones, and LAN wiring. The backup tapes might be useful if the secondary site were to have a server and client machines, although any work accomplished since the time of those backups might be inaccessible. If phone lines were still functioning in the primary site, a LAN-to-LAN update could speed resumption of operations without lost work. An astute organization would try to enable temporary call-forwarding or call-routing to a secondary location.

Although this is book is about Token-Ring networking *per se,* phone access is probably more important to most businesses than their networks. When billing operations are LAN-based, effected organizations can always move the servers, a handful of nodes, some jumpers, a MAU or two, some power strips, and the Rolodexes to a new site, and thus have operations online within a few hours. More involved operations with onsite mainframes and host-based linkages may still find operations hampered despite backup power supplies or generators for the mainframes since the other site failings prevent full use of the integrated computer operations. The message should be clear to many organizations: backup and redundancy is absolutely critical to the continued operation of an organization. Backup and redundancy may require a secondary site somewhat distant from the base operations. When disaster requires it, move the operation to the secondary site and put people in hotels until the primary site is restored.

## Redundancy

In prior chapters, maintaining equipment redundancy and a parts inventory were proposed as parts of an operationally astute policy. The issue here is backup, and when parts fail it becomes important to have replacement units available to solve the problem. This is particularly relevant for Token-Ring since it is a star-configured network. All nodes connect into a central MAU or hub. Failure of this central resource will disable the LAN. No amount of rewiring or inventive actions can bypass such critical components. Maintain a spare hub, or have plans to rewire master nodes into whatever hub units are still functioning. This same philosophy must be extended to other single sources on a LAN. This includes servers, server disk space, and any other critical devices. Failure of the database server or server for a client-server network will render the network dead. Loss of parts of striped files or total loss of files will render the network dead. When OCR, FAX, or printing are part of mission-critical operations, duplicate those nodes and their functionality.

Media backups, in part, provide a measure of security. The storage equipment and the device drivers are equally liable to fail and require replacement. Redundant parts are suggested. In addition, the people who maintain the network will occasionally be at home, on vacation, out sick, or leaving for a new job. The expertise to complete a repair should be available in duplicate to prevent a knowledge shortage. The level of redundancy maintained should factor in the level of risk an organization is willing to assume uninsured, since redundancy of parts and labor is an expense.

Parts cataloged as inventory and backups prepared and saved should be available and usable. Moreover, that inventory should be functional as well as available. Test the parts. Test the media. Prepared disaster recovery plans that fail are worse than having no contingency plans, since there is an expectation for an acceptable recovery. Such a failing tends to shorten careers suddenly.

Chapter

# 20

# Human Factors

Network communication has become a sophisticated management role. An organization inexperienced in communications technology faces a credibility problem because so much of business and management is based upon rapid and effective communication. Therefore, qualified people who can design, plan, install, and maintain a communications network are very important. The role is a difficult one because a network manager is a vendor to the user community. Responsibilities include responding to user and network problems, enhancing the information flow, and installing new applications, as well as maintaining network resources and costs within an established range.

There is never a lack of problems. There is always a lack of time to get things done and a shortage of staff to do all that needs to be done. Frequently, this results in a poor image and puts undue stress on the staff. The use of more people is unacceptable to upper management, or a reduction in the level of network service is unacceptable to everyone in the user community. Therefore, a significant part of any network management, including Token-Ring, is a clear understanding of these stresses and a means to cope with this supportive role.

The charters for network management, whether issued formally or developed over time and never verbally expressed, are compatibility, credibility, security, and stability. Figure 20.1 reiterates these charters fulfilled with a network team, experienced management, and administrative control of the network resources.

- Compatibility
- Credibility
- Security
- Stability

**Figure 20.1** The network management charter.

## Network Management

While a manager cannot control certain types of events, a manager can respond to events beyond control. Failure to accept events and responsibility for their impact, or reluctance to act and compensate for detrimental effects is a clear sign of management failure. Action, concerted and focused, is a clear sign of acceptance and control, whereas a reluctance to finalize decisions is an indication of a technical vacuum, a lack of clear lines of authority, or a basic interpersonal communication weakness. On the other hand, frantic and undirected action imparts disharmony to the user community. A network is a critical cog in the communications pathway; action and results consistent with the culture and requirements of the organization in time of crisis are imperative.

## Required Management Skills

The network manager's administrative abilities should encompass record-keeping, inventory-tracking, technical, diagnostic, interpersonal and analytical abilities. The ability to clearly explain complex ideas and reassure people at all levels in an organization is a key success factor. Little can overcome weak administrative control of resources. Figure 20.2 outlines these management needs.

## Administrative Control

Administrative control is an important factor for a large, growing, or critical network. Otherwise, self-taught experts or members of an *ad hoc* committee will provide such expertise. When a network provides development services, enterprise-wide communications, or critical services such as financial accounting, the network requires backup, daily maintenance, and a reliable team to control its operations. The network

- Administrative control
- Record-keeping skills
- Inventory-tracking skills
- Technical management skills
- Ability to make decisions
- Ability to establish priorities
- Means to cope with staff shortages and burnout
- Ability to provide recognition
- Skills to train and develop employees
- Team building skills
- Evaluation skills
- Ability to reassure people
- Effective communication skills

**Figure 20.2** Network management skill set.

administrator provides planning, network design and configuration expertise, maintenance and upgrade abilities, and also serves as the arbiter of file space, network access, and performance disputes. The most important role may be that of a clearinghouse for information and liaison to the user community.

Note, however, that responsiveness does not mean saying "yes" to everything. A negative reply is just as responsive as a positive one; no administrator can afford to forget this, nor the meaning of "yes" and "no." Resources are always limited. While this may often imply that a new file server, a bridging router, or a new hire will exceed available budget, limited resources could mean that one more meeting, one more evaluation, or even one more "of course I'll can take a look at it for you" will exceed the available time resources. Responsiveness is necessary, but it must be tempered with reality.

Lone wolves, the ruthless, aggressive types, are not effective managers despite the long-standing stereotype. A good administrator must be a team player. The traditional, autonomous "chief" is not effective in a service environment, and is counterproductive in today's workplace. This is particularly relevant when the responsibility for information systems and computer networks is guided by a pyramidal reporting structure while actual MIS and network management is a matrix obligation. Team orientation, responsiveness to subordinates, and a service ethic are personality traits that people welcome in an administrator today.

Distance from peers and subordinates results in an inability to hear constructive gossip. The gap also undermines administrative authority which should be based upon the nonegalitarian principle of information sharing and coordination rather than rank and command. The principle of "we are all in the same boat" is not a farce if actual rather than authoritarian control is desired.

## Record-Keeping and Inventory-Tracking Skills

Since the network is composed of many parts—hardware, software, data, and personal node equipment—accounting and inventory skills are required to track components and maintain an adequate inventory of spare repair parts. Records should indicate the status of software and hardware, and node configurations of all network components. A manager must know how to blueprint the network and track the status of work orders and job completions.

## Technical Skills

A serious issue for most organizations is finding a technical manager with the right mix of technical and organizational abilities. Often skilled technicians are elevated to management roles solely because of their demonstrated expertise, or skilled managers will find their talents at odds with the culture of a technical organization. These mismatches need to be corrected quickly for the good of all. Sometimes, when a qualified administrator is placed in the position of managing highly qualified technical personnel, the "troops" test and bait the manager in order to evaluate the manager's technical skills. When they find the technical ability lacking, they generally assume that the manager will not be competent. Network administration is a bifurcated need requiring both clear and ordered administration abilities and well-honed technical skills.

In the case of the technically competent manager, the administrative and interpersonal skills will present a valid challenge. This challenge must be confronted squarely, not avoided. A technical manager will certainly resolve the technical problems with ease, but may often fail to meet the expectations of subordinates and peers for handling issues, or disappoint the high expectations of network users. The solution, as proposed by copious managerial literature, is to map out the organizational interrelationships in order to understand the hidden needs, agendas, and expectations, and to build a power base within the organization. Listening to gossip is also suggested, although this implies a sufficiency of time to chat with and listen to people. Such a power base opens conduits of information, and provides for both formal and informal sources of answers, help, and organizational support.

In the case of the skilled manager who lacks the necessary technical skills, the problems will be in locating resources to solve problems and gaining the respect of the "troops." The skilled manager usually brings a power base and organizational contacts as a matter of course.

## Technical Managing Skills

Part of any job is regulating and influencing people. For the network team, this is a two-way process. Not only must the network manager manage the network team; all members of the network team must manage expectations company-wide, since the entire company is often the team's client. Management is not only from the top down, but also from the bottom up. The required skill set comprises more than the technical skills to maintain the physical and operative well-being of the network. Users must be satisfied that they are receiving adequate and equal (to any fee basis, if applicable) service. Because this skill set is so large, a single person might not succeed at the job. Perception of the workload usually determines who and how many people constitute the management team. If more than a single person is required—in fact, several might be required to provide hardware, software, maintenance, and administrative support—the internal dynamics of the group increase management workload. Adding more people to a problem does not always hasten the solution.

A good manager knows how to manage and control a situation. This does not imply that a good manager controls his or her team; rather, it means that the manager is able to control the situation and derive consensus goals and communicate them clearly to the team for implementation. The manager might feel distinctly out of control because of a dependence on the network team for implementation and technical skills. Here, as elsewhere, success will depend upon building consensus.

## Interpersonal Communication Skills

Organizations spend money on technology, not on the basic skills of how to be a good employee; this issue must be addressed. While technical skills are clearly necessary to resolve the technical network problems, a honed communication skill is a prerequisite. Reiterating an earlier point, there is a vendor-user relationship in the network maintenance role. A manager can do a top-notch job in the mechanical side of the network, but still fail if the targeted user community is ignored. People slated to use the system are often removed from the planning process and find that plans made for them really don't solve their problems. Exclusion from the planning process is also a political sleight that suggests that the users are neither intelligent enough nor important enough. Such ignorance rapidly erodes any manager's effective authority and ultimate success.

Additionally, a manager should know how to prepare all the paperwork that goes with being a manager. Honed presentation skills help convince others that you know how to design, plan, implement, and manage.

## Making Decisions

Think big: realize that the consequences of many decisions may not become apparent for a year or more. New administrators tend to err on the conservative side, finding it difficult to leap from their petty circumstances to the big picture. The game could be lost on this relative inaction.

Often the network administration team will be constrained to repair only those items that show clear failures. While individual problems may be innocuous, a number of marginal problems may combine to produce a global effect. Because the network management role is a repair, replace, and restore role, forward-thinking action is difficult to achieve. Upper management rarely encourages potentially disruptive risk taking. Radical changes are frowned upon, and network changes are filtered through a conservative screen of consensus. This policy can be the death of the success of a network manager, because growth, technological change, and proliferating problems may undermine that person's authority, perceived competence, and ability to institute large-scale repairs. It can also create a dead-end job. This tendency should be resisted. Not only will conservatism ultimately devalue the network manager and the team, but the organization as an entity may slip behind the competition, as new technology supersedes the old.

Conservatism boxes a manager into a suboptimal position and limits the options otherwise available. When decision making is indecisive and risk taking has been avoided as a matter of policy, taking even moderate chances raises eyebrows because others have become accustomed to the norm. Breach of the norm, no matter how risky or risk-adverse, will cause objections. Establish your credibility soon. The pattern of risk taking is established early on and success with those risks builds a consistent confidence in the network administration team.

## Setting Priorities

The best action is to negotiate with the user community. If users are denied a say in network management, you will have a poor user-vendor relationship. Users clearly will not get the type and level of service which they desire. The important point is that service is not merely network performance and computer resources, it also comprises personal reassurances, attention to people as individuals, and recognition of users' deadlines and problems. It is erroneous to assume that you or your team can determine needs and priorities. Users feel slighted and out of control when decisions are made for them. Certain projects or certain users may be key to the organization. For example, their network welfare is more critical than the welfare of other users. Unless this circumstance is communicated to the user community, other user groups might feel shortchanged when resources are applied to resolve problems not affecting them personally.

## Working around Staff Shortages

Extra staffing is always needed and difficult to obtain; staffing is always a real management issue. A high level of skill in small part counterbalances the paucity of staff. Good management, good organizational skills, and clear communication with the user community almost make up for threadbare resources. Involve the user community in the planning process; users know what they want. If consulted and apprised of events, they will help the process. If users are uncomfortable, they will reflect and magnify this insecurity over time. The users will understand resource limitations if clearly expressed. Involve them, and they will be part of your team.

## Burnout and Recognition

"Burnout" is a common result of understaffing. The level of network problems and the workload imposed are often beyond the control of the network team or the manager. Lack of control is a situation that can be rectified, but the daily pressures magnify the difficulty of the job. Without adequate recognition of accomplishments, the team members will feel frustrated, undervalued, and often, angry.

A manager who communicates well with the user community has solved part of this problem by explaining the limits of the resources within that manager's control and the level of service that can be provided. This will lessen the daily pressures, thus diverting episodic burnouts. More important, however, is attributing credit where it is due. Provide positive feedback to the team members and be certain that the user community is aware of the value of the services rendered.

## Employee Development Skills

Since staff shortages are a certainty, it is important to recognize the desires of the employees for technical achievement and accomplishment and help the employees to develop new skills. In order to construct an effective network management team it is important to provide a defined framework within which the group functions. Demonstrate policies by example and maintain a clear and concise model. Avoid sudden shifts in demands, needs, and policy. Practice and rehearse the policies until the group is competent and confident. By all means, provide feedback, demonstrate by example, reaffirm correct and incorrect procedures, reaffirm the developing skill sets, and fine-tune any newly acquired skills. Train on all levels. Role models acting differently will undermine any "positive" results. Figure 20.3 lists team development suggestions.

## Team Building Skills

It is a given that there will be staff shortages and that the staff will experience burnout. In order to cope with these problems it is imperative that the manager understand how to encourage the staff to develop new skills, and how to foster initiative and a team approach.

- Define a framework
- Demonstrate by example
- Practice for confidence and competence
- Provide immediate feedback
- Allow time for job-related education
- Express satisfaction with performance publicly
- Express dissatisfaction with performance privately
- Listen

**Figure 20.3** Team development steps.

### Evaluation Skills

Part of the job of manager includes hiring, firing, specifying the pay scale for each job, and evaluating the team members. Good evaluation skills are important for maintaining each team member's sense of fair pay for work performed. Effective evaluation encourages superior performance by outlining what the expected goals are, and how each team member has performed relative to these goals. Failure to present clear and concise goals will discourage good team spirit and confuse the team members and the user community. Additionally, inability to evaluate team performance will create disgruntled employees.

### The Network Team

Crucial to any Token-Ring is an experienced network team. A network team would not be needed if Token-Ring were a simple hook-up-and-run type of network. Instead, the link requires shared resources that offer both load limitations and a complex architecture. The simplified wiring of Token-Ring eases the burden of maintaining a network in contrast to the star-coupled mainframe environment. As a consequence, the skill set for the network team should be different from that of a mainframe support team. The network team must understand the diverse needs and varied equipment in use within the network community. It also must recognize the interrelationship that a network creates. A good team can make a crucial difference between a functioning network and an unmitigated disaster. A good team makes a manager look good.

### Team Skill Requirements

Several skill sets are required to keep the link of that network up and running. Figure 20.4 lists some of these needs. The physical layers of Token-Ring need to be maintained, and the software link layers need management. The node equipment, consisting of nonspecialized computer hardware, needs physical maintenance. The node equipment can range from simple and reliable personal computers to more fragile and complex engineering workstations, file servers, and print servers. This application layer requires software, physical, and preventive maintenance.

## Technical Knowledge

The network team applies mechanical and computer knowledge to plan, design, implement, and repair the network. Alternatively, if the group

- Technical knowledge
- Diagnostic skills
- Analytic skills
- Interpersonal communication abilities

**Figure 20.4** The network team skill set.

has a firm organizational charter, hired outside experts ease the load when problems exceed the abilities of the in-house crew.

## Diagnostic and Analytic Skills

As important as good technical skills for the success of a team member is the ability to uncover network problems in a Token-Ring environment. Problems are not solved with textbook knowledge. They often transcend the vendor manuals and the scope of any book. It is therefore important that all team members know how to think through a situation given the relevant facts, and apply their technical knowledge to solving the problem.

## Interpersonal Communication Skills

Organizations spend money on the people who bring to the company technical skills but not necessarily the basic skills of how to be a good employee. However, although technical skills are clearly necessary to resolve the technical network problems, a honed communication skill is prerequisite, not only for managers, but for the technicians as well. A technician can do a top-notch job in developing and repairing or implementing the mechanical side of the network, but still fail if the targeted user community is ignored. People slated to use the system are often removed from the repair process and find that plans made for them really don't solve their problems, or even negatively affect their work.

## Hierarchy

Organizations are political. Even nonprofit organizations are not immune to ambition. Hierarchical structures are established to achieve effective results and also to put people into controlled positions. No organization escapes the chains of authority. Authority is routed in the power of money, voting stock, seniority and titles, fear, knowledge, and expectations that develop over time. For example, the authority to reroute the network is based upon not only title but the expectation from users that since you have moved the cable before, you can do it now.

Electronic mail and fax services are useful tools to layer on top of a LAN. Electronic mail provides a useful capacity for people to share memos, schedule complex meetings, and sidetrack phone tag. Anyone can communicate with anyone else. Management may perceive this as a breach of the chain of command, an undermining of traditional authority, and a serious problem since they may not have the time or the knowledge to control the network. The network installation must not undermine the normal organization culture or threaten the reporting hierarchy of an organization—or else the network technology becomes a serious threat. LAN fax services provide network users with the ability to send an outgoing facsimile with less labor, or see incoming faxes automatically routed without a security breach, misplacement of the fax, or lost pages. Additionally, *optical character recognition* (OCR) provides the means to translate a facsimile into a data format with a minimal labor component.

## Fear of Technology

Networks represent a complex technical installation. More than that technology, they represent a profound organizational and management integration that is perceived as a complex technology. This results in a fear of change, distrust of technical innovation, and suspicion of the people who manage the computer systems and networks. Instinctively, this fear translates into a battle to remove, disrupt, and destroy the computer systems and the networks. While most users can merely disrupt and sabotage operations, top management can fire people and remove equipment. Disruptions and sabotage are annoying or expensive although resolvable problems.

Fear from top management can undermine network operations and your own personal success. These fears represent a serious nonverbal risk that must be recognized and addressed with effective communication skills. Users can be trained and helped so that the network doesn't threaten them. Top management can be trained in network lore, too, although more likely the need and time for it is minimal. Instead, top management must be shown that the network benefits them in the myriad of ways listed in Chapter 2. Any perceived threats must be addressed quickly and resolved.

## Squeaky Wheel versus Problem Resolution

Users shout and scream for their share of the pie. Each user wants more attention, faster service, and better results. Some shout louder than others, and clearly some users have more political clout as a consequence of their position, length of service, or network of friendships. While it often is necessary to resolve problems within a political framework, this should be moderated by clearly stated policies. A network by its design is an interrelated organism; thus certain problems need solutions as a prerequisite to repairing others. A service policy is a must.

Set up a policy. For example, respond to problems on global resources before those of user-specific workstations. Repair global failures that inhibit the work of a larger group before attending to a single user's complaint. Repairs or changes that are upgrades or minor modifications should command less priority than a total failure of a user workstation. Such a setting of priorities requires a clear policy from the network manager. Adhere to that policy.

## The Effects of Change

There are two successful ways of organizing a company: centralized and decentralized. There are valid reasons for going either way. Most managers and consultants know the textbook reasons: a decentralized company focuses the power in the hands of those who can best apply that power, whereas a centralized organizational structure returns control to a select few. But reasons for choosing a particular structure are irrelevant when facing problems. Sometimes, simply changing the organization from one structure to any other achieves results. Changes compel people to reconsider how they do things, indicate that performance is being evaluated, and also that their needs for attention are being fulfilled.

A network manager would do well to remember this concept when a situation seems out-of-hand: a simple change of organizational structure, policy, and reporting relationships may restore control.

## Political Feasibility

All networking tasks—whether new designs, fundamental implementations, upgrades and expansions, solutions for performance problems, or even mechanical repairs— are subjected to external scrutiny and political examination. Even the most basic repairs require a reallocation of resources, if only a technician is shifted from one ongoing project to the repairs. Although the repair might be as critical as restoring *some* network service to the entire organization, the reassignment is seen by those immediately affected as a loss. A typical response sounds like, "I guess I am not important enough!" Unfortunately, the answer really is "no" because the repairs are indeed more important to the organization as a whole. The real issue is how people within the organization perceive the allocation of the network manager's consideration to their own needs as it affects them.

Although this seems like a resource allocation problem, the communication of how and when resources are distributed is really a political problem. Technical questions such as network standards, physical media, acceptable protocols, and what is the best solution to fulfill the needs of an individual group are not always answered with the best technical answer. That may not be what people want to hear from the network manager. Technical evaluations are actually *loaded* questions that are tempered by judgment.

Successful network managers, ones who gain credibility and thrive, address every question with multiple answers, as Figure 20.5 prioritizes. There is the sensitive political answer, the technical qualification, the evaluation of utility and plausibility, a presentation of period time for implementation, and a response factoring in the availability of resources, including labor, equipment, and money.

- Politically viability
- Monetarily achievable
- Technically possible
- Skills congruent with objectives
- Realistically plausible
- Realizable within timetable

**Figure 20.5** The priorities of exigencies that conflict with networking projects.

Sometimes, complex and sensitive questions are answered bluntly with unfortunate political and interpersonal consequences. For example, "Every other department will aid the effort and wants to see this accomplished. But that backward DP department obstructs every effort to connect their precious mainframes into the proposed enterprise-wide network...."

Other times, answers will be, and must be, discreet. This tends to achieve better results and earns the respect and confidence of the DP department. The contemptuous overtones should not be expressed, rather cleverly skirted or masked. How remarkable or how backward the DP department actually is represents an relatively inconsequential issue. Furthermore, derisive remarks, though offered privately, often are rumored and embellished in the grapevine. Certainly, expressing personal views will tend to restrict any future success with the DP group and alienate the scorned individuals. Instead, consider, for example, "An FDDI backbone connecting all Token-Ring and Ethernet LANs is certainly the answer that matches your needs; it only needs the support and encouragement from the DP people." Both quotes reflect the same sentiment, the same technical evaluations, and plausibility within a timetable, but provide critically different political and interpersonal insights.

By the same token, the network manager should not respond to a network user with emotional statements or escalate an already heated discussion. If that happens, the disagreement is lost. Realize that the issue probably involves a resource allocation request that has not been fulfilled. Also, there might be a reason divorced from anything related to the network, and the network manager is an easy target or a person the user knows will argue needlessly; that may be very satisfying. The user may be under stress to perform up to par, to complete an overdue task, or be angry at a spouse. Assess the motivation for the user's hostility. Whatever that motivation, the user is angry at the *role* of network manager, but not personally at the network manager, per se. It is likely that the user would probably have the same discussion with any other person filling the role of network manager.

The outcome of the discussion in terms of emotional satisfaction for the user may be different even while the realities of time and resource limitations might not. In other words, the outcome may be the same regardless of how the discussion progresses, yet the user may feel that the network manager has listened to the stated complaints, understood these complaints, responded to these complaints and also to the underlying frustration, and defused any political or personal reasons for the controversy.

Additionally, emotional statements or gestures undermine the effectiveness of the manager. Respect is lost. Instead, respond to the anger and frustrations of the user. This does not mean that the network manager must concede; rather the manager must politely respond and explain the limitations imposed upon that network management and budgeting role. Solicit ideas. Ask what the user would like accomplished. Demonstrate the priorities and listen to any thoughts about reassessing those priorities. As the final word, nonetheless, that may mean saying "no." At least, the user's frustration might be rechanneled with the result that a once angry user becomes an ardent supporter and ally.

## Easier Said than Done. . .

Most plans are easily derailed, easily completed. Communication and negotiations with the user community establish a credible relationship, while priorities determine which problems will be resolved and when they will be resolved. Despite the best of intentions, the workload usually outstrips available resources and the complexity of network problems often taxes the technical expertise and time availability of the network team. Things just will not get done. As long as the user community is apprised of these delays and gets clear feedback, options for temporary solutions, and/or revised time schedules, the relationship will flourish. Communication is key to successful human interaction.

# Part 6

# Troubleshooting Reference

This part contains practical and concise information for the network manager to facilitate debugging Token-Ring network failures. Instead of text and graphics, this part uses charts to detail a methodology that progressively isolates the suspected component. The prescribed procedures encourage good work habits and help network managers develop a logical approach to solving network failures. Additionally, several chapters demonstrate the uses for network tools and include cross-referenced tables to use as aids in resolving network problems.

Chapter 21 iconically describes the network components and then, using tables with four different formats, matches symptoms of common network problems with the possible causes. This information is not available cross-referenced, nor completely accessible from other sources, including vendor documentation, the IEEE 802.5, or OSI specifications. Chapter 22 is a detailed troubleshooting manual that describes techniques to isolate hardware, software, and network overloading problems. Chapter 23 summarizes the contents of this book with a Token-Ring tool usage manual. This chapter supplies ideas and information on when to analyze the network with a multimeter, a pair scanner or TDR, and a protocol analyzer to solve network problems.

Chapter

# 21

# Troubleshooting Cross-Reference

This chapter presents five individual sections that cross-reference practical diagnostic information. Figure 21.1 lists these sections for the reader's benefit. They are useful both to provide diagnostic clues and to confirm that a hypothetical diagnosis does explain the observed symptoms of a network problem.

Components —> typical Failures
Causes —> symptoms
Possible causes —> symptoms
Transmission problems —> causes
Statistical inferences

**Figure 21.1** The troubleshooting reference tables.

The first section shows what can fail with each network component. Figure 21.2 illustrates the components included in the check list. Use it to narrow down a diagnosis when a problem has been localized to a specific component.

The second section lists common failures with each failure's characteristic symptoms. This table provides feedback as to whether a repair solution has correctly addressed the situation. Use it to confirm your diagnosis.

The third section matches characteristic symptoms with the possible causes, therefore providing valuable ideas when a problem defies solution and has stumped the administration team. This section is a reorganization of the second section. If the causes or symptoms which your network is exhibiting are not listed, look at related items. These lists are not exhaustive, but rather sufficiently comprehensive to provide insight into most network trouble.

The fourth section defines transmission errors and offers insight into likely causes. While it is specific to network transmission layer problems, the explanations do suggest hardware causes when pertinent.

The last section lists the prevalent network statistics trapped by protocol analyzers, and CMIP, SNMP, or network management software. Also included is the range of the possible and the normally expected values. Explanations are listed for statistics that are skewed outside the normal range.

## Typical Component Failures

- Twisted-pair . . . . . . . . . . . all types
- Genderless connectors . . . . IBM
- Modular connectors . . . . . . RJ-series
- NIC . . . . . . . . . . . . . . . . wireless
- Lobe cable (patch cord) . . . all types
- Token-Ring controller . . . . . all types
- MAU units . . . . . . . . . . all types
- Concentrators (hubs) . . . . . all types
- Network node . . . . . . . . . hardware unit
- Network node . . . . . . . . . workstation
- Network node . . . . . . . . . server
- Repeater . . . . . . . . . . . . all types
- Smart repeater . . . . . . . . . all types
- Gateway node . . . . . . . . . all types
- Bridge . . . . . . . . . . . . . . all types
- Brouter . . . . . . . . . . . . . all types
- Automatic ring wrap/recovery all types
- Software . . . . . . . . . . . . generic
- Network management tools . all types

**Figure 21.2** The Token-Ring components included in the checklist. *Note:* The component failures are listed in decreasing likelihood of failure.

## Components -> Typical Failures

**Twisted-pair . . . . . . . . . . . . . . all types**

Shorting at a punchdown block
Break at a punchdown block
Pair polarity reversed
Transmit-receive pairs crossed over
Interwired with live telephone circuits
Cable crushed
Wrong cable (wiring error)
Cable does not meet manufacturing specs
Cut through jacket exposing or shorting pairs
Wrong type of modular connector
Defective insulation (age)
Break in copper
Lobe too long
Controller set to wrong speed
Excessive number of sections in lobe or trunk
Defective cable
Crosstalk from excessive use of bundle
Overuse of wiring bundle
Mixed use of wiring bundle
Microfractures in wire
Stray voltage

**Genderless connectors . . . . . . . . . . . IBM**

Miswired
Metal fingers bent open
Metal fingers bent and shorting
Stripped wires shorting out
Connector not screwed onto cable tightly
Shield improperly secured to connector housing
Improper assembly—washer missing
Dirty or greasy fittings
Exposure to vibration from ventilation system

**Modular connectors . . . . . . . . . RJ-series**

Miswired
Incorrect connector size for wire gauge
Incorrect connector size or type
Stripped wires shorting out
Dirty or greasy fittings
Exposure to vibration
Corroded

Note: the component failures are listed in decreasing likelihood of failure.

**NIC . . . . . . . . . . . . . . . . . . wireless (IR)**

Not line-of-sight installation
Dirty transmitter or receiver
Particle-laden air
Incorrect infrared frequency
Frequency conflict with other wireless devices
Too many units sharing same frequency
Too far apart
Incomplete lobe connection to node
Wrong Token-Ring version for network
Defective electronics
Transmitter-receiver units not grounded
Stray voltage
Static electricity strike

**NIC . . . . . . . . . . . . . . . . . . wireless (RF)**

Frequency conflict with other wireless devices
Poor signal strength
Dirty transmitter or receiver
Incorrect frequencies
Spread-spectrum error
Too many units sharing same frequency
Too far apart
RF pollution
Incomplete lobe connection to node
Wrong Token-Ring version for network
Defective electronics
Transmitter-receiver units not grounded
Stray voltage
Static electricity strike

**Lobe cable . . . . . . . . . . . . . . all types**

Poor connection with node equipment
Poor connection with MAU or hub
Worn-out connectors
Transmit wires shorting to shield
Wire polarity reversed
Wires internally shorting
Defective dielectric insulation (age)
Cut through jacket exposing shield
Shield not grounded
Wire does not meet manufacturing specs
Wire too long
Not correctly grounded
Bad wire pin-out
Stray voltage

Note: the component failures are listed in decreasing likelihood of failure.

**Token-Ring controller . . . . . . . bus board**

- Mismatched with network Token-Ring version
- Jumpers improperly selected
- Set for wrong speed
- Buffer space insufficient for packet size
- Bad PROM
- Mismatched with node hardware
- Mismatched with other network equipment
- Not installed properly
- Not grounded
- Defective electronics
- Device driver missing
- Device driver incompatible
- Device driver not loaded into system boot
- System memory device conflict
- Network address missing

**Token-Ring controller . . . . . . . NAU type**

- Wrong speed configured
- Wrong IRQ
- Memory (buffer) overlap
- Not enough buffer space
- Incomplete connection to lobe cable
- Wrong Token-Ring version for network
- Set for wrong speed
- Defective electronics:
  - High or low signal strength
  - Out of phase
  - Bad clock (crystal) speed
  - Chatter
  - Jabber
  - Jitter
  - Misframed packets
  - Bad CRC
  - Packets too long or too short
  - Corrupted packets
  - Nondifferentiated signal
- Not grounded
- Static electricity strike
- Twisted-pair too long
- Twisted-pair connected to live telephone circuit
- Twisted-pair not crossed over
- Shorting at a punchdown block
- Break at a punchdown block
- Mismatched with network Token-Ring version
- Bad PROM
- Jumpers improperly selected
- Mismatched with other network equipment
- Not grounded
- Defective electronics
- Device driver missing
- Device driver incompatible
- Device driver not loaded into system boot
- System memory device conflict
- Network address missing
- Static electricity strike

Note: the component failures are listed in decreasing likelihood of failure.

**Token-Ring controller . . . . . multifunction**

Jumpers improperly selected
Wrong version
Bad PROM
Mismatched with network Token-Ring version
Mismatched with other network equipment
Twisted-pair too long
Twisted-pair connected to live telephone
Twisted-pair not crossed over
Shorting at a punchdown block
Break at a punchdown block
Not grounded
Defective electronics
Device driver missing
Device driver incompatible
Device driver not loaded into system boot
Device driver not configured properly
System memory device conflict
Network address missing
Static electricity strike

**MAUs (hubs) . . . . . . . . . . . . . . all types**

RI/RO cable missing
RI/RO wiring error
Dirty port contacts
Dirty relay contacts
Twisted-pair too long
Twisted-pair connected to live telephone
Twisted-pair not crossed over
Shorting at a punchdown block
Break at a punchdown block
Bad twisted-pair connectors
Electronics jammed (power cycle)
Defective electronics
Lobe cables not securely attached
Lobe cables exceed length specs
Not correctly grounded
Mismatched with network Token-Ring version
Cascaded too many deep
Too many network addresses
Phantom voltage
Stray voltage
Static electricity strike

Note: the component failures are listed in decreasing likelihood of failure.

**Concentrators (hubs) . . . . . . . . all types**

RI/RO cable missing
RI/RO wiring error
Dirty port contacts
Dirty relay contacts
Ring trunk or ARL too long
Twisted-pair connected to live telephone
Twisted-pair not crossed over
Shorting at a punchdown block
Break at a punchdown block
Bad twisted-pair connectors
Electronics jammed (power cycle)
Defective electronics
Lobe cables not securely attached
Lobe cables exceed length specs
Powered off (may require AC)
Not correctly grounded
Mismatched with network Token-Ring version
Cascaded too many deep
Too many network addresses
Phantom voltage
Stray voltage
Static electricity strike

**Network node . . . . . . . . . hardware unit**

Network node equipment not working
Poor lobe connection
Defective Token-Ring controller
Mismatched version of Token-Ring controller
Bad PROM
Defective lobe cable
Network overloaded
Controller set to wrong speed
Wrong controller drivers to match system or NOS
Improper Token-Ring address
Improper IPX address
Improper Internet address
Device driver missing
Device driver incompatible
Device driver not loaded into system boot
Device driver not configured properly
System memory device conflict
System configuration error
Software conflict
Memory conflict
Stray voltage
Static electricity strike

Note: the component failures are listed in decreasing likelihood of failure.

**Network node . . . . . . . . . . workstation**

Poor lobe connection
Defective Token-Ring controller
Mismatched version of Token-Ring controller
Defective lobe cable
Network overloaded
Mismatched network software
Controller set to wrong speed
Wrong controller drivers to match system or NOS
Overloaded workstation
Workstation not working
Workstation hardware component failure
Software "wedged"
Bad PROM
Improper Token-Ring address
Improper Internet address
Too many network addresses
Device driver missing
Device driver incompatible
Device driver not loaded into system boot
Device driver not configured properly
System memory device conflict
System configuration error
Software conflict
Memory conflict
Stray voltage
Static electricity strike

**Network node . . . . . . . . . . . . . server**

Poor lobe connection
Defective Token-Ring controller
Mismatched version of Token-Ring controller
Defective lobe cable
Network overloaded
Mismatched network software
Controller set to wrong speed
Wrong controller drivers to match system or NOS
Overloaded server
Server not working
Server hardware component failure
Software "wedged"
Device driver missing
Device driver incompatible
Device driver not loaded into system boot
Device driver not configured properly
System memory device conflict
System configuration error
Software conflict
Memory conflict
Bad PROM
Improper Token-Ring address
Improper Internet address
Too many network addresses
Stray voltage
Static electricity strike

Note: the component failures are listed in decreasing likelihood of failure.

**Repeater** . . . . . . . . . . . . . . . . **all types**
Defective design
Poor lobe connection
Cannot maintain network throughput
Configuration error
Mismatched Token-Ring version
Network overloaded
Powered off
Stray voltage
Static electricity strike

**Smart Repeater** . . . . . . . . . . . **all types**
Stray voltage
Static electricity strike
Configuration error
Routing table error
Defective design
"Missing" nodes
Cannot maintain network throughput
Fails to rout packets
Poor lobe connection
Mismatched version of transceiver
Mismatched Token-Ring version
Network overloaded
Powered off

**Gateway Node** . . . . . . . . . . . **all types**
Stray voltage
Static electricity strike
Defective design
Routing table error
Cannot maintain network throughput
Packet encapsulation errors
Poor lobe connection
Defective MAU port
Overloaded gateway server
Defective software
Network overloaded
Software "wedged"
Improper Token-Ring address
Improper Internet address
Token-Ring type errors
Too many network addresses
Powered off

**Bridge** . . . . . . . . . . . . . . . . . **all types**
Stray voltage
Static electricity strike
Defective design
Routing table error
Cannot maintain network throughput
Packet encapsulation errors
Configuration error
Token-Ring type errors
Poor transfer connection
Busy common carrier
Line dead
Overloaded destination network
Defective software
Powered off

**Brouter . . . . . . . . . . . . . . . . . . all types**

Too slow
Pathway too complex
Multiple pathways in conflict
Different forward and return paths
Difference in forward and return protocols
Protocols not supported
Routing path lost
Routing path error
Stray voltage
Static electricity strike
Defective design
Routing table error
Cannot maintain network throughput
Packet encapsulation errors
Configuration error
Token-Ring type errors
Poor transfer connection
Poor transmit connection
Busy common carrier
Line dead
Overloaded destination network
Defective software
Powered off

**Automatic ring recovery . . . . . . all types**

Does not recognize a network error
Defective design
System configuration error
Defective mechanism
Not installed correctly
Network trunk severed
Serious ring flaw

**Software . . . . . . . . . . . . . . . generic**

Stray voltage damages memory
Static electricity strike damages memory
Not applied correctly
Not installed correctly
Software bug
Wrong software revision
Shared files not read only (MS Windows)
Out of memory
Jammed into a nonfunctional state
Version incompatible with node system software
Version incompatible with server software
Version incompatible with node hardware
File server disk full
File server disk fragmented
Wrong controller drivers to match system or NOS
Software removed from network
Software corrupted on source media
Software overwritten in memory
Software overloaded by demand requests
Device driver missing
Device driver incompatible
Device driver not loaded into system boot
Device driver not configured properly
MS Windows not set up correctly
System memory device conflict
System configuration error
Software conflict
Memory conflict

**Network management tools . . . . all types**

Device not recognized as SNMP/CMIP agent
Packet protocol ignored
User does not understand usage
Not applied correctly
Not installed correctly
Software bug
Bad PROM
Too slow to perform necessary functions
Captures partial percentage of packets
Filter settings too restrictive
Monitoring process itself alters network traffic
Missing updated and/or corrected PROM for SMNP or CMIP
Wrong software revisions
Out of buffer memory
Jammed into a nonfunctional state
Version incompatible with system software
Version incompatible with server software
Version incompatible with node hardware
Disk full
Software removed from network
Software corrupted on source media
Software overwritten in memory
Software overloaded by demand requests
Cannot function across repeater
Cannot function across bridge
Cannot function across router
Cannot function across gateway
Device driver not configured properly
System memory device conflict
System configuration error
Software conflict
Memory conflict
Stray voltage damages memory
Static electricity strike damages memory

## Network Failures: Causes—>Symptoms

**Application running across bridge**

- Bridge overloaded
- Erratic file service
- Excessive waiting
- File server jammed
- Network ring open
- Overloaded network
- Poor performance
- Slow file service
- Slow response
- Software problems

**Application running across gateway**

- Erratic file service
- Excessive waiting
- File server jammed
- Gateway overloaded
- Network ring open
- Overloaded network
- Poor performance
- Slow file service
- Slow response
- Software problems

**Application running across router**

- Erratic file service
- Excessive waiting
- File server jammed
- Overloaded network
- Poor performance
- Router overloaded
- Slow file service
- Slow response
- Software problems

**Application running on server**

- Erratic file service
- Excessive waiting
- File server jammed
- Network ring open
- Overloaded network
- Poor performance
- Slow file service
- Slow response
- Software problems

**Bad interrupt request (DOS IRQ)**

- Bad packets
- Bridge overloaded
- Disk space fragmented
- Encapsulation error
- Erratic file service
- Excessive waiting
- File server jammed
- Gateway overloaded
- High error rate
- Network ring open
- Network tool stressing network
- Network undergoing maintenance
- No disk space
- No network service
- No remote file service
- Partial network response
- Partial system boot
- Poor performance
- Repeater overloaded
- Retransmissions
- Server undergoing maintenance
- Slow file service
- Slow response
- Software problems
- Workstation jammed

**Bridge overloaded**

Bad packets
Bridge overloaded
Encapsulation routing overloaded
Erratic file service
Excessive waiting
File server jammed
Network ring open
Network undergoing maintenance
No remote file service
Partial network response
Partial system boot
Poor performance
Retransmissions
Slow file service
Slow response
Software problems
Workstation jammed

**Brouter overloaded**

Erratic file service
Node dead
Nodes missing
Poor performance
Retransmissions

**Brouter routing error**

Erratic file service
Excessive waiting
Network ring open
No answer from a node
Node dead
Nodes missing
Partial network response
Poor performance
Retransmissions
Slow file service
Slow response
Workstation jammed

**Cable metal fatigue**

Bad packets
Excessive waiting
Network ring open
No file service
No network service
Partial network response
Slow response
Workstation jammed

**CMIP messages saturating network**

Bad packets
Erratic file service
Excessive waiting
File server jammed
Network ring open
No remote file service
Partial network response
Partial system boot
Poor performance
Retransmissions
Slow file service
Slow response
Software problems
Workstation jammed

**Corrupted database**

Bad packets
Encapsulation error
Excessive waiting
File server jammed
Files corrupted
No answer from a node
No network service
Nodes missing
Poor performance
Protocol error
Retransmissions
Slow response
Workstation jammed

**Corrupted distributed database**

Bad packets
Encapsulation error
Excessive waiting
File server jammed
Files corrupted
No answer from a node
No network service
Nodes missing
Poor performance
Protocol error
Retransmissions
Slow response
Workstation jammed

**Corrupted system files**

No remote system boot
Partial system boot

**Defective lobe cable**

Bad packets
Excessive waiting
Files corrupted
High error rate
Network ring open
No answer from a node
No remote system boot
Partial LAN access
Partial system boot
Retransmissions
Workstation jammed

**Defective system software**

Erratic file service
High error rate
No file service
No network service
Partial network response
Slow file service
Workstation jammed

**Device creating broadcast storm**

Erratic file service
Excessive waiting
File server jammed
Network ring open
No remote file service
Partial network response
Poor performance
Retransmissions
Slow file service
Slow response
Software problems
Workstation jammed

**Disk space fragmented**

Bridge overloaded
Erratic file service
File server jammed
Gateway overloaded
High error rate
Network ring open
No disk space
No free disk space
No network service
No remote file service
Partial network response
Partial system boot
Poor performance
Retransmissions
Server undergoing maintenance
Slow file service
Slow response
Software problems
Workstation jammed

**Driver configuration error**

Bad packets
Bridge overloaded
Disk space fragmented
Encapsulation error
Erratic file service
Excessive waiting
File server jammed
Gateway overloaded
High error rate
Network ring open
Network tool stressing network
Network undergoing maintenance
No disk space
No network service
No remote file service
Partial network response
Partial system boot
Poor performance
Repeater overloaded
Retransmissions
Server undergoing maintenance
Slow file service
Slow response
Software problems
Workstation jammed

**Drop cable not properly connected**

Bad packets
Excessive waiting
Files corrupted
High error rate
Network ring open
Network undergoing maintenance
No answer from a node
No remote system boot
Partial system boot
Retransmissions
Workstation jammed

**Drop cable polarity error**

Network ring open
No answer from a node
No remote system boot
Partial LAN access
Partial system boot
Workstation jammed

**Encapsulation protocol error**

Bad packets
Bridge overloaded
Encapsulation routing overloaded
Erratic file service
Excessive waiting
File server jammed
Gateway overloaded
Network ring open
Network tool stressing network
Network undergoing maintenance
No disk space
No network service
No remote file service
Partial network response
Partial system boot
Poor performance
Repeater overloaded
Retransmissions
Slow file service
Slow response
Software problems
Workstation jammed

**Excessive waiting**

Poor performance
Repeater overloaded
Retransmissions

**Fan-out jammed**

High error rate
Workstation jammed

**Faulty transceiver**

- Bad packets
- Excessive waiting
- Files corrupted
- High error rate
- No answer from a node
- No network service
- Workstation jammed

**File server disk too slow**

- Bad packets
- Erratic file service
- Excessive waiting
- File server jammed
- Network ring open
- No remote file service
- Partial network response
- Partial system boot
- Poor performance
- Retransmissions
- Slow file service
- Slow response
- Software problems
- Workstation jammed

**File server down**

- File server jammed
- High error rate
- No file service
- No network service
- No remote system boot
- Slow file service

**File server jammed**

- Bad packets
- Bridge overloaded
- Disk space fragmented
- Encapsulation routing overloaded
- Erratic file service
- Excessive waiting
- File server jammed
- Gateway overloaded
- Network ring open
- Network tool stressing network
- Network undergoing maintenance
- No disk space
- No network service
- No remote file service
- Partial network response
- Partial system boot
- Poor performance
- Repeater overloaded
- Retransmissions
- Server undergoing maintenance
- Slow file service
- Slow response
- Software problems
- Workstation jammed

**File server memory error**

- Bad packets
- Bridge overloaded
- Disk space fragmented
- Encapsulation routing overloaded
- Erratic file service
- Excessive waiting
- File server jammed
- Gateway overloaded
- High error rate
- Network ring open
- Network tool stressing network
- Network undergoing maintenance
- No disk space
- No network service
- No remote file service
- Partial network response
- Partial system boot
- Poor performance
- Repeater overloaded
- Retransmissions
- Server undergoing maintenance
- Slow file service
- Slow response
- Software problems
- Workstation jammed

**File server overloaded**

- Erratic file service
- High error rate
- No file service
- Slow file service

**Gateway overloaded**

- Bad packets
- Bridge overloaded
- Encapsulation routing overloaded
- Erratic file service
- Excessive waiting
- File server jammed
- Gateway overloaded
- Network ring open
- Network tool stressing network
- Network undergoing maintenance
- No disk space
- No remote file service
- Partial network response
- Partial system boot
- Poor performance
- Retransmissions
- Slow file service
- Slow response
- Software problems
- Workstation jammed

**Improper grounding**

- Excessive waiting
- High error rate
- Network ring open
- Network undergoing maintenance
- Slow response

**Improper shielding from noise**

- Bad packets
- Excessive waiting
- Files corrupted
- High error rate
- Network ring open
- Nodes missing
- Poor performance
- Software problems
- Wiring concentrator dead

**In excess of 72/136/250 nodes on network**

- Excessive waiting
- Network ring open
- Slow response

**Inconsistent network software**

- Bad packets
- Bridge overloaded
- Disk space fragmented
- Encapsulation error
- Erratic file service
- Excessive waiting
- File server jammed
- Gateway overloaded
- High error rate
- Network ring open
- Network tool stressing network
- Network undergoing maintenance
- No disk space
- No network service
- No remote file service
- Partial network response
- Partial system boot
- Poor performance
- Repeater overloaded
- Retransmissions
- Server undergoing maintenance
- Slow file service
- Slow response
- Software problems
- Workstation jammed

**Lack of SNMP agent**
- Incorrect waiting statistics
- Incorrect network statistics

**Malfunctioning bridge**
- High error rate

**Malfunctioning gateway**
- Bad packets
- File server jammed
- High error rate
- Network ring open
- No answer from a node
- Nodes missing
- Partial network response

**Malfunctioning repeater**
- Bad packets
- File server jammed
- High error rate
- Network ring open
- No answer from a node
- Nodes missing
- Partial network response

**Mismatched hardware**
- Bad packets
- Erratic file service
- Excessive waiting
- Files corrupted
- High error rate
- Network ring open
- No file service
- No remote system boot
- Node dead
- Partial network response
- Partial system boot
- Slow file service
- Software problems
- Workstation jammed

**Network audit functions enabled**
- Erratic file service
- Excessive waiting
- File server jammed
- Network ring open
- Poor performance
- Slow file service
- Slow response
- Software problems

**Network configuration error**
- Bad packets
- Bridge overloaded
- Disk space fragmented
- Encapsulation error
- Erratic file service
- Excessive waiting
- File server jammed
- Gateway overloaded
- Network ring open
- Network tool stressing network
- Network undergoing maintenance
- No disk space
- No network service
- No remote file service
- Partial network response
- Partial system boot
- Poor performance
- Repeater overloaded
- Retransmissions
- Server undergoing maintenance
- Slow file service
- Slow response
- Software problems
- Workstation jammed

**Network ring open**

Beacons
No network service
High error rate

**Network out-of-spec error**

Bad packets
Bridge overloaded
Erratic file service
Excessive waiting
File server jammed
Gateway overloaded
Network ring open
Network tool stressing network
Network undergoing maintenance
No disk space
No network service
No remote file service
Partial network response
Partial system boot
Poor performance
Repeater overloaded
Retransmissions
Server undergoing maintenance
Slow file service
Slow response
Software problems
Workstation jammed

**Network tool stressing network**

Bad packets
Bridge overloaded
Encapsulation routing overloaded
Erratic file service
Excessive waiting
File server jammed
Gateway overloaded
Network ring open
Network tool stressing network
Network undergoing maintenance
No disk space
No network service
No remote file service
Partial network response
Partial system boot
Poor performance
Repeater overloaded
Retransmissions
Slow file service
Slow response
Software problems
Workstation jammed

**Network undergoing maintenance**

Bad packets
Bridge overloaded
Disk space fragmented
Encapsulation routing overloaded
Erratic file service
Excessive waiting
Gateway overloaded
Network ring open
Network tool stressing network
Network undergoing maintenance
No disk space
No network service
No remote file service
Node dead
Partial network response
Partial system boot
Poor performance
Repeater overloaded
Retransmissions
Server undergoing maintenance
Slow file service
Slow response
Software problems
Workstation jammed

**NIC configuration error**

Excessive waiting
No network service
Node dead
Partial network service
Poor performance
Retransmissions

**No disk space**

High error rate

**No free disk space**

Bridge overloaded
Disk space fragmented
Erratic file service
File server jammed
Gateway overloaded
Network ring open
Network tool stressing network
Network undergoing maintenance
No disk space
No network service
No remote file service
Partial network response
Partial system boot
Poor performance
Repeater overloaded
Retransmissions
Server undergoing maintenance
Slow file service
Slow response
Software problems
Workstation jammed

**Open break on network**

Erratic file service
Network ring open
Network undergoing maintenance
No file service
No network service
Node dead
Nodes missing
Partial network response
Software problems

**Open short on network**

Erratic file service
Network ring open
Network undergoing maintenance
No file service
No network service
Node dead
Partial network response
Software problems

**Overloaded network**

Bad packets
Bridge overloaded
Disk space fragmented
Encapsulation routing overloaded
Erratic file service
Excessive waiting
File server jammed
Gateway overloaded
High error rate
Network ring open
Network tool stressing network
Network undergoing maintenance
No disk space
No network service
No remote file service
Partial network response
Partial system boot
Poor performance
Repeater overloaded
Retransmissions
Server undergoing maintenance
Slow file service
Slow response
Software problems
Workstation jammed

**Protocol analyzer creating traffic**

Bad packets
Erratic file service
Excessive waiting
File server jammed
Network ring open
No remote file service
Partial network response
Partial system boot
Poor performance
Retransmissions
Slow file service
Slow response
Software problems
Workstation jammed

**Protocol error**

Encapsulation error
Excessive waiting
Network ring open
No answer from a node
No network service
Node dead
Poor performance

**Remote query not optimized locally**

Erratic file service
Excessive waiting
File server jammed
Network ring open
Overloaded network
Poor performance
Slow file service
Slow response
Software problems

**Repeater overloaded**

Bad packets
Encapsulation routing overloaded
Erratic file service
Excessive waiting
File server jammed
Network ring open
Network tool stressing network
Network undergoing maintenance
No disk space
No remote file service
Partial network response
Partial system boot
Poor performance
Repeater overloaded
Retransmissions
Slow file service
Slow response
Software problems
Workstation jammed

**Router overloaded**

Bad packets
Encapsulation routing overloaded
Erratic file service
Excessive waiting
File server jammed
Network ring open
Network tool stressing network
Network undergoing maintenance
No disk space
No remote file service
Partial network response
Partial system boot
Poor performance
Retransmissions
Slow file service
Slow response
Software problems
Workstation jammed

**Router table address error**

- Bad packets
- Bridge overloaded
- Disk space fragmented
- Encapsulation error
- Erratic file service
- Excessive waiting
- File server jammed
- Gateway overloaded
- Network ring open
- Network tool stressing network
- Network undergoing maintenance
- No disk space
- No network service
- No remote file service
- Partial network response
- Partial system boot
- Poor performance
- Repeater overloaded
- Retransmissions
- Server undergoing maintenance
- Slow file service
- Slow response
- Software problems
- Workstation jammed

**Security functions enabled**

- Erratic file service
- Excessive waiting
- File server jammed
- Network ring open
- Overloaded network
- Poor performance
- Slow file service
- Slow response
- Software problems

**Server bus bandwidth overwhelmed**

- Bad packets
- Erratic file service
- Excessive waiting
- File server jammed
- Network ring open
- No remote file service
- Partial network response
- Partial system boot
- Poor performance
- Retransmissions
- Slow file service
- Slow response
- Software problems
- Workstation jammed

**Server I/O (input/output) bound**

- Bad packets
- Erratic file service
- Excessive waiting
- File server jammed
- Network ring open
- No remote file service
- Partial network response
- Partial system boot
- Poor performance
- Retransmissions
- Slow file service
- Slow response
- Software problems
- Workstation jammed

**Server undergoing maintenance**

- Bad packets
- Bridge overloaded
- Disk space fragmented
- Encapsulation routing overloaded
- Erratic file service
- Excessive waiting
- File server jammed
- File server jammed
- Gateway overloaded
- Network ring open
- Network tool stressing network
- Network undergoing maintenance
- No disk space
- No network service
- No remote file service
- Partial network response
- Partial system boot
- Poor performance
- Retransmissions
- Server undergoing maintenance
- Slow file service
- Slow response
- Software problems
- Workstation jammed

**SNMP messages saturating network**

- Bad packets
- Erratic file service
- Excessive waiting
- File server jammed
- Network ring open
- No remote file service
- Partial network response
- Partial system boot
- Poor performance
- Retransmissions
- Slow file service
- Slow response
- Software problems
- Workstation jammed

**Static electricity strike**

- Bad packets
- Disk space fragmented
- Encapsulation error
- Erratic file service
- File server jammed
- Gateway overloaded
- Network ring open
- Network tool stressing network
- Network undergoing maintenance
- No disk space
- No network service
- No remote file service
- Partial network response
- Partial system boot
- Poor performance
- Server undergoing maintenance
- Slow response
- Software problems
- Wiring concentrator dead
- Workstation jammed

**Store-and-forward message lost**

- Bad packets
- Encapsulation error
- Excessive waiting
- File server jammed
- Files corrupted
- No answer from a node
- No network service
- Nodes missing
- Poor performance
- Protocol error
- Retransmissions
- Slow response
- Workstation jammed

**Stray voltage corrupted memory**

- Bad packets
- Disk space fragmented
- Encapsulation error
- Erratic file service
- File server jammed
- Gateway overloaded
- Network ring open
- Network tool stressing network
- Network undergoing maintenance
- No disk space
- No network service
- No remote file service
- Partial network response
- Partial system boot
- Poor performance
- Server undergoing maintenance
- Slow response
- Software problems
- Wiring concentrator dead
- Workstation jammed

**Too many distributed processes**

- Erratic file service
- Excessive waiting
- File server jammed
- Network ring open
- No remote file service
- Partial network response
- Poor performance
- Retransmissions
- Slow file service
- Slow response
- Software problems
- Workstation jammed

**Too many wireless stations**

- Bad packets
- Encapsulation error
- Excessive waiting
- File server jammed
- Files corrupted
- No answer from a node
- No network service
- Nodes missing
- Poor performance
- Protocol error
- Retransmissions
- Slow response
- Workstation jammed

**Too much network traffic**

- Erratic file service
- Excessive waiting
- File server jammed
- Network ring open
- No remote file service
- Partial network response
- Poor performance
- Retransmissions
- Slow file service
- Slow response
- Software problems
- Workstation jammed

**Translation gateway too slow**

- Bad packets
- Erratic file service
- Excessive waiting
- File server jammed
- Network ring open
- Network tool stressing network
- Network undergoing maintenance
- No disk space
- No remote file service
- Partial network response
- Partial system boot
- Poor performance
- Retransmissions
- Slow file service
- Slow response
- Software problems
- Translation gateway overloaded
- Workstation jammed

**Translation protocol error**

- Bad packets
- Erratic file service
- Excessive waiting
- File server jammed
- Network ring open
- Network tool stressing network
- Network undergoing maintenance
- No disk space
- No remote file service
- Partial network response
- Partial system boot
- Poor performance
- Retransmissions
- Slow file service
- Slow response
- Software problems
- Translation gateway overloaded
- Workstation jammed

**Twisted-pair bundle overutilized**

- Bad packets
- Encapsulation error
- Excessive waiting
- File server jammed
- Files corrupted
- No answer from a node
- No network service
- Nodes missing
- Poor performance
- Protocol error
- Retransmissions
- Slow response
- Workstation jammed

**Twisted-pair crosstalk**

- Bad packets
- Encapsulation error
- Excessive waiting
- File server jammed
- Files corrupted
- No answer from a node
- No network service
- Nodes missing
- Poor performance
- Protocol error
- Retransmissions
- Slow response
- Workstation jammed

**Twisted-pair intermixed with RS-232**

- Bad packets
- Encapsulation error
- Excessive waiting
- File server jammed
- Files corrupted
- No answer from a node
- No network service
- Node dead
- Nodes missing
- Poor performance
- Protocol error
- Retransmissions
- Wiring concentrator dead
- Workstation jammed

**Twisted-pair not properly connected**

- Bad packets
- Excessive waiting
- Files corrupted
- Network ring open
- Network undergoing maintenance
- No answer from a node
- No remote system boot
- Partial system boot
- Retransmissions
- Workstation jammed

**Twisted-pair on live phone lines**

- Bad packets
- Encapsulation error
- Excessive waiting
- File server jammed
- Files corrupted
- No answer from a node
- No network service
- Node dead
- Nodes missing
- Poor performance
- Protocol error
- Retransmissions
- Wiring concentrator dead
- Workstation jammed

**Twisted-pair pairs reversed**

- Network ring open
- No answer from a node
- No remote system boot
- Partial system boot
- Workstation jammed

**Twisted-pair polarity error**

- Network ring open
- No answer from a node
- No remote system boot
- Partial system boot
- Workstation jammed

**Twisted-pair substandard**

- Bad packets
- Encapsulation error
- Excessive waiting
- File server jammed
- Files corrupted
- No answer from a node
- No network service
- Nodes missing
- Poor performance
- Protocol error
- Retransmissions
- Slow response
- Workstation jammed

**Twisted-pair wire metal fatigue**

- Bad packets
- Excessive waiting
- Network ring open
- No file service
- No network service
- Partial network response
- Slow response
- Workstation jammed

**Usage audit functions enabled**

- Erratic file service
- Excessive waiting
- File server jammed
- Network ring open
- Overloaded network
- Poor performance
- Slow file service
- Slow response
- Software problems

**User files corrupted**

- Erratic file service
- Partial network response
- Retransmissions
- Software problems

**Wireless RF frequency overlap**

Bad packets
Encapsulation error
Excessive waiting
File server jammed
Files corrupted
No answer from a node
No network service
Nodes missing
Poor performance
Protocol error
Retransmissions
Slow response
Workstation jammed

**Wireless signal conflict**

Bad packets
Encapsulation error
Excessive waiting
File server jammed
Files corrupted
No answer from a node
No network service
Nodes missing
Poor performance
Protocol error
Retransmissions
Slow response
Workstation jammed

**Wireless signal distorted by dust**

Bad packets
Encapsulation error
Excessive waiting
File server jammed
Files corrupted
No answer from a node
No network service
Nodes missing
Poor performance
Protocol error
Retransmissions
Slow response
Workstation jammed

**Wireless signal too weak**

Bad packets
Encapsulation error
Excessive waiting
File server jammed
Files corrupted
No answer from a node
No network service
Nodes missing
Poor performance
Protocol error
Retransmissions
Slow response
Workstation jammed

**Wireless stations too far apart**

Bad packets
Encapsulation error
Excessive waiting
File server jammed
Files corrupted
No answer from a node
No network service
Nodes missing
Poor performance
Protocol error
Retransmissions
Slow response
Workstation jammed

**Workstation undergoing maintenance**

No answer from a node
No remote file service
Node dead
Nodes missing
Partial network response
Poor performance
Retransmissions
Slow response
Workstation jammed

## Network Failures: Symptoms->Possible Causes

### Bad packets

Bad interrupt request (DOS IRQ)
Bridge overloaded
CMIP messages saturating network
Cable metal fatigue
Corrupted database
Corrupted distributed database
Defective lobe cable
Driver configuration error
Drop cable not properly connected
Encapsulation protocol error
File server disk too slow
Gateway overloaded
Improper shielding from noise
Inconsistent network software
Malfunctioning gateway
Malfunctioning repeater
Mismatched hardware
Network configuration error
Network out-of-spec error
Network tool stressing network
Network undergoing maintenance
Optical fiber clarity degradation
Optical fiber ends not polished
Overloaded network
Protocol analyzer creating traffic
Repeater overloaded
Router table address error
Server bus bandwidth overwhelmed
Server I/O (input/output) bound
Server undergoing maintenance
Signal injector creating traffic
SNMP messages saturating network
Static electricity strike
Store-and-forward message lost
Stray voltage corrupted memory
Too many wireless stations
Translation gateway too slow
Translation protocol error
Twisted-pair bundle overutilized
Twisted-pair crosstalk
Twisted-pair intermixed with RS-232
Twisted-pair not properly connected
Twisted-pair on live phone lines
Twisted-pair substandard
Twisted-pair wire metal fatigue
Wireless RF frequency overlap
Wireless signal conflict
Wireless signal distorted by dust
Wireless signal too weak
Wireless stations too far apart

### Bridge overloaded

Application running across bridge
Bad interrupt request (DOS IRQ)
Bridge overloaded
Disk space fragmented
Driver configuration error
Encapsulation protocol error
File server jammed
File server memory error
Gateway overloaded
Inconsistent network software
Network configuration error
Network out-of-spec error
Network tool stressing network
Network undergoing maintenance
No free disk space
Overloaded network
Router table address error
Server undergoing maintenance
TCP/IP protocol error

### Disk space fragmented

Bad interrupt request (DOS IRQ)
Driver configuration error
File server jammed
File server memory error
Inconsistent network software
Network configuration error
Network undergoing maintenance
No free disk space
Overloaded network
Router table address error
Server undergoing maintenance
Static electricity strike
Stray voltage corrupted memory
TCP/IP protocol error

### Encapsulation error

Bad interrupt request (DOS IRQ)
Corrupted database
Corrupted distributed database
Driver configuration error
Inconsistent network software
Network configuration error
Optical fiber clarity degradation
Optical fiber ends not polished
Protocol error
Router table address error
Static electricity strike
Store-and-forward message lost
Stray voltage corrupted memory
TCP/IP protocol error
Too many wireless stations
Twisted-pair bundle overutilized
Twisted-pair crosstalk
Twisted-pair intermixed with RS-232
Twisted-pair on live phone lines
Twisted-pair substandard
Wireless RF frequency overlap
Wireless signal conflict
Wireless signal distorted by dust
Wireless signal too weak
Wireless stations too far apart

### Encapsulation routing overloaded

Bridge overloaded
Encapsulation protocol error
File server jammed
File server memory error
Gateway overloaded
Network tool stressing network
Network undergoing maintenance
Overloaded network
Repeater overloaded
Router overloaded
Server undergoing maintenance

### Erratic file service

Application running across bridge
Application running across gateway
Application running across router
Application running on server
Bad interrupt request (DOS IRQ)
Bridge overloaded
Brouter overloaded
Brouter routing error
CMIP messages saturating network
Defective system software
Device creating broadcast storm
Disk space fragmented
Driver configuration error
Encapsulation protocol error
File server disk too slow
File server jammed
File server memory error
File server overloaded
Gateway overloaded
Inconsistent network software
Mismatched hardware
Network audit functions enabled
Network configuration error
Network out-of-spec error
Network tool stressing network
Network undergoing maintenance
No free disk space
Open break on network
Open short on network
Optical fiber break
Overloaded network
Protocol analyzer creating traffic
Remote query not optimized locally
Repeater overloaded
Router overloaded
Router table address error
Security functions enabled
Server bus bandwidth overwhelmed
Server I/O (input/output) bound
Server undergoing maintenance
Signal injector creating traffic
SNMP messages saturating network
Static electricity strike
Stray voltage corrupted memory
TCP/IP protocol error
Too many distributed processes
Too much network traffic
Translation gateway too slow
Translation protocol error
Usage audit functions enabled
User files corrupted

**Excessive waiting**

Application running across bridge
Application running across gateway
Application running across router
Application running on server
Bad interrupt request (DOS IRQ)
Bridge overloaded
Brouter routing error
CMIP messages saturating network
Corrupted database
Corrupted distributed database
Defective lobe cable
Device creating broadcast storm
Driver configuration error
Encapsulation protocol error
File server disk too slow
File server jammed
File server memory error
Gateway overloaded
Improper shielding from noise
In excess of 72/136/250 nodes
Inconsistent network software
Mismatched hardware
Network audit functions enabled
Network configuration error
Network out-of-spec error
Network tool stressing network
Network undergoing maintenance
NIC configuration error
Optical fiber clarity degradation
Optical fiber ends not polished
Overloaded network
Protocol analyzer creating traffic
Protocol error
Remote query not optimized locally
Router overloaded
Router table address error
Security functions enabled
Server I/O (input/output) bound
Server undergoing maintenance
Signal injector creating traffic
SNMP messages saturating network
Store-and-forward message lost
Too few buffers on controller
Too many wireless stations
Too much network traffic
Translation gateway too slow
Translation protocol error
Twisted-pair crosstalk
Twisted-pair intermixed with RS-232
Twisted-pair not properly connected
Twisted-pair on live phone lines
Twisted-pair substandard
Twisted-pair wire metal fatigue
Usage audit functions enabled
Wireless RF frequency overlap
Wireless signal conflict
Wireless signal distorted by dust
Wireless signal too weak
Wireless stations too far apart

**File server jammed**

Application running across bridge
Application running across gateway
Application running across router
Application running on server
Bad interrupt request (DOS IRQ)
Bridge overloaded
CMIP messages saturating network
Corrupted database
Corrupted distributed database
Device creating broadcast storm
Disk space fragmented
Driver configuration error
Encapsulation protocol error
File server disk too slow
File server down
File server jammed
File server memory error
Gateway overloaded
Inconsistent network software
Remote query not optimized locally
Repeater overloaded
Router overloaded
Router table address error
Security functions enabled
Server bus bandwidth overwhelmed
Server I/O (input/output) bound
Server offline
Server undergoing maintenance
Signal injector creating traffic
SNMP messages saturating network
Static electricity strike
Store-and-forward message lost
Stray voltage corrupted memory
TCP/IP protocol error
Too many distributed processes
Too many wireless stations
Too much network traffic
Translation gateway too slow

**File server jammed** (*continued*)

- Malfunctioning gateway
- Malfunctioning repeater
- Network audit functions enabled
- Network configuration error
- Network out-of-spec error
- Network tool stressing network
- No free disk space
- Optical fiber clarity degradation
- Optical fiber ends not polished
- Overloaded network
- Protocol analyzer creating traffic
- Translation protocol error
- Twisted-pair bundle overutilized
- Twisted-pair crosstalk
- Twisted-pair intermixed with RS-232
- Twisted-pair on live phone lines
- Twisted-pair substandard
- Usage audit functions enabled
- Wireless RF frequency overlap
- Wireless signal conflict
- Wireless signal distorted by dust
- Wireless signal too weak
- Wireless stations too far apart

**Files corrupted**

- Corrupted database
- Corrupted distributed database
- Defective lobe cable
- Drop cable not properly connected
- Improper shielding from noise
- Mismatched hardware
- Optical fiber clarity degradation
- Optical fiber ends not polished
- Store-and-forward message lost
- Twisted-pair bundle overutilized
- Twisted-pair crosstalk
- Twisted-pair intermixed with RS-232
- Twisted-pair not properly connected
- Twisted-pair substandard
- Wireless RF frequency overlap
- Wireless signal conflict
- Wireless signal distorted by dust
- Wireless signal too weak
- Wireless stations too far apart

**Gateway overloaded**

- Application running across gateway
- Bad interrupt request (DOS IRQ)
- Disk space fragmented
- Driver configuration error
- Encapsulation protocol error
- File server jammed
- File server memory error
- Gateway overloaded
- Inconsistent network software
- Network configuration error
- Network out-of-spec error
- Network tool stressing network
- Network undergoing maintenance
- No free disk space
- Overloaded network
- Router table address error
- Server undergoing maintenance
- Static electricity strike
- Stray voltage corrupted memory
- TCP/IP protocol error

**High error rate**

- Bad interrupt request (DOS IRQ)
- Defective lobe cable
- Defective system software
- Disk space fragmented
- Driver configuration error
- Drop cable not properly connected
- Fan-out jammed
- File server down
- File server memory error
- File server overloaded
- Improper shielding from noise
- In excess of 66/132/250 nodes
- Inconsistent network software
- Malfunctioning bridge
- Malfunctioning gateway
- Malfunctioning repeater
- Network jammed
- No disk space
- Overloaded network

### Incorrect waiting statistics

Lack of SNMP agent

### Incorrect network statistics

Lack of SNMP agent

### Network jammed

Application running across bridge
Application running across gateway
Application running on server
Bad interrupt request (DOS IRQ)
Bridge overloaded
Brouter routing error
CMIP messages saturating network
Defective lobe cable
Device creating broadcast storm
Disk space fragmented
Driver configuration error
Drop cable not properly connected
Drop cable polarity error
Encapsulation protocol error
File server disk too slow
File server jammed
File server memory error
Gateway overloaded
Improper shielding from noise
In excess of 72/136/250 nodes
Inconsistent network software
Network audit functions enabled
Network configuration error
Network out-of-spec error
Network terminator missing
Network tool stressing network
Network undergoing maintenance
No free disk space
Open break on network
Open short on network
Optical fiber break
Optical fiber clarity degradation
Overloaded network
Protocol analyzer creating traffic
Protocol error
Repeater overloaded
Router overloaded
Router table address error
Security functions enabled
Server bus bandwidth overwhelmed
Server I/O (input/output) bound
Server undergoing maintenance
Signal injector creating traffic
SNMP messages saturating network
Static electricity strike
Stray voltage corrupted memory
TCP/IP protocol error
Too many distributed processes
Too much network traffic
Translation gateway too slow
Translation protocol error
Twisted-pair not properly connected
Twisted-pair pairs reversed
Twisted-pair polarity error
Twisted-pair wire metal fatigue
Usage audit functions enabled

### Network tool stressing network

Bad interrupt request (DOS IRQ)
Driver configuration error
Encapsulation protocol error
File server jammed
File server memory error
Gateway overloaded
Inconsistent network software
Network configuration error
Network out-of-spec error
Network tool stressing network
Network undergoing maintenance
No free disk space
Overloaded network
Repeater overloaded
Router overloaded
Router table address error
Server undergoing maintenance
Static electricity strike
Stray voltage corrupted memory
TCP/IP protocol error
Translation gateway too slow
Translation protocol error

## Network undergoing maintenance

Bad interrupt request (DOS IRQ)
Bridge overloaded
Driver configuration error
Drop cable not properly connected
Encapsulation protocol error
File server jammed
File server memory error
Gateway overloaded
Inconsistent network software
Network configuration error
Network out-of-spec error
Network terminator missing
Network tool stressing network
Network undergoing maintenance
Open break on network
Open short on network
Optical fiber break
Overloaded network
Repeater overloaded
Router overloaded
Router table address error
Static electricity strike
Stray voltage corrupted memory
TCP/IP protocol error
Translation gateway too slow
Translation protocol error
Twisted-pair not properly connected

## No answer from a node

Corrupted database
Corrupted distributed database
Defective lobe cable
Drop cable not properly connected
Drop cable polarity error
Malfunctioning gateway
Malfunctioning repeater
Optical fiber clarity degradation
Optical fiber ends not polished
Protocol error
Store-and-forward message lost
Too many wireless stations
Workstation undergoing maintenance
Twisted-pair bundle overutilized
Twisted-pair crosstalk
Twisted-pair intermixed with RS-232
Twisted-pair not properly connected
Twisted-pair on live phone lines
Twisted-pair polarity error
Twisted-pair substandard
Wireless RF frequency overlap
Wireless signal conflict
Wireless signal distorted by dust
Wireless signal too weak
Wireless stations too far apart

## No disk space

Bad interrupt request (DOS IRQ)
Disk space fragmented
Driver configuration error
Encapsulation protocol error
File server jammed
File server memory error
Gateway overloaded
Inconsistent network software
Network configuration error
Network out-of-spec error
Network tool stressing network
Network undergoing maintenance
No free disk space
Overloaded network
Repeater overloaded
Router overloaded
Router table address error
Server undergoing maintenance
Static electricity strike
Stray voltage corrupted memory
TCP/IP protocol error
Translation gateway too slow
Translation protocol error

## No file service

Defective system software
File server down
File server overloaded
Mismatched hardware
Open short on network
Optical fiber break
Optical fiber clarity degradation
Twisted-pair wire metal fatigue

**No free disk space**

Disk space fragmented

**No network service**

Corrupted database
Corrupted distributed database
Defective system software
Disk space fragmented
Driver configuration error
Encapsulation protocol error
File server jammed
File server memory error
Inconsistent network software
Network configuration error
Network out-of-spec error
Network tool stressing network
Network undergoing maintenance
NIC configuration error
No free disk space
Open break on network
Open short on network
Optical fiber break
Protocol error
Router table address error
Server undergoing maintenance
Static electricity strike
Store-and-forward message lost
Stray voltage corrupted memory
Too many wireless stations
Twisted-pair bundle overutilized
Twisted-pair crosstalk
Twisted-pair intermixed with RS-232
Twisted-pair on live phone lines
Twisted-pair substandard
Twisted-pair wire metal fatigue
Wireless RF frequency overlap
Wireless signal conflict
Wireless signal distorted by dust
Wireless signal too weak
Wireless stations too far apart

**No remote file service**

Bad interrupt request (DOS IRQ)
Bridge overloaded
CMIP messages saturating network
Device creating broadcast storm
Disk space fragmented
Driver configuration error
Encapsulation protocol error
File server disk too slow
File server jammed
File server memory error
Gateway overloaded
Inconsistent network software
Network configuration error
Network out-of-spec error
No free disk space
Overloaded network
Protocol analyzer creating traffic
Repeater overloaded
Router overloaded
Router table address error
Server bus bandwidth overwhelmed
Server I/O (input/output) bound
Server undergoing maintenance
Signal injector creating traffic
SNMP messages saturating network
Static electricity strike
Stray voltage corrupted memory
TCP/IP protocol error
Too many distributed processes
Too much network traffic
Translation gateway too slow
Workstation undergoing maintenance

**No remote system boot**

Corrupted system files
Defective lobe cable
Drop cable not properly connected
Drop cable polarity error
File server down
Mismatched hardware
Twisted-pair not properly connected
Twisted-pair pairs reversed
Twisted-pair polarity error

**Node dead**

Brouter overloaded
Brouter routing error
NIC configuration error
Open break on network
Open short on network
Optical fiber break
Protocol error
Twisted-pair intermixed with RS-232
Twisted-pair on live phone lines
Workstation undergoing maintenance

**Nodes missing**

Brouter overloaded
Brouter routing error
Corrupted database
Corrupted distributed database
Improper shielding from noise
Malfunctioning gateway
Malfunctioning repeater
Open break on network
Optical fiber break
Optical fiber clarity degradation
Optical fiber ends not polished
Store-and-forward message lost
Too many wireless stations
Twisted-pair bundle overutilized
Twisted-pair crosstalk
Twisted-pair intermixed with RS-232
Twisted-pair on live phone lines
Twisted-pair substandard
Wireless RF frequency overlap
Wireless signal conflict
Wireless signal distorted by dust
Wireless signal too weak
Wireless stations too far apart
Workstation undergoing maintenance

**Overloaded network**

Application running across bridge
Application running across gateway
Application running across router
Application running on server
Remote query not optimized locally
Security functions enabled
Usage audit functions enabled

**Partial network response**

Bad interrupt request (DOS IRQ)
Bridge overloaded
Brouter routing error
CMIP messages saturating network
Defective system software
Device creating broadcast storm
Disk space fragmented
Driver configuration error
Encapsulation protocol error
File server disk too slow
File server jammed
File server memory error
Gateway overloaded
Malfunctioning gateway
Malfunctioning repeater
Mismatched hardware
Network tool stressing network
Network undergoing maintenance
No free disk space
Open break on network
Open short on network
Optical fiber break
Optical fiber clarity degradation
Overloaded network
Protocol analyzer creating traffic
Router overloaded
Router table address error
Server bus bandwidth overwhelmed
Server I/O (input/output) bound
Server undergoing maintenance
Signal injector creating traffic
SNMP messages saturating network
Static electricity strike
Stray voltage corrupted memory
TCP/IP protocol error
Too many distributed processes
Too much network traffic
Translation gateway too slow
Translation protocol error
Twisted-pair wire metal fatigue
User files corrupted
Workstation undergoing maintenance

**Partial network service**

NIC configuration error

**Partial system boot**

Bad interrupt request (DOS IRQ)
Bridge overloaded
CMIP messages saturating network
Corrupted system files
Defective lobe cable
Defective patch cable
Disk space fragmented
Driver configuration error
Drop cable not properly connected
Drop cable polarity error
Encapsulation protocol error
File server disk too slow
File server jammed
File server memory error
Gateway overloaded
Inconsistent network software
Mismatched hardware
Network configuration error
Network out-of-spec error
Network tool stressing network
No free disk space
Overloaded network
Protocol analyzer creating traffic
Repeater overloaded
Router overloaded
Router table address error
Server bus bandwidth overwhelmed
Server I/O (input/output) bound
Signal injector creating traffic
SNMP messages saturating network
Static electricity strike
Stray voltage corrupted memory
TCP/IP protocol error
Translation gateway too slow
Translation protocol error
Twisted-pair not properly connected
Twisted-pair pairs reversed
Twisted-pair polarity error

**Poor performance**

Application running across bridge
Application running across gateway
Application running across router
Application running on server
Bad interrupt request (DOS IRQ)
Bridge overloaded
Brouter overloaded
Brouter routing error
CMIP messages saturating network
Corrupted database
Corrupted distributed database
Device creating broadcast storm
Disk space fragmented
Driver configuration error
Excessive waiting
File server disk too slow
File server jammed
File server memory error
Gateway overloaded
Improper shielding from noise
Inconsistent network software
Network audit functions enabled
Network configuration error
Network out-of-spec error
Network tool stressing network
Network undergoing maintenance
Protocol analyzer creating traffic
Protocol error
Remote query not optimized locally
Repeater overloaded
Router overloaded
Security functions enabled
Server bus bandwidth overwhelmed
Server I/O (input/output) bound
Server undergoing maintenance
Signal injector creating traffic
SNMP messages saturating network
Static electricity strike
Store-and-forward message lost
Stray voltage corrupted memory
TCP/IP protocol error
Too many distributed processes
Too many wireless stations
Too much network traffic
Translation gateway too slow
Translation protocol error
Twisted-pair bundle overutilized
Twisted-pair crosstalk
Twisted-pair intermixed with RS-232
Twisted-pair on live phone lines
Twisted-pair substandard
Usage audit functions enabled

**Poor performance** (*continued*)

NIC configuration error
No free disk space
Optical fiber clarity degradation
Optical fiber ends not polished
Overloaded network
Wireless RF frequency overlap
Wireless signal conflict
Wireless signal too weak
Wireless stations too far apart
Workstation undergoing maintenance

**Protocol error**

Corrupted database
Corrupted distributed database
Optical fiber clarity degradation
Optical fiber ends not polished
Store-and-forward message lost
Too many wireless stations
Twisted-pair bundle overutilized
Twisted-pair crosstalk
Twisted-pair intermixed with RS-232
Twisted-pair on live phone lines
Twisted-pair substandard
Wireless RF frequency overlap
Wireless signal conflict
Wireless signal distorted by dust
Wireless signal too weak
Wireless stations too far apart

**Repeater overloaded**

Bad interrupt request (DOS IRQ)
Driver configuration error
Encapsulation protocol error
Excessive waiting
File server jammed
File server memory error
Inconsistent network software
Network configuration error
Network out-of-spec error
Network tool stressing network
Network undergoing maintenance
No free disk space
Overloaded network
Repeater overloaded
Router table address error
TCP/IP protocol error

**Retransmissions**

Bad interrupt request (DOS IRQ)
Bridge overloaded
Brouter overloaded
Brouter routing error
CMIP messages saturating network
Corrupted database
Corrupted distributed database
Defective lobe cable
Device creating broadcast storm
Disk space fragmented
Driver configuration error
Drop cable not properly connected
Encapsulation protocol error
Excessive waiting
File server disk too slow
File server jammed
File server memory error
Gateway overloaded
Inconsistent network software
Network configuration error
Network out-of-spec error
Network tool stressing network
Network undergoing maintenance
Protocol analyzer creating traffic
Repeater overloaded
Router overloaded
Router table address error
Server bus bandwidth overwhelmed
Server I/O (input/output) bound
Server undergoing maintenance
Signal injector creating traffic
SNMP messages saturating network
Store-and-forward message lost
TCP/IP protocol error
Too many distributed processes
Too many wireless stations
Too much network traffic
Translation gateway too slow
Translation protocol error
Twisted-pair bundle overutilized
Twisted-pair crosstalk
Twisted-pair intermixed with RS-232
Twisted-pair not properly connected
Twisted-pair on live phone lines
Twisted-pair substandard
User files corrupted

**Retransmissions** *(continued)*

- NIC configuration error
- No free disk space
- Optical fiber clarity degradation
- Optical fiber ends not polished
- Overloaded network
- Wireless RF frequency overlap
- Wireless signal conflict
- Wireless signal distorted by dust
- Wireless signal too weak
- Wireless stations too far apart
- Workstation undergoing maintenance

**Router overloaded**

- Application running across router

**Server undergoing maintenance**

- Bad interrupt request (DOS IRQ)
- Disk space fragmented
- Driver configuration error
- File server jammed
- File server memory error
- Inconsistent network software
- Network configuration error
- Network out-of-spec error
- Network undergoing maintenance
- No free disk space
- Overloaded network
- Router table address error
- Server undergoing maintenance
- Static electricity strike
- Stray voltage corrupted memory
- TCP/IP protocol error

**Slow file service**

- Application running across bridge
- Application running across gateway
- Application running across router
- Application running on server
- Bad interrupt request (DOS IRQ)
- Bridge overloaded
- Brouter routing error
- CMIP messages saturating network
- Defective system software
- Device creating broadcast storm
- Disk space fragmented
- Driver configuration error
- Encapsulation protocol error
- File server disk too slow
- File server down
- File server jammed
- File server memory error
- File server overloaded
- Gateway overloaded
- Inconsistent network software
- Mismatched hardware
- Network audit functions enabled
- Network configuration error
- Network out-of-spec error
- Network tool stressing network
- Network undergoing maintenance
- No free disk space
- Overloaded network
- Protocol analyzer creating traffic
- Remote query not optimized locally
- Repeater overloaded
- Router overloaded
- Router table address error
- Security functions enabled
- Server bus bandwidth overwhelmed
- Server I/O (input/output) bound
- Server undergoing maintenance
- Signal injector creating traffic
- SNMP messages saturating network
- TCP/IP protocol error
- Too many distributed processes
- Too much network traffic
- Translation gateway too slow
- Translation protocol error
- Usage audit functions enabled

### Slow response

Application running across bridge
Application running across gateway
Application running across router
Application running on server
Bad interrupt request (DOS IRQ)
Bridge overloaded
Brouter routing error
CMIP messages saturating network
Corrupted database
Corrupted distributed database
Device creating broadcast storm
Disk space fragmented
Driver configuration error
Encapsulation protocol error
File server disk too slow
File server jammed
File server memory error
Gateway overloaded
In excess of 72/136/250 nodes
Inconsistent network software
Network audit functions enabled
Network configuration error
Network out-of-spec error
Network tool stressing network
Network undergoing maintenance
No free disk space
Optical fiber clarity degradation
Optical fiber ends not polished
Overloaded network
Protocol analyzer creating traffic
Remote query not optimized locally
Repeater overloaded
Router overloaded
Router table address error
Security functions enabled
Server bus bandwidth overwhelmed
Server undergoing maintenance
Signal injector creating traffic
SNMP messages saturating network
Static electricity strike
Store-and-forward message lost
Stray voltage corrupted memory
TCP/IP protocol error
Too many distributed processes
Too many wireless stations
Too much network traffic
Translation protocol error
Twisted-pair bundle overutilized
Twisted-pair crosstalk
Twisted-pair substandard
Twisted-pair wire metal fatigue
Usage audit functions enabled
Wireless RF frequency overlap
Wireless signal conflict
Wireless signal too weak
Wireless stations too far apart
Workstation undergoing maintenance

### Software problems

Application running across bridge
Application running across gateway
Application running across router
Application running on server
Bad interrupt request (DOS IRQ)
Bridge overloaded
CMIP messages saturating network
Device creating broadcast storm
Disk space fragmented
Driver configuration error
Encapsulation protocol error
File server disk too slow
File server jammed
File server memory error
Gateway overloaded
Improper shielding from noise
Inconsistent network software
Mismatched hardware
Network audit functions enabled
Network configuration error
Open break on network
Open short on network
Optical fiber break
Overloaded network
Protocol analyzer creating traffic
Remote query not optimized locally
Repeater overloaded
Router overloaded
Router table address error
Security functions enabled
Server bus bandwidth overwhelmed
Server I/O (input/output) bound
Server undergoing maintenance
Signal injector creating traffic
SNMP messages saturating network
Static electricity strike
Stray voltage corrupted memory
TCP/IP protocol error
Too many distributed processes
Too much network traffic

**Software problems** (*continued*)

Network out-of-spec error
Network tool stressing network
Network undergoing maintenance
No free disk space
Translation gateway too slow
Translation protocol error
Usage audit functions enabled
User files corrupted

**Terminator missing**

Open short on network

**Translation gateway overloaded**

Translation gateway too slow
Translation protocol error

**Wiring concentrator dead**

Improper shielding from noise
Static electricity strike
Stray voltage corrupted memory
Twisted-pair intermixed with RS-232
Twisted-pair on live phone lines

**Workstation jammed**

Bad interrupt request (DOS IRQ)
Bridge overloaded
Brouter routing error
CMIP messages saturating network
Corrupted database
Corrupted distributed database
Defective lobe cable
Defective system software
Device creating broadcast storm
Disk space fragmented
Driver configuration error
Drop cable not properly connected
Drop cable polarity error
Encapsulation protocol error
Fan-out jammed
File server disk too slow
File server jammed
File server memory error
Gateway overloaded
Inconsistent network software
Mismatched hardware
Network configuration error
Network out-of-spec error
Network tool stressing network
Network undergoing maintenance
No free disk space
Optical fiber clarity degradation
Optical fiber ends not polished
Overloaded network
Protocol analyzer creating traffic
Repeater overloaded
Router overloaded
Router table address error
Server I/O (input/output) bound
Server undergoing maintenance
Signal injector creating traffic
SNMP messages saturating network
Static electricity strike
Store-and-forward message lost
Stray voltage corrupted memory
TCP/IP protocol error
Too many distributed processes
Too many wireless stations
Too much network traffic
Translation protocol error
Twisted-pair bundle overutilized
Twisted-pair crosstalk
Twisted-pair intermixed with RS-232
Twisted-pair not properly connected
Twisted-pair on live phone lines
Twisted-pair pairs reversed
Twisted-pair polarity error
Twisted-pair substandard
Twisted-pair wire metal fatigue
Wireless RF frequency overlap
Wireless signal distorted by dust
Wireless signal too weak
Wireless stations too far apart
Workstation undergoing maintenance

## Network Failures: Transmission Problems and Definitions

This section lists common Token-Ring transmission problems and their legal definitions. The numbered lists suggests the most likely causes for observed transmission problem in decreasing order of significance.

**Abnormal starting delimiter . . . . . . . . Frame start not identified**

1. The preamble pattern doesn't match the legal 8-byte Token-Ring synchronization pattern because a transmitter or a receiver does match specifications.

**Address error . . . . . . . . . . . . . . . . . . . . Packets not received**

1. Improper node address initialization.
2. Signal interference is disrupting communications.
3. A Token-Ring controller is not transmitting according to specification.

**Beacon . . . . . . . . . . . . . . . . . . . . . . . . Open break on network**

1. Bad connection on lobe or trunk.
2. A node is not retransmitting frames.

**Corrupt data . . . . . . . . . . . . . . . . . . . . . . . . Hardware failure**

1. A Token-Ring controller is not transmitting according to specification.
2. There are excessive jitter frames on the network.
3. A repeater, smart repeater, gateway, or bridge is not performing correctly.

**FCS error . . . . . . . . . . . . . . . . . . . . . . . . . . . Late collision**

1. A NIC has failed and is transmitting garbage packets.
2. Signal interference disrupted communications.
3. A Token-Ring controller is not transmitting according to specification.
4. The network wiring is improperly grounded.
5. Network lobes or trunks exceed length limitations.

**Incomplete transmission . . . . . Indicative of nonspecific problem**

1. Node not online.
2. Node failed.
3. Node overloaded.
4. Improper Internet address.
5. Address error.
6. Protocol mismatched.
7. Software failure.
8. Network overloaded.
9. Global network "state" lockup, software or hardware.
10. Application failure.
11. Interface problem.
12. Synchronization error.

**Interface problem . . . . . . . . . . . . . . . . No Token-Ring access**

1. Improper NIC speed.
2. Mismatched hardware.
3. Mismatched communication software.
4. A NIC has failed and is transmitting garbage packets.
5. The network cable is improperly grounded or connected.
6. A Token-Ring controller is not transmitting according to specification.

**Jitter frame . . . . . . . . . . . . Greater than maximum 1518 bytes**

1. A node is not transmitting according to specification.
2. A NIC has failed and is transmitting garbage packets.

**Misaligned frame . . . . . . . . . Uneven frame size and FCS error**

1. A NIC has failed and is transmitting garbage packets.
2. Hardware impedance mismatch is causing coaxial noise and internal reflection.

**No backoff error . . . . . . . . . . . . . . . . . . . . . . Late collision**

1. A NIC has failed and is transmitting garbage packets.
2. A Token-Ring NIC is not transmitting according to specification.

**No response . . . . . . . . Transmission confirmation not received**

1. Ring broken.
2. Node failed.
3. Node overloaded.
4. Improper Internet address.
5. Protocol mismatched.

**"Transmission error" . . . . . . Indicative of non-specific problems**

1. Network software.
2. Software.
3. Hardware.
4. Installation failure.
5. Network overloaded.
6. Ring broken.
7. Beacon.

## Statistical Inference

This section explores statistical information for isolating and understanding network problems. The first column, the actual statistic, is shown with a range, if applicable, and a "normal" value. When the statistic exceeds the normal range, an inference is listed in the last column.

### Packet Counts

| Statistic | 16 Mbits/s (4 Mbits/s) | Norm | Inference |
|---|---|---|---|
| Packets transmitted | 0 to 66,667 | * | statistical overloads |
| Packets received | 0 to 66,667 | * | statistical overloads |
| TRT | 4.5 to 260 (7.8 to 390) | 15 (18) | malfunctions, overloads |
| | | | faulty node or hub |
| | | | defective hardware |
| Packets per node | | prorated capacity | faulty transceiver, overloads |
| Source | | prorated capacity | faulty transceiver, overloads |
| Destination | | prorated capacity | improper segmentation |
| Source to destination | | prorated capacity | improper segmentation |
| Size distribution | 24 to 18,453 (24 to 4621) | * | design violations |
| | | | faulty software |
| | | | configuration error |

All failures are represented as packets per second. Percentages are a fraction of theoretical capacity.

## Packet Errors

| Statistic | Range | Norm | Inference |
|---|---|---|---|
| Alignment errors | * | 0 | defective hardware |
| Beacons | * | # nodes | node insertion noise |
| | | | broken ring |
| | | | defective node |
| | | | node at wrong speed |
| CRC errors | * | 0 | statistical overloads |
| | | | defective hardware |
| | | | defective software |
| Short frames | * | 0 | statistical overloads |
| | | | defective hardware |
| | | | defective software |
| Long frames | * | 0 | statistical overloads |
| | | | defective hardware |
| | | | defective software |
| Invisible packets | * | 0 | faulty NIC |
| Incompatible frames | * | * | mismatched hardware |
| Misaddressed frames | * | * | defective hardware |
| | | | defective software |

## Channel Utilization

| Statistic | Range | Norm | Inference |
|---|---|---|---|
| Throughput | 0 to 66,667 | 400 | statistical overloads |
| Peak rate | 0 to 66,667 | varies | overloads |
| | | | defective NIC |
| Utilization rate | 0 to 100% | K% | statistical overloads |

## Performance Statistics

| Statistic | 16 Mbits/s (4 Mbits/s) | Norm | Inference |
|---|---|---|---|
| Interarrival time | 1.5 x TRT | | statistical overloads |
| | | | software error |
| | | | user perpetrated |
| Latency time | | TRT or less | timing errors |
| | | | defective NIC |
| Packet size | 24 to 18,463 (24 to 4621) | * | defective software |
| | | | statistical overloads |

All failures are represented as packets per second. Percentages are a fraction of theoretical capacity.

Chapter

# 22

# LAN Troubleshooting Sequence

## Isolation Techniques

The first step when network failure occurs is to eliminate the obvious and isolate the problem for diagnosis. Figure 22.1 illustrates a logical step-by-step search pattern. The first step is to determine if failure is network software-, network hardware-, or node-specific. Unfortunately, experience with the reader's specific network provides the best basis for categorizing the failure. The only rule of thumb is that hardware failures are intermittent or transient and generally inexplicable, whereas software failures are reproducible and more logical. Software failures most often provide log messages which can help debug the trouble.

However, as network operating systems become more complex, supporting hot server activation, disk mirroring, disk striping, as well as multithreading and multiprocessing, the chances that memory could be overrun increase. Such sudden software failures are often inexplicable and not easily resolved. Any memory monitoring software or diagnostic tool to alter the memory mapping. As a result, such tools may not provide any insight into the failure. Additionally, the tools themselves may *stave off* the software failure. In either event, if a wrong assumption is made, the step-by-step isolation technique will eventually indicate that the reader incorrectly diagnosed the failure.

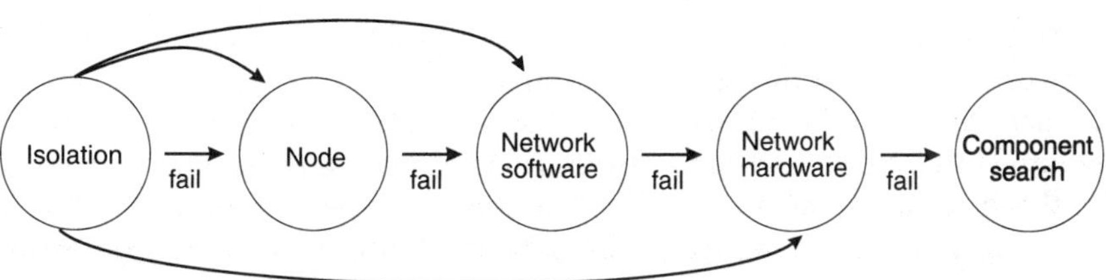


**Figure 22.1** The logical LAN troubleshooting sequence.

## Node Hardware and Software Failures

If the failure has been isolated to a single node, follow the steps to accomplish repair. The node may have failed, and this could cause network-wide failure. Assuming that the problem has been isolated to a failed node, follow the outlined steps in the tables. The sequence progresses with less likely causes of network failure. If all checks succeed, the problem is probably global, although individual nodes are more likely to fail than the entire Token-Ring network and consequently they should be tested first. In fact, a failed node and an irate user are usually the first indicators of a global network problem. If the network fails as a unit, even though hardware is a more frequent cause of network loss than software, software should be explored first, if at all possible, because the diagnostic tools are comprehensive.

If all nodes seem to be working independently, ascertain if network-level devices are suspect. While Token-Ring, IPX, TCP/IP, and many other upper-level communication software are supposed to be "stateless," some condition has likely occurred to lock the software into a perpetual waiting cycle. Assuming that the problem has been isolated to failed network software, follow the steps outlined in the accompanying tables. The sequence progresses with less likely causes of Token-Ring failure. Should all software, both node-local and global, seem to be functioning correctly, it is probably a hardware malfunction that is causing the inconvenience. The "server" side of a link shouldn't retain "state" before or after a transaction, although it frequently does. Therefore, every network transaction implies an open and close of a file and the network link. (This is not always true for client-server database transactional processing, or, when transaction commit and rollback features are enabled for SQL, DB2, and similar full-featured relational databases.) If state is maintained, the system is said to be jammed. Not only can this process halt the network; it can also cause a gradual and progressive degradation in normal network performance as network operating software create gratuitous loading.

## Network Hardware Failures

At this stage in the isolation process, the problem is probably a global network hardware problem. For example, a main connection is broken, or a crucial router or bridge has failed. Assuming that the problem has been isolated to a failed network hardware component, follow the steps outlined in the accompanying tables. The sequence progresses with less likely causes of Token-Ring failure. If the network defies these standard debugging strategies, there may be a hidden component that is at fault.

## Progressive Search for Hidden Component Failure

If all network components and devices appear to meet Token-Ring specifications, the final alternative is to power down the network piece by piece, section by section, until the problem is uncovered. If the problem can't be resolved quickly and the user community is willing to endure a complete network shutdown, a sequential shutdown of the network in conjunction with a binary or sequential search pattern will ultimately uncover any network problem. Note that the binary search is more efficient than random, guesswork methods networks. Follow the steps outlined. This is a last resort, and should be performed only with cooperation from the user community.

## Isolation Techniques for Enterprise-Wide Network Failures

### For either hardware or software problems, isolate the location:

- ☐ Apply binary search method or apply sequential search method.
- ☐ Check for failed segment operation.
- ☐ Check MAU or hub mechanisms for correct functioning.
- ☐ Check bridge mechanisms and sustained capacity.
- ☐ Check gateway mechanisms and sustained capacity.
- ☐ Check the network management statistics (SNMP or CMIP).
- ☐ Check the software indicators.
- ☐ Apply the multimeter or continuity tester.
- ☐ Apply the ring scanner, pair scanner, or TDR.
- ☐ Gather statistics and diagnose with protocol analyzer.

### On location:

- ☐ Verify operation of all subsegments or rings (networks in isolation).
- ☐ Check to confirm that components are plugged in.
- ☐ Jiggle components in case of short circuit or corrosion.
- ☐ Trace a beacon signal upstream (lower numbers) on MAU or hub.
- ☐ Check for electrical shorts or breaks.
- ☐ Replace failed components or interchange suspected components.
- ☐ Reroute traffic through other bridges, routers, or gateways.
- ☐ Check for failed packet encapsulation or translation.
- ☐ Check for overloaded components (bridges, routers, gateways).

Note: Step through each check. If the test shows correct network operation, proceed to the next item. Each item is progressively less likely to occur. If all checks succeed, widen the search pattern to a larger subset of the network. If a node has failed without clear reason, check the network. If the network has failed without clear reason, check the network software.

**For a software problem, isolate the location:**

- ☐ Check the network management statistics (SNMP or CMIP).
- ☐ Gather statistics and diagnose with the protocol analyzer.
- ☐ Analyze the network software.
- ☐ Locate failed or nonoperative nodes in the ring.
- ☐ Check the software indicators.
- ☐ Root out nonfunctional nodes and physically remove them from ring.

**On location:**

- ☐ Isolate segments.
- ☐ View node memory maps.
- ☐ View software state.
- ☐ Reboot nodes or workstations selectively.
- ☐ Restart software.
- ☐ Replace software.
- ☐ Debug and/or fix software.
- ☐ Check for overloaded components (bridges, routers, and gateways).
- ☐ Power down MAUs, hubs, bridges, gateways, routers.
- ☐ Power cycle individual hardware components.
- ☐ Reroute traffic and bypass failed sections or components.

Note: Step through each check. If the test shows correct network operation, proceed to the next item. Each item is progressively less likely to occur. If all checks succeed, widen the search pattern to a larger subset of the network. If a node has failed without clear reason, check the network. If the network has failed without clear reason, check the network software.

## Isolation Techniques for Network Failures

**For either hardware or software problems, isolate the location:**

- ☐ Apply binary search method or apply sequential search method.
- ☐ Check for failed, nonoperative node.
- ☐ Check the software indicators.
- ☐ Apply the multimeter.
- ☐ Apply the pair scanner, TDR, or ring scanner.
- ☐ Gather statistics and diagnose with the protocol analyzer.

**On location:**

- ☐ Check to confirm that components are plugged in.
- ☐ Jiggle components in case of short circuit or corrosion.
- ☐ Check for electrical shorts or breaks.
- ☐ Replace failed components or interchange suspect components.

**For a software problem, isolate the location:**

- ☐ Gather statistics and diagnose with the protocol analyzer.
- ☐ Analyze the network software.
- ☐ Locate failed or non-operative node.
- ☐ Check the software indicators.
- ☐ Root out nonfunctional nodes.

**On location:**

- ☐ Reboot nodes and workstations selectively.
- ☐ View node memory maps.
- ☐ View software state.
- ☐ Restart software.
- ☐ Replace software.
- ☐ Debug and/or fix software.
- ☐ Power cycle individual hardware components.

Note: Step through each check. If the test shows correct network operation, proceed to the next item. Each item is progressively less likely to occur. If all checks succeed, widen the search pattern to a larger subset of the network. If a node has failed without clear reason, check the network. If the network has failed without clear reason, check the network software.

## Decreasing Likelihood Search: Node Failed

**If a node has failed, check that:**

- ☐ The workstation or node unit is plugged in.
- ☐ The workstation has electrical power.
- ☐ The workstation is functioning.
- ☐ The workstation inserts into ring (ring noise on protocol analyzer).
- ☐ The workstation sees Token-Ring and NOS.
- ☐ The lobe cable connections are secure.
- ☐ The MAU connection is correct.
- ☐ The Token-Ring controller electronics function at the right speed.
- ☐ The Token-Ring address is correct.
- ☐ The Internet or IPX address is correct.
- ☐ All other nodes are working.
- ☐ Some other nodes are working.
- ☐ That Token-Ring versions and variations match.

**If all checks succeed =>**

........you have a network software failure or
........you have a network hardware failure or
........you have a device driver conflict or
........you may have experienced electricity spikes or stray voltage, or
........you have a hidden component failure.

## Decreasing Likelihood Search: Network Software Failed

**If network software has failed, check that:**

- ☐ The network software is correct.
- ☐ The network is not overloaded with traffic.
- ☐ The "state" of Token-Ring is not jammed.
- ☐ All nodes are set to the same speed.
- ☐ Each software node is compatible and repeats tokens and data packets.
- ☐ Token-Ring specifications are met.
- ☐ Token-Ring versions and protocols (ETR and burst mode) are uniformally supported.
- ☐ The network software is performing tasks.
- ☐ The operating network software is not corrupted.
- ☐ The software is compatible with physical devices.

**If all checks succeed =>**

.......you have a network hardware failure or
........you have a device driver conflict or
........you may have experienced electricity spikes or stray voltage, or
.......you have a hidden component failure.

Note: Step through each check. If the test shows correct network operation, proceed to the next item. Each item is progressively less likely to occur. If all checks succeed, widen the search pattern to a larger subset of the network. If a node has failed without clear reason, check the network. If the network has failed without clear reason, check the network software.

## Decreasing Likelihood Search: Network Hardware Failed

**If network hardware has failed, check that:**

- ☐ The network software is correct.
- ☐ The network print and file servers are online.
- ☐ The network is not overloaded with traffic.
- ☐ Terminators are in place.
- ☐ Lobes are correctly installed.
- ☐ MAU connectors are tightly connecting.
- ☐ No lobe sections are broken.
- ☐ There are no cable breaks, cuts, or abrasions.
- ☐ The "state" of Token-Ring is not jammed.
- ☐ Token-Ring is not connected to a live telephone circuit.
- ☐ Token-Ring wiring is not crossed over.
- ☐ Token-Ring wiring bundle also does not support RS-232.
- ☐ Token-Ring wiring bundle also does not support serial communication.
- ☐ Token-Ring wiring polarity is maintained properly.
- ☐ The gateways and routers are functioning.
- ☐ MAUs and hubs units are not jammed.
- ☐ Individual network rings are functioning.
- ☐ Repeated segments (rings) are functioning.
- ☐ Gateway segments (rings and other structures) are functioning.
- ☐ Individual network wiring sections are operational.
- ☐ Controller components are functioning.
- ☐ Controllers are not jabbering, jittering, or chattering.
- ☐ Controller electronics are operational.
- ☐ There are no software node incompatibilities.
- ☐ Token-Ring versions and variations match.
- ☐ There is no outside electrical or radio-frequency interference.

**If all checks succeed =>**

........you have a device driver conflict or
.......you may have experienced electricity spikes or stray voltage, or
.......you have a hidden component failure.

Note: Step through each check. If the test shows correct network operation, proceed to the next item. Each item is progressively less likely to occur. If all checks succeed, widen the search pattern to a larger subset of the network. If a node has failed without clear reason, check the network. If the network has failed without clear reason, check the network software.

## Progressive Search for Hidden Component Failure

**To shut down the entire network, follow these steps:**

1. Power down all nodes.
2. Power down all MAUs, hubs, bridges, routers, and gateways.
3. Power down all file servers, print servers, and auxiliary devices.
4. Disconnect all network segments.
5. Check specification on all individual trunks, lobes, or auxiliary segments.
6. Electrically test wiring components for electrical incompatibilities.
7. Electrically test controllers for electrical incompatibilities.
8. Disconnect all network sections and rings (institute binary search).
9. Electrically test wire components for electrical incompatibilities.
10. Electrically test controllers for electrical incompatibilities.
11. Power up each individual network ring or section.
12. Complete to specification all individual components.
13. Reconstitute rings.
14. Power up each individual network ring or segment.
15. Electrically test wiring components for electrical incompatibilities.
16. Electrically test lobe lines for electrical incompatibilities.
17. Power up all nodes on each individual ring.
18. Power up all file servers, print servers, and auxiliary devices.
19. Power up MAUs and hub concentrators.
20. Power up bridges.
21. Power up routers.
22. Power up gateways.
23. Reconstitute network and reconnect all rings.
24. Power on all nodes.

**If all checks succeed and the network remains dysfunctional =>**

........you have traffic overload or
........you have a device driver conflict or
........you may have experienced electricity spikes or stray voltage, or
........you may have experienced an act of vandalism

**If all checks succeed and network now provides complete service =>**

........you had traffic overload or
........you had a network "state" problem or
........you had corrupted memory or
........you had a user application crashed network software or
........you may have experienced electricity spikes or stray voltage, or
........you had software incompatibilities or
........you may have experienced an act of vandalism

Chapter

# 23

# Tool Usage Reference

The four network tools—network hardware indicator lights (on hubs), the multitester, the twisted-pair scanner or time domain reflectometer, and the protocol analyzer—have overlapping functionality. The accompanying tables coach the network management team in the hour(s) of crisis by suggesting appropriate uses for each tool. These uses and the listed sequences direct the reader to a careful investigation; the aim is to discover the causes of possible network malfunction. The ideal values are repeated here for the reader's convenience.

Additionally, there are two sections detailing the sequence of tools and the best tool to apply in cases of hardware or software failures. While hardware problems are often easier to locate and repair than software problems, search for problems at the highest, most comprehensive, level; this is often a statistical search with a protocol analyzer, or a software search. Note also that software-level searches are generally noninvasive.

As each test succeeds, select a more basic component until the problem is traced. Certain types of problems, including hardware malfunctions, may be clearly pinpointed with this software search. A software search with a protocol analyzer or network management software like SNMP or CMIP is apt to provide comprehensive diagnosis. In some serious cases network faults necessitate TDR, scanner, or multitester testing because the network traffic is halted, precluding the use of the protocol analyzer. Check the network globally first. Contrast any visible conditions with experienced events or network statistics. Check if any nodes are functioning in a stand-alone mode, or analyze any patterns of failed nodes. Check key servers for functionality. Localize the search to a common area, or common subset of possible problems, and test accordingly.

If the problem cannot be localized, consider the possibility of a hardware malfunction and, as with the software tests, start with a major component and select progressively more basic components until the problem is traced. Unresolved problems may necessitate a complete shutdown and network restart as detailed in the preceding chapter.

## Functionality of Network Tools

### Indicator lights (on intelligent hubs)

- ☐ Is network functioning?
- ☐ Check network device receiving electrical power.
- ☐ Check for correct network device installation.
- ☐ Check for proper transmission speed settings.
- ☐ Does device transmit?
- ☐ Does device receive?
- ☐ Does device recognize token?
- ☐ Does device jabber, jitter, or chatter?
- ☐ Does device pass loop-back test (may need scanner)?

### Multimeter

- ☐ Check network voltage: 0 V on halted network, within -4.5 V to +4.5 V when transmitting.
- ☐ Check network resistance (negligible).
- ☐ Check network impedance (approximately 16 Ω/100 m).
- ☐ Check connector conductivity.
- ☐ Check network wiring for continuity and polarity.
- ☐ Check probes for conductivity and pairwise isolation.
- ☐ Check lobe pinout continuity.

### Pair scanner or time domain reflectometer (TDR)

- ☐ Check network lobe conductivity (16 Ω/100 m).
- ☐ Check lobe cable continuity.
- ☐ Check controller and connector installation.
- ☐ Check controller repeats signal.
- ☐ Perform a signal spectrum analysis.

### Protocol analyzer and network managemet software (SNMP, CMIP, and CMOT)

- ☐ Check for network traffic overload (>80% channel utilization).
- ☐ Check for exceptionally busy nodes (>20% network load).
- ☐ Check for chattering or jabbering controllers.
- ☐ Check for long TRT (> 25 ms).
- ☐ Check for high CRC error rates.
- ☐ Check for small or oversized packets.
- ☐ Check for nonsense packets.
- ☐ Check for interconnectivity device failures and overloads.

Note: Step through each check. If the test shows correct network operation, proceed to the next Item. Each item is progressively less likely to occur. If all checks succeed, widen the search pattern to a larger subset of the network. If a node has failed without clear reason, check the network. If the network has failed without clear reason, check the network software.

## Troubleshooting Sequence for Software Failures

If the network is functioning:

**Indicator lights (on intelligent hubs)**

- ☐ Check that node is online.
- ☐ Perform loop-back tests.
- ☐ Check that network is online and available.
- ☐ Check for operational dial-up, PBX, or PDN interconnectivity.
- ☐ Check that node is transmitting.
- ☐ Check that node is receiving.
- ☐ Check that node is detecting token and retransmitting the packet as received (no overruns).
- ☐ Check that node is not jabbering, chattering, or jittering.

**Protocol analyzer: partial network service**

- ☐ Perform a network-wide statistical evaluation:
  - Traffic load
  - Packet counts
  - Packet defect rate
  - TRT times
  - Rates of beacon exceeding number of ring insertions
  - Missing packet addresses
  - Jittering twisted-pair NICs
  - Nonresponsive MAUs or hubs
- ☐ Check for interconnectivity device failures and overloads.

**Server software functioning with partial network service**

- ☐ Perform a network software and hardware evaluation:
  - Check for any new changes
  - Software functioning
  - Version numbers
  - Version compatibility
  - File service
  - Memory levels
  - Source
  - Check for overloads

If node subset halted:

**Indicator lights (on intelligent hubs)**

- ☐ Check that nodes are online.
- ☐ Check that nodes are tokens.
- ☐ Perform loop-back tests or check ring for integrity.
- ☐ Check that network is online and available.
- ☐ Check that nodes are transmitting.
- ☐ Check that nodes are receiving.
- ☐ Check that any node is not jabbering, chattering, or jittering.

Note: Step through each check. If the test shows correct network operation, proceed to the next Item. Each item is progressively less likely to occur. If all checks succeed, widen the search pattern to a larger subset of the network. If a node has failed without clear reason, check the network. If the network has failed without clear reason, check the network software.

## Troubleshooting Sequence for Software Failures *(continued)*

**Protocol analyzer: partial network service**

- ☐ Perform network-wide statistical evaluation:
  - Traffic load
  - Packet counts
  - Packet defect rate
  - TRT and TTRT
  - Missing packet addresses
  - Nonresponsive nodes, nodes upstream from beaconing nodes

**Node software functioning with partial network service**

- ☐ Perform a node software and hardware evaluation:
  - Check for any new changes
  - Software functioning
  - Version numbers
  - Version compatibility
  - File service
  - Memory levels
  - Source
  - Overloads

If network halted and no network service is available:

- ☐ Power down hub concentrators and remove lobes.
- ☐ Power down network and restart all nodes individually.
- ☐ Check hardware for proper installation and functionality.
- ☐ Or, as a last resort, apply a progressive search.

Note: Step through each check. If the test shows correct network operation, proceed to the next Item. Each item is progressively less likely to occur. If all checks succeed, widen the search pattern to a larger subset of the network. If a node has failed without clear reason, check the network. If the network has failed without clear reason, check the network software.

## Troubleshooting Sequence for Hardware Failures

If the network is functioning:

### Indicator lights (on intelligent hubs)

- ☐ Check that node is online.
- ☐ Perform loop-back tests.
- ☐ Check that node is receiving and retransmitting.
- ☐ Check that node is not jabbering, chattering, or jittering.

### Protocol analyzer: partial network service

- ☐ Perform a network-wide statistical evaluation:
  - Traffic load
  - Packet counts
  - Packet defect rate
  - TRT
  - Missing packet addresses
  - Jittering twisted-pair NICs
  - Nonresponsive nodes

If a node subset is halted:

### Indicator lights

- ☐ Perform loop-back tests.
- ☐ Check that node is online.
- ☐ Check that network is online and available.
- ☐ Check that node is receving and retransmitting.
- ☐ Check that node is not jabbering, chattering, or jittering.

### Protocol analyzer: partial network service

- ☐ Perform statistical evaluation on suspect nodes if possible:
  - Traffic load
  - Packet counts
  - Packet defect rate
  - TRT and TTRT
  - Missing packet addresses
  - Jittering twisted-pair NICs
  - Nonresponsive nodes

Note: Step through each check. If the test shows correct network operation, proceed to the next Item. Each item is progressively less likely to occur. If all checks succeed, widen the search pattern to a larger subset of the network. If a node has failed without clear reason, check the network. If the network has failed without clear reason, check the network software.

## Troubleshooting Sequence for Hardware Failures *(continued)*

### Scanner and TDR: erratic or no network service

- ☐ Check the cable for continuity in terms of:
  - Breaks
  - Shorts
  - Abrasions
  - Parity errors and cable crossovers
  - Misspecified cable
  - Excessive bends
  - Impedance errors
  - RFI/EFI errors
  - Excessive crosstalk
- ☐ Check the connectors for:
  - Poor installation
  - Shorts
  - Breaks
  - Genderless contacts with metal fatigue and non-release
  - Dirty or greasy fittings
- ☐ View the twisted-pair NICs for:
  - Jabbering or jittering electronics
  - Signal interference
  - Poor installation
  - A signal spectrum that is out of specification

If the network is halted:

### Indicator lights (on intelligent hubs)

- ☐ Check that node is online.
- ☐ Check that node is receiving and retransmitting.
- ☐ Perform loop-back tests.
- ☐ Check that node is not jabbering, chattering, or jittering.

Note: Step through each check. If the test shows correct network operation, proceed to the next Item. Each item is progressively less likely to occur. If all checks succeed, widen the search pattern to a larger subset of the network. If a node has failed without clear reason, check the network. If the network has failed without clear reason, check the network software.

## TDR: no network service

- ☐ Check the cable for continuity in terms of:
  - Breaks
  - Shorts
  - Abrasions
  - Misspecified cable
  - Impedance errors
  - RFI/EFI errors
  - Excessive crosstalk
  - Excessive bends
  - A signal spectrum that is out of specification
- ☐ Check the connectors for:
  - Poor installation
  - Shorts
  - Breaks
  - Upside-down installation
  - Genderless contacts with metal fatigue and non-release
  - Dirty or greasy fittings
- ☐ View the transceivers for:
  - Jabbering or jittering electronics
  - Poor installation
- ☐ Test the lobe cables for:
  - Bad pin-out
  - Misspecified cable
  - Impedance errors
  - Shorts
  - Breaks
  - Crossover
  - Connection with live phone lines (48 V, 96 V when ringing)
  - Dirty or greasy fittings
  - Poor installation

## Multimeter: for serious cabling failures or isolated testing

- ☐ Test the cable for:
  - Breaks and shorts
  - Misspecified cable
  - Impedance errors
- ☐ Test the connectors for:
  - Poor installation
  - Breaks and shorts
  - Crossover
  - Wrong connectors
  - Genderless contacts with metal fatigue and non-release
  - Dirty or greasy fittings

Note: Step through each check. If the test shows correct network operation, proceed to the next Item. Each item is progressively less likely to occur. If all checks succeed, widen the search pattern to a larger subset of the network. If a node has failed without clear reason, check the network. If the network has failed without clear reason, check the network software.

# Part 7
## Appendices

Appendix A is a glossary with local area network and Token-Ring terms defined and cross-referenced by their all-too-common acronyms.

Appendix B is a bibliography of reference materials and some suggested additional readings.

Appendix

# A

# Glossary

**AC:** Alternating current. Electricity.

**ARL:** See **Adjusted Ring Length.**

**AUI Cable:** Attachment Unit Interface cable that connects a workstation to a transceiver or fan-out box. Often called a **drop cable.**

**ANSI:** See **American National Standards Institute.**

**Active Monitor:** A random network node, usually the first unit to attach to the LAN, which initiates **Ring Polls** every seven seconds per the 802.5 protocol, and **Ring Purges** when the ring is perceived to be broken or the token has been lost for longer than the TTRT.

**Adapter Board:** A PC board that plugs into any computer, including mainframe, minicomputer, personal computer, or workstation. Within the networking context it often refers to the network access unit, network interface card (NIC), or a network controller adapter.

**Address:** A reference to a source station or destination station on a network.

**Address Error:** A packet is improperly labeled with either source or destination information.

**Adjusted Ring Length:** The driving transmission path length for a ring architecture when a node or segment fails, and the ring wraps to provide network service without interruption.

**Alignment Error:** A packet that has not been synchronized correctly. It usually is uncovered as a packet that is not a multiple of 8 bits.

**American National Standards Institute:** A governmental agency that maintains standards for science and commerce that include a list of acceptable standards for computer languages, character sets, connection compatibility, and many other aspects of the computer and data communications industries. Also known by the ANSI acronym.

**Analog:** Something that bears a similarity to something else.

**Analog Signal:** A transmission in which information is represented as physical magnitudes of electrical signals.

**Application Level:** The seventh layer of the **OSI Reference Model** which supports identification of communicating partners, establishes the authority to communicate, transfers information, and applies privacy mechanisms and cost allocations. It may be a complex layer. The application layer supports file services, print services, and electronic mail.

**Average:** The statistical value representing the middle point in a sample distribution. Also, the sum all sample values divided by the number of samples.

**BAT:** Abbreviation for a batch file; usually refers to an MS-DOS or OS/2 script containing commands to execute. The file extent for an MS-DOS or OS/2 script file.

**BMP:** See **Burst Mode Protocol.**

**Bandwidth:** The range (band) of frequencies that are transmitted on a channel. The difference between the highest and lowest frequencies is expressed in hertz.

**Baseband:** A transmission channel which carries a single communications channel, on which only one signal can transmit at a given time.

**Beaconing:** A term used to describe a malfunctioning node on a Token-Ring network that has not isolated itself from the ring. A constant signal which collapses the ring.

**Benchmark:** A measuring standard. LAN performance benchmarks include **Mbits/s, throughput, error rates**, and other less formal definitions.

**Bits Per Second (bits/s):** Rate at which data is transmitted over a communications channel. Sometimes abbreviated as bps.

**Bits/s:** Rate at which data is transmitted over a communications channel. See **Bits Per Second.**

**Bit Time:** The time for a network to transport 1 bit of data. It is equivalent to the reciprocal of the network transmission rate, and is a convenient measurement in performing network performance calculations.

**Break:** A physical break (electrical or optical) in the network media that prohibits passage of the transmission signal. See also **Open.**

**Bridge:** A device that interconnects networks using *similar* protocols. The bridge provides service at level 2 of the **OSI Reference Model.** See also **Gateway** and **Router**.

**Broadband:** A transmission cable with a wider frequency range (than baseband) that carries individual multiplexed communications channels.

**Broadcast:** The transmission from one node on a LAN to two or more nodes on a LAN, or a packet with a destination broadcast address.

**Brouter:** Combination or hybrid derived from **bridge** and **router**. A device that performs the function of a bridge while filtering protocols and packets specifically destined for a node on another interconnected network.

**Buffers:** A temporary memory structure allocated for containing data. Usually refers to a memory structure for containing a block read or written to a hard disk.

**Burst Mode Protocol:** A NOS enhancement implemented in Novell NetWare that optimizes the performance of intensive file transfer operations.

**Bus:** A network topology in which nodes are connected to a linear configuration of cable. The data transfer path with a computer.

**Bus Master:** A specialized CPU and interface unit that controls the data transfer path and bypasses the computer CPU.

**Bus Width:** Refers to the size of the data units that the computer system needs to move through **I/O**. Usually represented by 8, 16, 32, or 64 byte units.

**CCITT:** See **Consultative Committee for International Telephone and Telegraph.**

**CDMA:** See **Code-Division Multiple Access.**

**CI:** See **Confidence Interval.**

**CMIP:** See **Common Management Information Protocol.**

**CMOT: CMIP on TCP/IP.**

**COM:** The file extent for an MS-DOS executable command application.

**CSMA/CD:** See **Carrier Sense Multiple Access with Collision Detection.**

**CRC:** See **Cyclic Redundancy Check.**

**CRC Error:** See **Cyclic Redundancy Check Error.**

**Cable Tester:** A testing tool which verifies the integrity and performance of network wiring and cable. It tests for electrical breaks, shorts, impedance, capacitance, as well as for signal crosstalk and signal attenuation. These tools are sometimes called pair or ring scanners when designed for Token-Ring.

**Cache:** A temporary memory structure that **buffers** data movement in computer system to provide faster access to information and improve overall performance.

**Caching Controller:** A storage interface device that improves disk performance. See **cache.**

**Capacitance:** The electrical properties of the network cable and hardware.

**Carrier Sense Multiple Access with Collision Detection (CSMA/CD):** A communications protocol in which nodes contend for a shared communications channel and all nodes have equal access to the network. Simultaneous transmissions from two or more nodes results in random restart of those transmissions.

**Chained Files:** Files on disk stored in discontiguous **blocks.**

**Channel:** An individual path that carries signals.

**Channel Logic:** The logical functions between the transceiver cable and the data link layer which support the defined interface between the system and the hardware,

**Chatter:** The condition resulting when NIC electronics fail to shut down after a transmission, and the NIC floods the network with random signals.

**Claim Token:** The signal propagated by a station which determines that a token is overdue, lost, or corrupted.

**Client:** A network "user," often a device or workstation.

**Client Layer:** The collective term that is used to refer to the data link and physical layers of the **OSI Reference Model.**

**Client-Server Processing:** The establishment of a host computer (server) to provide end-user (client) services.

**Code-Division Multiple Access:** Wireless transmission technology that employs a range of radio-frequency wavelengths to transport multiple channels of communication signals. See also **spread-spectrum technology.**

**Common Carrier:** Companies which provide communication networks (like AT&T).

**Common Management Information Protocol:** A network management protocol compatible with the OSI Reference Model. Also called **CMIP**.

**Common Network Interface Protocol:** A contender for standard network management protocols specified by **ISO**. This protocol provides a standard for managing large networks across bridges, routers, and gateways. See also **Simple Network Management Protocol.**

**Computer Virus:** Man-made software designed to disable, damage, or destroy computer hardware or read/write storage systems. Sometimes called incorrectly *worms*, *trojan horses*, and *trap doors*.

**Concentrator:** A wiring hub.

**Confidence Interval:** A statistical range surrounding the average value.

**Congestion:** A slowdown in a network due to a bottleneck.

**Consultative Committee for International Telephone and Telegraph:** An international organization that makes recommendations for networking standards like X.25, X.400, and CCITT facsimile data compression standards.

**Contiguous File Blocks:** Storage units in a hard drive that are logically positioned next to each other.

**Corrupt Data Error:** Condition resulting when hardware components fail.

**Crosstalk:** A technical term indicating that stray signals from other wavelengths, channels, communication pathways, or twisted-pair wiring have polluted the signal. It is particularly prevalent in unshielded twisted-pair networks or when telephone and network communications share wiring bundles.

**Cyclic Redundancy Check:** A checksum—an error checking algorithm—that the transmitting station includes within a packet. The receiving station generates its own CRC to check against the transmitted CRC. If the results are different, the receiver usually requests a retransmission of the packet. This encoded value is appended to each frame by the data link layer to allow the receiving NIC to detect transmission errors in the physical channel. Also **Frame Check Sequence** (q.v.).

**Cyclic Redundancy Check Error:** An error caused by alignment errors, 8-bit-multiple shortages, under- or oversized packets.

**Cylinder:** Refers to a collection of tracks within a hard disk that are co-located on multiple platters.

**DAS:** See **Dual Access Station.**

**DC:** Direct current. Electricity.

**DCE:** Abbreviation for **Distributed Computing Environment.**

**DDE:** Abbreviation for **Dynamic Data Exchange.**

**DDL:** Abbreviation for **Dynamic Link Library.** The file extent for an MS-Windows or OS/2 application overlay and executable code library.

**DP:** Acronym for **Data Processing.**

**DTE:** Acronym for **Data Terminal Equipment.** A computer terminal.

**Data Compression:** A method of reducing the space required to represent data, either as bits, characters, or graphic images.

**Data Link Layer:** The second layer of the **OSI Reference Model**. It manages transmissions and error acknowledgment and recovery. Technically, the mechanical devices map data units to data link units, provide physical error detection and notification, and link activation and deactivation.

**Data Processing:** Computer operations which are geared to the entry, manipulation, and dissemination of information.

**Data Terminal Equipment:** A computer terminal which connects to a host computer. It may also be a software session on a workstation or personal computer attaching to a host computer.

**Decouple:** A gateway (OSI application layer) process to notify an application that transmission will not be completed within the roundtrip delay limitations a LAN protocol. Instead, a completion message (for transmission success or failure) is given at some later time. This feature is critical for WANs, heterogeneous networks, and enterprise-wide facilities.

**Defragment:** The process of rewriting files stored on disk in discontiguous **Blocks** into a contiguous format to improve disk performance.

**Delni Unit:** A type of fan-out box.

**Destination Address:** The receiving station's address. See **Address.**

**Device:** Any item on the network. This includes logical addresses that refer to software or hardware processes. It is refers to any physical node, including a PC, **workstation**, mainframe, minicomputer, **bridge**, **router**, **gateway**, remote probe, **repeater**, or **protocol analyzer**.

**Digital:** A representation of information by a unit of length or size.

**Digital Transmission:** A transmission of information represented by electrical units.

**Disk Head Seek Time:** The average time required for the read/write heads on a hard drive to reach a random **block** and **sector.**

**Disk Transfer Time:** Average time required to read or write a block to a hard disk.

**Distributed Computing:** The technique of maintaining application software and data files on a centralized server for access by individual users on network nodes. See also **File Server.**

**Distributed Computing Environment:** See **Distributed Computing.**

**Downsizing:** The replacement of computer equipment (and the operating environment) with a less expensive version.

**Driver:** A software program to control a physical computer device (q.v. NIC, printer, disk drive, or RAM disk).

**Drop Cable:** Generally an 802.3 Ethernet trabsceiver cable. May also refer to the Token-Ring lobe cable.

**Dropped Packets:** Packets lost in transmission.

**Dual Acccess Station:** An FDDI station which attaches to dual FDDI rings.

**Duplex:** The method in which communication occurs, either two-way as in full-duplex, or unidirectional as in half-duplex.

**Dynamic Data Exchange:** Also called **DDE**. A method introduced by Microsoft with MS Windows to link cell information into a master document, spreadsheet, or other compound process running within the same CPU processor and memory stack. The cell content is not altered or duplicated, merely temporarily inserted for the master.

**Dynamic Link Library:** Code overlays loaded into memory as requested by application programs or operating systems.

**EMI:** See **Electromagnetic Interference.**

**EMS:** Abbreviation for *either* **Enhanced Memory Services** or **Expanded Memory Services.** Refers to a remapping and utilization of memory beyond the 640 K normally accessible to MS-DOS.

**ESDI:** Abbreviation for **Enhanced Small Device Interface.** A disk storage specification.

**ETR:** Abbreviation for **Early Token Release.**

**Early Token Release:** An enhancement for Token-Ring allowing a station to release a token upon completion of frame transmission.

**Electromagnetic Interference:** Signal noise pollution from radio, radar, or electronic instruments.

**Enhanced Memory Services:** A MS DOS memory specification allowing memory mapping for addresses above 640 K.

**Enhanced Small Device Interface:** A specification for attaching subservient computer devices to a computer processor bus.

**Enterprise Networks:** A wide area network that services all (or most) organizational sites. See **Enterprise-Wide Networks.**

**Enterprise-Wide Networks:** A wide area network that interconnects LANs at multiple sites.

**Error:** A functional violation of a LAN protocol.

**Error Rate:** The number of errors during a period of time divided by the number of *packets* tranmitted during that same interval. Errors may be reflected as a single bit error, but the rate should reflect errors as a basis not of bit throughput, but rather of packet throughput. See also **Throughput.**

**Ethernet:** A popular example of a **local area network** from which the IEEE 802.3 standard was derived. Ethernet applies the IEEE 802.2 MAC protocols and uses the persistent CSMA/CD protocol on a **Bus** topology. Transmission rate is a maximum of 10 Mbits/s. Ethernet is a persistent transmission protocol.

**EXE:** The file extent for an MS-DOS or OS/2 executable application.

**FAT:** Abbreviation for **File Allocation Table.** Refers to the MS-DOS, OS/2, or Unix table structures that maintain file directory information (q.v. size, name, placement, and block chaining).

**FOIRL:** See **Fiber Distributed Optical Interface.**

**FCS:** See **Frame Check Sequence.**

**FCS Error:** See **Frame Check Sequence Error.**

**FDDI:** See **Fiber Data Distributed Interchange.**

**ft:** Abbreviation for an SAE foot.

**Facility:** A WAN connection provided by a common carrier (such as Sprint, MCI, or AT&T).

**Fiber Data Distributed Interchange:** Optical fiber network based upon the ANSI X3.139, X3.148, X3.166, X3.184, X3.186, or X3T9.5 specifications. FDDI provides 125 Mbits/s signal rate with 4 bits encoded into 5-bit format for a 100-Mbit/s transmission rate. It functions on single or dual ring and star local area network with a maximum circumference of 4 km, although copper-based (CDDI) hardware is an option.

**Fiber Distributed Optical Interface:** The interconnection protocol required to access FDDI optical fiber networks.

**Fiber Optics:** Thin glass or plastic cables that transmit data by modulating light pulses.

**File Allocation Table:** Refers to the MS-DOS, OS/2, or Unix table structures that maintain file directory information (q.v. size, name, placement, and block chaining).

**File (Buffers):** A temporary memory structure allocated to contain names, locations, sizes, and other information about a file residing on a hard disk.

**File Server:** A device that provides file services for other nodes. It is a shared resource often with higher speed, larger capacity, or better economies-of-scale than remote data storage.

**Firewall:** A mechanism to protect network stations, subnetworks, and channels from complete failure caused by a single point.

**Firmware:** Software which is encoded into a ROM BIOS or PROM chips.

**Frame:** See **Packet.**

**Frame Check Sequence:** A checksum value to verify correct receipt of the data packet. The checksum is based upon a cyclic redundancy formula. The encoded value is appended to each frame by the data link layer to allow receiving controllers to detect transmission errors in the physical channel. Also called a **Cyclic Redundancy Check.**

**Frame Check Sequence Error:** The condition occurring when the encoded value appended to each frame specifies the received frame as corrupt. See also **Cyclic Redundancy Check Error.**

**Frame Relay:** A packet switching device. See **Packet Switching Network.**

**Frame Relay:** A switching interface to get **frames** or **packets** over parts of the network as quickly as possible.

**Framing:** The process of assigning data bits into the network time slot.

**Full-Duplex:** A two-way transmission method that echoes characters to ensure proper reception.

**GIS:** Abbreviation for **Graphical Information System.** Generally refers to a database of graphical data, although it also can refer to an image storage and retrieval system.

**Gateway:** A device that routes information from one network to another. It often interfaces between dissimilar networks and provides protocol translation between the networks. A gateway is also a software connection between different networks; this meaning is not implied in this book. The gateway provides service at level 7 of the **OSI Reference Model.** See also **Bridge** and **Gateway.**

**Gauss Meter:** A device that measures the strength of a magnetic field.

**Global Resource:** Any hardware, software, server, or other resource generally available to all processes and users on a network.

**Graphical Information System:** Generally refers to a database of graphical data, although it also can refer to an image storage and retrieval system.

**HLLAPI:** Abbreviation for **High Level Language Application Programming Interface.** An IBM standard for interconnecting processes running on host computers for data transfer and user display.

**HMA:** See **High Memory Area.**

**Half-Duplex:** A one-way transmission method that does not support characters' echoes.

**Handshaking:** The exchange of signals between transmitting and receiving devices or their associated modems to establish that each is working and ready to communicate, and to synchronize timing. See also **Protocol.**

**Hertz (Hz):** A unit of frequency that is one cycle per second. Token-Ring is 8 or 32 million hertz, or 8 or 32 million cycles per second. Two cycles are required to represent a bit transition.

**High Level Language Application Programming Interface:** Also called **HLLAPI**. An IBM standard for interconnecting processes running on host computers for data transfer and user display.

**High Memory Area:** An MS-DOS memory region generally corresponding to any memory above 640 KB and below 1024 KB. Device controllers and VGA drivers can be loaded into this area for PC performance enhancement.

**Hub:** A network interface that provides star connectivity for Token-Ring nodes. See **MAU**.

**Hub Adapter:** A network interface board that provides access for additional network nodes. This **Network Interface Unit** essentially doubles as a concentrator unit.

**Hunt Group:** A series of telephone numbers in sequence that permits the calling party to connect with the first available line.

**IDE:** Abbreviation for **Integrated Drive Electronics.** A composite unit consisting of a disk drive and controller components.

**IEEE:** The **Institute for Electrical and Electronic Engineers.**

**IEEE 802:** An IEEE standard for interconnection of local area networking computer equipment. The IEEE 802 standard describes the physical and link layers of the **OSI Reference Model.**

**IEEE 802.2:** A specification for media-layer communication typified by Ethernet and Token-Ring. See also **Logical Link Control.**

**IEEE 802.3:** An Ethernet specification derived from the original Xerox Ethernet specifications. It describes the CSMA/CD protocol on a bus topology using baseband transmissions.

**IEEE 802.5:** A token ring specification derived from the original IBM Token-Ring LAN specifications. It describes the token protocol on a star/ring topology using baseband transmissions.

**IES:** An acronym for **Inter-Enterprise network System.** See **Enterprise-wide Networks.**

**I/O:** Abbreviation for input and output from a computer. Refers to all memory movement with the **bus**, data moved to and from disks, user and screen presentations, and data packets placed to and from the network channel.

**IPX:** See **Internet** and **Internet Packet Exchange.**

**ISO: International Standards Organization** which created the **OSI Reference Model.**

**Impedance:** The mathematical combination of resistance and capacitance that is used as a measurement to describe the electrical properties of the coaxial cable and network hardware.

**In:** Abbreviation for an SAE inch.

**IPX:** Abbreviation for **Internet Packet Exchange.** A Novell specification for OSI level 3 data exchange.

**Inductance:** The property of electrical fields to induce a voltage to flow on the coaxial cable and network hardware. It is usually a disruptive signal that interferes with normal network transmissions.

**Institute for Electrical and Electronic Engineers:** An membership-based organization based in New York City that creates and publishes technical specifications and scientific publications.

**Integrated Drive Electronics:** Also abbreviated as **IDE.** A composite unit consisting of a disk drive and controller components.

**Intelligent hub:** A hub device that connects Token- Ring nodes and manages nodes and traffic while it also isolates failing lobes, trunks, and nodes.

**Interface:** A device that connects equipment of different types for mutual access. Generally, this refers to computer software and hardware that enable disks and other storage devices to communicate with a computer. In networking, an interface translates different protocols so that different types of computers can communicate together. In the OSI model, the interface is the method of passing data between layers on one device.

**Interface Error:** A condition indicative of hardware or software incompatibilities.

**International Standards Organization:** Abbreviated as **ISO.** An international organization that sponsors the development of unified standards for measurements and data communication.

**Internet:** A government-sponsored mail communication network that gave rise to TCP/IP protocols.

**Internet Address:** An address applied at the TCP/IP protocol layer to differentiate network nodes from each other. This is in addition to the station hardware or protocol address.

**Internet Packet Exchange:** A common network-level protocol proposed and applied by vendors, including Novell. IPX is based upon the original Xerox **XNS** frame specifications.

**Internet Protocol:** See **Transaction Control Protocol/Internet Protocol.**

**Internetworking:** Communication between two or more different networks through a bridge, a gateway, a modem, or other routing equipment.

**Interoperability:** The process of different network protocols, network hardware, and host mainframe systems to communicate.

**Jabber:** To talk without making sense. The condition when a NIC's timing electronics malfunction, and the unit broadcasts in excess of the specified token holding timer limit and creates an oversized frame.

**Jitter:** A network failure that occurs when a Token-Ring network segment preamble and the packet signal are out of phase. The jitter shows up as transmission signal distortion, decay, frequency, and timing errors on a token-based LAN.

**Jitter budget:** The allowed range for signal distortion on a token-based LAN.

**k:** Abbreviation for a metric kilometer, or a unit representing a 100 **Meters.** It also may be represented by km.

**KB:** Abbreviation for kilobytes (1024 bytes) of memory.

**LAM:** Acronym for **Lobe Attachment Module** (q.v.).

**LAN:** Acronym for **Local Area Network** (q.v.).

**LAN Operating System:** See **Network Operating System.**

**LLC:** See **Logical Link Control.**

**Latency:** The waiting time for a station desiring to transmit on the network.

**Learning Bridge:** A smart device that interconnects two local area networks using similar protocols. It learns what nodes are on each connecting segment and routes only that information which is destined for the other segment, therefore improving network performance. The learning bridge is a simple router that provides service at level 3 of the **OSI Reference Model.**

**Lease Line:** A dedicated common carrier circuit providing point-to-point or multipoint network connection. Also called a private line.

**Link Control Field:** A data field contained within an an Ethernet packet as part of the Internet Protocol.

**Linkage Product:** Any unit that provides an interface between network segments. This includes gateways, bridges, and other specialty components.

**Load Balancing:** A technique to equalize the workload over peer and client network components. This includes workstations, storage disks, servers, network connectivity devices, and network transmission channels.

**Lobe:** A section of cable or wire extending from a MAU, hub, or concentrator to a network station.

**Lobe Attachment Module:** a type 3 media filter which provides signal retiming and filtering so that 16 Mbits/s Token-Ring will function correctly on unshielded twisted-pair media.

**Local Area Network:** Also referred to by the acronym, **LAN.** A network limited in size to a floor, building, or city block.

**Logical Device:** A description that lists how the network references **Physical Devices** (q.v.).

**Local Echo:** A host implementation for capturing and display individual keystrokes on terminal or serial network (sic) connections.

**Logical Link Control:** A data link control field occupying the first few bytes of the data field that initiates, maintains, and terminates any communication.

**Long Packet:** A packet that exceeds the specified protocol length maximum of the Token-Ring maximum hold timer.

**Loop-back Test:** A test for faults over a transmission medium where received data is returned to the sending point (thus traveling a loop) and compared with the data sent.

**Low-Level Format:** A process which creates (or overwrites) the pattern of **Tracks** and **Sectors** on a hard or floppy disk while the disk head is moving across the spinning media.

**M:** Abbreviation for a metric **Meter** (39.25 SAE in).

**MB:** Abbreviation for a megabyte (1024 kilobytes) of memory.

**Mbits/s:** Abbreviation for a megabits per second. Sometimes abbreviated as Mbps.

**MAN:** Abbreviation for **Metropolitan Area Network.** A network that spans buildings, city blocks, a college or corporate campus. Optical fiber repeaters, bridges, routers, packet switches, PDN and PBX services usually supply the network links.

**MAU:** See **Media Access Unit.** Also called a **hub.**

**MFM:** Abbreviation for **Modified Frequency Modulation** encoding method used for storing data on a hard disk. A disk storage specification.

**MPS:** Megabits (1,000,000 decimal units) per second (Mbits/s). This is a channel bandwidth. See also **Bandwidth** and **Mbits/s.**

**ms:** Abbreviation for a **millisecond.**

µs: Abbreviation for a **millisecond.**

**Manchester Encoding:** A digital encoding technique in which there is a transition in the middle of each bit time period. A "1" is represented by a high level during the first half of the bit time period whereas a "0" is represented by a low level during the first half of the bit time period.

**Mean:** See **average.**

**Media:** The physical material used to transmit the network transmission signal. It is either some form of copper wire or optical fiber. However, wireless networks use infrared, microwaves, or radio frequency signals through the ambient air as the media.

**Media Access Control:** A hardware-level protocol for networking corresponding to ISO level 1.

**Media Access Unit:** Media Access Unit connects directly to a lobe and broadcasts and receives information over that cable and switches the signals to the next active downstream node. It is often called a **MAU** or **hub.**

**LMedia Filter:** a passive (unpowered) electrical device which provides signal retiming and filtering so that Token-Ring will function correctly on unshielded twisted-pair media.

**Memory Paging:** The process of moving memory within the CPU or temporary computer memory to other parts of memory, to screen, or to a disk.

**Meter:** Unit of measurement equivalent to 39.25 SAE in, or 3.27 ft. Meter is abbreviated as **m**.

**Metrics:** A formal measuring standard or benchmark. LAN performance metrics include **Mbits/s, throughput, error rates**, and other less formal definitions.

**Metropolitan Area Network:** Abbreviated as **MAN.** A network that spans buildings, city blocks, a college or corporate campus. Optical fiber repeaters, bridges, routers, packet switches, PDN and PBX services usually supply the network links.

**Millisecond:** $1 \times 10^{-6}$ seconds.

**Misaligned Frame:** A frame that trails a fragmentary byte (1 to 7 residual bits), and has an FCS error, or a packet that was framed improperly by the receiving station and therefore a **Synchronization Error** (q.v.).

**Modem:** A device which converts digital to analog signals and restores analog signals back into digital signals for transmission over a network.

**Modified Frequency Modulation:** Abbreviated as **MFM.** This is an encoding method used for storing data on a hard disk. A disk storage specification.

**Monte Carlo Experiments:** Repetitive experiments using sophisticated variance reduction techniques to approximate the behavior of a random process.

**Monitor:** See **Protocol Analyzer.**

**Multicast:** The ability to broadcast to a select subset of nodes.

**Multimeter:** A test tool that measures electrical voltages (units in V) and resistances (units in Ω). It is also called **multitester.** It is sometimes called an **ohmmeter**.

**Multitester:** A test tool that measures electrical voltages (units in V) and resistances (units in Ω).

**Multithreading:** A concurrent processing of messages commonly implemented in OS/2, UNIX, and VMS operating systems.

**NAU: Network Access Unit.** This term represents the network controller as found in most Token-Ring adapter boards. See also **Controller.**

**NDIS:** See **Network Device Independent Specification.**

**NIC:** See **Network Interface Card.**

**NOS:** See **Network Operating System.**

**ns:** Abbreviation for **Nanosecond.**

**NetBEUI:** Abbreviation for network **NetBIOS Extended User Interface.** A version of NetBIOS from Microsoft (LAN Manager).

**NetBIOS:** Abbreviation for **Network Basic Input Output System.** The first level of network software which controls network hardware. A specification for OSI level 1 data exchange.

**NETBLK: Network Block Transfer Protocol.**

**NIC:** See **Network Interface Card.**

**NIDL:** See **Network Interface Definition Language.**

**NIU:** Abbreviation for **Network Interface Unit.** See **Ethernet Controller.**

**Nanosecond:** $1 \times 10^{-10}$ seconds.

**NetBIOS Extended User Interface.** Abbreviated as **NetBEUI.** A version of NetBIOS from Microsoft (LAN Manager).

**Network:** Hardware and software that allow computers to transmit data over both local and long distances.

**Network Computing:** The ability of underutilized workstations to broadcast their status and provide automatic, parallel computing power.

**Network Access Unit.** Another term that represents the network controller as found in most Token-Ring adapter boards. See also **Controller.**

**Network Basic Input Output System:** Abbreviated as **NetBIOS.** The first level of network software which controls network hardware. A specification for OSI level 1 data exchange.

**Network Block Transfer Protocol:** A protocol used to transfer large units of data at the operating system level over a LAN. Abbreviated as **NETBLK.**

**Network DDE:** See also **Dynamic Data Exchange:** A method for linking cell information (such spreadsheet cells, text blocks, audio or graphic elements) into master documents, spreadsheets, or other compound processes accessible by LAN, WAN, or enterprise-wide networks. These TSR or shell processes define the location of the cell, type of information, method of access, complete address, or frequently the means to establish remote links and initiate remote processes to fetch the cell contents.

**Network Device Independent Specification.** Some vendors define it as Network Driver Interface Specification. An effort to create a standard for bridging different types of network adapter cards and multiple protocol stacks. This network-level protocol is supported by IBM LAN Manager and new Microsoft networking products.

**Network Interface Card:** The network access unit which contains the necessary hardware, software, and specialized PROM information for a node to communicate across the network.

**Network Interface Definition Language:** IEEE proposed model for parallel processing and logical process partitioning across a distributed network. See also **Network Computing.**

**Network Interface Unit:** See **Ethernet Controller.**

**Network Layer:** The third layer of the **OSI Reference Model** which activates the routing with network address resolution and flow control in terms of segmentation and blocking. Also, this layer provides service selection, connection resets, and expedited data transfers. The **Internet Protocol (IP)**, or **IPX**, both common LAN softwares, runs at this level.

**Network Monitor:** See **Protocol Analyzer.**

**Network Operating System:** A platform for networking services that combines operating system software with network access. This is typically not application software, but rather an integrated operating system.

**Node:** A logical, nonphysical interconnection to the network that supports computer workstations or other types of physical devices on a network. Alternatively, a node may connect to a fan-out unit providing network access for many devices. A device might be a terminal server, or a shared peripheral such as a file server, printer, or plotter.

**Noise:** Electrical signal interference on a communications channel that can distort or disrupt data signals. Generally, this refers to **electromagnetic interference (EMI)** or **radio-frequency interference (RFI)**.

**ODI:** See **Open Data-Link Interface.**

**OLE:** See **Object Linking and Embedding.**

**OSI Reference Model: Open Systems Interconnection Reference Model** defined by the International Standards Organization (ISO), which has determined a data communication architectural model for networking.

**OTDR:** See **Optical Time Domain Reflectom.**

**Object Linking and Embedding:** Also called **OLE.** A method introduced by Microsoft with MS Windows not merely to link specific data cells but also to include the latest versions of entire documents, graphic images, full-motion video, and sounds into a master document, spreadsheet, or other compound process or object. Changes made to objects linked thusly within this master framework are simultaneously reflected and updated within the individual and original cells, processes, or objects. Additionally, other masters, including objects with multiple OLE links, would see such changes simultaneously. See also **Dynamic Data Exchange** and **Network DDE**.

**Ohmmeter:** See **multimeter.**

**Open:** A partial physical break (electrical or optical) through one or more signal conductors in the network media that prohibits passage of the transmission signal. Open circuits usually do not refer to a complete cut of the media. See also **break.**

**Open Data-Link Interface.** Also called **ODI.** An interoperability standard. Novell has proposed this network-level protocol and built IPX/SPX with this protocol specification. This is the LLC control standardized by Novell.

**Open Systems Interconnection Reference Model:** A specification defination from the International Standards Organization (ISO). It is a data communication architectural model for networking.

**Operating System:** The software required to control basic computer operations (q.v. disk access, screen display, and computation).

**Optical Fiber:** A glass or plastic material drawn into a cable that carries data communications via light modulation.

**Overhead:** CPU, disk processing, and/or network channel bandwidth allocated to the processing and/or packaging of LAN data.

**Oversized Packet:** A packet that exceeds the maximum packet size defined by a protocol.

**PBX:** See **Private Branch Exchange.**

**PDN:** See **Public Data Network.**

**PROM:** Abbreviation for programmable read-only memory. A computer chip with software designed into its structure.

**PVC:** Polyvinyl Chloride. An extensively used insulator in cable coatings and coaxial cable foam compositions.

**Packet:** A self-contained group of bits representing data and control information. The control information usually includes source and destination addressing, sequencing, flow control, and error control information at different protocol levels. Token-Ring packet length is variable.

**Packet Buffers:** A structure created in computer memory to build, disassemble, or temporarily store network data packets.

**Packet Burst:** An overwhelming broadcast of packets requesting LAN and station status information, source or destination addresses, or indicating panic error messages.

**Packet Switching Network:** A network transmission methodology that uses data to define a start and length of a transmission for digital communications. A process of sending data in discrete blocks.

**Paging:** See **Memory Paging.**

**Peer-to-Peer Exchange:** The ability of computer workstations from the same or different vendors to interconnect and communicate.

**Persistance:** A statistical term refering to a protocol's method of accessing the network. Ethernet is *persistent* in transmitting, while other protocols are *non-persistent* and wait for a permission token.

**Phantom Voltage:** The voltage applied between the transmit and receive wire pairs in a Token-Ring network to activate the mechanical relays in **MAUs** or **hubs.**

**Physical Address:** The unique address associated with each workstation on a network. A physical address is devised to be distinct from all other physical addresses on interconnected networks. A worldwide designation unique to each unit.

**Physical Channel:** The actual wiring and transmission hardware required to implement networking.

**Physical Device:** Any item of hardware on the network.

**Physical Layer:** Level 1 of the **OSI Reference Model** which insulates the data link layer from the medium-dependent physical characteristics.

**Ping:** A protocol request to poll a subset of network stations for an active status. See **Ring Poll.**

**Polling:** An access method involving a central node asking each node in a predetermined order if it has data to send. This is often used in mainframe environments, and the order is often determined as a function of priority.

**Position-Dependent Unfairness:** A situation common to LANs where some stations receive better service due to proximity to other stations or a central location in a bus-structured LAN.

**Premises Network:** See **Enterprise-Wide Network.**

**Presentation Layer:** This is the sixth layer of the **OSI Reference Model** which transfers information from the application software to the network session layer of the operating system. At this level, software performs data transformations, data formatting, syntax selection (including ASCII, EBCDIC, or other numeric or graphic formats), device selection and control, and data compression or encryption.

**Print Server:** A device that provides print services for other nodes. It is a shared resource often with higher speed, larger capacity, or better economies-of-scale than local printers.

**Private Branch Exchange:** Also called a PBX. A telephone system used to connect calls between offices in the same complex, and to switch calls between the site and a larger phone network.

**Protocol:** A formal set of rules by which computers can communicate. This includes session initiation, transmission maintenance, and termination.

**Protocol Analyzer:** Test equipment that transmits, receives, and captures data packets to verify proper network operation.

**Public Data Network:** Also called a **PDN.** An analog or digital wide-area communication link. This term usually refers to a common carrier such as AT&T, Sprint, or MCI.

**Queueing Model:** A statistical model describing a system of event arrivals (q.v. packets or transmission requests) and service times (q.v. tranmission delivery times, network channel loading, and performance levels). Also *Queuing Model.*

**RAM Disk:** A temporary disk created in memory that functions as a fast disk drive.

**RF:** Acronym for **Radio-Frequency** (q.v.).

**RFI:** Acronym for **Radio-Frequency Interference** (q.v.).

**RLL:** Abbreviation for the run length limited data encoding method used for storing data on a hard drive. A disk storage specification.

**ROM:** Abbreviation for read only access memory. Refers the basic information required by most computers to check memory, initialize the bootstrap, and load operating systems and networks.

**RS-232:** A standard for interfacing data communications between peripheral devices and the computer.

**Random:** A statistical term referring to a process with outcomes in a defined sample space. Random does not mean chaotic, indiscriminate, or arbitrary.

**Random variable:** A numerically valued function defined over a sample space.

**Radio-Frequency Interference:** Electronically propogated noise from radar, radio, or electronic sources. See **Electromagnetic Interference.**

**Radio-Frequency Switch:** A remote radio-frequency trigger relay that electrically switches sections of network wiring or coaxial cable and alters network topology. Sometimes called an isolation switch or a **Firewall.**

**Redirector:** A software driver that diverts commands to access local devices and routes them to network devices for data storage, retrieval, and printing.

**Repeater:** A device that boosts a signal from one network lobe or trunk and continues transmission to another similar network lobe or trunk. Protocols must match on both segments. The repeater provides service at level 1 of the **OSI Reference Model.**

**Resistance:** The measurement of the electrical properties of the wiring and network hardware that describes their ability to hinder the passage of electrons.

**Ring:** A network topology that has nodes in a circular conflguration.

**Ring Poll:** A Token-Ring protocol whereby the **Active Monitor** sends out a broadcast signal to every active node to see if it is functioning correctly.

**Ring Purge:** A Token-Ring protocol operation where a node initiates a request to create a new token.

**Router:** A device that interconnects networks that are either local area or wide area. Routers often provide intercommunication with multiple protocols. Routers provide service at level 3 of the **OSI Reference Model.** See also **bridge** and **gateway**.

**s:** Abbreviation for a second.

**SCSI:** Abbreviation for **Small Computer System Interface.** A hardware device controller specification.

**SEF:** See **Source Explicit Forwarding.**

**SNA: System Network Architecture.** IBM host mainframe connection protocol.

**SNMP:** See **Simple Network Management Protocol.**

**SPX:** Abbreviation for **System Packet Exchange.** A Novell specification for OSI level-4 data exchange.

**SQE:** See **Signal Quality Error** heartbeat.

**SST:** See **Spread-Spectrum Technology.**

**STA:** See **Spanning Tree Algorithm.**

**STP:** See **Shielded Twisted-Pair.**

**Sector:** A pie-shaped structure on a hard disk.

**Server:** A dedicated processor performing a function such as printing, file storage, or tape storage. See also **File Server** and **Print Server.**

**Session Layer:** The fifth layer of the **OSI Reference Model**. It recognizes the nodes on the LAN and sets up the tables of source and destination addresses. It also establishes, quite literally, a hand-shaking for each session between different nodes. Technically, these services are called *session connection, exception reporting, coordination of send-receive modes,* and of course, the actual *data exchange*.

**Service Address Point:** A data link status value contained within the logical link control field of each frame data field that initiates, maintains, and terminates any communication.

**Shield:** A barrier, usually metallic, within a wiring bundle that is intended to contain the high-powered broadcast signal within the cable. The shield reduces **electromagnetic interference (EMI)** and **radio-frequency interference (RFI)**, and signal loss.

**Shielded Twisted-Pair:** Pairs of 22 to 26 gauge wire clad with a metallic signal shield.

**Short:** A physical discontinuity (usually electrical, rarely optical) such that one or more signal conductors in the network media leaks signal into other conductors. Usually, a short refers to an electric short circuit between signal conductor and the shield or grounds. It can also refer to a short between receive or transmit pairs.

**Signal:** A transmission broadcast. The electrical pulse that conveys information.

**Signal Quality Error:** A background indicator, or "heartbeat," signal that provides a carrier signal.

**Simple Network Management Protocol:** A contender for standard network management protocols becoming widely implemented by NIC hardware and software vendors to provide management of heterogeneous networks. See also **Common Network Interface Protocol**.

**Simplex:** A transmission standard that does not echo characters.

**Simulation:** A technique to model or represent a real-world situation using computerized tools (q.v. *LANModel*).

**Single access station:** An FDDI station which connects into a concentrator, but not into the dual optical fiber ring.

**Small Computer System Interface:** A hardware device controller specification. Abbreviated as **SCSI.**

**SONET:** See **Synchronous Optical Network.** A common carrier fiber optic transmission link providing basic bandwidth in blocking units of 50 Mbits/s. Multiple streams can support bandwidths up to 18 billion bits per second.

**Source Address:** The transmitting station's logical address.

**Source Explicit Forwarding:** A security feature provided by a bridge, router, or gateway that permits only packets from a specified list to be forwarded to another network.

**Spanning-Tree Algorithm:** IEEE 802.1 standard that detects and manages logical loops in a network. When multiple paths exist, the **bridge** or **router** selects the most efficient one. When a path fails, STA automatically reconfigures the network with a new active path.

**Spectrum Analysis:** A technique that tests the radio, electrical, or optical signal frequencies to ascertain that the transmission signal conforms to requirements.

**Spread-Spectrum Technology:** Wireless radio-frequency signal transmission that utilizes multiple frequencies to transmit an identical signal to defeat jamming, background noise, and lower the required power requirements.

**Stable:** A description of the consistency for a network protocol, infrastructure, or application subject to error condition and traffic loading levels.

**Star:** A network topology where nodes join at a central location.

**Station:** A single addressable node on Token-Ring, generally implemented as a stand-alone computer or a peripheral device such as a printer or plotter. This sometimes refers to a **Node** or **Workstation**.

**Stochastic:** A process that is random, or probabilistic.

**Subnet:** A ring that is a portion of a larger network.

**Swap File:** A temporary file established on a local workstation to buffer network data access, provide rapid storage for image displays and work files, and to provide a linearly mapped memory for construction of database views and complex data processing.

**Synchronization:** The event occurring when transmitting and receiving stations operate in unison for very efficient (or inefficient) utilization of the communications channel.

**Synchronization Error:** A Token-Ring packet that is framed improperly by the receiving station or overruns the controller.

**Synchronous Optical Network: SONET.** A common carrier fiber optic transmission link providing basic bandwidth in blocking units of 50 Mbits/s. Multiple streams can support bandwidths up to 18 billion bits per second.

**TCP/IP:** Acronym for **Transaction Control Protocol/Internet Protocol.** Although commonly referred to as TCP/IP, a complete implementation of this networking protocol includes Transaction Control Protocol (TCP), Internet Protocol (IP), Internetwork Control Message Protocol (ICMP), User Datagram Protocol (UDP), and Address Resolution Protocol (ARP). Standard applications are File Transfer Protocol (FTP), Simple Mail Transfer Protocol (SMTP), and TELNET which provides a virtual terminal on any remote network system.

**TDR:** See **Time Domain Reflectometer.**

**TSR:** See **Terminate and Stay Resident.**

**TRT:** See **Token Rotation Time.**

**TTRT:** See **Target Token Rotation Time.**

**Target Token Rotation Time:** The expected time in which a station can next acquire the token after transmitting.

**Teflon:** Trade name for fluorinated ethylene propylene. A nonflammable material used for cable foam and jacketing.

**Telco:** A reference to modular telephone wiring.

**Terminal Server:** A computer device that provides low-speed DTE network access. A device for connecting terminals to a network.

**Terminate and Stay Resident:** Also called **TSR.** A PC- and MS-DOS program that is permanently loaded into memory for access by a unique key-stroke sequence or event sequence. It can be likened to an extension to the operating system functionality.

**Throughput:** A measurement of LAN work accomplished. Measurements are presented in percentages, bits/s, packets/s, or other user-defined gauges.

**Time Delay Reflectometer:** An incorrect reference to a device called a **Time Domain Reflectometer.**

**Time-Division Multiplexer:** A method using specific time slots to access a communication link. This is accomplished by combining data from several devices into one transmission.

**Time Domain Reflectometer:** Test equipment that verifies proper functioning of the physical components of the network with a sequence of time-delayed electrical pulses. Primarily, this tool checks for contiguity and isolation of STP and UTP wiring.

**Time Domain Reflectometry:** The process of testing transmission lines for proper electrical functioning.

**Token:** The protocol-based permission that is granted to a station in a predetermined sequence. The permission allows that station to transmit on network.

**Token Acquisition Time:** The waiting time for a station awaiting permission to transmit to acquire the token.

**Token Hold Timer:** The time measurement and measuring device that sets the time a station may hold a token (while transmitting data), and thus implicitly refers to the size of the longest possible legal packet.

**Token-Ring:** A popular example of a **local area network** from which the IEEE 802.5 standard was derived from original IBM working papers. Token-Ring applies the IEE 802.2 MAC protocols and uses the non-peristent token protocol on a logical ring, although a physical star topology. Transmission rate is a 4 Mbits/s, with upgrades to 16 Mbits/s and an early token release or burst mode option.

**Token-Ring:** An IBM network protocol and trademark.

**token ring:** A physical networking configuration.

**Token-Ring Address:** The hardware address contained within a NIC PROM. The logical ring position relative to position 1 on a MAU.

**Token Rotation Time:** The time for a token to circulate once around the network. See **Token.**

**Topology:** Layout of a network. This describes how the nodes are physically joined to each other.

**Track:** A circular (ring-shaped) structure on a hard disk.

**Traffic:** A measure of network load which refers to the packet transmission rate (frames per second or frames per hour).

**Transaction Control Protocol/Internet Protocol:** Common communication protocol servicing the network and transport layers that provides transmission routing control and data transfer. This represents logical connectivity at levels 2 and 3 of the **OSI Reference Model,** although the protocol does not conform in fact to this model. Also known by its acronym, **TCP/IP**.

**Transmission Error:** Catch-all term for a CRC Error. Such errors are caused by **Alignment Errors, Undersized Packets,** or **Oversized Packets** (q.v.), plus a variety of application, system software, or hardware failures.

**Transport Layer:** The fourth layer of the **OSI Reference Model** which controls data transfer and transmission control. This software level is called **Transaction Control Protocol (TCP)**, the common LAN software.

**Twisted-Pair:** Telephone-type wire twisted over its length to preserve signal strength and minimize **Electromagnetic Interference.**

**Type Error:** A packet that is improperly labeled with protocol information.

**UDP:** User Datagram Protocol. A simplified version of the **Transmission Control Protocol (TCP)** for application-level data.

**UMB:** See **Upper Memory Blocks.**

**UPS:** Uninterrupted Power Supply. A backup power supply in case the main electrical source fails.

**UTP:** See **Unshielded Twisted-Pair.**

**Undersized Packet:** A packet that contains less than 64 bytes, including address, length, data, and CRC fields.

**Unshielded Twisted-Pair:** Pairs of 22 to 26 gauge wire usually in bundles of 25 pairs installed for telephone service and occasionally for data networks.

**Upper Memory Blocks:** An MS-DOS memory area that is accessible above 1024 KB. MS Windows and some application software can be loaded into this memory when special memory access software is installed. Both *enhanced* and *expanded* memory services reside within UMB. Expanded memory tends to provide the better MS-DOS performance, although it provides the more restricted utility.

**VSAT:** Very-Small-Aperture Terminal. Synonomous with satellite data communication.

**Virus:** See **Computer Virus.**

**WAN:** Wide Area Network. A network that spans cities, states, countries, or oceans. PBX services usually supply the network links.

**Wiring Concentrator:** See **Wiring Hub.**

**Wiring Hub:** Central wiring concentrator for a series of Token-Ring nodes.

**Workstation:** A single addressable site on Token-Ring, generally implemented as a stand-alone computer or a peripheral device, connected to the ring with a controller. Also termed a **Station.**

Appendix

# B

# Additional Reading and Bibliography


Bickel, Peter J., and Kjell A. Doksum, *Mathematical Statistics: Basic Ideas and Selected Topics,* Holden-Day, San Francisco, CA, 1977.

Haller, Ted, *Cookbook Approach to Troubleshooting in the Token-Ring Environment*, 1992 Communication Test Symposium, Hewlett-Packard.

Hiller, Frederich S., and Gerald J. Lieberman, *Operations Research,* Holden-Day, San Francisco, CA, 1974.

*IEEE Standards for Local Area Networks: Logical Link Control Procedures,* IEEE, New York, 1985.

*Internet Protocol Transition Workbook,* March 1981, SRI International, Menlo Park, CA.

Shannon, C. E., *The Mathematical Theory of Communications,* University of Illinois Press, Urbana, IL, 1964.

The Seybold Report on Publishing Systems, Vol. 20, No. 10/11, Autumn 1990.

*Time Domain Reflectometry Applications for Token Ring Networks,* Tektronix, Inc. Redmond, OR.

*Token Ring Network Planning Guide,* Andrew Corporation, Torrance, CA 90503.

# Index

## ABOUT THE AUTHOR

Martin A. W. Nemzow is president of SST, Inc., a consulting firm, and executive vice president of ValueFinders, Inc., a database publishing company. He is the author of the first and second editions of *The Ethernet Management Guide* and *LAN Performance Optimization*, all published by McGraw-Hill.